Introduction to
Information Technology Law

Visit the *Introduction to Information Technology Law, sixth edition*
Companion Website at **www.mylawchamber.co.uk/bainbridgeIT**
to find valuable **student** learning material including:

- Weblinks to useful further resources online
- Regular updates on major legal changes affecting the law

Introduction to
Information Technology Law

Sixth Edition

David Bainbridge

BSc, LLB, PhD, C Eng, Chartered IT Professional, MBCS

Professor of Intellectual Property Law,
Aston Business School, Aston University

Barrister, Honorary Member of Hardwicke Building, Lincoln's Inn

PEARSON

Longman

Harlow, England • London • New York • Boston • San Francisco • Toronto • Sydney • Singapore • Hong Kong
Tokyo • Seoul • Taipei • New Delhi • Cape Town • Madrid • Mexico City • Amsterdam • Munich • Paris • Milan

Pearson Education Limited
Edinburgh Gate
Harlow
Essex CM20 2JE
England

and Associated Companies throughout the world

Visit us on the World Wide Web at:
www.pearsoned.co.uk

First published 1990 as *Computers and the Law*
Second edition published 1993 as *Introduction to Computer Law*
Third edition published 1996
Fourth edition published 2000
Fifth edition published 2004
Sixth edition published 2008

ISBN: 978-1-4058-4666-0

British Library Cataloguing-in-Publication Data
A catalogue record for this book is available from the British Library.

10 9 8 7 6 5 4 3 2 1
11 10 09 08

Typeset in 10/12pt Minion by 3
Printed by Ashford Colour Press Ltd, Gosport

The publisher's policy is to use paper manufactured from sustainable forests.

Brief contents

Contents

Contents

Contents

Contents

Supporting resources
Visit **www.mylawchamber.co.uk/bainbridgeIT** to find valuable online resources

Companion Website for students
- Weblinks to useful further resources online
- Regular updates on major legal changes affecting the law

For instructors
- An Instructor's Manual containing feedback and answer guidance on the multiple choice and exam style questions contained in the book, along with copies of selected diagrams from the book

For more information please contact your local Pearson Education sales representative or visit **www.mylawchamber.co.uk/bainbridgeIT**

Preface

The first edition of this book was published in 1990. It was a relatively slim volume, indicative of the fact that computer law was only really starting to develop as a subject in its own right. Since that time, computer law has grown enormously, reflecting the continual growth of the use of computers and the new and emerging uses that computer technology has been and will be put to. Over the years, in line with technological development, the scope of the book has widened to include information technology and communications technology to take account of the growth of the internet and online activities. The wider scope is reflected in the change of title of this edition of the book to refer to information technology law rather than computer law.

The technological development having the most impact has been the phenomenal rise of the internet, leading to a whole range of issues having legal and other implications and stimulating legislative responses on a national and international scale. These issues include the use of the internet for access to massive amounts of information, its use for transactions, such as buying goods and services online, participating in online auctions and online banking. It has posed particular challenges to intellectual property rights such as copyright and raised privacy and freedom of expression issues. It has provided opportunities for criminal activities, from fraud to the distribution of pornographic materials to the dissemination of viruses and denial of service attacks.

On the whole, the legal responses have been quick and proportionate in the light of the threats posed. For example, in the UK, the maximum penalty in respect of child pornography was raised to imprisonment for 10 years and/or a fine. New fraud offences were introduced to overcome difficulties with the old deception offences which were of doubtful application to computer fraud. The need for legal intervention is clear when one considers that the 'I Love You' computer virus was reckoned to have cost a total of $8.75 bn worldwide. Significant legislative action has come from the European Parliament and Council to ensure that Europe is not disadvantaged by a lack of appropriate regulations and that there is a level playing field in Europe in terms of establishing information society services and carrying out electronic commerce. Other European initiatives concerned data protection laws, freedom of information in respect of environmental information and overhauling intellectual property laws to strengthen copyright in electronic works and bringing in a special form of protection for databases.

Information technology law covers a wide and diverse spectrum, which is reflected in the structure of this book. After a brief introductory chapter, **Part 1** of the book concentrates on intellectual property rights. These are the rights associated with creative, innovative and inventive works. Particular areas covered include the protection of computer programs and computer databases, copyright in the information society and the patenting of software. Design law and trade mark law are also relevant. Design law was transformed by a European Directive and Regulation and it is now possible to register computer graphics and icons as designs. There have been numerous cases involving trade marks on webpages and the registration of famous names as internet domain names, often described as 'cybersquatting'. There is a new chapter on criminal offences and intellectual property to reflect the seriousness with which piracy and counterfeiting are now perceived.

Part 2 deals with information technology contracts and looks at contracts for the writing of software, the acquisition of ready-made software, open source software, website development contracts, outsourcing and hardware contracts. There is also a chapter on the liability for defective hardware and software which includes material on the lawfulness of exemption clauses.

Part 3 focuses on electronic contracts and torts. It looks at developments in the formation of contracts over the internet, electronic commerce and regulations relevant to distance selling, for example, where a person orders a product or service over the internet. As regards torts, there is a chapter on a range of subjects including defamation on the internet and liability for negligent misstatements. A further issue is the position of intermediaries, such as internet service providers, with respect to illegal material made available or transmitted through their services.

Part 4 looks at information and communications technology crime, including fraud, unauthorised access ('hacking') and associated offences and causing damage to computer programs or data, for example, by the malicious spread of computer viruses or the deliberate erasure of programs or data. There is a chapter on computer pornography, harassing e-mails and incitement. A new chapter is included on computer evidence in criminal proceedings and computer forensics.

Part 5 of the book deals with data protection and freedom of information law. There have been many developments in this field of law which impacts of some of the important rights and freedoms enshrined in the Council of Europe Convention for the Protection of Human Rights and Fundamental Freedoms. There is a new chapter on freedom of information, an important area of law now fully in force in the UK giving a right of access to much information held by public authorities. Significant use has already been made of this law, for example, by journalists seeking information about the government and local authorities. A further chapter looks at privacy in electronic communications which covers telecommunications, including mobile phones, and internet communications.

The last part of the book, **Part 6**, is new and looks at other issues relating to the use of information and communications technology. This includes consideration of the position, responsibilities and obligations of computer professionals, the impact of ICT on fundamental rights and freedoms and on property rights. Wider social issues are also discussed.

A feature of this new edition is the use of summaries and self-test questions at the end of each chapter. The correct answers to the multiple choice questions are at the rear of the book. The answers will also be made available on the companion website with some explanation. The companion website will include updates to this book, links to useful websites and advice as to finding cases and legislation and other materials to help supplement the book. There will also be an instructor's manual, available to lecturers and teachers, on the companion website which will include outline answers to the 'essay style' questions at the end of chapters, together with further multiple choice questions and other useful information and materials.

It has been my intention to make the subject matter accessible and practical, and of interest to students and those involved in the field of computer and information and communications technologies. The sixth edition has been fully updated to take account of new legislation and case law since the previous edition and the scope has been widened where appropriate to reflect recent developments in technology. Each new edition of this book involves a considerable amount of research but this has proved an enjoyable exercise in such a fast-moving, vibrant and important field of study. I hope readers will find the book interesting, stimulating and useful.

I am indebted to those who have helped me in researching for and writing this book. My own students have often asked questions that have driven me to find out more and suggestions from students and practitioners alike have been and always will be most welcome. I would like to thank my wife, Lorraine, for all her help and support and all at Pearsons who have helped with the preparation for and publication of this edition.

I have endeavoured to state the law as it was at 1 March 2007.

David Bainbridge

Glossary of computer, information technology and legal terms

Computer and information technology terms

Note: terms that have fallen into common use are not included unless the meaning is significant.

Algorithm – a structured set of rules or operations defining a logical solution to a problem or a methodology to achieve some end result. An algorithm may be expressed in the form of a flow chart.

Blog – a diary or log on an internet website, derived from 'web' and 'log'.

Chip – sometimes referred to as 'silicon chip' or, more correctly, integrated circuit. A small piece of semiconducting material, such as silicon, which, with layers of conducting and insulating materials, makes up a micro-electronic circuit incorporating numerous semiconductor devices (such as transistors, resistors and diodes). The contents of some chips are permanently fixed (called ROM chips – *read only memory*) while the contents of others are volatile and can be changed (called RAM chips – *random access memory*). Another form of chip is the EPROM – *erasable programmable memory*. The central processing unit (CPU) of a computer is contained on an integrated circuit; this chip is the 'brains' of the computer and carries out the machine language instructions derived from computer programs.

Compiler – a program which converts a computer program written in a high-level language (source code) into machine language code (object code). The operation is known as compiling and the reverse operation, converting machine language code into a higher-level language code, is known as decompiling.

Computer – a programmable machine which can store, retrieve or process data automatically, usually electronically. Section 5(6) of the Civil Evidence Act 1968, now repealed, gave a statutory definition of a computer as 'any device for storing or processing information'.

Computer forensics – specialised techniques used to recover, verify and preserve computer data, typically to be used in evidence in criminal proceedings.

Computer program – a series of instructions which control or condition the operation of a computer. Programs may be contained permanently in the computer, on integrated circuits or the computer's hard disk, or stored on optical or magnetic disks, etc. to be loaded into the computer's memory as and when required. The Export of Goods, Transfer of Technology and Provision of Technical Assistance (Control) Order 2003 defines 'programme' as '. . . a sequence of instructions to carry out a process in, or convertible into, a form executable by an electronic computer'. Legislation having a direct bearing on computer or information technology law, such as the Computer Misuse Act 1990, the Copyright, Designs and Patents Act 1988 and the Data Protection Act 1998, do not attempt to define 'computer program'. The United States Copyright Act 1976, as amended, in §101 (the definitions section) defines a computer program as 'a set of statement or instructions to be used directly or indirectly in a computer in order to bring about a certain result'.

Cookies – small files placed on a person's computer which contain information, such as user preferences, to make website use more efficient. May contain username and passwords to make access quicker. There are privacy issues with cookies as they transmit information to host websites. In many cases, individuals can choose to disable cookies but this can compromise browser capabilities.

Cybersquatting – this refers to the practice of registering names of celebrities or large corporations as domain names in the hope that those persons or corporations will pay large sums of money to have the domain names transferred to them.

Data and database – data comprises information, which may be stored in a computer or on computer storage media such as optical or magnetic disks. A database is a structured set of data – for example, a list of clients' names and addresses, or a list of employees and their details – typically stored in a computer file. A database is usually associated with computer programs used to store, access, manipulate or retrieve the data contained in it. In terms of copyright and data protection laws, databases may also include manual systems such as a card index or set of structured paper files. A data warehouse is a massive collection of data, often obtained from various sources and pooled together to form a rich repository of information.

Domain name – the name of a website, being a unique identifier of that website, for example, **www.pearsoned.co.uk**. An e-mail address is a personal identifier placed before a website address, for example, **anyone@www.pearsoned.co.uk**. Generic top level domains (gTLDs) include **.com, .net, .org or .info**. There is also a system of country code top level domains (ccTLDs) such as **.uk, .de** or **.fr**. Hence, UK government domains tend to finish with .gov.uk, such as **www.dca.gov.uk** for the Department for Constitutional Affairs.

Expert system – a computer system designed to provide advice at, or approaching, the level of an expert. These systems (and other similar systems known as KBS – knowledge-based systems or decision-support systems) usually contain knowledge in a database of rules and facts and details of the internal structure of the knowledge, an inference engine which manipulates and resolves an enquiry from a user, together with a user interface to control interaction with the user including the ability to provide justifications for any advice suggested by the system. The thought of developing expert systems looked very exciting some years ago but, generally, they failed to meet the expectations of researchers in the field. Decision-support and automated decision-taking systems are commonly used though lacking the refinement and sophistication of expert systems.

Facilities management – this is where a contractor takes responsibility for a particular set of operations or functions for the client. It is common in respect of information technology and data processing. For example, a contractor may be appointed to run the client's IT systems. This may require the contractor to develop the IT systems, designing new systems and making recommendations for IT policies and strategies. The facilities management work may be carried out on the client's premises, using the client's equipment and software or it may be carried on off-site at the contractor's premises. Often, when a client first awards a facilities management contract to a contractor, there will be a transfer of staff, equipment and software. Facilities management, sometimes known as **outsourcing**, is common in relation to the development and maintenance of websites.

Firmware – computer programs, which are permanently 'wired' into the computer, are often referred to as firmware or as being 'hard-wired'. These programs are permanently stored on integrated circuits ('silicon chips').

Hacker – a computer hacker is a person who gains access to a computer system without authorisation, usually by guessing or surreptitiously discovering which passwords will allow him access. A hacker may simply inspect the contents of the system he has 'broken into' or may go on to alter or erase information stored in the system or place a computer virus on the system.

Hardware – the physical pieces of equipment in a computer system; for example, a computer, printer, monitor and disk drive. Hardware devices usually incorporate software.

High-level language – a programming language which is relatively remote from the computer's machine language. A high-level language statement is equivalent to several machine language instructions. High-level languages often resemble a mixture of written English and conventional mathematical notation and are easier to use for writing and developing computer programs than are low-level languages or machine language. A program in a high-level language is often referred to as a source code program. Examples of high-level languages are BASIC, COBOL, FORTRAN, PASCAL and C.

HTML – HyperText Markup Language, used to create webpages. It is used to control the format of a webpage, for example, font size, type and colour, tables, lists, the insertion of pictures and internal and external links.

Low-level language – a programming language which is very close to the computer's machine language. Each instruction in a low-level language has a direct equivalent in machine language.

Machine language – the set of instructions and statements which control the computer directly. Many computer programs are written in high-level languages and have to be converted into machine language code by the use of an interpreter or compiler program. An interpreter produces a temporary translation while a compiler produces a permanent translation into machine language which can be used on its own without the presence of the original program.

Meta-tag – a tag used in HTML (HyperText Markup Language, the mark up language used to create webpages). Some meta-tags describe the contents of the website and are displayed in a list of 'hits' following a search on the internet. Others are invisible in normal use, such as keyword meta-tags which are used by search engines to find relevant sites following a search. Sometimes famous names and trade marks have been used without permission in keyword tags for some webpages to increase the likelihood of their being retrieved following a search, with the potential of capturing business or for other deceptive uses.

Object code and source code – a program which must be converted into a different form, such as machine language, before it will operate a computer is known as a source code program. Source code is the version of the program as it is written by the programmer and must be converted, temporarily or permanently, into object code before a computer can execute it. Most commercially available computer programs are distributed in object code form only.

Open source software – source code made available to the public allowing anyone to build it into his or her software or to develop new applications based on it. The conditions under which such software is made available often include a duty to freely distribute software developed using open source software. A number of standard licence agreements are used for distributing open source software.

Operating system – a program or set of programs which control and organise the operation of applications programs in addition to managing memory and providing certain facilities such as loading, saving, deleting files, etc. An operating system sets up the computer so that applications programs, such as word processing and spreadsheet programs, can be used. Examples are UNIX and Microsoft Windows and Vista.

Shrink-wrap licence – originally, a licence agreement exposed for view under a clear wrapper on the outside of a box containing software in an attempt to draw the licence terms to the attention of the buyer of the copy of the software. This was designed to overcome the problem that it is not possible to introduce new terms into a contract after the contract comes into being. Nowadays, it is more common for the media carrying the software to be in a sealed container carrying a notice to the effect that breaking the seal signifies acceptance of the terms of the licence agreement.

Software – software includes computer programs and data stored in a computer, preparatory design materials and also associated documentation such as user guides and manuals. Software may be obtained ready-made ('off-the-shelf'), as in the case of popular word processing and spreadsheet packages, or it may be specially written or adapted for a client ('bespoke' software). Applications software is software designed to perform a particular applied function required by the user such as word processing, the preparation of accounts, the design and use of a database or the preparation of a drawing. In contrast, operating system software provides the basic platform upon which applications software can operate.

Spam – unsolicited e-mails, often described as junk e-mails. It is thought that the name derives from the famous Monty Python sketch about Spam (a tinned meat product containing mainly ham, originally an abbreviation of 'spiced ham').

Spyware – software surreptitiously placed in computer storage which can transmit information back to the person responsible, hoping to obtain sensitive information, such as usernames and passwords. In some cases, spyware records keystrokes to transmission.

Virus – a program that attaches to other programs and files and is self-replicating and causes damage to computer programs and files. Easily transmitted from computer to computer, often as an e-mail attachment. The damage caused can be considerable with files and programs deleted or modifications made to operating system programs causing a computer to continually crash. Some viruses are specially written to take advantage of weaknesses in operating systems to spread themselves. Some have been spread by automatically forwarding themselves to all the addresses in a person's e-mail address book.

Web-wrap licence – sometimes referred to as a click-wrap licence. A licence agreement used in the context of obtaining software, music or other works in digital form online. The usual procedure is for the licensee to signify acceptance of the terms of the licence agreement by clicking on a button on a website at which a copy of the licence agreement is also available for inspection. Normally, the transaction cannot be completed until such positive assent to the licence is given. By these means, the licensor ensures that the licence is incorporated into the contract.

Legal and other terms

Note: legal terms are explained when first introduced in the book but it may help readers who are not lawyers to have a brief glossary of legal and associated terms they may not be familiar with.

Assignment – the transfer of the ownership of a right, for example a copyright. The person transferring the right is known as the assignor and the person acquiring the right is known as the assignee. An assignment need not be in relation to the entire right and may be partial, for example, in respect of certain acts, such as copying but not for the purpose of performing the work in public or rental of copies, or an assignment may be limited geographically, such as the right to make copies and sell those copies in the UK only.

Brussels and Lugano Conventions and the Brussels Regulation – these former two Conventions are, in the European Community, largely replaced by a regulation known as the Brussels Regulation and govern questions of jurisdiction and the enforcement of judgments in civil and commercial matters. They are important in determining the jurisdiction in which a legal action may be brought and provide for the recognition and enforcement of judgments in the courts of the EC and other EEA countries.

Directive – a Directive is a form of legislation of the European Union which must be implemented by the Member States using their own domestic laws. There are many Directives mentioned in this book. They range from matters such as copyright to data protection and electronic contracting to trade marks. Sometimes a provision in a Directive is optional and Member States can choose whether or not to implement it. Most provisions are not optional. Where this is so, Member States are required to implement them accurately and faithfully.

European Court of Human Rights – a judicial body set up under the Council of Europe which hears cases involving rights and freedoms under the Council of Europe Convention for the Protection of Human Rights and Fundamental Freedoms. Examples include the right to a fair trial, the right to privacy and the right of freedom of expression.

European Economic Area (EEA) – the EEA consists of the countries of the European Community together with Norway, Iceland and Liechtenstein. Some of the European Community legal initiatives apply also to the other EEA countries, for example, in the field of copyright and data protection.

European Union (EU) and European Community (EC) – The EU was established by the Treaty of Maastricht 1992. It comprises the 'three pillars', being the European Communities (European Community, formerly the European Economic Community, Euratom and the European Coal and Steel Community), a common foreign and security policy and cooperation in justice and home affairs. In terms of the content of this book, it is the European Community that we are concerned with. EC law has been very influential in the areas of intellectual property rights, e-commerce law and data protection law. There has been significant harmonisation of laws in Member States in these fields and there are now also some Community-wide rights, for example, the Community trade mark and design. There are 25 Member States of the EC, being Austria, Belgium, Cyprus, the Czech Republic, Denmark, Estonia, Finland, France, Germany, Greece, Hungary, Ireland (Republic of), Italy, Latvia, Lithuania, Luxembourg, Malta, the Netherlands, Poland, Portugal, Slovenia, Slovakia, Spain, Sweden and the UK.

European Court of Justice (ECJ) and Court of First Instance (CFI) – in the context of the subject matter of this book, the European Court of Justice is important for its judgments in relation to preliminary references where the court is asked to rule upon uncertainties or ambiguities in European Community law, such as where the meaning of a provision in a Directive or Regulation is uncertain. Where such a question arises in a national court, it may (in some cases must) refer the matter to the ECJ. The ECJ's ruling then is applied by the national court to the particular case in hand. The Court of First Instance hears appeals against decisions of the Office for the Harmonisation of the Internal Market (Trade Marks and Designs) (OHIM) in respect of the Community trade mark and the Community design.

Exhaustion of rights – a doctrine whereby the owner of an intellectual property right such as a patent or a trade mark loses the right to subsequent commercialisation of products subject to the right after those products have been put on the market in the European Community by or with the consent of the owner of the right. For example, the proprietor of a trade mark used for laptop computers might sell 100 of those computers in France. He cannot thereafter use his trade mark rights to stop a third party, who has lawfully come into possession of those particular computers, from further commercialising them such as by importing them into another Member State and re-selling them. The doctrine does not apply in relation to products placed for the first time on the market outside the European Community.

Ex parte – a hearing on behalf of someone not a direct party to the action.

Forum non conveniens – a rule of jurisdiction under which a court may decline jurisdiction on the basis that the courts in another jurisdiction are more appropriate to hear the case, because it is more convenient for the parties and it is in the interests of justice. This is now of very limited application, if any, because of the Brussels Regulation.

Injunction – an order of the court, typically requiring a party to refrain from doing something, for example, to stop the defendant from continuing to infringe a copyright or disclosing personal data in breach of the Data Protection Act 1998. An important form of injunction is the interim injunction (formerly known as the interlocutory injunction) and which applies until the full trial of the issue at hand. It can be used to prevent continuing damage caused by an alleged wrong, such as an infringement of copyright, until the full trial which might not be recoverable, for example, if the defendant is unlikely to have sufficient assets to pay an award of damages. A balance of convenience is used to determine whether or not to grant an interim injunction. Usually, an interim injunction will not be granted if it would put the defendant out of business.

Inter alia – amongst other things.

Licensor and licensee – the licensor grants permission to the licensee allowing him to do certain acts in relation to the subject matter of the licence. For example, the owner of a computer database may grant a licence to an end-user allowing the latter, the licensee, to access the database and retrieve data from it for specified purposes.

Mutatis mutandis – with necessary changes. May be used where a body of law is applied to similar subject matter, such as where provisions on copyright are applied to the database right, but modified as appropriate to take account of the differences between the two rights.

Rescission and repudiation – rescission is a remedy whereby a contract is set aside because of misrepresentation. Repudiation occurs where one party to a contract indicates that he will not perform his obligations under the contract. This might occur, for example, where a party repudiates a contract because he considers that the other party is in breach of an important term of the contract entitling the first to repudiate the contract.

Search order – a search order is an order of the court allowing a claimant, in the company of solicitors, to search the defendant's premises for evidence of the alleged wrong and to take copies of or remove alleged infringing material or other evidence as appropriate. Now carefully governed to prevent abuse, its main purpose is the preservation of evidence that might otherwise be destroyed or concealed. Search orders, formerly known as *Anton Piller* orders, are to be distinguished from search warrants under criminal law and other forms of civil search powers, typically provided for by legislation.

Abbreviations

The following list gives the full name of the law reports and other publications for which abbreviated references are used in the text of the book, in line with the usual conventions.

AC	Appeal Cases
AIPC	Australian Intellectual Property Cases
All ER	All England Reports
All ER (D)	All England Reports Digests
ALR	Australian Law Reports
BCLC	Butterworths Company Law Cases
BGHZ	Bundesgerichtshof (Civil) (German Federal Court)
BLR	Building Law Reports
Ch	Chancery (Chancery Division of the High Court)
CMLR	Common Market Law Reports
Con LR	Construction Law Reports
Const LJ	Construction Law Journal
Cr App R	Criminal Appeal Reports
Crim LR	Criminal Law Review
ECR	European Court Reports
EG	Estates Gazette
EHRR	European Human Rights Reports
EIPR	European Intellectual Property Review
EPOR	European Patent Office Reports
EWCA	England and Wales Court of Appeal cases, suffixed by (Civ) for Civil Division or (Crim) for Criminal Division
EWHC	England and Wales High Court cases, suffixed depending on the Division of the court, for example, (Ch) Chancery Division, (QB) Queen's Bench Division, (TCC) Technology and Construction Court
Fam	Family Division (High Court)
FCA	Federal Court of Australia
FLR	Family Law Reports
FSR	Fleet Street Reports
HCA	High Court of Australia
HC Deb	Hansard, House of Commons debates
HL Deb	Hansard, House of Lords debates

IRLR	Industrial Relations Law Reports
KB	King's Bench (High Court)
LEXIS	Computer database of cases and legislation, part of LEXIS-NEXIS service provided in the United Kingdom by LexisNexis Group, part of Reed Elsevier (UK) Ltd
Lloyd's Rep	Lloyd's Reports
Med LR	Medical Law Reports
NI	Northern Ireland Law Reports
OJ	Official Journal of the European Union
QB	Queen's Bench (High Court)
RPC	Reports of Patent, Design and Trade Mark Cases
RTR	Road Traffic Reports
S Ct	Supreme Court (US)
Sol J	Solicitor's Journal
STC	Simon's Tax Cases
TLR	Times Law Reports
US	Supreme Court (US) – see also S Ct, above
USPQ	United States Patents Quarterly
WLR	Weekly Law Reports

Table of cases

Table of statutes

1 Introduction to information technology law

Information technology continues to have an ever-growing impact upon society and the way that society conducts its affairs. Information and communications technologies have permeated almost every professional, commercial and industrial activity and most organisations would find it difficult, if not impossible, to function without relying heavily on these technologies. As far as the law is concerned, computers and electronic communications networks have been a mixed blessing. They have become indispensable tools, allowing the use of massive information storage, processing, dissemination, searching and retrieval. On the other hand, information and communications technologies have posed and continue to pose novel and complex social and legal problems. Frequently, the law has been found wanting when dealing with the issues raised by these constantly evolving technologies, and legislators and the courts have often struggled to come to terms with the challenges raised by them.

An understanding of the legal issues involved remains of key importance to persons and organisations concerned with information and communications technology, and it is only armed with such understanding that they can satisfactorily address and cater for the problems raised by the development and use of these technologies. For example, when drawing up a contract for the acquisition of computer hardware or software, the legal implications associated with the technology require careful consideration by lawyers and computer professionals alike. One of the purposes of this book is to bridge the gap between law and information and communications technologies so that effective legal arrangements can be made governing the use and exploitation of these technologies, dealing robustly with misuse and abuses, providing an equitable framework within which the various persons and organisations involved can operate fairly and efficiently. It is hoped that this book can help by indicating various ways of avoiding expensive and lengthy litigation by suggesting suitable legal measures, using the law constructively, as a tool. A practical approach is adopted in the book, giving advice of a proactive and preventative nature, where appropriate. If litigation is inevitable, however, such as when it is suspected that the copyright subsisting in a computer program has been infringed, knowledge of the legal implications should point the way to the most appropriate legal remedies and improve the likelihood of a successful outcome.

Six areas of particular importance to computer and information technology professionals are emphasised in this book: intellectual property (which includes copyright, patents and trade marks), computer contracts, electronic contracts and torts, criminal law, data protection law and professional, social and ethical aspects of information and communications technologies. Other areas of law are brought into the discussion where appropriate. For example, in negotiating a contract for the writing of software it is important to address the issue of liability for defects and an understanding of the law of negligence is important in this respect. When discussing the practical implications of computer crime, the admissibility and status of computer documents as evidence in a criminal trial must be taken into account.

Intellectual property law is important because it is the key to protecting innovation in computer hardware and software in its widest sense. Intellectual property rights, which include copyright, the law of confidence, design rights, trade marks, patents and regulations to protect integrated circuits, are first described in general terms in Chapter 2. These rights provide a basic framework of protection from piracy and plagiarism for computer programs, databases and works created using a computer and works or other information created, stored, made available online and transmitted digitally. The enormous scale of computer software piracy resulted in a general recognition of the desirability of effective laws in this area. Special attention is paid to computer software and copyright, the protection of databases, problems associated with electronic publishing and dissemination and the patentability of software inventions. Intellectual property law has striven to adapt and keep pace with technology to provide the protection necessary but there remain some difficulties which are discussed in detail in Part 1.

Much of the impetus for changes to and the strengthening of intellectual property law comes from the European Community and the need for harmonised law throughout Europe is very real in the context of rights such as copyright and patent law. This is also true on a wider international scale, resulting from international treaties and agreements, such as the Agreement on the Trade Related Aspects of Intellectual Property Rights, the 'TRIPs' Agreement. As a result, intellectual property law has developed rapidly and there have been numerous European initiatives aimed at dealing with specific issues raised by the use of information technology. A prime example is the European Directive on copyright and related rights in the information society which, *inter alia*, affords specific protection for electronic rights management information (such as a copyright notice and details of acceptable uses of a work made available electronically) and provisions to deal with the circumvention of technological measures designed to protect copyright works and other rights such as rights in performances and rights in databases.

Part 2 of the book is concerned primarily with computer contracts. In terms of the acquisition or modification of computer hardware and software, satisfactory contractual provisions are important to deal with problems which may arise both during the performance of the contract and subsequently. A well considered contract can provide effective machinery for determining responsibilities and resolving disputes without recourse to the courts. The special nature of contracts for the writing of computer software (bespoke software) or for the purchase of ready-made software is discussed together with a description of the implications of licensing and maintenance agreements and the scope and effectiveness of statutory controls on such agreements. Other forms of contractual agreements include 'shrink-wrap' licences and 'web-click' licences and the legal nature of these licences is still not entirely beyond doubt. Website development and maintenance contracts raise particular issues as do the use, modification and distribution of open source software. The utility and content of terms in various forms of licence agreements and related contractual agreements are analysed and described in the context of computer contracts.

Electronic contracting is an area that has become very important and is now a settled and major way of doing business, after the initial 'dot.com' euphoria. It is also an area that has attracted significant legislation dealing with issues such as electronic contracting generally, consumer protection and the admissibility of electronic signatures. A number of European Directives have been instrumental in shaping this area of law in Europe and, certainly in the UK, the emphasis has been to facilitate this form of contracting and also in terms of other forms of doing business, such as e-conveyancing and the submission of forms and documents electronically. Another important issue concerns the liability of service providers in the information society, for example, in respect of any illegal material passing through or made available through their services. Applicable law and jurisdiction are also important and there are Regulations and Conventions that provide the rules for determining both of these aspects within Europe but, elsewhere, the position is variable. Liability for electronic torts, for example, defamation on the internet is also considered in Part 3 of the book, which covers electronic contracts and torts.

Information and communications technology crime is dealt with in Part 4 of this book. It is a major concern to computer professionals, especially when the high incidence of computer-related crime is considered and related to the apparently poor security record of computer and information systems. At one time, the criminal law was perceived by many computer professionals and financial institutions as lacking teeth and being largely ineffective in the face of some very worrying threats and dangers which could seriously compromise the security of computer systems and undermine confidence in the use of computer technology. Activities which attracted a great deal of attention were hacking (that is, gaining access to a computer system without permission), computer fraud and damaging or erasing computer programs or data. The spread of computer viruses was alarming and relatively few organisations running large computer systems can claim to have been unaffected. The Computer Misuse Act 1990 was enacted specifically to deal with these problems and to tighten up the law in other areas where computer crime was involved. Three offences were created by the Act and these are described in detail together with the related practical issues in Part 3. Computer fraud is an area of growing concern with new threats such as 'phishing' (obtaining personal data to carry out fraud, for example, by means of an e-mail purporting to come from a bank asking for confirmation of passwords and account details). The old deception offences, such as the dishonest obtaining of property by deception, were unsuited to information technology and have been replaced by new fraud offences, set out in the Fraud Act 2006. These offences no longer need proof of deception, being based on dishonesty alone. As the courts had come to accept that it was not possible to deceive a machine, this had been a significant problem when prosecuting persons carrying out fraud by computer.

A major problem has been that of pornography, particularly child pornography, available over the internet. Maximum penalties for these and related offences have been significantly increased as has been the scope and reach of the offences. Another recent issue has been that of grooming children for sex, particularly through internet chat-rooms or by e-mail. An offence has been brought in specifically to deal with this problem. Other areas of criminal law are still useful in the fight against information and communications technologies crime such as the law of conspiracy to defraud, theft, blackmail and offences related to electronic communications networks.

Part 5 of the book deals with privacy and information, in particular, with the provisions of the Data Protection Act 1998. It also looks at the Freedom of Information Act 2000 and Regulations on privacy in electronic communications. The Data Protection Act 1998 imposes a considerable body of regulation on the processing of personal data on those who decide the means and purposes of the processing (data controllers). The 1998 Act marked a significant change in data protection law in the UK and gave individuals far more rights than they had under the previous legislation. Existing rights were enhanced. As well as a right of access, individuals have rights to prevent processing of personal data relating to them in certain circumstances, and rights in respect of automated decision taking, for example, where computer software is used to make decisions as to whether the individual will be given credit, or other decisions which significantly affect the individual. Data controllers also have to provide individuals with more information than was previously the case. It is obviously important for organisations and individuals processing personal data to know how the new data protection law impacts upon their processing activity, especially as there are several criminal penalties in the Act, and the Information Commissioner has strong powers of enforcement and criminal prosecution.

Access to information held by public authorities is given under the Freedom of Information Act 2000. This can be seen as parallel legislation to data protection law but is based on the principle of open government rather the privacy issue. There is an inevitable overlap with data protection law which was modified to address this. Rights to privacy in electronic communications extends to landlines and mobile phones. The amount of personal data that can be recorded, stored and further processed carries risks for privacy. For example, it is possible to locate the geographic location of a call from a mobile phone, the time and duration of the conversation, the number dialled and even the conversation itself. Another concern is the use of information and communications technologies to deliver unwanted marketing material.

Data protection is an area where good security is vitally important and obligations are placed on data controllers and those who process data for them such as an outsourcing company providing information technology facilities management. Indeed, a common thread running throughout the subject matter of this book is the need for good security and good housekeeping systems, the application of which will prevent or minimise many of the legal problems which can result from the use of information technology.

Although the main areas covered in this book appear to be quite distinct, it should be noted that there is considerable overlap. Contractual provisions can affect copyright issues and vice versa. Computer hackers can interfere with information which is confidential and which may be subject to copyright protection; additionally, hackers can cause difficulties for the owners and managers of computer systems with respect to their responsibilities and duties under the Data Protection Act 1998. There are clear links between electronic contracting and intellectual property and data protection. For example, a commercial website might contain material which infringes copyright and the capture of personal data from a person visiting the site has data protection implications. Employees, working under a contract of employment, may commit computer fraud, commit offences under data protection law and make pirate copies of computer programs, thereby infringing copyright, and so on. Social and ethical issues concern matters such as the ownership and dissemination of information, rights to privacy and freedom of expression.

A common theme in this book is the manner in which computer technology affects relationships between individuals in terms of rights and duties. Intellectual property endows rights on the owners of works of copyright or proprietors of patents to exploit their works or inventions while imposing a correlative duty on others not to do certain acts in relation to the subject matter of the rights. Contracts, whether conventional or electronic, are all about reciprocal rights and duties. The criminal law governing computer misuse imperfectly provides rights to computer owners not to have certain acts carried out in relation to the hardware or software while punishing those who fail in their duty to abide by this arm of criminal law. Data protection law imposes obligations on data users and grants rights to individuals who have their personal data stored on computer by others. Thus, an employed computer programmer has a duty not to copy his employer's software without permission, and has duties and rights flowing from his contract of employment. He has a duty not to engage in computer hacking, fraud or similar activities and a right to process personal data stored on his employer's computer in accordance with his contract of employment.

Another theme of a more practical nature is the importance of organisations developing policies with respect to the use of computer technology. For example, systems of auditing should be drawn up to check for unauthorised software, to check for computer viruses and fraud, and to verify that the use of personal data is lawful and in accordance with data protection law. Electronic commercial websites need to have clear and accessible terms and conditions of use and privacy policies, providing a good measure of transparency for persons visiting the sites. Policies and procedures should also be drawn up to deal with the acquisition and use of computer software, and educating users and employees should be a priority. Effective and responsible use of computer technology can only come through an understanding of the legal setting in which it takes place.

The last part of this book explores the professional, social and ethical issues underlying the use and exploitation of information and communication technologies. This brings a fresh perspective to examine the legal and practical implications of these technologies and the duties and responsibilities of professionals working on the development and application of them and those who make use of them, whether for personal or business purposes.

Diagrams and tables are included in this book at appropriate places to help with the identification and summarisation of the legal position and the practical implications. In line with standard legislative practice, as confirmed by section 6 of the Interpretation Act 1978, the masculine form, used throughout this book, should be taken to include the feminine form unless the contrary is stated.

Apart from this chapter, all chapters end with a brief summary followed by self-test questions, including up to four multiple choice questions and, in most cases, an essay-type question. The correct answers to the multiple choice questions are given towards the end of the book. The instructor's manual for the book contains more explanation of the correct answers together with outline answers to the essay-style questions, along with other materials including presentation slides with figures, charts and tables.

Part 1

Information technology and intellectual property

This part of the book deals with the branch of law known as 'intellectual property', which includes copyright law, patent law, trade marks, designs and related areas. The rights associated with intellectual property are of immense importance to those involved in the development, exploitation and use of computer hardware and software, and information technology generally. Legal remedies are available against those who unfairly seek to take advantage of the efforts and investment of someone else. However, the law strives to balance competing interests and the rights given by intellectual property law are not absolute.

Copyright law protects computer programs, databases and other works created using computers or stored in computers. Amending legislation passed in 1985 made it clear that computer programs were protected by copyright law and the current legislation, the Copyright, Designs and Patents Act 1988, confirms that computer programs, preparatory design material for computer programs and databases are literary works for copyright purposes. This Act also uses wide and flexible definitions to make sure, hopefully, that future technological development will not defeat copyright protection.

The law of confidence is a very useful supplement to other areas of intellectual property law and is particularly important in the context of research and development and in matters relating to employees, consultants and freelance workers.

New forms of computer hardware, large or small, usually fall within the province of patent law. Computer programs, as such, are specifically excluded from the grant of a patent but it appears that a program can still be part of a patent application if there is some technical effect which is more than just a software implementation of 'mental steps' or methods of doing business. As a patent is generally considered to be a more desirable form of intellectual property than copyright, there have been numerous attempts to protect computer programs, algorithms and other software inventions by patent law, meeting with varying degrees of success. There are, however, many patents for software in Europe and, in particular, in the US and other countries such as Japan and Australia.

Trade mark law, the law of passing off and design law are very important in terms of the commercial exploitation of products, including computer hardware and software. Integrated circuits have their own form of protection by virtue of regulations passed in 1989 which apply an amended form of the design right to semiconductor products.

2 Overview of intellectual property rights

INTRODUCTION

'Intellectual property' is the name given to legal rights which protect creative works, inventions and commercial goodwill. Basically, intellectual property rights are designed to provide remedies against those who steal the fruits of another person's ideas or work. For example, if a person writes a novel, a piece of music or a computer program, he will be able to take legal action to obtain an injunction preventing third parties from using it or otherwise exploiting it together with an award of damages or an account of profits and other remedies in respect of any unlawful use of the novel, music or computer program. In view of the large investment required to finance research, design and development in respect of computer hardware and software, these intellectual property rights are of vital importance to the computer industry and anyone involved in information technology in its widest sense. Without such protection, there would be little incentive to invest in the development of new products. Why spend large sums of money to develop a computer program that could be copied freely without recompense?

What are these intellectual property rights? Some will sound familiar – for example, *copyright, patents* and *trade marks* – while others will be less familiar – for example, the *law of confidence, design rights* and *passing off*. The scope of these rights differs but sometimes overlaps. Different rights may be appropriate at different times during the lifespan of a product from inception through development to marketing and subsequent modification and updating.

Primarily, intellectual property law is civil law and infringements are dealt with by the civil courts which also have important powers to grant interim remedies and preliminary orders before trial. These include search orders, interim injunctions and orders freezing a defendant's assets. Failure to comply with these orders is treated seriously as contempt of court and can result in imprisonment. There are also some criminal offences related to intellectual property rights, for example, in respect of software piracy and counterfeit goods bearing trade marks. Some of the offences now carry massive penalties, up to 10 years' imprisonment in some cases. This is a mark of the seriousness with which piracy and counterfeiting is now viewed by Parliament. The criminal offences under intellectual property law and associated offences are described in Chapter 14 in Part 2 of the book. At this stage, by way of introduction, it will be useful to describe briefly the various intellectual property rights.

COPYRIGHT LAW

As its name suggests, copyright protects works from being copied without permission. Copyright goes beyond mere copying, however, and extends to other activities such as making an adaptation of the work in question, performing or showing the work in public, communicating the work to the public (for example, by broadcasting it or placing it on a website from where it can be downloaded) and dealing with infringing copies of the work. The types of works protected by copyright are:

- literary works (including computer programs, preparatory design material for computer programs and databases);
- dramatic, musical and artistic works;
- sound recordings, films, broadcasts; and
- typographical arrangements of published editions.

Copyright protection has a long duration, the general yardstick being the life of the author (normally the creator of the work) plus 70 years or, depending on the type of work, 50 or 70 years from the end of the year during which the work was created or published. The major attractions of copyright as a form of protection are that it is free and that no formalities are required; it is automatic upon the creation of the work in question. Additionally, copyright law is practical in nature and has developed to take account of technological changes and advances. In short, most things, if they have been recorded in some tangible form (for example, by writing or printing or by storing the work on a magnetic or optical disk), are protected by copyright, subject to some basic requirements being satisfied. Copyright law is of vital importance to the computer software industry and to people who prepare, record or transmit all sorts of works (for example, literary works such as books, reports, letters or musical works) using computer technology and to those developing or operating websites. Copyright law is governed by the Copyright, Designs and Patents Act 1988, the main provisions of which came into force on 1 August 1989, and subsequent amendments, together with a wealth of case law.

Until the Copyright and Rights in Database Regulations 1997 came into force on 1 January 1998, databases were protected as compilations, being a form of literary work. Now, there are two forms of protection for databases. Those that are the 'author's own intellectual creation' have copyright protection as databases which also protects the structure of the database, while databases that are the result of a substantial investment are protected by a 'database right' which is of shorter duration than copyright. Strictly speaking, database right is a unique form of right and not a copyright as such though it has some similarities with copyright. The duration of database right is significantly less than for copyright, the basic term for protection being based on 15 years though modifications to a database can result in a new term of protection arising. Although the tests for subsistence of copyright and database right are different, in many cases, databases will be subject to both rights.

Some significant changes to copyright law were made to implement a Directive on copyright in the information society,[1] including specific provisions aimed at protecting electronic rights management information, such as the names of the copyright author and owner and details of the permitted uses of the work and in relation to the circumvention of technological measures designed to protect copyright works, for example, from unlawful copying or access. Regulations implementing the Directive made numerous other amendments to the Copyright, Designs and Patents Act 1988.

---

[1] Directive 2001/29/EC of the European Parliament and of the Council of 22 May 2001 on the harmonisation of certain aspects of copyright and related rights in the information society, OJ L 167, 22.06.2001, p. 10 (the 'Directive on copyright in the information society').

THE LAW OF CONFIDENCE

The law of confidence protects information which is not in the public domain. Unlike copyright and patent law, the law of confidence is not defined by statute and derives almost entirely from case law. The scope of this branch of intellectual property is considerable and it protects trade secrets, business know-how and information such as lists of clients and contacts, information of a personal nature and even ideas which have not yet been expressed in a tangible form (for example, an idea for a new dramatic play, an idea for a new computer program or a new method of doing business using e-commerce). The law of confidence will protect the contents of many databases. However, the major limitation is that the information concerned must be of a confidential nature and the effectiveness of the law of confidence is largely or completely destroyed if the information concerned falls into the public domain: that is, if it becomes available to the public at large or becomes common knowledge to a particular group of the public such as computer software companies. Nevertheless, the law of confidence can be a useful supplement to copyright and patent law as it can protect ideas before they are sufficiently developed to attract copyright protection or to enable an application for a patent to be made. Being rooted in equity, the law of confidence is very flexible and has proved capable of taking new technological developments in its stride. It is particularly important in the context of contracts with consultants, contractors and sub-contractors in the computer and information technology industries. It is also important in respect of employees and ex-employees and there is often a tension between a previous employer's confidential information and an ex-employee's right to make use of his own skill and experience including what he has learnt during his previous employment. The law of confidence attempts to protect employer's confidential information from unfair use but will draw short of protecting that employer from fair competition.

PATENT LAW

Patent law is concerned with new inventions such as a new type of computer hardware, or a new process for use in the manufacture of integrated circuits. For an invention to be protected by a patent formal application must be made to the relevant patent office, an expensive and lengthy process and, if granted, the patent can be renewed for a total period of up to 20 years. Three routes are open to the potential patentee: a UK patent; a European Patent Convention (EPC) patent applying in respect of three or more of the Member States of the Convention; or a Patent Co-operation Treaty (PCT) patent designating some or all of the countries covered by the treaty. The choice of countries in which to obtain protection is obviously of fundamental importance and requires careful planning and timing. One proviso is that a resident of the UK may not, under certain circumstances, file an application outside the UK for an invention relating to military technology or if its publication would be prejudicial to national security or public safety.

The relevant statute dealing with patent law in the UK is the Patents Act 1977. This Act was passed primarily as a response to the EPC and the basic requirements for patentability are consequently the same in the UK as in all other members of the Convention. Consequently, decisions at the European Patent Office (EPO) are very persuasive and there have been a number of influential decisions there concerning computer software inventions.

To be patentable, an invention must be new, involve an inventive step, be capable of industrial application and not be excluded. Most things which are protected directly by copyright law such as a literary work are excluded from patentability *as such*: therefore, a new computer program *as such* cannot normally be protected by a patent. The same applies to methods of doing business and performing a mental act. If there is an associated technical effect, however, a patent may be a possibility. For example, a new computer-controlled industrial process may be patentable even though the inventive step resides in the computer program. A patent is the form of intellectual property *par excellence* giving the nearest thing to an outright monopoly although there are provisions in UK law and European Community law (and US law) to prevent abuses of patents and other intellectual property rights.

A proposed Directive[2] could have had the effect of facilitating the patenting of software inventions if they made a non-obvious technical contribution to the state of the art in a technical field. Some countries, such as the US, have no specific restrictions for patenting software inventions. However, the proposed Directive was rejected by the European Parliament by a substantial majority and the status quo in Europe looks set to continue for some time.

TRADE MARKS AND PASSING OFF

Everyone is familiar with trade marks; they are very common and there are many examples in the computer industry: for example, the Apple logo, the terms 'Microsoft', 'Windows' and 'Adobe Acrobat' and the Dell monogram. Trade marks are often in the form of a word (sometimes stylised) or a symbol or both and registration is provided for by the Trade Marks Act 1994. Marks may be registered in respect of goods or services. To be registrable as a trade mark, the mark must be distinctive and capable of being represented graphically. Distinctiveness requires that the mark must be capable of distinguishing the goods or services of one undertaking from those of other undertakings. ('Undertaking' is the modern word used to describe a trader.) In other words, trade marks must function as 'badges of origin': their fundamental purpose is to indicate the origin of the goods or services in respect of which they have been used or applied. Trade marks are very important as they become associated with successful products and purchasers will often buy or order goods or services by reference to the mark. Marks such as 'Hoover' and 'Hovis' are examples which have become very closely associated with the products concerned. However, trade marks are in danger of being revoked if they become a generic name (common name) for goods or services as a result of the acts or inactivity of the proprietor. Business goodwill and reputation is protected by trade mark law and this has a secondary effect of also protecting the buying public from deceptive practices.

Trade marks are registered for specified goods and services. There is a classification system comprising 34 classes of goods and 11 classes for services. Data processing and computers are in Class 9 and the development of computer hardware and software falls in Class 42. Other classes may be relevant for information technology such as Class 35 for advertising, business management, business administration and office functions. There is no particular difficulty in registering graphic symbols, including moving images, displayed on computer screens and the like provided that they are distinctive. Colours and sounds may also be registrable as trade marks, though registration of a single colour may be quite difficult to achieve.

Apart from registering a trade mark in individual countries, there is also a Community trade mark which, like the Community design, has a unitary character and has effect throughout the European Community. As with the Community design, the Community trade mark is administered by the Office for the Harmonisation of the Internal Market (Trade Marks and Designs) ('OHIM'). The OHIM first started accepting applications to register trade marks at the begin-

---

[2] Proposal for a Directive of the European Parliament and of the Council on the patentability of computer-implemented inventions, COM(2002) 92 Final, Brussels, 20.02.2002.

ning of 1996 and the Community trade mark has proved to be very popular. The basic requirements are equivalent to those for the national trade mark, except on a Community-wide scale.

An area of law related to trade mark law is the law of passing off. This derives from the common law and gives a right of action against anyone who 'passes off' his goods or services as being those of someone else. If a trader uses a particular name or mark or has a particularly unusual method of doing business, he can obtain legal redress against others who use similar names or marks or business methods, especially if there is a serious possibility that the buying public will be deceived and the trader's business goodwill damaged as a result. The law of passing off is independent of trade mark law and will often be useful where a mark has not been registered as a trade mark. For the law of passing off to be effective, however, the trader concerned must have established a goodwill associated with the name or mark or business method. The agreeable alcoholic drink known as champagne affords an example. The French producers of champagne were able to prevent products called 'Spanish Champagne' and 'Elderflower Champagne' from being marketed under those names. In some respects, the law of passing off is wider than trade mark law where, to be registrable, the mark must conform to the requirements of the Trade Marks Act 1994 or the Community Trade Mark Regulation as appropriate. There is no such restriction with passing off, which can apply to marks which fall outside the scope of trade mark law and can also apply to other aspects of business and marketing.

Both trade mark law and the law of passing off have proved very important in the context of cybersquatting and the internet generally, for example, in terms of the territorial scope of infringement of a registered trade mark by placing a similar sign on a webpage and the use of trade marks in hidden meta-tags.

THE LAW RELATING TO DESIGNS

The statutory provisions covering rights in new designs are complicated and have been subject to considerable change and development. Essentially, under UK law there are two types of right: *registered designs* and a *design right* which is not subject to registration. The former is available for designs which are new and have an individual character, the latter being measured by the overall impression it produces on an informed user. For registered designs, a 'design' is the appearance of the whole or a part of a product resulting from the features of, in particular, the lines, contours, colours, shape, texture or materials of the product or its ornamentation. For designs subject to the design right, 'design' means the 'design of any aspect of the shape or configuration (whether external or internal) of the whole or part of an article'. This area of law is complex and this is compounded by the fact that the distinction between the rights is not easy to draw, as there is considerable overlap as regards the rights *inter se* and with respect to copyright law.

The durations of the rights are different, being a maximum of 25 years for registered designs and a maximum of 15 years for the design right (but limited to 10 years of commercial exploitation). For the last five years of the design right, licences of right are available. That means that anyone is entitled to a licence to copy the design. The licence will be subject to terms agreed between the parties or, failing agreement, to be fixed by the Comptroller of Patents, Designs and Trade Marks (the head of the Patent Office).

These two forms of rights in designs might be appropriate for items such as a new design for a computer mouse or a new design of laptop computer, keyboard or printer. Design rights and the exceptions to them also have implications for the manufacturers of spare parts, where the design is dictated by the shape of the article with which the spare part must fit or match, as we shall see. The registered design system is important especially in terms of the design of computer hardware as is, to some extent, the unregistered design right. However, the latter is particularly important in relation to the design of semiconductor products as a version of that right protects the topography or layout of such products. The appropriate statutes are the Registered Designs Act 1949 (as amended) and Part III of the Copyright, Designs and Patents Act 1988. The most significant recent amendment, implementing a Directive on the legal protection of designs[3] took place on 9 December 2001. This made major changes to the UK law on registered designs. These changes mean that typefaces and graphic symbols, including computer icons and other images, may now be registered as designs. This was not generally the case previously and represents a significant change for the computer software industry. Computer programs, however, may not be protected by either form of right.

To further complicate matters, a system of Community-wide design rights was introduced in 2003.[4] This provides for two forms of protection, a registered monopoly right very similar to the UK registered design and which also can be renewed for up to 25 years maximum, and an informal unregistered right which lasts for three years only. The unregistered right is subject to the same basic requirements as the registered right and is very different to the UK's unregistered design right. Consequently in the UK, it is possible to register a design under the UK's Registered Designs Act 1949, to register the design as a Community design, to claim a UK unregistered design right in the design and also to claim an unregistered Community design in it. Even without taking any action whatsoever, software 'designs' such as computer icons and fonts will have three years' protection throughout the European Community providing they are new and have individual character.

The Community design has a unitary character. This means that it cannot be assigned except in its entirety and if it is revoked it will be revoked in its entirety. It has effect throughout the European Community and is administered by the OHIM, which is based in Alicante, Spain.

SEMICONDUCTOR REGULATIONS

Integrated circuits are protected by virtue of the Design Right (Semiconductor) Regulations 1989 which apply a modified version of the design right to semiconductors. They are given 15 years' maximum protection (15 years from creation or 10 years from commercial exploitation, whichever is the lesser). As with the UK's unregistered design right generally, there is no requirement for registration in the UK and there are a number of similarities with copyright law. It is the 'topography' of the chip which is protected, that is, the patterns fixed in or upon the layers of the semiconductor or the arrangement of the layers of the semiconductor product.

Before looking at each of the intellectual property rights in more detail in the following chapters, Table 2.1 summarises the scope, duration and formalities associated with the various intellectual property rights.

---

[3] Directive 98/71/EC of the European Parliament and of the Council of 13 October 1998 on the legal protection of designs, OJ L 289, 28.10.1998, p. 28 (the 'Directive on the legal protection of designs').
[4] Council Regulation (EC) No 6/2002 of 12 December 2001 on Community designs, OJ L 3, 05.01.2002, p. 1 (the 'Community design Regulation').

Table 2.1 Intellectual property rights

Right	Types of works protected	Examples with respect to computers	Duration	Formalities (UK only)
Copyright	• Original literary, dramatic, musical or artistic works; • Sound recordings, films or broadcasts; • Typographical arrangement of published editions. (Computer programs, preparatory design material for computer programs and databases are literary works)	Computer programs and preparatory design material. Databases, other types of work made using a computer or generated by a computer: e.g. a weather forecast automatically made by a computer linked to weather satellites or a computer-aided design or music made using a computer. Almost any form of work in digital form	Generally 70 years from the end of the calendar year during which the author dies for the original works and films. For most of the other works the period is 50 years from a specific event	None Copyright is automatic upon the work being created. However, there are tests for subsistence, such as originality or that the work is the author's own intellectual creation
Confidence	Almost anything of a confidential nature (such as a trade secret or commercially important information not already in the public domain)	Idea for a new computer program or for a new invention (prior to patent), secret algorithm, lists of customers, business methods, contents of databases	Until subject matter falls into the public domain	None
Patent	New inventions including products and industrial processes	New type of printer or computer, new method of making integrated circuits, industrial process controlled by software	Renewable up to a maximum of 20 years	Formal application to the Patent Office with detailed specification, subject to search and examination to ensure requirements complied with
Registered trade marks	Any sign capable of being represented graphically which is capable of distinguishing goods or services of one undertaking from those of other undertakings	'Dell', 'Microsoft', 'Oracle', the Apple logo, 'Adobe Acrobat', 'Netscape'	Initially for 10 years and renewable in 10-year periods indefinitely	Formal application to register at the UK Trade Marks Registry

2

Overview of intellectual property rights

Table 2.1 continued

Right	Types of works protected	Examples with respect to computers	Duration	Formalities (UK only)
Passing off	Trade names and marks, product 'get-up' or style	Names of software and get-up around which a reputation associated with goodwill has been acquired and internet domain names	Indefinite as long as the name, get-up or style still associated with goodwill (e.g. by continued use)	None
Registered design (UK or Community registered design)	New designs, having an individual character through the eyes of the informed observer	The appearance of the whole or a part of a product resulting from the features of, in particular, the lines, contours, colours, shape, texture or materials of the product or its ornamentation: e.g. laptop computer, mouse, computer peripherals and accessories, computer fonts and icons	Initially 5 years renewable by 5-year periods up to a maximum of 25 years	Registration by application to the Design Registry at the Patent Office
Community unregistered design	As for registered designs	As for registered designs	3 years	None – automatic as with copyright
UK unregistered design right	Original designs, being any aspect of shape or configuration (external or internal) of the whole or part of an article. Applies to functional and aesthetic designs. Spare parts and surface decoration excluded	CD or DVD storage system (partly), keyboard design, mouse, internal components if not commonplace	15 years from creation or 10 years from first marketing (licences of right available during last five years)	None – automatic as with copyright
Semiconductor Regulations (modified form of the UK design right)	Topography (patterns or arrangements of layers within integrated circuit)	Original design of integrated circuit which is not commonplace	15 years from creation or 10 years from commercial exploitation (licences of right not generally available during the last five years)	None

Note: as far as periods for protection are concerned, for copyright, the design right and the Semiconductor Regulations, these periods are measured from the end of the calendar year during which the relevant event occurred, for example, the creation of the work or the death of the author.

SUMMARY

- Copyright can protect computer programs, their preparatory design material and databases.
- The law of confidence protects trade secrets, confidential technical and commercial information.
- New software inventions may be patentable in some cases.
- Trade marks for computer hardware and software companies can be registered as trade marks.
- The law of passing off can be useful in the fight against cybersquatting.
- Some forms of design law can protect graphic images and software fonts.
- The topography of semiconductor products is protected if original and not commonplace.

SELF-TEST QUESTIONS

Note: there is only one correct answer to each multiple choice question.

1   **Which one of the following statements is NOT CORRECT?**

   (a) Copyright protection for computer programs endures until 70 years after the end of the year in which the author of the program dies.

   (b) A computer program can never be part of a patentable invention.

   (c) If they are new and have individual character, computer icons and symbols displayed on computer screen can be protected by registration as a design.

   (d) To be registrable as a trade mark, a sign must be capable of being represented graphically and capable of distinguishing the goods and services of one undertaking from those of other undertakings.

2   **Which one of the following statements is CORRECT in relation to databases?**

   (a) Databases are protected by copyright as literary works, being compilations.

   (b) To be protected by copyright, a database must be novel and the result of a substantial investment.

   (c) To be protected by copyright, a database must be the author's own intellectual creation.

   (d) A database can never be protected by both copyright and the database right.

3   **Which one of the following statements is NOT CORRECT?**

   (a) The fundamental purpose of a trade mark is to indicate the origin of goods or services.

   (b) A trade mark cannot be registered for software development services as such services do not fall within the classification of goods and services for which trade marks may be registered.

   (c) It is possible for a graphic symbol to be protected by both the Community design and by registration as a trade mark.

   (d) The law of passing off protects a trader's goodwill.

4   **Which one of the following statements is CORRECT?**

   (a) The topography of a semiconductor product is protected by a modified version of the UK's unregistered design right.

(b) The topography of a semiconductor product is protected by registration as a UK registered design.

(c) The topography of a semiconductor product is protected by copyright as a form of literary work.

(d) The topography of a semiconductor product is not protected by any intellectual property rights.

For further resources and updates please go to the Companion Website accompanying this book at **www.mylawchamber.co.uk/bainbridgeIT**

3 Basic principles of copyright

Note: in Chapters 3 to 7, unless otherwise stated, section numbers quoted refer to the Copyright, Designs and Patents Act 1988, as amended.

FUNDAMENTALS

Copyright protects a wide range of works and has developed enormously since its early beginnings as an important intellectual property right. Copyright has a pragmatic approach and it extends to a wide range of works regardless of quality, subject to some basic requirements, which are usually easily satisfied. Since the end of the nineteenth century, tables, compilations and even codebooks have been the subject matter of copyright law. During the twentieth century, copyright law flourished and it now includes under its umbrella the following: photographs, films, broadcasts, sound recordings as well as computer programs, preparatory design material for computer programs, databases and all manner of works in digital form and works created by or with the aid of a computer. The first developments in the twenty-first century were to address issues relating to copyright and neighbouring rights (for example, rights in live performances) associated with the information society. The practical development of copyright has been supported by the judges who have usually been sympathetic to the principle of protecting the results of a person's skill, effort or judgment. As Peterson J said in *University of London Press Ltd* v *University Tutorial Press Ltd* [1916] 2 Ch 601:

> ... what is worth copying is *prima facie* worth protecting.

However, this may go too far and the first work must be the result of skill and judgment. As Pumfrey J said in *Cantor Fitzgerald International* v *Tradition (UK) Ltd* [2000] RPC 95:

> ... it is possible that entirely mechanical labour may be saved by copying something produced by entirely mechanical labour, involving no skill.

Taking a photograph of an object will usually require some degree of skill expended by the photographer even if the object photographed is fairly mundane. Skill may derive from the choice of angle, lighting and positioning of the object. These factors may endow the photograph with sufficient skill in its making to attract copyright protection. However, subsequently reducing the object in the photograph to a simplified outline, for example, as use as a watermark on a webpage, will not result in a new work of copyright as it is unlikely that any of the original aspects of the photograph would be carried through into the watermark and it would be doubtful that the process of creating the watermark would require the necessary skill to make it original for copyright purposes. So it was held by Neuberger J in *Antiquesportfolio.com plc* v *Rodney Fitch & Co Ltd* [2001] FSR 23.

COPYRIGHT WORKS

Copyright is declared to subsist (that is, 'exist') in the following works by virtue of section 1 of the Copyright, Designs and Patents Act 1988:

(a) original literary, dramatic, musical or artistic works;

(b) sound recordings, films or broadcasts; and

(c) the typographical arrangement of published editions;

provided that the requirements for qualification are met: for example, that the author of an original literary work is a British citizen or has certain other nationality or residential qualifications, or that the work was first published in the UK. Literary works include computer programs, preparatory design material for computer programs and databases.

The first category of works is expressed as being 'original'. This does not mean that the work must be unique or special in any way. It is sufficient that the work is the result of the skill or judgment on the part of the creator of the work and that it has not been copied from another work. In other words, it has *originated* from its creator. For one of these original works, the test is qualified and for copyright databases, they are required to be the author's own intellectual creation, as discussed in more detail in Chapter 5. Technically, this should also be the test for computer programs as stated in the Directive on the legal protection of computer programs,[1] but the UK did not include that definition in the Copyright, Designs and Patents Act 1988 when implementing that Directive.

Databases may also be protected by a right known as the database right which can be described as a right related to copyright. The database right was introduced as a means of protecting databases that are the result of a substantial investment even though they might not otherwise meet the requirements for copyright protection. Nevertheless, the two rights are not mutually exclusive and, in some cases, databases will be protected by both copyright and the database right. This can be useful as the scope and protection afforded by both rights is different. The database right is the result of the Directive on the legal protection of databases,[2] where it was described as a *sui generis* right, meaning it is a right of its own kind or unique. The database right is described further in Chapter 5 along with copyright in relation to databases.

OWNERS AND AUTHORS

The owner of the copyright in a work is then given the exclusive right to do certain specified *restricted acts* in relation to the work, described below. The basic rule is that the first owner of a copyright is the author of the work (the person creating it). A major exception applies in the case of a work made by an employee in the course of his employment. Where this is so, the employer will be the first owner of the copyright, unless otherwise agreed (section 11). There are other exceptions to the basic rule, such as in the case of Crown copyright and copyright belonging to certain international organisations such as the United Nations. The Copyright, Designs and Patents Act 1988 usually refers to the creator of a work as the 'author' of the work, thus a person writing a piece of music is the author of the music and a photographer is the author of his

---

[1] Council Directive 91/250/EEC of 14 May 1991 on the legal protection of computer programs, OJ L 122, 17.05.1991, p. 42 (the 'Directive on the legal protection of computer programs').

[2] Directive 96/9/EC of the European Parliament and of the Council of 11 March 1996 on the legal protection of databases, OJ L 77, 27.03.1996, p. 20 (the 'Directive on the legal protection of databases').

photographs. For sound recordings and computer-generated works, the author is the person who makes the arrangements necessary for the making or creation of the work (section 9), so the author of a report produced automatically by a computer will normally be the person who loads and operates the software in order to create the work. In many cases, ownership, as distinct from authorship, will reside initially with an employer.

DURATION OF COPYRIGHT

Regardless of who the present owner of a copyright is, the identity of the author is important because the duration of copyright in original literary, dramatic, musical or artistic works (not being computer-generated) is determined by the life of the author, irrespective of ownership. The copyright in such works lasts for 70 years from the end of the calendar year during which the author dies. This was increased from the life of the author plus 50 years as a result of the Directive on the term of copyright.[3] The duration of copyright in films is now also based on life plus 70 years, measured from the end of the calendar year during which the last of a number of persons, including the principal director, involved in the creation of the film, dies.

The US also increased its term of protection to 'life plus 70 years' by the Copyright Term Extension Act 1998. This Act is referred to as the Sonny Bono Copyright Term Extension Act out of respect for Sonny Bono (originally part of the Sonny and Cher singing duo), a congressman who died in a skiing accident but who had supported the extension of the term of copyright for songs and films. The increase in protection to 70 years was subject to a challenge that, in terms of published and existing works, it was unconstitutional as being contrary to the First Amendment (free speech) and the Copyright Clause in Article I, section 8, cl. 8 of the Constitution which states that Congress has the power, *inter alia*, to secure to authors for *limited times* the exclusive right to their writing. The Supreme Court rejected these claims in *Eldred v Ashcroft, Attorney General*, 537 US 186 (2003). The increase of 20 years' protection for existing works did not prevent the protection being for *limited times* and as the First Amendment and the Copyright Clause were adopted closely together this indicates that the view of those framing these provisions was that the limited monopoly provided by copyright was compatible with free speech principles.

If the work in question is one of joint authorship (a collaborative work in which the contribution of each author is not distinct from that of the other authors), as many computer programs and other computer works are, the 70-year period starts to run from the end of the calendar year during which the last surviving author dies. This generosity in terms of duration of copyright might seem disproportionate in a fast-moving technology but can be justified on the basis that, generally, copyright does not give a true monopoly, just a right to prevent others copying the work or doing certain other acts in relation to it. A rough and ready rule of thumb is that copyright does not protect ideas, merely the expression of an idea.

For other works, except films where the 70-year period is used, the duration is set at 50 years from the end of the calendar year during which the work was created, made available to the public or released, as appropriate. For sound recordings the situation is fairly complex and the copyright lasts for:

- 50 years from the end of the calendar year during which the sound recording was made;
- if published during that period, 50 years from the end of the calendar year when it was first published; or

---

[3] Council Directive 93/98/EEC of 29 October 1993 harmonising the term of protection of copyright and certain related rights, OJ L 290, 24.11.1993, p. 9 (the 'Directive on the term of copyright').

- if not so published but it is made available to the public by playing it in public or communicating it to the public (this includes making it available online on a website) during that 50 year period, the copyright lasts for 50 years from the end of the calendar year when it was made available to the public.

There are some exceptions to the basic rules and copyright in typographical arrangements of a published edition lasts for 25 years from the end of the calendar year during which the edition was first published and certain commercially exploited artistic works have effective protection for 25 years only (other exceptions apply to Crown copyright and Parliamentary copyright and to original works of unknown authorship).

The author's identity may also be important for determining whether a work qualifies for protection. It should be noted, however, that there are two international conventions affording, in effect, reciprocal protection to foreign works of copyright and which also protect UK works in other countries. In general terms, nationals of other convention countries are afforded the same rights as those of the country in question which, under the conventions, extend their copyright to nationals of other countries which are members of the conventions.

THE ACTS RESTRICTED BY COPYRIGHT

Copyright functions by granting specific rights to the owner of the work: only the copyright owner is allowed to perform, or authorise others to perform, certain types of activity in relation to the copyright work. These activities are referred to as the acts restricted by copyright, and are set out in section 16 of the Copyright, Designs and Patents Act 1988. The following are the acts restricted by the copyright and only the owner can do or authorise others:

(a) to copy the work;

(b) to issue copies of the work to the public;

(ba) to rent or lend the work to the public;

(c) to perform, show or play the work in public;

(d) to communicate the work to the public;

(e) to make an adaptation of the work or do any of the above in relation to an adaptation.

Section 16(ba) was inserted by the Copyright and Related Rights Regulations 1996 to comply with the Directive on rental right and lending right.[4] Section 16(b) was also modified to cover all forms of copyright work and section 16(d) was changed to include broadcasting the work and making it available by electronic transmission such that persons can access the work at a place and time of their choosing (typically, by accessing the work from a website). This was a result of implementing the Directive on copyright and related rights in the information society.[5]

---

[4] Council Directive 92/100/EEC of 19 November 1992 on rental right and lending right and on certain rights related to copyright in the field of intellectual property, OJ L 346, 27.11.1992, p. 61 (the 'Directive on rental right and lending right').

[5] Directive 2001/29/EC of the European Parliament and of the Council of 22 May 2001 on the harmonisation of certain aspects of copyright and related rights in the information society, OJ L 167, 22.06.2001, p. 10 (the 'Directive on copyright in the information society').

INFRINGEMENT

A person infringes the copyright in a work if he does one of these restricted acts, or authorises another to do one of the acts, in relation to a substantial part of the work without the permission of the copyright owner and such a person may be sued by the copyright owner (or an exclusive licensee of the owner or even a non-exclusive licensee who has been granted a right of action by the owner) for the infringement. The infringing act may be direct (for example, making a photocopy or a disk to disk copy) or indirect (for example, making a clay model of a sculpture from a photograph of the sculpture,

The similarities and differences between the first work and the alleged infringement may be important in finding whether the defendant had copied the first work (copying is one form of infringement though all forms of infringement require that some use has been made of the first work). The independent creation of a work which happens to be similar to an existing work does not infringe the copyright in that existing work. Whether the part taken is substantial is a question of fact but once it is accepted that the defendant's work was copied from that of the claimant, it is no longer relevant to consider the differences between the two works (to do so would be to revisit the question of whether copying had taken place). The question then becomes whether the sum of the parts copied represent a substantial part of the claimant's work. A visual comparison of the two works at this stage is unnecessary and may be misleading. The majority of the House of Lords judges took this view in *Designers Guild Ltd* v *Russell Williams (Textiles) Ltd* [2001] FSR 113, a leading case on copyright infringement set in the context of artistic works, though of wider application. However, Lord Scott of Foscote distinguished a case of altered copying where he suggested that the similarities between the two works could help determine which side of the dividing line, between permissible borrowing of an idea and impermissible piracy, the activity fell, accepting that it is not an infringement of copyright to borrow an idea. Another important principle is that substantiality must focus on the claimant's work not that of the defendant. It may be that a substantial part of the claimant's work has been incorporated into the defendant's work but, because of the inclusion of further additional material, it does not represent a substantial part of the defendant's work. Essentially, to prove copyright infringement by copying, all the following four questions must be answered in the affirmative.

- Is the claimant's work protected by copyright?
- Has the claimant the entitlement to sue, for example, as the owner of the copyright or a licensee with entitlement to sue?
- If so, has the defendant copied from the claimant's work?
- If so, does that part of the claimant's work copied represent a substantial part of the claimant's work?

EXCEPTIONS TO INFRINGEMENT AND THE PERMITTED ACTS

There are some defences to copyright infringement at common law, such as public interest and where the copyright owner has acquiesced in the infringement. For example, it might be in the public interest to copy information concerning a computer virus for circulation to the appropriate authorities and organisations. The same would apply to copying material, such as e-mail correspondence between two organisations engaged in illegal price-fixing, to send to the Competition Commission. Acquiescence would apply where the copyright owner impliedly consented to an infringement he later complained about. Another defence is estoppel, an example, being where a copyright owner, with full knowledge, encouraged and allowed someone to carry out infringing acts in relation to his copyright work.

The Copyright, Designs and Patents Act 1988 also contains a large number of exceptions to copyright infringement called the permitted acts. These are contained in sections 28 to 76 of the Act and cover a vast range of acts that may be done without the copyright owner's licence and without infringing copyright. Of course, these permitted acts are only relevant if the activity complained of would otherwise infringe copyright. Take the following examples:

- Alan lends his paper copy of a novel to his friend Barry to read – this does not infringe copyright as lending a book to a friend is not a restricted act.

- Alan copies out a few paragraphs from the novel using his word processor. This does not infringe as a few paragraphs are unlikely to be considered to be a substantial part of the novel.

- Alan is a student who copies a few pages from a journal article for the purposes of his own private study. Although a few pages from an article may constitute a substantial part of the article, Alan can rely on the permitted act of fair dealing for research or private study. (Note: if the article is in the library of the college attended by Alan, he may be permitted to copy the whole article under a licensing scheme if the college has taken a licence from a collecting society such as the Copyright Licensing Agency.)

- Alan decides to record an entire television programme broadcast at a time when he is at college so he can watch it later at his convenience. He uses his own equipment at his home to do so. This does not infringe as it is covered by the permitted act of 'time-shifting'.

In respect of the last permitted act 'time-shifting', this only applies where the recording is made on domestic premises for private and domestic use. An internet café which operated a CD burning service for its customers in return for payment of a fee could not rely on the defence as confirmed in *Sony Music Entertainment (UK) Ltd* v *Easyinternetcafe Ltd* [2003] EWHC 62 (Ch). This case also confirms that liability for infringement applies even if the person responsible for copying was not aware the work being copied was protected by copyright. The defendant's employees were instructed not to look at the content of the downloaded files they copied on to CDs for customers.

There are some important permitted acts for computer programs introduced by the Copyright (Computer Programs) Regulations 1992 which implemented the Directive on the legal protection of computer programs. These permitted acts allow a lawful user of a computer program to:

- 'decompile' a computer program under certain circumstances in order to create a new independent program that will operate with the program decompiled or another program;

- make back-up copies of computer programs if necessary for lawful use of the program;

- observe, study and test the functioning of a computer program in order to determine the program's underlying ideas and principles (confirming that copyright does not protect ideas) whilst carrying out certain acts the lawful user is entitled to do;

- copy or adapt the computer program if necessary for lawful use providing the act is not prohibited by the agreement regulating the lawful use. This could apply, in particular, to copying or making adaptations for the purposes of error correction.

There is also a permitted act covering databases. This allows a person having a right to use a database (or part of a database) to access and use the contents of that database or part thereof.

An intermediary, such as an internet service provider, in the process of transmitting material through its equipment, makes temporary copies of works of copyright. These may be held for a short period of time in a cache or other form of storage. As even making a transient copy of a work of copyright infringes that copyright, there is a special permitted act which applies in such cases. The permitted act covers the original works of copyright (apart from computer programs and databases) sound recordings and films and typographical arrangements. The copyright in these works is not infringed by making a transient or incidental copy, for example, for the purpose of onward transmission, providing that making the copy has no independent economic significance.

These permitted acts relating to computer programs, databases and copies made by intermediaries are considered in more detail in the following two chapters.

SECONDARY INFRINGEMENT AND CRIMINAL OFFENCES

There are additional ways of infringing copyright, known as secondary infringements, which typically apply where someone is dealing in infringing copies (such as selling unauthorised copies of software) and there are also some criminal offences which now carry a maximum penalty of a term of imprisonment not exceeding 10 years and/or a fine. Some of the criminal offences are very similar to the equivalent form of secondary infringement. For example, a trader who is selling unauthorised copies of copyright software, knowing or having reason to believe that they are infringing copies, is liable under civil law for secondary infringement and also commits a criminal offence under copyright law.

Distributing an article which is an infringing copy of a work of copyright to such an extent as to prejudicially affect the owner of the copyright is a secondary infringement of copyright and a criminal offence. This is so even if the person responsible is not distributing the article in the course of business provided he knows or has reason to believe that it is an infringing copy. This could apply where a person places an infringing copy of a work of copyright on a website so that it can be accessed or downloaded by large numbers of third parties.

Until the 1980s, the criminal offences under copyright law did not attract liability for imprisonment, the maximum penalty being a modest fine. The reason the penalties have been increased is a reflection of the damage done to copyright owners by counterfeiting operations and, more lately, the involvement of organised crime in such activities. As copyright is a form of property, it can fairly be said that deliberately infringing copyright is tantamount to theft. Interestingly, for a conviction for theft the prosecution has to prove, *inter alia*, dishonesty. The threshold for copyright offences is lower, being that the accused knew or had reason to believe that the copy he was dealing with was an infringing copy, that is, that its making infringed copyright or, where it has been imported into the UK, it would have infringed copyright had it been made in the UK or it was made in breach of an exclusive licence agreement.

REMEDIES FOR INFRINGEMENT

If the owner of a copyright successfully sues a person for infringement of that copyright, there are a number of potential remedies available. In particular, an injunction, damages or, as an alternative to damages, an account of profits might be appropriate and these are provided for by section 96. The basic purpose of an award of damages is to put the claimant in the position he would have been in but for the infringement, as far as a money award can do that. The award should reflect the natural and foreseeable consequences of the infringing acts. Copyright damages may be assessed as the estimated loss resulting from the infringement: for example, where the copyright owner grants licences in respect of the work, damages may be based on the licence fee or royalties that the copyright owner would have expected to receive had he given permission for the acts complained of.

If a computer software pirate makes and sells 1,000 copies of an item of computer software each valued at £500, the copyright owner might expect damages equivalent to a 10 per cent royalty: that is, 10% × 1,000 × £500 = £50,000. This is somewhat of an oversimplification and other factors may affect the final award, such as the impact on the copyright owner's business (for example, if he also sold copies and lost sales as a result or had to reduce prices to compete with the infringer). Interest will also usually be awarded, based on the quantum of damages and the time elapsed since the infringement and costs usually follow the event. The losing party will usually have to pay his own legal costs and those of the other party. In some cases, these costs can outweigh the award of damages.

Damages are not available if the defendant did not know or had no reason to believe that the work was protected by copyright. The meaning of 'having no reason to believe that copyright subsisted in a work' requires an objective test: that is, whether the reasonable person, having knowledge of the facts known to the defendant, would have believed that copyright subsisted in the work; confirmed in a case involving sportswear shoes: *LA Gear Inc* v *Hi-Tec Sports plc* [1992] FSR 121. An infringer of computer software copyright cannot escape an award of damages merely by turning a blind eye to the question of whether the software is protected by copyright or being indifferent to the possibility. In any case, an account of profits, as an alternative to damages, may be available regardless of the defendant's knowledge and could be awarded even where the person infringing copyright has done so innocently. Of course, software piracy can attract criminal penalties also (see Chapter 12).

Injunctions are very important because they prevent a continued or anticipated infringement of copyright. An injunction is a court order requiring the defendant to do something or to refrain from doing something. For example, an injunction would be appropriate to stop a computer software pirate continuing to sell unauthorised copies of computer programs. A particularly useful type of injunction is an interim injunction (previously known as an interlocutory injunction). If a person is sued for infringing copyright, it may be a considerable time before the case comes to trial and, in the meantime, significant damage may be done to the copyright owner's business. This is very relevant in the context of a fast-moving technology like computer technology and, to deal with this problem, the court may be willing to accede to a request for an interim injunction pending the full trial. However, an interim injunction will be granted to a claimant only if there is a serious question to be tried and the claim does not appear to the court to be frivolous or vexatious. Additionally, the balance of convenience must be satisfied, meaning that the damage likely to be done to the claimant if the alleged infringement continues is greater than the harm that will be done to the defendant if the injunction is granted (see *NWL Ltd* v *Woods* [1979] 1 WLR 1294). This balance of convenience is of particular importance if the granting or refusal of an interim injunction would have very serious consequences for either party. In any case, an interim injunction will not usually be granted if the payment of damages by the defendant if he loses at the full trial would be an adequate remedy and the defendant is likely to have the means to pay, not being a 'man of straw'.

For an interim injunction to be a possibility, the courts used to require that the claimant showed a serious issue to be tried. However, since the case of *Series 5 Software Ltd* v *Clarke* [1996] FSR 273, the courts have been more willing to consider the relative strengths of the parties' cases as they appear at that stage. If there is material before the court to allow the court to assess the strength of the parties' cases, it should be taken into account in deciding whether or not to grant an interim injunction. In *Series 5 Software*, the defendant removed software belonging to the claimant allegedly in order to encourage the latter to make payment owing to the defendant. The injunctions sought were refused but the judge continued an order for the defendant to deliver up any materials he had which belonged to the claimant. If the defendant had any such materials in his possession and failed to deliver them, he would be in contempt of court.

A distinction between an honest and a dishonest trader might be relevant in determining the terms of any interim injunction and any ancillary relief granted. In *Microsoft Corporation* v *Plato Technology Ltd* [1999] FSR 834, the defendant had sold five copies of counterfeit Windows 95 software infringing the claimant's copyright and trade marks. It was accepted that the defendant had no reason to believe that the copies were counterfeit (he could be liable only for primary infringement and neither secondary infringement nor the criminal offences were relevant) and an interim injunction was granted restraining the defendant from dealing with software which it knew or ought upon reasonable enquiry to know was counterfeit. The defendant was also required to deliver up all copies in its possession which it knew or ought upon reasonable enquiry to know was counterfeit.

Apart from an award of ordinary damages, the courts also have a discretion to award additional damages under section 97(2), having regard to the flagrancy of the infringement and the benefit accruing to the defendant. This is akin to punitive damages though, strictly speaking, technically distinguishable. Additional damages are suitable in cases where normal damages would not be appropriate: for example, where the defendant has blatantly infringed copyright thinking that he can make a profit far in excess of any normal damages he might have to pay. Another possible use for additional damages is where the claimant has not suffered purely economic loss. This might be the case if the infringement concerned some material which the claimant did not want to publish such as the contents of his diary. In *Williams* v *Settle* [1960] 1 WLR 1072, additional damages were considered suitable when a professional photographer, without permission of the copyright owner, supplied the press with a wedding photograph showing a man who had been murdered.

Additional damages may also be appropriate where a normal award of damages still left the defendant in a favourable position, enjoying the fruits of his infringement, especially where those fruits were non-economic and not recoverable on the basis of an account of profits. Furthermore, such damages could be used to deprive a defendant of the benefit of deliberate wrongdoing when they would not be awarded against someone who did the same thing in innocence. In *Nottinghamshire Healthcare National Health Service Trust* v *News Group Newspapers Ltd* [2002] RPC 49 a photograph of a patient at Rampton Hospital was copied without permission and published by the defendant with a sensationalistic article. An award of £450 for ordinary damages was made together with an award for additional damages to bring the overall total up to £10,000. This was justified on the basis that the defendant had reaped a significant economic benefit from publication of a photograph that was obviously 'stolen' and the lack of an apology, together with the degree of upset to the claimant, which had taken over control of Rampton Hospital and been responsible for the medical records from which the copy of the photograph had been taken without permission.

Recently, claimants seem more prepared to ask for additional damages. In relation to computer software, such damages may be relevant in the case of blatant infringement, for example, by deliberately using someone else's specialised computer software to gain a competitive edge over that other person. Another example is where a person deliberately makes use of another person's database of highly sensitive information. It has been confirmed that additional damages may only be awarded alongside ordinary damages and not an account of profits. A claimant has to elect between damages and an account of profits and cannot ask for both.

In addition to the remedies mentioned above, the claimant may apply to the court for an order for the infringing copies to be delivered up to him or for those copies to be destroyed.

Although relatively unusual in this context, there is nothing to prevent a copyright owner later bringing a civil action against a person convicted of criminal offences under copyright law. In such a case section 11(2)(a) of the Civil Evidence Act 1968 applies and states that, in civil proceedings, evidence of a conviction is proof that a person has committed the offence unless the contrary is proved. Section 11(2)(b) makes admissible in evidence the contents of the indictments to identify the facts on which the convictions were based. In *Microsoft Corporation v Alibhai* [2004] EWHC 3282 (Ch), the defendants had been convicted of a conspiracy to defraud by distributing counterfeit copies of Microsoft software. Microsoft later brought a civil action. Summary judgment was given in favour of Microsoft but the judge refused to grant an interim order for payment of damages pending a full inquiry into damages as Microsoft had not adduced sufficient evidence of its loss. Microsoft had claimed over £11 million in damages. The software pirates had been sentenced to 4½ years' imprisonment in 2002.

COPY PROTECTION AND ELECTRONIC RIGHTS MANAGEMENT INFORMATION

Before implementing the Directive on copyright and related rights in the information society, the Copyright, Designs and Patents Act 1988 contained remedies against persons who where instrumental in overcoming copy-protection for computer programs, for example, by selling devices designed or adapted to overcome copy-protection or publishing relevant information to enable individuals to overcome copy-protection. The Directive provided a whole raft of provisions to deal with this issue in relation to all forms of copyright works and the database right, and rights related to copyright. There were exceptions, especially in relation to computer programs which continued to be dealt with under the Directive on the legal protection of computer programs.

The Copyright and Related Rights Regulations 2003 implemented the Directive on copyright and related rights in the information society with effect from 31 October 2003 and provide two forms of protection against overcoming technological measures aimed at protecting works from unauthorised use. One set applies to works other than computer programs whilst the other set of provisions applies otherwise.

Another feature of the Directive implemented by the Regulations was the protection of electronic rights management information. This includes information identifying the author and owner and the uses to which the work might lawfully be put to. The perceived danger was that a person might make a copy of a work and, after removing such information, make it widely available for others to access, for example, by placing it on or linking to it, from a webpage. Third parties accessing it might think they could copy or distribute it as they wished with the result that the economic interests of the owner and the moral rights of the author could be seriously prejudiced. These particular provisions are explored in more depth in Chapter 7.

MORAL RIGHTS

Moral rights were a relatively new concept in the UK when introduced by sections 77–89 of the Copyright, Designs and Patents Act 1988. These rights, which have long been recognised in some European countries, are independent and distinct from ownership of copyright and give the author of a literary, dramatic, musical or artistic work and the director of a film the right:

- to be identified as the author (or director) of the work;
- to object to a derogatory treatment of the work (for example, if someone rewrites a serious play in the form of a smutty farce without the author's permission); and

- to not have a work falsely attributed to him (this right previously existed under the Copyright Act 1956).

There is also a right to privacy with respect to photographs and films made for private and domestic purposes.

These moral rights last as long as the copyright in the work, with the exception of the false attribution right which lasts for 20 years after the death of the person falsely attributed. The rights are designed to give the creator of the work, who may no longer be the owner of the copyright itself, a degree of recognition and control in respect of the work. By section 103, infringements of moral rights are treated as a breach of statutory duty, injunctions and damages being appropriate remedies. There is no provision for additional damages. However, the claimant may also have a claim in defamation, particularly in respect of a derogatory treatment of his work or the false attribution of a work.

As computer programs are considered to be literary works, it is surprising that the first two of the moral rights mentioned above are stated not to apply to computer programs. Less surprisingly, nor do they apply to computer-generated works. These exceptions may be justified because of the commercial nature of most computer programs and other software and because of the need to prevent ex-employees from attempting to interfere with any future changes to the software they had previously worked on. Problems could arise if computer programmers, systems analysts or software developers demanded to be recognised as authors. Much computer software is the result of teamwork, involving many individuals, both in its original development and creation and in respect of subsequent alterations and upgrades.

Moral rights will exist in relation to other forms of original works created using a computer, such as a report or computer-aided design (unless a computer-generated work), and in respect of many other types of work stored in a computer in digital form, for example, in a database of artistic works. However, employee-created works are excepted in relation to things done by or with the licence of the copyright owner and the author must positively assert his moral right to be identified. Furthermore, an author may waive his moral rights.

DEALING WITH COPYRIGHT

It is important to appreciate that copyright is a property right and it can be dealt with as with other forms of property. It can be sold or licences may be granted in respect of it. It can even be used as security for a loan. Often, the owner of a copyright will want to use someone else to exploit that copyright for him. It might be more attractive financially to use an established publisher to market and sell copies of the work, because the latter will have the marketing expertise and distribution facilities necessary to sell the work in large numbers. The usual way is for the copyright owner to grant a licence to the publisher. In terms of copyright, a licence is a permission to do one or more of the acts restricted by copyright and licences are usually contractual in nature: that is, the publisher will pay a licence fee or royalties in return for the permission. In many cases, the licence will be exclusive, which means that permission will be granted to one publisher only. In the case of marketing computer programs, the copyright owner might grant an exclusive licence to a software publisher who will then grant non-exclusive user licences to 'purchasers' of copies of the program. The users will need licences because loading a program onto a hard disk or into computer memory involves making a copy or adaptation of the program, acts restricted by the copyright. By section 92(1), an exclusive licence must be in writing and signed by or on behalf of the owner of the copyright. No formalities are required for non-exclusive licences but it is sensible to make a written record of the agreement.

Non-exclusive software licences are very common and are used where the copyright owner wishes to retain ownership but wants to allow several or many other persons to use the software. This is the way a great deal of popular software is made available, such as operating systems software, word processing, database management and spreadsheet software. Each person acquiring a copy of the software obtains a non-exclusive licence permitting certain uses. Of course, a licence is only required in as much as the use of software is controlled by copyright but the agreement will include additional terms dealing with other issues such as liability for defects. An important consideration that applies to software is that simply using it is a restricted act as making transient copies falls within the meaning of copying. Thus, loading software into a computer's random access memory is making a copy of it even though that copy no longer exists once the application is closed or the computer switched off.

As an alternative to licensing the copyright, the owner may *assign* the copyright (that is, transfer ownership of the copyright) to another person and an assignment must be distinguished from a licence. With an assignment, the copyright owner transfers all or part of his rights to another person, whereas a licence is a permission given to another person authorising him to do certain specified things in relation to the copyright work. Furthermore, ownership in copyright can pass under a will or by way of intestacy or as a result of the bankruptcy of the copyright owner. Moral rights cannot be assigned (section 94) but will pass under a will or by way of intestacy (by section 95).

Assignments and exclusive licences, to be effective at law, must be in writing and signed by or on behalf of the assignor (person making the assignment) or licensor (person granting the licence) as the case may be. If these requirements are not complied with the courts may be prepared to use the concept of beneficial ownership or to imply a licence giving the acquirer the right to do what, in the view of the court, was intended by the parties. Nevertheless, it is obviously more satisfactory to make sure that the formalities are complied with.

It is possible to deal with a future copyright; that is, copyright in a work yet to be created (section 91). The prospective owner can assign the future copyright or grant licences in respect of it. These provisions are useful where a self-employed consultant is engaged to create a new item of software. The agreement under which he is engaged should contain a term to the effect that he assigns the future copyright in any work created under the agreement to the person engaging him. This agreement must then be signed by or on behalf of the consultant and, on the work coming into existence, the assignment will automatically take effect. This simple expedient is very important in the software industry, where many persons are self-employed or freelance, and can prevent a bitter dispute later as to ownership of copyright.

SUMMARY

- Copyright is a property right which protects a wide variety of works.
- The owner has the exclusive right to perform or to authorise the performance of the restricted acts.
- Copyright law protects original literary works which include:
  - computer programs;
  - preparatory design material for computer programs; and
  - databases.
- Copyright computer programs and databases must be the author's own intellectual creation.
- Databases may be protected by the database right.

- The person creating a work of copyright is known as its author.
- Employers will usually own the copyright in works created by employees.
- Copyright for computer programs and databases last for 'life plus 70 years'.
- A person infringes copyright by:
  - performing, or authorising another to perform, one of the acts restricted by copyright;
  - in relation to a substantial part of the work, directly or indirectly;
  - without the permission of the copyright owner.
- There are a number of defences to copyright infringement and numerous permitted acts.
- Dealing with pirate copies can attract both civil and criminal liability.

SELF-TEST QUESTIONS

Note: there is only one correct answer to each question.

1   Which one of the following statements is CORRECT?

(a) A computer program is a *sui generis* work and is protected by copyright only if it is the result of a substantial investment.

(b) Preparatory material for a computer program is protected as an artistic work, especially if it includes diagrams.

(c) Computer programs can only be protected by copyright as computer-generated literary works.

(d) A computer program is a literary work and is required to be original, meaning it is the result of the author's own intellectual creation.

2   Who is the AUTHOR of a computer-generated work?

(a) The person who owns the computer used to generate the work.

(b) The person who made the arrangements necessary for its creation.

(c) The person who is entitled to use the software used to generate the work.

(d) No one as a computer-generated work cannot, by definition, have a human author.

3   Abdul is a self-employed computer programmer. He was engaged to write a computer pro-gram for Excel Logistics Ltd ('Excel') and was paid a large fee for this work. The contract between Abdul and Excel made no mention of who would own the copyright in the program. In relation to the copyright subsisting in the computer program, which one of the following statements is CORRECT?

(a) Abdul and Excel are joint owners of the copyright.

(b) Excel is the sole owner of the copyright at law as Excel paid Abdul to write the program.

(c) Abdul is the owner of the copyright at law but the courts may be prepared to grant beneficial ownership or an implied licence to allow Excel to use the program.

(d) Excel will not be able to use the program until after it has a written assignment of copyright from Abdul for which Excel will have to pay the market value of the program.

4   How LONG does copyright in a computer program, not being computer-generated last, for?

(a) For 50 years after the end of the calendar year during which the author dies.

(b) For 50 years after the end of the calendar year during which it was first made available to the public.

(c) For 70 years after the end of the calendar year during which it was first made available to the public.

(d) For 70 years after the end of the calendar year during which the author dies.

For further resources and updates please go to the Companion Website accompanying this book at **www.mylawchamber.co.uk/bainbridgeIT**

4 Copyright and computer programs

INTRODUCTION

Now that the basic principles of copyright law have been described in Chapter 3, the protection of computer programs by copyright law can be examined. Subsequent chapters are concerned with the protection of databases by copyright and the database right and copyright in computer-generated works. The final chapter on copyright law looks at developments in copyright in the information society.

Copyright law protects computer software, whether it be computer programs, databases, computer files or printed documentation. The distinction between computer hardware and software is sometimes difficult to determine. For example, does a 'dongle' contain a computer program? A dongle is a device which was popular some time ago and which was inserted into a computer port enabling certain programs to be used. Its prime purpose was as a form of copy protection, limiting the use of a program to one computer at any given time. In the Australian case of *Dyason* v *Autodesk Inc* (1990) 96 ALR 57 it was held that the dongle together with the program used to write digital information into it were, in combination, a computer program for copyright purposes.

Some confusion as to whether a single word in a computer program was itself a program was resolved in the Federal Court of Australia which held that a single statement in a high-level programming language was not a program but was merely the cipher or key to access a set of instructions: *Powerflux* v *Data Access Corp* [1997] FCA 490. In the United Kingdom there was some judicial confusion as to whether 'hard-wiring' a computer program in a ROM chip allows the algorithm it represents to be patented on the basis that this constituted a technical effect, contrary to the case where the program resided on a magnetic disk (see *Gale's Application* [1991] RPC 305).

It is now beyond doubt that computer programs are protected by copyright, save perhaps only in respect of the most trivial programs requiring little skill or judgment in their creation. Current issues concern the scope of the protection, for example, whether it is permissible to create a new program to emulate the operation and functionality of an existing program, the circumstances under which a computer program may be analysed to determine its underlying ideas and principles and whether a computer program can be decompiled to access interface details. Other matters dealt with in this chapter include the lawfulness of error correction by a person having use of a computer program and whether a computer programming language is protected by copyright. Finally, the thorny issue of the ownership of copyright in computer programs is considered. Given the fact that many computer programmers are self-employed, freelance or operate under the umbrella of a small limited company or limited liability partnership, this is a perennial problem often exacerbated by the lack of any formal provision as to ownership. Before looking at the current state of copyright law in the context of computer programs it will be useful to look at the historical development of this important area of law.

HISTORICAL DEVELOPMENT OF COPYRIGHT FOR COMPUTER PROGRAMS

The United States amended its Copyright Act in 1980 to specifically include computer programs, defining a computer program as 'a set of statements or instructions to be used directly or indirectly in a computer in order to bring about a certain result'. In the United Kingdom, before 1985, it was not at all clear whether computer programs were protected by copyright. The then current Copyright Act of 1956 made no mention of computer programs. One view was that a listing of a computer program, printed out on paper, was protected as a literary work. An analogy could be drawn with codebooks which had been accepted as literary works towards the end of the nineteenth century. Also, program listings, at least in source code, resembled written English to some extent.

On the whole, the courts appeared to be sympathetic towards the notion that computer programs were protected. For example, in *Sega Enterprises Ltd v Richards* [1983] FSR 73, which concerned alleged copies of the computer game 'FROGGER' (the object of which was to get a frog across a busy road without it being squashed by a lorry), the trial judge was of the opinion that the source code program was protected by copyright and the object code program was protected indirectly as an adaptation of the source code version. However, this was an interim hearing only and the case did not go to a full trial, so the point was not finally decided. Indeed, there were a number of cases involving copying of computer programs but these were dealt with by summary judgment and none went to a full trial. In most cases, the judge granted an interim injunction preventing further copying by the alleged infringer who did not seek to challenge the injunction or take the case further. Usually the copying was quite blatant and, presumably, the defendant moved on to some new venture.

The lack of a full trial with the benefit of counsels' detailed arguments and submissions with a fully considered judgment being handed down increased serious concerns amongst the software industry. These fears reached a climax following a case in Australia involving the computer programs in the Apple II computer in *Apple Computer Inc v Computer Edge Pty Ltd* [1984] FSR 481. The defendant imported clones of the Apple II personal computer into Australia. His initial claim that his computers, appropriately called 'Wombats', did not contain the Apple operating system and start-up programs was rejected when it was discovered that the programs in the 'Wombat' chips had the names of the Apple programmers embedded within them. The defendant's second line of defence was that the programs were not literary works in the copyright sense, being object code programs. This was accepted by the trial judge but rejected by a 2:1 majority in the Federal Court of New South Wales. However, this decision was unsatisfactory in many respects and the Australian Parliament acted very quickly, passing amending legislation (the Australian Copyright Amendment Act 1984) to put the matter beyond doubt. This did little to assuage concerns in the United Kingdom; it merely highlighted the uncertainty concerning object code programs. (There was a subsequent appeal by the defendant in the *Apple* case to the High Court of Australia which held, by a 3:2 majority that the object code programs were not literary works, nor where they adaptations of literary works: *Computer Edge Pty Ltd v Apple Computer Inc* [1986] FSR 537. Of course, this appeal was based on the Australian Copyright Act prior to its amendment by the Australian Copyright Amendment Act 1984 and is of academic interest only.)

Following considerable pressure from the computer industry, notably from the lobby group FAST (the Federation Against Software Theft), the Copyright (Computer Software) Amendment

Act 1985 was passed which made it clear that computer programs were protected as if they were literary works. The Copyright, Designs and Patents Act 1988 placed computer programs firmly within the literary work category for the purposes of copyright law under section 3 together now also with preparatory design material for computer programs and databases. Neither the word 'computer' nor the term 'computer program' is defined in the Act. This is sensible in view of the rapid rate of change in the computer industry as attempts to offer precise definitions would probably prove to be unduly restrictive in the light of technological development. It is better to allow the judges to use their discretion sensibly, permitting a degree of flexibility in this respect. There should be no difficulty in a court deciding that copyright subsists in a program written in assembly language or in a computer program in object code form.

On a European scale, it has proved necessary to harmonise protection for computer programs throughout the European Community and also spell out in detail the scope of exceptions to copyright infringement in relation to computer programs and, to this end, the 1988 Act was amended by the Copyright (Computer Programs) Regulations 1992, as described later in this chapter. The Regulations implemented the Directive on the legal protection of computer programs[1] and also specifically placed preparatory design material for computer programs in the literary work category. However, the Directive did not treat preparatory design material in the same manner and simply said that the term 'computer programs' shall include their preparatory design material: Article 1(1).

SUBSISTENCE OF COPYRIGHT IN COMPUTER PROGRAMS

Under section 3 of the Copyright, Designs and Patents Act 1988, for copyright to subsist in a computer program it must be 'original' and it must be 'recorded' (all literary, dramatic and musical works are required to be 'recorded in writing or otherwise'). The qualification requirements must also be satisfied. Each of these elements, originality, recorded in writing or otherwise and qualification are discussed below.

Originality

Literary, dramatic, musical and artistic works have to be 'original' for copyright. A significant amount of case law explained what this requirement meant in practice, particularly in relation to literary works. Generally, the courts looked for the expenditure of skill, labour or judgment in the creation of the work and a parallel or even supplementary rule developed which denied copyright to works which were trivial or very small. This could be seen as a simple application of the basic requirement for skill, labour or judgment as a very small item such as a name (for example, 'Kojak' or 'Elvis') a title for a novel or film or a simple slogan could not really be said to conform to the test of originality.

As regards computer programs, the requirement for originality was qualified by the Directive on the legal protection of computer programs, Article 1(3) of which stated:

> A computer program shall be protected if it is original in the sense that it is the author's own intellectual creation. No other criteria shall be applied to determine its eligibility for protection.

The Copyright (Computer Programs) Regulations 1992 which implemented the Directive failed to insert an equivalent provision into the Copyright, Designs and Patents Act 1988. As this

---

[1] Council Directive 91/250/EEC of 14 May 1991 on the legal protection of computer programs, OJ L 122, 17.05.1991, p. 42 (the 'Directive on the legal protection of computer programs').

4

Copyright and computer programs

provision in the Directive was not optional and is quite clear and unambiguous, it can be said to have direct effect. Consequently, all the prior case law on the meaning of 'original' either must be the same in effect as the test of the 'author's own intellectual creation' or the courts must have recourse to that term rather than the case law on what the word 'original' means in the context of computer programs. In practice, this has not proved to be an issue and there have been no reports of challenges to the subsistence of copyright in a computer program on the basis that it was not the author's own intellectual creation. Before considering this issue further, it will be useful to look at the case law on the meaning of 'original'.

The requirement of originality has not been applied by judges in a strict way and it does not require that the computer program must be novel or unique in some respect. It simply has been construed as requiring that the work in question has been the result of a modest amount of skill, labour or judgment and that it 'originates from the author' (Peterson J in *University of London Press Ltd v University Tutorial Press Ltd* [1916] 2 Ch 601). Although judges in the past have used a variety of different formulations of the requirement for skill, labour or judgment, it is tolerably clear that the better approach is to look for skill or judgment as a work that is the result of labour only will not be protected by copyright. Compilations of existing information as in a street directory may be the proper subject matter of copyright. In *Macmillan & Co Ltd v K & J Cooper* (1923) 40 TLR 186, it was held that, although many compilations have nothing original in their parts, the sum total of a compilation may be original for the purposes of copyright. There could be skill or judgment in deciding what type of data to include, what its form should be and how it should be arranged, for example. However, the courts will draw a line somewhere and in *G A Cramp & Sons Ltd v Frank Smythson Ltd* [1944] AC 329, a diary which contained the usual information contained in diaries, such as a calendar, tables of weights and measures, postal information and the like, failed to attract copyright protection. The reason given was that the commonplace nature of the information left no room for taste or judgment in the selection and organisation of the material. In the light of these cases, virtually all computer programs but for the most trivial will meet the requirement of originality. This will be so even if the program comprises little more than an arrangement of commonly used sub-routines, providing the selection and arrangement of those sub-routines involved a reasonable amount of skill or judgment.

In the United States, the position is not necessarily different and the expenditure of labour alone is unlikely, without some intellectual contribution, to confer copyright protection on a work (the 'sweat of the brow' doctrine put to rest by the US Supreme Court in *Feist Publications Inc v Rural Telephone Service Co Inc* 499 US 340 (1991), discussed in more detail in the following chapter). It is difficult to conceive of a computer program which does not involve skill and judgment in its creation regardless of the amount of effort or labour involved. However, standards varied internationally and, in Germany, it was once said that, to be protected by copyright, a computer program must be the result of creative achievement exceeding the average skills used in the development of computer programs (*Sudwestdeutsche Inkasse KG v Bappert und Burker Computer GmbH* (1985) Case 5483, BGHZ94, 276). This would have meant that a computer program which simply automated an existing process using no special programming techniques would be unlikely to be the subject of copyright. In the light of the Directive on the legal protection of computer programs (a key goal of the Directive was to harmonise the requirements for, and scope of protection for, computer programs) this case must now be viewed as laying down too stringent a test and, indeed, this was confirmed by the Federal Supreme Court of Germany in the *Buchhaltungsprogram* case (unreported) 14 July 1993 which concerned an accounts program.

It is arguable that the test of a computer program being the author's own intellectual creation is the same as the way the courts have interpreted, and are likely to interpret in the future, the term 'original', particularly as the trend has been to look for skill and judgment in the creation of a work and the rejection of labour or effort alone being enough to attract copyright protection. The point is likely to be academic in relation to computer programs apart from one thorny question. Is it possible to have a computer-generated computer program? This is a computer program which is created in circumstances such that there is no human author. If that is so, wherein lies the necessary act of intellectual creation? The only way this can be fulfilled is to consider the skill and judgment of the person who wrote the software used to create the computer-generated program. However, as we shall see in Chapter 6, it is debatable whether there can be such a thing as a computer-generated work. The Directive on the legal protection of computer programs did not mention computer-generated computer programs and no other copyright Directives provided for computer-generated works generally nor, as far as the author of this book is aware, does any copyright legislation anywhere else other than the UK. Computer-generated works are a 'home-grown' provision and it is arguable that provisions relating to them in the Copyright, Designs and Patents Act 1988 should be repealed.

Recorded in writing or otherwise

In the United Kingdom, another requirement for computer programs (and other literary, dramatic and musical works, though not artistic works) is that they must be recorded in writing or otherwise: section 3(2). This has a very wide meaning and 'writing' is defined by section 178 as including:

> ... any form of notation or code, whether by hand or otherwise and regardless of the method by which, or medium in or on which, it is recorded.

Storage of a computer program in a computer memory or on computer storage media such as magnetic or optical disks or 'memory sticks' should present no problems as the above definition in section 178 is sufficiently wide to cover any existing form of storage and any new forms which might be invented in the future. Furthermore, given the spirit of the Act, it is unlikely that the courts will attempt to narrow the requirement that a work be recorded. It is even arguable that a work that exists only in a computer's RAM is recorded in writing or otherwise. This view is reinforced by the fact that, for the purposes of the restricted acts of making a copy of a work, copying includes making a copy which is transient.

Qualification

Section 1(3) of the Act requires that, to be protected by UK copyright, a work must qualify for protection. A work may qualify by reference to the author of the work or by virtue of the country of first publication. These provisions are complex but, essentially, if the author was a British citizen (there are other forms of British 'nationality' status as well) or was domiciled or resident in the UK or other countries to which the provisions apply, then the work will have UK copyright, no matter where the work was created. Qualification by publication in the UK or other country to which the provisions extend still applies even if the work was first published elsewhere provided that did not happen more than 30 days previously.

The impact of the Berne Convention for the Protection of Literary and Artistic Works 1883 and other conventions and agreements is to extend the qualification provisions to many other countries. The Copyright and Rights in Performances (Application to Other Countries) Order 2006 lists those countries in the Schedule to the Order. Consequently, qualification for copyright subsistence will rarely be an issue.

4

Copyright and computer programs

PREPARATORY DESIGN MATERIAL FOR COMPUTER PROGRAMS

Copyright protection extends beyond the computer program itself and will cover written or printed listings of programs, flow charts, specifications and notes. Section 3(1)(c) includes preparatory design material for a computer program in the literary work category. Prior to the Copyright (Computer Programs) Regulations 1992, these materials would generally be protected as literary works although flow charts and diagrams would have been protected as artistic works. The artistic work category of copyright includes paintings, drawings, diagrams, maps, charts and plans which are all protected irrespective of artistic quality. As a result of the Regulations which implemented the Directive on the legal protection of computer programs, however, preparatory design material is deemed to be a literary work, irrespective of whether such material might previously have been protected as graphic works and, hence, artistic works. In practice, this should not be of any significance although there are some differences in the provisions for literary and artistic works. Preparatory design material must be original in the sense already discussed for copyright protection of computer programs. Because copying includes copying by indirect means, it is possible that making an unauthorised copy of a computer program, or elements associated with a computer program such as a screen display, infringes the copyright subsisting in the preparatory design material in addition to any question of infringement of the copyright in the computer program or screen display, *per se*.

There is one slight caveat to all this which results from the manner in which the UK implemented the Directive on the legal protection of computer programs. The Act appears to classify preparatory design material as a form of literary work separate from the computer program it is associated with whereas Article 1(1) of the Directive states that the term 'computer programs' shall include their preparatory design material. The implication of this is that the computer program and its preparatory design material should be looked at in the round as together constituting the entire work. To infringe by indirectly copying preparatory design material, such as a diagram showing the design of a screen display, it must be a substantial part of the computer program (including the preparatory design material) as a whole. The manner in which the UK imperfectly implemented the Directive in this respect possibly gives too much prominence to preparatory design materials and, arguably, computer programs by treating the two separately. Again, there is no case law which addresses the distinction between the Act and the Directive on this. Although, in *Nova Productions Ltd* v *Mazooma Games Ltd* [2006] RPC 379, the judge considered that the ideas taken by the defendant from the claimant's video game based on the game of pool did not constitute a substantial part of the preparatory design materials for the game. He dealt with the preparatory design materials as if they constituted a work of copyright separate to the computer programs.

RESTRICTED ACTS FOR COMPUTER PROGRAMS

Of the acts restricted by copyright, four are worthy of special mention as far as computer programs are concerned. These are:

- copying the work;
- issuing copies of the work to the public;
- communicating the work to the public; and
- making an adaptation of the work.

All of these restricted acts have a particular meaning which is only partly explained by the language of the Act. Copying and making an adaptation have fairly technical meanings and both of these restricted acts have been extended to take account of computer technology. Copying includes copying electronically. A particular difficulty for copyright law is where a person, without the copyright owner's permission, makes a copy of a work but without taking any or much of the literal text, for example, by creating a work based on the structure or architecture of the first work. This might cover the situation where a person copies the plot of a play or story without taking the actual words used. In terms of computer programs, a person may study an existing program and write a new program to emulate the operation and functions performed. He may use a different computer programming language. The resultant program will have no textual similarity with the first (or only minimal textual similarity). The question is whether such use of a computer program to create a new computer program should be allowed or whether it should be prohibited on the basis that there has been a non-textual or non-literal infringement of copyright. Just how close to the actual code of the first program can one get without infringing? There have been a number of important cases on this in the US and in the UK. This reflects the greater prominence of the restricted act of copying in the following parts of this chapter.

The restricted acts of issuing copies to the public and communicating copies to the public are relatively straightforward but a special doctrine applies in respect of issuing copies of works on physical media. This is to the effect that subsequent dealing with copies put on the market within Europe by or with the permission of the copyright owner cannot be prevented by the copyright owner. Thus, if Smita buys a legitimate copy of a computer program on a CD-ROM in Spain, the copyright owner cannot object if she imports it into the UK and re-sells it there. This doctrine is known as exhaustion of rights. It is limited and, if Smita made one or more copies which she kept for herself or sold, those would be infringing copies. Neither would she be allowed to rent or lend the copy to the public unless she had the copyright owner's permission to do this.

The restricted act of making an adaptation, concerned first of all with translations of literary works and arrangements of musical works, now has to deal with the process of converting source code into object code and vice versa. In terms of computer programs it means converting a program into or out of a computer language or code or into a different computer language or code. The restricted acts that have particular relevance for computer programs are now examined in more detail.

Copying

Copying in relation to a literary, dramatic, musical or artistic work means, by section 17(2), reproducing the work in any material form which includes storage in any medium by electronic means: for example, by making a copy of a computer program on a magnetic disk. Additionally, in relation to all forms of copyright work, copying includes making copies which are transient or incidental to some other use of the work: section 17(6). This implies that the act of loading a computer program into a computer's random access memory for the purpose of running the program will be considered to be making a copy of the program, even though this copy will be lost as soon as the computer is switched off. In this way, any unauthorised use of a computer program will infringe the copyright in that program. This is why a licence is required in order to use another person's computer program or database, or indeed, any other work in digital form which will be accessed by computer.

The Directive on the legal protection of computer programs reinforces this and states under Article 4(1)(a) that the copyright owner has the exclusive right to authorise:

... the permanent or temporary reproduction of a computer program by any means and in any form, in part or in whole. Insofar as loading, displaying, running, transmission or storage of the computer program necessitate such reproduction, such acts shall be subject to authorisation by the rightholder.

In terms of copying computer programs the copy may be a duplicate such as where a copy is made from disk to disk. In some cases, the copy may be subject to some modification, for example, where the person making the copy then carries out further work on the program such as by re-writing parts of it or adding new routines to it. Alternatively, the copy may be made without copying the actual code of the first program. It may be that the person making the copy does so without seeing the code of the first program but creates his program by studying the operation of the first to gain an insight into what functions it performs and its structure and sequence of events. Mathematical formulae, logic and algorithms in the first program may be discovered by submitting test data to it and checking the results. This form of copying is referred to a non-literal or non-textual copying. Similar considerations apply to some other forms of work, particularly literary and artistic works. Whether and to what extent non-literal copying is permitted is examined below but first issues relating to literal copying are discussed.

Literal copying

Where an exact duplicate is made of a computer program, the question of infringement will be an easy matter to decide. Many such cases will involve secondary infringement and the criminal offences under copyright law, for example, where duplicate copies are made and sold. Providing the program is protected by copyright, to prove 'primary' infringement it simply needs to be shown that the defendant had made the copies in question (or authorised their making). For secondary infringement and the criminal offences it must further be shown that the defendant was responsible for the relevant act (for example, by making, importing or selling the copies in the course of trade) and that he knew or had reason to believe that the copies were infringing copies. It is very rare that a defendant will argue that the claimant is not the person entitled to sue. This is because there are some useful presumptions that apply to works of copyright. In the case of a computer program issued to the public in electronic form, a statement that a named person was the copyright owner when the copies where issued is admissible in evidence and presumed correct unless the contrary is shown: section 105(3). In *Microsoft Corp* v *Electrowide Ltd* [1997] FSR 580 it was held that, because of this presumption Microsoft did not have to prove that it owned the copyright in software such as Windows 95. The judge thought it would be highly unlikely that Microsoft would not have owned all the relevant copyrights by ensuring that it took an assignment of the copyright in any elements of the software that the company did not generate itself. Piracy in relation to computer software is discussed in more detail in Chapter 12.

Literal copying has another main form. A typical example is where an employee takes a copy of his employer's computer program (usually in source code form), usually also taking copies of preparatory design material, and uses the program and other material as a basis to write his own program. This might be done for a new employer or a client where the employee has decided to strike out and work for himself. Of course, by making the copy of the computer program and preparatory design material, there will be a straightforward infringement of copyright, assuming the copies were made without the permission of the employer or copyright owner if it is owned by someone other than the employer. However, the question arises as to whether the new program infringes the copyright in the first. It may be that only part of the first program has been incorporated in the new program. The new program may be significantly larger and contain a number of new features and routines.

Where only part of the claimant's program has been taken and included in the defendant's program, there are four things that must be proved, if the defendant contests them all. They are:

- Is the claimant's computer program protected by copyright?

- Is the claimant the copyright owner or a licensee with a right to sue for infringement (being either an exclusive licensee or a non-exclusive licensee who has been expressly granted a right of action by the copyright owner)?
- Has the defendant copied from the claimant's program?
- Does the part taken by the defendant represent a substantial part of the claimant's program?

A defendant will not usually argue that the claimant's program is not protected by copyright. All but the most trivial computer programs will be protected by copyright and there is no point in arguing a hopeless point as this would increase the legal costs of the trial. A losing defendant normally has to pay the claimant's legal costs as well as his own.

Where a defendant has only made minor changes to a program, there are likely to be a number of similarities that can only be explained on the basis of copying. Examples include errors in remark lines, quirky routines and even redundant routines. If only part of the claimant's program has been taken, the last question will be relevant. That is, does the part taken by the defendant represent a substantial part of the claimant's computer program? Substantiality is a question of quality rather than quantity and is tested against the claimant's program rather than the defendant's program. Otherwise a defendant who took a substantial part of a claimant's program and incorporated into a much larger computer program might escape an infringement action.

Before looking at the case law on literal copying, it is worth bearing in mind that the same person may have been involved in the creation of both computer programs where, for example, he wrote the first program as an employee for his employer. Where this is so and the two programs objectively bear a substantial similarity, the burden of proof may 'shift' so that the claimant does not have to prove copying, rather it is for the defendant to explain the similarities between the programs, in other words, to show on a balance of probabilities that he did not copy from the first program.

There are two instructive cases on literal copying, both of which involved the same programmer or programmers in the creation of the claimant's and defendant's computer programs and a degree of modification, re-writing or writing a significant amount of new code.

The *IBCOS Computers* case

In *IBCOS Computers Ltd* v *Barclays Mercantile Highland Finance Ltd* [1994] FSR 275, one of the defendants, Mr Poole, wrote a suite of programs and files to handle accounts and payroll for agricultural machinery dealers. He further developed this software for the claimant and when he left the claimant company, he signed a note agreeing to the fact the company owned the copyright in the software and agreeing not to write competing software for two years. Mr Poole then wrote another software package, which performed similar functions, for the first defendant, Barclays. The new software was not marketed until the two-year period in restraint of trade had expired. Nevertheless, the claimant sued for copyright infringement and breach of confidence. Both suites of programs were written in similar programming languages, being variants of COBOL.

When the code of the two suites of programs was examined, common errors were noticed. These were primarily to do with spelling and punctuation in the comment lines in the programs. The same mistakes tended to occur in the same places. The same piece of redundant code was also present in both suites of programs. The judge, therefore, had little difficulty in finding that there had been copying, showing the usefulness of including deliberate mistakes or redundant elements in copyright works. He held that copyright subsisted not only in the individual programs but also in the whole suite of programs as a compilation because the selection and arrangement of the programs required skill and judgment. On this latter point the judge, Mr Justice Jacob, disagreed with Judge Paul Baker who said, in *Total Information Processing Systems*

Ltd v *Daman Ltd* [1992] FSR 171, that linking several programs together could not constitute an original compilation. In view of the increasing structural complexity of software products, Jacob J's approach should be welcomed by the software industry as strengthening the copyright protection of computer programs.

Jacob J held that the defendant had infringed copyright in a number of individual programs in addition to an infringement of the copyright subsisting in the overall structure of the software comprising 335 programs, 171 record layout files and 46 screen layouts. Mr Poole argued that similarities were the result of his programming style and the re-use of well-known routines but he was unable to convince the judge on these points. In other words, he was unable to offer a satisfactory explanation for the similarities. It was also held that Mr Poole was guilty of a breach of confidence in respect of the claimant's source code programs.

In his judgment, Jacob J discussed previous case law and was critical of some aspects of it (see the section on non-literal copying later in this chapter). Some other important points made by Jacob J included:

- Modifying a computer program could give rise to a fresh copyright (presumably if the work in making the modifications was the result of skill or judgment).

- The fact that the program, or parts of it, was constrained by the program's function did not weaken or compromise copyright protection.

- The data division of a COBOL program (being the part defining the variables and database structures) can be a substantial part of a program; and a file record, though not a computer program as such, could be a compilation.

- Where the evidence clearly indicates copying but the defendant denies this, the court should infer that similarities are the result of copying and not due to programming style unless independent evidence suggests otherwise.

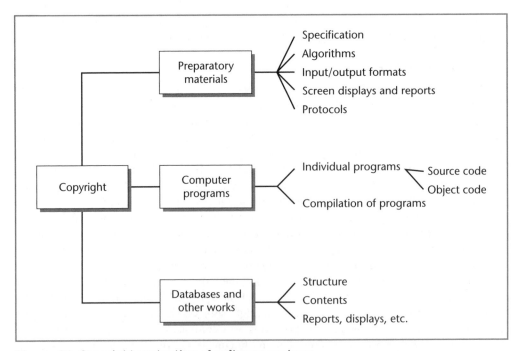

Figure 4.1 Copyright protection of software package

The *IBCOS* case is an important step in the application of copyright law to computer programs. Bearing in mind that preparatory design material is now expressly subject to copyright, the width of protection afforded to software is quite strong. Strictly speaking preparatory design material should be considered to be part of the computer program in accordance with the Directive on the legal protection of computer programs. Figure 4.1 shows this in relation to a typical software package including a suite of programs, databases and data files. The protection of databases by copyright and the database right is the subject of the following chapter.

The *Cantor Fitzgerald* case

Cantor Fitzgerald International v *Tradition (UK) Ltd* [2000] RPC 95 concerned copying in a number of ways. First, there was an allegation of copying the whole of the claimant's programs by loading the source code into the defendant's computer. This was admitted by the defendant. Secondly, allegations of copying parts of the code of the claimant's program code were made. The defendant admitted including relatively small parts of the claimant's code in its programs. This accounted for just under 4 per cent of the entire code of the claimant's programs. The defendant had written a considerable amount of code as part of developing its own system. Although the judge, Mr Justice Pumfrey, accepted that the architecture of a computer system could be protected by copyright, no allegation had been made in respect of that.

The main parties to the dispute were independent bond brokers. A further defendant had been the claimant's managing director. He had been dismissed and obtained employment with the first defendant, Tradition (UK) Ltd ('Tradition'). He took a number of other employees of the claimant with him, including programmers who had worked on the claimant's software system. Within a relatively short period of time, the first defendant had a bond broking software system which the claimant alleged was a copy of its system. Eventually, the first defendant admitted that a small proportion of its software had been copied from the claimant's software.

In finding that the defendants had infringed the claimant's copyright, Mr Justice Pumfrey noted the following points::

- Tradition accepted that the whole of the claimant's software had been loaded onto its computer. This was itself an infringement of copyright.

- The expression of thought in a human language differed to a program for a computer written in a computer programming language. There was a danger in adapting principles developed in the context of traditional literary works and applying them uncritically to computer programs which, although literary works in the copyright sense, had the sole purpose to control the operation of a machine.

- Although every part of a computer program might be essential to its performance, it was too simplistic to regard every part however small as a substantial part of the program. The fact that a program might not function properly or at all without that part did not mean that it was a substantial part of the program. According to Pumfrey J, substantiality must be judged against the program or programs as a whole in the light of the 'skill and labour in design and coding which went into the piece of code which is alleged to be copied'. In that case, the defendant admitted copying some 2,952 lines of code from the claimant's programs which comprised 77,000 lines of code. The judge found the claimant's case made out in part but he went on to say that substantiality was not to be determined by whether the system would work without the part copied nor by the amount of use made of the code in question during the running of the program.

- The function of copyright was to protect the relevant skill and labour expended by the author of the work and a copyist infringed if he took a part of the work upon which a substantial part of the author's skill and labour was expended.

4

Copyright and computer programs

■ A substantial part of the author's skill and labour might reside in the plot of a novel or play and to take it without taking any part of the particular manner of its expression might be sufficient to amount to copying (a case of non-literal copying – see later in this chapter). The architecture of a computer program (either the overall structure of the system at a high level or allocation of functions between various programs) was analogous to a plot and capable of protection if it represented a substantial part of the author's skill, labour and judgment. However, in this particular case, similarities at the architectural level were no more than could be accounted for by the fact that both systems were written by the same programmers and, in any case, the claimant did not pursue this aspect. The judge did seem surprised that, although the architecture of the two programs were similar, less than 4 per cent of the code of the claimant's program could be detected in Tradition's program code.

■ In terms of the decisions taken as to how the programs should be modularised, where the content of each module was largely arbitrary or was not based on considerations concerned with the program as a functional unit but was related to extraneous matters such as the availability and skill of programmers or convenience in terms of debugging and maintenance of the program, it was unlikely, though not impossible, that the skill and labour expended in making such a choice could ever amount to a substantial part of the copyright subsisting in the program.

■ If the copied program code had been disguised to hide its origins, this showed that the person copying knew what he was doing was wrong and if this was done in blatant disregard of the claimant's rights, this might be the basis of a claim for additional damages.

■ The judge accepted that the actual proportion of code copied and used in Tradition's program was very small and Tradition's programmers had wanted the claimant's code as a record of what they had done before. It was intended to build a system which was a substantial improvement on that of the claimant's.

One of the main uses of the claimant's code made by the programmer working for Tradition was to use it for debugging purposes. This was also a breach of confidence. In such a case, it would be appropriate to calculate damages based on a reasonable fee for the use of code for those purposes.

Overall, it was held that there had been an infringement of copyright by loading the claimant's programs into the defendant's computer and that there had been an infringement of copyright in respect of some of the allegations admitted by the defendant. In some cases, the judge held that some parts of code admitted to have been copied did not represent a substantial part of the relevant program. One example was two lines of code in a program, being:

```
SYS_RET=SYS$ASSIGN(TPF_IN_PORT,FEED_CHAN,,,)

SYS_RET=SYS$ALLOC(TPF_IN_PORT,,,)
```

Clearly, these two lines did not represent a substantial part of the programmer's skill and labour in writing the program.

The facts of this case are not unusual in practice. Computer programmers tend to move from job to job and create similar programs for different clients or employees. It is tempting for them to use earlier programs and designs for programs subsequently. Many programmers build up a toolkit of useful routines and modules to save them time writing them from scratch in the future. It is also likely that programmers working on new programs with functions similar to those they have written before will try to improve upon them and expand their functionality. To draw a line between what is acceptable and what is not is notoriously difficult to do. However, simply making a copy of a previous employer's program without permission infringes copyright as will any subsequent use involving loading the program into a computer. On the other hand, simply remembering the basic ideas and algorithms underlying the programs and writing new programs on the basis of those ideas and algorithms should not infringe copyright (and will not be a breach of confidence unless the functions performed by those programs were in the nature of trade secrets protected by the law of confidence).

On the whole, Mr Justice Pumfrey's judgment in *Cantor Fitzgerald* is sound and builds on the principles expounded by Jacob J in *IBCOS*. The fact that relatively little of the claimant's program code found its way into the defendant's program does not lessen the finding of infringement (providing substantiality is found nonetheless) but might be relevant to the quantum of damages awarded and whether a permanent injunction is granted. One criticism of the judgment is that the judge frequently referred to the author's labour in a way that suggested that it might be sufficient on its own to give rise to copyright. The better view is that the author must expend skill or judgment or both. The test for originality in the Directive on the legal protection of computer programs was that they must be the author's own intellectual creation (the same applies to copyright databases).

Mr Justice Pumfrey's judgment in this case is also referred to in the following section on non-literal copying together with another very important judgment of his in *Navitaire v easyJet* [2006] RPC 111.

Non-literal (non-textual) copying

Non-literal copying, sometimes described as non-textual copying where literary works are concerned, occurs where the actual text of the first work has not been copied. Rather the copyist has made use of aspects of the work at a level of abstraction from the actual text. Thus, in terms of a literary novel, the plot may have been taken by a person writing the novel in the form of a screenplay for a film. This could mean that the events and occurrences, the sequence of them and other aspects such as the characterisation of the *dramatis personae*, have been taken. There may be little or no direct copying of the actual text of the novel. Consequently, there may be very limited if any similarity in the literal text of the two works.

The dilemma for copyright is to what extent non-literal elements should be protected. On the one hand, if copyright protection is limited to an investigation of the amount of actual text the defendant has copied from the claimant's program, it would be too easy to overcome copyright by re-writing the text of the first using a different programming language. A person might use a computer program extensively to fully understand what it does and its underlying ideas, principles and architecture. From that knowledge but using a different programming language, he might write another computer program to emulate the operations and functions performed by the first program. On the other hand, copyright is not supposed to protect ideas and principles. Indeed, the Directive on the legal protection of computer programs makes this explicit. If a balance is to be struck between protecting only the literal text and protecting basic ideas, the problem is where to draw the line. This has proved quite elusive in relation to computer programs, as will be seen.

It is a well-established aphorism that copyright does not protect ideas but protects the expression of ideas. But how do we separate the two? As Lord Hailsham accepted in *LB Plastics Ltd v Swish Products Ltd* [1979] RPC 551, quoting the late Professor Joad, 'it all depends on what you mean by "ideas" '. At what level of abstraction from the literal text does copyright protection come to an end? Taking a basic idea may be acceptable but taking a very detailed plot for a play or novel and re-writing it without copying the actual text of the original play or novel may infringe copyright. It would seem clear that it is quite acceptable to write a novel about a secret agent in the style of Ian Fleming as long as it does not follow closely the plot, events and their sequence, and character portrayals used in a particular James Bond novel. The late Ian

Fleming did not have a monopoly in tongue-in-cheek, humorous adventures about secret agents licensed to kill, but a novelist might commit the tort of passing off if he changes his name to Ian Fleming or uses the name James Bond or the 007 code in his novel. Copyright protection does not extend, however, to ephemeral things such as skeletal plots for novels or ideas for computer programs unless and until they are recorded in some form or another and, even then, it is the ideas as expressed that are protected, not the ideas themselves or the underlying concepts.

Making a duplicate of a computer program in which copyright subsists infringes that copyright if made without the consent of the copyright owner. However, copying is not necessarily limited to duplication of substantial parts and it is possible to copy a computer program in a wider sense. For example, the structure, flow and sequence of operations expressed in a computer program may be copied and, if a different computer programming language is used, a printout of the second program will look dissimilar to a printout of the first program. Should the use of one program to assist with the writing of a second program in such a way be within the ambit of copyright protection even though the codes of the two programs look dissimilar? In other words, should copyright extend to non-literal elements which are not directly perceivable? This question is of such fundamental importance because, if answered in the negative, copyright protection for computer programs would be considerably weakened.

This issue is also relevant in respect of the look and feel of composite works which may contain literary and artistic works, such as a glossy magazine or a website. In the latter case, there are other elements to consider. A website may include audio-visual works. It will also have a structure in how the pages are interlinked and other structural elements such as internal and external links.

The United States progressed much faster than the United Kingdom in determining this question but the basic legal principles are broadly similar: copyright protects expression but not idea. Nevertheless, expression goes beyond the immediate literal form. For example, in the UK case of **Glyn** v **Weston Feature Film Co** [1916] 1 Ch 261, in which it was argued (unsuccessfully) that a film infringed the copyright in a novel, it was acknowledged that copyright can extend beyond the literal text of a book to the dramatic scenes and incidents contained within it.

Because expression may exist at various levels of abstraction (for example, in the program's architecture, structure or algorithms) the courts have to be able to distinguish between idea and expression. This has not proved easy and the following US cases give an indication of the development of tests that may be appropriate. (Of course, US law has no binding effect on the United Kingdom courts but it may be of persuasive authority, particularly in the field of information technology.)

Non-literal copying in the United States

In the US, non-literal copying has been described as taking a computer program's 'look and feel'. The first major case was **Whelan Associates Inc** v **Jaslow Dental Laboratory Inc** [1987] FSR 1. The computer programs in question were designed to assist with the administration of dental laboratories. The same person was involved in the development of each program but they were written in different computer languages: the first was written in EDL and the second, attempting to infiltrate the microcomputer market, was written in BASIC. Thus, there was no substantial literal similarity between the listings of the two programs. The US Court of Appeals (3rd Circuit) distinguished between idea and expression by reference to the purpose of the program. The purpose of a utilitarian work is the idea of the work whereas everything pertaining to the work which is not necessary to the purpose is expression. If there are several ways of achieving the desired purpose, none of which is necessary to the purpose, then the way chosen is expression and, consequently, protected by copyright.

The purpose of the original program in *Whelan* v *Jaslow* was to assist in the running of dental laboratories. There were several different methods which could be employed to achieve that same purpose, and therefore the structure of that original program was not essential to the purpose and, hence, the structure was expression and not idea. The purpose itself, being the idea, was not protected by copyright; it is quite acceptable for others to write programs to help with the running of dental laboratories. In this case the structures of the two programs were similar, the programs had a similar look and feel even though written in different computer programming languages and this, coupled with the fact that the same person had been involved in the two programs, raised a strong presumption that there had been copying and, hence, an infringement of copyright. The distinction between idea and expression has been applied in the context of screen displays. In the 'Pac-Man' computer games the maze and dots were deemed to be idea, being necessarily dictated by the program function, but the 'Pac-Man' and 'ghost monsters' characters were considered to be expression as different graphical representations could have been used.

Another important case involved the spreadsheet program Lotus 1-2-3 and a compatible spreadsheet program called VP-Planner. In *Lotus Development Corp* v *Paperback Software International* 740 F Supp 37 (D Mass 1990), the defendant claimed that he had not copied the Lotus program code but had used a similar menu system to achieve compatibility (especially with respect to spreadsheet files and macros) and to enable people to change to VP-Planner from Lotus 1-2-3 without requiring retraining. The similarities between the programs were the menu command system (two-line moving cursor menu) and the grid system (letters and numbers arranged in a 'rotated L'). It was held by Judge Keeton that the defendant had infringed copyright by copying the two-line moving cursor menu. Various spreadsheet programs used different menu systems showing that the system used by Lotus was expression and not idea. He confirmed, however, that there was no infringement of the rotated 'L' grid as this was idea, it being almost inevitable that a spreadsheet program would use such a system.

In a later spreadsheet case, *Lotus Development Corp* v *Borland International Inc* [1997] FSR 61, in the 1st Circuit Court of Appeals, the decision of Judge Keeton along the lines of his *Lotus* v *Paperback* judgment was reversed by the Court of Appeals which found that the menu command hierarchy in the Lotus 1-2-3 spreadsheet was not a work of copyright. Therefore, by using the 1-2-3 menu command system in its Quattro spreadsheet, Borland had not infringed copyright. The rationale was that the menu command system was a method of operation which is excluded from copyright protection by section 102(b) of the US Copyright Act. The court likened the menu system to the buttons on a video recorder. The distinction in *Whelan* between idea and expression was considered unhelpful by the court which confirmed that the fact that the Lotus designers could have designed the system differently was immaterial to the question of whether it was a method of operation. The case was then appealed to the US Supreme Court but there was no substantive judgment as the court reached a split decision, and the finding of the Court of Appeals stands.

The *Lotus* v *Borland* case can be seen as a further weakening of copyright protection for interfaces (in this case, the interface with the user) and facilitates the pursuit of compatibility in software from an operational point of view. However, it could discourage investment in novel forms of software and major software companies may be encouraged to allow someone else to make the investment in developing innovative software in the knowledge that they can copy the ideas and interfaces to produce similar competing software providing that they do not copy the program code or other protected non-literal elements.

Prior to the *Lotus* v *Borland* case, the authority of *Whelan* v *Jaslow* was already looking shaky and that case was strongly disapproved of by the United States Court of Appeals (2nd Circuit) in *Computer Associates International Inc* v *Altai* (1992) 20 USPQ 2d 1641. The defendant had produced a program called 'Oscar', a job-scheduling program for controlling the

4

Copyright and computer programs

order in which tasks are carried out by a computer. It incorporated a common interface component allowing the use of different operating systems and this part had been added by a former employee of the claimant who had a similar program and interface. The claimant's former employee was very familiar with the interface element (known as 'Adapter') which was part of the claimant's 'CA-Scheduler' program and had even been allowed to take a copy of the 'Adapter' source code home while working on it. When the claimant issued a summons and complaint, the defendant rewrote 'Oscar', using different programmers in an effort to avoid infringing the claimant's copyright in 'Adapter'. The claimant still proceeded even though the defendant had agreed not to challenge an award of $364,444 damages in respect of the earlier version of 'Oscar'. The trial judge held that the later version of 'Oscar' did not infringe the 'Adapter' copyright and the claimant appealed to the Court of Appeals which confirmed the decision of the trial judge.

In a far-reaching judgment, the Court of Appeals laid down a new test for the determination of the question of non-literal copyright infringement, that is, whether there has been an infringement of copyright in non-literal elements such as program structure. The test requires a three-step procedure as follows:

■ *Abstraction* – discovering the non-literal elements by a process akin to reverse engineering, beginning with the code and ending with the program's ultimate function. The designer's steps are retraced and mapped. This produces structures of different detail at varying levels of abstraction.

■ *Filtration* – the separation of protectable expression from non-protectable material. Some elements will be unprotected being idea, dictated by considerations of efficiency (therefore necessarily incidental to idea), required by external factors (*scènes à faire* doctrine), or taken from the public domain. These elements are filtered out leaving a core of protectable material (this is the program's 'golden nugget').

■ *Comparison* – a determination of whether the defendant has copied a substantial part of the protected expression, that is, ascertaining whether any aspect has been copied and, if so, assessing the copied portion's relative importance in respect of the claimant's overall program.

Of course, this test only applies to non-literal copying and the actual code remains fully protected against direct (literal) copying. The test was thought likely to reduce significantly the strength of protection for program structure, menu command systems and interfaces. In many cases, it is possible that, after the process of filtration, there will be no 'golden nuggets' left, that is, no protectable expression, to take forward to the process of comparison. However, the judges in the Court of Appeals recognised that their test would be difficult to apply and would need further case law before its application could be predicted with any certainty but nothing significant has thus far been forthcoming.

Non-literal copying in the United Kingdom

Old cases such as *Corelli* v *Gray* [1913] TLR 570, in which copyright was infringed by taking the plot of a novel, demonstrate that non-literal infringement of copyright is a possibility. However, in *Cantor Fitzgerald International* v *Tradition (UK) Ltd* [2000] RPC 95, discussed above, Pumfrey J cautioned about using old precedents from cases involving conventional literary works in computer program cases. He said (at para. 77):

> The closest analogy to a plot in a computer program lies perhaps in the algorithms or sequences of operations decided on by the programmer to achieve his object. But it goes wider. It seems to be generally accepted that the 'architecture' of a computer program is capable of protection if a substantial part of the programmer's skill, labour and judgment went into it. In this context,

'architecture' is a vague and ambiguous term. It may be used to refer to the overall structure of the system at a very high level of abstraction.

The first case on the non-literal copying of computer programs borrowed from the US test in the *Computer Associates* case. The facts of ***John Richardson Computers Ltd* v *Flanders*** [1993] FSR 497 were difficult and provide an object lesson in how not to manage the development of computer software, with scant regard being paid to record-keeping and ownership of copyright. Essentially, the claimant had a computer program for use by pharmacists to print labels for drug prescriptions and to monitor stock levels. The driving force behind the claimant company was Mr Richardson, a pharmacist, who had originally written a rudimentary program in BASIC and had later engaged computer programmers, both on an employee and consultancy basis and including the defendant, to refine and enhance the program. Eventually it was rewritten in assembly language for the BBC computer (and is referred to below as 'the BBC program').

The defendant then wrote a program called 'Chemtec' to perform the same functions as the claimant's program written in QUICK-BASIC for the IBM personal computer. The claimant sued for copyright infringement and breach of confidence though the latter claim was not pursued at the trial. The judge, Mr Justice Ferris, had to consider the claim for copyright infringement in the context of two computer programs written in different languages and bearing no significant literal similarities and with very little English case law to assist him. He identified the following issues raised by the case.

- Does copyright subsist in a computer program?
- If it does, does the copyright in the BBC program belong to the claimant?
- If the above questions are answered in the affirmative, what should the court's approach be to a claim of 'non-literal' copying?
- Are there any objective similarities between the BBC program and the Chemtec program enabling the Chemtec program to be regarded in any respect as a copy of the BBC program?
- Were any such similarities in fact copied from the BBC program?
- Is any copying thus found, copying of a substantial part of the BBC program?

The issue of copyright subsistence was easily dealt with by the judge and ownership of copyright in the BBC program was resolved in favour of the claimant. Although the defendant may have been the legal owner of those parts of the program he had written as a self-employed consultant, the claimant was the owner in equity (the 'beneficial owner') and, as the claimant had joined the legal owner in the action (by suing him), the full range of remedies was available to the claimant should infringement be proved.

After reviewing the English and United States authorities on non-literal copying and discussing the *Computer Associates* case at length, Mr Justice Ferris said that there was nothing in any English decision which conflicted with the general approach adopted in that case. However, he said that, in preference to seeking the 'core of protectable expression' in the claimant's program, an English court would:

- decide whether the claimant's program as a whole is entitled to copyright protection, and then
- decide whether any similarity in the defendant's program resulting from copying amounts to a substantial part of the claimant's program.

Ferris J went on to say that the approach to separation of idea and expression as expounded in *Computer Associates* was appropriate and a similar approach should be adopted in England. This would be relevant to issues of substantiality of copying and originality. Thus, the non-literal elements of a computer program are to be taken into account. In testing for infringement, the judge concentrated on objective similarities in the non-literal elements of the programs and he classified them in four ways:

- similarities that were the result of copying a substantial part of the claimant's program, being the line editor, amendment routines and drug dose codes;

- similarities that were the result of copying but not in relation to a substantial part of the claimant's program – for example, the date option, operation successful message;

- similarities which may have been the result of copying but which, in any case, did not involve copying substantial parts of the claimant's program – for example, the vertical arrangement of entry prompts;

- similarities that were not the result of copying including the use of the escape key, position of label on screen, etc.

It was held that the defendant had infringed copyright in respect of three non-literal elements. This would mean that it might be a relatively simple matter for the defendant to rewrite the offending parts of his program, notwithstanding any award in damages in respect of the infringement.

The judgment in *Richardson* v *Flanders* attracted a fair amount of criticism. In particular, Mr Justice Jacob in his judgment in *IBCOS* v *Barclays* (a case on literal copying) was particularly critical of a blind allegiance to the US approach, pointing out that UK copyright law is different, being based on a different statute. He said that the US approach was not helpful. It must be noted, however, that Jacob J was dealing with a more straightforward case of copying and the two cases are distinguishable, one being predominantly based on literal copying (*IBCOS*), the other on non-literal copying (*Richardson*). Consequently, it is possible to reconcile the two cases and the judgments can be seen as complementary. Where *Richardson* is weak is, arguably, in the abstraction to non-literal expression. Furthermore, there was no serious attempt to filter out unprotected elements but this is more likely to be due to differences between UK and US law than a failure on the part of the judge.

Finally, it should be noted that the defendant in *Richardson* v *Flanders* had made significant additions and enhancements to his program, which was substantially larger than the claimant's program and had more features. Nevertheless, when comparing programs for copyright infringement it was confirmed that more attention should be paid to the parts claimed to be the same or similar than the other parts of the program.

For some time, there was nothing further of note in case law on non-literal copying of computer programs. In *Cantor Fitzgerald*, Pumfrey J suggested that the architecture of a computer program could be protected but he did not have to rule on non-literal copying as no such allegation had been made that the architecture had been copied. Later, in *Navitaire* v *easyJet*, Pumfrey J got his opportunity to fully consider and apply the concept of non-literal copying of computer programs. This case must now be seen as the leading case on non-literal copying of computer programs. Following this is a brief discussion of another non-literal copying allegation made in relation to computer programs: *Nova* v *Mazooma Games* [2006] RPC 379.

The *Navitaire* v *easyJet* case

Navitaire Inc v *easyJet Airline Co Ltd* [2006] RPC 111 involved a deliberate attempt to write new computer programs designed to emulate the operation and functioning of an existing software system used for ticketless airline bookings. The first defendant, easyJet Airline Co Ltd ('easyJet') acquired the system, called OpenRes, from Open Skies Inc in 1996 under a licence agreement and used it for some time. Part of the system (a program called TakeFlight) was integrated into easyJet's website. The copyright in OpenRes was eventually transferred to its present owner

Navitaire Inc ('Navitaire'). By 1999, it became clear to easyJet that the part of the system integrated with its website needed enhancing with further airline routes and special offers being added together with different language versions. No satisfactory agreement could be reached with the copyright owner and easyJet commissioned the second defendant, BulletProof Technologies Inc ('BulletProof') to write a similar software system, which was called eRes. It was important that the new software should appear the same in use as OpenRes and that the existing data in the databases built up using OpenRes could be migrated to eRes. BulletProof worked in conjunction with easyJet's IT department to create eRes.

Apart from TakeFlight neither defendant had access to the OpenRes source code and did not reverse engineer the OpenRes code. In creating eRes, in effect, the operation and functionality of the OpenRes software was emulated. Navitaire sued for non-textual infringement of its copyright, *inter alia*, on the basis of the copyright in the commands used in OpenRes (simple and complex commands) individually and collectively as a compilation, in screen displays and reports and in respect of the 'business logic' underlying the OpenRes software.

The commands were those entered by the person using the software. Some were simple. An example was the command NP. If this was entered on its own, it gave access to notepad built into the software. If followed by a hyphen, it allowed the user to modify the contents of the notepad. More complex commands involved a command followed by syntax relating to a particular enquiry or activity. For example, the command A13JUNLTNAMS asked for the availability of flights from Luton to Amsterdam on the 13 June. Some were more interactive in that the initial entry triggered a request for further input.

Pumfrey J said that a single word could not be a work of copyright, regardless of whether skill or judgment was expended in its derivation. Of the complex commands, he doubted whether these could be works of copyright as they were not recorded in the program code but simply recognised by it. However, he went on to say that they were excluded from protection as being a computer programming language or user interface as the Directive on the legal protection of computer programs expressly excludes from copyright protection both computer programming languages and interfaces including user interfaces. Considering the commands as a set, Pumfrey J said he did not think they were a compilation as they had not been put together as part of some overall design. Individual commands had been written by different persons and it was possible to identify the author of each but it was not possible to identify the author or joint authors of the entire set. He also said that the set of commands was not protected as it probably was also a programming language.

Navitaire also argued that the set of commands was akin to the plot of a novel and protected in that way. That was also rejected as the user interface was not part of the computer programs themselves. Any other permutation of commands could have been made to work equally as well. The independence of the set of commands from the functions performed by the computer programs meant it was legitimate to separate them out from the program code and not give them a separate protection.

As for the screen displays, there were two types. Some were simple and consisted of text in the form of printable characters that provided a static framework for the input or display of dynamic data. These were excluded from protection on the basis that they were ideas underlying the program's interfaces. The fact that such displays could be considered to be tables (a form of literary work) was of no consequence. However, some screen displays contained graphic symbols (graphic user interfaces, or GUIs). Pumfrey J accepted that these were artistic works and protected by copyright and even the icons in the form of buttons bearing symbols were individually protected as artistic works, there being sufficient skill or labour in creating the original drawings from which they were made. To the extent that these displays had been copied by the defendants, there was infringement of copyright.

The most interesting aspect of the allegations of infringement was that Navitaire alleged that the defendants had taken the 'business logic' of OpenRes. To the end user, the functions performed by both software systems were identical. The claimant's case was that by emulating the functions and operation of its software to produce new software that worked in the same way and produced the same outputs amounted to non-textual infringement, notwithstanding that source code of the defendants' software must be different. Navitaire used the analogy of taking the plot of a literary work as a form of infringement.

Pumfrey J described this as a claim to copying without access to the thing copied, directly or indirectly. By emulating existing software, using it, observing what it does, how it handles inputs and what it outputs, the creator of the second software system saves himself the trouble of carrying out systems analysis and producing a functional specification. But this did not release the claimant from the need to show that the defendant had taken something not simply inherent in the nature of the business function. The claimant had to show that the defendant had taken something over and above that. A factor in this case was that the functions carried out by the software were common to flight booking systems. The judge noted that two completely different computer programs can produce results identical at any level of abstraction. This is so even though the creator of the second program does not have access to the source code of the first. For this reason, the analogy with the plot of a literary work was not appropriate. A computer program does not really have a plot or any narrative flow. A computer program has a series of predetermined operations directed to a desired result in response to requests from the person using the program.

Once the interfaces had been stripped away, all that was left was the business function performed by the software. The source code of the claimant's software was neither read nor copied by the defendants. Consequently, Pumfrey J held that there was no infringement by non-textual copying. He said he did not regret this conclusion which he thought to be in tune with the Directive on the legal protection of computer programs and the exclusion of protection for computer programming languages and interfaces.

An allegation was made in relation to the TakeFlight software. This served pages to customers in a predetermined sequence and had been integrated with easyJet's website. Unlike the case with the OpenRes software, easyJet had been given a copy of the source code of this program. EasyJet copied and modified this software outside the scope of its licence and the claimant was entitled to relief in respect of such activities. Finally, a claim that the defendants had infringed the copyright in databases in OpenRes was dismissed except to the limited extent that easyJet had supplied extracts of the databases to Bulletproof.

As he acknowledged, the decision of Pumfrey J accords with the House of Lords decision in *Designers Guild Ltd* v *Russell Williams (Textiles) Ltd* [2001] FSR 113 where Lord Hoffmann identified two distinct propositions concerning the distinction between ideas and the expression of ideas. First, a work may express some ideas that are not protected because they have no connection with the literary, dramatic, musical or artistic nature of the work. Thus, a literary work describing an invention does not give the author a claim to protect the invention as such. Secondly, certain ideas expressed in a copyright work may not be protected even though they are of a literary, dramatic, musical or artistic nature, because they are not original or are so commonplace as not to form a substantial part of the work.

Of the allegation of infringement of the business logic of OpenRes, Pumfrey J said (at para. 129):

> Navitaire's computer program invites input in a manner excluded from copyright protection, outputs its results in a form excluded from copyright protection and creates a record of a reservation in the name of a particular passenger on a particular flight. What is left when the interface aspects of the case are disregarded is the business function of carrying out the transaction and

creating the record, because none of the code was read or copied by the defendants. It is right that those responsible for devising OpenRes envisaged this as the end result for their program: but that is not relevant skill and labour.

He added that he thought the extension of protection to business logic through the medium of copyright in the computer program was an inappropriate extension of copyright.

The *Nova* v *Mazooma Games* case

In *Nova Productions Limited* v *Mazooma Games Limited* [2006] RPC 379 the claimant created a video game, called 'Pocket Money' based on the game of pool. Apart from being able to adjust the horizontal angle of the cue, players had to choose the timing of their shot as the 'power' of the cue hitting the ball fluctuated. The first defendant, Mazooma, created a similar video game called 'Jacket Pool'. A number of claims of copyright infringement were made (including that the video game was an artistic work and a dramatic work) but for the present purposes the important claim related to non-literal infringement of copyright in a computer program and preparatory design material for a computer program. In terms of the latter, it was argued that a substantial part of the skill and labour of the person who had designed the claimant's game was in devising the appearance and operation of it. The preparatory design materials were mainly in the form of design notes. No allegation was made that the defendants had access to or copied directly either the computer programs or the preparatory design material.

Mr Justice Kitchen held, *inter alia*, that the copyright in the computer programs and preparatory design materials for Pocket Money had not been infringed. The elements alleged to have been copied (such as similarities in how the cue was moved, values associated with each pocket and having the balls arranged in a specific pattern) were at such a level of abstraction that they could not be a substantial part of a computer program. Kitchen J said that they were '… ideas which have little to do with the skill and effort expended by the programmer and do not constitute the form of expression of the literary works relied upon'. He said that he would come to the same conclusion applying the principles from *Navitaire* v *easyJet*. Nothing had been taken in terms of program code or program architecture.

The judge then went on to say that the claimant's difficulties were even worse in relation to the preparatory design material. The materials were a series of jottings and ideas. There was nothing in the materials which looked like sketches of the screen displays alleged to have been copied. Essentially, the claim was to ideas at a high level of abstraction, and even then, those ideas were not embodied in the preparatory design materials.

Kitchen J fell into error by considering the preparatory design material as separate to the computer program to which they related. He treated preparatory design material as a work of copyright independent of the computer program. This was unlikely to have had any practical impact on the decision concerning computer programs and preparatory design material. However, the Directive on the legal protection of computer programs, as noted earlier in this chapter, makes it clear that computer programs *include* their preparatory design material. Application was made to the Court of Appeal for a reference to the European Court of Justice for a preliminary ruling in *Nova* v *Mazooma* on this point. That application was turned down but an appeal against the decision of Kitchen J is pending at the time of writing.

The future of non-literal copying of computer programs in the UK

With *Navitaire*, the position in the UK now looks somewhat different to that in the US where *Computer Associates* v *Altai* still provides the relevant test to apply. The denial of protection to computer programming languages and interfaces by the Directive on the legal protection of computer programs (at least in so much as they are idea and principles) removes significant elements of the non-literal elements of computer programs. Often what is left is not worthy of protection. The function of a computer program will not normally represent enough of the programmer's skill and judgment expended in the creation of the computer program to be considered to be a substantial part of it.

The decision in *Navitaire* must be put in the context of the allegations made in the case. There is a danger of reading more into the decision than is supported by the facts. The claimant had great difficulty in specifying just what the 'business logic' was as a non-literal element of the computer programs in question. It might be different if a claimant is able to spell out a detailed architecture or structure alleged to have been copied at a level of abstraction only one step away from the source code. This will depend on the complexity of the program or suite of programs. It could be argued that Jacob J, in finding infringement in a suite of programs as a compilation in *IBCOS*, was dealing with a non-literal aspect of the software.

The judge in *Nova v Mazooma* appeared to accept that preparatory design materials could be infringed by non-literal copying. Thus, regardless of any other copyright issues, copying a screen display could infringe the copyright in original drawings and sketches of the screen display made before any program code is written. A better way of viewing this would be to see it as a form of indirect copying. Non-literal copying might be relevant where the preparatory design material set out the program's architecture in some detail. However, in *Nova v Mazooma*, there was no evidence that anything had been copied beyond very generalised ideas.

The difficulty claimants have in specifying non-literal elements is not limited to computer programs. In *Baigent v Random House Group Ltd* [2006] EWHC 719, an allegation was made that the defendant, the publisher of the *Da Vinci Code* novel, had infringed the copyright in an earlier literary work, *The Holy Blood and the Holy Grail*. The claim was based on non-textual copying and the textual similarities were not relied on. The claimants (two of the three authors of the work alleged to have been copied) argued that the 'central theme' of their work had been copied. The claim was very unsatisfactory and the particulars of claim had been subject to extensive modification. Rather than identify the non-textual aspects of their program as a first step before comparing them to the defendant's novel, it appeared that the claimants had identified parts of the defendant's novel that had similarities with their work and then they had attempted to construct their central theme based on those similarities. The allegations were dismissed.

To summarise, it still seems possible to infringe the copyright in a computer program in the UK by taking non-literal elements. These elements must be:

- sufficiently detailed (perhaps no more than one step away from the actual code of the program);

- not excluded as being ideas or principles, for example, in relation to interfaces; and particularly user interfaces; and

- represent sufficient of the programmer's skill and judgment to be regarded as a substantial part of the computer program as a whole (bearing in mind that the preparatory design material must, in accordance with the Directive on the legal protection of computer programs, be seen as part of the computer program and not as a separate form of literary work as the Copyright, Designs and Patents Act 1988 erroneously suggests).

Emulating the functions of existing computer programs without access to the source code of the programs will not infringe if the studying and testing of the existing programs is itself permitted (for example, by being performed by a lawful user) and the creation of the new programs does not otherwise infringe. This might be so where the person creating a new program does not attempt to replicate the detailed architecture of an existing program except to the extent that it represents unprotected ideas and principles.

Issuing copies to the public

Under section 18, issuing copies of a work to the public is a restricted act and will infringe copyright if done without the permission of the owner of the copyright. However, the right to control the issue of copies to the public only applies to the first issue of individual copies within the European Economic Area ('EEA'). The EEA comprises all the Member States of the European Community together with Iceland, Liechtenstein and Norway. Thus, once a particular copy of a computer program has been issued to the public, for example on a CD-ROM, by or with the consent of the copyright owner, he can no longer use that right to control subsequent dealings with *that* particular copy, apart from rental and lending to the public. This principle is known as 'exhaustion of rights'. The rights of the copyright owner to control further distribution and sale are said to be exhausted. The owner still has the right to issue other copies to the public, of course. Importantly, the principle of exhaustion of rights does not apply to works delivered electronically, for example, by online delivery.

Exhaustion of the right to issue copies to the public would apply where, for example, a software company has sold copies of its programs on tangible media to one dealer in Germany and, at a lower price, to another dealer in France. A third party might be able to buy copies in France and import them into Germany in order to resell them, undercutting the German dealer. The software company would not be able to use its copyright to prevent this.

Communicating to the public

This restricted act was brought in to comply with the Directive on copyright in the information society.[2] The purpose was to specifically address the situation where copies of a work were made available online but it also extends to making a work available by means of a broadcast.

The restricted act of communicating a work to the public applies to all forms of copyright work with the exception of typographical arrangements of published editions. Communication to the public means, by section 20 of the Act, communication by electronic transmission which includes broadcasting the work or making it available by electronic transmission in such a way that members of the public may access the work from a place and at a time individually chosen by them. This covers, for example, the situation where a work may be accessed or downloaded from a website. The doctrine of exhaustion of rights does not apply to this means of making a work available to the public even if a charge is made for access. Therefore, a person who downloads a work from a website cannot subsequently make it available to the public, for example, by selling it or placing it on his website so that others may download it.

The Directive on the legal protection of computer programs does not have a restricted act of communication to the public and the Directive on copyright in the information society states that it does not affect the former, which it leaves intact. However, the restricted acts in the Directive on the legal protection of computer programs are stated in a non-exhaustive way by use of the phrase 'shall include the right to do or authorise' before the list of restricted acts. This would seem not to preclude the addition of further rights. When the Directive on the legal protection of computer programs was drafted, online delivery of computer programs was not a practical option.

---

[2] Directive 2001/29/EC of the European Parliament and of the Council of 22 May 2001 on the harmonisation of certain aspects of copyright and related rights in the information society, OJ L 167, 22.06.2001, p. 10 (the 'Directive on copyright in the information society).

Rental or lending copies to the public

By virtue of section 18A (which was inserted by the Copyright and Related Rights Regulations 1996) the rental or lending of copies of a work to the public is an act restricted by the copyright. This provision applies to literary, dramatic and musical works, to artistic works (except works of architecture and works of applied art) and films and sound recordings. 'Rental' and 'lending' do not include a number of specific acts such as communicating the work to the public.

Making an adaptation

Making an adaptation of a literary, dramatic or musical work is a restricted act. In terms of a musical work, a new arrangement of a song is an adaptation of the original. Changing a cartoon strip into a story told by words only is also making an adaptation, as is a translation of a literary or dramatic work, for example, from one language to another. An adaptation is made when it is recorded in writing or otherwise. Doing any of the restricted acts in relation to an adaptation, including making an adaptation of an adaptation, also infringes if done without the copyright owner's permission. This could apply where a person translates into German a novel in French which was translated from the original English.

For a computer program, making an adaptation means making an arrangement or altered version of the program or a translation of it: section 21(3)(ab). 'Translation' has a special meaning for computer programs, by section 21(4), and includes:

> ... a version of the program in which it is converted into or out of a computer language or code or into a different computer language or code.

The Directive on the legal protection of computer programs includes in the restricted acts making a translation, adaptation, arrangement and any other alteration of a computer program and the reproduction of the results thereof, without prejudice to the rights of the person who alters the program. There is no definition of translation as there is in the Act. Despite these differences, it is at least as likely as not that the provisions on making adaptations of computer programs in the Act are equivalent to those in the Directive.

If a high-level, source code computer program is compiled (converted) into an object code program, this will be an adaptation of the source code program and, therefore, a restricted act.

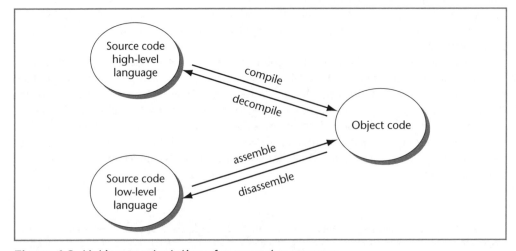

Figure 4.2 Making an adaptation of a computer program

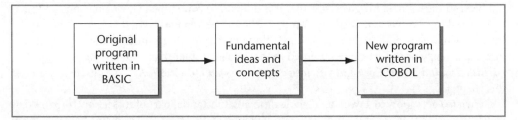

Figure 4.3 Conversion of a computer program

This provision is aimed at controlling the compilation, decompilation, assembly and disassembly of computer programs – that is, the conversion of source code programs into object code and vice versa as shown in Fig. 4.2. This would seem to be a reasonable activity to be controlled by copyright, especially as the reverse engineering of an object code program will make the techniques, ideas and principles underlying a computer program more accessible. As we shall see later, however, under certain circumstances this is expressly permitted under copyright law where the purpose is to create a new program which can be operated with that or another program. Furthermore, underlying ideas and principles are not protected by copyright. This is confirmed by the Directive on the legal protection of computer programs and certain acts can be carried out to access those ideas and principles though not decompilation or disassembly.

Source code programs are protected by copyright provided they are 'original' – that is, they are the result of skill, labour or judgment. (Strictly speaking the test should be that the computer program is the author's own intellectual creation.) The position is less clear as far as object code programs are concerned because they may not be deemed to be the author's own intellectual creation or even original in the sense described above. In most cases, an object code program will have been created by submitting the source code program to a compiler program or assembler program. This process may require little effort or skill on the part of the person creating the object code unless there are several errors detected which need correction before a suitable executable version of the object code is obtained. Even if an object code program is not itself an original literary work, it will be protected by copyright as an adaptation of such a work and the restricted acts extend to an adaptation as they do to the original work. Thus, it is an infringement of copyright to copy an adaptation of a program or even to make an adaptation of an adaptation.

It could be argued that the meaning of translation is too wide as it might catch a version of a source code program written in a different high-level language from that used for the original program. If a computer program is written using BASIC and someone then rewrites the program in COBOL, is the latter an adaptation of the BASIC program because it has been converted into a different computer language? To produce a program in a different high-level language, however, is not merely a question of translating the program instructions from one language to another as with spoken languages. The programmer would have to reduce the original program to its underlying concepts and ideas and from those concepts and ideas (not from the computer program itself) develop a new version of the program in another high-level language, as shown in Fig. 4.3.

The differences between the two programs could be as those between *Romeo and Juliet* and *West Side Story* and, as a basic principle, copyright should not protect ideas as such, only the expression or recording of those ideas. However, it seems that the new version of a program in a different high-level language could be seen as a translation of the original program and, hence, an adaptation of it. This is regardless of the considerable amount of skill and effort required to 'translate' the program in such a way. This could be a way to catch non-literal copying of computer programs but there has been no case law on this. Where the code of the first program has not been studied, a major drawback is that it is difficult to contemplate how a person can translate something he has not seen. However, it should be remembered that copyright can be infringed indirectly and the House of Lords thought it possible to infringe the copyright in a drawing by copying the article represented in the drawing rather than copying the drawing itself (*British Leyland Motor Corp Ltd* v *Armstrong Patents Co Ltd* [1986] AC 577, discussed later in this chapter).

Restricted acts apply to a work as a whole or to any substantial part of it (section 16(3)). What is substantial is a matter of fact and the courts will look to quality as well as quantity (see *Hawkes & Sons (London) Ltd* v *Paramount Film Service Ltd* [1934] Ch 593). Therefore, a computer program which includes parts (such as sub-routines) copied from another program will infringe the copyright in that other program if the copied parts represent a substantial part of the original program (including its preparatory design material) and they may be substantial if they go to the root of the other program or capture its essence, even though they are small in terms of quantity.

Theoretically, it might seem possible to increase copyright protection by modularising a single program into a number of separate sub-programs which, if each individually is the result of skill, labour and effort, will all be independently protected in addition to any copyright in the suite of programs as a compilation. Substantiality, in terms of infringement, will be measured by comparison with a sub-program rather than the unified whole. However, there are limits to this and the part copied must represent a substantial part of the author's skill or judgment used in creating that part. Furthermore, the judgment in *Cantor Fitzgerald International* v *Tradition (UK) Ltd* [2000] RPC 95, discussed earlier in this chapter, suggests that it is unlikely that decisions made in respect of how to modularise a program or suite of programs will, *per se*, be the result of sufficient skill or judgment for the purposes of copyright subsistence. In that case, Pumfrey J said (at para. 160):

> ... the division of source code into modules and so on is as much a result of pressures extraneous to writing the software (such as debugging, maintenance and convenient building) as it is a result of deliberate design. Indeed, some methods of writing software may decide the modules for the programmer. I attach no importance to such divisions ...

Pumfrey J said that there was a temptation to break down copyright works into smaller parts because a substantial part of the small work may not be a substantial part of a larger work. This ignored the fact that substantiality was a matter of quality rather than quantity. However, computer programmers might take issue with the view that decisions as to how to modularise computer software including computer programs lacks the basic requirement for skill or judgment. In any case, the question should be whether such decisions can be said to be the programmer's own intellectual creation.

PERMITTED ACTS FOR COMPUTER PROGRAMS

When it was decided in 1985 to classify computer programs as literary works for copyright purposes, the usual exceptions to copyright infringement applied. The Act contains a great many exceptions, called the 'permitted acts': for example, fair dealing for research or private study or for criticism, review or news reporting. The purpose of the Directive on the legal protection of computer programs was to provide for a fair, balanced and uniform protection of computer programs throughout the European Community. UK law was already well developed and complied in some respects with the Directive's provisions but changes to the Act were necessary to fully implement the Directive. We have seen that the implementation in respect of subsistence was defective and the courts should turn to the text of the Directive rather than the equivalent provisions in the Act.

In order to ensure the scope of protection was balanced, the Directive provided for some specific permitted acts for computer programs (described as exceptions to the restricted acts in the Directive). These permitted acts were transposed into UK law by the Copyright (Computer Programs) Regulations 1992 and are:

- 'decompiling' an existing computer program for interoperability;
- making necessary back-up copies;
- copying and adapting for lawful use including error correction;
- observing, studying or testing a computer program to determine the underlying ideas and principles.

These four important exceptions to copyright infringement apply only if carried out by a lawful user of the computer program (for example, a person having the right to use the program under a licence agreement) and are described and examined in detail below. But first, it should be pointed out that the previous law may have covered the above acts in some circumstances. For example, fair dealing for research purposes might have allowed decompilation to achieve interoperability, though now fair dealing for research is limited to non-commercial purposes. Implied licences might have been appropriate in some cases involving error correction and the making of back-up copies. The final permitted act above is required to enable lawful users to gain access to underlying ideas and principles as ideas and principles, including those underlying the program's interfaces, which are expressly excluded from protection by the Directive.

Decompilation of computer programs

Article 6 of the Directive on the legal protection of computer programs provides an exception to the restricted acts, known as decompilation, being where a person reproduces program code or makes a translation of it to obtain the information necessary to achieve the interoperability of an independently created computer program with other computer programs (including, presumably, the one which has been the subject matter of the acts of reproduction and/or translation). The acts must be carried out by or on behalf of a licensee of the program or some other person having a right to use it. Furthermore, the information necessary to achieve interoperability must not be readily available to the persons carrying out the acts and the acts themselves must be confined to the parts of the original program which are necessary to achieve interoperability. The latter point is a difficult one as it may not be easy or even possible to determine which parts of the program contain the relevant information.

The Directive imposes further conditions and the information so obtained must not be used for goals other than to achieve the interoperability of the independently created computer program and must not be given to others, except when necessary for the interoperability of the independently created computer program. The information must not be used for the development, production or marketing of a computer program substantially similar in its expression, or for any other act which infringes copyright. Finally, Article 6 is not to be interpreted in such a way so as to unreasonably prejudice the copyright owner's legitimate interests or to conflict with a normal exploitation of the computer program.

As was common in those days, the UK implementation attempted to make the provision more precise by rewriting the wording of the Directive rather than simply write it out in the relevant parts of the Act. This can only lead to potential difficulties in interpreting the UK provision although in case of doubt, the wording of the Directive should be followed.

4

Copyright and computer programs

Section 50B was inserted into the Act and 'decompilation' is defined as converting a copy of a computer program expressed in a low-level language into a version expressed in a higher-level language. Copying incidental to such conversion is also permitted. The restricted act of making an adaptation includes decompilation (and will also involve making at least a temporary copy of the program) and infringes copyright unless allowed by the decompilation permitted act. By section 50B(1), a lawful user (being a person having a right under a licence or otherwise to use the program: section 50A(2)) may decompile the program if necessary to obtain the information necessary to achieve the interoperability of any independently created program with the decompiled program or another program. In other words, it is permissible for a lawful user to decompile or disassemble a computer program to determine its interfaces if this is a necessary step in creating a new program which will interoperate (interact) with that or some other program.

Typically, a software developer might want to write a word processing program which will be compatible with another company's spreadsheet program (Spreadsheet A) so that data and files can be passed between the two programs (see Fig. 4.4). This form of compatibility is certainly desirable and should not cause any great concerns, unless the spreadsheet company was hoping to make its own compatible word processor in the future. Once the compatible interoperable program has been created there seems no reason why the interface details cannot be used subsequently to create competing, replacement programs (Spreadsheet B) as long as a substantial copy is not made of the original program.

The Copyright, Designs and Patents Act 1988, as amended, attempts to deal with this situation by making the use or supply of the information for any other objective, or in the development, production or marketing of any computer program substantially similar in its expression to the original program, an infringement of copyright (section 50B(2)). However, re-using of interface details will not necessarily result in a substantially similar expression and, in the example in Fig. 4.4, the expression (program listings and structure) may be quite different. Interface details may be qualitatively insubstantial; after all the program is a spreadsheet program, not an interface

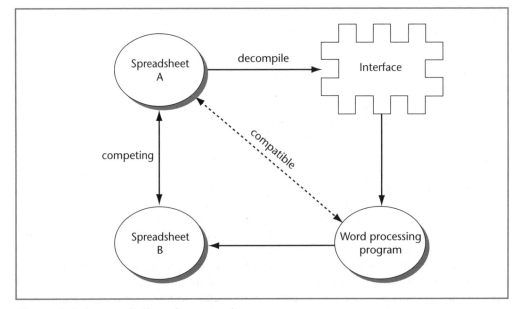

Figure 4.4 Decompilation of a computer program

program, and may be written in different code to achieve the same purpose. In practice, these provisions will be very difficult to apply but the preamble to the Directive may give some assistance as it talks about the European Community being fully committed to the promotion of international standardisation. The permitted act of decompilation does not apply if the information required has been previously readily available (section 50B(3)): for example, the interface details have been published or made available at reasonable cost. A further point is that there is no need to rely on the right unless the decompilation is carried out to a substantial part of the original program (there is no infringement to excuse otherwise). The decompilation permitted act cannot be prohibited or restricted by a term in a licence agreement, any such term being void and unenforceable at law (section 296A).

Back-up copies of computer programs

It is essential that back-up copies of computer programs be made. A back-up copy will be needed if the original copy of the computer program becomes damaged or corrupted in any way. The original may be physically damaged, for example, if the surface of the magnetic or optical disk on which the program was delivered has been scratched or damaged in other ways. The original program, if stored on re-writeable media, may become contaminated with a computer virus. If a computer program has been obtained for use in a commercial environment, whether it is a word processing package, accounts system or spreadsheet, the chances are that the software will fail at the worst possible moment. If a back-up copy is available, a potential disaster can be averted and the urgent document, spreadsheet or whatever can still be completed on time.

The Act, as amended, makes specific provision for the making of back-up copies of computer programs. Before the amendments made by the Copyright (Computer Programs) Regulations 1992, there was no such provision although the courts may have been prepared to imply an appropriate term into a software licence where the making of a back-up copy was a reasonable thing to do in the circumstances. Of course, many software companies make express provision for the user to make a back-up copy.

Section 50A states that copyright is not infringed by a lawful user making an additional copy of a computer program for back-up purposes if doing so is necessary to the lawful use. This right cannot be taken away by any terms in a licence agreement but there may be some difficulty with deciding when making a back-up copy is truly necessary. It might not be so if a licence agreement includes terms to the effect that the licensor will himself make a further copy available to the licensee in the event of failure of the original copy.

The Act recognises the possibility that back-up copies may have been made and deals with the situation where copies of a work obtained in electronic form have been lawfully made and the original is then transferred to another person. In such circumstances, section 56 makes any copies so made and not transferred infringing copies.

Copying and adapting for lawful use including error correction

By section 50C, a lawful user is permitted to copy or adapt a computer program providing that it is necessary for his lawful use and not prohibited by the agreement regulating the use (for example, a licence agreement). Section 50C(2) provides a specific example of when this may be necessary, that is, where it is for the purpose of error correction. A licence agreement may specifically prohibit error correction so that all this provision does is to raise a presumption in favour of the lawful user. For example, if disassembling a computer program in order to correct errors is necessary to the lawful use and there are no express terms prohibiting this, then it can be done without infringing copyright.

All of this broadly accords with the Directive on the legal protection of computer programs which allows, in the absence of specific contractual provisions, the performance of acts of reproduction and making adaptations, etc. if necessary for the use of the computer program by a lawful acquirer in accordance with its intended purpose, including error correction. Again, the meaning of 'necessary' may be at issue but the important factor is that the presumption that a lawful acquirer may correct errors can be and, in many cases in practice, will be negated by express terms. Many software companies are reluctant to allow licensees or third parties to modify their computer programs. Any such modifications could be carried out badly, resulting in unfavourable publicity for the software company through no fault of its own. A more telling factor is that software companies developing specialised software for clients like to reserve for themselves the ongoing maintenance of the software including error correction.

Even though a licence agreement may prohibit error correction by the licensee or a third party acting on the licensee's behalf, it is possible that other areas of law may apply to defeat the prohibition. The common law principle of non-derogation from grant was used in *British Leyland Motor Corp Ltd* v *Armstrong Patents Co Ltd* [1986] AC 577 to stop British Leyland enforcing its copyright in drawings of exhaust systems for cars so as to prevent a free market in spare parts. The same argument holds true for computer programs. A licensee should have access to a free market in maintaining the programs and there are signs that judges might accept this in appropriate circumstances.

European Community or domestic competition law may also impinge on terms prohibiting error correction by anyone other than the licensee on the basis that this is restrictive of trade between Member States under Article 81(1) of the EC Treaty.[3] Alternatively, where the licensor is a major software company, a restriction on third party maintenance could be seen as an abuse of a dominant position under Article 82. UK competition law also has equivalent provisions under the Competition Act 1998. The major difference is that the European Community provisions apply where the activity concerned may affect trade between Member States or competition within the Community whereas, the Competition Act controls relevant activities where the effects are within the United Kingdom. Competition law provisions are described in more detail in Chapter 15.

Observing, studying or testing to determine underlying ideas and principles

Section 50BA of the Copyright, Designs and Patents Act 1988 permits a lawful user of a computer program to observe, study or test the functioning of a computer program in order to determine the ideas and principles underlying any element of the program. There is a proviso that in doing so the lawful user may only perform acts of loading, displaying, running, transmitting or storing the program that he is entitled to do. There is no mention of making an adaptation for the purpose of determining the underlying ideas and principles.

Any term or condition in an agreement which purports to prohibit or restrict acts permitted under section 50BA is void by virtue of section 296A to the extent that it does purport to prohibit or restrict such acts. This latter section also applies to terms which attempt to interfere with the permitted acts of decompilation and making necessary back-up copies. Therefore, the right to observe, study and test cannot be prejudiced by means of contractual terms, such as a term in the licence agreement under which a person has a right to use a computer program.

These provisions reinforce the idea/expression dichotomy in copyright (ideas are not protected, only the expression of ideas is capable of protection) but is unlikely to be welcomed by

---

[3] The Treaty Establishing the European Communities (Consolidated Version, OJ C 325, 24.12.2002, p. 33).

software producers. It would, for example, excuse the form of reverse engineering used in the case of *Dyason* v *Autodesk* [1992] RPC 575 (measuring the electrical signals passing between the dongle and the computer program). The permitted act could also be used to facilitate the creation of a computer program designed to emulate the operation and functionality of an existing computer program.

PROGRAMMING LANGUAGES AND INSTRUCTION SETS

A computer program is written using a specific computer programming language. Languages vary enormously from the basic instruction set of the central processing unit to high-level languages, such as BASIC and C++, and languages used for programming logic. A great deal of skill, imagination and effort goes into the design of a new programming language and the development of new languages will be encouraged if some form of protection is afforded to them. However, the exercise of rights in languages could seriously interfere with the licensing and distribution of computer programs and databases. In principle, there is a strong argument for saying that programming languages are ideas and, as such, cannot be protected by copyright. Therefore a person who writes an original program in COBOL infringes no copyright in the process of writing the program. There is an analogy with natural language and it would be ridiculous to suggest that writing an article or report using 'Esperanto' infringed any copyright subsisting in the language. Of course, making an unauthorised copy of an Esperanto–English dictionary would infringe copyright, if only that subsisting in the typographical arrangement.

The Directive on the legal protection of computer programs recognises that programming languages, at least to the extent that they comprise ideas and principles, should not be protected by copyright. Given that this is so one might wonder wherein lies the incentive to create a new language. The answer lies in the fact that, usually, the program, once written, can only be run on a computer if it is converted into object code whether temporarily, using an interpreter program, or permanently, using a compiler program. The licensing of these interpreter and compiler programs, together with appropriate documentation describing the syntax, semantics and use of the language, is the method by which financial reward is usually sought. These programs are, of course, protected by copyright.

Some languages and program development tools (languages in a wide sense including database development software and programs to generate code for screen displays and moving images) require 'run-time' licences to be acquired before application programs and systems may be distributed. These generally permit the copying and distribution of a cut-down version of the language, tool or shell sufficient to run the application.

A computer's instruction set represents a language at its most basic level and, at this level, it is nearest to idea and, when used to write small programs, it has been argued that there is a merger of idea and expression – in which case protection will be denied. This happened in the US case of *NEC Corp* v *Intel Corp* (1989) 10 USPQ 2d where it was held that Intel's microcode programs were dictated by the instruction set of the microprocessors and, as there were no alternative ways of expressing the ideas incorporated, reverse analysis of the microcode programs did not infringe copyright. However, it was also accepted that such programs could be protected if not dictated by idea.

In the UK, the question of copyright protection for an instruction set was considered in *Microsense Systems Ltd* v *Control Systems Technology Ltd* (unreported) 17 June 1991, Chancery Division. The claimant made traffic control systems and controllers for pelican crossings, which were programmed using a set of mnemonics (a set of three-letter symbols) which were in turn used to monitor the controllers. The defendant made similar controllers and used a total of 49 of the claimant's mnemonics arguing that there was no copyright in them because, once the functions had been decided, there was no room for skill and labour in devising the mnemonics. This was an interim hearing so no final decision was taken but the judge thought that there was an arguable case that the list of mnemonics was protected by copyright because of the work in designing the controller in the first place. This seems to contradict the *NEC* v *Intel* case although, being an American case, it is not binding on the courts in the UK. However, the defendant's argument that the list was effectively idea reflects the desirability of standardisation in traffic controllers as, otherwise, there could be catastrophic mistakes.

The facts of the *Microsense* case occurred before the Directive on the legal protection of computer programs was implemented and must be viewed with some suspicion now. Recital 14 to the Directive confirms that, to the extent that logic, algorithms and programming languages comprise ideas and principles, those ideas and principles are not protected by copyright. That being so, it would seem unlikely that the decision would now be the same.

OWNERSHIP, EMPLOYEES AND FREELANCE PROGRAMMERS

The basic rule is that the author of a work is the first owner of the copyright in the work. An exception which applies to literary, dramatic, musical or artistic works (and films) is where the work is made by an 'employee in the course of his employment', in which case the employer becomes the first owner of the copyright in the work, subject to any agreement to the contrary (section 11(2)). Further exceptions apply in the case of Crown copyright, Parliamentary copyright and copyright of certain international organisations. These latter exceptions are not considered further.

The main issues in terms of writing computer programs and other items of software is whether a work has been made by an employee in the course of his employment or, if not, whether there are any provisions concerning ownership of copyright. If there is no agreement as to ownership of copyright where, for example, a person creates a computer program as a self-employed consultant, can the law step in to resolve any potential difficulties? This is a problem that is very common. All too often, a company commissioning the creation of a work of copyright assumes that it will own the copyright because it has paid for the creation of the work. That assumption is wrong.

This raises the following questions.

- Who is an employee and what is meant by 'in the course of employment'?
- What is the position regarding self-employed computer programmers?
- What is the position where a program is created by employees of a software development company?

The Copyright, Designs and Patents Act 1988 does not specifically define these terms but states that 'employed', 'employee', 'employer' and 'employment' refer to employment under a contract of service or apprenticeship (section 178). The question of ownership of computer programs created by employees is considered first.

The employee and the course of employment

Deciding whether a person is an employee is not an easy question. It depends on a number of factors, such as whether income tax is stopped at source, whether the person is paid during holidays, who pays pension contributions and national insurance payments, what degree of control there is over the employee's work and, if the work is defective, does the person have to put it right at his own expense? A couple of points can be made in relation to persons creating computer programs and other items of software:

■ The degree of control over what a person does is less relevant where computer programs are being written as a computer programmer may have specialised knowledge and expertise that the employer and employer's managers may not have.

■ The status of computer programmers has become clouded as a result of tax legislation: the notorious IR 35 tax regime. Many self-employed computer programmers worked under the auspices of limited companies to take advantage of the tax rules. The main thrust of IR 35 was to treat as employees, for tax purposes, such persons where they worked for one client at a time in circumstances such that they would otherwise be treated as employees. This anti-tax avoidance legislation has clouded the issue of whether a person is an employee for copyright purposes (this is discussed in the section on self-employed programmers).

The basic distinction between a person who is an employee and one who is not is whether the contract under which he is engaged can be seen as a contract of service (employee) or a contract for services (not an employee). As with any doubts as to whether the work in question was created in the course of employment, the safest course where there is any doubt is to provide contractually for this. It is important to ensure that contracts of employment have appropriate terms and job descriptions are kept up to date to reflect changes in duties. Where it is doubtful whether a person is an employee, a letter of engagement should contain an acknowledgement as to copyright ownership or an express assignment of copyright and be signed by the person engaged to create the work.

As regards persons who can safely be classified as employees, their employers cannot assume that they will own the copyright in everything produced by those employees. If a person employed as an accountant writes a computer program to help with his work, his job is not to write computer programs and his employer cannot necessarily assume that he will own the copyright in the computer program. A lecturer normally owns the copyright in any book or article he writes because he is primarily employed as a teacher and not as a writer of books and articles, even though his employer may encourage this.

A person employed as an accountant who writes a computer program to help with the production of financial accounts will own the copyright in that program if he wrote it in his own time, using his own equipment. Initially, this may create no problems because the accountant may have been motivated by interest and a desire to improve his own efficiency at work but problems could arise later if the accountant moves to another firm or discovers that his program is commercially viable. If an employer is faced with the situation where an employee has, in his own time and using his own equipment, developed a useful computer program, then the employer should immediately try to reach agreement as regards questions of ownership and use of the program with the employee concerned, rather than allowing the program to be used without such agreement.

If an employee, whose job description does not extend to writing computer programs, creates a computer program then he will be the first owner of the copyright unless he has already assigned the copyright. This is so even if he used his employer's computer to write the program and did so during normal working hours. The only possible exception could be where the employer knew about this and encouraged it. In these circumstances, it could be argued that the contract of employment was modified by implied mutual consent.

In *Stephenson Jordan & Harrison Ltd* v *MacDonald & Evans* [1952] RPC 10, an employed accountant gave some lectures, which he later incorporated into a book. Some parts of the book had been typed by the employer's typists. It was held that, even though his employer had provided secretarial help, the copyright in the lectures belonged to the accountant because he was employed as an accountant to advise clients, and not to deliver public lectures. However, part of the book was based on a report that the accountant had written for a client of his employer, so the copyright in this part belonged to his employer.

Self-employed programmers

It is essential when employing self-employed computer programmers, or anyone else who is not employed under a permanent contract of employment, to make contractual provision for determining ownership of copyright. The organisation hiring the programmer may want to own the copyright so that it can exploit the resultant program itself, or it may simply want to prevent its competitors from obtaining a copy of it. In either of these situations, the contract should specifically state that the ownership of the copyright belongs to the organisation and not to the programmer and, furthermore, there should be a written assignment of copyright, signed by the programmer. Of course, the fee charged will probably be greater as a result because the programmer might have envisaged making use of the program elsewhere; he may know of other businesses which would be interested in what he produces. On the other hand, if the commissioning organisation does not itself contemplate commercially exploiting the software or preventing others from using it, then it is important that a term is included in the contract granting a licence for the continued use of the program, specifying the use that may be made of the program.

One issue for a self-employed programmer asked to assign his copyright is that he may wish to retain rights in certain modules that he uses in other software he creates. These may be part of the programmer's toolkit and he may want to consider an appropriate reservation in any assignment of copyright to the client.

If the contract is silent on ownership of copyright, the programmer may later decide to test his ownership of the program by offering it to others or ask the client for an additional fee to assign the copyright to the client. These difficulties may arise especially when the program in question turns out to be more useful and successful than the parties originally envisaged. There is a danger that a programmer will try to hold his client to ransom if he later realises that the value of the software he has produced is out of proportion to the payment he received for creating it.

Where the programmer is a freelance, in practice, he may be employed by an agency. In this case the same precautions apply. In the absence of an assignment of copyright, it is unlikely that the copyright in the program will be deemed to belong to the agency. It is unrealistic to say that the programmer created the program in the course of his employment by the agency. The programmer could be the legal owner of the copyright unless developments in relation to tax law can be transposed into the copyright arena. Of course, the safest solution is to consider who the owner will be at the outset and make proper provision for this by way of an assignment or licence.

It became common for computer software professionals to set up small limited companies or partnerships, perhaps with a spouse as co-director or partner. This was advantageous for the purposes of calculating tax liability. However, where the circumstances are such that the individual would otherwise be deemed to be an employee of the client, for example, where he or she works for a single client for a prolonged period of time, such persons are now deemed as employees for tax purposes. In such cases, the distinction between self-employed consultants and employees has become blurred by the changes to tax law made by the notorious IR 35 'anti-tax avoidance' provisions in the Finance Act 2000. The basic difference between a self-employed consultant and an employee is that the former works under a *contract for services* whereas employees work under a *contract of service*.

In *Synaptek Ltd* v *Young (Inspector of Taxes)* [2003] ICR 1149, a consultant software engineer carried out work under the auspices of a company, the only directors being the engineer and his wife. He carried out work for a government department for a period of six months. It was held that the tax commissioners were correct in deciding that, had the engineer worked directly for the government department, he would have been an employee. A number of factors were put forward in favour of a finding that the contract was a contract for services rather than a contract of service. They were that the client had only limited control of the time and manner in which the engineer performed his duties, his company provided training and computer facilities at his own premises, the contract with the client contained provisions dealing with intellectual property rights and the engineer was required by the client to provide professional indemnity insurance. On the other hand, the minimum working hours were broadly equivalent to a normal working week, the engineer's only financial risk was that the client might become insolvent (extremely unlikely in the particular circumstances), the duration of the contract was six months, the engineer worked with other staff of the client and his work was sufficiently integrated with the other workers for him to have a line manager and the fact that he agreed to comply with the client's instructions. On balance, the court thought that the commissioners had not been mistaken in law and confirmed that the IR 35 provisions applied.

The decision in this case, makes it very difficult to predict whether a person, working on his/her own behalf or under the auspices of a company or partnership, is an employee of the client. What, for example, if the software engineer worked for the client for only three months or worked more irregular hours or where the work was not integrated with that of employees of the client? This makes it even more important to expressly provide for ownership of copyright and any other intellectual property rights subsisting in the programs and other items of software created by the person engaged by the client.

The final point that can be made is that *Synaptek* was a tax case and it does not necessarily provide a precedent that would apply in relation to the question of whether a computer programmer is an employee for the purpose of determining copyright ownership. However, it is submitted that it might well be applicable to the copyright provisions on computer programs created by employees.

Programs created by employees of software development companies

Where a computer program is created by employees of a software development company (not being a company set up by a self-employed programmer to attempt to take advantage of the tax system) in the absence of any agreement otherwise, the copyright will belong to the software development company. Software development companies normally make specific provision for ownership of copyright and, in many cases, they want to retain ownership and grant the client a licence. This will permit the software development company to licence the program or a similar program to other clients. If the client wants an assignment of copyright, this should be made clear and provided for by the normal rules for a legal assignment (in writing and signed by or on behalf of the person granting the assignment).

The position could become more complex where the software development company engages self-employed programmers to carry out the work although such companies are usually alert to the need to provide for copyright ownership. An example of the difficulties that can arise in relation to copyright ownership and software development companies is given in the case of *Cyprotex Discovery Ltd* v *University of Sheffield* [2004] RPC 887, discussed in Chapter 15.

OPEN SOURCE SOFTWARE AND COPYRIGHT

A person may write some software such as a computer program and be quite happy to allow others to use, modify, copy and distribute it free of charge. A significant amount of 'free' software (often referred to as 'freeware') is available. There also exists software called 'shareware' which is often freely available but on a trial basis only and continued use sometimes attracts a licence fee. Open Source Software (for example, Linux) is the term used for software distributed freely under the Open Source Initiative's requirements for licensing arrangements. A number of organisations, individuals and software companies distribute software in this way under licences controlling the distribution and use of open source software and many such licences are available. One example is the GNU General Public Licence which operates a 'Copyleft' system enabling the distribution of free software and ensuring all modified and extended versions of the software are also available free of charge. Copyleft operates by using a licence to control the use and further distribution of free software.

The fact that software is made freely available does not mean that it is not subject to copyright or other intellectual property rights, if applicable. The normal rules apply as to subsistence of copyright and the identity of the author and owner of the copyright. Furthermore, in some jurisdictions such as the UK, except in relation to computer programs, the author will enjoy the moral rights to be identified as the author and to object to a derogatory treatment of the software (for example, in relation to copyright databases and other works, such as audio-visual works and documents, included in the software).

If a person, being the owner of copyright in software, wishes to allow others to use it free of charge, a number of technical and legal issues arise. First, the rationale behind open source software is that it should be freely available to others who may use it, modify it and/or include it in an overall software package containing other items of software (whether free or otherwise) and freely distribute it in its original or modified form without charging end users. For this to work effectively, the source code should also be readily available free of charge (or for a small charge reflecting the cost of distributing it). One of the aims is to encourage the evolution, development and spread of good software. A danger is that someone who has obtained a copy of open source software modifies it and then claims proprietary rights in it and then distributes the modified version only in return for a substantial licence fee. Another concern is that liability might attach to the originator or persons subsequently modifying the software if it proves defective or if it interferes with a third-party intellectual property right. It is usual, therefore, to include a written licence with the software to deal with such matters. A US company, SCO Group Inc, has made numerous claims that some implementations using Linux infringe SCO's copyright. In one such case, SCO claimed that IBM had infringed SCO's copyright by IBM's Unix-like Linux operating system. The case rumbles on in the US District Court for Utah. In a hearing on 8 February 2005 to dismiss or stay certain claims and to ask for summary judgment on certain aspects Judge Kimball said:

> Viewed against the backdrop of SCO's plethora of public statements concerning IBM's and others' infringement of SCO's purported copyrights to the Unix software, it is astonishing that SCO has not offered any competent evidence to create a disputed fact regarding whether IBM has infringed SCO's alleged copyrights through IBM's Linux activities.

It is always advisable to include a copyright notice on the software (preferably also displayed on screen when the software is operated) with the familiar copyright symbol ©, the name of the owner of the copyright and the year of first publication. If there are any moral rights these should also be spelt out, for example, by a notice stating that the author asserts his moral right to be identified as author of the work.

The licence should spell out precisely what rights are being granted and, if it is desired that the software can be modified and redistributed, that relevant copyright notices are placed on such copies. It may be sensible to include all such information and, indeed, the licence itself within the software.

In many countries, anyone removing or modifying such information without permission will be liable as if they had infringed the copyright (see the section on electronic rights management information in Chapter 7 on copyright in the information society).

If the software is modified by subsequent users, they should be required to indicate on the software that this has happened, when it happened and that they have copyright in the modification. If possible, some indication of the nature of the modifications should also be given. The originator of the software may require to be informed of modifications and may even require a copy to be made available.

SUMMARY

- Copyright protects as literary works computer programs that are:
  - the author's own intellectual creation;
  - recorded in writing or otherwise;
  - non-trivial; and
  - qualifying.
- Computer programs include their preparatory design materials.
- Infringement of copyright by literal copying of a computer program requires that:
  - copyright subsists in the computer program;
  - the defendant copied from the computer program;
  - the part copied represents a substantial part of the computer program.
- Copyright does not protect the ideas and principles underlying computer programs.
- Infringement of copyright by non-literal copying remains a possibility but is difficult to show because:
  - ideas and principles are not protected including those underlying program interfaces; and
  - the claim must be carefully formulated to properly identify the architecture alleged to have been copied.
- Computer programming languages, to the extent they comprise ideas and principles, are not protected by copyright.
- There are a number of special permitted acts that apply to computer programs.
- Ownership problems may arise where computer programs are created by persons who are not employees creating the programs in the course of their employment.

SELF-TEST QUESTIONS

Note: there is only one correct answer to each multiple choice question.

1   **In relation to the Directive on the legal protection for computer programs, which one of the following statements is NOT CORRECT?**

   (a) Ideas and principles underlying any element of a computer program are not protected by copyright.

   (b) The term 'computer programs' does not include their preparatory design material.

   (c) Computer programs are protected as literary works.

   (d) A computer program is protected if it is original in the sense that it is the author's own intellectual creation.

2   **Copying is an act restricted by copyright. In relation to copying a computer program, which one of the following statements is NOT CORRECT?**

   (a) For infringement of copyright by copying, the part copied by the defendant must be a substantial part of the claimant's computer program but need not be a substantial part of the defendant's computer program.

   (b) Copying includes making copies that are transient or incidental to some other use of the computer program.

   (c) Copying may be direct or indirect.

   (d) Non-executable parts of computer programs, such as the data division in a COBOL program, and remark lines in programs are ignored when addressing the question of copying.

3   **The Directive on the legal protection of computer programs denies protection to ideas and principles underlying any element of a computer program, including its interfaces. In which one of the following ways does the Copyright, Designs and Patents Act 1988 make underlying ideas and principles ACCESSIBLE to others.**

   (a) By providing a permitted act allowing a lawful user to decompile a computer program in order to determine the ideas and principles underlying any element of the computer program providing this is necessary in order to determine those ideas or principles.

   (b) By providing that an exclusive licensee of a computer program in object code may call upon the copyright owner to release a copy of the program's source code, subject to an implied obligation of confidence in respect of the source code.

   (c) By providing a permitted act allowing a lawful user to observe, study and test the functioning of a program to determine the ideas and principles underlying any element of the program if he does so by performing any of the acts of loading, displaying, running, transmitting or storing the program which he is entitled to do.

   (d) By providing a permitted act allowing a lawful user to copy or adapt the computer program if necessary for his lawful use, including error correction subject to this not being prohibited by a term or condition of an agreement regulating the use of the program.

4   **Which one of the following statements is CORRECT in relation to a computer program created by an employee?**

   (a) In the absence of any valid assignment of the copyright in the computer program, the employee will be the first owner of the copyright.

(b) If the computer program was created in the course of the employee's employment, the employer will be the first owner of the copyright, subject to any agreement to the contrary.

(c) Technically, the employee will be the first owner of the copyright at law but the employer will be the beneficial owner of the copyright.

(d) The employee and the employer will be joint first owners of the copyright unless there is a term in the contract of employment stating that the employer will automatically own all the intellectual property rights in anything created by the employee in the course of his employment.

5   The US test for non-literal infringement of computer programs set out in *Computer Associates* v *Altai* no longer has any relevance to cases in the UK on non-literal infringement of computer programs. Discuss.

For further resources and updates please go to the Companion Website accompanying this book at **www.mylawchamber.co.uk/bainbridgeIT**

4

Copyright and computer programs

5 Database copyright and the database right

INTRODUCTION

Until changes to copyright law which took effect on 1 January 1998, it was generally accepted that computer databases were protected by copyright as literary works as they could be considered to be compilations. This was, of course, without prejudice to any individual copyrights subsisting in the individual items or works contained within the database. For example, consider a database of modern romantic poems. Each poem would be protected by copyright as an original literary work and, providing sufficient skill or judgment was expended in selecting and arranging, indexing or annotating the poems, there would be a separate copyright in the database as a whole. There could be other copyrights also, such as in respect of any index, cross-referencing system or annotations. Some of these elements could be protected as non-literal elements such as, for example, any hypertext links or the indexing system itself.

The legal protection of databases was significantly changed by the Copyright and Rights in Databases Regulations 1997, which came into force on 1 January 1998. These Regulations were made in order to comply with the Directive on the legal protection of databases.[1] A particular concern, following developments in the US in *Feist* v *Rural Telephone* 499 US 340 (1991) (discussed below), was that some databases that might be commercially valuable would fail to attract copyright protection in some Member States of the European Community. Thus, a dual approach to protection was taken in the Directive. First, if a database, by reason of the selection or arrangement of the contents of the database, can be regarded as the author's own intellectual creation, it will have copyright protection. This is without prejudice to any rights subsisting in the contents of the database. If the database can be regarded as the result of a substantial investment, it will attract a right, known in the Directive on the legal protection of databases as a *sui generis* right but referred to in the Regulations as the database right. In many cases, databases will enjoy both a copyright and a database right. However, the database right was intended specifically to protect commercially valuable databases which failed to reach the requirement of being regarded as the author's own intellectual creation for copyright protection.

Before looking at the provisions for the protection of databases by copyright and the database right it will be useful to look at the basic position before the changes brought about by the Regulations and the position in the US where database protection appears to be much weaker.

---

[1] Directive 96/9/EC of the European Parliament and of the Council of 11 March 1996 on the legal protection of databases, OJ L 77, 27.03.1996, p. 20 (the 'Directive on the legal protection of databases').

COPYRIGHT DATABASES IN THE UK BEFORE 1 JANUARY 1998

Databases were not expressly mentioned in the Copyright, Designs and Patents Act 1988 but were potentially protected by copyright as compilations, provided they were original in the sense of being the result of skill or judgment. Copyright might have subsisted at two levels if the database was a collection of individual works, as mentioned earlier. Each work contained in a database might have had its own copyright in addition to a separate copyright in the database as a database. If the individual contents of the database were small pieces of information, such as in the case of a database of customers' names and addresses, these would not be protected by copyright independently to the database which could still be subject to copyright providing it was the result of skill or judgment expended, for example, in the overall design of the database, including the design of its structure.

If the work involved in designing a database was a simple matter, not requiring skill and judgment, then it would not have its own copyright. In such a case, the House of Lords decision in *G A Cramp & Sons Ltd* v *Frank Smythson Ltd* [1944] AC 329 would be applicable. Nonetheless, the UK approach to compilations in the past was a generous one and compilations of non-original matter can be protected providing that some skill or judgment had been expended in their making (see *Macmillan & Co Ltd* v *K & J Cooper* (1923) 40 TLR 186). In reported cases on copyright and databases, including cases on the copyright in a database of lawyers, the question of whether the databases were protected by copyright was not put into issue; see, for example, *Waterlow Directories Ltd* v *Reed Information Services Ltd* [1992] FSR 409. It could have been claimed in the past that the UK provided very strong protection for databases.

THE US AND THE 'SWEAT OF THE BROW' PRINCIPLE

The 'sweat of the brow' principle, affording copyright protection to works which are the result of labour only, was roundly rejected in the US Supreme Court in *Feist Publications Inc* v *Rural Telephone Service Co Inc* 499 US 340 (1991). In that case, it was held that the 'white pages' in a typical telephone directory were not protected by copyright because of a lack of creativity, as they did not owe their origin to an act of authorship. The court did recognise, however, that a compilation of facts could be the subject of copyright because the author has to choose which facts to include and in what order to place them. The court went on to suggest that the 'yellow pages' section of a telephone directory could be protected because of the presence of original material such as drawings in advertisements. There is also some skill in devising the classification system used. Subsequently, however, it was held in the US that taking a large amount of data from a classified directory did not infringe copyright (see *BellSouth Advertising & Publishing Corp* v *Donnelley Information Publishing Inc* 999 F 2d 1436, US Court of Appeals 11th Circuit, 1993). The arrangement or appearance of the claimant's directory had not been copied and, although the amount of material taken by the defendant was substantial in a purely quantitative sense, it did not take what original elements might arguably exist in the claimant's directory. The court noted that the protection of compilations of factual information was 'thin'. One judge in the Court of Appeals dissented and he thought that the defendant had infringed copyright, for example, by using substantially similar headings and listings under the headings.

The US Court of Appeals, 3rd Circuit, considered whether a database of part numbers for fastening devices was protected by copyright in *Southco Inc* v *Kanebridge Corp* (unreported) 22 May 2003. Southco complained when Kanebridge used 51 of Southco's part numbers in a comparative advertisement. In denying that copyright subsisted in the part numbers individually or collectively as a compilation, the court held as follows.

- Short phrases and words are not protected by copyright (an example of a part number was 47–10–202–10). An example of a phrase previously denied protection on this basis was 'Good morning Detroit. This is JP on JR in the AM. Have a swell day'. The part numbers were not protected even if they were creative.

- Under US copyright law compilations are protected. A compilation is '. . . a work formed by the collection and assembling of pre-existing materials or of data that are selected, coordinated, or arranged in such a way that the resulting work as a whole constitutes an original work of authorship' (§101 of the US Copyright Act). Although a compilation of part numbers could be the proper subject matter of copyright if it was the result of an act of sufficient authorship, the protection thus afforded did not extend to the part numbers themselves but only to the arrangement and selection of the part numbers. In this case only 51 out of 1,000 part numbers had been taken by the defendant.

- Even if a compilation has copyright protection, that cannot protect individual part numbers not themselves protected by copyright.

The upshot of these cases is that the protection by copyright of databases comprising of entries that are not themselves protected by copyright is very weak or even non-existent in terms of protecting those entries. This is so even if the databases are the result of a substantial investment and would, otherwise, be commercially valuable. To some extent, these developments have been influenced by the US Constitution, Article 1 §8 cl. 8 of which states that the object of copyright is 'to promote the progress of science and the useful arts'. Although denying copyright protection to new ideas and even newly discovered facts 'may seem unfair', it encourages others to build freely upon the ideas and information conveyed by a work, as confirmed in *Feist*.

PROTECTION OF DATABASES IN THE UK AND EUROPE

In view of the lack of harmonisation of database protection throughout Europe and the dangers of commercially valuable databases being left with no protection following developments in US case law, it was considered important to take action on a European scale. There was a fear that the makers of databases which were made available online by subscription or sold on magnetic or optical media would go unprotected. This would remove the incentive to invest in the making of new databases which, although requiring substantial investment to make, would fail to attract copyright protection.

The Directive on the legal protection of databases was the result of these concerns and now the position in Europe appears to be more satisfactory from the perspective of persons creating databases. The twin track approach of a copyright for databases which are the result of the author's own intellectual creation and a database right for databases which represent a substantial investment looks strong. Copyright databases are a form of literary work and, apart from some differences, are treated much the same. The database right is arguably more controversial. Although it can be described as a quasi-copyright, there are some significant differences between copyright and the database right which uses tests for subsistence and infringement which are very different to those applicable to copyright. Rulings from the European Court of Justice in cases involving football fixture lists and a database of horse-racing data have helped in understanding the nature and scope of the right.

Database copyright and the database right both apply equally to electronic and non-electronic databases. This is in line with the desire of not to distinguish between electronic and manual databases. Both rights are without prejudice to copyright or other rights, if any, subsisting in the contents of the database. Thus, where a database contains individual works of copyright, those works will retain their own copyright in addition to any copyright or database right in the database as a whole. For example, consider a database of recipes. If a person copies one of the recipes without permission, he will infringe the copyright in it. If he copies numerous recipes without permission, he will infringe the copyright in each individual recipe and may also infringe the copyright in the database and/or the database right, depending upon the circumstances.

It should also be noted at this stage that the author of a copyright database may have moral rights in respect of it although there are no moral rights in respect of a database only protected by the database right (ignoring any copyright in the constituent parts). Music collections on compact discs are expressly excluded from the provisions of databases. They continue to be treated as compilations for copyright purposes.

Meaning of database

For both copyright purposes and the database right, the meaning of 'database' is the same and is also the same for electronic and non-electronic databases. Databases are no longer treated as compilations and this is made explicit in section 3(1)(a) of the Copyright, Designs and Patents Act 1988.

There is a detailed definition of 'database', which follows that in the Directive on the legal protection of databases. Section 3A of the Act defines a 'database' as

> . . . a collection of independent works, data or other materials which –
> (a) are arranged in a systematic or methodical way, and
> (b) are individually accessible by electronic or other means.

The use of the phrase 'other means' confirms that the provisions apply equally to non-electronic databases. The recitals to the Directive confirm this. A card index containing customer details arranged by name will be a database for the purposes of copyright and the database right. Although the Act, as modified, is silent on the point, the Directive on the legal protection of databases makes it clear that the copyright protection for a database does not extend to any computer program used in the making or operation of an electronic database. This could cause some issues if the database contains executable code. A database containing only program sub-routines should not, on this basis, be considered to be a database but should, instead be classed as a compilation.

The meaning of 'database' came up for consideration in a ruling made by the European Court of Justice in a case involving fixture lists for football games in the English and Scottish leagues. In Case C-444/02 *Fixtures Marketing Ltd* v *OPAP* [2004] ECR-105 49, the claimant complained that the defendant, in Greece, was making use of its fixture lists without permission and brought an action for infringement of the database right. The European Court of Justice confirmed that a database was:

> . . . any collection of works, data or other materials, separable from one another without the value of their contents being affected, including a method or system of some sort for the retrieval of each of its constituent materials.

The court went on to confirm that a fixture list such as the one in issue was a database within the meaning in the Directive. Although the case concerned the database right, as the definition of database is also the same for copyright databases, this must also apply to the latter. The ruling confirms, in effect, the importance of the individual constituent parts being independent from each other.

COPYRIGHT DATABASES

Section 3(1) of the Copyright, Designs and Patents Act 1988 was amended and 'database' was added to the non-exhaustive list of works that are literary works. As databases are no longer compilations for copyright purposes, there are now some differences as to how databases and compilations are treated. Of course, many of the provisions are the same for both but it should be noted that there is a difference in the fair dealing provisions and there is a special permitted act that applies to databases.

For copyright databases, a gloss is added to the test of originality and a database is original for copyright purposes if and only if, by reason of the selection or arrangement of its contents, the database constitutes the author's own intellectual creation; section 3A(2). This is similar to the test that should now apply to computer programs but is qualified by the expression 'by reason of the selection or arrangement of its contents'. The creativity must, therefore, relate to the work of selecting or arranging the contents of the database and this implies that it does not extend to the creation of those contents. Rather, it is a case of collecting together existing materials and arranging them in a database. However, by the use of the disjunctive 'or', it is at least arguable that there can be the necessary creativity in arranging newly created materials in a database. This would seem possible, especially as the recitals to the Directive on the legal protection of databases confirm that the structure of a database can be protected by copyright.

The usual restricted acts apply to databases as they do for literary works generally except that the restricted act of making an adaptation is redefined for databases in terms of an adaptation being an arrangement or altered version or a translation of the database. Examples of this are:

- a version in which the information contained in the database has been sorted into a different order (arrangement);
- a version in which some of the information is suppressed or deleted (either records or fields or both) (arrangement or altered version);
- a version in which the database is converted to be used with a different program to access the contents or where it is converted from 8 bit to 7 bit code or where it is imported into a word processing or spreadsheet program (altered version or translation).

The Directive on the legal protection of databases left Member States with some discretion as to which permitted acts they implemented for copyright databases. The approach in the UK was to apply the traditional permitted acts that apply to literary works except that section 29(1A) was inserted into the fair dealing provisions in the Act. In respect of fair dealing for research or private study, the source is required to be indicated. Furthermore, under section 29(5), it is not fair dealing to do anything in relation to a database for a commercial purpose. This was in line with the changes made to fair dealing generally.

A permitted act specifically for databases is included under section 50D of the Act. This applies to any person having a right to use a database or part of a database, whether under a licence to do any of the acts restricted by the copyright or otherwise. Such a person does not infringe copyright if, in the exercise of that right, he does anything which is necessary for the purposes of his access to and use of the contents of the database, or part of the database, as the case may be. This prevents a person from licensing a database including terms in the licence agreement which purport to hinder the right of access to and use of the database. This could be the case where the licence grants permission to carry out acts restricted by copyright but includes other terms which prejudice the exercise of those rights. It is no easy matter to think of examples. One might be where the licence grants the right to access and consult the contents of an electronic database but contains a term stating that transient copies cannot be made of the database.

The provision is essentially an example of non-derogation from grant. As section 50D accepts, it is possible to grant a right to use only part of the contents of a database, for example, by restricting access to certain records or fields within the database. In respect of, say, a database of potential customers, a licensed user may be restricted to customers living in the south of England only or it may be that the user can retrieve names and addresses only and not data relating to individuals' financial standing. The right under section 50D cannot be prohibited or restricted and section 296B makes void any term or condition in an agreement in so far as it purports to prohibit or restrict those acts permitted under section 50D or any act necessary for the exercise of the rights granted by the agreement.

Database structure

We have seen in the previous chapter that, potentially, some of the non-literal (or non-textual) elements of a computer program, such as its structure or architecture, may be protected by copyright. We have also seen that it is difficult to succeed in a claim of non-literal infringement. This may be more a reflection of the idiosyncrasies of the case law where such claims were or could have been made. Furthermore, the protection of non-literal elements of computer programs is further constrained by the denial of protection to a computer program's underlying ideas and principles.

There is little case law on the protection by copyright on the structure of databases in the UK. The structure of a database used by a COBOL program could be taken to be the field and record specifications in the data division of the program. In *Total Information Processing Systems Ltd* v *Daman Ltd* [1992] FSR 171, it was held that the data division of a COBOL program was not protected because, in this form, the information in it concerning the field and record specifications did not form a substantial part of the computer program as a whole. However, in *IBCOS Computers Ltd* v *Barclays Mercantile Highland Finance Ltd* [1994] FSR 275, Mr Justice Jacob made a number of criticisms of the judgment in the *Total Information Processing Systems* case and he said that there may well be a considerable degree of skill in devising the data division and so it could be considered to be a substantial part of a program as a whole.

The Copyright and Rights in Databases Regulations 1997 which implemented the Directive on the legal protection of databases made no mention of the structure of a database. However, recital 15 to the Directive expressly states that copyright protection should cover the structure of a database. The only major requirement for protection, therefore, apart from the qualification provisions (for example, that the author was a British citizen at the time of creation or that the work was first published in the United Kingdom), is that the database is original. This is so if, and only if, by reason of the selection or arrangement of the contents of the database, it constitutes the author's own intellectual creation. Therefore, that being so, if someone copies the database structure but not its contents without the permission of the owner, this will infringe the copyright if the database structure represents a substantial part of the database in terms of the author's own intellectual creation. It must be the case that here we are concerned with the arrangement of the contents of the database rather than their selection. The work in deciding how to arrange the contents, rather than that in selecting the contents, must count as an intellectual creation. That arrangement must be reflected in the structure of the database, for example, by representing the structure of the fields applied to the records in the database.

THE DATABASE RIGHT

The *database right* is a right given to the *maker* of a database which is the result of a *substantial investment* to prevent the unauthorised *extraction and/or reutilisation* of the contents of a database (the meaning of the highlighted terms will be discussed later, as appropriate). The right is described in the Directive on the legal protection of databases as a *sui generis* right, meaning it is a right of its own kind or unique. The right is provided for in the UK by Part III of the Copyright and Rights in Databases Regulations 1997. The database right can be described as a right related to copyright but it is a mistake to think that it is very similar in its nature to copyright. The rules for subsistence of the database right are quite different to those that apply to a work of copyright and infringement is differently defined (and is narrower). The duration of the database is significantly less than for copyright. Even the test for substantiality is different to that for copyright. Having said that, there are some points of similarity, including:

- the definition of database is the same as for copyright;
- some of the acts which do not infringe the database right are similar to the equivalent permitted acts under copyright;
- the provisions for assignment, licensing and remedies, for example, are the same as for copyright;
- provisions on circumventing effective technical measures that apply to copyright works (other than computer programs which have their own separate protection) also apply, with necessary modification, to the database right. These provisions protect measures taken to prohibit or restrict unauthorised access and are described in Chapter 7 on copyright in the information society.

The database right was designed to protect a substantial investment in obtaining, verifying or presenting the contents of a database. Investment is defined in terms of financial, human or technical resources. Recital 39 to the Directive on the legal protection of databases talks of protecting the makers of databases from the misappropriation of the results of the financial and professional investment in obtaining and collecting the contents of the database.

The database right is of limited duration compared to copyright but the right is not restricted to non-copyright databases and many databases will be subject to both copyright and the database right. As with the copyright provisions, the database right is unaffected if the database contains works which are themselves subject to copyright or other rights. Take, for example, a database of original maps or charts which was the result of the author's own intellectual creation in selecting the maps or charts to include in the database but which was also the result of a substantial investment in obtaining, verifying or presenting the contents of the database. The individual maps or charts will be works of artistic copyright; the database as a whole will be a work of copyright and it will also be subject to the database right.

The interpretation of terms used for the database right are particularly important as some of them have no parallel under copyright law. Some of the terms have been subject to clarification by the European Court of Justice in cases on a database of racehorses and related information and football fixture lists, it will be worthwhile first briefly reflecting on these cases before looking at the database right in further detail.

European Court of Justice cases on database right

On 9 November 2004, the European Court of Justice handed down important rulings on questions submitted to it under Article 234 of the EC Treaty[2] for preliminary rulings. The most expansive set of rulings was handed down in a case referred to the Court of Justice by the English Court of Appeal concerning a database operated on behalf of the British Horseracing Board. The three other cases were referred to the European Court of Justice from Finland, Greece and Sweden respectively. In all these cases, the claimant was Fixtures Marketing Ltd, a company which exploited the fixture lists for the English and Scottish football leagues outside the UK.

In Case C-203/02 *British Horseracing Board Ltd* v *William Hill Organisation Ltd* [2004] ECR I-10415 (the '*BHB* case'), the British Horseracing Board ('BHB') a company on behalf of BHB maintained a very large database of racehorses and associated information and compiled lists of runners and riders for horse races. The operation cost around £4 million a year. The defendant started an internet betting service and placed information about races and horses taking part in them on its website. Some of the information had been derived indirectly from the BHB database via lists of runners and riders published in newspapers. The amount of information from the BHB database used by the defendant each day was a very small proportion of the entire database. The European Court of Justice made rulings on the meaning of investment, extraction and reutilisation of the contents of a database, substantiality and under what circumstances the database right could be infringed by the repeated and systematic taking of insubstantial parts of a database. Those rulings and their impact are mentioned below where appropriate.

In the *Football Fixtures* cases,[3] the claimant complained about the defendants making use of the football fixture lists for games in the English and Scottish leagues. Apart from commenting on the meaning of 'database' in one of those cases, as discussed earlier, the meaning of investment was considered. The rulings are, to all intents and purposes the same as in the *BHB* case on this point. The European Court of Justice confirmed, however, that a football fixture list such as the one exploited by the claimant was a database within the meaning of the Directive on the legal protection of databases.

In applying the rulings of the European Court of Justice, the Court of Appeal subsequently confirmed that the database right did not protect the BHB database.

Basic requirement for subsistence of database right

First, it must again be stressed that the meaning of 'database' is the same as applies to databases subject to copyright and as interpreted by the European Court of Justice in the *Fixtures Marketing* v *OPAP* case, discussed earlier.

The database right is defined in Regulation 13(1) of the Copyright and Rights in Databases Regulations 1997 as a property right which subsists in a database if there has been a substantial investment in obtaining, verifying or presenting the contents of the database. Substantiality is defined for this and other purposes, as meaning substantial in terms of quality or quantity or a combination of both. This must mean that whether an investment is deemed to be substantial is measured by the relative importance and/or relative proportion of the part of the database to which the investment relates. The Directive places the burden of proving the database right subsists in accordance with this basic requirement on the maker of the database under Article 7(1). The Regulations are silent on this matter.

---

[2] The Treaty Establishing the European Communities (Consolidated Version, OJ C 325, 24.12.2002, p. 33).

[3] Case C-46-02 *Fixtures Marketing Ltd* v. *Oy Veikkaus AB* [2004] ECR-I-10365; Case C-444/02 *Fixtures Marketing Ltd* v *Organismos Prognostikon Agonon Podosfairou* [2004] ECR-105 49; Case C-338/02 *Fixtures Marketing Ltd* v *Svenska Spel AB* [2004] ECR-I-10497.

In the *BHB* case, the European Court of Justice confirmed that the investment in 'obtaining' meant the investment in seeking out existing materials and collecting them into the database. It did not mean the investment in creating the materials to be included in the database. Similarly, the investment in 'verifying' the contents of a database referred to the resources used in checking the accuracy of the materials collected when the database was created and during its operation. Resources used in the verification process when the contents were created does not fall within that definition.

The court also ruled that the resources used to draw up a list of horses for a race and carrying out checks in connection with that did not constitute an investment in the obtaining or verification of the contents of the database in which the list appears for the purposes of the database right. In other words, it is envisaged that the investment must be in connection with seeking out and collecting and/or verifying pre-existing materials. As any one of the three forms of investment, obtaining, verifying or presenting the contents of a database, can be sufficient to give rise to the database right providing the investment is substantial, the same must hold true in relation to the investment in presenting the contents of the database. Those contents must have been made up of pre-existing materials for the investment in their presentation to give rise to the database right.

The court considered that the recitals to the Directive supported its interpretation. Recital 39 mentions the investment in 'obtaining and collecting the contents of the database' as being an object of protection by the *sui generis* right. The ruling seems harsh as one might think that creating the contents of a database would be more deserving of protection than collecting existing materials together in a database.

Maker of a database

The identity of the maker of a database is important for two reasons. First, the maker will be the first owner of the database right. Secondly, a database must qualify for the database right and this depends on who the maker was. For example, one of the ways a database will qualify is if the maker was, at the material time, a resident of or habitually resident in a European Economic Area state.

The maker is defined in Regulation 14(1) as the person who takes the initiative in obtaining, verifying or presenting the contents of a database and assumes the risk of investing in that obtaining, verification or presentation. That person will be considered to be the maker of the database and as having made it. To this basic rule there are exceptions. Where a database is made by an employee in the course of his employment, the employer is regarded as the maker of the database, subject to any agreement to the contrary. There are also provisions for Her Majesty to be regarded as the maker of a database where it is made by an officer or servant of the Crown in the course of his duties, subject to the maker being regarded as either or both of the Houses of Parliament in relation to databases made under the direction or control of either or both. Equivalent provision is made for the Scottish Parliament.

It is debatable whether special provision should be made for databases made by employees and other situations as the definition of the maker is in terms of taking the initiative in making the database and assuming the risk of investment. Where a database is made by an employee, surely it is the employer who takes the initiative and assumes the risk of investment.

A database is made jointly if two or more persons collaborate in making the necessary investment. Where a database has joint makers, references in the Regulations to the maker is to all the makers unless as otherwise provided.

Qualification

For the database right to subsist, it must satisfy the qualification requirements. These are set out in Regulation 18, and require that, at the 'material time' (the time the database was made or, if its making extended over a period of time, a substantial part of that period), the maker was:

- an individual who was a national of an EEA state or the Isle of Man ('IoM'), or habitually resident in an EEA state or the IoM;

- a body incorporated in an EEA state or the IoM, having its central administration or principal place of business in an EEA state or the IoM or registered office in the EEA or IoM and the body's operations linked on an ongoing basis with the economy of an EEA state or the IoM; or

- a partnership or other unincorporated body formed under the law of an EEA state or the IoM, having at that time its central administration or principal place of business within the EEA or the IoM.

The inclusion in the qualification provisions of the Isle of Man was the result of an agreement between the UK on behalf of the Isle of Man and the European Community so as to extend the database right to the Isle of Man, with effect from 1 November 2003.

Where the database has joint makers it will qualify for protection if one or more of them fall within the qualification requirements. For example, if a database is made by a French woman and a Chinese man resident in China, working collaboratively (in terms of taking the initiative and assuming the risk of investment), it will qualify for the database right even if only one of the makers satisfies the qualification requirements. As we will see later, however, the Chinese man, being a joint maker will be the joint first owner of the database right.

The qualification requirements do not apply in the case of Parliamentary database right although there is no express exception for Crown database right nor in relation to the Scottish Parliament.

Duration

The Directive on the legal protection of databases emphasised that the database right was to be limited in time, subject to a new right arising if a database undergoes substantial change so as to be considered a new substantial investment. Consequently, the term of protection afforded by the database right is 15 years from the end of the calendar year during which the making of the database was completed; although, if it was made available to the public before the end of that period, the right will continue to endure for 15 years from the end of the calendar year during which it was first so made available: regulation 17.

Many databases are subject to continual or periodic modification. A new period of protection arises if changes to the database are substantial and this *includes* any substantial change resulting from an accumulation of successive additions, deletions or alterations, which would result in the database being considered to be a substantial new investment. The use of the word *includes* suggests that a substantial investment in subsequently verifying the contents or presenting them in a new or improved manner could suffice in appropriate circumstances. Whether a change is substantial is to be evaluated qualitatively and/or quantitatively.

It is possible, therefore, that a new term of protection could come about because the owner of the database makes a substantial investment in writing new, or modifying existing, computer programs responsible for presenting the contents of the database. In another case, the owner may put significant resources into verifying the accuracy of the contents. This could be the case where the contents are likely to become inaccurate over time, for example, in the case of a database of

5

Database copyright and the database right

customers. A yet further case, is where additional records are included in the database, existing records are checked and brought up to date and obsolete records are deleted.

There are some transitional provisions to protect the interests of the owners of databases that were previously protected by copyright but which might not be so protected under the changed regime for copyright. In such cases, the copyright continues to endure in the database. If the database in question was made on or before 1 January 1983 and the database right subsisted in the database immediately on 1 January 1998 (or 1 November 2003 in the Isle of Man), the database right will last for 15 years beginning with 1 January 1998. This provision was intended to protect the interests of owners of older databases which have protection until 1 January 2013.

Ownership and dealing with the database right

The rule as to ownership is surprisingly simple. Under Regulation 15, the maker of the database is the first owner of the database right in it. As the definition of the maker of a database takes account of databases made by employees and Crown and Parliamentary database right, there is no need to make special provision in such cases for the ownership of the database right. This is unlike the position with copyright where the author is, in most cases concerning original literary, dramatic, musical or artistic works, simply the person who creates the work. Therefore, for copyright a set of rules is needed to determine the identity of the owner. The database right simply puts things the other way round but this is probably a result of how the Directive is worded.

Where a database has joint makers, they will, of course, be the joint first owners. This is so even though not all of them fall within the qualification requirements.

The rules for assignment and licensing of databases subject to the database right are the same as for copyright. This is helpful because, otherwise, it could prove very inconvenient to have different rules for the database right where the database in question happens to be subject both to copyright and the database right. Thus, assignments must be in writing and signed by or on behalf of the person assigning the right and exclusive licences must be in writing and signed by or on behalf of the owner of the database right. As with copyright, it is also possible to deal with the database right prospectively, for example, by granting licences in respect of databases that have not yet been made.

Rights and infringement

The rights of the owner of the database right are not spelt-out. Rather they can be determined negatively by reference to the acts that infringe the right and the exceptions to infringement of the right. Infringement is described in terms of *extraction* or *reutilisation* of the contents of the database. These terms are defined as follows:

- 'extraction', in relation to any contents of a database, means the permanent or temporary transfer of those contents to another medium by any means or in any form; and
- 'reutilisation', in relation to any contents of a database, means making those contents available to the public by any means (the Directive goes on to define making the contents available to the public by the distribution of copies, by renting, by online or other forms of transmission).

Note that reutilisation does not mean, as the word might suggest, re-use in the sense that a person is simply using the contents for his own purposes, for example, by consulting the contents extracted from the database. It might have been simpler to describe the act as making the contents available to the public by any means. The reason why reutilisation is important, in addition to extraction, is to cover the situation where a person has a right to use a database for consultation purposes only but then decides, without the owner's permission, to make a substantial part of the contents available to the public.

In the *BHB* case, the European Court of Justice ruled that extraction and reutilisation did not imply direct acts only. To take an example, say that a newspaper prints part of the contents of a database, such as a list of runners and riders in a horserace or a football fixture list with the permission of the owner of the database. If a third party takes those lists and copies them and publishes them he will have extracted and reutilised the relevant contents of the database even though he has not had direct access to the database. Furthermore, the fact that the owner of a database himself makes the database, or parts of it, available to the public does not prevent him exercising his rights to prevent others extracting or reutilising those contents. This is subject to the doctrine of exhaustion of rights where a copy of a database is sold on tangible media in respect to the resale of that copy. This is described below in the context of exceptions to infringement.

Infringement by extracting or reutilising a substantial part

Infringing acts are defined in Regulation 16 in terms of the extraction or reutilisation of all, or a substantial part of, the contents of the database without the consent of the owner. There is a slight difference in the Directive which uses 'extraction and/or reutilisation' rather than 'extraction or reutilisation'. This is unlikely to be an issue. If a substantial part is extracted and the whole of that part is reutilised, then a substantial part is reutilised. If only a small part of the part extracted is reutilised then there will still be an infringement because a substantial part was extracted in the first place.

As with the meaning of investment, substantiality for the purposes of extraction or reutilisation is also determined qualitatively or quantitatively or by a combination of both. The meaning of substantiality is considered further below together with what constitutes an insubstantial part of a database.

Infringement by the repeated and systematic extraction or reutilisation of insubstantial parts

Reflecting the special nature of databases and the damage that may be done to the owner's interests by a systematic course of unauthorised extraction or reutilisation of small parts of the database, a further form of infringement is provided for. The repeated and systematic extraction or reutilisation of insubstantial parts of the contents of a database may also infringe. This may amount to the extraction or reutilisation of a substantial part of those contents. The curious use of the word 'may' makes it difficult to predict whether or not infringement will be found. Fortunately, the Directive is more helpful and it states under Article 7(5) that:

> ... the repeated and systematic extraction and/or re-utilization of insubstantial parts of the contents of the database implying acts which conflict with a normal exploitation of that database or which unreasonably prejudice the legitimate interests of the maker of the database shall not be permitted.

Guidance as to the scope of the prohibition under Article 7(5) was given in the *BHB* case by the European Court of Justice. It is intended to catch situations which might otherwise escape infringement by extracting and/or reutilising *substantial* parts of the database. Acts of repeated and systematic extraction and/or reutilisation of insubstantial parts which are cumulatively equivalent to taking a substantial part infringe. It is implied that such acts do indeed conflict with the normal exploitation of the database or unreasonably prejudice the legitimate interests of the owner of the database. Article 7(5) is intended to deal with the situation where the whole or a substantial part of the database is reconstituted or made available to the public. Two points can be made. If the parts of the database extracted or reutilised when put together do not cumulatively amount to a substantial part of the database (qualitatively and/or quantitatively) there can be no infringement. The second point is that it appears that the claimant simply will have to show that, cumulatively, a substantial part has been extracted or reutilised. He will not have to show that the acts complained of conflict with the normal exploitation of the database or that his legitimate interests have been prejudiced. Based on the judgment of the European Court of Justice in the *BHB* case, the effects may be presumed.

Substantial and insubstantial

Whether the part of a database extracted or reutilised is substantial is critical to a finding of infringement of the database right. The *BHB* case again is interesting as the European Court of Justice attempted to flesh out what substantial meant qualitatively and quantitatively and also what insubstantial meant.

The court ruled that substantiality, evaluated quantitatively, referred to the volume of data extracted or reutilised assessed in relation to the total volume of the contents of the database. Evaluated qualitatively, a substantial part of the contents of a database referred to the scale of investment of obtaining, verifying or presenting the contents extracted or reutilised regardless of whether it was a substantial part of the general contents of the database.

Finally, the court came to a conclusion that can only be described as stating the obvious. It ruled that any part which did not fulfil the definition of a substantial part, evaluated either quantitatively or qualitatively, was an insubstantial part.

Exceptions to infringement

Lending a copy of a database (not for direct or indirect commercial advantage) by an establishment accessible to the public does not constitute extraction or reutilisation of the contents of a database but this exception does not extend to making the database available for on-the-spot reference use which could, therefore, fall within the meaning of extraction or reutilisation.

The doctrine of exhaustion of rights within the European Economic Area (EEA) applies to copies sold within the EEA by or with the consent of the owner of the database right to the extent that any subsequent sale of *those* copies does not constitute extraction or reutilisation of the contents of the database. Therefore, if a person lawfully buys a copy of a database, that person can resell that copy elsewhere in the EEA without infringing the database right. The fact that a database has been made available online for consultation by members of the public does not, however, exhaust the maker's right of reutilisation. It is only the sale of copies, for example on magnetic or optical discs, which exhausts any right to control resale of *those copies*. The exhaustion of rights provision now also applies in respect of copies sold in the Isle of Man.

Regulation 19 contains what is basically a 'non-derogation from grant' provision. This prevents the owner of the database right interfering with the subsequent extraction or reutilisation of insubstantial parts by a lawful user. A lawful user, in relation to a database, means any person who (whether under a licence to do any of the acts restricted by any database right in the database or otherwise) has a right to use the database. A lawful user of a database, which has been made available to the public, cannot be prevented from extracting or reutilising insubstantial parts of the database for any purpose. Any term in an agreement, under which the right to use a database or part of a database has been granted, which attempts to prevent this is void.

There is a fair dealing exception to infringement in Regulation 20. Where the database has been made available to the public in any manner, fair dealing with a substantial part of the contents does not infringe if:

- the part is extracted by a person who is otherwise a lawful user;
- the part is extracted for the purposes of illustration for teaching or research (but not for a commercial purpose); and
- the source is indicated.

Further exceptions are set out in Schedule 1 to the Regulations and relate to Parliamentary and judicial proceedings, Royal Commissions and statutory inquiries, material open to public inspection or on official register, material communicated to the Crown in the course of public business, public records and acts done under statutory authority. These mirror the equivalent permitted acts for copyright. However, apart from these exceptions and the others mentioned here, none of the other permitted acts that apply generally to literary works under copyright apply to the database right. For example, there is no provision for fair dealing for criticism or review or for reporting current events.

Presumed expiry of database right

Where it is reasonable to assume that the database right has expired and the identity of the maker (or each of the makers in the case of a database made jointly) cannot by reasonable enquiry be ascertained, the right will not be infringed by the extraction or reutilisation of a substantial part of the contents: Regulation 21. It is important, therefore, for the owner of databases to indicate the identity of the maker on copies of the database and the year during which it was first published. If the database is made available online, this information should appear on the title screen or other appropriate place. This is also worth doing so as to raise useful presumptions as discussed below.

Deposit libraries

Copies of published books are required to be deposited at certain libraries, such as the British Library. By the Legal Deposit Libraries Act 2003 this obligation was extended to cover works in digital form of a description to be prescribed. Regulation 20A was inserted by the Legal Deposit Libraries Act 2003 into the Regulations to make provision for this in relation to the database right where a database is published on the internet by a person connected with the UK in a manner to be prescribed, subject to conditions also to be prescribed.

Where deposit is required of non-print publications, a copy of a computer program required to access and display the publication may also be required together with any manual. It may be possible to deposit the materials electronically. Thus far, Regulations to bring these provisions into effect have not been made.

The 'British Leyland' defence

The first reported case to involve the database right was *Mars UK Ltd* v *Teknowledge Ltd* [2000] FSR 138 in which the claimant designed and made coin operated machines which contained discriminators designed to detect whether or not a coin was genuine. The claimant brought out a new discriminator known as 'Cashflow' which was programmed for new coin data and contained an EEPROM (electronically erasable programmable read only memory) which could be reprogrammed in the future with new data. This was important so as to allow the discriminator to be recalibrated to accept new types of coin and reject new forms of blanks or foreign coins. The claimant wanted to keep to itself the work of reprogramming these EEPROMs and the data contained within them was encrypted. The defendant managed to overcome the encryption and was then able to recalibrate Cashflow machines itself. The claimant commenced proceedings for infringement of copyright and the database right in the computer programs and data in the computer chips in the discriminators. Breach of confidence was also alleged but this claim failed, for which see Chapter 8.

The defendant eventually admitted carrying out acts that would otherwise infringe copyright and the database right but claimed the *British Leyland* defence applied. In **British Leyland Motor Corp Ltd v Armstrong Patents Co Ltd** [1986] AC 577, the defendant made exhaust systems for the claimant's motor cars without permission. It was held that this had been a technical infringement of the copyright subsisting in the drawings of the exhaust systems by indirect copying. However, the House of Lords refused to enforce that copyright because persons buying motorcars had a right to access a free market in spare parts. This 'spare parts' defence has been largely overtaken by the Copyright, Designs and Patents Act 1988 and changes to design law.

Mr Justice Jacob doubted whether recalibration of discriminators fell within the *British Leyland* spare parts defence anyway but considered the situation if it did. He noted that no provisions equivalent to a spare parts defence were contained in Directives on the legal protection of computer programs and the legal protection of databases. Nor was there any overriding public policy in having such a defence in this context. Although the Directive on the legal protection of databases permitted individual Member States to adopt defences traditionally authorised under national law, Parliament had chosen not to provide for such a defence in relation to the database right. That being so, it would be wrong for judges to introduce such a defence. The *British Leyland* defence has all but disappeared, and its further development has been effectively disapproved of by the Privy Council in **Canon Kabushiki Kaisha v Green Cartridge Co** [1997] AC 728 (an appeal from Hong Kong) where it was held that a company refilling toner cartridges for photocopiers and laser printers could not avail itself of the defence. However, the defence may yet have a residual role to play in very limited circumstances such as in terms of software maintenance and error correction.

Presumptions

There are some presumptions which apply to the database right and which may be helpful to the owner in an action for infringement. They are not dissimilar to the equivalent presumptions which apply in relation to copyright works. Under Regulation 22, where a name purporting to be that of the maker of the database appears on copies of the database as published, it is presumed that that person is the maker and the database was not made in circumstances where the employer would be the first owner and that the database is not subject to Crown or Parliamentary database right. Where copies of a database as published bear a label or mark stating that a named person was the maker and that it was first published in a specified year, the label or mark shall be admissible as evidence of those facts and presumed correct until the contrary be proved.

Where a database has been made jointly, these provisions apply in relation to each person alleged to be one of the makers. Under copyright law, the usefulness of the equivalent presumptions was seen in the case of **Microsoft Corp v Electrowide Ltd** [1997] FSR 580 where, in the absence of any evidence submitted by the defendant, the Microsoft Corporation did not have to prove that it owned the copyright subsisting in software such as 'Windows 95'.

Other provisions

The provisions which apply to dealing with rights in copyright works, the rights and remedies of the owner of copyright and of an exclusive licensee under the copyright are all applied without modification to the database right.

Remedies are the same as for copyright and include damages, injunctions, accounts or otherwise as is available for infringement of any other property right, and additional damages are also possible in the case of flagrant infringement. Exclusive licensees have rights concurrent to those of the owner and may bring an action themselves. As is usual, the owner would be expected to be joined in the action, for example, as co-claimant or defendant. It would appear that section 101A of the Copyright, Designs and Patents Act 1988 also applies to the database right. This gives a right of action to a non-exclusive licensee where there is a written licence signed by or on behalf of the owner granting the non-exclusive licensee a right of action.

Schedule 2 to the Regulations contains provisions for licensing schemes and in relation to licensing bodies and the referral of licensing schemes to the Copyright Tribunal. An example of a licensing scheme would be where the owner of a database right sets out the types of case where the scheme applies, the persons to whom he is prepared to grant licences and the terms of those licences. A licensing body is one which negotiates or grants licences on behalf of owners of database rights. These provisions are equivalent to those in sections 116–129 and 144 of the Copyright, Designs and Patents Act 1988 which apply to copyright works. The jurisdiction of the Copyright Tribunal is enlarged accordingly to give it jurisdiction over the database right.

SUMMARY

- Databases can be protected by copyright and/or the database right.
- The contents of a database may be subject to other rights such as copyright.
- A database is protected by copyright if, by reason of the selection or arrangement of its contents, it constitutes the author's own intellectual creation.
- Protection of a database by copyright may extend to its structure.
- A database is protected by the database right if its making was:
  - the result of a substantial investment in human, financial or technical resources;
  - in obtaining, verifying or presenting the contents of the database.
- The maker of a database subject to the database right is the person:
  - who takes the initiative in obtaining, verifying or presenting the contents; and
  - who assumes the risk of the investment in doing so.
- For the database right:
  - there are qualification requirements;
  - the basic term of protection is 15 years;
  - infringement is by extracting and/or reutilising a substantial part of the contents;
  - an accumulation of insubstantial extractions and/or reutilisations may infringe;
  - there are a number of exceptions to infringement; and
  - there are presumptions in relation to the name of the maker and year of publication.

5

Database copyright and the database right

SELF-TEST QUESTIONS

Note: there is only one correct answer to each multiple choice question.

1   **Which one of the following statements is NOT CORRECT in relation to a database protected by copyright?**

(a) A database is protected by copyright as a database providing it is original in the sense that it is the result of a substantial investment.

(b) Making an adaptation of a database is an act restricted by the copyright.

(c) Databases may be protected by copyright if, *inter alia*, the independent works, data or other materials contained in the database are individually accessible by electronic or other means.

(d) Copyright protection for a database extends to the structure of the database.

2   **Artemus lives in Wales and is a keen amateur photographer. He decided to make a database of photographs of Welsh civic buildings for his own amusement. He went all over Wales taking photographs for this purpose and then converted the photographs into digital form and put them in a database he had created. It is possible to search the database by location and building type to retrieve particular photographs. Artemus has not made the database available to the public and has no intention of so doing. Which one of the following statements is CORRECT?**

(a) The database is not protected by copyright or the database right for the sole reason that the contents, the photographs, each have their own copyright.

(b) Although Artemus went to considerable lengths and spent much time travelling Wales, taking his photographs and assembling them in a database, the database can have no protection independent of the photographs simply because he has not made a substantial investment as, being an amateur photographer, he made his database as a hobby.

(c) The database will be protected by copyright as a compilation independent to the copyright subsisting in the individual photographs.

(d) The database will not be protected by the database right on the basis of a substantial investment in obtaining the contents.

3   **Isambard was an academic who put together a database of details of the families and lineage of Saxon kings. It took a considerable amount of research to assemble this information from libraries and archives. It is searchable by name and date. This database was useful to historians interested in the subject matter and Isambard grants licences to historians to use his database which he delivers on CD-ROM. Isambard then wrote an article for a journal which included substantial extracts from the database. Kane, an academic historian saw the journal article and, without asking permission, he entered the extracts from the article into a computer database which he has now made available free of charge from his own website. In respect of Kane's activities, which of the following statements is most likely to be CORRECT?**

(a) Isambard's database is not subject to copyright or the database right as Isambard created it as an academic and not in the course of a business.

(b) Isambard's database is subject to the database right as it involved a substantial investment in obtaining the materials (at least in human resources) and Kane has infringed the right by indirectly extracting a substantial part of the contents and also by reutilisation.

(c) Isambard's database is subject to the database right as it involved a substantial investment in obtaining the materials (at least in human resources) but Kane has not infringed the right as he obtained the extracts indirectly from the journal article.

(d) Isambard's database is subject to the database right as it involved a substantial investment in obtaining the materials (at least in human resources) but as he published extracts in the journal article he will be taken to have waived his rights in respect of those extracts.

4 **In respect of infringement of the database right by the repeated and systematic extraction or reutilisation of insubstantial parts of the contents of the database, which one of the following statements is CORRECT?**

(a) Such acts will infringe if cumulatively a substantial part of the database, determined qualitatively or quantitatively (or by a combination of both) is extracted or reutilised.

(b) As each individual act does not infringe the right, an accumulation of such acts cannot infringe otherwise, how can one infringe by carrying on not infringing for long enough?

(c) Such acts can never infringe a database subject to continual modification as each day it is a different database.

(d) Simply extracting or reutilising an insubstantial part can infringe if that part is important qualitatively in terms of the investment in the making of the database as a whole.

5 **To what extent does the protection of databases in the US differ from the protection now afforded to databases in the UK and Europe?**

For further resources and updates please go to the Companion Website accompanying this book at **www.mylawchamber.co.uk/bainbridgeIT**

5

Database copyright and the database right

6 Computer-generated works

INTRODUCTION

The Copyright, Designs and Patents Act 1988 expressly recognises that works produced by or with the aid of a computer are worthy of copyright protection. Such works were protected before the 1988 Act but there were difficulties in determining the identity of the author of the work for copyright purposes. Grids of random numbers selected by computer for a newspaper competition called 'Millionaire of the Month' were held to be protected by copyright in *Express Newspapers plc* v *Liverpool Daily Post & Echo plc* [1985] 1 WLR 1089. It was argued that there was no human author and, consequently, the lists of numbers drawn by the computer were not protected by copyright. This was rejected by Mr Justice Whitford who said that such a claim was as silly as saying that a pen could be the author of a literary work. The human expertise in computer-derived works could be found to reside in the programs which, in this case, produced the lists of random numbers.

In works produced by or with the aid of a computer, human skill can reside in the person who enters information into the computer to produce the output or in the programmer who writes the program used or a combination of them both. Section 178 of the Act defines a work as 'computer-generated' when it is generated by a computer in circumstances such that there is no human author of the work. Section 9(3) states that, in the case of a literary, dramatic, musical or artistic work which is computer-generated, the author is the person by whom the arrangements necessary for the creation of the work are undertaken. This could be the person or persons who wrote the programs and created the other materials used collectively to generate the work in question.

The definitions of a computer-generated work and the author of such a work are tautologous when taken together: a computer-generated work is one created in circumstances such that there is no human author but if we attribute authorship to a human it cannot be computer-generated. The only way round this dilemma is to determine authorship *after* the creation of the work but this seems illogical. Normally, creation and attribution of authorship are coincident in time.

The approach taken in the Act can lead to difficulties because in many cases of works produced *with the aid of a computer* it will not be possible to say with any certainty whether the work has a human author. At one end of the spectrum a work will be produced using a computer as a tool, just as a writer uses a pen or a typewriter, while, at the other end, the computer will produce its works with little or no direct human effort. Neither of these situations should cause any great difficulty, but in between these two extremes lay a great many types of work which are the result of a modest amount of direct human input and classifying such works will not be easy. In order to consider this question further, works which involve computers in their production will be categorised as follows:

- works created using a computer;
- works created by a computer; and
- intermediate works.

In all these cases 'computer' means a programmed computer.

WORKS CREATED USING A COMPUTER

Examples of works which fall into this category are: documents produced using a word processing system; CAD (computer-aided designs) such as plans for a house or a new car body panel; music written using a program designed to assist with the composition of the music (as opposed to a program designed to write music); and an accounts report created using a spreadsheet program. In all these cases, the person operating the system is using the computer to achieve the results that he wishes to obtain. The programmed computer is merely a tool that allows the operator to use his creativity and imagination to the fullest extent and efficiency. Such works are not computer-generated; the skill and expertise (or at least the greatest part of these) derives from the user of the system. Word-processed documents, drawings, music and reports produced using packages which facilitate the making of these works are protected by copyright as original literary, dramatic, musical or artistic works in their own right. Indeed, section 51 of the Act recognises that copyright can subsist in data stored in a computer representing a design as a form of design document.

The person using the computer to create the work provides the expertise necessary for the making of the work and is, for copyright purposes, the author of the work. That expertise may be applied directly or indirectly: for example, a person writing a report may draft it out on paper and then hand it to a typist who enters it into the computer. In these circumstances, the author is not the operator but the person writing the report. It is similar to the process of amanuensis in which a person dictating a letter will be the author of that letter; the person who writes the dictation down is merely his agent.

The person who wrote the computer program used to assist in the creation of the types of works described above has no rights in the work because, although the programmer may control or influence the *format* of the finished work, he has no control or influence on the *content*. The fact that many works in this category may be produced directly using a computer before any other tangible form exists presents no serious problems because these works will exist, in terms of copyright protection, the instant they are recorded; that is, as soon as they are stored on a computer disk or printed out on paper.

WORKS CREATED BY A COMPUTER

These works, which may be literary, dramatic, musical or artistic, are those in which there is 'no human author' (section 178). This implies that the direct degree of human intervention in the making of the work is lacking or minimal. Examples might include:

- the automatic generation of weather forecasts by a computer communicating with satellites;
- the selection of lists of random numbers for a competition or for the Premium Bond draw;
- programs which produce artistic designs or music automatically, being based upon a set of rules or algorithms built into the program;
- a program designed to simulate some particular environment, such as climate, monetary systems, battle scenarios, etc. and to produce reports based on that simulation;

- works resulting from the application of fractal theory (it is claimed that fractal theory has a growing number of industrial and commercial uses, for example, to accurately measure a coastline).

Many of these systems operate with no human effort or skill apart from switching the equipment on and checking that there is sufficient paper in the computer printer or plotter and so on. The human operator has very little or no control over the *format* or *content* of the output produced by the computer. The author of such a work is the person who makes the arrangements for the work to be created. There are two possible interpretations of this. First, it could be the person who obtains the equipment and software to generate such works. Secondly, it could be the person or persons who wrote the software used to generate such works.

An example of the first alternative is where a business organisation buys and installs computer equipment and software to generate works of copyright which owe nothing (or nothing beyond the trivial) in terms of their authorship to the person operating the software. The Act contemplates non-human authors as, by section 154, an author can be a qualifying person if, *inter alia*, it is a body incorporated in the United Kingdom, such as a limited company. In the case of an unincorporated body, such as a partnership, the partners will be considered to be the joint authors of the work. As, theoretically, a company can be an author of a computer-generated work, there has to be a special rule for determining the duration of copyright in such works: the copyright expires at the end of the period of 50 years from the end of the calendar year in which the work was made; section 12(7).

The second alternative, giving authorship to the persons writing the software used to generate the work conforms to the position before the 1988 Act, for example, as shown in the *Express Newspapers* case. There has been only one case where a judge considered the authorship of computer-generated works. It was *Nova Productions Ltd* v *Mazooma Games Ltd* [2006] RPC 379 in which it was held that composite frames displayed on screen during the playing of a computer game based on pool were computer-generated artistic works. It was also held that the person who designed the appearance of the various elements displayed, devised the rules and logic by which each frame was generated and wrote the computer program was the person by whom the arrangements necessary to generate the frames were undertaken. He was, therefore, the author of the frame images. The judge discounted the role of the player in generating the frames as his input was not of an artistic character and he '. . . contributed no skill or labour of an artistic kind'. Nor did he undertake any of the arrangements necessary to create the frame images.

This decision in *Nova* v *Mazooma* may be satisfactory if limited to the facts of the case. The owners of the computer game had claimed that the defendant had copied the claimant's game in making its own game. However, there are other situations where it might lead to unacceptable results. Consider the situation where a company makes complex metal shapes by a process of casting. Once a shape is designed, it is a lengthy and complex process to decide how to break down the shape for ease of casting, the individual parts later being assembled to form the whole article to that shape. Say that the company obtains a licence to use software that automates the process of deciding how to break down a complex shape for efficient casting. Who is the author of that information? Is it the company which bought the software or the person or persons who wrote the software? What if the software was written in circumstances such that the employer of the persons writing the software was the owner of the copyright?

These issues are largely unresolved. Perhaps the identity of the person making the arrangements necessary for the creation of a computer-generated work depends on the nature of the work. In *Nova* v *Mazooma* the frame displays generated during the video game had no intrinsic value outside the context of playing the game. If the computer-generated work has a value in its own right and its creation is the reason why the person obtaining the software wanted it in the first place, it might be easier to accept that that person should be the author. By running the software, it is he who has made the arrangements necessary for the creation of the work.

Faced with this uncertainty, not really resolved in *Nova v Mazooma*, it is arguable that the provisions on computer-generated works should be repealed, so that the basic rules for determining authorship apply. It would then be a question of considering who it was that provided the act of authorship in the creation of the work. If it is the person writing the computer programs expressing the logic and rules and other software elements used, the law can adequately deal with that by looking at the licence under which the software has been made available by implying appropriate terms in that licence or using the concept of beneficial ownership. In any case, the licence itself may expressly cover the ownership of works created using the software. The inclusion of special rules on computer-generated works is an unnecessary complication which could have unexpected results.

INTERMEDIATE WORKS

These works lie in the area between computer-generated works and works made using the programmed computer as a tool. The *content* of the output produced is the result of the skill and effort of the person using the computer *and* the skill and effort of the person who wrote the computer program and/or the person who produced any database used in conjunction with it. There are many examples of these intermediate works, such as a specialised accounting system for a particular type of business, builders' estimating systems, or a music synthesiser designed to produce music from a basic framework of notes entered by the user and expert and decision-support systems.

A great deal of specialised software falls into this category where the skill required to produce the finished results is contained partly within the program, the remainder being provided by the user of the computer system. In some systems, the skill may come from more than two sources. For example, consider a computer system designed to be used to estimate the cost of building work. The system itself will comprise a suite of computer programs, which include routines to provide analyses and breakdowns of the costs derived, and a database of standard prices, based on sets of resources and labour outputs. The person using the system to work out the cost of a building brings a substantial degree of skill by deciding whether the standard prices are applicable and, if not, by building up new prices and entering them into the database. As Fig. 6.1 shows, the resulting computer output has three sources of expertise: that of the programmer, of the persons responsible for developing the database of standard prices, and of the person using the system. Who is the author of the finished work? Because the person using the system brings an amount of skill to the task, it would not be unreasonable to suggest that he is the author. Indeed, the user has the most direct link with the finished product and has ultimate control but may, nevertheless, rely to a great extent on the programs and information contained in the database. It could be argued that the finished work is partly created by human author and partly computer-generated. Alternatively, all three persons – programmer, database developer and user – might be considered to be joint authors. In the absence of any clear guidance in the Act and until we have a judicial precedent which clarifies the meaning of 'computer-generated', it is important that contractual provisions are made to cover the ownership of rights in the output of such intermediate works. In some cases, because all the persons involved are employees of the company developing and using the software, there will be little difficulty, but if outsiders are involved at any stage, terms should be inserted in contractual agreements dealing with ownership and use of the computer output.

The same considerations apply to expert and decision-support systems. These computer systems, which are intended to emulate the thought processes, analytical reasoning and advice of

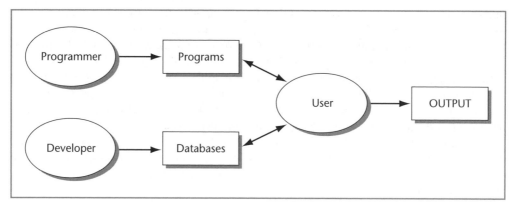

Figure 6.1 Authorship of intermediate works

experts, contain a great deal of skill and expertise within the systems themselves. An expert system, in basic terms, contains three main elements: a knowledge base (rules and facts provided by experts), an inference engine (a computer program which manipulates the knowledge base and applies it to a particular problem) and a user interface to make the system 'user-friendly' and to provide explanations of the reasoning adopted and advice given by the expert system. When an expert system is used to produce some advice or a report, the expertise underlying the output comes from the following sources:

- the experts who provided the knowledge;
- the persons (sometimes called 'knowledge engineers') who refined the knowledge and formalised it so that it could be installed in the knowledge base;
- the persons who wrote the inference engine and the user interface (or adapted existing ones); and
- the user of the system.

The user of the system provides expertise because he will have to understand and respond to the system, and he will have to interpret the questions asked by the system and know what the scope and limitations of the system are. Most, if not all, expert and decision-support systems cannot be used by naive users; a reasonable general knowledge of the area of expertise covered by the system (its knowledge domain) is essential if the output produced is to be taken seriously, just as the scope, limitations and difficulties presented by a new piece of legislation can only be predicted with any certainty by a lawyer and, even then, not always correctly.

What will the law make of the output of expert and decision-support systems when it comes to deciding the authorship and ownership of the copyright in that output? To argue that it is computer-generated and has no human author runs counter to common sense. To say that the user of this system is its sole author might be convenient but is unrealistic. To attribute authorship to the experts and knowledge engineers who developed the knowledge base is unsatisfactory because they cannot predict how the system will be used and what responses will be made by the user; they have no control over its use. In reality, all the persons listed above are the joint authors, in differing proportions, of the output resulting from the use of the system. It must be said, however, that, if the courts follow this interpretation, it will lead to all manner of complications regarding the commercial use of expert systems and other 'intermediate' systems. Although the courts might be willing to imply terms – for example, that the licensee or 'purchaser' of such systems owns the copyright in any output – it is obviously more sensible to recognise the difficulties associated with this part of the Act and to make suitable contractual provision for ownership (as opposed to authorship) of computer output. Better still, the provisions relating to computer-generated works ought to be repealed. It is notable that the United States has no provisions for determining the authorship of computer-generated works and that does not seem to have caused any particular problems in practice though there are some concerns, particularly as utilitarian works are less likely to attract protection under United States copyright law.

In spite of the doubtful value and uncertainty surrounding the authorship of computer-generated works, it is surprising that, apart from *Nova* v *Mazooma*, there are no cases in the UK on the authorship of computer-generated works following the commencement of the Copyright, Designs and Patents Act 1988. Incredibly, the only two cases on this issue were decided under the previous legislation, the Copyright Act 1956, which had no provisions whatsoever on the matter. There may be a number of explanations for this. Either the provisions are well understood and work effectively in practice (which seems unlikely) or the question of ownership of computer-generated works or intermediate works has been dealt with by way of licences and assignments. Another possibility is where several persons might have a claim to authorship, they are all employees of the same employer. A final possibility is that the software industry has not yet woken up to the potential uncertainties regarding authorship. It may simply need just one case where the output from an intermediate work proves to be very valuable commercially in a situation where ownership has not been fully tied up that we see some serious litigation in this area.

SUMMARY

- A computer-generated work is one created in circumstances such that there is no human author.
- The author of a computer-generated work is the person by whom the arrangements necessary for its creation are undertaken. That person could be either:
  - the person who decides to run the software used to create the work; or
  - the person who wrote the software used to create the work.
- The position is even more complex where the work is the result of the person using the software and the persons who wrote the software.
- The courts may be prepared to imply appropriate terms in software licences.
- Better still, express provision should be made for ownership of copyright in works that are, or could be considered to be, computer-generated.

SELF-TEST QUESTIONS

Note: there is only one correct answer to each multiple choice question.

1 **Which one of the following CORRECTLY describes the classes of copyright work that fall within the provisions on computer-generated works?**

   (a) Literary works.

   (b) Any work in which copyright may subsist.

   (c) Literary, dramatic, musical or artistic works.

   (d) Broadcasts, films and sound recordings.

2   According to the judge in *Nova Productions* v *Mazooma Games*, which one of the following CORRECTLY describes the author of the frames displayed on screen during the playing of a video game?

   (a) The person who devised the various elements displayed on screen, the rules, logic and computer program used to create the frames.

   (b) The person playing the game.

   (c) The person who devised the various elements displayed on screen, the rules, logic and computer program used to create the frames and the person playing the game, as joint authors.

   (d) The person who owned the games machine.

3   The provisions on computer-generated works are a complete anachronism and can only lead to uncertainty as to the identity of the author or authors of such works and should be repealed. Discuss.

For further resources and updates please go to the Companion Website accompanying this book at **www.mylawchamber.co.uk/bainbridgeIT**

7 Copyright in the information society

INTRODUCTION

All manner of works can be stored and made available electronically. Literature, music, works of art, audio-visual works and industrial designs can all be represented in digital form. Three-dimensional works and moving images can be expressed digitally and, using appropriate software, displayed on screens, copied, manipulated or transmitted anywhere in the world 'at the touch of a button'.

The ease with which all forms of creative expression can be exploited digitally has far-reaching consequences as regards the dissemination of information and opened up the exciting prospect of a global information village. The term generally accredited to Al Gore, the then Vice-President of the United States, of 'The Information Super-Highway' is very apt to describe the technology, and the rate at which the largely unregulated internet has grown and continues to grow is impressive.

The internet and also tangible media such as DVDs and CDs have been a mixed blessing for publishers. They can expose their works to a massive worldwide consumer audience with the exception, perhaps, of some repressive countries which cling on to a forlorn hope that they can control what is made available to their citizens. On the other hand, the internet can facilitate piracy and unauthorised copying and dissemination.

In terms of copyright and related rights, such as the database right, the internet has had a profound effect, so much so that a Directive[1] was adopted to try to deal with the issues raised which include the danger of a proliferation of copyright infringement on an unprecedented scale. The Directive also addressed a number of other concerns, such as the protection of access control technologies applied to copyright works and the dangers of works being made available online with information as to matters such as the copyright status and permissible uses having been removed.

One issue that the Directive did not adequately deal with was the phenomenon of peer-to-peer file sharing but, to some extent, this has subsequently been addressed by the courts and there has been an important US Supreme Court decision on this.

Copyright and related intellectual property rights may be used negatively so as to prevent the dissemination of information, for example, by threatening intermediaries such as internet service providers with copyright infringement actions or by obtaining injunctions against them. An early example of this involved the Church of Scientology which took legal action against a former member of the Church who posted on the internet extracts from the writings of L. Ron Hubbard,

---

[1] Directive 2001/29/EC of the European Parliament and of the Council of 22 May 2001 on the harmonisation of certain aspects of copyright and related rights in the information society, OJ L 167, 22.06.2001, p. 10 (the 'Directive on copyright in the information society').

the founder of the Church. The service provider was threatened with legal action if it did not remove the extracts.[2] The law has to reach a balance between freedom of expression and other rights where the two impinge. Copyright law reflects this to some extent by the provision of permitted acts, such as fair dealing for criticism or review or for reporting current events. These, and other, permitted acts can be compromised where technological access controls are applied to works made available electronically or where intermediaries are threatened with legal action.

This chapter looks at these issues and also other aspects of the implementation of the Directive on copyright in the information society.

THE INTERNET

Internet publishing looks very attractive at first sight. It is a really effective way of making a work available to a wide audience at minimal expense. Many academic writers were quick to seize the opportunity to spread their work on a worldwide scale. Numerous academic journals are now available online. Countless other works are available freely such as online encyclopaedias (such as Wikipedia), online health information (such as NHS Direct) and online language translation services (such as Babel) to name but a few. Many works available online contain marketing material or are provided as part of an information service.

Whilst many authors and copyright owners may be happy to distribute their work in this way, without direct recompense, they might complain if the works are further used. An example may be where a rival company lifts material from a commercial website to re-publish on its own website, passing it off as its own material. In other cases, authors and their publishers depend on the income they receive from publishing. The view that the internet is equivalent to the public domain and anything available there can be freely copied and distributed is misguided.

Typically, individuals gain access to works on the internet, which are stored on host computers, via an access provider (see Fig. 7.1).

Simply put, the internet is made up of public telecommunications systems which are used to carry information from host computers to recipients. The technology makes use of the most effective path through the system at the time of transmission, breaking down the materials transmitted into small packets and routing the packets to avoid busy lines. Different packets of information sent from one server to one recipient may take different routes through the telecommunications networks, to be re-assembled when received. No one is in overall control of the internet.

Individual works available on the internet will normally have their own copyright which may well be a foreign copyright. In most cases, the copyright country and the recipient country will be Contracting Parties to the Berne Convention for the Protection of Literary and Artistic Works. In these cases, the recipient country will extend its copyright protection to the work in question. Thus, for example, if a work subject to French copyright is accessed online in the UK and copies made there without permission, the owner of the French copyright will be able to sue for copyright infringement on the basis of UK copyright.

The works may also be subject to other rights such as moral rights, performance rights and recording rights. Contrary to the view that the internet is equivalent to the public domain, this does not affect the fact of subsistence of copyright and other rights. A copyright owner may choose to make his work available freely but it will remain a work of copyright and will not affect the copyright position of other works. It is advisable for owners of copyright works to make it clear whether the work can be printed or downloaded or used in other ways which would other-

[2] BBC2, *The Net*, 15 May 1995.

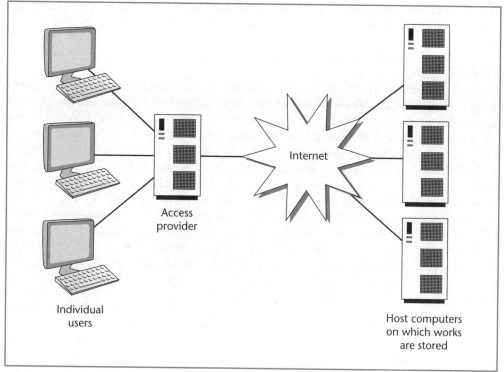

Figure 7.1 The internet

wise infringe copyright. The copyright position, including moral rights, should be spelt out. There is now specific protection for such information, as described later in the chapter.

Peer-to-peer file sharing

Companies like Napster distributed software that enabled individuals to share music and video files. These were the so-called 'peer-to-peer' ('P2P') networks. Whilst some of the files may have been copied without infringing copyright the majority did involve copyright infringement. When Napster ran into legal troubles, others took over, including Grokster and Streamcast. These latter companies' software allowed file sharing on networks linking individual computers without going through a central server, hoping to avoid Napster's problems. It was estimated that billions of files (mainly music and video files) were shared in this way each month. Using the software, one person could download a file from another person's computer. Of course, by downloading a copy of a file without authorisation, each individual doing this would infringe copyright but, in order to tackle the problem, copyright owners needed to prevent the distribution of P2P software.

In the days of the video recorder, film companies in particular were concerned at the use of video recorders to make unauthorised copies of films. In *Sony Corp of America* v *Universal City Studios Inc* 464 US 417 (1984), the US Supreme Court held that Sony was not liable for contributory infringement of copyright even though the company knew that it was highly likely that purchasers of the video recorders would use them to make infringing copies of television programmes or films broadcast on television. The video recorders could be used for non-infringing uses, for example, playing films on video tape that had been purchased or rented lawfully, for recording works out of copyright or for time-shifting (recording a programme to watch it at a more convenient time). Furthermore, Sony did not have knowledge of specific infringements, nor was there any evidence to suggest that the company encouraged infringing uses of its video recorders.

Napster Inc became famous (or, perhaps, infamous) in facilitating file sharing by the use of its software. In *A & M Records Inc v Napster Inc* 239 F 3d 1004 (9th Cir 2001) the US Court of Appeals for the 9th circuit confirmed that contributory liability may be imposed only to the extent that Napster received reasonable knowledge of specific infringing files, knowing that such files were available on the Napster system (or where Napster should have known this) and where it failed to act to prevent distribution of these works. After Napster was sued, other companies came along offering Napster alternatives. They included Streamcast and Grokster. They were sued by a number of companies including Metro-Goldwyn-Meyer Studios Inc.

The US Supreme Court distinguished the *Sony v Universal Studios* case in *Metro-Goldwyn-Meyer Studios Inc v Grokster Inc* 545 US 913 (2005), in which it was held that Grokster and Streamcast were guilty of contributory infringement of copyright. The difference here was that the defendants had actively encouraged copyright infringement, for example, by advertising their software as suitable for making copies of films or music and instructing users how to engage in infringing use. Although the software could be used for non-infringing purposes (some musicians keen to promote themselves are happy to have their music distributed freely) it had been made available with the object of promoting infringement. The defendants had incited or encouraged infringement and profited by the use of their software (through selling advertising space which was streamed to the users of the software) and they made no attempt to prevent infringement.

The position in *Sony v Universal* was reflected in the UK in cases involving Amstrad's twin cassette tape 'music centres' which permitted copying from one cassette tape to another. However, the machines could be used lawfully and there was nothing to suggest that Amstrad was authorising infringement of copyright: *Amstrad Consumer Electronics plc v The British Phonograph Industry Ltd* [1986] FSR 159. There was a possibility that technological development could be hindered had the courts held otherwise.

Copyright owners concerned about the impact on their business by file sharing technology began to bring legal proceedings against individuals using file-sharing software to infringe copyright. In particular, the British Phonograph Industry Ltd ('BPI') mounted a campaign of legal actions against persons infringing copyright using P2P software. In *Polydor Ltd v Brown* [2005] EWHC 3191 (Ch), it was held that a father who installed P2P software on his computer with around 400 audio files in a shared directory was a primary infringer of copyright by making the files available to the public by electronic transmission in such a way that members of the public could access the files at a time and place chosen by them (this falls within the restricted act of communication to the public under section 20 of the Act). Mr Brown also infringed copyright by authorising the infringement by those persons who downloaded copies from the shared directory. The claimants in the case were recording companies, some of which were members of the BPI which had downloaded sample files from Mr Brown's computer as evidence. Mr Brown was identified by means of court orders requiring internet service providers to identify him through his account with them. He claimed that he was unaware that he was distributing music. He said he had had the software on his computer for about a year and that his children used it to download music.

▨ Website content

Publishing material on a website has parallels to traditional forms of publishing or making works available to the public. There are, however, a number of differences. Placing a work on a website will necessitate making a copy of it by copying a work already in digital form or by digitising a work in other forms, such as by scanning. A work or performance placed on or made available through a website can be accessed and a permanent copy made without any tangible medium being involved in the distribution or transmission of the work. Simply accessing a work or performance online is to make a transient copy of it. This alone would normally be sufficient to infringe copyright. The Directive on copyright in the information society attempted to deal with these and other issues. Specific provision was made to:

■ Grant the owner of copyright (or related right, such as a performance) the exclusive right to authorise or prohibit the direct or indirect temporary or permanent reproduction of their work by any means and in any form.

■ Grant the owner of copyright the exclusive right to communicate the work to the public by wire or wireless means.

■ Provide for an exception for temporary acts of reproduction, for example, where a work is transmitted through an intermediary such as an internet service provider or where the use is otherwise lawful.

Placing a work of copyright on a website without the permission of the copyright owner infringes copyright by making a copy of the work and communicating the work to the public. It may also amount to infringement by authorising others to infringe copyright. These forms of infringement (particularly the latter two) were recognised in relation to music files on a computer for file sharing using peer-to-peer software in *Polydor Ltd* **v** *Brown* [2005] EWHC 3191 (Ch), discussed above.

The concept of authorisation for copyright infringement does not require that the authorisation is express and it may be implied where a person turns a blind eye or even fails to warn of copyright infringement: *Moorhouse* **v** *University of New South Wales* [1976] RPC 151, discussed in more detail later in this chapter in the context of the liability of internet service providers. However, that case was set in the context of photocopying facilities in a university library and does not necessarily translate to materials placed on a website which can be accessed by anyone. But, it is probable that placing a work of copyright on a website without any notice about its copyright status or other information about permissible uses is equivalent to giving implied consent to the work being accessed and copied. Of course, to infringe by authorisation, the act authorised must itself infringe copyright and it might not do so if it involves no more than temporary reproduction as covered by section 28A of the Copyright, Designs and Patents Act 1988.

Accessing works from a website and temporary reproduction

Making a transient copy of a work of copyright infringes that copyright if done without the permission of the copyright owner. This could mean that persons visiting websites or otherwise accessing information on the internet would inadvertently infringe copyright in anything they accessed which had been placed there without the copyright owner's permission. Although 'innocent' infringers may not have damages awarded against them, their innocence does not prevent them infringing. They could be subject to an injunction and other remedies.

Section 28A of the Copyright, Designs and Patents Act 1988 contains a permitted act that should avoid infringement of copyright in such circumstances. Copyright is not infringed (except in the case of computer programs, databases and broadcasts) by making temporary copies that are transient or incidental, which is an integral and essential part of a technological process the sole purpose of which is, *inter alia*, to enable a lawful use of a work and which has no independent economic significance. Whilst 'lawful use' obviously covers acts authorised by the copyright owner, recital 33 to the Directive on copyright in the information society includes also uses not restricted by law. Certain acts are not restricted by copyright. They include the act of reading a literary work or viewing an artistic work. Therefore, it would seem that simply accessing and viewing material on a website, without making a permanent copy or retransmitting it, does not infringe copyright in the work. The proviso that there should be no independent economic significance should apply where private individuals access works for their private and domestic purposes.

This does not prevent infringement by a person uploading a work onto a website by making the copy to upload and by communicating the work to the public. Equivalent provisions on temporary reproduction also apply to rights in performances.

Exhaustion of rights

The doctrine of exhaustion of rights applies generally to prevent the owner of an intellectual property right using that right to interfere with further commercialisation of goods subject to those rights which have been placed on the market within the European Community by him or with his consent. For example, if a person sells in Italy music CDs subject to copyright, rights in performances and to which his trade marks are applied, he cannot use those rights to prevent a third party from buying those CDs, importing them into the UK and re-selling them there. If it were otherwise, the objective of a single market in Europe would be compromised as it would enable owners of intellectual property rights selling the same goods at different prices in different Member States. However, the Directive on copyright in the information society makes it clear that the doctrine of exhaustion of rights does not apply to works and other protected subject matter made available online. This is also the case where a material copy has been made with the consent of the rightholder, for example, where the owner of the copyright in a document made available online allows persons accessing it to make a permanent copy on disk or on paper. If that person then sells the copy, he will infringe the copyright.

The European Court of Justice has made it clear that exhaustion of rights only applies to goods put on the market within the European Community. It does not apply where the goods are put on the market outside Europe. Under the European Free Trade Association, the principle of exhaustion of rights extends to the Member States of the European Economic Area, being the 25 EU Member States, Norway, Iceland and Liechtenstein.

Blogs (web logs)

A 'blog' (derived from 'web log') is an entry in an electronic form of a journal or diary hosted on a website. In many cases, individuals can add entries which are usually displayed in reverse chronological order. They often relate to news or political topics but can cover anything. Most blogs are text based but some also contain images such as photographs or video and may also contain audio. As with podcasts (typically audio files which may be downloaded to a computer or a device such as an MP3 player) there are a number of legal issues. For example, the content may be defamatory (see Chapter 23) or may amount to a criminal offence such as incitement (see Chapter 28). Here, we are concerned with infringement of intellectual property rights, in particular, in the context of copyright.

Individuals uploading their blogs (or contributing to newsgroups and the like) often do so with scant regard to legal implications. Sometimes, the material is too small to have any copyright significance. Where it is more substantial, the person adding the material may have created it himself and be the owner of the copyright in it. However, it may be tempting to add third-party materials, particularly images, music or audio-visual works. What has been said above in relation to website content applies equally here. The main difference is that the informal nature of blogs makes it easier to overlook issues of copyright and related rights. Building a website involves more planning and, usually, more thought about the legal implications.

Website architecture

There is nothing exceptional about copyright protection for works available on websites or for protection of databases through the database right. Placing a copyright work on a website is to make it available by electronic transmission in such a way that members of the public can access it from a place and at a time individually chosen by them, an act restricted by copyright under section 20. This will infringe the copyright if done without the licence of the copyright owner. There may also be issues of infringement of moral rights in relation to the work. Furthermore, as indicated in *Polydor* v *Brown* above, there could be liability for authorising persons accessing the work to infringe copyright. It should be remembered that innocence is not a defence to copyright infringement though it can prevent an award of damages being made.

The architecture of a website can be described as the selection and arrangement of individual webpages and their overall structure and inter-relationships: how they are linked together. There are also likely to be links to external websites. The architecture can be quite complex where numerous pages are set in a hierarchy with a number of links on each page to the home page and main pages and subsidiary pages. One has only to reflect on the number of times one is forced to refer to the site map to find what one is looking for. The question is whether the architecture is protected by copyright independently to the content on the webpages.

It has been accepted that it is possible to infringe the copyright in a work, particularly, a literary or dramatic work, by non-textual copying. It is theoretically possible to infringe the copyright in a computer program by non-textual copying. For example, in *Cantor Fitzgerald International* v *Tradition (UK) Ltd* [2000] RPC 95, Pumfrey J accepted that the architecture of a computer program could be infringed by non-textual copying (although this had not been alleged in that case, discussed in Chapter 4). Jacob J accepted that a compilation copyright could subsist in a suite of computer programs in *IBCOS Computers Ltd* v *Barclays Mercantile Highland Finance Ltd* [1994] FSR 275 (also discussed in Chapter 4).

Can these views be translated into the context of websites? It seems quite likely. However, it would have to be shown that the architecture of a website was the result of skill and judgment sufficient for copyright subsistence directed to designing and expressing that architecture. It would have to be more than the result of technical or efficiency considerations. The fact that another website has a similar 'look and feel' will not usually be sufficient for a finding of infringement. Any claim of infringement must be supported by detailing the architecture of the website alleged to have been copied, showing that it is the result of skill and judgment. It must also be shown that the defendant copied that architecture and that it represented a substantial part of the claimant's website. Similarity in look and feel can be explained in other ways. For example, the authors of each website may have worked independently, deriving much of their material from common sources and used common design techniques. This possibility was mentioned by Laddie J in *IPC Media Ltd* v *Highbury-SPL Publishing Ltd* [2004] EWHC 2985 (Ch) in respect of a claim of infringement of copyright in a glossy magazine 'Ideal Home' by a rival magazine called 'HOME'. Laddie J failed to find copying but said that, even if he was wrong as to that, and the defendant had been 'inspired' in some of its design choices by what it saw in 'IDEAL HOME', this would have been at far too high a level of generality to amount to copyright infringement. At least on some levels, a glossy magazine can be seen as analogous to a website and what Laddie J had to say in the *IPC Media* case should be applicable to websites.

If the architecture of a particular website was the result of the relevant skill and judgment, the question then becomes one of deciding what type of work it is. Two, mutually exclusive, possibilities exist. The first is that architecture or overall structure is a compilation (as in *IBCOS*, though this case preceded the express inclusion of databases as a form of literary work) and the second possibility is that it is a database with the individual webpages being the contents of that database.

A database is protected by copyright if it is original in the sense of being, by reason of the selection and arrangement of its contents, the author's own intellectual creation. The definition of 'database' requires, *inter alia*, that it is a collection of individual works, data or other materials. That would seem to exclude most websites as the works included therein are usually intended to form a whole homogeneous entity. If that is the case, it would seem most likely that the website is a compilation and will be protected by copyright as such, providing skill and judgment went into its making and the other requirements for copyright subsistence are present.

Domain names and hypertext links

A domain name, *per se*, is unlikely to be considered to be a work of copyright on the basis that it is too small, lacking in sufficient skill and judgment. Names, titles and phrases have usually been denied copyright protection, examples being 'Kojak', 'Elvis', 'The Man Who Broke the Bank at Monte Carlo' and 'Beauty is a Social Necessity, not a Luxury'. It appears that even if a name or short phrase is the result of substantial work and, possibly, judgment, it will not be protected by copyright. In *Exxon Corporation* v *Exxon Insurance Consultants International Ltd* [1982] Ch 119, it was argued that 'EXXON' was an original literary work because it was original (not having been thought of before), literary (being composed of letters which were written, typed or printed) and that it was a work (being the result of the work and effort that went into its invention). The Court of Appeal rejected that argument saying that the phrase 'original literary work' was a composite expression which could not be satisfied by breaking it down into its constituent parts. The phrase required that the work provided information, instruction or pleasure in the form of literary enjoyment. However, that explanation of what an original literary work is, deriving from a nineteenth-century case, must now be seen as too limiting, given that copyright protection now extends to computer programs, including programs in object code form.

A Scots case on copyright infringement where headlines were used to link to the pages of another website cast some doubt on the above principle that titles and phrases are too small for copyright protection. In *Shetland Times Ltd* v *Dr Jonathan Wills* [1997] FSR 604, the claimant (known as the pursuer in Scottish law) ran a newspaper business and had a website carrying articles from the newspaper which could be accessed by clicking on the headline to the article. It was intended that the front page of the website would carry advertising. The defendant (known as the defender in Scottish law) also operated a website which carried verbatim copies of the claimant's headlines which, when clicked on, would link to the articles on the claimant's website thereby missing the front page and any advertising that would be carried on it. This is known as 'deep linking' though in this case it was not very deep! The judge said that it was arguable that at least some of the headlines were works of copyright. Each contained several words put together for the purpose of imparting information, an example being: 'Bid to save centre after council funding "cock up"'. This probably goes too far. The judge was not referred to any authorities on the issue and that part of the judgment must be treated with extreme caution. The better view is that headlines such as the example above are not protected by copyright. Similar considerations apply to domain names and addresses to pages within websites (an example being the address to the Companion Website for this book, being **www.pearsoned.co.uk/bainbridge**). Of course, where a link on a website is indicated by an icon or other image, there may be a copyright in the icon or image. It was accepted in *Navitaire Inc* v *easyJet Airline Co Ltd* [2006] RPC 111, discussed in Chapter 4, that icons and screen images could be protected as artistic works, providing they were the result of skill and judgment.

The main issue in the *Shetland Times* case was whether the defender had infringed copyright in the website on the basis that it was a cable programme service.[3] Cable programs no longer exist as a work of copyright in their own right and now the question would be whether the defender had infringed copyright by communicating the newspaper articles to the public. His linking to the articles avoiding the front page of the pursuer's website was clearly done without the pursuer's permission. To remind ourselves, the restricted act of communication to the public includes making available to the public of the work by electronic transmission in such a way that members of the public may access it from a place and at a time individually chosen by them: section 20. This would seem to apply to the *Shetland Times* case although making the works available to the public in this way was indirect, that does not matter as copyright can be infringed indirectly. There is a problem, however. It could be argued that the defender was not making the articles available to the public: he simply provided an alternative means of access to the articles. It was not as if the defender had copied the articles and placed them on his own website (as in *Union des Associations Européenes de Football* v *Briscomb* [2006] EWHC 1268 (Ch) in which broadcasts of football matches were captured digitally and made available on the defendant's website – the judge gave summary judgment to the claimant in respect of the allegations of copying and communicating to the public). On the other hand, the language of section 20 seems to suggest that even providing an alternative means of access is caught as, by doing so, the defender was making the articles available to the public who could access them indirectly via his website. Members of the public who might otherwise not access the articles, for example, being unaware of the existence of the *Shetland Times* website, might access them by visiting the defender's website. Article 3(1) of the Directive on copyright in the information society reinforces this view as it states that the rightholder should have the '… exclusive right to authorise or prohibit *any* communication to the public …' (emphasis added).

If we accept, on balance, that the activity of linking to another person's website is covered by the restricted act of communication to the public, what are the consequences of this? By placing material on a website generally accessible to all (not being a subscription website which can be fully accessed only on payment of a fee) the owner of the rights in the content can be taken to impliedly consent to persons accessing the content, at least to view it on screen. That is, assuming the owner of the rights has agreed to it being made available in this way in a case where the owner of the rights is someone other than the website owner. It can also be assumed that the owner of the website is taken to have agreed to others linking to that website. At least, in relation to the front page. It cannot be assumed, however, that such implied consent extends to deep linking. It will depend on the particular circumstances, including the nature of the website. A website owner may have placed a notice on the website expressly specifying what is and is not permissible. This may cover the use of the content, for example, whether it may be printed out, stored or further distributed. It may also set out what is acceptable in terms of linking to the website. If the front page carries advertising, it is unlikely that the owner will want others to deep-link directly to other webpages on the website. Even if all or most pages carry advertising, deep linking is unlikely to be acceptable as the front page advertising can be expected to be charged at a premium price. Of course, whether the website owner can legally control deep-linking depends on the scope of the restricted act of communication to the public, as discussed above.

---

[3] For a discussion of this aspect of the case, see the fifth edition of this book at pp. 79–80.

Electronic mail ('e-mail')

Short e-mail messages (and text messages on mobile phones) will usually be too small to attract copyright protection. However longer e-mails and attachments may be subject to copyright and related rights (for example, in a case where an attachment is an audio-visual file subject to rights in performances). Where a work is an infringing copy, the person sending the e-mail infringes copyright by making a copy of it but unless he sends it to a large number of persons, he will not infringe by communicating the work to the public. If a student at a university or college sends an infringing copy to all the other students at the institution, this could be considered to be communicating the work to the public even though it is communicated to a discrete set of persons. In an old case on public performances, *Ernest Turner Electrical Instruments Ltd* v *Performing Right Society Ltd* [1943] 1 Ch 167, it was accepted that playing music to 600 employees in a factory was a public performance. This could be seen as a policy decision as the right to control such performances could be seriously compromised if playing music before such audiences were permitted. There seems to be no valid reason why this finding should not apply equally to the act of communicating a work to the public.

The only issue remaining is the position of a person who receives an e-mail which contains, or has attached to it, an infringing copy. If that person encouraged, perhaps even tacitly, the sending of the work, he may be liable for authorising the infringement of copyright by the person who made the copy to send to him. Otherwise, the recipient should be covered by section 28A which allows temporary reproduction in accordance with lawful use, for example, where the person simply reads or views the contents of an e-mail and no independent economic significance is involved. However, if that person makes a permanent copy, section 28A no longer applies and there is a technical infringement of copyright. Where the offending material is sent as an attachment, this will usually entail saving the file first by downloading it. This is not a temporary copy and the copyright will be infringed before the file is even read or viewed. Unless the recipient knows or has reason to believe that the attached file infringes copyright or any rights related to copyright, he will have a defence to damages, without prejudice to any other remedies available. A sensible approach for the law to take where the recipient has no idea that an attached file he is about to save contains infringing material is to permit the recipient to view the contents without attracting any liability, provided he erases infringing material as soon as he realises it does infringe copyright or where, in the circumstances, it would be reasonable to assume that it does. This approach found favour with the judge in a case on computer pornography sent as an e-mail attachment (*R* v *Porter*, discussed in Chapter 28).

MULTIMEDIA

A CD or DVD typically may contain a whole range of works. For example, a multimedia product on the topic of romantic poems may include among other things:

- the text of poems to be displayed on screen;
- the sound of poems being recited;
- a commentary comprising an oral and/or textual description of material relating to the poets and their poems;
- film sequences showing the poets at work or relaxing;
- photographs of the poets' birthplaces, homes, relatives and acquaintances; and
- introductory and background music.

A feature of multimedia is that the person using the product can move about it at will. The information is, therefore, structured and may have hypertext links. In terms of copyright subsistence, all the works above may be subject to copyright in addition to the whole as a compilation or database. The following example gives some idea of the complexity of rights in such a work.

MultiMega, a multimedia publisher, decides to produce a DVD containing selected poems written by Andrew, Belinda and Clarence. Andrew is still alive, Belinda died some 20 years ago and Clarence has been dead for 80 years. Diana, a famous self-employed literary critic has been commissioned by MultiMega to select the poems to include in the DVD and to write some material giving a critical appraisal of each poem. MultiMega's editing manager, Edward, selects some music written by Frances, who died 62 years ago, to use as background music. George, an actor, is commissioned to recite the poems in front of a studio audience. A selection of modern photographs of the poets' homes and favourite haunts, taken by Harriet, is to be included in the work, with her permission. There is also some old footage of Belinda being interviewed live on ICE television. MultiMega's employees created the computer programs to access and display the works and the hypertext links.

Assuming that there has been no subsequent transfer of the various copyrights except on the death of a copyright owner, the following permissions will be required by MultiMega:

■ a licence from Andrew and from Belinda's estate (as she is now deceased) allowing for the copying, performance and issue to the public of their poems;

■ an assignment (or exclusive licence) from Diana in respect of the compilation copyright and the material she has written;

■ an exclusive licence from George in respect of his live performance and that of the recording company which first recorded the performance (these are rights in performances, such rights being similar to copyright, often described as rights related to copyright or neighbouring rights); and

■ a licence from ICE in respect of the broadcast.

No permission is required in respect of Clarence's poems which are now out of copyright but care must be taken as far as Frances's music is concerned as the copyright in it might be revived as a result of the extension of the term of copyright to life plus 70 years (this will be so if her music was still protected in any Member State of the European Community). As Edward presumably is an employee, none of his efforts will result in a copyright that belongs to him rather than MultiMega. Another problem for MultiMega is that some of the persons involved will have moral rights (in particular, Andrew, Diana and Harriet), and it must take account of moral rights, either by acknowledging the authors as such or seeking a waiver in respect of the right to be identified. It is clear that, in most cases, obtaining the necessary permissions for a work of multimedia will be difficult, drawn out and, probably, expensive!

The ensuing multimedia product probably will be considered to be a database rather than a compilation. The definition of a database is a collection of independent works, data or other materials which are arranged in a systematic or methodical way and are individually accessible by electronic or other means. This would certainly seem to be the case with MultiMega's DVD. However, one proviso is that it may be that not all the works included are 'individually accessible'. For example, a particular piece of music may be played only when a specific film sequence is accessed and it may not be possible to access that music entirely on its own. This may seem overly pedantic but, if the DVD does not qualify as a database, it almost certainly will as a compilation. As far as copyright is concerned, there is not a great deal of difference between copyright in a database and copyright in a compilation. In particular, databases must be personal intellectual creations to attract copyright whereas the requirement for originality for compilations is not further explained.

On balance, it seems most likely that such DVD and CD products will be classified as databases, except in the case of music compilations which are excluded by the Directive on the legal protection of databases:[4] these continue to be protected as compilations. If a DVD or CD like that made by MultiMega is a database, the next question is whether it is a copyright database or whether it is only subject to the database right. As seen in the preceding chapter, this is a question as to whether its making was the result of the author's own intellectual creation and/or whether it required a substantial investment. In the above example, it is possible that both of these rights subsist. Of course, whether the entire work is classed as a copyright database or one subject to the database right or both does not affect the copyright and other rights subsisting in the individual works and performances contained within it.

A further issue is whether the hypertext links built into the software are protected by copyright. These may be considered to be a structural element of the database protected as a non-literal element. As the Directive on the legal protection of databases makes clear, the protection of copyright databases extends to their structure. It seems entirely reasonable to assume that a person copying the structure of hypertext links from one multimedia product to another, different, product may infringe the copyright in the first if those parts taken represent a substantial part of the first, provided that it is a copyright database. Of course, it would be rare that much would be gained simply by copying the structure of hypertext works alone.

LEGAL LIABILITY OF INTERNET SERVICE PROVIDERS

Internet service providers (ISPs) enable and facilitate access to material on the internet as well as providing a range of other services including e-mail services, bulleting boards, chat-rooms and hosting websites. Some organisations provide a full range of services whilst others may specialise, for example, in relation to website hosting. All these activities have serious copyright implications and this part of the chapter considers the liability of ISPs generally for infringement of copyright and related rights.

Through their agreements with persons to whom they provide services, ISPs have some measure of control, for example, by requiring their subscribers to adhere to copyright law and not to make infringing material available to others, whether on a bulletin board, website, transmission by e-mail or otherwise. ISPs may even seek indemnities from their subscribers for copyright infringement attributable to their actions.

ISPs are not liable for temporary reproduction where it is in accordance with the permitted act under section 28A of the Copyright, Designs and Patents Act 1988. This provision was inserted into the Act by the Copyright and Related Rights Regulations 2003 to comply with the Directive on copyright in the information society. This states that copyright is not infringed by the making of a temporary copy which is transient or incidental, which is an integral and essential part of a technological process and the sole purpose of which is to enable (a) a transmission of the work in a network between third parties by an intermediary; or (b) a lawful use of the work; and which has no independent economic significance. It applies in respect of all forms of copyright work (except computer programs, databases and broadcasts) and rights in performances. Typically, in the context of ISPs, this prevents ISPs being liable for infringement where a work (or performance) is transmitted by one person to another and which passes through the

---

[4] Directive 96/9/EC of the European Parliament and of the Council of 11 March 1996 on the legal protection of databases, OJ L 77, 27.03.1996, p. 20 (the 'Directive on the legal protection of databases').

ISPs equipment. It would seem to allow straightforward transmission as well as temporary storage such as by caching data during web browsing. A cache is a temporary storage area where frequently accessed data is stored. For example, when browsing a website, data already accessed (such as the front page) will be stored temporarily so that it can be retrieved again quickly rather than being loaded up again from the website.

Apart from the permitted act of temporary reproduction and special defences for ISPs in relation to illegal material, discussed later, ISPs may be vulnerable for copyright infringement in a number of ways:

- by being secondary infringers;
- by authorising infringement; or
- by joint infringement.

Secondary infringement

Under section 24(2) of the Copyright, Designs and Patents Act 1988 it is an infringement of copyright to transmit a work, without the licence of the copyright owner, by a telecommunications system (otherwise than by communicating to the public), knowing or having reason to believe that infringing copies will be made by means of the reception of the transmission in the United Kingdom or elsewhere. Although it matters not where the reception takes place, the definition of 'infringing copy' provides territorial constraint as, in relation to infringing copies made outside the United Kingdom, the copy must either have been imported or is proposed to be imported into the United Kingdom. Also, had it been made in the United Kingdom that would have been an infringement of the copyright in the work or a breach of an exclusive licence agreement relating to the work.

A serious limitation is that the transmission must be otherwise than by communicating to the public. This covers broadcasting and making available by electronic transmission in such a way that members of the public may access it from a place and at a time individually chosen by them. Therefore, placing material on a website so that persons can access it where and when they choose is outside this form of infringement. It probably does not apply to e-mails either, including e-mails sent by ISPs to their subscribers, as the recipient can still choose when and where to access an e-mail. It could apply to pop-ups and instant messaging. However, the scope for infringement is not particularly great and, in terms of ISPs, it is highly unlikely that this form of infringement would ever apply, notwithstanding the requirement of knowledge or reason to believe that infringing copies will be made.

Authorising infringement

Section 16(2) of the Copyright, Designs and Patents Act 1988 states that copyright in a work is infringed by a person who, without the licence of the copyright owner does, *or authorises another to do*, any of the acts restricted by the copyright. If the act which infringes is done in the UK, it does not matter if the authorisation comes from elsewhere. In *ABKCO Music & Records Inc* v *Music Collection International Ltd* [1995] RPC 657, a Danish company granted a licence to an English company to make and issue to the public recordings of the claimant's sound recordings in the UK and Eire. It was held that it did not matter where the authorisation was given as long as the restricted act was carried out within the jurisdiction of the courts of the UK. Thus, if an Australian ISP authorises someone in Scotland to make infringing material available on the internet from a server in Scotland, the ISP is caught by section 16(2) and is liable for the infringement together with the person responsible for making the material available.

It is important to understand what is meant by authorisation. It has been construed by the courts in a fairly wide sense and turning a blind eye can amount to authorisation. Indifference or even failing to inform persons of the implications of copyright law may suffice. In *Moorhouse* v *University of New South Wales* [1976] RPC 151, a failure to inform users of a library with photocopying facilities as to copyright law and to supervise the use of the copiers was held to be authorising infringement of copyright. In the UK, judges have equated authorisation with '... the grant or purported grant, which may be express or implied, of the right to do the act complained of'.

An ISP could be said to authorise infringement if it fails to inform its clients of copyright law and the need to avoid infringement of copyright. However, the specific defence available to ISPs in respect of illegal material, discussed later, generally does not require vigilance on the part of the ISP and there is no duty imposed on an ISP to police what is available through his service.

Joint infringement

It is possible that an ISP could be claimed to be a joint infringer along with the client responsible for making infringing material available through its service. Joint infringement occurs where two or more persons act in concert pursuant to a common design to infringe. In terms of stereo equipment having dual cassette tape players, in *Amstrad Consumer Electronics plc* v *The British Phonograph Industry Ltd* [1986] FSR 159, it was held that supplying machines which would be likely to be used to unlawfully copy pre-recorded cassettes subject to copyright protection was not authorising infringement of copyright. Nor was it sufficient to make Amstrad a joint infringer. Amstrad had no control over the way the machines were used once sold.

In the case of ISPs, it could be argued that things are different. They do have some control. They can monitor and check what is being made available through their service. They can erase or block infringing material. The problem they have is that the sheer volume of material involved makes effective control and policing almost impossible. The best they can do is to warn their clients about the dangers of copyright infringement. But if they encourage, even implicitly, a disregard for copyright laws, this could be seen as authorisation or even joint infringement. A sensible approach for an ISP is to inform their clients and to carry out a reasonable level of policing and checks on what material is being made available and transmitted through their service, the only difficulty being that they may then be accused of invasion of privacy.

What has been said above in relation to ISPs also applies to others who facilitate access to material over the internet. Thus, libraries with online facilities or employers who allow or encourage employees to make use of the internet should be careful as regards copyright infringement by their clients or employees. Education and vigilance seem to be the key words in respect of the internet.

Injunctions against ISPs

An injunction is an important remedy for infringement of intellectual property rights. The courts have discretion as to whether to grant an injunction but an injunction will normally follow a finding of infringement. It may be difficult to obtain an injunction against an ISP, where the service is being used to infringe copyright, because the ISP may not itself be liable for the infringement as a primary or secondary infringer or by authorising the infringement.

Bearing this difficulty in mind and the problem of ISPs effectively policing activities by those using their services, section 97A of the Copyright, Designs and Patents Act 1988 has special provisions covering the grant of injunctions against ISPs and other service providers in a case of copyright infringement. The court has the power to grant an injunction against a service provider where the service provider has actual knowledge that someone is using the service to infringe copyright. In determining whether the service provider has actual knowledge, a court shall take into account all matters which appear in the particular circumstances to be relevant. Amongst other things, regard shall be had to whether the service provider has received a notice in accordance with Regulation 6(1)(c) of the Electronic Communications (EC Directive) Regulations 2002. This requires the service provider to make available to the recipient of the service (and any relevant enforcement authority) in a form and manner which is easily, directly and permanently accessible, the details of the service provider, including his electronic mail address, making it possible to contact him rapidly and to communicate with him in a direct and effective manner. The court must also have regard to the extent to which any such notice includes the full name and address of the sender of the notice and details of the infringement in question.

A 'service provider' is anyone providing an information society service, being any service normally provided for remuneration, at a distance, by means of electronic equipment for the processing (including digital compression) and storage of data, and at the individual request of a recipient of a service. A fuller definition is given in two Directives on the provision of information in the field of technical standards and regulations. It certainly covers ISPs and a number of other services provided online. These forms of injunction could be useful where the infringing material is on a computer server outside the jurisdiction of the courts of the UK.

The courts have the power to grant injunctions in such cases but they are not required to do so. A court may refuse to grant an injunction, for example, where the complainant has not identified himself properly or where the details of the alleged infringement are vague or sketchy or where the allegation is overly optimistic with no real foundation. Other factors may be taken into account and this could include, for example, the possibility that the acts complained of do not infringe by reason of the permitted acts or other defences such as public interest.

ISPs and illegal material

One of the issues dealt with by the Directive on electronic commerce[5] was the potential liability of information society service providers for any illegal material that passed through or was stored on their computer systems. The head of one ISP had been prosecuted in Germany in respect of pornographic images made available through the ISP's services. The decision was taken to provide information society service providers, which include ISPs, with a defence, not just in respect of pornographic images but also in terms of illegal material generally. These provisions, which were implemented in the UK by the Electronic Commerce (EC Directive) Regulations 2002, came into force on 21 August 2002 (with the exception of Regulation 16 which modified the law relating to Stop Now Orders which came into force on 23 October 2002). The defences relevant for ISPs apply to all forms of illegal material and this covers material infringing copyright and other intellectual property rights. It is in terms of copyright and liability for infringement of copyright that this section is directed. For a more general in-depth view of these regulations, see Chapter 24.

Under Regulation 17 (the 'mere conduit' defence), where the service consists of the transmission in a communication network of information provided by a recipient of the service or the provision of access to a communication network, the service provider will not be liable for damages or other financial remedy if it did not initiate the transmission, did not select the receiver of the transmission and did not select or modify the information contained in the transmission.

---

[5] Directive 2000/31/EC of the European Parliament and of the Council of 8 June 2000 on certain legal aspects of information society services, in particular, electronic commerce, in the Internal Market, OJ L 178, 17.07.2000, p. 1 (the 'Directive on electronic commerce'). This Directive is discussed in more detail in Part 3 of this book.

Automatic, intermediate and transient storage is permitted provided it is for the sole purpose of the transmission and the information is not stored for longer than necessary for that transmission.

Regulation 18 applies to caching (that is, temporary storage for quick access). The service provider will not be liable for damages or other pecuniary remedy if the sole purpose is to make more effective the onward transmission of the information to other recipients of the service upon their request. The service provider must not modify the information and comply with conditions on access to the information and with any rules regarding the updating of the information, specified in a manner widely recognised and used by industry. Furthermore, the service provider must not interfere with the lawful use of technology, widely recognised and used by industry, to obtain data on the use of the information and must act expeditiously to remove or to disable access to the information he has stored upon obtaining actual knowledge of the fact that the information at the initial source of the transmission has been removed from the network, or access to it has been disabled, or that a court or an administrative authority has ordered such removal or disablement. In other words, once the service provider knows that the information has been removed or disabled at source or a court has so ordered, the service provider must remove or disable access to that information.

Regulation 19 applies to storage of information supplied by the recipient of the service (for example, where the service provider hosts a subscriber's webpages). Again, the service provider will not be liable for damages or any other pecuniary remedy if he does not know (actual knowledge is required) of unlawful activity or information and, where a claim for damages is made, is not aware of facts or circumstances to put him on notice that the activity or information was unlawful. If the service provider obtains such knowledge or awareness, he must act expeditiously to remove or to disable access to the information. A further requirement for the defence to apply is that the recipient of the service (that is, the person subscribing to the service) was not acting under the authority or the control of the service provider.

Actual knowledge, for the purposes of Regulations 18 and 19 is a matter of taking into account all matters which appear to the court in the particular circumstances to be relevant. This may include whether a service provider received notice from any person through a means of contact required to be made available by the service provider (for example, e-mail address) and the extent to which the notice includes the full name and address of the sender, details of the location of the information in question and details of the unlawful nature of the activity or information in question.

The mere conduit defence is a complete defence if the conditions apply. However, in respect of the caching and hosting defences, they do not provide complete immunity to a copyright infringement action (nor in respect of other civil wrong) but operate to protect the service provider for a claim in damages or for some other pecuniary remedy, such as a claim for an account of profits. The service provider may still be subject to a finding of infringement (again, noting that innocent infringement is no defence) but the only appropriate remedy available to the copyright owner would be an injunction which may, in such circumstances, require the service provider to remove the offending material.

In the Directive on electronic commerce, Article 15 states that the service provider does not have a general obligation to monitor the information he transmits or stores, or any general obligation to actively seek facts or circumstances indicating illegal activity.

CIRCUMVENTION OF 'COPY-PROTECTION'

Works subject to copyright and other rights which are made available in electronic form are sometimes encrypted or have other forms of protection applied to them to prevent or restrict access not authorised by the owner of the rights. When computer games were distributed on cassette tape in copy-protected form, it was not long before third parties marketed software designed to overcome the copy-protection enabling the making of multiple copies. The Copyright, Designs and Patents Act 1988, when it came into force on 1 August 1989, already had provisions giving remedies to copyright owners against persons helping to overcome copy-protection of computer programs: section 296. The Directive on the legal protection of computer programs[6] also contained provisions dealing with copy-protection of computer programs which were seen as compatible with those already provided under law in the UK.

The Directive on copyright in the information society required Member States to provide adequate legal protection against the circumvention of technical measures applied to prohibit or restrict unauthorised acts in relation to works of copyright and other materials subject to related rights, such as rights in performances and database right. The legal protection of computer programs was unaffected by this Directive. The result of all this has been that there are two forms of control over 'copy-protection'. One applies to computer programs only (set out in section 296). The other set of controls apply to works of copyright other than computer programs and subject matter protected by related rights: contained in sections 296ZA to 296ZF.

Computer programs

A new section 296 was substituted for the old section and applies in relation to computer programs to which a technical device has been applied, intended to prevent or restrict unauthorised acts that would otherwise infringe the copyright.

The technical device does not have to be incorporated in the program itself and may reside in hardware. This was confirmed in *Sony Computer Entertainment Inc v Ball* [2004] EWHC 1738 (Ch) in which the defendants were involved in the manufacture, sale and installation of computer chips, called 'Messiah2' which, when installed in Sony Play-Station consoles, enabled Sony's games imported from other parts of the world to be played. Sony's CDs and DVDs containing the games had embedded codes which were recognised by the consoles – a sort of lock and key system. Copying the CDs and DVDs using standard copying equipment did not copy the embedded codes. Because of different television standards in the world (Europe uses the PAL system, unlike the US and Japan) Sony was able to use different forms of code in different areas which meant that it could prevent parallel importation into Europe from the US and Japan. A game sold in Japan, for example, would not work on a console bought in the UK. The Messiah2 chips overcame this technical form of copy-protection by tricking the console into believing that the CD or DVD contained the relevant embedded codes. Not only could games imported from other parts of the world be played but unauthorised copies of the games could also be played. A defence submission that the technical device had to be contained in the computer program rather than the hardware was rejected by the judge. He said that there was nothing in the wording of section 296 which limited where the device should be. The device was applied to the computer program whether it was on the program or the hardware which read it or both.

---

[6] Article 7(3) of Council Directive 91/250/EEC of 14 May 1991 on the legal protection of computer programs, OJ L 122, 17.05.1991, p. 42 (the 'Directive on the legal protection of computer programs').

Before amendment, section 296 applied to all forms of copyright work, not just computer programs, and was clearer in that all it required was that the work was issued to the public in electronic form which was copy-protected. Copy-protection was defined as including any means intended to prevent or restrict copying of a work. Now, of course, forms of copyright works other than computer programs are covered by the provisions in sections 296ZA to 296ZF.

A person is liable under section 296 if, knowing or having reason to believe that it will be used to make infringing copies, he:

(i)   manufactures for sale or hire, imports, distributes, sells or lets for hire, offers or exposes for sale or hire, advertises for sale or hire or has in his possession for commercial purposes any means the sole intended purpose of which is to facilitate the unauthorised removal or circumvention of the technical device; or

(ii) publishes information intended to enable or assist persons to remove or circumvent the technical device.

The persons who have the right to bring an action against such a person have the same rights against that person as does the copyright owner in respect to an infringement of the copyright. The identity of the persons having the right to bring an action are:

(a)   a person issuing to the public copies of, or communicating to the public, the computer program to which the technical device has been applied;

(b)   the copyright owner or his exclusive licensee, if he is not the person specified in (a);

(c)   the owner or exclusive licensee of any intellectual property right in the technical device applied to the computer program.

The rights are concurrent and all have the same rights as regards delivery up or seizure as regards any means intended to remove or circumvent the technical device. As previously, the presumptions under sections 104 to 106 of the Act apply as does the withdrawal of the privilege against self-incrimination in intellectual property matters. The presumptions are useful evidentially. For example, if a copy of a computer program contains a notice stating the name of the author, it will be presumed that he is the author of the work and was the first owner of the copyright unless the contrary is proved. In other words, the defendant would have the burden of proving that he was not the author and first owner of the copyright.

There is a rule of law that a person has a right not to incriminate himself in respect of a criminal offence (the privilege against self-incrimination). There are some exceptions to this rule, in particular in intellectual property matters. Section 72 of the Supreme Court Act 1981 (and equivalent legislation in Scotland and Northern Ireland) removes the privilege in proceedings for infringement of intellectual property rights or passing off including proceedings for disclosure or to prevent an apprehended infringement of intellectual property rights or passing off. For example, a person subject to a court order in relation to civil infringement of copyright cannot refuse to disclose materials which tend to show that he has committed offences on the basis that to comply may incriminate him for a criminal offence.

Other works and subject matter

The Copyright and Related Rights Regulations 2003 inserted new sections 296ZA to 296ZF into the Act. They apply where effective technological measures have been applied to a copyright work other than a computer program and, with necessary modifications, the subject matter of related rights. Again, in *Sony* v *Ball*, above, it was accepted that this does not require the technological measures to be applied to the work itself and the measure could reside in, for example, a games console rather than in the game itself. Apart from computer programs, Sony's games consisted also of other copyright works including artistic works.

The interpretation section for the purposes of these provisions is section 296ZF. This defines 'technological measures' as 'any technology, device or component which is designed, in the normal course of its operation, to protect a copyright work other than a computer program'. Such measures are 'effective' if the:

> ... use of the work is controlled by the copyright owner through
> (a) an access control or protection process such as encryption, scrambling or other transform-ation of the work, or
> (b) a copy control mechanism,
> which achieves the intended protection.

References to the protection of a work is to the prevention or restriction of acts not authorised by the copyright owner that are restricted by copyright and references to use of a work do not extend to any use outside the scope of the acts restricted by copyright.

Under section 296ZA, a person who circumvents effective technological measures applied to a copyright work other than a computer program, knowing, or with reasonable grounds to know, that he is pursuing the objective of circumventing the measures is liable as if he had infringed copyright. The identity of the persons having the right to bring an action is the same as in the case of computer programs above and the presumptions apply also as does the withdrawal of privilege against self-incrimination.

These provisions also apply, with necessary changes, to rights in performances, the publi-cation right (rights in respect of the publication of previously unpublished works which are themselves out of copyright) and the database right.

An important exception is in section 296ZA(2) and applies where a person does anything cir-cumventing effective technological measures for the purposes of research into cryptography. This does not give rise to a cause of action under section 296ZA unless by doing so, or in issuing information from that research, the rights of the copyright owner are prejudicially affected. This is not expressly limited to non-commercial research and there is no requirement that the act itself is fair dealing.

Criminal offences associated with technological measures

The act of circumventing technological measures does not, *per se*, give rise to criminal liability. However, under section 296ZB, a number of activities give rise to offences being committed. Section 296ZB(1) states that a person:

> ... commits an offence if he –
> (a) manufactures for sale or hire, or
> (b) imports otherwise than for his private and domestic use, or
> (c) in the course of a business –
>   (i)   sells or lets for hire, or
>   (ii) offers or exposes for sale or hire, or
>   (iii) advertises for sale or hire, or
>   (iv) possesses, or
>   (v) distributes, or
> (d) distributes otherwise than in the course of a business to such an extent as to affect prejudi-cially the copyright owner,
> any device, product or component which is primarily designed, produced, or adapted for the pur-pose of enabling or facilitating the circumvention of effective technological measures.

A person also commits an offence if he provides, promotes, advertises or markets:

(a) in the course of a business, or
(b) otherwise than in the course of a business to such an extent as to affect prejudicially the copyright owner,
a service the purpose of which is to enable or facilitate the circumvention of effective technological measures.

The offences are triable either way and the maximum penalty, if tried summarily, is a fine not exceeding the statutory maximum and/or imprisonment for a period not exceeding three months. On conviction on indictment, the maximum penalty is a fine and/or imprisonment not exceeding two years.

The offences are of strict liability and there is no requirement for *mens rea* ('guilty knowledge') but it is a defence for the accused to show that he did not know and had no reasonable grounds for believing that the device, product, component or service enabled or facilitated the circumvention of effective technological measures. Note that there is no equivalent offence for circumventing technical devices applied to computer programs. The offences in section 296ZB do not appear to apply to the database right, publication right and rights in performances. The absence of any express mention of the offences applying to these rights taken together with the express mention of the copyright owner in the specific offence under section 296ZB(1)(b) confirms this.

Activities of the law enforcement agencies and intelligence services in the interests of national security or for the prevention or detection of crime, the investigation of offences or the conduct of prosecutions are excluded from criminal liability. There are provisions for search warrants and forfeiture as apply to unauthorised decoders under sections 297B to 297D.

Separate civil remedy in respect of making, importing, etc.

In some cases, acts that fall within the criminal offences under section 296ZB may also attract civil liability. Civil liability under section 296ZD applies where –

(a) effective technological measures have been applied to a copyright work other than a computer program; and
(b) a person ... manufactures, imports, distributes, sells or lets for hire, offers or exposes for sale or hire, advertises for sale or hire, or has in his possession for commercial purposes any device, product or component, or provides services which –
 (i)   are promoted, advertised or marketed for the purpose of the circumvention of, or
 (ii) have only a limited commercially significant purpose or use other than to circumvent, or
 (iii) are primarily designed, produced, adapted or performed for the purpose of enabling or facilitating the circumvention of, those measures.

In *Sony* v *Ball*, discussed above, the judge had no doubt that Mr Ball distributed, offered, exposed or advertised for sale and had the chips in his possession for commercial purposes. He also noted that liability under section 296ZD was strict and it was not necessary to show that he knew or had reason to believe that the Messiah2 chips would be used to overcome the technical measures applied by Sony so as to facilitate the making of infringing copies. As the purpose of the technical measures was to prevent unauthorised use of Sony's copyright works in a way which would amount to an infringement of copyright, those measures were within section 296ZD. Although he did not decide the matter, the judge considered that the circumvention itself must take place within the jurisdiction of the courts of the UK. Subsequently, Mr Ball was fined £2,000 for contempt of court as a result of false statements he had made which had been supported by a signed statement of truth in *Sony Computer Entertainment Inc* v *Ball* [2004] EWHC 1984 (Ch). Had it not been for Mr Ball's personal and financial circumstances, the judge would have imposed a much more severe penalty.

Concurrent rights are provided for as are rights of delivery up or seizure and the presumptions apply. Liability also extends to rights in performances, the publication right and the database right. The privilege against self-incrimination is withdrawn as is usual with certain intellectual property proceedings. One difference to the other civil remedies in relation to overcoming protection measures is that the test for the unavailability of damages for innocent infringement is slightly changed and the test is whether the defendant knew or had reason to believe that his acts enabled or facilitated an infringement of copyright.

Remedy where effective technological measures prevent permitted acts

If copyright owners prevent access to their works by, for example, encryption, scrambling or password systems, this could have the effect of prejudicing the permitted acts. To overcome potential conflicts, section 296ZE provides for voluntary measures or agreements enabling a person to carry out a permitted act. Where a person is prevented from carrying out a permitted act he, or a representative of a class of such persons, may issue a notice of complaint to the Secretary of State who may give directions to the copyright owner or exclusive licensee.

The purpose of the directions may be to establish whether a relevant voluntary measure or agreement exists or where an appropriate measure or agreement does not exist, requiring the copyright owner or exclusive licensee to make available the means of carrying out the permitted act that is the subject of the complaint. This imposes a duty owed to the complainant and failure to act is treated as a breach of statutory duty. Directions must be in writing and may be varied or revoked by subsequent directions. These provisions also apply, with necessary changes, to rights in performances, the publication right and the database right but do not apply to computer programs. They do not apply, however, where a copyright work is made available to the public on agreed contractual terms such that members of the public can access the work at a place and time individually chosen by them.

A new Schedule 5A lists the permitted acts covered by section 296ZE. Significantly, permitted acts not included are fair dealing for criticism or review and fair dealing for reporting current events and the permitted act of incidental inclusion.

The *Gowers Review of Intellectual Property* was published in December 2006.[7] Many submissions have been submitted to the Review which was published on the Review's website at the time of writing. The Electronic Frontier Foundation ('EFF'), a US based non-profit legal services and consumer advocacy organisation, has submitted a response[8] suggesting, *inter alia*, that UK legislation should either (in paras 2 to 4, not verbatim):

- provide a complete defence for manufacture and supply of circumvention technologies to libraries and archives; or

- require content producers to provide the relevant DRM (digital rights management) keys or decryption information to deposit libraries at the time a work is added to a library or archive collection, or require deposit of copies of digital works without any technological protection measures applied for the purposes of digital preservation and to enable such institutions, as intermediaries, to make accessible copies available for disabled people, or to otherwise enable readers to avail themselves of the statutory exceptions and limitations to copyright.

---

[7] Andrew Gowers was asked to lead an independent review of intellectual property rights in the UK by the Chancellor of the Exchequer in December 2005. The Review was published by HMSO on 6 December 2006.

[8] Electronic Frontier Foundation, *Electronic Frontier Foundation Submission to the Gowers Review of UK Intellectual Property Law*, San Francisco, 2006.

The EFF points to the negative effects that the Digital Millennium Copyright Act 1998 has had in the US in respect of lawful activities and suggests that a defence be introduced to monetary and criminal penalties where a person who, acting for non-commercial purposes had a reasonable, good faith belief that his activity did not infringe and was within the exemptions applicable to circumvention.

ELECTRONIC RIGHTS MANAGEMENT INFORMATION

Where a work is made available electronically, particularly online, the copyright owner may well have included a copyright notice which, apart from the usual familiar notice, © together with the owner's name and year of publication, may include other information, typically, limiting what can be done with the work. If that information is removed, in whole or in part, anyone accessing the work subsequently may think that they are allowed to carry out other acts. They may think that they can make it freely available for others. Apart from these and similar dangers, there may be other issues such as where the name of the author has been removed, compromising his moral rights. The Directive on copyright in the information society attempted to protect such information, known as rights management information, where works were made available in electronic form. The relevant provisions are contained in section 296ZG of the Copyright, Designs and Patents Act 1988. It defines rights management information as:

> ... any information provided by the copyright owner or the holder of any right under copyright which identifies the work, the author, the copyright owner or the holder of any intellectual property rights, or information about the terms and conditions of use of the work, and any numbers or codes that represent such information.

A person who knowingly and without authority removes or alters electronic rights management information knowing or having reason to believe that by doing so he is enabling, facilitating or concealing an infringement of copyright is liable as if that person had infringed the copyright subsisting in the work. That liability is owed to the person issuing copies to the public or communicating the work to the public or the copyright owner or his exclusive licensee, all of whom have concurrent rights. For these purposes 'electronic' has the same wide meaning as in section 178.

Furthermore, a person will similarly be liable if he knowingly and without authority distributes, imports for distribution or communicates to the public copies of a copyright work from which such information, associated with the copies or appearing in connection with the communication to the public of the work, has been removed or altered without authority. The form of knowledge required is that the person knows or has reason to believe that by so doing he is inducing, facilitating or concealing an infringement of copyright.

The usual presumptions apply and the privilege against self-incrimination in intellectual property proceedings is withdrawn. These provisions also apply, with necessary changes, to rights in performances, the publication right and the database right.

SUMMARY

- Making music files available for copying with peer-to-peer file sharing software infringes copyright by:
  - communicating the musical works to the public; and
  - authorising infringement of copyright.

- Placing a copyright work on a website falls within the restricted act of communicating the work to the public.
- Temporary reproduction of a copyright work is allowed under certain circumstances:
  - by ISPs in transmitting a work from one third party to another; and
  - where the use of the work is otherwise lawful.
- The architecture of a website may be protected as a non-literal element.
- Domain names are unlikely to be works of copyright.
- Many rights may exist in a multimedia product.
- ISPs have potential liability for infringement but:
  - they have some special defences; although
  - injunctions may be granted against them in respect of infringing material.
- Legal protection is given to:
  copy-protection devices applied to computer programs; and
  - technical measures applied to other works which prevent or
  - restrict unauthorised acts.
- Rights management information applied to works in electronic form is protected.

SELF-TEST QUESTIONS

Note: there is only one correct answer to each multiple choice question.

1   In *Metro-Goldwyn-Meyer* v *Grokster*, the US Supreme Court held that Grokster was guilty of contributory infringement by distributing its peer-to-peer file sharing software. ON WHAT BASIS did the Supreme Court distinguish its earlier decision in *Sony* v *Universal City Studios* in which it held that the sale of video recorders did not infringe copyright?

   (a) Grokster's software could only be used for infringing purposes.

   (b) There was no real difference between the cases from a copyright perspective but there had been a change in policy at the Supreme Court since *Sony* v *Universal*.

   (c) Grokster actively encouraged infringement.

   (d) The Sony Betamax video recorder was quickly being overtaken by the VHS system and, consequently, the threat to copyright owners was diminishing quickly contrary to the position with Grokster.

2   Making a temporary copy of a work of copyright which is transient or incidental, which is an integral and essential part of a technological process, is permitted under certain circumstances. Which one of the following statements is NOT CORRECT in respect of the permitted act?

   (a) The permitted act applies to all works of copyright except films and broadcasts.

   (b) There must be no independent economic significance.

   (c) The purpose must be to enable the transmission of the work in a network between third parties by an intermediary.

   (d) The purpose must be to enable a lawful use of the work.

3   Injunctions are available against service providers in respect of infringing material under s97A of the copyright, Designs and Patents Act 1988. Which of the following statements is CORRECT?

(a)   The service provider must have actual knowledge of another person using his service to infringe copyright.

(b)   The service provider must be implicated in the infringement, for example, by being a joint infringer.

(c)   The service provider must know or have reason to believe that his service is being used to infringe copyright.

(d)   If a person informs a service provider that another person is using his service to infringe copyright, the courts must grant an injunction requiring the service provider to take appropriate action to prevent further infringement.

4   Of the provisions relating to the circumvention of technical devices applied to computer programs, which of the following statements is NOT CORRECT?

(a)   The technical device can be contained in the computer program or the hardware that reads the computer program or contained in both, analogous to a lock and key.

(b)   The technical device must prevent or restrict acts not authorised by the copyright owner and not restricted by the copyright.

(c)   The provisions extend to persons publishing information intended to enable or assist persons to remove or disable the technical device.

(d)   The technical device must be part of the computer program itself.

5   The provisions on the circumvention of protection measures are unnecessary and may compromise the permitted acts under copyright law and also prejudice the right of freedom of expression. Discuss. [Note: some research into this issue will be helpful.]

For further resources and updates please go to the Companion Website accompanying this book at **www.mylawchamber.co.uk/bainbridgeIT**

8 The law of confidence

INTRODUCTION

The law of confidence is concerned with the protection of secrets whether they are trade secrets, secrets of a personal nature or concerning the government of the country. The fundamental rationale underlying the law of confidence is that it can prevent a person divulging information which has been given to him in confidence, on an express or implicit understanding that the information should not be disclosed to others or otherwise used by the recipient of the information. Alternatively, if the information has already been disclosed or used in breach of confidence, damages or an account of profits may be awarded against the person divulging or using the information. The roots of the law of confidence lie in equity and it is almost entirely based on case law. With the Human Rights Act 1988 bringing into effect the Council of Europe Convention for the Protection of Human Rights and Fundamental Freedoms, the law of confidence has developed to assimilate the rights of privacy and freedom of expression.

The law of confidence is given statutory recognition in the Copyright, Designs and Patents Act 1988, section 171, which states:

> ... nothing in this Part [the part dealing with copyright] affects ... the operation of any rule of equity relating to breaches of trust or confidence ...

Although of older pedigree, the modern law of confidence developed quickly in the nineteenth century and then lay relatively dormant until the middle of the twentieth century. It soon became clear that breach of confidence was actionable *per se*, and did not require a contractual relationship between the parties. An important case, *Prince Albert v Strange* [1849] 1 Mac & G 25, helped to establish this area of law and concerned etchings made by Queen Victoria and her consort, Prince Albert. The Queen and Prince made etchings for their own amusement, intended only for their own private entertainment, although they sometimes had prints made to give to friends. Etchings were sent to a printer to make some impressions and someone surreptitiously made copies which he passed on to the defendant who intended to display them in an exhibition which the public could attend on payment of an admission charge. It was held that relief would be given against the defendant even though he was a third party. He had argued that the prints were not improperly taken but it was said that his possession must have originated in breach of trust, confidence or contract and, therefore, an injunction was granted preventing the exhibition.

The law of confidence can be a very useful adjunct to other intellectual property rights. Copyright protects the expression of an idea, but the law of confidence is wider and can protect the idea itself. In *Andersen Consulting v CHP Consulting Ltd* (unreported) 26 July 1991, Chancery Division, a case concerning a dispute about maintenance of computer software by third parties, it was said by Mr Justice Harman that confidence is frequently used in connection with copyright material as it is:

... of course notorious that copyright protects only the expression of ideas and does not protect the idea itself ...

The law of breach of confidence can supplement copyright and patent protection especially in the early stages when there is nothing tangible or substantial enough for copyright law or patent law to protect. Additionally, the law of confidence can be useful for certain types of secrets for which other rights are inappropriate such as secret recipes, secret research techniques and secret industrial processes which have not been patented.

BASIC REQUIREMENTS

A good working formula for the application of the law of confidence was laid down in *Coco v AN Clark (Engineers) Ltd* [1969] RPC 41, by Mr Justice Megarry (as he then was). This involved a moped engine designed by the claimant who entered into informal negotiations with the defendant; no contract was executed. Megarry J held that the defendant owed the claimant an obligation of confidence (although he doubted the confidential quality of the information) and said that, apart from contract, an action for breach of confidence will require three elements:

1 The information must have the necessary quality of confidence about it.
2 The information must have been imparted in circumstances importing an obligation of confidence.
3 There must be an unauthorised use of that information to the detriment of the party communicating it.

The third of these elements is self-evident, but the first two require further discussion.

Quality of confidence

To be protected by the law of confidence, the information must have the quality of confidence about it. If the information is commonplace or is common knowledge to a class of persons (for example, it is well known to computer programmers as a useful technique or 'wrinkle') or to the public at large, it cannot be confidential: instead, it will be considered to be in the public domain. Often, it will be obvious whether the information is or is not confidential. The concept of confidentiality was considered in the case of *Thomas Marshall (Exports) Ltd v Guinle* [1976] FSR 345, in which the defendant, who was the managing director of the claimant company, resigned halfway through his 10-year service contract to set up a rival business. The information involved sources of supply and the names of officials and other contacts in Europe and the Far East. Sir Robert Megarry VC found for the claimant and he said that four elements were necessary in testing for confidential quality.

1 Release of the information would injure the owner of the information or benefit others.
2 The owner must believe the information to be secret and not already in the public domain.
3 The owner's belief in 1 and 2 above must be reasonable.
4 The information must be judged in the light of usages and practices of the particular trade or industry concerned.

To come within the scope of the law of confidence, the information does not have to be particularly special and, as in the above case, ordinary and mundane information can be the proper subject matter of confidence as long as it is private to the person who has compiled the information, even though others could gather similar information if they took the trouble to do so. In this way, the law of confidence prevents others from gaining benefit from the work of the person who accumulated the information in the first place. As a result, a great deal of material related to the running of a business will fall within the ambit of the law of confidence. Examples of information relevant to computers which may be the subject matter of confidence include:

- ideas for a new or improved computer system, hardware and software (programs, databases or other works in digital form) and research and development work generally;
- details of existing computer systems as would be known by computer analysts or programmers or even users of the system (in terms of users, the system would have to be uncommon in some respect);
- databases of customers, suppliers or contractors and associated information – for example, what customers' credit ratings are, what they have ordered in the past and how they paid, what goods or services do suppliers or contracts provide and what are their prices;
- a company's strategy for future research and development, production and marketing.

In *Gorne* v *Scales* [2006] EWCA Civ 311, a seed-processing business had a card index containing information about customers, their addresses, telephone numbers, details of seeds processed for them in the past and prices they paid was accepted to be confidential and to be an asset of the business. It was wrongfully taken by a partner in the business for use in a new seed-processing business and, at first instance, the card index was estimated to be worth nearly £½ m (although the Court of Appeal remitted the case back as it considered the method of calculating the value was defective).

Usually, software companies treat their source code programs as being confidential and, in most circumstances, only make available to clients object code versions of the programs. It is generally accepted that source code programs are confidential unless published. In *Cantor Fitzgerald International* v *Tradition (UK) Ltd* [2000] RPC 95, the defendant made use of the claimant's source code programs when developing its own bond-broking software. It was held that the claimant's copyright had been infringed by the defendant which had loaded the claimant's programs into its computers and had adapted some of the claimant's modules in its own programs. Accepting that the source code was confidential, the judge confirmed that the defendant's use of the claimant's programs for the purposes of debugging its own programs was a breach of confidence. Some of the techniques and 'wrinkles' developed by the defendant's programmers whilst they were employed by the claimant were held not to be trade secrets as such and were the sort of thing an ex-employee would be expected to be free to use after cessation of his employment, in the absence of a covenant in restraint of trade. However, had the programmers disclosed this sort of information to a third party during their employment by the claimant that would have been a breach of their employment contracts and a breach of confidence.

Obligation of confidence

An obligation of confidence will not be imposed on everyone. A person who is given confidential information and is unaware of its confidential nature (and has no reason to be aware) will be able to use the information freely. This is a major weakness of the law of confidence as it is largely ineffective against innocent third-party recipients of the information. For example, if A tells B something in confidence and B (without A's permission) passes the information on to C, who has not been told that it is confidential and the circumstances are such that an obligation of confidence cannot be imputed to C, then C will be able to use the information freely although B himself can be prevented from using the information or divulging it further. However, it may still be possible for A to obtain an injunction against C in respect of future disclosure or use by C if the information has not yet entered the public domain. C will not, of course, be liable for any acts that he may have carried out innocently before notification that B had divulged the information in breach of his obligation of confidence to A.

Obviously, an obligation of confidence can arise by express agreement: for example, where a self-employed freelance computer programmer is engaged to carry out some work under a contract which contains a term stating that the programmer will not use or divulge details of the client's business or software. An obligation of confidence may also be implied by the courts where there is a duty of good faith as in the relationship between a client and a solicitor, patent agent or bank manager. Another situation where the obligation will be imposed is where a person discusses his ideas with business organisations with a view to the commercial exploitation of those ideas: for example, if a computer analyst has an idea for a new computer system and discusses that idea with software houses interested in developing and marketing the system. However, where the subject-matter is such that one would expect it to have been protected by applying for a patent or registered design, it is better to impose an express obligation of confidence if it is not so protected.

Using technical means to make it difficult to gain access to confidential information will not necessarily be sufficient to impose an obligation of confidence. In *Mars UK Ltd* v *Teknowledge Ltd* [2000] FSR 138, the claimant designed and manufactured mechanisms for receiving coins in vending machines and the like. The mechanisms contained computer programs, algorithms and databases of acceptable parameters for coins (to distinguish genuine coins from foreign coins and blanks). The programs, algorithms and databases where stored in encrypted form on EEPROM computer chips ('electronically erasable programmable read only memory'). These could be recalibrated with new data. When the defendant reversed engineering the chips so that it could offer a re-calibration service, it was claimed that this was a breach of confidence (apart from breach of copyright and database right; see Chapter 5). As the machines containing the mechanisms were freely available on the market, the encrypted information did not have the necessary quality of confidence about it. There was nothing to prevent a purchaser of the machines from dismantling them to find out how they worked and the fact that the information was encrypted did not, *per se*, impose an obligation of confidence. The message sent out by encryption was that the owner did not want others to access the information rather than imposing an obligation of confidence. Of course, it might have been different if an express obligation of confidence had been imposed on persons acquiring the machines but there is some doubt that even that would be effective unless the contract under which the ownership of the machines passed imposed duties not to dismantle the machines or reverse engineer the chips inside them. This might not be enough, however, to impose an obligation on third parties, perhaps who obtained the machines after subsequent re-sale.

Photographs and other images of individuals

As a basic rule it is a breach of confidence to publish a photograph or film of an individual (or for that matter information of a personal nature about an individual) without that person's consent. A major exception to this rule is where publication is in the public interest or the right of freedom of expression is engaged. Even celebrities who court publicity can expect some measure of privacy. For example, in *von Hannover* v *Germany* [2005] 40 EHRR 1, the European Court of Human Rights confirmed that even famous people like Princess Caroline of Monaco have a legitimate expectation of protection for their private life, even if they appeared in places where they can be seen by the public. It would be different, of course, if celebrities, politicians and other famous persons were in situations where it would be reasonable for them to expect to be photographed or filmed, such as where they attended the opening of a new film or play, carried out activities associated with their fame or performed official duties. In other circumstances, publication might be acceptable if it showed illegal or reprehensible conduct.

In *Campbell* v *MGN Ltd* [2004] 2 AC 457, the House of Lords held, by a 3:2 majority, that the publication of details of the model Naomi Campbell's treatment for drug addiction, including a photograph of her leaving a meeting of Narcotics Anonymous, was a breach of confidence. Although the Mirror Newspaper (owned by the defendant) was free to publish the fact that she had a drug problem which she had previously denied, the publication of the details of the treatment and photograph was an unwarranted invasion of her privacy. [1]

The same considerations apply to publishing on a website images of persons or other private information concerning them. In such cases, however, the potential for causing distress is greater. There are also data protection issues in respect of such publication and there may be remedies under the Data Protection Act 1998. As yet, there have been no reported cases of breach of confidence in relation to publication on websites in the UK but the cases above, together with the Michael Douglas case, below, give some indication of how the law might apply in that context.

In *Douglas* v *Hello! Ltd* [2006] QB 125, Michael Douglas and Catherine Zeta-Jones, the film stars ('the Douglases') were married in the New York Plaza Hotel. They had made a contract with the proprietor of *OK!* magazine (OK! Ltd), granting it exclusive rights to publish and syndicate photographs of the wedding and reception. Photographers were engaged by the Douglases and, under the contract, they were responsible for ensuring that no other photographs were taken. Very rigorous security arrangements were put into place to restrict those attending to invited family and friends, to prevent unauthorised photographs being taken and to preserve the exclusivity of the photographs to be given to *OK!* magazine. The Douglases were each paid £500,000 together with a share of any income from syndicating the photographs made by *OK!* magazine in excess of £1 m. As part of the arrangement, the Douglases were to select which photographs would be published and syndicated by *OK!* magazine.

Unknown to the Douglases, a paparazzo photographer had somehow gained access to the event and he surreptitiously took a number of photographs of the couple, most of which were poor quality and blurred. The photographs found their way to the owners of *Hello!* magazine and arrangements were made to publish the photographs in the next issue. When the Douglases found out about the planned publication of the unauthorised photographs, they obtained an interim injunction preventing publication but this was lifted by the Court of Appeal which considered that damages would be an adequate remedy if the claimants were successful at full trial.

In the ensuing action in the Chancery Division of the High Court, numerous claims were put forward by the Douglases and *OK!* magazine, including a claim for breach of confidence. In holding that the defendants had been guilty of a breach of confidence, Mr Justice Lindsay confirmed that, in a situation where it had been made clear, expressly or impliedly, that photographs were not to be taken by the guests, their actual or imputed knowledge was sufficient to impose a duty of confidence upon them, even though there were in excess of 300 guests. That duty also extended to the defendants. By the strict security arrangements, which included searching guests for cameras and camcorders the Douglases had sent a message to the guests which placed them under a duty of confidence. The Douglases were awarded £14,600 in damages and OK! Ltd was awarded £1,033,156 in damages.

Eventually, the Court of Appeal allowed Hello! Ltd's appeal against the finding that it had a 'commercial confidence' which had been breached. The Court of Appeal said that all OK! Ltd had was an exclusive licence to publish the photographs and that it had no rights under the law of confidence. Speaking of the award to the Douglases, the Court of Appeal described it as inadequate and the court also considered that discharging the injunction by a differently constituted

---

[1] There were also data protection issues in this and the *Douglas* case, for which see further this chapter and Part 5.

Court of Appeal was wrong as the Douglases had a very strong claim. OK! Ltd successfully appealed to the House of Lords which, by a 3:2 majority, confirmed that it did have a 'commercial confidence' which was breached by the publication of the photographs in Hello! magazine ([2007] UKHL 21).

An interesting point made by the Court of Appeal is that although the Douglases had authorised photographs for publication in OK! Magazine, this did not compromise their expectation of confidence in respect of any photographs taken without authorisation.

Mars UK Ltd v *Teknowledge Ltd* was not mentioned in the *Douglas* case (nor in the Court of Appeal earlier) and it is hard to reconcile the two decisions in respect of an imposition of a duty of confidence. It could be argued that encrypting information to make it very difficult to access sends a similar message to that of letting persons attending a wedding ceremony and reception know in clear terms that they are not allowed to take photographs.

To conclude, it is tolerably clear that permission should be sought before placing personal information, including images, on a website. Otherwise, there is likely to be a breach of confidence in addition to any issues under data protection law. The fact that dissemination could potentially be on a very large scale could be reflected in a proportionately large award in damages.

Employees

The employee–employer relationship is a special case and may be governed by express terms, as incorporated in the contract of employment, or implied terms or both. Generally, the duty of confidence owed by ex-employees will be less than for current employees who should always act in their employer's best interests. A present employee must respect the confidentiality of his employer's information even to the extent that he should not pry into information he has been told not to look at. In *Denco Ltd* v *Joinson* [1991] IRLR 63, an employee who had a right of access to certain information in his employer's computer system used another employee's password to gain access to other parts of the computer system – something he was not entitled to do. It was held that the employer was entitled to dismiss the employee summarily for his unauthorised use of the password.

Ex-employees have to make a living and much of the ex-employee's skill will involve what he learnt while in his previous employment, thus providing the courts with a dilemma. In many cases, to complicate matters, there may be an overlap with copyright law. However, the courts have developed rules for resolving the conflict which strike a reasonable balance between the interests of employee and employer alike.

When there are no express terms, the employer will not be protected to any great extent. If the ex-employee simply remembers details of some of the previous employer's customers, there is nothing to stop him using this information. Of course, it would be different if he deliberately memorised the customers' names or made a copy of them. In the absence of an express term in the contract of employment dealing with confidentiality, it was said, in *Printers and Finishers Ltd* v *Holloway* [1965] RPC 239, that there would be nothing improper in the employee putting his memory of particular features of his previous employer's plant at the disposal of his new employer. Even if there is an express term the employer would have to show that the information was over and above the employee's normal skill in the job and amounted to a trade secret. The nature of a trade secret was considered in *Lansing Linde Ltd* v *Kerr* [1991] 1 WLR 251, in which it was recognised that it was not confined to secret formulae or processes but could, in appropriate cases, extend to names of customers and the goods which they buy.

In *Northern Office Microcomputer (Pty) Ltd* v *Rosenstein* [1982] FSR 124, a South African case, the problem of where to draw the line between the employer's and employee's interests was considered. In this case, a computer programmer developed a computer program which was similar to one he had written for his previous employer. The case involved copyright matters in addition to the law of confidence and is notable in that the court recognised that computer programs were protected by South African copyright law as literary works. The trial judge agreed that the computer programs were protected by confidence but said that the protection should be of a limited nature. Although the defendant programmer would not be allowed simply to copy the programs in question, he would not be required to 'wipe clean the slate of his memory' because to do so would unduly restrict his use of his own training, skill and experience. There would be nothing, in principle, to prevent an ex-employee computer programmer writing a similar program by the exercise of his own mental effort provided he did not simply plagiarise his previous employer's program. To some extent, an important factor is the computer program itself, whether it is a commonplace program, carrying out mundane operations, or whether it is designed to do something novel, that is, whether the purpose of the program can be said to be in the nature of a trade secret.

In many cases, the employer's 'trade secrets' may be no more than the result of the application by an employee of his own skill and judgment, but if the employee was engaged specifically to produce that information then it can still amount to a trade secret. If the material were commonplace, however, there would be nothing to stop an ex-employee deriving the same or similar material again as long as he did not simply copy his employer's material. In such circumstances, all that would be protected would be the employer's 'lead time', the advantage of getting his product to the market place first.

An important case laying down principles which can be applied to the employer–employee relationship was *Faccenda Chicken Ltd* v *Fowler* [1986] 1 All ER 617. The employer's business was supplying fresh chickens and it was alleged that the employee had made wrongful use of sales information such as customers' names and addresses. The employer's action failed, but the following guidelines were laid down in the Court of Appeal.

1 If there is a contract of employment, the employee's obligations were to be determined from the contract.

2 If there were no express terms, the employee's obligations would be implied.

3 While still in employment, there was an implied term imposing a duty of good faith. This duty might vary according to the nature of the contract of employment but would be broken if the employee copied or deliberately memorised a list of customers.

4 The implied term imposing an obligation on the employee after the termination of his employment was more restricted. It might cover secret processes and trade secrets.

5 Whether information fell within this implied term to prevent its use or disclosure by an ex-employee depended on the circumstances, and attention should be given to the following:

   – the nature of the employment;
   – the nature of the information;
   – whether the employer stressed the confidential nature of the material;
   – whether the information could be easily isolated from other material the employee was free to use.

An ex-employee is thus allowed to make use of his own memory of the work he has carried out in his previous employment unless it involves genuine secrets or is covered by an express term in the contract of employment. Computer programmers and analysts will be allowed to make use of programming techniques and skills which they have learnt and which have become part of their own skill and experience, unless there is something very special about them or they have expressly agreed not to make further use of them. However, a very restrictive express term which tries to prevent an ex-employee making use of mundane skills will be struck out by the courts as being in restraint of trade. The same fate will await any terms which restrict the ex-employee's future employment prospects to any great extent – for example, a term which states that a computer programmer cannot work for computer software companies in the United Kingdom for five years following the termination of his employment. Such restrictive terms will be upheld by the courts only if they are reasonable, such as when a computer programmer working for a bank agrees not to work for another similar bank within a five-mile radius for the first year following the termination of his employment. The purpose of a covenant in restraint of trade should be to protect the employer's legitimate interests rather than simply preventing competition. Essentially, to be enforceable, the term should be aimed at protecting the employer's genuine business interests rather than trying to prevent lawful competition.

It is not easy to lay down an all-purpose formula based on time and geographical area as each case will turn on its own facts. For example, in *Office Angels Ltd* v *Rainer-Thomas* [1991] IRLR 214, it was held that a covenant precluding an ex-employee from opening an employment agency anywhere in an area only within a 1,000-metre radius of the previous employer's agency for a period of only six months was inappropriate and would do little to protect the employer's interests because clients usually placed orders over the telephone and the geographical location of the office was of no consequence to them. In that case, the Court of Appeal also confirmed that, where a covenant in restraint of trade was ambiguous, the narrower construction would be taken. This is even more so where organisations are engaged in e-business and trade online. Geographic area is largely irrelevant in terms of deciding whether a covenant in restrain of trade is or is not reasonable.

Whistle-blowing by employees

The Employment Rights Act 1996 has provisions protecting employees making certain types of disclosures to his employer or another responsible person. For examples, disclosures showing a breach of a legal obligation or the commission of a criminal offence. This is often referred to as whistle-blowing. Such types of disclosures are defined as qualifying disclosures under section 43B(1) of the Act and, where the disclosure is made in good faith to an employer or, where applicable, some other person having responsibility, the disclosure is a protected disclosure under section 43A. This means, for example, an employee making a protected disclosure in good faith in the reasonable belief that the disclosure is a qualifying disclosure is protected from dismissal or other detriment as a result of the disclosure, providing he does not commit a criminal offence by making the disclosure. If an employee is dismissed for making the protected disclosure (or that is the principal reason for the dismissal) the dismissal is regarded as unfair. Protected disclosures may involve what would otherwise be a breach of confidence. This could be the case where an employee makes a disclosure to a responsible person other than the employer.

In *Bolton School* v *Evans* [2006] IRLR 500, a school-teacher thought that the school's network of computers was not sufficiently secure from unauthorised access. This would mean that the school was in breach of data protection law. The teacher proved the lack of security by decoding passwords and accessed user accounts belonging to some members of staff which he disabled. He informed a member of staff to whom concerns about security should be directed but was disciplined for his actions and resigned. He claimed that he was constructively dismissed. The Employment Appeal Tribunal confirmed that his disclosure was a qualifying disclosure but the Employment Rights Act 1996 did not cover anything done to investigate concerns, for example, that there is a breach of a legal obligation or a criminal offence has been committed.

Computer hackers

A computer hacker is a person who gains access to a computer system without permission. Computer hackers pose a serious threat to the security of computer systems and some of the activities in which they engage are potentially criminal in nature. These activities are fully discussed in Chapter 26. However, computer hackers also might be liable under the law of confidence, depending on the circumstances. If a hacker gains access to confidential files stored on a computer, the law of confidence might be used to prevent the hacker from making use of the information or further disclosing it, assuming, of course, that he can be identified. In many cases, information stored in computer systems is highly confidential. It might, for example, concern medical records, creditworthiness, employment or lifestyle details. But will an obligation of confidence attach to a computer hacker? The case of *Prince Albert* v *Strange*, discussed above, suggests that an action might lie in breach of confidence even if the information was obtained surreptitiously. The court in that case was quite happy to imply an obligation of confidence even though it was not possible to say how the confidential information (that is, the prints taken from the engravings) came into the defendant's hands. It could only be assumed that the prints had been obtained in a clandestine manner. In principle, this is very similar to the position of a computer hacker. The case of *Douglas* v *Hello! Ltd*, discussed above, reinforces this notion. A hacker must know that there is a strong possibility that the information he accesses will be confidential and, therefore, he will be fixed with an obligation of confidence. If the information turns out to have a quality of confidence, then there is no reason in principle why the hacker should not be sued for breach of confidence if he uses that information or discloses it to others.

If the information is accidentally overheard or intercepted in circumstances where the owner of the information utters it or transmits it by insecure means (for example, by telling it to someone in a crowded room or by transmitting the information by a public telecommunications system, by telephone or by fax) an obligation of confidence might not be imposed on the person obtaining the information in this manner. In *Malone* v *Metropolitan Police Commissioner* [1979] Ch 344, information overheard during an authorised telephone tapping operation by the police was held not to have been disclosed in confidence. However, the law on the matter of unauthorised interception of information is not clear. In most circumstances, unless authorised by a judge or senior police officer, an offence may be committed under the Regulation of Investigatory Powers Act 2000 and any evidence contained in any information obtained may not be admissible in court.

Spyware

Information obtained through the use of spyware, software placed surreptitiously on a computer which then transmits or enables the transmission of the information to another person, will be obtained in breach of confidence if the information itself has the necessary quality of confidence about it. It may also be a breach of data protection law if the information contains personal data.

In *Ashton Investments Ltd* v *OSJC Russian Aluminium* [2006] EWHC 2545 (Comm), it was alleged that the defendant had placed spyware on the claimant's computer which was situated in London. The information appeared to have been used to compromise the claimant's contract with a third party. The court accepted that this may have been a breach of confidence and also the tort of unlawful interference with business. Although the defendant had accessed the information from Russia, it was held that the breach of confidence and the tort (if indeed they were proved at a full trial) would have been committed in London as that was from where the information was accessed. The defendant had claimed that the alleged wrongful acts would have been committed in Russia and also challenged the jurisdiction of the English courts. That challenge was unsuccessful and the court confirmed that the English courts would be the most appropriate forum to hear the case.

PUBLIC INTEREST AND FREEDOM OF EXPRESSION

Disclosure of confidential information in the public interest has long been a defence to a breach of confidence action. It could apply, for example, to information showing that a company was involved in an illegal price fixing arrangement with others or where an internal company report indicated that its products were defective or unsatisfactory in some way. Another example would be a secret test report showing that a radar device used by the police to catch speeding motorists was inaccurate. However, it must be noted that what is interesting to the public is not necessarily in the public interest. This is particularly so in respect of famous persons and although those who seek publicity and foster a particular image of themselves to the public must expect publication of information tending to show this image is false, a line has to be drawn even so. See, for example, the *von Hannover* and *Campbell* cases discussed earlier.

The law of breach of confidence has developed to incorporate the rights of privacy and freedom of expression in the Council of Europe Convention for the Protection of Human Rights. These rights, which are often in conflict, both contain exceptions. For example, the right of freedom of expression under Article 10 of the Convention may be subject to restrictions preventing the disclosure of confidential information but the right of privacy under Article 8 (actually the right to respect for private and family life, home and correspondence) may be subject to the rights and freedoms of others. This will include the right of freedom of expression. A balance has to be made between the two rights.

In terms of computer-held information, public interest or freedom of expression would be engaged where the information discloses some iniquity or criminal offence or contradicts a false statement made publicly. It would also apply to information about computer viruses, hacking and other computer misuse.

Public interest and freedom of expression were used as defences, at first instance, in *Douglas* v *Hello! Ltd*, discussed earlier in this chapter. The court accepted that the law of breach of confidence has been somewhat modified by the adoption of the above Convention rights but there is no separate right to privacy. The law of confidence, as amended by these rights, is the appropriate means to protect privacy. Mr Justice Lindsay rejected the defence and the claim by the defendant, that by publishing their own selected photographs of their wedding, Michael Douglas and Catherine Zeta-Jones had waived their right to prevent publication of surreptitiously taken photographs. In any case, the defendant had violated the Privacy Code of the Press Complaints Commission, something which, under section 12 of the Human Rights Act 1998, must be taken into account.

REMEDIES FOR BREACH OF CONFIDENCE

The most important remedy for breach of confidence is an injunction preventing the use or disclosure of the information. If the information has been divulged to sufficient people so that it can be said to be no longer confidential, an injunction will not be of any help; it would be like locking the stable door after the horse has bolted. If this has happened and the information has been used to the detriment of the person to whom it 'belongs', however, damages will be available against the person responsible and a limited injunction may be granted against that person. Where the information is used commercially and is of the type that could be sold as a company asset, the method of calculating damages is on the basis of what a willing seller and buyer would agree it was worth.

As an alternative to damages, an account of profits may be available and this may be more advantageous to the claimant, especially if the defendant has made substantial profit from his use of the information. Being an equitable remedy it is discretionary and the claimant must have 'clean hands' and have acted promptly in enforcing his rights. An example of the use of this remedy is the case of *Peter Pan Manufacturing Corp* v *Corsets Silhouette Ltd* [1963] RPC 45, which involved the use of confidential information, after the expiry of a licence agreement, in the manufacture of brassières. The claimant asked for the whole of the profits on the brassières but the defendant said that the account of profits should only be based on the profit resulting from the wrongful use of the confidential information; that is, the profit relating to the parts of the brassières incorporating the confidential information. The difference between the two sums was substantial and the claimant was awarded the higher sum because the defendants would not have been able to make the brassières at all without using the confidential information.

It can be seen that the law of confidence is very useful at an early stage when ideas are being formulated and discussed. Although the law of copyright gives some protection at this stage by protecting plans, specifications and notes, the protection does not extend to the ideas behind them. Confidence is particularly important during the development of inventions before they are granted patents because a patent will be refused if details of the invention have been made available to the public, as we shall see. In the computer industry, as with any other, ideas have to be discussed with various persons and organisations with a view to raising finance and granting licences to use or reproduce the resulting invention or copyright work. Many licences for the use of patented inventions include permission to use 'know-how', the confidential information needed to work the invention to best effect. Some licences may be purely for know-how where there is no patent involved. In most circumstances, during negotiations, an obligation of confidence will be implied but it is sensible to impose it expressly in writing, for example, by stating that the information is confidential and must not be used or disclosed to anyone else without the owner's express written permission.

COURT ORDERS AND BREACH OF CONFIDENCE

Apart from the usual orders for injunctions and delivery up of confidential information taken illegally, the courts may have to consider other forms of order such as an order for disclosure of the identity of the person responsible for passing on confidential information to a third party who publishes the information. Where information has been divulged in breach of confidence and there is a danger that there will be more such breaches in the future, this could be a factor in whether a court identifies the person responsible. In *Ashworth Security Hospital* v *MGN Ltd* [2003] FSR 17 an unknown person who presumably worked at the hospital disclosed confidential information taken from a hospital database about Ian Brady to the defendant, Mirror Group Newspapers. The hospital sought an order forcing the defendant to identify the culprit who might be in breach of his contract of employment, in breach of confidence, notwithstanding any criminal offences under the Data Protection Act 1998. It was argued that ordering that the defendant identify the person responsible for the disclosure of information was a breach of the right of freedom of speech under Article 10 of the European Convention for the Protection of Human Rights and Fundamental Freedoms. However, the Court of Appeal and the House of Lords confirmed that the order was lawful and did not breach Article 10. In particular, Article 10(2) permits derogation from the basic principle, *inter alia*, to prevent the disclosure of information received in confidence. The House of Lords held that the disclosure of patients' records from a secure hospital was an exceptionally serious matter and, to deter further disclosures in the future, it was necessary, proportionate and justified to order disclosure of the source so that he could be punished. Section 10 of the Contempt of Court Act 1981 was not incompatible with the

Convention. Section 10 prevents a court from ordering such disclosure except in the interests of justice, national security or the prevention of crime and disorder.

If it is suspected that a person has taken copies of confidential information or copyright material, for example, on magnetic or optical media, there may be a suspicion that the information will be erased or destroyed once the defendant is aware that legal proceedings are likely to be initiated against him. The 'without notice search and seizure order' (formerly known as an *Anton Piller* order) may be particularly valuable in this respect and has the purpose of preserving evidence where there is a danger it may be destroyed. In *Elvee Ltd* v *Taylor* [2002] FSR 738 some ex-employees of the claimant, a company designing computer graphics, left to join another company (which had been incorporated whilst two of the defendants were still employed by the claimant). It was later discovered that about 200 blank CDs belonging to the claimant were missing. The claimant thought that data relating to its customers which was confidential or subject to copyright had been copied by the defendants and, fearing the evidence would be destroyed, sought a without notice search and seizure order against the defendants' company. A specialist data recovery company was engaged by the claimant and made images of the computer hard disks at the defendants' company's premises. An application by the defendant to discharge the order on the grounds of a material non-disclosure was refused. The judge making the original order had not been told about the fact that, in parallel proceedings, the defendants had entered a defence and counter-claim. A further reason was that the judge who granted the order was in the Queen's Bench Division and he should have been told that such an application in an intellectual property case should be made to the Chancery Division.

SUMMARY

- The three ingredients of breach of confidence are:
  - the information must have the quality of confidence;
  - the defendant must be under an obligation of confidence;
  - there must be an unauthorised use of the information (or a threatened use).
- Information protected by confidence can include:
  - source code for computer programs;
  - databases of customers.
- An obligation of confidence may be express or implied.
- Encrypting data, *per se*, does not impose an obligation of confidence.
- Placing personal information and images of individuals on websites without their permission will be a breach of confidence in most cases.
- The duty of confidence owed by current employees is very high but:
  - will not prevent them, after termination of their employment, making use of learnt skills and techniques unless they are trade secrets.
- If the information so accessed is confidential, it will be a breach of confidence to:
  - hack into a computer;
  - place spyware on a computer.
- Public interest and freedom of expression may excuse what would otherwise be a breach of confidence.
- A court may order disclosure of the identity of a person responsible for a breach of confidence.

SELF-TEST QUESTIONS

Note: there is only one correct answer to each multiple choice question.

1 In respect of making a copy of a previous employer's software without permission and using it to verify that software written for a competitor operates properly (that is, for the purpose of debugging the new software), which one of the following statements is NOT CORRECT?

(a) There will be an infringement of copyright in the previous employer's software by making a copy of it.

(b) There will be a breach of confidence providing the previous employer's software had the necessary quality of confidence.

(c) If the copy was taken by a person whilst still employed by the previous employer, he will be in breach of his fiduciary duty to that employer.

(d) The new software will inevitably infringe the copyright in the previous employer's software.

2 If a company which makes and sells articles which include information stored in encrypted form and subject to the database right, a third party which lawfully acquires an article and reverse engineers it to gain access to the information is liable to which ONE of the following legal remedies, assuming there is no contractual obligation not to decrypt the information?

(a) An action for breach of confidence.

(b) An action for breach of contract.

(c) An action for breach of a licence agreement.

(d) An action under copyright law for circumventing effective technological measures.

3 Prince Ferdinand is the heir to the throne of Bradavia. He attends numerous public and official functions at which photographs are taken and published. However, recently, he was photographed by one of the paparazzi whilst he was in a restaurant in London, enjoying a meal with Peter and Erik. Peter is a psychoanalyst and it has been rumoured that the Prince has experienced some bouts of depression (which he has denied). The photograph found its way onto the website of a UK newspaper, *The Daily Rag*, together with a sensational story about the Prince's state of mind. The story included details of the conversation between the Prince and Peter which had been given to the newspaper by Erik. The Prince was furious when he found out and sued *The Daily Rag* for breach of confidence. Which one of the following statements is CORRECT?

(a) *The Daily Rag* is in breach of confidence simply by questioning the Prince's state of mind.

(b) *The Daily Rag* is in breach of confidence by publishing the photograph and the details given to it by Erik.

(c) *The Daily Rag* was not acting in breach of confidence as the Prince is a public figure and must expect photographs of him in places where the public have access to be published.

(d) *The Daily Rag* has a defence to a breach of confidence action based on the right of freedom of expression which takes precedence over the right of privacy.

4 Whilst carrying out a check on its computer systems, Pinacle SA, a large French construction company, discovered spyware on its main computer server. It transpired that an English company, Peak plc, was responsible for the spyware and had accessed information relating to Pinacle's bids for major construction projects throughout Europe. Which one of the following statements is CORRECT?

(a) By placing the spyware on Pinacle's main server and accessing the information, Peak is in breach of confidence, notwithstanding there may also be other breaches of civil and criminal law by Peak.

(b) Peak is not in breach of confidence as owners of computer systems are responsible for ensuring they are secure from spyware.

(c) Peak is not in breach of confidence as information as to placing bids for major construction contracts does not have the necessary quality of confidence.

(d) Technically, Peak is in breach of confidence but may have a defence based on public interest as it is in the public interest that information as to bids for construction projects is in the public domain.

5   To what extent does the law of confidence prevent an ex-employee from exercising his learnt skill and experience for either himself or a new employer?

For further resources and updates please go to the Companion Website accompanying this book at www.mylawchamber.co.uk/bainbridgeIT

9 Patent law

INTRODUCTION

Patents are granted for new, non-obvious inventions that have an industrial application. A patent is a very desirable form of intellectual property because it gives to the owner a monopoly in his invention, enabling him to exploit the invention for a number of years to the exclusion of all others (subject to provisions designed to prevent abuse of the monopoly granted). Patent law has a long history and has developed as a means of protecting innovation, which has a benefit to innovator and public alike. Inventors are encouraged to invent and investors are more likely to risk money in the development of new inventions if a monopoly right is available for inventions. Society reaps a benefit because the invention will eventually fall into the public domain and because, in the meantime, commercial enterprise is stimulated.

The availability of patents for software inventions has been, and continues to be, a subject of some controversy. A particular problem is that under the European Patent Convention ('EPC'), of which the UK and another 30 countries are party to, computer programs, *as such*, are excluded from the meaning of 'invention'. Also excluded are schemes, rules or methods of performing mental acts, playing games or doing business. Again the exception applies only to the extent that the patent application related to the thing *as such*. This does not prevent the patenting of software inventions altogether and many such inventions have been patented in Europe. But patent law in Europe, as it presently stands, can only be described as confused. This is made worse by the fact that patent law in some other countries, notably the US, carries no equivalent exclusion for computer programs and business methods and patents for inventions in those fields are freely granted, provided that the other requirements for a patent (novelty, inventive step and industrial application) are present.

It was hoped that the position regarding the patentability of software inventions would be significantly improved in Europe following a proposed Directive.[1] However, that proposal was roundly defeated by the European Parliament on 6 July 2005 and there seems little chance that it will be resurrected. After looking at patent law generally, this chapter then focuses on the patentability of computer programs and other forms of software inventions, such as computer implemented business methods.

---

[1] Proposal for a Directive of the European Parliament and of the Council on the patentability of computer-implemented inventions, Commission to the European Communities, Brussels, 20.02.2002, COM(2002) 92 final, 2002/0047 (COD) (the 'proposed Directive on the patentability of computer-implemented inventions').

BASIC CONSIDERATIONS

There are two types of patentable invention – a product invention and a process invention – and it has been said that an invention is a new way of making something old or an old way of making something new. A patentable invention could relate to a new piece of computer hardware such as a new and inventive storage medium or a new process for making integrated circuits. There have been many patent applications for computer hardware and other electronic materials: for example, the invention of the printed circuit board, the transistor and the integrated circuit have all been subject to patents. Sometimes, other forms of protection may be available such as design law or copyright. These may run in parallel with patent protection or might give protection to things that fail to meet the rigorous standards for patent protection. For example, the design right may protect a new layout of components on a printed circuit board even if there is no inventive step for patent purposes. Subject to a general but not complete exclusion, some computer programs and other software inventions may be patentable, such as a new and inventive digital image processing system or a computer program which, when run in a computer, controls an industrial process.

An application for a UK patent is filed at the UK Patent Office. If the application is successful, a patent will be granted for four years initially and may be renewed, annually, up to a maximum of 20 years from the date the application is first filed (the priority date). The renewal fees become progressively steeper throughout the life of the patent and most patents do not run the full 20 years. A system of priority applies so that applications for patents for the same invention can be made at other patent offices within the next 12 months claiming the priority of the first application and those subsequent applications will be judged in the light of the circumstances at the date the first application was filed (which is known as the priority date). Intervening events will be ignored in determining whether the invention was new and involved an inventive step.

Apart from applying for patents at individual national patent offices, it is possible to apply through the European Patent Office ('EPO') designating some or all of the contracting states. Through a single application it is possible to obtain a bundle of national patents. Another route is via the Patent Cooperation Treaty which is administered by the World Intellectual Property Organisation, based in Geneva. There are presently 133 contracting states to that treaty.

Obtaining a patent is a complex, expensive and lengthy process and the services of a patent agent are desirable because the drafting of the patent specification and claims is extremely important as regards the future scope of the patent. In some circumstances, it may be preferable simply to keep the idea secret and rely on the law of confidence; this costs little or nothing and there is no requirement that the invention must eventually fall into the public domain. Examples of the effectiveness of this approach are the recipes and processes used in many familiar drinks and foodstuffs. In many cases, however, the invention cannot be kept secret, especially if articles made to the invention are to be marketed commercially or if a large number of employees know of the invention, in which case obtaining a patent may be the only realistic way of protecting the invention.

PROCEDURE

Obtaining a patent usually involves a lengthy process and this seems to be unsuited to a fast-moving technology as it can take several years from initial application before a patent is finally granted. However, the reason it can take so long is that patent applications are subject to stringent search and examination to ensure that all the requirements are satisfied. It is also common for amendments to be made during the process. These may be the result of what has been found as a result of the initial search or because of objections raised by the examiners at the Patent Office. It is important that inventions which fail to meet the requirements for patentability are not granted patents, although it is not unusual for patents to be revoked later, usually as a result of a challenge to validity raised in infringement proceedings.

Simply put, the procedure for obtaining a patent in the UK is as follows:

1 The application is filed together with a specification describing the invention, an abstract (the title for the invention and concise summary) and the claims (defining the scope of the monopoly claimed). Drawings will usually be included in the specification.

2 The Patent Office will carry out a search for patents and other documents which may be relevant to the invention. Typically, this will find previous patents in the same field which might have a bearing on the patentability of the invention. It is common for the application to be amended following the search.

3 Eighteen months following the first filing of the patent it is published. This is referred to as 'A' publication.

4 The Patent Office examiners then carry out an extensive examination of the patent application to check for conformity with the requirements of the Patents Act 1977. Again, some amendments may be necessary at this stage, though it should be noted that the monopoly claimed cannot be widened.

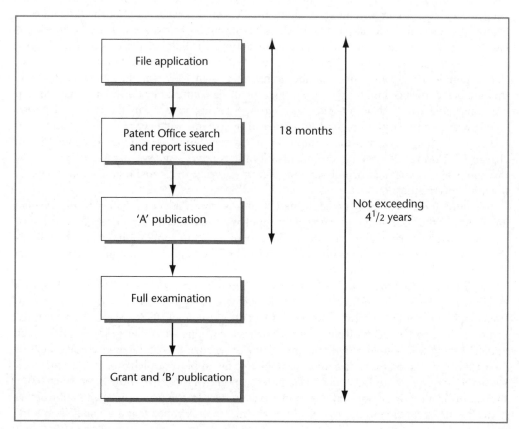

Figure 9.1 Patent procedure (simplified)

5 Finally, the patent will be granted (all being well) and it will be published again – 'B' publication.

The procedure is shown in Fig. 9.1. It is greatly simplified and assumes no problems are encountered. Since 1995, the UK Patent Office has offered a speedier procedure whereby the applicant can request a combined search and examination and earlier publication. This procedure may be suitable for straightforward applications but is unlikely to be appropriate for software inventions.

The proprietor's monopoly dates back, effectively, to the date of 'A' publication. Although he cannot bring legal proceedings for infringement of the patent until the time that the patent is granted, he will be entitled to damages in respect of any infringement carried out after that publication.

The date when the patent application is first filed becomes its priority date if applications are made elsewhere subsequently in respect of the same invention.

The main legislation governing patents is the Patents Act 1977 and the Patents Rules 1995. Both have been subject to substantial modification, the former specially by the Patents Act 2004. The 1977 Act was passed to bring UK patent law in line with the EPC in relevant respects. Some of the provisions of the Patents Act 1977 are stated to have, *inter alia*, the same effect as the equivalent provisions of the EPC. These include, importantly, the provisions on patentability.

The EPO is not an EC institution although it will administer the Community Patent Convention which, if it ever comes into force, will provide for a Community-wide patent, which will have effect throughout the EC. This system was first on the drawing board in the 1960s but still has not yet come to fruition. In many respects this is a great pity as the availability of a single patent in force throughout the EC could prevent some of the difficulties of enforcing equivalent national patents for the same invention across a number of countries. A basic rule of jurisdiction is that, if in patent litigation the validity of the patent is challenged, only the courts in the country where the patent is registered have jurisdiction to hear the case. If, for example, a company owns a number of national patents covering the same invention and they are being infringed in, for the sake of argument, six countries by defendants that are economically linked to each other (such as a group of companies or in the case of a parent company and subsidiary companies) the owner of the patents will have no option but to commence proceedings in each of those countries unless the validity of each national patent is not challenged. Normally, however, a defendant will raise issues of validity, after all, if he can show that the patent is not valid or not valid in relevant respects, that provides a complete defence to an infringement action.

It is normal for a company based in the UK or a person resident in the UK to file a patent application at the UK Patent Office first before applying elsewhere. In fact, in designated circumstances, it can be a criminal offence for a UK resident to file an application outside the UK less than six weeks before filing an application in respect of the same invention in the UK or where security directions are still in force.

In addition to the Patents Act 1977, there are a number of rules and regulations dealing with details such as registration procedure, fees and the Patents County Court in London. The comptroller (full title is the Comptroller-General of Patents, Designs and Trade Marks) also has jurisdiction to hear certain patent disputes if the parties are willing and to hear other matters, such as determining who should be the true proprietor or whether an employee inventor should be awarded compensation for an invention belonging to his employer which is of outstanding benefit to the employer. Since 1 October 2005, under section 74A (inserted by the Patents Act 2004), the comptroller can issue non-binding opinions as to the infringement of a patent and whether it satisfied the requirements of novelty and inventive step. It is hoped that this will help to settle disputes.

Not all inventions are capable of supporting a patent. The Patents Act 1977 lays down several requirements which must be satisfied before a patent can be granted and, furthermore, certain things are specifically excluded from patentability. The basic requirements for the grant of a patent will now be explained.

BASIC REQUIREMENTS

The basic requirements for the grant of a patent are stated in section 1(1) of the Patents Act 1977 as follows:

> A patent may be granted only for an invention in respect of which the following conditions are satisfied, that is to say:
> (a) the invention is new;
> (b) it involves an inventive step;
> (c) it is capable of industrial application;
> (d) the grant of a patent for it is not excluded by subsections (2) and (3) below . . .

Section 1(2), referred to in (d) above, declares that certain things are not inventions if the application relates to that thing as such. Section 1(3) excludes from patentability inventions where the commercial exploitation of them would be contrary to public policy or morality.

Invention

The word 'invention' is not defined in the Act but its meaning is really a matter of common sense and it can be used in a fairly wide sense. It is, in effect, circumscribed by the other requirements and exclusions for patentability. Industrial application suggests that an invention is something that can be put to practical use, for example. It has to be more than a mere idea. Furthermore, section 1(2) states that the following (amongst other things) are not inventions for the purposes of the Act:

(a) a discovery, scientific theory or mathematical method;
(b) a literary, dramatic, musical or artistic work or any other aesthetic creation whatsoever;
(c) a scheme, rule or method for performing any mental act, playing a game or doing business, or a program for a computer;
(d) the presentation of information;
but the foregoing provision shall prevent anything from being treated as an invention for the purposes of this Act only to the extent that a patent or application for a patent relates to that thing *as such* [emphasis added].

The exclusions in (a) would prevent Einstein patenting his law of relativity, $E = mc^2$ and Newton his law of gravity. In any case these would not be patentable because any claim to them, as such, would be too vague. Patents are directed to industrial or commercial activity and laws and theories on their own do not relate to such activities.

Note that the above exclusions apply only to the extent that a *patent or application for a patent relates to that thing as such*. This means that the presence of these particular things is not necessarily fatal to a patent application. For example, a new and inventive computer-controlled industrial process being a means of operating a production line used in a manufacturing process should be patentable providing the claims are not directed to the computer programs as such.

Some are more controversial. For example, is a claim to computer-controlled means of presenting information on a conventional display device a claim to a computer program as such, a claim to the presentation of information as such, both or neither? Is a claim to an online auction system a claim to a method of doing business as such? We will consider these issues in more detail later in the section on software inventions.

Novelty

A patent should not be granted for anything which is not new, something which is already in the public domain, otherwise the grant of the patent could make illegal an act which was previously legal. For example, if a company has been making integrated circuits by a special process for several years but failed to apply for a patent, a second company which uses the same process, perhaps coincidentally, and applies for a patent for the process will be refused a patent on the grounds that the invention is not new unless the first company's use of the process was not such as to make it available to the public. In that case, the second company may be able to obtain a patent for the process but there is a special 'defence' for the first company under section 64 of the Patents Act 1977 and it will be allowed to continue to use the process. The same would apply if the first company had not necessarily used the process before the application for a patent had been filed but had made serious and effective preparations to use the process by the filing date.

Section 2 of the Act expands on the meaning of 'new' and says that an invention is new if it does not form part of the 'state of the art'. This expression comprises all matter which has been made available to the public in the UK or elsewhere, by written or oral description, by use or in any other way. Matters contained in patent applications published after the priority date but which have earlier priority dates are also included in the state of the art. Something which is part of the state of the art is often described as prior art. It will mean that an invention is not new if it is anticipated by the prior art. An invention is anticipated if the prior art contains an enabling disclosure, meaning that it discloses the invention and gives sufficient information to enable a person skilled in the relevant art to perform, work or make the invention, as the case may be.

There is no need for the prior art to have been made widely available to the public and, in *Windsurfing International Inc* v *Tabur Marine (GB) Ltd* [1985] RPC 59, it was held that a 12-year-old boy, who had made his own sailboard which he used at Hayling Island on summer weekends, had made the invention available to the public with the effect that a patent later granted to the claimant for a sailboard was declared invalid after the defendant had challenged its validity on the grounds of lack of novelty and lack of inventive step.

The inventor must resist any temptation he might have to publish details of his invention before the first filing date (the priority date), otherwise he could inadvertently add his invention to the state of the art and anticipate his own patent. Similarly, the inventor must be careful when discussing his invention with potential manufacturers and the like. The law of confidence is very important at this stage. However, if details of the invention are disclosed by a person acting in breach of confidence or who has obtained details unlawfully, that disclosure will be disregarded in determining the state of the art if such breach occurs no earlier than six months preceding the filing of the patent.

As technology advances and the pool of knowledge in the public domain grows, it is increasingly difficult to devise something which is absolutely 'new'. Indeed, it is not an easy task to find out if the invention has been anticipated and is already part of the state of the art, given the massive world-wide volume of published work, and it is possible that a publication which anticipates the invention will not be discovered. If that material is subsequently found and shows that the invention was not new when the patent was applied for, the patent is in danger of being revoked. A number of patents may be on shaky ground as far as novelty is concerned if sufficient time and effort were expended on trying to trace anticipatory materials or prior use. This is particularly the case in respect of software inventions where the size of the prior art is enormous. A person who is being sued for infringing a patent will try to find such material and, in the case of a challenge to a software patent, the enquiry is likely to go far beyond looking at prior patents and will cover other published material and software products put on the market prior to the first filing date of the software patent.

Inventive step

By section 3 of the Patents Act 1977 an invention involves an inventive step if it is not obvious to a person skilled in the art. This test, known as the 'notional skilled worker test', takes account of the complexity of technology, hence the reference to a skilled person rather than the ubiquitous reasonable person, so often used as a benchmark by judges. The reason is that a great many 'inventions' would not be obvious to a layperson but would be to someone who knew something of the technology involved. It has been accepted that the 'skilled person' may be a team of highly qualified research workers such as a team of systems analysts, software development engineers and computer programmers. When it comes to applying the test, the skilled person is not endowed with any inventive faculties himself, a somewhat artificial premise, but to hold otherwise would mean that all inventions could be deemed to be obvious and not patentable.

'Obvious' has no special meaning but is judged by looking at the invention as a whole and considering the entire state of the art. Whether the invention is obvious is a question of fact. In the *Windsurfing* case discussed earlier in connection with novelty, Lord Justice Oliver suggested the following four-stage test for determining whether an invention is obvious.

1 Identify the inventive concept embodied in the patent.
2 The court then assumes the mantle of the normally skilled but unimaginative person in the art at the priority date of the patent and imputes to him what was, at that date, common general knowledge in the art.
3 Identify what, if any, differences exist between that knowledge and the patented invention.
4 Consider whether, without knowledge of the invention, those differences constitute steps which would have been obvious to the person skilled in the art or whether they require any degree of invention.

When considering whether an invention contains an inventive step, the danger of using hindsight must be avoided. It is so easy for expert witnesses and, sometimes, the judge, to fall into that trap. What might seem obvious now with the benefit of hindsight might not have seemed obvious at the time the application for the patent was filed. Step 2 of the *Windsurfing* test guards against this danger by reminding the judge to put himself in the position of the skilled person *at the priority date* of the patent.

Commercial success is a factor which can be taken into account in determining obviousness though it is not conclusive. In ***Technograph Printed Circuits Ltd* v *Mills & Rockley (Electronics) Ltd*** [1969] RPC 395, a case involving a patent for a method of making printed circuits, Harman J said:

> It was objected that in fact it was not until ten years after the invention was published that it was commercially adopted ... and it was argued from this that it was not a case of filling a long felt want. I do not accept this argument. In the years immediately following the war, manufacturers could sell all the machines they wanted using the old point-to-point wiring and had no need to trouble themselves with anything better.

Computer technology spreads into all kinds of other technologies and this may lead to patentable inventions and, even though the computer technology used itself is not new, the application of the technology to provide a solution to a technical problem may be new. In principle there is nothing to prevent the application of well-known technology to a particular problem from being the proper subject matter of a patent. This may not be obvious if there has been a major problem and a solution has evaded many attempts to reach it. Again, the commercial success of the invention is a useful guide. In *Parks-Cramer Co* v *G W Thornton & Sons Ltd* [1966] RPC 407, the invention was a method of cleaning floors between rows of textile machines. There had been many unsuccessful attempts to find a satisfactory solution but none of them, unlike the present invention, actually worked. Essentially, all the invention consisted of was an overhead vacuum cleaner which moved back and forth between the textile machines and which had attached to it a long vertical tube, reaching almost to the floor. It was argued that this was obvious because 'every competent housewife' knows that dust can be removed from a floor by the passage of a vacuum cleaner. This argument was rejected and the patent was held to be valid as the many unsuccessful attempts by inventors to find a solution coupled with the immediate commercial success of the present invention denied the possibility of a finding of obviousness.

The courts have to draw a line somewhere when it comes to obviousness although it is difficult to lay down hard and fast rules. It is clear, however, that there must be a sufficient inventive step and merely taking two older inventions and sticking them together, described by patent lawyers as a mere collocation, will not necessarily be regarded as an inventive step. However, in *Storage Computer Corp* v *Hitachi Data Systems Ltd* [2002] EWHC 1776 (Ch), a case involving patents for a system for compensating for and overcoming hard errors common in writing to and reading from computer hard disks, Mr Justice Pumfrey confirmed that there is no separate law of collocation. The statutory test, being whether the invention is obvious to a person skilled in the art, remains the same. In some cases, it may well be inventive to combine two separate pieces of prior art.

Industrial application

Another requirement for the grant of a patent is that the invention must have an industrial application but this is widely defined by section 4 of the Patents Act 1977 which states that the invention must be capable of being made or used in any kind of industry, including agriculture. However, a method of treatment of the human or animal body by surgery or therapy or a method of diagnosis practised on the human or animal body is not capable of industrial application although this does not prevent the patenting of drugs to be used in any such treatment or diagnosis.

The need for industrial application shows the practical nature of patent law, which requires that the invention should be something which can be produced or that it relates to some sort of industrial process.

Examples of refusal on the grounds that the invention does not have an industrial application are rare, but one example is provided by *Hiller's Application* [1969] RPC 267. This case concerned an improved plan for underground service distribution schemes for housing estates; that is, the layout of the gas, sewerage and water pipes and electricity cables. It was held that this could not constitute a 'manner of manufacture' (the phrase used instead of 'industrial application' prior to the 1977 Act). Therefore, if someone develops a new form of layout for the components in a computer or a new configuration for printed circuit boards, these are unlikely to be granted patents. However, the layout of components and the configuration of a printed circuit board may be protected by copyright through any drawings which have been made indicating the layout or by the design right. Methods or principles of construction are excluded from the design right. The physical layout of the circuitry in a semiconductor chip may be protected by a variation of the unregistered design right which protects the topography of semiconductor products.

ENTITLEMENT

The basic rule is that the inventor is entitled to the grant of a patent (or, as the case may be, the joint inventors) under section 7 of the Act. The owner of a patent is known as its proprietor. This is subject to others who are entitled, for example, by virtue of an enforceable term in an agreement entered into by the inventor before the invention was made. Section 39 contains special provisions to deal with the situation where the inventor is an employee. In such a case, if the invention was made in the course of his normal duties or duties specifically assigned to him and the circumstances are such that the invention would be reasonably expected to result from the performance of those duties, the employer is entitled to the patent. Also, if the employee is under a special obligation to further the interests of his employer's undertaking because of the responsibilities arising out of his normal duties, the employer is entitled to the patent.

What we can say about these provisions is that there is a presumption that the inventor is entitled to the grant of a patent for his invention. He may have agreed beforehand that someone else is entitled, for example, in a case where, as a self-employed person, he has been working for a client to seek a solution to a particular problem and the contract contains an appropriate term as to entitlement of any inventions that may result from his work. In terms of employee inventors, the following points are important:

Either:

(a) the invention must result from the employee's normal duties or specially assigned duties, in other words he is 'paid to invent'; and

(b) the invention must be one which could reasonably be expected to result from the employee's performance of such duties.

Or:

(a) the employee must have particular responsibilities arising from his normal duties imposing a special obligation to further his employer's undertaking (for example, in the case of a managing director of a company); and

(b) the invention was made in the course of those duties.

The fact that an employee's contract of employment may encourage him to carry out research work (rather than require him to do so) is likely to mean that the employee will be entitled to be granted the patent in any invention which results from him carrying out research. Also, a senior executive, who is not paid to invent, and who is working his redundancy notice, is unlikely to have a special obligation to further his employer's undertaking.

Employee compensation

A great many inventions come from the work of employees and it could be said that the salary drawn by the employee is his reward for making the invention. In some cases, the employee may be given a bonus or some *ex gratia* payment as a result of making the invention. This may seem parsimonious if the invention turns out to be very significant. Where an employee invention turns out to be of outstanding benefit to his employer then, under section 40 of the Patents Act 1977, compensation may be payable to the employee. Outstanding benefit is gauged in relation to the size and nature of the employer's undertaking. Section 40 was modified as from 1 January 2005 with the intention that it should be easier for employees to obtain compensation. Compensation may also be payable if an employee has made an invention to which he was entitled but he has subsequently assigned it to his employer (or granted his employer an exclusive licence) and the benefit he has obtained as a result is inadequate compared with the benefit accruing to the employer.

INFRINGEMENT

A patent is infringed if a person does one of certain things in relation to the invention in the United Kingdom without the permission of the proprietor (owner) of the patent. Section 60 of the Patents Act 1977 defines what does and what does not constitute infringement. The nature of the infringement depends on whether the invention is a product (for example, a new type of computer printer) or a process (for example, a new method of making integrated circuits). If the invention is a product, the patent is infringed by making, disposing of or offering to dispose of, using, importing or keeping the product. Similar provisions apply to a process: for example, using the process infringes but, additionally, the patented process may be infringed by using or disposing of, etc. any product obtained directly from that process. Another difference between products and processes relates to the knowledge of the infringer. For a process, knowledge that a patent is being infringed is required. However, 'knowledge' is used in a special way and a person can still be deemed to have the requisite knowledge if it would be obvious to a reasonable person that a patent was being infringed. There is no requirement for knowledge as regards a product and, therefore, in the absence of a defence, liability for infringement is strict.

Under section 60(2), a patent is also infringed if a person supplies or offers to supply some other person with any of the means, relating to an essential element of the invention, for putting the invention into effect. Knowledge is required in that the person supplying knows, or it is obvious to a reasonable person, that those means are suitable for putting the invention into effect and that person so intends. This 'supplying the means' infringement is useful as it applies to persons who supply products in kit form. For example, if a person supplies a computer in kit form which, when assembled, infringes a patent, then the supplier of the computer kit infringes the patent even if he is just an intermediary as long as he has the requisite knowledge. This prevents a possible loophole in patent law such as where a person imports components made in a foreign country to be sold as a kit. The person assembling the kit computer will not be liable under patent law, however, if he assembles and uses the computer privately and for non-commercial purposes. To give a practical example of infringement, consider the following situation.

An inventor **A** has invented a new type of computer chip, which works in a different and inventive way compared with prior art chips, and **A** has also invented a new process which will be used for making those chips. He has taken out patents for the process and for the chips. **B** finds out about the process and decides to build a similar process for making these computer chips. **B** asks **C** to supply equipment which is essential to the process. **B** then makes some computer chips and sells them to **D**, a trade supplier.

The position is:

B, if he knows, or it would be obvious to a reasonable man, that the process was patented, has infringed the patent for the process. Even if **B** had no actual knowledge it would be most likely that he would be fixed with knowledge on the basis of the reasonable person test. (Patent specifications are available for public inspection – would a reasonable person check first?)

B has infringed the patent for the computer chips even if he did not know or could not be expected to know of the patent.

C has infringed the patent for the process if he knows, or it would be obvious to a reasonable person, that the equipment he supplied was suitable for putting the process into effect and the equipment was intended to do so.

D infringes the patent for the computer chips, regardless of knowledge.

The fact that some infringements do not require any form of knowledge may seem unduly harsh, but knowledge is required for some of the remedies and the situation is not as inequitable as it might appear, bearing in mind the need to protect the patent.

Variants and the 'Protocol questions'

A person may make something or use a process which is similar to a patented product or process but there may be some differences compared with the invention itself. The second is a variant of the first. The question then is whether the variant second infringes the patent. Does it fall within the penumbra of protection afforded by the patent? To determine whether there has been an infringement, the claims, interpreted in accordance with the specification and any drawings, must be examined to determine the scope and limits of the invention as protected by the patent. Although judges tend to interpret Acts of Parliament and legal documents literally (unless this leads to an absurd result), patent specifications are interpreted purposively, that is, in line with the presumed intention of the person who wrote it.

In *Catnic Components Ltd* v *Hill & Smith Ltd* [1982] RPC 183, the claimant obtained a patent for a load-bearing lintel, the main strength of which came from a vertical metal rear face. The specification and claims in the patent referred to the rear face as being vertical. Claim 1 described the rear face as '. . . a second rigid support member extending vertically from or from near the rear edge of the first horizontal plate . . .'. The defendant made a similar lintel but with a rear face inclined at six degrees from the vertical. The House of Lords adopted a test which has since been refined into a three-stage test which can be briefly summarised as follows:

1 if the variant does not have a material effect on how the invention works; and

2 this would have been obvious to a skilled person at the time of publication of the specification; and

3 the skilled person would understand that the proprietor of the patent did not intend to limit his invention to the strict wording of the claim;

then the variant infringes the patent.

Effectively, the House of Lords interpreted the relevant claim by taking the word 'vertical' to mean, in effect, 'vertical or nearly vertical' and held that the patent had been infringed. The important feature was the metal rear face, the purpose of which was to support the load. The defendant's slightly sloping rear face had a minimal impact on the load-bearing qualities of the lintel. This approach is in line with both common sense and prevents others from flouting patent law by making minor changes to details of an invention while retaining the underlying principles involved, and is justified on the basis that patent specifications and claims are directed to technical people, not lawyers. It also shows the different scope of patent law compared with copyright law, because patent law can protect purpose and the embodiment of a principle whereas, generally, copyright law cannot. The so-called *Catnic* test survived an attack upon its validity during 1995 when it was claimed by one judge to be inappropriate under the 1977 Act, *Catnic* being a case under the Patents Act 1949, and that the provision in the EPC should be used instead where an approach to interpretation of patent claims is based on a middle way between a strict literal meaning and using the claims as a guideline only.

Article 69 of the EPC states that the extent of protection conferred by a European patent should be determined by the terms of its claims as interpreted by the description and drawings. The Protocol on Article 69 goes on to confirm that this does not require a strict literal interpretation, the description and drawings only being used to resolve ambiguities. Nor should the claims be used as a guideline, the actual protection extending to what, on consideration of the description and drawings by a person skilled in the art, the patentee has contemplated. The extent of the protection is a position between these two extremes, combining a fair protection for the patentee with a reasonable degree of certainty for third parties.

Subsequently, the *Catnic* test, reformulated and now referred to by judges as the Protocol questions has been confirmed to be the correct way of applying Article 69 in the UK. A recent example of the use of the Protocol questions in the context of computers was *Storage Computer Corp v Hitachi Data Systems Ltd* [2002] EWHC 1776 (Ch) which concerned patents for a system for compensating for and overcoming hard errors common in writing to and reading from computer hard disks. The defendant used a system which was a variant of that described in the first patent (the second patent was held invalid in its entirety). However, there were some differences in how the claimant and defendant's inventions worked even though they did the same thing. In particular, the claimant's invention used a dedicated disk to write parity blocks to, whereas the defendant's system used distributed parity (writing parity blocks to different disks). This resulted in the variant having, in fact, a material effect on how the invention worked. Even if it did not, Mr Justice Pumfrey held that the claimant had made it clear in his claims that an essential element of the invention was that it used a fixed parity disk. Therefore, the defendant did not infringe the patent. In any event, it was also held that the first two claims of the first patent were invalid for lack of inventive step.

DEFENCES AND REMEDIES

There are a number of defences or exceptions to infringement of a patent set out in section 60(5) of the Patents Act 1977: for example, if the act is done privately and for non-commercial purposes or for experimental purposes (on the basis that the proprietor's interests are not harmed by such use). It has long been accepted that there is a right to repair defence at common law. This might be applicable where an error in a software invention has been discovered. However, the House of Lords has confirmed that this defence is very narrow and does not allow a patented product to be rebuilt under the pretence that it is being repaired. There are some other defences, such as use on certain aircraft or ships temporarily or accidentally in the United Kingdom and some special defences in relation to agriculture.

A patent, once granted, can be revoked if it is subsequently shown to fail to meet the requirements for patentability. An example, is if it was not novel at its filing date (or priority date if subject to the priority of an earlier application) or if it did not involve an inventive step, did not have an industrial application or if it was not granted to the person entitled to it. The fact that a patent has been granted is not conclusive proof that the invention has satisfied all the requirements and the discovery of a prior publication disclosing the invention can result in the patent being revoked. Often, a person sued for infringement of a patent will attack the validity of the patent. If it is found to be invalid wholly or in a relevant part, that will provide a complete defence.

The remedies available for infringement of a patent are injunctions, delivery up or destruction of infringing articles, damages or an account of profits and a declaration that the patent is valid and infringed by the defendant. Damages and accounts of profits are alternatives. If the defendant proves that he was not aware and had no reasonable grounds for supposing that the patent existed, then neither damages nor accounts of profits are available. If a product carries the word 'patent' or 'patented' or similar, this does not automatically mean that the defendant knows of the patent unless the number of the patent also appears on the product concerned. This enables anyone to look up and inspect the patent specification to determine its scope.

The proprietor of a patent must be careful how he warns alleged infringers. There is a remedy under section 70 in respect of groundless threats of infringement proceedings. A person aggrieved by the threat may bring an action, unless the person making the threat can show that the acts in respect of which the threats were made were or would constitute an infringement of the patent, and the patent is not shown to be invalid by the person bringing the action (or, if shown to be invalid, the defendant shows that at the time of making the threats he did not know and had no reason to believe that the patent was invalid in a relevant respect). The remedies available are a declaration that the threats are unjustified, an injunction against a continuance of the threats, and damages for any loss sustained by the person aggrieved who has brought the action. Groundless threats actions do not apply to all forms of infringement (making or importing a product or using a process) and simply notifying any person of the existence of the patent does not constitute a groundless threat. Making enquiries for the sole purpose of whether, or by whom, a patent has been infringed and making assertions about the patent for the purposes of such enquiries does not constitute a groundless threat.

An example where a groundless-threats action might be appropriate can be seen below:

It is alleged that a computer imported into the UK by Acme Importers Ltd infringes a UK patent belonging to Esoteric Computers plc. The computers are sold by Acme to Krafty Computer Sales Ltd, a retail outlet. Esoteric sends a letter to Krafty threatening to sue Krafty for patent infringement unless it ceases selling the computers forthwith. Krafty will be a perso n aggrieved' and, if Krafty stops buying computers from Acme, so may be Acme. Either should be able to bring an action for groundless threats and will be entitled to remedies unless Esoteric can show that the sale of the computers infringes the patent (subject to a reasonable belief that that is so) and, if a challenge has been made on the validity of the patent, or any relevant part of it, that it is valid.

SOFTWARE INVENTIONS

The term 'software inventions' covers a range of inventions which are implemented by means involving a programmed computer. The ill-fated proposed Directive on the patentability of computer-implemented inventions defined a 'computer-implemented invention' as:

> any invention the performance of which involves the use of a computer, computer network or other programmable apparatus and having one or more *prima facie* novel features which are realised wholly or partly by means of a computer program or computer programs.

The term software invention is synonymous with this definition and includes inventions which produce effects which may or may not be themselves among the list of things declared not to be inventions under section 1(2) of the Patents Act 1977. For example, a programmed computer may control an industrial process such as an automatic painting plant for vehicle bodies or it may control a business method such as a method of buying and selling company shares electronically.

It has to be said that the law on the patentability of software inventions is in a mess. The Boards of Appeal at the EPO (which hear appeals from decisions of the EPO's patent examiners) have handed down a number of contradictory decisions. It is as if they have been making up how the exclusion of computer programs and business methods should be interpreted 'on the hoof'. This recipe for confusion is made worse by the fact that, although decisions of the Boards of Appeal at the EPO are of persuasive authority, they are not binding on the courts of the UK.[2] In England, for example, the Court of Appeal is bound by decisions of the House of Lords and, subject to limited exceptions not really relevant in this context, its own previous decisions. The High Court is bound by decisions of the House of Lords and Court of Appeal. The courts in the UK are required to take judicial notice of decisions of the Boards of Appeal at the EPO under section 91 of the Patents Act 1977. This is not to say that they must follow those decisions, however.

Recently, the Court of Appeal considered the case law in the UK and at the EPO in *Aerotel Ltd v Macrossan* [2006] EWCA Civ 1371. In spite of the requirement to take judicial notice of the decisions of the Boards of Appeal at the EPO, the Court of Appeal decided it had no option but to apply the law as it had developed in previous Court of Appeal cases such as *Merrell Lynch*, *Gale* and *Fujitsu* (all discussed below). These cases treated with the greatest respect an earlier case on the patentability of computer programs at the Board of Appeal at the EPO in *Vicom* (also discussed).

Taking into account recent developments at the EPO's Boards of Appeal, the structure of the remainder of this section of the book is to look at the position in the UK as regards (a) computer programs, and (b) matter declared not to be inventions, particularly mental acts and business methods, implemented by computer. There follows a description of the recent decisions of the Boards of Appeal at the EPO and then a description of the decision in *Aerotel* v *Macrossan* and possible implications. First, however, it might be worth setting out the relevant parts of Article 52 of the EPC on which section 1(1) and (2) of the Patents Act 1977 is modelled.

Article 52

(1) European patents shall be granted for any inventions which are susceptible of industrial application, are new and which involve an inventive step.

(2) The following in particular shall not be regarded as inventions within the meaning of paragraph 1:
    (a) discoveries, scientific theories and mathematical methods;
    (b) aesthetic creations;
    (c) schemes, rules and methods of performing mental acts, playing games or doing business, and programs for computers;
    (d) presentations of information.

(3) The provisions of paragraph 2 shall exclude patentability of the subject-matter or activities referred to in that provision only to the extent to which a European patent application or European patent relates to such subject-matter or activities as such.

Section 1 of the Patents Act 1977 is one of those provisions declared to have, as near as practicable, the same effect as the equivalent provisions in, *inter alia*, the EPC. There has been some criticism of the fact that the UK chose to rewrite these provisions. For example, in *Markem Corp v Zipher Ltd* [2005] EWCA Civ 267, the Court of Appeal said (at para. 94):

> In a peculiarly cack-handed way the draftsman chose to re-number and re-write some of these and then say, in s.130(7) in effect that his re-writing does not count – that the relevant provision is 'so framed as to have, as nearly as practicable, the same effect in the UK as it has in the EPC'. No one has ever identified any difference in meaning between a 1977 Act provision and the meaning of a corresponding provision of the EPC and we do not suppose anyone ever will.

Similar criticism has been made in relation to the UK's implementation of other Directives, particularly the Directive to approximate the laws of Member States in relation to trade marks, dis-

---

[2] This is unlike the position in respect of decisions of the European Court of Justice, the decisions and rulings of which are binding on the courts in the UK.

cussed in the chapter in trade marks and passing off. Where provisions in Directives are required to be implemented without variation, judges in the UK now tend to go straight to the text of the Directive rather than the UK implementing legislation.

Computer programs

The exclusion from patent of computer programs reflects international trends. Copyright is seen as the proper vehicle for the protection of computer programs although, when the current Patents Act was passed in 1977, it was far from clear whether copyright did protect computer programs. Even before the 1977 Act, computer programs were not generally patentable *per se*, but there were cases, both in the UK and in the US, where computer programs were the subject-matter of granted patents, usually as being part of a piece of machinery or an industrial process. For example, in *Diamond* v *Diehr* [1981] 209 USPQ 1, the US Supreme Court confirmed that a computer-controlled process used in rubber curing was patentable. Since that time, the US has become much more liberal in granting patents for software inventions generally and the courts there now accept that computer programs and business methods are patentable in principle. One reason for this is that the US Patents Act 1952 does not have specific exceptions for them. It also has a wide definition of what a patentable invention is under § 101 which states:

> Whoever invents or discovers any new and useful process, machine, manufacture, or composition of matter, or any new and useful improvement thereof, may obtain a patent therefor, subject to the conditions and requirements of this title.

In the UK, under the previous patent legislation, the Patents Act 1949, an invention was defined in section 101 (the interpretation section) as 'any manner of manufacture ... and any new method or process of testing applicable to the improvement or control of manufacture ...'. In *Gever's Application* [1970] RPC 91, data processing apparatus was arranged to work in a certain way associated with punched cards inserted into it. The purpose of the apparatus was to file world trade marks in such a way that they could be easily produced to check for similarity and prior registration. The patent application, which concerned a piece of machinery which functioned in a certain way because of the punched cards, was allowed to proceed. The cards were described by the judge as a 'manner of manufacture' because he thought that a punched card was analogous to a cam for controlling the cutting path of a lathe. This was distinguished from a card which merely had written or printed material on it, intended to convey information to the human eye or mind, and not meant to be ancillary to some machine by being specially shaped for that purpose. However, because of subsequent technological developments, integrated circuits, magnetic disks and tapes and optical character readers now are used to enter information into a computer or to store the programs which control the computer. The analogy with a mechanical process no longer rings true and it is unlikely that this case will be followed.

In another case, *Burrough's Corporation (Perkin's) Application* [1974] RPC 147, computer programs controlled the transmission of data to terminals from a central computer (a communications system). The system, including the computer programs, was held to be the proper subject matter of a patent because the programs were embodied in physical form; they were 'hard-wired' – permanently embedded in the electronic circuits of the equipment. In many respects the significance of the physical form of a program, whether hard-wired on a silicon chip or stored on magnetic disks, is an irrelevance and should not affect patentability.

The distinction between modes of storage and their effect on patentability was considered under the 1977 Act in *Gale's Application* [1991] RPC 305, concerning an application for a method of calculating square roots by program instructions contained in a ROM chip. The application was rejected but the applicant's appeal to the Patents Court was allowed by Aldous J who said that the claimed invention related to a product (the ROM chip) and was, therefore, patentable. He then said that the program would not have been patentable had it been stored on a floppy disk. This decision would have had the effect of making a software designer's choice of storage medium crucial to the question of patentability but it was, fortunately, quickly overruled in the Court of Appeal where Lord Justice Nicholls said:

> It would equally be nonsense, if a floppy disc containing a computer program is not patentable, that a ROM characterised only by the instructions in that program should be patentable.

The Court of Appeal's decision conforms to common sense and the simple expedient of hardwiring a computer program should not, *per se*, make the program patentable. Something else must be present such as a technical contribution to the art.

Technical effect or contribution

Two alternative approaches have been made to the question of the patent protection of inventions which include a computer program. The first is that the patent application should be considered without the contribution of the excepted thing. For example, if a machine includes a computer program it is then a question of whether the machine, without taking the computer program into account, adds anything to the state of the art. Does the machine, ignoring the computer program, meet the requirements for patentability? If the only novel and inventive step concerns the computer program itself, then the machine as a whole is not patentable. The case of *Re Merrill Lynch, Pierce Fenner & Smith Incorporated's Application* [1988] RPC 1, illustrates this approach. The invention related to an improved data processing system for implementing an automatic trading market for securities. The system received and stored the best current bids, qualified customer buy and sell orders, executed orders as well as monitoring stock inventory and profit. On appeal to the Patents Court, it was held that where an invention involves any of the materials excluded from the meaning of 'invention' in section 1(2), the proper construction of the qualification in that subsection requires an enquiry into whether the inventive step resides in the contribution of the excluded matter alone. If the inventive step comes only from the excluded material, then the invention is not patentable because of section 1(2). The judge, Falconer J, said that the novel and inventive effect must reside outside the computer program even though it may be defined by the program.

On appeal to the Court of Appeal (*Merrill Lynch's Application* [1989] RPC 561), the approach taken by the EPO in *Vicom*, as described below, was approved. However, the Court of Appeal still confirmed that the invention in *Merrill Lynch* was not patentable but on the ground that there was no technical contribution as the invention was entirely software based.

In Case T208/84 *VICOM/Computer-related invention* [1987] 2 EPOR 74, an application was made to obtain a patent for a new digital image processing system, the process steps being expressed mathematically in the form of an algorithm. The Board of Appeal at the EPO said that if a claim is directed to a technical process which is carried out under the control of a program (whether implemented in the hardware or the software), then the claim cannot be regarded as related to a computer program as such. It is an application of the program for determining the sequence of steps in the process and it is the process for which protection is sought. In the present case, the subject matter of the invention was the practical application of a computer program, the technical effect resulting from the operation of the programmed computer and not the computer program itself. The Board of Appeal also made a number of other important points.

- A computer of a known type which is set up to operate according to a new program cannot be considered to be part of the state of the art.

- It would be illogical to grant protection for a technical process controlled by a suitably programmed computer but not to protect the computer itself when set up to execute the control.
- A process carried out under the control of new hardware and/or software is not necessarily capable of industrial application, an example being in the case of a game.

For some time, the decision in *Vicom* was followed in the courts in the UK and treated with great respect. For example, in *Genentech Inc's Patent* [1989] RPC 147, it was held, *inter alia*, in the Court of Appeal that a patent which claimed the practical application of a discovery did not relate to the discovery as such and was not excluded by section 1(2) of the Patents Act 1977 even if the practical application might be obvious once the discovery had been made. *Gale's Application* [1991] RPC 305, discussed above, confirms this as the correct approach.

In *Fujitsu Ltd's Application* [1997] RPC 608, discussed later, Aldous LJ in the Court of Appeal said (at 614):

> It would therefore seem that as a matter of words, if for instance the patent was not confined to a computer program, then it could not be excluded under subsection (2), as to an extent the patent would not relate to the computer program as such. However it is and always has been a principle of patent law that mere discoveries or ideas are not patentable, but those discoveries and ideas which have a technical aspect or make a technical contribution are. Thus the concept that what is needed to make an excluded thing patentable is a technical contribution is not surprising. That was the basis for the decision of the Board in *Vicom*. It has been accepted by this court and by the EPO and has been applied since 1987. It is a concept at the heart of patent law.

It would seem that the technical effect or contribution does not have to be external to the computer and, in principle, operating systems are patentable because they determine how a computer operates technically. Indeed, there are many patents in the UK, Europe and the US in respect of operating systems.

With applications programs it is more difficult to achieve a technical advance where the whole process is software based. In *Wang Laboratories Inc's Application* [1991] RPC 463, an application for a patent for an expert system shell was rejected because there was no new technical effect. Aldous J said that the computer (being a conventional machine) and the program combined did not produce a new computer. In *Hitachi Ltd's Application* [1991] RPC 415, an application in respect of a compiler program was rejected by the Patent Office as being no more than an application for a computer program as such.

While a patent will be refused for a computer program as such it will be allowed if the purpose of the program is to bring about some technical effect and it is that effect which is the subject matter of the patent application. The subject matter should make a technical contribution to the state of the art.

Mental acts, business methods and the presentation of information

The operation of a novel computer program may produce a technical effect which is itself caught by the exceptions to patentability. If that is so, and this was accepted in Vicom, then the subject matter should not be deemed to be an invention. Simply put, the subject matter must make a technical contribution to the art which is not excluded from the meaning of invention. Thus, where running a computer program produces a technical effect which is a method of doing business or the presentation of information only, then it should not be patentable. In *Re The Computer Generation of Chinese Characters* [1993] FSR 315, an application for a patent in respect of a method of storing, processing, displaying and printing Chinese characters was turned down in Germany. It was said that the subject matter neither solved a technical problem by a technical method nor did it make a technical contribution to the state of the art.

The EPO has, however, moved away somewhat from the simple premise that the technical contribution must be not itself excluded, as will be seen later. In the meantime, the position in the UK in respect of three particular things excluded from the meaning of invention is discussed, with reference to the EPO Board of Appeal decision in *IBM/Card reader* which appears to have been overtaken by subsequent cases at the EPO but probably best represents the current position in the UK (and possibly also in other countries such as Germany).

Mental acts

In the UK, a patent was refused for a software means of identifying ships by comparing the silhouette of an unknown ship with a database of ships' silhouettes in *Raytheon Co's Application* [1993] RPC 427. The fact that the equivalent mental act in the human mind would not be a deliberate conscious process did not bring the application out of the exception. Recognition of shapes by humans is almost instantaneous, whereas a computer program doing this would be based on algorithms that may operate quite differently, in logical terms, to the human brain. The deputy judge was not prepared to read the exception in a narrow sense. Thus, it appears that a computer program that simply does something that can be done by mental acts in the human brain will not be patentable even though the program may do it differently and in a totally new way. The same must apply to the other exceptions such as methods of doing business.

The refusal of software inventions where the technical contribution related to a mental act became even more ingrained in UK patent law. *Fujitsu Ltd's Application* [1997] RPC 608 involved an application for a patent in relation to software which was developed to help chemists design new chemical compounds. A computer screen displayed the crystalline structure of two known chemicals and these images could be rotated and manipulated so as to align one face of one crystal to be aligned with the complementary face of the other crystal. This then formed the blueprint for a new hybrid 'designer' chemical.

It was held that the application was for a method of performing a mental act as such. In the Court of Appeal, Lord Justice Aldous rejected the submission that, as it was not possible to perform a mental act using a computer, a claim for a method of using a computer could not be a claim to a method of performing a mental act. He stressed that it was important to look at the substance of an application. Thus, a claim for a computer program operating in a particular way is no more than a claim to a computer program. Furthermore, a claim to a method of carrying out a calculation, which is a method of performing a mental act, can never become more patentable simply because the calculation is being performed by a computer rather than being done manually on a piece of paper.

It was also accepted by the Court of Appeal that the application was for a computer program as such and not patentable on this ground also. The invention used a conventional computer to do what was previously done using plastic models. The only advance was that of using a computer to enable the result to be portrayed more quickly. Aldous LJ said that this was just the sort of advantage to be obtained by the application of a computer program. In other words, there was nothing special in it.

In the context of computers, the exception for methods of doing business and performing mental acts is potentially very wide. Many programs automate business methods that were carried out previously without the use of computer technology or operations that used to be performed by the human mind, even if a computer does it on the basis of completely different algorithms. Although not really discussed in the *Fujitsu* case, it was highly arguable that the application would also have failed for lack of novelty (the exercise was done before but by using physical models) or through lack of inventive step. It is fairly obvious that advantages can be achieved by automating existing processes. This is why most computer programs would fail to be patentable. However, there are some programs that make new and effective technical contributions and it is for these that the patent system is important. Incidentally, the Fujitsu patent appears to have been granted in Japan.

Business methods

In Case T854/90 *IBM/Card Reader* [1994] EPOR 89 the Board of Appeal dismissed an appeal against a refusal to grant a patent in relation to an invention whereby an automatic card-reading machine could read any card. This would allow the use of any bank card with a machine such as an automated teller machine (ATM or cashpoint machine) to carry out a transaction. The Board of Appeal confirmed that the subject matter of a patent must have a technical character and be industrially applicable. It also went on to say that applying technical means to perform a business activity does not mean that the business activity has a technical character and is thus an invention.

Fujitsu failed to obtain a patent for an invention involving a reservation management system for scheduling meetings based on an algorithm to resolve conflicting reservation requests which were based on a number of criteria and which would, if appropriate, reschedule a particular meeting. Further embodiments of the invention concerned prioritising queues processed by computer and the management of database entries designed to prevent mutually exclusive entries in the database. In *Fujitsu Limited's Patent Application* (unreported) 23 August 2000, in the Patent Office, the hearing officer held that the invention was a method of doing business and, although he accepted that automating the system would make it quicker, more accurate, more easily accessible to users and, in a network version, more widely available, these were the usual benefits of computerisation. There was nothing to produce a new technical result. The hearing officer also confirmed that he considered the invention also to be excluded as a program for a computer.

A claim to a method of online wagering was rejected in *CFPH LLC's Application* [2006] RPC 259 as a claim to a method of doing business. Peter Prescott QC, sitting as a Deputy Judge of the High Court, spoke of the difficulty in deciding whether a claim was to subject matter or activities excluded from the meaning of an invention. He noted that many things are now controlled by a programmed computer, for example, the automatic pilot of an aircraft or a process for making canned soup and, in principle, a better way of doing those things ought to be patentable. He said (at para. 104):

> The question to ask should be: is it (the artefact or process) new and non-obvious merely *because* there is a computer program? Or would it still be new and non-obvious in principle even if the same decisions and commands could somehow be taken and issued by a little man at a control panel, operating under the same rules? For if the answer to the latter question is 'Yes' it becomes apparent that the computer program is merely a tool, and the invention is not about computer programming at all. It is about better rules for governing an automatic pilot or better rules for conducting the manufacture of canned soup.

Peter Prescott QC referred to the EPO Board of Appeal in Case T258/03 *HITACHI/Auction method* [2004] EPOR 548, discussed later. One way of looking at a computer-implemented invention is to first find out what the problem is that the invention seeks to overcome. Then ask whether the solution uses technical means to overcome the problem or whether it uses, for example, a new business method to overcome the problem. This does not, however, appear to fully agree with the above quote or the decision in *HITACHI/Auction method*. Surely the question should be not about new rules *per se* but, rather, about how those rules are implemented. Are they implemented in a technical way which is new and non-obvious.

In *Shoppalotto.com Ltd's Patent Application* [2006] RPC 293, which involved a claim to a lottery game played through the internet, Mr Justice Pumfrey said that the correct approach was to ask whether there was a relevant technical effect, being one over and above 'that to be expected from the mere loading of a program into a computer'. What did the claimed programmed computer invention contribute over and above the fact that it involved a computer program? It would be patentable if there was a contribution not within the subject matter and activities declared to be 'non-inventions' as then it would not be an application for the excluded matter *as such*.

Finally, in *Crawford's Patent Application* [2006] RPC 345, a display system designed to prevent bus grouping was also held to be not an invention as it was, *inter alia*, a method of doing business.

Presentation of information

Computers and the internet are used for many things but a significant use is providing information. According to the EPC, presentations of information are not inventions if a patent application relates to presentations of information as such. New ways of presenting information may be patentable, for example, a new form of screen display or environment for displaying information on websites.

In *Townsend's Patent Application* [2004] EWHC 482 (Pat), an application was made to patent an advent calendar having additional information printed on the doors on the calendars which when opened revealed a treat such as a small toy or small chocolate. The particular problem was where an advent calendar was shared by two children and the solution was to include information so each would know when it was their turn to open the door and retrieve the treat. The application was rejected as being simply the presentation of information. A distinction between the expression of information and the provision of information failed to impress the judge.

Other applications rejected on this basis (and also on the basis that they were essentially claims to methods of doing business) were *Shoppalotto* and *Crawford*, mentioned above. In *Crawford*, the heart of the invention was a display system mounted on buses which operated in two modes, one being that the bus was available for both picking up and dropping off passengers. In the other mode, the bus would only drop off passengers and not pick up new passengers. It was said that this would lessen the problem of bus grouping caused by the first bus having to pick up passengers with the second bus not having to pick up as many passengers. The flow of buses would be made more regular and consistent. The judge held that the only new and inventive element was the nature of the information to be displayed on the outside of the bus and the method of operating the bus in 'exit mode'. This did not have a technical nature. The information to be displayed was a presentation of information and the method of operating a bus in exit mode was a method of doing business. There was no technical contribution to the art that was not otherwise excluded matter.

Developments at the EPO

For a while, the EPO remained loyal to the technical effect approach. Another example was provided by the case of *IBM/Card Reader*, discussed above. However, there has been something of a sea change at the EPO. One example was Case T935/97 *IBM/Computer programs* [1999] RPC 861. IBM applied to patent a data processing system used to display information in windows such that any information displayed in one window and obscured by a second window is moved automatically to a new position so that it was no longer obscured. The first few claims concerned the process and had been accepted by the EPO as having a technical effect but some subsequent claims were rejected. Some of these focused on a computer program product (that is, a storage device on which the program was stored) and which, when run, caused the computer to execute the process.

The Board of Appeal at the EPO held that a computer program product was not excluded, *per se*. It confirmed that computer programs must have a technical character, for example, in the effects resulting from the running of the program, to be patentable. Furthermore, a claim for a computer program product may have a technical character resulting from the potential technical effect which will be revealed when the program is run on a computer. The same applies to the apparatus adapted for carrying out the technical effects. Therefore, in principle, a patent may be available for:

■ a computer program which has a technical character because, when run, it causes technical effects;

■ a computer when so programmed to create those technical effects; and

■ a computer program product containing the program which, when run in a computer, creates the technical effects.

If a computer program, when run in a computer, produces a new and inventive effect which is itself excluded from patentability, does this mean that a patent cannot be granted under any circumstances? This certainly seems to have been, and continues to be, the approach in the UK but later cases at the EPO suggest it may be a matter of precisely what is claimed, for example, a business method or an apparatus to perform that business method. In Case T931/95 *PBS Partnership/Controlling pensions benefits system* [2002] EPOR 522, the Board of Appeal confirmed that it was implicit that an invention had to have a technical character to be patentable. The board further stated that methods only involving economic concepts and practices of doing business are not inventions for the purposes of the EPC and a feature of a method which concerned the use of technical means for a purely non-technical purpose and/or for processing purely non-technical information does not necessarily confer a technical character to such a method. However, an apparatus constituting a physical entity or concrete product, suitable for performing or supporting a business or economic activity, is an invention within the meaning of the EPC. The Board then rejected the notion that the question of whether the invention made a technical contribution to the art was relevant to whether it was an invention for the purposes of the EPC, though, of course, it might be relevant to whether it was new or involved an inventive step. The invention was held not to involve an inventive step.

In *PBS Partnership*, the Board of Appeal distinguished *Vicom*, without saying that it was wrong but the *PBS Partnership* case departed from *Vicom* in a significant way. It seemed to diminish the exclusion of computer programs as such from inventions almost to vanishing point. However, although a programmed computer could be an invention, the state of the art included the idea of using computer technology in the economic sector. The notional skilled computer programmer would think the invention obvious.

In Case T258/03 *HITACHI/Auction method* [2004] EPOR 548, there was a further change. The alleged invention was a method of conducting online auctions. One problem was that of delays in computer networks when persons placed bids. This was overcome by using a Dutch auction system in which a bidder placed two bids, the desired bid price and the maximum bid price. The patent was refused. The Board of Appeal confirmed that a method using technical means, as well as the apparatus itself was an invention. The question was whether the subject matter had a technical character and technical character can be implied from:

■ the physical features of an entity;

■ the nature of an activity; or

■ conferred on a non-technical activity by use of technical means.

A purely abstract concept devoid of technical implications would not be an invention, being caught by Article 52(2). The consequence of the decision is that anything carried out by a programmed computer, whether it is claimed in that way, as a concrete entity, or the activity performed by the programmed computer, has a technical character and is an invention. In this respect the Board of Appeal differed from the decision in *PBS Partnership* which focused on claims to a concrete entity rather than the method itself.

The Board of Appeal in *Hitachi* realised that its interpretation of 'invention' was very broad and would include '... activities which are so familiar that their technical character tends to be overlooked, such as the act of writing, using pen and paper'. The Board also noted that it had long been accepted that the exclusion of things as such, meant that a mix of technical and non-technical features may be patentable. Of course, *Hitachi* does not mean that all methods using technical means are patentable. They still have to satisfy the other requirements, in particular, novelty and inventive step.

In *Hitachi*, the invention did not solve the problem by technical means. It simply circumvented it by adapting a Dutch auction system for use on a computer. Therefore, it did not involve an inventive step. The system as adapted could just as easily be conducted using a system of postal bids. Furthermore, the invention was the mere automation of a non-technical activity. However, the Board of Appeal went on to say that if a step in such a method was designed to be particularly suitable for being performed on a computer then, arguably, it had a technical character. It is perhaps noteworthy that *Vicom* was not referred to in *Hitachi*.

The Microsoft Corporation applied to patent inventions concerning the use of clipboard formats to transfer non-file data between software applications. The Board of Appeal cases were Case T424/03 *MICROSOFT/Clipboard format I* and Case T411/03 *MICROSOFT/Clipboard format II*, both decisions handed down on 23 February 2006. In both cases, the Board of Appeal, following *Hitachi*, confirmed that a method using technical means was an invention and a computer system including a memory (a clipboard in the present case) was a technical means. A method implemented in a computer system represents a sequence of steps actually performed and achieving an effect, and not a sequence of computer-executable instructions (that is, a computer program) which only have the potential of achieving such an effect when loaded into, and run on, a computer. The claims in the application were not, therefore, claims to a computer program as such. Even though a method of operating a computer may be put into effect by means of a computer program, a claim to such a method does not claim the computer program as such.

The Board of Appeal went on to say that the steps in the claimed method solved a technical problem by technical means as functional data structures (clipboard formats) were used independently of any cognitive content in order to enhance the internal operation of a computer system with a view to facilitating the exchange of data among various application programs. The claimed steps thus provide a general purpose computer with a further functionality. The computer thus programmed assists the user in transferring non-file data into files. Finally, a computer program on a technical carrier is not a computer program as such and may contribute to the technical character of the subject matter of what is claimed to be a patentable invention.

This is a very wide meaning of invention and it is arguable that now, at the EPO, it seems that the focus is more on whether the alleged invention is new and involves an inventive step. The Board of Appeal confirmed that the Microsoft inventions were new and inventive over the prior art (the closest available prior art was Windows 3.1). There is one major difference between *Microsoft* and the *PBS* and *Hitachi* cases. The technical character was not directed to other material declared to be non-inventions such as business methods and the presentation of information as such.

To summarise these important cases at the EPO which may reflect an incremental narrowing of the exception for computer programs, business methods and the like:

- simply using a business method to overcome a technical problem is not an invention (*Hitachi*);

- the emphasis is on whether the alleged invention has a technical character (*PBS*, *Hitachi* and *Microsoft*);

- a mix of technical and non-technical features may be patentable (*Hitachi* – originally so held in Case T26/86 *Koch & Sterzel/X-ray apparatus* [1988] EPOR 72);

- carrying out a business method by technical means is an invention (*PBS*);

- using concrete apparatus (that is, a programmed computer) to perform a business method is an invention (*PBS*);

- claiming the technical activity (not just the concrete apparatus) is also an invention (*Hitachi*);

- inventive step may be an issue and it is not inventive to automate a known process (*PBS* and *Hitachi*);

- a computer-implemented method which represents a sequence of steps which, when performed achieves an effect is not a computer program as such (*Microsoft*);

- a claim to a technical carrier containing a computer program is not a claim to a computer program as such (*Microsoft*).

The *Aerotel* v *Macrossan* case

Aerotel Ltd v *Telco Holdings Ltd; Macrossan* [2006] EWCA Civ 1371 concerned two inventions. One was to a telephone system allowing pre-payment from any available telephone ('Aerotel'). The other was to a method of automatically acquiring the documents required for the formation of a company ('Macrossan'). In the Court of Appeal, Lord Justice Jacob reviewed the case law on patentability of software inventions at the EPO, in the UK and in the US. The previous Court of Appeal decisions in *Merrill Lynch*, *Gale* and *Fujitsu* (all discussed above) had taken the *Vicom* approach. There must be a technical contribution which is not itself within the matter excluded from the meaning of 'invention'. Jacob LJ noted the developments at the EPO but said that he had no option but to follow the previous Court of Appeal decisions under the doctrine of binding precedent.

In Aerotel, it was held that the patent was valid. It used a new combination of existing apparatus and, thus, was not a business method as such. In Macrossan, in essence, the alleged invention was to an interactive system to do the work normally done by a solicitor or company formation agent. Jacob LJ held that this was a business method as such and the method was also a claim to a computer program as such.

The end result would probably be the same at the EPO however, there, it would be more likely that the Macrosson application would be rejected on the basis that it was not new or did not involve an inventive step, being no more that the automation of an existing process.

Implications

Patenting software is big business. Perhaps billions of pounds sterling ride on how the exclusion in Article 52(2) of the EPC is interpreted. It is regrettable that the Court of Appeal has, in effect, chosen to ignore recent developments at the EPO. In many cases, it appears that the UK courts and the Boards of Appeal at the EPO will come to the same conclusions as to whether a particular invention is patentable though it is likely that, in many cases involving computer programs and business methods, the reasons will differ. Of course, criticism can be levelled at the EPO and the movement away from *Vicom*, which has never been expressly overruled. But the EPO does not appear to adhere to a strict doctrine of precedent although earlier cases are usually referred to. The only way in which the present uncertainty can be resolved is by the Enlarged Board at the

9

Patent law

EPO. That Board which rules on cases of significant importance only hears a handful of cases each year. Its decisions are of some importance. The time is now ripe for the Enlarged Board to look at the application of Article 52(2). It is unlikely that changes can be made to the EPC itself to clarify the exclusions but some guidance as to interpretation would be welcome. Even if this happens, only the House of Lords could overrule the previous Court of Appeal decisions (unless that court could adopt a new exception to its application of binding precedent).

The uncertainty as to the scope of the exclusions has reached new heights and the Patent Office now has around four hearings a week on software inventions, whereas years ago it was only one or two a year. This is a reflection of both the difficulty in interpreting and applying the statutory provision and also the desirability of having a patent for a software invention. This gives the proprietor a monopoly whereas copyright protection requires the owner to show that the defendant has copied the computer program or made some other use of it.

The shift in the application of Article 52(2) at the EPO as regards software inventions could be explained by the recognition that software inventions should, perhaps, be more freely patentable. This was the aim of the now defunct proposed Directive on the patentability of software inventions. There is no evidence, however, of any policy changes at the EPO. There is a lot to be said for the approach in other countries, particularly, the US where there are no specific exclusions for computer programs and business methods. The focus there is on novelty and inventive step, although the US Patent and Trademark Office has been subject to the criticism that it grants computer programs and business method patents too freely.[3] A significant proportion of these may prove to be invalid if challenged.

One thing is clear. Something must be done to harmonise the patentability of software inventions on a world scale. The Agreement on the Trade Related Aspects of Intellectual Property Rights (TRIPs Agreement) carries no equivalent exceptions and Article 27(1) of that Agreement states that patents should be available in any field of technology.

PATENT INFRINGEMENT AND THE INTERNET

The internet presents two particular problems in the case of software patents. First, the use in the UK of a software invention on a webpage or an offer to deliver software advertised on a webpage (whether or not delivered online) could infringe patents in other jurisdictions even if there are no relevant patents in the UK. Bearing in mind the apparent ease with which some dubious software inventions are granted patents in the US, there are serious dangers of infringing software patents there from web-based activities in the UK. If readers think this fanciful in the extreme, the author suggests looking up US patent number 4,646,250 for a data entry screen and US patent number 6,272,493 for a system and method for facilitating a windows based content manifestation environment within a WWW browser.

Infringement of a patent includes using a patented product or process and offering to sell a patented product or process in the relevant jurisdiction. Thus, taking the above example, collecting data using a similar design of data entry screen could infringe in the US as could using windows in a web browser. Placing an advertisement on a webpage for a product and including a reference to a price in US$ could infringe. For a court in the US to accept jurisdiction, however, the particular activity would have to be targeted at individuals in the particular state where legal proceedings are commenced. If patent infringement was found in a US court against a person resident in the United Kingdom who has no physical presence in the US, the proprietor could find it very difficult to enforce that judgment in the UK, unless the defendant put in a defence to

[3] *The Economic Impact of Patentability of Computer Programs*, Intellectual Property Institute, London, March 2000.

the action in the US. The proprietor would have to ask a court in the UK to enforce the judgment which it would be unlikely to do if the defendant put in an appearance and challenged the validity of the patent in question. These difficulties of enforcement do not apply to European countries and most Commonwealth countries and a few others because of Conventions and Regulations covering jurisdiction and the enforcement of judgments.

As patent rights are territorial in nature, to infringe a UK patent, the infringing act must be done within the territory of the UK. A rudimentary application of this simple rule in the context of computer networks and the internet could result in a person who puts to work a software invention without permission escaping an infringement action by placing the most significant part of the invention outside the territory of the UK. However, in such a case a sensible approach is to consider where the person or persons making use of the invention are located. In *Menashe Business Mercantile Ltd v William Hill Organisation Ltd* [2002] RPC 47, Dr Julian Menashe was the proprietor of a patent in respect of a system for playing an interactive casino game. The patent claimed a computer terminal connected to a host computer by communication means. For example, a gambler could use his own computer to access the host computer on which the gambling software was located by means of the internet. Menashe Business Mercantile Ltd had an exclusive licence to work the patent.

The defendant was a bookmaker who decided to operate a gaming system. Gamblers were supplied with CDs containing a computer program which they installed on their own computers. This enabled the gamblers' computers to communicate via the internet with the defendant's host computer which was situated first in Antigua and, later, in Curaçao. The claimants sued the defendant on the basis of section 60(2) of the Patents Act 1977 alleging that the defendant had supplied and/or offered to supply in the UK the means, relating to an essential element of the invention, for putting the invention into effect, knowing or where it would be obvious to a reasonable person in the circumstances that those means were suitable for putting, and were intended to put, the invention into effect in the UK. The defendant argued that it did not infringe the patent because its host computer and part of the communication means were situated outside the UK. The court had to determine a preliminary question concerning whether the fact that the host computer and part of the communication system which were located outside the UK was a defence to an infringement action under section 60(2).

The Court of Appeal noted that infringement of a patent under section 60 can only occur if a person does an act within the UK without the proprietor's consent. However, that does not assist with the meaning of the phrase in section 60(2) '... to put, the invention into effect in the United Kingdom'. The court said that where the invention is an apparatus what is required is that the means are intended to put the apparatus into effect so that the apparatus becomes effective. Therefore, in the present case, the means, being the CDs, must be suitable for putting the apparatus into a state of effectiveness: that is, to put it into an infringing state in the UK. The Court of Appeal held that where an invention is an apparatus, it is irrelevant to the question of infringement if part of the apparatus is situated outside the UK and it is wrong to apply old notions of location to inventions such as that in the present case. The answer in such a case is to consider who is making use of the system and where he is located when he makes that use. As the gamblers used the system in the UK they could be said to use the host computer in the UK even though it was physically situated outside the UK. Therefore, supplying gamblers with CDs in the UK to enable them to use the gambling system was supplying the means relating to an essential element of the invention, intended to put the invention into effect in the UK and was not a defence to an infringement action under section 60(2).

This is a very sensible decision and overcomes the danger of defendants avoiding infringement by taking a significant part of an invention outside the jurisdiction of the UK and relying on cross-border problems. Similar circumstances are likely to become more common, especially with the potential growth in numbers of software patents which will have a relevance to activities carried out over the internet.

SUMMARY

- To be patentable an invention must:
  - be new;
  - involve an inventive step;
  - be capable of industrial application.
- Certain things are excluded from the meaning of invention if the patent or application relates to that thing 'as such'. They include:
  - a scheme, rule or method for performing a mental act, playing a game or doing business or a program for a computer;
  - the presentation of information.
- An invention is not new if it forms part of the state of the art.
- An invention involves an inventive step if it is not obvious to a person skilled in the art.
- An invention is capable of industrial application if it can be made or used in any kind of industry including agriculture.
- Software inventions may be patentable according to the Court of Appeal if they include a technical contribution to the art which itself is not excluded from the meaning of invention.
- At the EPO, a software invention must possess a technical character and, that being so, the emphasis is more likely to be on whether the alleged invention is new and inventive.
- Because of the apparent ease with which computer programs and business methods are patentable in the US, there is a danger that running an e-commerce website could infringe a US patent.

SELF-TEST QUESTIONS

Note: there is only one correct answer to each multiple choice question.

1   Certain matter is excluded from patentability if the patent or the application for a patent relates to that thing as such. Which one of the following statements is CORRECT regarding that exclusion?

   (a) The matter is not an invention.

   (b) The matter is deemed not to involve an inventive step.

   (c) The matter is not patentable on the basis that it is contrary to public policy.

   (d) The matter is not capable of industrial application.

2   The state of the art for testing the novelty of an invention subject to a patent application includes which ONE of the following?

   (a) Patent applications which were withdrawn before publication but which have an earlier priority date than that of the application in question.

(b) New inventions that would, at the priority date of the patent in question, be considered obvious to a person skilled in the art.

(c) Non-obvious combinations of inventions which were in the public domain before the priority date of the patent in question.

(d) Patent applications published on or after the priority date of the application but which have an earlier priority date.

3   Enrico is employed as a project manager by Sagacious Software plc. He is not a director of the company nor does he hold any shares in it. His normal duties are to manage new software projects through to final testing and acceptance by clients. He assigns duties to analysts and programmers and oversees their work, ensuring that projects are completed to specification and on time. He does not have any programming or software design duties himself: his job is as a team leader and manager. Enrico came up with the idea of a new software based system of data transformation which appears to be patentable. Which of the following statements is CORRECT in relation to any patent that might be granted for the data transformation system?

(a) Enrico is entitled to the patent providing he had not been assigned any special duties to make the invention.

(b) As an employee, Enrico's employer, Sagacious Software plc is automatically entitled to the patent.

(c) Sagacious Software plc is entitled to the patent but will be required to pay Enrico compensation, equivalent to a reasonable royalty, in respect of any income it derives from the patent.

(d) Enrico and Sagacious Software plc are jointly entitled to the patent as, although Enrico did not make the invention in the course of his normal duties, he was under a special obligation to further his employer's interests.

4   Which of the following statements concerning the decision of the Board of Appeal in *Hitachi/Auction method* is NOT CORRECT?

(a) A method involving technical means is an invention for the purposes of Article 52(1) EPC.

(b) Using a known business method to solve a technical problem does not contribute to the technical character of the claimed subject matter.

(c) Claims must be directed at concrete apparatus rather than activities when assessing whether something is an invention.

(d) The comparatively wide definition of 'invention' accepted by the Board of Appeal will include activities so familiar that their technical character tends to be overlooked such as the act of writing using a pen and paper.

5   The application of the exclusions from the meaning of invention in section 1(2) of the Patents Act 1977 (Article 52(2) and (3) EPC) now differs between the Court of Appeal and the Boards of Appeal of the EPO. Describe the present position and how the inconsistency of approach could be resolved.

For further resources and updates please go to the Companion Website accompanying this book at **www.mylawchamber.co.uk/bainbridgeIT**

9

Patent law

10 Design law

INTRODUCTION AND BACKGROUND

Design law was originally concerned with the protection of aesthetic designs applied to articles, for example, a new design of furniture, telephone, lamp, linen, cutlery, writing instrument, etc. The scope of articles for which designs could be protected was enormous but, apart from being able to protect new designs applied to hardware, design law had little relevance for the computer industry and information technology generally. That is no longer the case and design law can now protect computer graphics and icons, software fonts as well as the shape and appearance of computer hardware and semiconductor chips such as CPUs.

Significant changes were made to design law by the Copyright, Designs and Patents Act 1988, the relevant provisions of which came into force on 1 August 1989. This Act made changes to the UK registered design (provided for under the Registered Designs Act 1949) and also introduced a new form of protection for features of shape or configuration: the UK unregistered design right. This latter right was intended to protect functional designs but was not limited to such designs. A variant of the UK unregistered design right is used to protect the 'topography' of semiconductor products. Later, in 2001, as a result of a Directive harmonising registered design law throughout the European Community,[1] the Registered Designs Act 1949 was again modified (so much so that it would have been better to pass a new Act of Parliament rather than make further changes to the 1949 Act which now bears little resemblance to its original form). Then in 2003, a Community design protection was introduced. This provides for two forms of protection, one through registration, the other by means of an informal unregistered design right, not to be confused with the UK unregistered design right which bears no resemblance whatsoever to the Community design. The basic requirements for protection by the Community design, whether registered or unregistered, are virtually identical to those for the UK registered design. There are, of course, some differences. The Community design has a unitary nature and is effective throughout the European Community. The UK registered design only has effect within the UK (and other territories that it has been extended to, such as the Isle of Man).

There are now four ways in which a design may be protected. They are not mutually exclusive and there is some overlap between them. They are:

- registration in the UK under the Registered Designs Act 1949;
- protection by the UK unregistered design right;

---

[1] Directive 98/71/EC of the European Parliament and of the Council of 13 October 1998 on the legal protection of designs, OJ L 289, 28.10.1998, p. 28 (the 'Directive on the legal protection of designs').

■ registration as a Community design;

■ protection as an unregistered Community design.

In some cases, a design may be protected by all four rights. This might apply, for example, in the design of a new piece of hardware which has been registered in the UK and as a registered Community design. Some designs cannot be protected by all of the rights, such as the design of the topography within a semiconductor product or the internal features not seen during the normal use of a product. Surface decoration and computer images such as icons and screen displays may be protected by all the rights apart from the UK unregistered design right.

First, the Community design is described then, so far as is relevant, aspects of the UK registered design followed by the UK unregistered design right. Finally, the modified version of the latter as applies to the topography of semiconductor products is discussed.

COMMUNITY DESIGN

The Community design regime provides for two forms of protection:

■ the registered Community design ('RCD'), acquired by registration at the Office for Harmonisation of the Internal Market (Trade Marks and Designs) ('OHIM'), presently situated in Alicante, Spain (registration lasts for five years and may be renewed for a further four five-year periods, making a total possible protection of 25 years); and

■ the unregistered Community design ('UCD') which comes into being when products to the design are first made available to the public but only lasts for three years from that date.

In both cases, the design right has a unitary nature and is of equal effect throughout the European Community. It can only be transferred, surrendered, made subject to a declaration of invalidity or its use prohibited in respect of the entire Community. The Community design rights are provided for by the Community Design Regulation[2] and OHIM commenced accepting applications for the registered Community design on 1 January 2003. The protection afforded by the unregistered Community design has been available as from 6 March 2002. Registration of designs as Community designs has proved very popular. One reason is the fee structure which is fairly modest. Currently, the registration fee is €230 and the publication fee is €120. There are reduced fees for additional registrations. Renewal fees vary from €90 to €180. Applications can be made direct to the OHIM or through the UK Patent Office which charges a £15 handling fee. The examination process is minimal and there are no provisions for opposition but, once a design has been registered and published, an application for invalidity may be made. It is also possible to apply for a registered Community design online.

Definitions

The definitions of 'design', 'product' and 'complex product' are important in determining what designs can be registered and/or protected by the UCD. They are set out in Article 3 as follows.

(a) 'Design' means the appearance of the whole or a part of a product resulting from the features of, in particular, the lines, contours, colours, shape, texture and/or materials of the product itself and/or its ornamentation.

(b) 'Product' means any industrial or handicraft item, including *inter alia* parts intended to be

---

[2] Council Regulation (EC) No. 6/2002 of 12 December 2001 on Community designs, OJ L 3, 5.1.2002, p. 1.

assembled into a complex product, packaging, get-up, graphic symbols and typographic typefaces, but excluding computer programs.

(c) 'Complex product' means a product which is composed of multiple components which can be replaced permitting disassembly and re-assembly of the product.

It can be seen that these definitions are quite wide and can apply to computer icons and displays and to software fonts (computer-generated images and icons are discussed in more depth later in the chapter). These could be said to be applied to a tangible product, being a computer or mobile telephone, for example. The inclusion of graphic symbols and typographic typefaces in the meaning of product makes this plain. In any case, the inclusion of graphic symbols indicates that products are not limited to physical entities. However, some of the exclusions from protection by Community design appear to apply only to physical products, such as an exclusion for features enabling mechanical connectivity.

The exclusion of computer programs from the meaning of product is simply because they are protected by copyright law which has been harmonised throughout Europe for computer programs. This exclusion does not extend to other forms of software and the fact that a computer program generates a graphic symbol does not prevent protection of the graphic symbol, as such. Otherwise, copyright protection for designs, where available in each Member State, is not prejudiced and designs may also be protected by other laws, where appropriate, such as trade marks, patents, unfair competition laws and national unregistered design rights such as that available in the UK.

Apart from complying with the definitions, designs must be new, have individual character and not be excluded to be protected by registration or by the UCD.

Novelty and individual character

Article 4 of the Community Design Regulation states that a design shall be protected by the Community design to the extent that it is new and has an individual character. This means that a design may comprise a combination of elements that are not new or do not have individual character provided other elements are new and have individual character. Of course, where this is the case, protection will only extend to the parts which are new and have individual character.

If the product to which the design has been applied is a component part of a complex product it is not considered to be new and have individual character if the parts which remain visible during normal use are new and have individual character. Therefore, 'under-the-bonnet' component parts, for example, parts of the engine of a car, are not protected. Normal use is use by the end user and does not include maintenance, servicing or repair work.

Novelty

A design is new if it, or a design differing only in immaterial details, has not been made available to the public: Article 5. For the RCD, the date at which this is tested is the date the application to register was filed. However, if the priority of an application previously made in the preceding six months is claimed, novelty is tested at the priority date (that is the date of filing that previous application). Typically, for example, a designer may apply to register the design in the UK under the Registered Designs Act 1949 and then he will have six months to file applications elsewhere, claiming the priority of that first application. For the UCD, the date is date the design was first made available to the public.

Article 7 of the Community Design Regulation expands upon the meaning of novelty. A design has been made available to the public if it has been published (following registration or otherwise), exhibited, used in trade or otherwise disclosed to the public before the filing date or priority date, if there is one, for the RCD or the date the UCD was first made available to the public. However, such disclosures will be ignored in certain situations, including if the design could not reasonably have become known in the normal course of business to persons carrying on business in the Community and specialising in the sector concerned or if the disclosure was made in confidence or if the disclosure was made by the designer himself in the 12-month period before filing the application. This latter provision allows a designer to market products made to the design for up to 12-months before applying to register his design without compromising novelty. This allows designers to test their designs on the market before deciding whether it is worthwhile applying for registration. In the meantime, protection by the UCD is available to bring infringement proceedings against copyists. The advantage of registration is that it does not require proof of copying. The 12-month period of grace also applies if a design has been made available to the public as a consequence of some abuse in relation to the designer. This must extend to situations such as where there has been a breach of confidence and other situations, for example, where a designer has contracted with a manufacturer to make products to the designs and the designer has placed them on the market earlier than provided for by the contract.

Individual character

Whether a design has an individual character is assessed by considering if the overall impression it produces on the informed user differs from the overall impression produced on such a user by any design which has been made available to the public. The degree of design freedom of the author in creating the design is taken into account. Therefore, where the designer has little design freedom, a design in which some small details are different from what has previously been made available may suffice for registration. When a design is made available to the public is the same as for novelty.

The informed user is not defined but can be taken to be someone who takes an interest in products of the type to which the design has been applied. The OHIM has said that the informed user is someone familiar with the basic features of the design in question who will pay more attention to dissimilarities than to similarities and who will be aware of the prior art in the business sector.

Exclusions

Features of the appearance of a product that are solely dictated by technical function are excluded under Article 8. Note the use of the word 'solely'. Even though some features may fall within the technical function exclusion, other features of the appearance of a product may be protected as a design can apply to the whole or part of a product. Also excluded are features of the appearance of a product which relate to interconnections or positioning against other products but that does not prevent the registration of component parts of modular systems. Designs which are contrary to public policy or morality are also excluded from protection by the Community design.

There is a transitional provision in that component parts of complex products, used for the purposes of repair so as to restore the original appearance of the complex product, are not protected: Article 110. Typically, this prevents protection of replacement body panels for vehicles. This may be subject to an amendment to the Community Design Regulation although it is now unlikely that there will be any change to this. Under the harmonised national registered design laws, this was an area of some controversy and Member States were allowed to retain their previous laws on whether such spare parts could be protected by registration. The UK does not protect such 'must-match' spare parts unlike some countries, such as France. There is a proposal to prevent protection through national registered design law for must-match spare parts.

10

Design law

Entitlement to and dealing with a Community design

The designer or his successor in title is entitled to the right in a Community design: Article 14. Where the design has been developed by two or more persons, the right in the design vests in them jointly. Where the designer is an employee who developed the design in the execution of his duties or following instructions given by his employer, the employer will be entitled to the right in the design, unless otherwise agreed or specified under national law.

There are no provisions for entitlement of designs created under a commission. This is unlike the position under the Registered Designs Act 1949, section 2 which states that, where the design was made in pursuance of a commission for money or money's worth, the commissioner is entitled to be the first proprietor. There is similar provision in respect of the UK's unregistered design right. Should an issue concerning entitlement to a Community design created under a commission come before the courts of England and Wales, it is likely that the person commissioning the creation of the design would be deemed to be the beneficial owner of it.

The right to a Community design is a property right and may be dealt with accordingly as with other intellectual property rights. Dealing with a Community design is subject to the relevant national law as regards the formalities. For example, if the holder of a Community design is an English or Welsh company, it will be the law of England and Wales. The Community design may be assigned (but only in respect of the whole Community), though it may be licensed separately. For example, a Community design may be licensed to X for the UK and Ireland and to Y for the remainder of the Community. Certain forms of transaction involving the RCD must be entered on the register (for example, transfer of ownership) and the OHIM requires certain formalities to be complied with to prove the transaction has taken place.

Infringement, remedies and limitation of rights

Article 19 spells out what acts infringe the Community design. For the RCD a person infringes the design is he uses the design without the consent of the proprietor. Use means in particular, making, offering, putting on the market, importing, exporting or using a product in which the design is incorporated or stocking a product for those purposes.

For the UCD, the same acts infringe but proof of copying is also required. Copying is not to be inferred where the design in question was an independent work of creation and it is reasonably thought that its designer was not familiar with the design made available to the public by the holder. Copying also must be shown where publication of the RCD has been deferred until such time as it is published. Deferred publication reduces the initial fees and allows the designer to keep his design private for up to 30 months. This might be useful where there is likely to be a delay between filing for registration and the launch of the products to which the design will be applied.

For both the RCD and UCD, the scope of protection includes any design which does not produce on the informed user a different overall impression. Design freedom is taken into consideration.

Some remedies are spelt out in the Community Design Regulation such as an order prohibiting the acts complained of (an injunction in England, Wales and Northern Ireland or interdict in Scotland) and an order to seize infringing products. Other remedies are left to Member States. In the UK, this will include damages or an account of profits. Interim relief is also a possibility, such as an interim injunction prohibiting certain acts until the full trial of the issues.

As with patents and trade marks (and the UK unregistered design right) there is an action for remedies where groundless threats of infringement actions are made. This is provided for by the UK's Community Design Regulations 2005. In *Quads 4 Kids* v *Colin Campbell* [2006] EWHC

2482 (Ch), the judge accepted that it was seriously arguable that statements made to eBay through its VeRO service (standing for Verified Rights Owner) constituted a threat of infringement proceedings. Dr Campbell had registered 16 designs as Community designs but had deferred publication of them. This reduces the fees until publication which can be up to 30 months later. Dr Campbell informed eBay through VeRO that quad bikes listed by the claimant infringed his Community designs. eBay has a policy of removing listings following such notification. This was described as an institutionalised avoidance of litigation. The judge considered that, in view of the arguable case that there was a groundless threat the granting of an injunction against continuation of the threats was appropriate. Dr Campbell, described by the judge as being of modest means, had indicated that he would be reluctant to commence proceedings for infringement.

Article 20 sets out limitations to the rights of the holder of a Community design. The following do not infringe the Community design:

- acts done privately and for non-commercial purposes;
- acts done for experimental purposes;
- acts of reproduction for the purposes of making citations or teaching if compatible with fair trade practice, do not unduly prejudice the normal exploitation of the design and mention is made of the source;
- acts of repairing ships and aircraft registered in countries outside the Community which are temporarily within the territory of the Community, including importing spare parts for this purpose.

The doctrine of exhaustion of rights applies so that the holder of a Community design cannot use his right to prevent the further commercialisation of products which have been placed on the market within the territory of the Community by him or with his consent.

Invalidity and surrender

A Community design may be declared invalid as a result of an application or by way of a counterclaim in infringement proceedings. The grounds for invalidity are set out in Article 25 of the Community Design Regulation and are:

- if the design does not conform to the definition of design;
- if it does not fulfil the requirements of Article 4 to 9 (novelty, individual character and not excluded);
- if because of a court decision, the rightholder is not entitled to it under Article 14;
- in the case only of the RCD, if it is in conflict with a prior design which was not published at the filing date or priority date (if there was one) of the design in question (includes national prior designs);
- where there is a conflicting earlier distinctive sign (for example, a trade mark) and Community law or national gives the rightholder or the sign the right to prevent use of the Community design;
- if the design is an unauthorised use of a work of copyright protected in a Member State;
- if the design constitutes an improper use of any of the items listed in Article 6ter of the Paris Convention for the Protection of Industrial Property (for example, armorial bearings, flags and State emblems and hallmarks) or of badges, emblems and escutcheons other than those covered by the Article 6ter and which are of particular public interest in a Member State.

10

Design law

Where invalidity is based on the existence of an earlier conflicting right, generally, the ground can only be invoked by the holder of that right. The effect of a finding of invalidity are that the design is deemed never to have been protected. There are some provisions to deal with past infringement actions and transactions.

A RCD can be surrendered at any time and takes effect when entered on the register: Article 51. Any person having a right under the design which has been entered into the register must consent (for example, a mortagee) and any licensee entered on the register must be informed of the intention to surrender the design.

UK REGISTERED DESIGNS

The UK registered design is provided for under Registered Designs Act 1949, as amended, together with subordinate legislation. To all intents and purposes it is virtually the same as the RCD in terms of registrability and duration except of course, it only applies to the territory of the UK and other territories to which it has been extended such as Gibraltar and the Isle of Man.

It has already been noted that the provisions on entitlement are different in that particular mention is made of commissioned designs, for which the person commissioning the design is entitled to be the first proprietor. Any other differences are generally minor in nature and beyond the scope of this book.[3]

COMPUTER-GENERATED IMAGES AND ICONS

Before changes made to UK registered designs law under the Directive on the legal protection of designs, a 'design' was defined in the Registered Designs Act 1949 as being '. . . features of shape, configuration, pattern or ornament applied to an article by any industrial process . . .' and 'article' was defined as '. . . any article of manufacture and includes any part of an article if that part is made and sold separately'. These definitions, together with the requirement that a design be applied to an article by an *industrial process* appeared to rule out the registrability of computer-generated images, such as computer icons and graphical user interfaces (GUIs). The UK Designs Registry practice at the time was that a graphic symbol displayed on a computer screen, *per se*, was not an article and, hence, not registrable as a design. However, a distinction was made in one case. In *Suwa Siekosha's Design Application* [1982] RPC 166, icons displayed on digital watches were held to be registrable as the symbols were built into the watches (that is, the code to produce them was in an integrated circuit built into the watch). Nevertheless, this was the exception and the number of registrations for computer-generated images in a wide sense was negligible.

Under the old law, the question came up again in *Apple Computer Inc's Design Applications* [2002] FSR 38. In that case, an application was made to register computer icons as designs. The application was stated to be in relation to a 'set of user interfaces for computer display'. The hearing officer at the Designs Registry considered that applying a design to a computer screen by a computer program did not involve an industrial process and, furthermore, a user interface was not an article. On appeal to the Registered Designs Tribunal, Mr Justice Jacob thought the issue was basically one of semantics and modifying the description of the article to which the design was applied might overcome the objection. A suggestion was 'a computer with an operating system which displays the icons concerned'. Jacob J's view was that, where icons are inherently built into a computer's operating system, the requirement for industrial application would be

---

[3] Further description of the UK registered design is given in Bainbridge, D. (2007) *Intellectual Property*, 6th edn, Longman.

satisfied, as opposed to the display of icons produced by running a particular computer program. Apple eventually was able to obtain registration of the icons by describing the articles as 'computer display screens with computer-generated icon'.

As a result of the *Apple* case, the position immediately preceding the significant changes made by the Registered Designs Regulations 2001 (which made substantial changes to the 1949 Act to bring it in line with the Directive on the legal protection of designs) was that graphic symbols including icons and other forms of GUIs were potentially registrable as designs providing they were:

- produced by the computer's operating system; and
- were permanently and inherently built into the computer (or mobile telephone or other item of hardware for that matter).

On the other hand, graphic symbols and images produced by applications software were not registrable, as they were not built into the computer: they were not an intrinsic part of the computer.

The position is very different now. We have seen the definitions of 'design' and 'product' in the Community Design Regulation which mirror those in the Directive on the legal protection of designs. These definitions are considerably wider than under the old law. The provisions now relating to the UK registered design and, of course, the Community design clearly permit the registration of images generated on computer screen displays and mobile telephones, digital watches, digital cameras and so on. Even though computer programs are excluded from the definition of 'design', this does not extend to images such as icons generated by running computer programs, whether operating system or applications programs. Providing the other requirements, such as novelty and individual character, are satisfied, there should be no difficulty in registering computer-generated images, icons and even webpage designs. The computer and information technology industry and companies with e-business operations were at first quite slow off the mark to realise that such things can be protected by registration. At the time of writing there are on the UK register of designs 106 registrations for icons (Locarno class 14.02.13) and 66 for interfaces and webpages, etc. (Locarno 14.02.14). A few are scattered about in other classes. ('Locarno' refers to the Locarno Agreement Establishing an International Classification for Industrial Designs, 1968, and is administered by the World Intellectual Property Organisation. At the time of writing, 45 states apply the Locarno classification.) Relatively few applications (no more than a few dozen) have been made at the OHIM to register icons and graphic symbols as Community designs.

An inspection of those computer icons and screen displays, including webpages, that have been registered in the UK gives some cause for concern. Many of the icons registered seem very simple or commonplace and it is questionable whether they possess an individual character. Some registrations include numerous representations, for example, showing different variants of a screen display or sequential steps in a series of screen displays. In this way, very strong monopolies are being obtained, relatively easily and at little expense. Quite a few screen displays for games have been registered. Unlike the case with trade mark law (and in respect of graphic symbols, the overlap between trade marks and designs is particularly strong) there is no requirement that the design is put to use. There is a danger that speculative designs may be registered in the hope that computer companies and e-commerce organisations may have to 'buy' conflicting registered designs or redesign the images they use. The danger of such conflicts is all the greater because, unlike the case with registered trade marks, it is less likely that searches of registered designs will be made before committing to a particular set of icons or webpage designs.

As will be seen in the following chapter, the law of passing off is effective against those who registered famous names as internet domain names, hoping to sell them on for a large profit. However, registered design law is different and provides more opportunity for pre-emptive registrations of designs which are not similar to existing designs but which may turn out to be similar to designs later created for use as graphic images. In the *Apple* case mentioned above, Mr Justice Jacob thought that the fact that registration of computer icons and the like as designs under the new law meant that the legislators did not think that registration of icons and other graphic images used with computers, mobile telephones, etc. would lead to a 'floodgates disaster' situation. It remains to be seen whether he was right to so conclude. To give an insight into the dangers that might lie ahead, consider the Windows operating system environment, first invented by the Xerox Corporation at its Palo Alto Research Center. Had that been newly developed and registered as a Community design competitors could have been kept out of the field throughout the European Community for 25 years, something copyright would not have been able to do as effectively providing only the basic idea of such a system was used to develop other Windows systems.

THE UK UNREGISTERED DESIGN RIGHT

The UK unregistered design right (hereafter the 'design right') can usefully protect the shape of items of computer hardware such as laptop computers, handheld devices such as personal playstations and palmtops and other items of electronic goods including mobile phones. In many cases, however, these will be subject to registered design rights (UK and Community design) as well as the unregistered Community design. A modified version of the UK design right protects topographies of semiconductor products if they were original and not commonplace when created.

Like copyright, the design right is automatic and does not depend on registration but, unlike registered designs, there is no requirement for the design to relate to the appearance of a product, although if it does, it is not barred from protection by the design right. The result is that there is an overlap with registered designs but not all designs that are registrable are subject to the design right and not all designs in which design right subsists are registrable under the Registered Designs Act 1949 or under the Community Design Regulation. Where there is an overlap, the potentially longer duration of registered designs is the main reason why a design should be registered. Another reason is that a registered design gives a monopoly right while infringement of a design right depends on proof of copying. The design right does not apply to designs created prior to 1 August 1989.

Subsistence

A 'design' in the context of the design right is, by section 213 of the Copyright, Designs and Patents Act 1988:

> ... the design of any aspect of the shape or configuration (whether external or internal) of the whole or part of the article.

It might be thought that the article to which a design subject to the design right is applied must be three-dimensional but this is not necessarily the case. For example, a shape might be formed by cutting it out of a piece of card. A configuration could be an arrangement of parts, for example, components placed on a printed circuit board or even the printed circuit itself without the components fixed into position. An arrangement of 'colourways' in a garment, however, has been held not to be a configuration in *Lambretta Clothing Co Ltd* v *Teddy Smith (UK) Ltd* [2005] RPC 88.

The design right applies to all manner of industrial designs whether functional or not and whether visible in normal use or not. A design must be original and section 213(4) states that a design is not original if it is commonplace in the design field in question at the time of its creation. It has been held, in *C & H Engineering* v *F Klucznik & Sons Ltd* [1992] FSR 421, that this requires a two-stage test. First, is the design original in a copyright sense; that is, did the design originate from the author? If the answer is 'yes', then secondly it must be determined whether the design is commonplace (at the time of its creation). The design, therefore, must be the independent work of the designer which was not commonplace in the relevant field when created.

The test for originality was once more considered in *Ocular Sciences Ltd* v *Aspect Vision Care Ltd* [1997] RPC 289. Mr Justice Laddie pointed out that the word 'commonplace' was new to English law and could be traced back to the Directive on the legal protection of semiconductor topographies,[4] discussed later in the chapter. He accepted as plausible a definition that any design which is 'trite, trivial, common-or-garden, hackneyed or of the type which would excite no peculiar attention in those in the relevant art is likely to be commonplace'. Nevertheless, that did not mean that a design which is made up of such commonplace features must necessarily itself be commonplace. A new and exciting design could be produced from the most trite of ingredients providing the combination itself is not commonplace.

The *Ocular Sciences* case is also authority for the view that the design right could protect detail differences, which may be too small to be readily distinguished by the naked eye. In that case, it was accepted that, in principle, the design right could apply to details of a range of soft contact lenses, although, in the event, Mr Justice Laddie decided that the designs, as a whole, were commonplace.

Exceptions

There are a number of exceptions to design rights and design right does not subsist in a method or principle of construction. Also excluded are features of shape or configuration of an article which:

- enable the article to be connected to, or placed in, around or against, another article so that either article may perform its function (a 'must-fit' exception); or
- are dependent upon the appearance of another article of which the article is intended by the designer to form an integral part (a 'must-match' exception).

These exceptions are significant for manufacturers and suppliers of spare parts. The former part of the exception applies to 'functional' spare parts which have to be a particular shape to fit another article. An exhaust pipe for a car will fall into this exception. Any piece of computer equipment which has to be fitted to some other equipment, such as a replacement 'card' (printed circuit board containing integrated circuits) which has to be a certain shape, or have a certain type of connector, in order to fit into a computer, will also fall into the first part of the exception.

The 'must-fit' exclusion is directed at rationalising the *British Leyland* case and it allows for the fact that persons who buy items of equipment which eventually may need replacement or additional parts should be able to obtain those parts in a free market at reasonable cost. If a design right monopoly were to be granted to spare parts, manufacturers of cars, washing machines, computers, etc. would be able to control the supply and price of spare parts and might be tempted to charge exorbitant prices for them. However, the *British Leyland* principle, sometimes referred to as a 'right to repair' has been shown to be of very limited scope and it is unlikely that it will be further developed by the courts. In *Canon Kabushiki Kaisha* v *Green Cartridge Co (Hong Kong) Ltd* [1997] FSR 817, the defendant made replacement toner cartridges for laser printers and photocopying machines. The Judicial Committee of the Privy Council held that this

[4] Council Directive 87/54/EEC of 16 December 1986 on the legal protection of topographies of semiconductor products OJ L 24, 27.01.1987, p. 36 (the 'Directive on the legal protection of topographies of semiconductor products').

went beyond the concept of repair. In a patents case, the House of Lords confirmed that the concept of repair was a narrow one and did not permit the replacement of so much of a product being the subject matter of a patent such that it could be said that the effect was that a new product was made; *United Wire Ltd* v *Screen Repair Services (Scotland) Ltd* [2001] FSR 24. In terms of the design right, the better view is that the *British Leyland* principle is no longer applicable leaving the scope of the right to be determined only in the light of the specific exclusions in the part of the Copyright, Designs and Patents Act 1988 covering design right.

The second part of the exception would apply typically to spare parts such as replacement body panels for cars where the design is dictated by the appearance of the car, but it is unlikely that many computer spare parts will fall into this category, although it could apply in respect of replacement parts for items of computer equipment, having visual significance, intended to replace some worn out or damaged part. A further exception to design right protection is surface decoration, being more appropriately protected by registration as a design.

The surface decoration exception was considered in *Mark Wilkinson Furniture Ltd* v *Woodcraft Designs (Radcliffe) Ltd* [1998] FSR 63, a case concerning fitted kitchen furniture. It was said, in that context, that the exclusion was not restricted to features lying on the surface which were essentially two-dimensional such as a painted finish but could extend to other features such as small grooves. However, other features might not be excepted where, for example, they themselves were subject to surface decoration. A cornice or recessed door panel might be subject to the right. In *Lambretta Clothing Co Ltd* v *Teddy Smith (UK) Ltd* [2005] RPC 88, the Court of Appeal accepted that a coloured pattern which ran right through the material of a garment was surface decoration.

Ownership and duration

With registered designs, the person creating the design is known as the author but, and for no explicable reason, the person creating a design which is subject to a design right is known as its designer. The owner of a design right is the designer unless he creates the design in the course of his employment or has been commissioned to create it. A computer-generated design belongs to the person making the arrangements necessary for the creation of the design. Design right lasts for 15 years from the end of the calendar year in which it was first recorded in a design document (which includes storage in a computer) or an article was made to the design, unless articles have been made available for sale or hire within the first five years, in which case the right lasts only a further 10 years.

The result of the provisions relating to duration is that the owner of the right can only have a maximum of 10 years to exploit the design commercially. This period will be reduced if the owner fails to market articles made to the design within the first five years. Effectively, and in a commercial sense, the right lasts for 10 years with the owner being given a five-year breathing space within which to bring articles made to the design to the market place. The right is further diluted because licences are available as of right during the last five years. This means that anyone can exploit the design during its last five years subject to the payment of a royalty to the design right owner. Failing agreement of the terms of the licence, the Comptroller-General of Patents, Designs and Trade Marks will settle the terms.

Infringement and remedies

Infringement occurs when a person makes articles to the design or makes a design document recording the design for the purpose of enabling such articles to be made. This covers identical articles and articles made to substantially the same design. There are also secondary infringements where a person 'deals' with infringing articles, for example, by importing, selling or hiring. Remedies for infringement are as for copyright but there are no criminal penalties for dealing with infringing articles. In *C & H Engineering* v *F Klucznik & Sons Ltd* [1992] FSR 421, the defendant claimed his design right in a pig fender, a three-sided box structure, had been infringed. The 'original' part of the design was a round bar welded around the top. Aldous J said the question of infringement involved an objective test through the eyes of a person to whom the design is directed (in this case, a pig farmer). There was no infringement here because the claimant's and defendant's articles were not exactly or substantially the same. Although a design can relate to a part of an article, it seems that the whole article must be looked at when deciding infringement.

SEMICONDUCTOR TOPOGRAPHIES

Integrated circuits, commonly known as 'silicon chips' or, simply, 'chips', are of tremendous importance to the computer industry and to other areas of industry and commerce which rely heavily on information technology. The simplest integrated circuit consists of three layers, one of which is made of semiconductor material. A semiconducting material, in terms of its ability to conduct electricity, is one which lies between a conductor such as copper and an insulator such as rubber. Examples of semiconducting materials include silicon, germanium, selenium and gallium arsenide.

The patterns formed by the processes of etching and/or evaporation of the conducting layer of chip makes its electrical circuitry. These patterns represent the circuit design. The processes involved in the making of integrated circuits fall within the province of patent law and the first patents for integrated circuits were filed in the late 1950s, the most important one being developed by Noyce of the Fairchild Semiconductor Corporation in 1959. Licences were readily available and in 1961 the first chips were available commercially. Since the early patents expired some time ago, much of the know-how lies in the public domain. It is essential that the considerable effort that goes into the design and development of new integrated circuits is protected. In some cases, new designs of integrated circuits may be patentable as could be a new process for the manufacture of integrated circuits (which indirectly protects the product derived from using that process). Finally, a computer program product (being a computer program installed on an integrated circuit) could be claimed in a patent application if, when run in a computer, it produces a technical effect.

Semiconductor design right

It was once thought that integrated circuits were protected by copyright through drawings or photographs as most of the masks used in the manufacturing process were produced photographically and would be protected as photographs. However, protection varied throughout Europe and eventually there was a Directive on the legal protection of the topographies of semiconductor products. In the UK this was implemented by the Semiconductor Products (Protection of Topography) Regulations 1987. However, it was decided to replace these Regulations with an amended version of the new design right by the Design Right (Semiconductor Regulations) 1989, which came into force on 1 August 1989. The result was that the 'semiconductor design right' is protected by a modified version of Part III of the Copyright, Designs and Patents Act 1988 which provides for the design right.

The 1989 Regulations are similar to the 1987 Regulations in several respects: for example, it is the topography of a semiconductor which is protected, being, by Regulation 2, a design which is either:

  (a) the pattern fixed, or intended to be fixed, in or upon
      (i) a layer of a semiconductor product, or
      (ii) a layer of material in the course of and for the purpose of the manufacture of a semiconductor product, or
  (b) the arrangement of the patterns fixed, or intended to be fixed, in or upon the layers of a semiconductor product in relation to one another.

A semiconductor product is defined as:

> ... an article the purpose, or one of the purposes, of which is the performance of an electronic function and which consists of two or more layers, at least one of which is composed of semiconducting material and in or upon one or more of which is fixed a pattern appertaining to that or another function.

These definitions are not very helpful being somewhat tautologous but despite that it is fairly plain that all original integrated circuits will be covered by the Regulations. If the description of integrated circuits given earlier is now considered, it can be seen that the requirements are met: there are two or more layers (usually three), one layer is made of a semiconducting material and a pattern is fixed upon it for the purpose of performing an electronic function. Normally, the ingenuity which requires protection is in the circuitry represented by the patterns formed by the conducting materials, but the Regulations are wider in the sense that they will apply in situations where the ingenuity lies not so much in the horizontal patterns themselves but in the vertical arrangement of layers.

Subsistence and ownership

To be protected, the semiconductor topography must be original and it is not original if it is commonplace in the design field in question at the time of its creation: section 213 of the Copyright, Designs and Patents Act 1988. What has been said above about the meaning of 'original' and commonplace in respect of the design right generally applies here also. Incidentally, this test which also applies to the design right generally derives directly from the Directive on the legal protection of topographies of semiconductor products, Article 2(2) of which states:

> The topography of a semiconductor topography shall be protected in so far as it satisfies the conditions that it is the result of its creator's own intellectual effort and is not commonplace in the semiconductor industry.

Note the preferred European definition of originality being the creator's own intellectual effort, a similar test to that used in respect of copyright databases and, although not expressly stated in the Copyright, Designs and Patents Act 1988, computer programs. It is arguable that the UK model of protection for semiconductor topographies is unsatisfactory as the first part of the test remains that of originality not intellectual effort. The traditional UK approach to originality has been fairly generous, as discussed in Chapter 5 in relation to databases.

Article 2(2) goes on to confirm that where a topography comprises commonplace elements, it may still be protected if, taken as whole, the conditions of intellectual creation and not being commonplace are satisfied. Apart from being required to be original (and not commonplace), the design has to qualify for protection. Qualification is based on the citizenship or domicile of the creator of the topography (or his employer or commissioner) or the person by whom and country in which semiconductors containing the topography are first marketed.

The qualification requirements are similar to those that apply in respect of the design right but there are a number of differences. In particular, the rule that a commissioned design qualifies by virtue of the commissioner (if he is a qualifying person) is subject to any agreement in writing to the contrary. This proviso is missing from the basic design right model. The same applies to designs created in the course of employment. There is also a change with respect to semiconductor designs which qualify by virtue of the first marketing, in that the person must be exclusively authorised to put the semiconductor products on the market in every Member State of the European Community, whereas for other designs the exclusivity relates to the UK only. There are a number of other differences concerning territorial scope for qualification purposes. Protection is also afforded to semiconductor topography designs to persons from the Isle of Man, the Channel Islands and any colony and to firms or companies formed under the law of Gibraltar and to firms or companies having a substantial business activity in a number of other countries including the other states of the European Economic Area, Japan, Switzerland and the US.

Ownership of the semiconductor design right is dealt with by amending section 215 of the 1988 Act. The first owner of the right is the designer unless the design is created in pursuance of a commission or in the course of employment in which cases the commissioner or the employer respectively is the first owner of the right, subject to any written agreement to the contrary. If the right arises by reference to the first marketing of the article, such as where a semiconductor topography is designed by a Brazilian in Brazil but is marketed in the UK by an importer who is exclusively authorised to put articles made to the design on the market in every Member State of the European Community, then the importer will be deemed to own the semiconductor design right. By section 214 of the 1988 Act, the designer is the person who creates the design and in the case of a computer-generated design, the designer is the person by whom the arrangements necessary for the creation of the design are undertaken. The recognition of computer-generated topographies was added by the 1989 Regulations.

Duration

The duration of the semiconductor design right depends on if and when the topography is commercially exploited. Normally, by section 216 of the 1988 Act, the right endures for 10 years from the end of the year in which it was first commercially exploited (anywhere in the world). If the right is not commercially exploited within 15 years of the creation of the topography, however, the right expires 15 years from the time the topography was first recorded in a design document or the time when an article was first made to the design, whichever is the earlier. Unlike the case with other designs subject to the design right, under Regulation 9 of the 1989 Regulations, licences of right are not available in relation to semiconductor topographies.

Rights and infringement

The semiconductor design right is, by section 226(1) of the 1988 Act as substituted for semiconductor topographies, the exclusive right to reproduce the design by making articles to that design or by making a design document (which includes data stored in a computer) recording the design for the purpose of enabling such articles to be made. A person doing either of the above infringes the right whether he does it in relation to the whole or a substantial part of the topography. There are important exceptions to infringement connected with research, non-commercial or educational purposes. The regulations have one very unusual effect in that it is permissible to make a reproduction of a topography for the purpose of analysing or evaluating that topography or the concepts, processes, systems or techniques embodied in it by section 226(1A) of the 1988 Act as substituted. Furthermore, by Regulation 8(4), it is not an infringement of the semiconductor design right to create another original topography as a result of such analysis or evaluation or to reproduce that other topography. Therefore, a form of 'reverse engineering' is positively encouraged allowing the knowledge gained from an inspection of an existing topography to be used in the design of a new topography. In practice, a limiting factor will be the requirement for the new topography to be original and not commonplace. On reflection, this exception is probably justified on the grounds that to provide otherwise might inhibit innovation in this very fast-moving field where the existing technology is being built upon all the time while property rights still subsist in that existing technology.

If an infringement of a topography right also infringes copyright, the semiconductor design right is suppressed leaving remedies to be pursued under copyright law only, by section 236 of the 1988 Act. This is the same as with other designs. Regard must be had to section 51 of the Copyright, Designs and Patents Act 1988, however, which removes from the scope of copyright infringement the making of articles to designs recorded in design documents (or embodied in models) unless the design is for an artistic work. It is highly unlikely that semiconductor designs will be considered to be artistic works. Design documents include drawings, photographs and computer data and the effect of section 51 is to suppress copyright protection from semiconductor topographies leaving the modified design right with its limited duration as the only form of legal protection, apart from the law of confidence which will protect until, at least, the semiconductor products are made available to the public.

Remedies for infringement

Remedies for infringement are as for the design right generally and are injunctions, damages and accounts of profits 'or otherwise': section 229 of the 1988 Act. Additional damages are also provided for as they are for copyright infringement and the unregistered design right generally. Orders for delivery up and destruction are also available. In the case of innocent infringement (if the defendant did not know and had no reason to believe that the semiconductor design right subsisted in the article) damages are not available although other remedies may be, such as an account of profits.

SUMMARY

- There are four forms of design law:
  - registered Community design (can last for up to 25 years);
  - unregistered Community design (only lasts three years);
  - UK registered design (can last for up to 25 years);
  - UK unregistered design right (can last up to 15 years but only 10 years of commercial exploitation).
- For the Community design (both forms) and the UK registered design:
  - the designs must be new and have individual character;
  - there are a number of exclusions, such as 'under-the-bonnet' parts, spare parts to restore the original appearance of a complex article, technical function and interconnections.
- The Community design (both forms) and the UK registered design can protect graphic symbols, such as computer images and icons.
- Registered designs gives a monopoly protection (unless during deferred publication).
- The unregistered Community design and the UK unregistered design right give protection against copying (as does registered designs subject to deferred publication).
- The UK unregistered design right protects shape and configuration of original designs which were not commonplace in the design field in question at the time of their creation.
- A modified version of the UK unregistered design right protects the topographies of semiconductor products.

- Licences of right are available for the UK unregistered design right during the last five years but not for semiconductor topographies.

- There is a remedy of groundless threats of infringement proceedings for all design rights.

SELF-TEST QUESTIONS

Note: there is only one correct answer to each multiple choice question.

1   Smita lives in England and designed a set of new icons for mobile phone screens which had individual character. She immediately showed her new design to Eric, a friend who normally lives in France. She told him the design was secret. Six months later Smita licensed the icons to VIP Telecomms Ltd which applied them to its mobile phones and put them on sale in the UK within the next month. It is now 14 months since Smita developed her new design but she has just discovered that FranceTel SA has been selling mobile phones in France which bear her icons for the last 10 months. FranceTel SA obtained the designs of the icons from Eric. Which one of the following statements is CORRECT in relation to Community design? Smita had not applied to register the designs anywhere previously.

(a) Smita's designs can be registered as Community designs as they are still new because the abuse in relation to her by Eric and the commercialisation by VIP Telecomms Ltd both happened within the last 12 months and the period of grace applies.

(b) Smita's designs cannot be registered as Community designs because, being graphic symbols, they do not fall within the meaning of 'product' for the purposes of the Community Design Regulation.

(c) Smita's designs are no longer novel as the 12-month period of grace only applies if Smita herself put the mobile phones bearing the designs on the market.

(d) Smita cannot register the design as Community designs as they are no longer novel but she can sue FranceTel SA in France on the basis of the UK unregistered design right which will subsist in her original designs.

2   Which one of the following CORRECTLY describes the test for individual character for the Community design and the UK registered design?

(a) Individual character is assessed from the perspective of the consumer who is taken to be reasonably well-informed and circumspect but has an imperfect recollection of designs already on the market.

(b) To have individual character, a design must be original and not commonplace in the design field in question at the time of its creation.

(c) Individual character requires that a design must be novel, involve an inventive step and be capable of industrial application and not be excluded from the grant of a registered design.

(d) A design has individual character if the overall impression it produces on the informed user differs to the overall impression produced on such a user by any design which has been made available to the public.

3   Which one of the following features or designs is NOT expressly excluded from protection by Community design?

(a) Designs which are contrary to public policy or morality.

(b) Features which are methods or principles of construction.

    (c) Features of the appearance of a product dictated by technical function.

    (d) Features of the appearance of a product which must necessarily be reproduced in their exact form and dimensions in order to permit the product in which the design is incorporated or to which it is applied to be mechanically connected to or placed in, around or against another product so that either product may perform its function.

4   **Which one of the following statements in relation to the protection of topographies of semi-conductor products by the modified version of the design right in line with the Directive is NOT CORRECT?**

    (a) It is permissible to make a reproduction of a semiconductor topography for the purpose of analysing or evaluating that topography or the concepts, processes, systems or techniques embodied in it.

    (b) The Directive on the legal protection of topographies on semiconductor products requires that the topography must be the result of the creator's own intellectual effort and is not common-place in the semiconductor industry.

    (c) The topography of a semiconductor product that consists only of elements that are common-place in the semiconductor industry can be subject to the semiconductor design right if the combination of those elements is itself an intellectual creation and not commonplace.

    (d) Licences of right are available during the last five years of the subsistence of protection.

5   **If the design of graphic symbols may be protected by the Community design and the UK registered design, bearing in mind that they are created by the operation of computer programs, is there any justification for excluding computer programs from the meaning of 'product', thus preventing their protection by these forms of design law?**

For further resources and updates please go to the Companion Website accompanying this book at **www.mylawchamber.co.uk/bainbridgeIT**

Trade marks, passing off and malicious falsehood

INTRODUCTION

Marks have been used to identify the makers of goods for thousands of years. Individual marks become associated with a particular product and with the quality of that product. As regards the value of a trade mark to a trader (for example, a manufacturer of goods or a provider of services), two factors are important: the buying public's familiarity with the mark and its experience of reasonable quality or value for money in the past associated with the mark. A trade mark which is used with a successful product, is of tremendous value to the owner of the mark and he will want to prevent others from using the mark or a similar one to capture some of his trade. From the perspective of a consumer, the association between a trader (referred to as an 'undertaking' in the legislation) and his goods or services allows the consumer to repeat a buying experience that has proved positive or to avoid repeating one that has proved unsatisfactory.

The primary function of a trade mark is to distinguish the goods or services of one trader from those of other traders, that is, to act as a 'badge of origin'. By fulfilling this function, trade mark law serves two main purposes: first it protects the goodwill and reputation which a trader has built up around the mark involved and, second, it prevents the public from being deceived as to the origin of goods or services. Trade mark law establishes a property right in the mark in question and requires that the mark be used (failure to use a mark for five or more years may result in it being revoked).

A trader who makes or sells goods or provides services may register a sign as a trade mark for specified goods or services in one or more classes of goods or services. This will give the owner of the mark a monopoly in the use of that mark in the goods or services for which the mark has been registered. There is a total of 34 classes of marks for goods (for example, chemicals, electrical goods and scientific apparatus, vehicles, clothing, fancy goods and smokers' articles) and a further 11 classes for services (for example, advertising and business, insurance and financial, telecommunications, transport, education and medical services). Trade marks for computers and software may be registered in Class 9 which includes data processing equipment and computers. A person providing services by designing and developing computer hardware and software would register a mark in Class 42 which includes installation, maintenance and repair of computer software, computer consultancy services, website design and keeping registers of domain names. Providing access to internet or portal services is covered in Class 38 which applies to telecommunications.

If anyone else uses the mark, or one deceptively similar, in the course of trade without the owner's permission, that person can be sued for infringement of the trade mark. Depending on the circumstances, a criminal offence may also be committed, as mentioned in Chapter 12. The remedies available to the owner of the trade mark are as usual: injunctions, damages or an account of profits as an alternative to damages, plus removal of offending marks. The infringing articles may be ordered to be destroyed if the offending marks cannot be removed.

In the computer industry, the power of trade marks can readily be seen as, in a relatively short space of time, names such as 'Apple', 'IBM', 'Oracle', 'Java', 'Windows' and 'Microsoft' became very well-known names. Trade marks are especially important in a fast-moving industry and it is very comforting to buy goods with familiar names when so many products and businesses come and go in rapid succession, as happened with microcomputers in the early 1980s. A familiar name or mark is very influential as many who buy computer hardware and software will look for a product which is likely to be of reasonable quality and will be supported in years to come. There have been few examples of trade mark infringement in the world of computers and most counterfeiters have used different names or marks: for example, copies of the Apple computer imported into Australia were called 'Wombats'. Other Apple look-alikes have been called 'Pineapples' and 'Microprofessors'. Perhaps this is a testimony to the effectiveness of trade mark law.

Until 1994 trade mark law was provided for by the Trade Marks Act 1938 which was widely recognised as being difficult, outdated and obscure in parts. The present law is contained in the Trade Marks Act 1994 which is a result of a trade marks Directive.[1] The 1994 Act marks a significant change in trade mark law and only a little of the case law under the 1938 Act and previous trade mark legislation is still relevant. Although the 1994 Act was seen as a welcome and much awaited improvement of trade mark law, that Act and the Directive have not been without their difficulties and together, they have generated an impressive amount of case law before the courts in the UK and the European Court of Justice.

An area of law related to trade marks is that of passing off. This applies where one trader passes off his goods or services as being those of another trader, typically hoping to 'cash in' on the goodwill and reputation of that other trader. It can be described loosely as a law protecting unregistered trade marks. Another area of law that might be relevant in terms of trade is that of malicious falsehood, sometimes referred to as trade libel. This could apply, for example, where one trader alleges that another trader's goods are defective. This chapter looks at all these three areas of law with reference, where appropriate, to information technology, in particular, the internet. There have been a surprising number of cases involving trade mark issues on the internet and cybersquatting, that is where someone registers a famous name as a domain name.

TRADE MARKS

Registered trade marks are a vital part of the intellectual property rights of most commercial and industrial undertakings. Protection of a trade mark by registration can be obtained by applying for a UK registered trade mark, a Community trade mark or through the Madrid System for the International Registration of Marks which allows trade marks to be obtained in a number of countries by means of a single application.[2] In this part of the chapter the focus is on the UK registered trade mark, with reference to other jurisdictions, as appropriate. Unlike the case with the UK registered design right, the UK registered trade mark system remains very popular. But first, it is worth mentioning the Community trade mark.

---

[1] First Council Directive 89/104/EEC of 21 December 1988 to approximate the laws of the Member States relating to trade marks, OJ L 40, 11.2.1989, p. 1 (the 'trade marks Directive').

[2] There are two parts to the Madrid System: the Madrid Agreement (which, at the time of writing has 55 Member States), and the Madrid Protocol (which has 70 Member States including the UK, the US and the European Community).

Community trade mark

Apart from the national systems of trade marks (substantially but not completely harmonised by the trade marks Directive), there is also a Community trade mark ('CTM') which gives the proprietor of the trade mark a single registration at the Office for Harmonisation of the Internal Market (Trade Marks and Designs) ('OHIM') which has effect throughout the European Community. The CTM is described as having unitary effect, that is, validity throughout the Community. The OHIM commenced accepting applications to register Community trade marks on 1 January 1996 and the provisions governing the registrability, infringement and validity of a CTM are, to all intents and purposes, the same as those applicable to the UK registered trade mark, the main difference being, of course, that the latter only has effect in the UK and any other country to which it has been extended to apply, such as the Isle of Man.

The OHIM has its own Boards of Appeals to hear appeals against decisions of the trade mark examiners at the OHIM. Subsequent appeals are brought before the European Court of First Instance from where appeals may be brought before the Court of Justice of the European Communities (the European Court of Justice). In terms of trade mark law in Member States, references for preliminary rulings on the interpretation of the harmonising Directive are submitted to the European Court of Justice. This is where there is some doubt as to the meaning of a provision in the Directive arising in a national court.

Although the main aspects of the CTM look very similar to those for the harmonised national trade mark systems, it has been made clear that it is a completely separate system and decisions in cases on the harmonised national trade marks before the national courts and the European Court of Justice are not binding on the OHIM. Nor is it bound by decisions taken in national trade mark offices, such as a decision to permit or reject registration of a particular type or form of mark, such as an olfactory mark. However, the Court of First Instance and Court of Justice, when deciding cases on the CTM often refer to rulings of the Court of Justice on the harmonised national trade mark and the Court of Justice, when making rulings on the harmonised national trade mark often refers to its decisions on the CTM. As the requirements for registrability are, to all intents and purposes, identical, this is not surprising.

From a trader's point of view, the CTM is a very attractive proposition, a single registration giving validity throughout the Community and the possibility of bringing legal proceedings in respect of infringement occurring anywhere in the Community. However, in some cases, whilst a trade mark might be registrable in some Member States, it may not be in others because of pre-existing conflicting national registrations or other rights. Such a position could prevent the OHIM accepting registration as the unitary nature of the CTM requires it to be registrable in every part of the Community. Thus, for example, an application to register 'COMPSERV' as a CTM will be refused if it is already registered in Germany for the same goods or services.

In practice it is not uncommon for traders based in one of the Member States to apply to register in their own country and at the OHIM and, in some cases, to apply for registration in other countries through the Madrid System.

The following description is based on the UK registered trade mark but the same principles apply also to the CTM generally, unless otherwise stated.

Registration of a trade mark in the UK

Initial registration of a trade mark is for 10 years and the renewal period is also 10 years. There is no upper limit to the duration of a trade mark, which can be renewed again and again providing it is still used. A trade mark that has not been used for a period of five years is vulnerable to revocation. Some trade marks first registered under the Trade Marks Registration Act 1875, when

11

Trade marks, passing off and malicious falsehood

registration became possible in the UK, are still registered and in use today, demonstrating the importance of trade marks, including Britain's Number 1 trade mark, the BASS 'red triangle' mark.

Following receipt of the application, it is examined by the Trade Marks Registry to determine whether it is acceptable under the Trade Marks Act 1994. If it is it will be advertised in the *Trade Marks Journal*. This allows others to object to the application by raising grounds of opposition to registration or by making observations. Opposition must be filed within three months of the publication of the trade mark in the journal. If opposition is based on an earlier trade mark which has been registered for five or more years, the proprietor of that earlier trade mark must prove that it has been used within the previous five years. Opposition proceedings take place in the Patent Office, subject to appeal. The most common grounds of opposition are on the basis that the mark applied for is identical or similar to an earlier trade mark and is intended to be used for identical or similar goods or services. Bad faith is frequently used also but does not succeed very often.

The fee for registration is £200 covering goods or services in one class of goods or services. For each additional class the fee is £50. The renewal fee is £200 for one class and £50 for each additional class. The fee for filing an opposition to a trade mark application is £200.

What is a trade mark?

By section 1(1) of the Trade Marks Act 1994, a trade mark is:

> . . . any sign capable of being represented graphically which is capable of distinguishing goods or services of one undertaking from those of other undertakings.

The section goes on to say that a trade mark may, in particular, consist of words (including personal names), designs, letters, numerals or the shape of goods or their packaging. This is quite a wide definition and much wider that under previous trade mark legislation in the UK. It allows the registration of colours, sound and shape marks, providing the basic requirements for registrability are satisfied. Even a small number of smells marks have been accepted for registration though this is very controversial and the better view is that they are not registrable as it has not proved an easy matter to represent olfactory marks graphically with sufficient precision. There should be no difficulty for software companies to register as trade marks signs embedded in software such as a moving image produced on a screen when a computer game is being loaded together with any associated distinctive musical motif, computer icons and other computer-generated images, providing they are distinctive and not otherwise excluded, for example, because they are descriptive or deceptive.

Under the previous trade marks Act in the UK it was said that a mark was capable of distinguishing if it would become distinctive through use; in other words, if it was not incapable of becoming distinctively associated with the goods of the trade mark proprietor: *Davies v Sussex Rubber Co* (1927) 44 RPC 412, a case involving 'Ustikon' for stick-on rubber soles for shoes,

This approach was accepted as also being appropriate under the 1994 Act in *AD2000 Trade Mark* [1997] RPC 168. In that case an application to register AD2000 as a trade mark failed. A combination of two letters and four numbers could be capable of distinguishing if it was idiosyncratic. However, that was not the case here as AD2000 naturally referred to the year 2000 and was not idiosyncratic. Mr Geoffrey Hobbs QC, the Appointed Officer hearing the case, refused to be swayed by the fact that the word 'MILLENNIUM' had previously been accepted for registration as a trade mark.

As regards a sign being capable of being represented graphically, the European Court of Justice ruled that this meant that the sign must be represented visually, particularly by means of images, lines or characters, so that it can be properly identified. The representation must be clear, precise, self-contained, easily accessible, intelligible, durable and objective.

Unregistrable trade marks

The fundamental purpose of a trade mark is to distinguish goods or services of one undertaking from those of other undertakings. In other words the mark must serve as an indicator of trade origin. If it does not do this, it is not registrable. For example, 'TARZAN', 'ELVIS' and 'ELVIS PRESLEY' were held to be unregistrable. By the time the applications were received, these names were so well known as 'household' words that they could not serve the function of indicating a connection in the course of trade between a trader and his goods. Although 'three-dimensional' signs are now potentially registrable, the same principle applies. One problem for shape marks if is that consumers do not generally recognise shapes as serving a trade mark purpose.

Apart from the basic requirement that a trade mark must serve as a badge of origin, by being capable of being represented graphically and capable of distinguishing the goods or services of one undertaking from those of other undertakings, there are two types of grounds for refusal of registration – absolute grounds and relative grounds – the latter being so called because refusal depends on the mark's similarity with other marks.

Absolute ground for refusal of registration

The absolute grounds for refusal are, by section 3 of the Trade Marks Act 1994, where the sign or mark in question:

- does not satisfy the requirements of section 1(1) (is not capable of graphical representation or not capable of distinguishing goods or services of one undertaking from those of other under-takings);
- is devoid of any distinctive character;
- consists exclusively of signs or indications which serve in trade to designate the kind, quality, quantity, intended purpose, value, geographical origin, time of production of goods or rendering of services, or other characteristics of goods or services (in other words, they are descriptive or laudatory (praiseworthy) – for example, 'Superb Computers' or 'Cheap Software' or 'Yorkshire Computer Services' or 'Personal Computers' or 'Internet Services';
- consists exclusively of signs or indications that have become customary in the current language or in the *bona fide* and established practices of the trade – for example, 'Software Bug' or 'Website' or 'Applet';
- consists exclusively of:
  - a shape which results from the nature of the goods themselves – for example, the shape of a silicon chip; or
  - the shape of goods which is necessary to obtain a technical result – for example, the shape of a CD; or
  - the shape which gives substantial value to the goods (it is very difficult to know where the boundaries of this exception lie though a possible example is a computer mouse with a new ergonomic shape);
- is contrary to public policy, accepted principles of morality or deceptive (for instance, as to the nature, quality or geographic origin of the goods or services) – for example, where a dating agency that does not possess or use a computer wishes to register the mark 'ComputaDate'.

Also excluded are certain flags, emblems, the Royal Arms, representations of the Royal family, etc. These are listed in section 4. In some cases, registration may be possible if consent is given. Registration is not allowed where, or to the extent that, the use of the trade mark would be prohibited in the UK by any enactment, rule of law or any provision of Community law. The latter could apply, for example, where the trade mark is a designation of geographical origin used in connection with wines and spirits.

An example of a challenge to validity of a trade mark on the basis that it was descriptive was in *International Business Machines Corp v Web-Sphere Ltd* [2004] EWHC 529 (Ch). In that case, the IBM Corporation had registered 'WEBSPHERE' as a CTM for a number of goods and services, including computer software for website development and for providing services in relation to website development and maintenance. The registration was challenged as being invalid. The judge said that the trade mark was a neologism not previously existing in the English language. WEB alluded to the internet (especially the world wide web) but went no further and SPHERE might allude to the world but neither alone described the goods or services for which the trade mark had been registered. The word WEBSPHERE as a whole was greater than the sum of its two parts and there was no doubt that the registration was valid. Nor was there any evidence to show that WEBSPHERE had acquired a special trade meaning so as to have become customary in the current language or bona fide practices of the trade.

The meaning of 'bad faith' under the Trade Marks Act 1994 was not entirely clear at first. In *Road Tech Computer Systems Ltd v Unison Software (UK) Ltd* [1996] FSR 805, the claimant traded in computer software for the transportation business and was the registered proprietor of the trade mark 'Roadrunner', which was registered in respect of 'computer software and programs; all included in Class 9 but not including any such goods relating to birds'. The reason for the latter exception was that an American bird, the paisano, is also known as a roadrunner. The defendant claimed that the registration was not *bona fide* as the claimant had no intention of using the mark. The claimant argued that bad faith was more restrictive and required dishonesty. The judge pointed to the difficulty of determining the meaning of bad faith under the 1994 Act, which was not helped by looking at the trade marks Directive. Accordingly, he granted the defendant leave to defend the claimant's action for infringement as he considered that the claimant's argument was not sufficiently clear to allow it summary judgment against the defendant. He added that if the hearing had been a full trial, he would have considered referring this issue to the European Court of Justice for a preliminary ruling.

Later, in *Gromax Plasticulture Ltd v Don & Low Nonwovens Ltd* [1999] RPC 367, Mr Justice Lindsey, whilst avoiding formulating a comprehensive definition said that bad faith plainly includes dishonesty and some dealings that 'fall short of the standards of acceptable commercial behaviour observed by reasonable and experienced men in the particular area being examined'. This case has become the authority for the meaning of bad faith in trade mark cases.

Applying to register a trade mark, having no intention to use the mark in respect of the goods or services applied for, could give rise to an allegation of bad faith. The form used to apply to register a sign as a UK trade mark carries a declaration that the trade mark is being used by applicant or with his consent in relation to the goods or services covered by the application or that there is a *bona fide* intention that it will be so used. Another form of bad faith could be where a person applies to register as a trade mark a name or mark already used by an established trader who has failed to register the name or mark himself, perhaps in the hope of selling the registration to the trader. An extreme example was in the case of *Baywatch Trade Mark Application* (unreported) 12 November 1999. The applicant had nothing to do with the producers and owners of the rights in the Baywatch television series, Baywatch Production Company, but applied to register the name in respect of various fast-food items. When challenged, the applicant offered to sell the trade mark for £15 m plus royalties. The production company opposed the application and it was held to be unregistrable, *inter alia*, on the ground that the application was made in bad faith as the applicant failed to convince the hearing officer that he had a *bona fide* intention to use the mark. The applicant claimed that he intended to use the mark with a restaurant he intended to open but he failed to adduce convincing evidence of business plans to that effect.

Relative grounds for refusal of registration

The relative grounds of refusal of registration are set out in section 5 of the Trade Marks Act 1994 and depend on the relationship of the mark applied for and earlier trade marks, or other rights. First of all, a trade mark will be refused registration if it is identical to an earlier trade mark and the goods or services for which the trade mark is applied for are identical to those for which the earlier trade mark is protected. If this is the case, registration will be refused without having to prove anything else, such as a likelihood of confusion. Where the trade mark applied for is identical to or similar to the earlier trade mark and is to be used for similar goods or services, or where the trade mark applied for is similar to the earlier trade mark and is to be used for identical goods or services (in other words, where there is not identity of trade marks *and* goods or services), then it will not be registered if there exists a likelihood of confusion on the part of the public. A likelihood of confusion is stated to include a likelihood of association but this seems to add little or nothing to the test and it has been confirmed that there must be confusion as to the origin of the goods or services. The fact that seeing a trade mark applied to goods might bring another trader to the mind of a consumer without causing the consumer to be misled as to the origin of the goods is not enough. In terms of deciding whether two trade marks are identical, the fact that there are minor changes or additions does not prevent the marks being identical for these purposes if they incorporate differences that are so minor as to go unnoticed by the average consumer. Some latitude in whether goods or services are identical is also possible.

The fact that goods are advertised under a registered trade mark but it is made clear that they are imitations of the genuine goods does not prevent there being a likelihood of confusion. In *Rolex Internet Auction* [2005] ETMR 255, a court in Germany (the Bundesgerichtshof) confirmed that selling counterfeit and imitation Rolex watches on an internet auction site, where the watches were described as imitations, did not prevent there being a risk of confusion for trade mark purposes.

A further relative ground for refusal of registration is where the trade mark applied for is identical or similar to an earlier trade mark which has a reputation in the UK (or European Community in the case of a CTM or trade mark registered under the Madrid Protocol entitled to protection in the European Community). However, for this to apply, the use of the mark applied for must be such, without due cause, as to take unfair advantage of or be detrimental to the distinctive character or repute of the earlier trade mark. An example might be if someone other than the Microsoft Corporation applied to register 'Windows XP' for double-glazing or mobile telecommunications services. The trade marks Directive described this ground for refusal in terms of goods or services that were not similar, the European Court of Justice has ruled that it also applied to identical or similar goods or services in Case C-292/00 *Davidoff & Cie SA* v *Gofkid Ltd* [2003] ECR I-389. The Trade Marks Act 1994 was modified to make this clear.

Causing detriment to a well-known trade mark may dilute its attractive force by a process of 'blurring'. An example of this was *Sihra's Trade Mark Application* [2003] RPC 789 in which registration was sought for 'INTER-TEL' in respect of 'hand-held constructional toys being puzzles'. The Intel Corporation Inc, makers of the famous Intel computer chips, opposed registration on the basis of its registration of 'INTEL' for computer games, apparatus and software. It was held, *inter alia*, that the use of the applicant's trade mark would undoubtedly dilute the strength of the 'INTEL' mark and reduce the distinctive character of it, causing detriment to it. A desire by the

11

Trade marks, passing off and malicious falsehood

applicant to increase sales of its puzzle was no justification for needing to use a mark incorporating the word 'INTEL'.

For the purposes of the above relative grounds for refusal, an earlier trade mark means one which is a UK registered trade mark, a CTM or one entitled to protection under the Paris Convention for the Protection of Industrial Property or the World Trade Organisation Agreement (1994), being a trade mark well-known in the UK even though the person to whom the mark belongs does not carry on business in the UK and does not have any goodwill there. Also included are trade marks registered under the Madrid Protocol entitled to protection in the European Community and certain trade marks having a valid claim to seniority. This might apply, for example, where an application for a UK trade mark has been converted from an earlier application for a CTM. This could be the case where it has been found that the CTM application might fail because of a conflicting trade mark in a country other than the UK.

The further relative grounds for refusal of registration are based upon the relationship with signs and trade marks protected by other rights, such as copyright, design right or registered designs. Registration will be refused if the use of mark applied would be liable to be prevented by virtue of any rule of law, in particular, the law of passing off. This might be the case where the trade mark applied for is in conflict with a well-known trade mark which has never been registered as a trade mark but in which substantial goodwill has been built up. In terms of copyright, an example of refusal on this ground is where someone has applied without the consent of the copyright owner to register a trade mark which includes a computer icon protected by copyright as an artistic work.

Rights and infringement

The registered proprietor of a trade mark has, by section 9 of the Trade Marks Act 1994, the exclusive right to use the mark in the UK. Use of a sign by another without the proprietor's consent will infringe if the act or acts complained of fall within section 10. Infringing use must be in the course of trade. For the purposes of infringement, a person is taken to use a sign in a number of situations including fixing it to goods or their packaging, offering or supplying services, offering or exposing goods for sale, importing or exporting under the sign or using it on business papers or in advertising.

With that in mind, the infringing acts set out in section 10 closely follow the relative grounds of refusal that apply in respect of earlier trade marks or other rights (except now the reference is to registered trade marks or other earlier rights). Using a sign identical to a registered trade mark in relation to identical goods or services infringes *per se*. Where there is not complete identity of the sign and the registered trade mark *and* the goods or services then infringement depends on the existence of a likelihood of confusion. This applies in the following situations:

- use of a sign identical to the registered trade mark for similar goods or services;
- use of a sign similar to the registered trade mark for identical or similar goods or services.

Trade marks having a reputation in the UK are infringed if a sign identical or similar to the trade mark is used such that, without due cause, it takes unfair advantage of, or is detrimental to, the distinctive character or repute of the registered trade mark. This form of infringement applies where the goods or services are identical, similar or even not similar.

In respect of whether goods or services are similar, Mr Justice Jacob laid down some guidelines based on an old test under the 1938 Act which he said was still applicable under the 1994 Act. In *British Sugar plc* v *James Robertson & Sons Ltd* [1996] RPC 281, he said that respective uses and users, the physical nature of the goods or services, the respective trade channels, whether goods are sold alongside each other in supermarkets and the extent to which the goods compete are all useful factors to consider.

Practice as developed at the Trade Mark Registry may also be a factor. In *Avnet Inc v Isoact Ltd* [1998] FSR 16, the defendant used the word 'Avnet' for his internet service for the aviation industry. This service also allowed subscribers to place advertisements on their own webpages. The claimant had registered 'AVNET' for advertising and promotional services and complained of the defendant's use of the word. However, summary judgment was refused. An important factor was that, at the time, Registry practice was to classify the claimant's activities and defendant's activities in different classes of the trade marks register.

The more stronger the distinctive character or reputation of the registered trade mark alleged to have been infringed, the easier it may be to accept that there is a likelihood of confusion. The degree of similarity between the allegedly infringing sign and the registered trade mark and the goods or services for which they are used are also factors. The perspective of the average consumer is important and such a consumer will make a global appreciation of the visual, aural or conceptual similarity of the marks based on the overall impression given by them, bearing in mind their distinctive and dominant components. The main question is whether the average consumer would think that the claimant's and defendant's goods or services came from the same or economically linked undertakings.

In *Ellerman Investments Ltd v C-Vinci* [2006] EWHC 1442 (Ch), the claimant owned the Ritz Hotel in London and a number of trade marks including the name 'Ritz' which was registered, *inter alia*, for gaming services and online gaming services. From 2002, the claimant had also registered as domain names 'ritzclublondon.com' and 'ritzclublondon.co.uk'. The defendants registered 'ritzpoker.net' as a domain name which had links to online gambling sites. In granting summary judgment to the claimant, the judge accepted that there was no real prospect that it would fail to establish at full trial that there was a likelihood of confusion.

Comparative advertising

Comparative advertising occurs where a trader advertises his goods or services in comparison with those of another trader in a way which includes a reference to that other trader's registered trade mark. It used to infringe under the 1938 Act and may still do so under the 1994 Act. However, under section 10(6) of the 1994 Act comparative advertising will not infringe if it is in accordance with honest practices in industrial or commercial matters. Otherwise, it will infringe if, without due cause, it takes unfair advantage of, or is detrimental to, the distinctive character or repute of the trade mark. Comparative advertising may take place on a commercial website in a similar way as with any other form of advertising and the same principles should apply. The important question is whether the particular form it takes would be regarded as in accordance with honest practices. It could be said that if it is not, then it can be assumed that unfair advantage or detriment will follow as a rule. However, the purposes of an advertisement which attempts to show that the advertiser's goods are better than those of a competitor must be intended to be detrimental to the competitor. But consideration must be given to the fact that consumers are not so naive to know that there may be some selectivity in choosing what features to compare and how to compare them. After all, consumers know that advertisements are unlikely to be completely unbiased and objective.

Under the 1938 Act the case of *Compaq Computer Corp v Dell Computer Corp Ltd* [1992] FSR 93 gives an example of comparative advertising. Dell advertised its computers with a photograph showing its computer and a Compaq computer with both makers' names (including the word 'Compaq', a registered trade mark) and the price of the machines. The claimant, Compaq, sued for trade mark infringement, passing off and trade libel. The court granted an interlocutory injunction to Compaq. It was at least highly arguable that Dell infringed the Compaq mark through its advertising. However, there was some doubt as to whether the Compaq mark should have been accepted for registration because of its phonetic similarity with 'Compact', an every-day word.

The 1994 Act marked a sea change in legal responses to comparative advertising and it was not long before traders were exploring the boundaries of what was permissible. In *Barclays Bank plc v RBS Advanta* [1996] RPC 307, the defendant advertised its new credit card by reference to the Barclaycard trade mark with a list of features comparing both cards. Of course, the features selected were designed to show the defendant's card in the best light. The judge said that it was for the proprietor of the trade mark to show that the use was not in accordance with honest practices. Further, persons reading the advertisement would realise that the advertiser would be selective in choosing which features to compare and would also expect a certain amount of hyperbole. What an advertiser can get away with would depend to some extent on the nature of the goods or services concerned.

In *Vodafone Group plc v Orange Personal Communications Ltd* [1997] FSR 34, where the defendant advertised by stating that on average subscribers would save £20 per month by switching to its service, the judge accepted that the public would expect some elasticity of price and usage in relation to the quoted average saving. However, if the information is clearly untrue or misleading, comparative advertising is likely to infringe as in *Emaco & Aktiebolaget Electrolux v Dyson Appliances* [1999] EWHC 260 (Patents).

Section 10(6) is not limited to comparative advertising (the term is not even mentioned) but applies where a trade mark is used to identify goods or services as those of the proprietor of the trade mark, providing such use is in accordance with honest practices in industrial or commercial matters and does not, without due cause, take unfair advantage of, or is detrimental to, the distinctive character or repute of the trade mark. In *Tesco Stores Ltd v Elogicom Ltd* [2006] EWHC 403 (Ch), discussed in more detail later, registering domain names including the word 'Tesco' and linking them into Tesco's own websites for the purposes of generating income by trading on Tesco's goodwill without the knowledge of Tesco was held not to be within section 10(6). Whether the practice was honest was held to be an objective test. Whether the defendant thought it in accordance with honest practices was not relevant.

Exceptions to infringement

There are a limited number of exceptions to trade mark infringement which may be set up as a defence. They include, by section 11:

- use by a person of his own name or address;
- use of indications of the kind, quality, quantity, intended purpose, value, geographical origin, the time of production of goods or rendering of services, or other characteristics of goods or services;
- use, where it is necessary, to indicate the intended purpose of a product or service, in particular, as accessories or spare parts (for this and the exceptions above to apply, the use must be in accordance with honest practices in industrial or commercial matters); or
- use of an earlier right (such as an unregistered mark protected by the law of passing off) in a particular locality.

The own-name defence does not apply where the name is that of a newly-formed company. In *IBM v Web-Sphere*, mentioned above, it seemed that the defendant's name had been deliberately chosen in order to take advantage of IBM's goodwill in the name. Although far from certain, it appears that the own-name defence is available to a company as well as an individual. The defendant in *Reed Executive plc v Reed Business Information Ltd* [2004] RPC 767 could avail itself of the defence in relation to the use of Reed Business Information on its jobs website. It was held that its use of its own name was in accordance with honest practices. In particular, it had taken steps to reduce the possibility of confusion with the claimant's website when it discovered that there had been some confusion with the claimant's employment agency business.

The third exception (actually, its equivalent under section 4(3) of the Trade Marks Act 1938) was considered in *IBM Corp v Phoenix International (Computers) Ltd* [1994] RPC 251. Phoenix supplied computer equipment including 'reworked' memory cards which contained IBM components. Phoenix advertised these cards as 'IBM manufactured' and IBM sued for trade mark infringement and for passing off. Phoenix argued, as far as the trade mark infringement was concerned, that it had IBM's implied consent or that the use indicated that the boards were adapted from IBM components. The judge refused to strike out this defence. However, this does not mean that the defence would succeed at a full trial. The wording of section 11 in the 1994 Act is much simpler and, provided the use of the mark in such cases is necessary to indicate the intended purpose (for example, that the cards will work in IBM mainframe computers) and such use accords with honest practices, the defence ought to succeed. It is submitted that the use of the phrase 'manufactured from IBM components' would be more likely to be acceptable than simply 'IBM manufactured'.

Advertising an accessory or spare part for one's own goods whilst making it clear it can also be used with or fit a competitor's goods may come within this exception. In Case C-228/03 *Gillette Company v LA-Laboratories Ltd Oy* [2005] ECR I-2337, the European Court of Justice ruled that this was so in respect of razor blades advertised as being suitable for the razors made by a competitor as well as those of the advertiser.

Where goods bearing a trade mark have been placed on the market within the European Economic Area ('EEA') by or with the consent of the proprietor of the trade mark, he cannot use his trade mark rights to prevent the further commercialisation of them. This is a result of the doctrine of exhaustion of rights. The proprietor's rights are said to be exhausted by the first consensual sale within the EEA. There is a proviso to this and the proprietor's rights to enforce the trade mark are not exhausted if there exist legitimate reasons to oppose further dealing with the goods. This could apply, for example, where the condition of the goods have been impaired or altered. Exhaustion of rights does not apply where the goods have been placed on the market outside the EEA. For example, if computers made by Alan and sold by him in Japan under his trade mark were bought there by Brian, Alan could prevent their import into the UK if Alan's trade mark was registered in the UK.

In *Sun Microsystems Inc v Amtec Computer Corp* [2006] EWHC 62 (Ch), the court confirmed that there was no distinction between new and secondhand goods in applying the doctrine of exhaustion of rights. In that case, it had been alleged that some computer servers made by the claimant had been sourced from Israel. The proprietor's rights would not be exhausted in such a case as some of the computer servers in question had been placed on the market outside the EEA and it made no difference whether they were new or used.

As with patents and designs, there is a remedy in respect of groundless threats of infringement proceedings. This was introduced into trade mark law by the 1994 Act. An example of a successful action was *Prince plc v Prince Sports Group Inc* [1998] FSR 21 in which the defendant, a US company with a UK registration in respect of the word 'Prince', threatened the claimant, which had registered 'prince.com' as its internet name, with legal proceedings if it did not transfer the domain name to the defendant. The court held that the threats were unjustified and granted an injunction against their continuance.

TRADE MARKS AND THE INTERNET

A number of issues have arisen in relation to trade marks and the internet, in particular where trade marks have been used on websites. Before looking at these issues in detail, it is worth making a few points about trade marks which apply generally to trade mark law, whatever the country.

- Is it possible to register domain names as trade marks, for example, 'acmetrading.com'?
- Is a trade mark on a website used in relation to goods or services made available through the website?
- Does the test for a likelihood of confusion differ where a sign, alleged to infringe a registered trade mark, appears on a website?
- What is the position in relation to banner advertisements triggered by reserved keywords?
- Can invisible keyword meta-tags infringe registered trade marks?
- Can placing a sign on a website bring the potential of infringing registered trade marks all over the world?

These issues are now dealt with below.

Registration of domain names as trade marks

The fact that a trade mark is also a domain name is neutral as far as its registrability as a trade mark is concerned. What is important is whether the domain name functions as a trade mark. It is not enough that they function as domain names; they must have trade mark significance. In other words, would a person coming across the domain name think it also functioned as a trade mark? This was confirmed in *Digeo Broadband Inc's Trade Mark Application* [2004] RPC 638 which involved an application to register a series of 308 marks, all including the word 'DIGEO'.

Examples included DIGEO, DIGEO.COM, DIGEO.CO.UK and DIGEO.FR. The objection in that case was that, for marks to be registrable as a series, under section 41(2), the differences must be such as not to substantially affect the identity of the trade mark. That does not mean to say that the marks may have each been registrable individually.

The defining elements of a domain name as such, the example, the prefix ('www') and suffix ('.com', for example) cannot be ignored but it is the overall effect that is important. Would it be perceived as a trade mark instead of or as well as a domain name, rather than just seeing it as an internet address? There are examples of domain names which have been accepted for registration as trade marks. For example, in the UK: TESCO.com, ORANGE.COM and CAN AND WILL.COM. However, the OHIM refused an application to register 'BUY.COM'. It was descriptive of an internet site at which persons could buy goods or services. It is submitted that the more knowledgeable the public become as regards domain names, the more difficult it will become to argue that simply adding a domain code, such as a generic or country code, as a suffix will transform an indistinct mark into a distinctive and registrable one.

Use as a trade mark in relation to goods or services?

Simply placing a sign on a website does not necessarily infringe a registered trade mark. Apart from the usual requirements for infringement (for example, that the sign is identical or similar to the registered trade mark), the use must be in the course of trade and must be used in relation to the relevant goods or services. 'Trade' includes any business or profession. A private individual with his own website who uses it solely for the purposes of a hobby or his own entertainment or amusement, and who does not sell goods or provide services (other than making the content available for others to see) is not using any of that content, including any signs that might look like registered trade marks, in the course of trade.

Where the website is commercial in nature, then it does not automatically follow that any sign displayed there is being used in relation to any goods or services provided through the website. Apple Computer Inc starting making music tracks available on its iTunes website. These could be downloaded onto iPods. This resulted in litigation commenced by Apple Corps Ltd, a company that managed music by The Beatles and other musicians. Both companies used apple logos. Some years, appreciating that their apple trade marks might clash, the companies entered into an agreement restricting the use of each of their trade marks. The purposes were to prevent potential conflicts. Apple Computer Inc. would restrict its use to computers and computer systems whilst Apple Corps would restrict its use of its trade mark to the field of music. The agreement was later modified to allow Apple Computer to uses its trade mark for data transmission services.

In *Apple Corps Ltd* v *Apple Computer Inc* [2006] EWHC 996 (Ch), Apple Corps complained about Apple Computer's iTunes Music Store ('ITMS') available online and from which music tracks could be downloaded. Apple Computer's apple logo appeared in monochrome at the top centre of the ITMS screen display. It was visible at the beginning and at most other times. However, during certain operations, it was replaced by other graphic symbols, for example, when a music track was being listened to.

It was alleged that the use of the logo and other aspects of the iTunes operation, such as in advertising for iTunes and Apple Computer's iPod infringed Apple Corps' trade mark and was a breach of the trade mark agreement. Complaint was also made in relation to the use of the logo with Computer's gift cards (which included the phrase 'Remember – iTunes isn't just the #1 music download store. It's also the best jukebox around').

The judge held that the agreement must be construed from the perspective of use of a trade mark in a trade mark sense, that is, as a badge of origin. Mr Justice Mann said that the correct test to apply to determine whether there had been an infringement of a trade mark was that given by the European Court of Justice in Case C-342/97, *Lloyd Schuhfabrik Meyer & Co GmbH* v *Klijsen Handel BV* [1999] ECR I-3819. It that case, the court ruled that it was relevant to consider how things would appear to the average consumer who 'is reasonably well-informed and reasonably observant and circumspect'.

Mann J said that the use of the apple logo on the website was not such as to make an unfair or unreasonable association between the logo and the musical content. The apple logo was used in relation to providing a music downloading service but it was not used to 'frank' the music itself. There was no doubt as to who the owners of the rights in the music were. The use of the logo related to the iTunes music store and not to the music itself or, if not, it related to a data transmission service which Apple Computer was allowed to provide under the agreement as modified some years before.

Domain name providing a pathway as a service in the course of trade

It is possible to register a domain name such that when a person enters it into a search engine, that person will be diverted to a website located somewhere else. The domain name simply serves as a pathway. Two issues are whether doing so is using the domain name in relation to a service and whether, if so, in appropriate circumstances, it is done in the course of trade.

In *Tesco Stores Ltd* v *Elogicom Ltd* [2006] EWHC 403 (Ch), the famous Tesco supermarket company had a number of registered trade marks including 'TESCO' and 'TESCO.com'. Apart from its substantial bricks and mortar businesses, it also did business online through a number of websites. Tesco also ran an affiliate scheme through an intermediary. Affiliate companies generated business for Tesco by having advertisements on their websites which, when clicked on, took the user to one of Tesco's websites. Affiliates earned fees according to the business they generated through their websites.

The defendant, Elogicom, had two affiliate websites: (**www.Avon4me.co.uk** and **www.Avonlady.co.uk**). These had been accepted by or on behalf of Tesco. However, it also registered a large number of domain names which included the word 'tesco', for example, **www.tescodiet.co.uk**, **www.jerseytesco.com** and **www.tesco-opticians.com**. Any person entering these domain names in their browser would be diverted to one of the Tesco websites without going through either the **Avon4me.co.uk** or the **Avonlady.co.uk** website. It had been arranged by Elogicom that persons accessing Tesco's websites using the domain names including the word 'tesco' would generate fees for Elogicom. The judge said (at para. 32):

> Elogicom was seeking to benefit from use of domain names which incorporated the word 'tesco' by 'fishing' for persons browsing the internet who might be searching for goods or services provided by Tesco and, being unsure of the precise address for a Tesco website, might by guesswork enter in the address bars on their computers names closely associated with Tesco in the hope that those addresses would take them to the Tesco website they were searching for.

The judge held that the use of an internet domain name is a service provided to the public and by registering the domain names and providing a pathway to Tesco's sites was using the signs (domain names) in the course of trade. He confirmed that Elogicom infringed the Tesco trade marks under section 10(2) (there being a likelihood of confusion) and section 10(3) because of an unfair advantage was taken of the Tesco trade marks as the domain names had been registered for the purpose of taking advantage of the distinctive character and reputation of the Tesco trade marks. That was both unfair and detrimental to the distinctive character and reputation of the latter. The judge also held that a claim in passing off succeeded on the basis of *BT v One in a Million*, discussed later in the section on passing off. Tesco was given summary judgment and injunctive relief.

Likelihood of confusion and websites

For some forms of trade mark infringement, it must be shown that the use complained of is such as to cause to exist a likelihood of confusion on the part of the public. This is where there is not complete identity of the sign and the trade mark or the goods or services for which the sign has been used and the goods or services covered by the registration. The way in which this is tested is to consider the question from the viewpoint of the average consumer of the relevant goods or services and who is taken to be reasonably well-informed and reasonably circumspect and observant but who rarely has the opportunity of comparing the marks side by side and relies instead on his somewhat imperfect recollection of them. The visual, aural and conceptual similarities of the sign and the trade mark are assessed globally by reference to the overall impression made by them. Furthermore, a greater similarity between the sign and the trade mark might be offset by a lesser similarity between the goods or services in question and vice versa.

Based on the above and other guidelines, most of which emanate from the European Court of Justice, the national courts and trade mark offices now have a reasonable amount of experience in applying such tests and guidelines in relation to conventional forms of trade marks, for example, as fixed to goods or their packaging or as used in newspaper and magazine advertisements. But it is debatable whether such approaches to the likelihood of confusion are the same or have similar outcomes in the case of signs placed on websites which are similar to registered trade marks.

In the US, in *Brookfield Communications Inc v West Coast Entertainment Corp* 174 F 3d 1036 (9th Cir 1999) the claimant owned databases of information concerning the entertainment industry. It had previously used the name 'MovieBuff' but without having registered it as a trade mark. Later, the claimant wanted to register 'moviebuff.com' as its domain name but discovered that it had already been registered as a domain name by the defendant so it registered 'moviebuff-online.com' as its domain name instead. Subsequently, the claimant registered 'MovieBuff' as its trade mark used for its database and sued the defendant for infringing the trade mark by offering a database in a similar field on its website. The US Court of Appeals held that the defendant infringed the trade mark. The judge cautioned against rigidly applying previously accepted tests for infringement in the context of the internet. He went on to say that 'web surfers are more likely to be confused as to ownership of a website than the traditional patrons of a brick-and-mortar store would be of the store's ownership'. The fact that both parties used the internet as a marketing tool and provided access to their respective databases on line was likely to increase the likelihood of confusion. This factor was also influential in *GoTo.com Inc v Walt Disney Corp* (unreported) 27 January (9th Cir 2000) where the defendant's use of a sign similar to the claimant's registered trade mark infringed it.

The significant difference between the internet and traditional 'brick-and-mortar' establishments is that there are fewer clues to help the consumer discriminate between different traders. This is exacerbated by the fact that many websites are relatively transient and web-traders can appear and disappear with greater rapidity than conventional traders having a physical presence such as offices, factories, retail outlets or simply goods stacked on supermarket shelves. A further factor is that it is not always possible to confirm the location of a web-trader, for example, where a country-neutral domain name is used. On the other hand, it is likely that most people ordering goods or services over the internet will exercise a greater degree of caution because of the increased dangers of fraud and scams or being deceived as to origin, ending up being supplied with sub-standard goods or services.

Most people carrying out a search using the internet appreciate that they are likely to retrieve any spurious or unwanted hits. Consequently, most people have become used to discriminating between those which are likely to be relevant and of interest and those that are not. The approach in *Brookfield* above is less likely to be appropriate now. This is particularly so when one bears in mind that the case is now some eight or more years old and, generally, persons in the UK, the US and Europe are likely to be even more circumspect when confronted with websites than they might have been in the past.

In *Reed Executive plc v Reed Business Information Ltd* [2004] RPC 767, the claimant was a well-known employment agency which had registered 'Reed' as a trade mark for employment agency services. In 1995, it stated advertising vacancies on its website, **www.reed.co.uk.** The identity of potential employers was not given so potential applicants would have to proceed through the claimant to be put in touch with the employer.

The defendant was part of a large publishing organisation (Reed Elsevier). A number of its publications, carried job advertisements placed by employers and recruitment consultants. During 1999 the defendant created a dedicated jobs website **www.totaljobs.com** which could also be linked to from the defendant's online publications. The name **totaljobs.com** appeared prominently on the top of the webpages which also carried the Reed Elsevier logo and the Reed Business Information logo (use of these logos on the website was eventually abandoned as it was accepted that they infringed the claimant's trade mark). There was also a banner advertisement and copyright notice.

It was alleged that the defendant's use of 'Reed' on its website infringed the claimant's trade mark. An argument that the sign was identical to the trade mark and used for identical services under section 5(1) of the Trade Marks Act 1994 was rejected. The question was whether 'Reed

Business Information' was identical to 'Reed'. In Case C-291/00 *LTJ Diffusion SA v Sadas Vertbaudet SA* [2003] ECR I-2799, the European Court of Justice held that the equivalent provision in the trade marks Directive must be interpreted as meaning that a sign is identical with the trade mark where it reproduces, without any modification or addition, all the elements constituting the trade mark or where, viewed as a whole, it contains differences so insignificant that they may go unnoticed by an average consumer. In the present case, the Court of Appeal held that the average consumer would not fail to notice the additional words. Therefore, the signs were not identical. Furthermore, there was also a difference in the services offered by the parties. The defendant was simply providing information unlike the case with the claimant's business.

As regards an allegation of infringement under section 5(2) by the use of 'Reed' in the copyright notice on the defendant's website, it was noted that the 'global assessment' test was relevant to whether there was a likelihood of confusion. However, where a common surname was used, the average consumer would be more alert to differences. Furthermore, there was no direct evidence of confusion arising from the use of the copyright notice containing the name of the defendant company and, therefore, there was no infringement. In any case, it would have been at least arguable that the use of a name in a copyright notice was not used in a trade mark sense.

Banner advertisements and reservation of keywords

A related issue in the *Reed* v *Reed* case was in respect of the reservation of keywords with search engines which trigger banner advertisements. The defendant reserved a number of keywords with the Yahoo! search engine. These words included 'job', 'jobs', 'vacancies', 'careers' and 'employment'. However, a free extra word was added by Yahoo! which happened to be 'Reed'. Carrying out a search using any of these words automatically triggered the display of the totaljobs.com banner advertisements. Clicking on the banner advertisements took the user directly to the defendant's website.

In the Court of Appeal, Lord Justice Jacob said (at para. 140):

> The banner itself referred only to totaljobs – there was no visible appearance of the word Reed at all. Whether the use as a reserved word can fairly be regarded as 'use in the course of trade' or not (as to which I express no opinion), I cannot see that causing the unarguably inoffensive-in-itself banner to appear on a search under the name 'Reed' or 'Reed jobs' can amount to [infringement requiring a likelihood of confusion]. The web-using member of the public knows that all sorts of banners appear when he or she does a search and they are or may be triggered by something in the search. He or she also knows that searches produce fuzzy results – results with much rubbish thrown in. The idea that a search under the name Reed would make anyone think there was a trade connection between a totaljobs banner making no reference to the word 'Reed' and 'Reed Employment' is fanciful. No likelihood of confusion was established.

Jacob LJ said that this did not mean to say that there could not be infringement under section 5(1) (identical sign and identical services) as there is no requirement for a likelihood of confusion for this. However, in view of what he said about the use of the sign on the website, this would not apply in this case.

In respect of searches, where a person enters a name which is a trade mark, it is the person carrying out the search who initially uses the trade mark. If the only use the owner of the website which is accessed by clicking through a banner retrieved following a search is invisible by having the trade mark as a keyword, it is arguable whether this is infringing use. The possibility of infringement by invisible use is discussed in the next section on meta-tags.

Meta-tags

Webpages on the internet contain meta-tags. These are HTML (Hyper-Text Mark-up Language) tags that do not affect the normal appearance of the webpage with which they are associated but have a number of uses such as describing the contents of the webpage when it is retrieved in a list of 'hits' following a search. Another form of meta-tag is the keyword meta-tag. In this a list of keywords is placed which will be used by search engines looking for sites that match the search criteria. When a person builds a webpage in HTML it is sensible to include appropriate keywords which will attract hits from persons carrying out searches who will be interested in the content on that webpage and other pages linked to from there. Persons carrying out searches and visiting websites do not see the keyword meta-tags as they are visible only when the page is viewed as source code, which a person visiting a website is unlikely to do.

It might be tempting for a person building a commercial website to include trade mark names belonging to rival traders in an attempt to divert visitors to that site rather than to a rival's site. Can such use of a trade mark infringe even though consumers visiting the site do not see the trade mark in the meta-tags?

As is often the case, the question first arose for consideration by the courts in the US. In *Playboy Enterprises Inc v Calvin Designer Labels* 985 F Supp 1220 (ND Cal 1997) the defendant inserted the claimant's trade marks 'Playboy' and 'Playmate' in meta-tags. Although invisible to persons visiting the defendant's website, this was held to infringe the trade marks. However, to infringe, the use must be use as a trade mark. In *Playboy Enterprises Inc v Welles* 7 F Supp 2d 1098 (SD Cal 1998), the defendant, the model Terri Welles advertised the fact that she was a former Playmate of the Year. This was held not to infringe as the use of the trade marks was minimal and there were a number of disclaimers on the website. Her use of the trade marks was a descriptive use and was her way of indexing the content of her website.

The first case in the UK on the use of trade marks in meta-tags was *Roadtech Computer Systems Ltd v Mandata Ltd* [2000] ETMR 970, where the defendant inserted the claimant's trade mark 'Roadrunner' and its name 'Roadtech' in meta-tags. Before the trial, the defendant removed the names from the meta-tags but the court confirmed that this use of a trade mark infringed and that the defendant was also guilty of passing off. In *Pfizer Ltd v Eurofood Link (UK) Ltd* [2001] FSR 3, the defendant which marketed a drink called 'Viagrene', included the claimant's registered trade mark 'Viagra' in the keyword meta-tags. However, the court did not need to find that this infringed as it was held that there had been an infringement by the use of 'Viagrene' in connection with the drink.

Finally, in the *Reed* v *Reed* case mentioned above, the defendant used the name 'Reed' in its meta-tags. To infringe, the offending sign must be *used* in the course of trade. At first instance, Mr Justice Pumfrey, accepted that invisible use of a trade mark was 'use' for the purposes of infringement. Although he did not mention it, section 103(2) of the Trade Marks Act 1994 states that use includes use otherwise than by means of a graphic representation and, providing the use is in the course of trade, there seems no reason to take a restrictive view of the meaning of use. A possible way of looking at the question of whether an invisible use is caught is to look at the effect of that use. If it has real and commercial effects than that should be sufficient, for example, if the invisible use is such as to divert potential customers from the trade mark proprietor's site.

In the appeal to the Court of Appeal, Jacob LJ said that, even assuming meta-tag use is use on a trade mark sense, there simply was no confusion for the purposes of infringement under section 5(2). Thus, there was no infringement. However, for the purposes of section 5(1) (identical mark used for identical services), there is no requirement of confusion. Jacob LJ did not have to decide this and reserved his judgment on this point and whether the own-name defence could apply to meta-tags. Difficult issues arose. For example, if invisible use counted for infringement it also ought to count for allegations of non-use, being a ground for revocation. It would be strange if an application to revoke a trade mark on the basis of non-use for five or more years could be defeated by showing invisible use in meta-tags only. Also, using another undertaking's trade mark in a meta-tag could be seen by some as legitimate competition providing no one was deceived but others might think it unfair.

To summarise, whether use of another's trade mark in keyword meta-tags is use in a trade mark sense which could potentially infringe is not yet resolved in the UK. But even if it is, it seems that the forms of infringement requiring a likelihood of confusion may not be applicable. Other forms of infringement might apply, such as where there is identity of trade marks and goods or services. It would seem possible that there could be infringement under section 5(3) by taking unfair advantage of a registered trade mark but this has not been considered by the courts in the UK where trade marks have been used in meta-tags.

Jurisdiction – potential world-wide infringement?

To infringe a registered trade mark, the offending sign or mark must be used in the course of trade. In other words, it must be used as a trade mark. Furthermore, that use must be use within the territory in which the trade mark is registered. The use must, therefore, be targeted at consumers within the territory where the trade mark has legal effect. In the US, a trade mark registered there has effect throughout the territory of the US but an action for infringement must be commenced in a state where the infringement is alleged to have occurred. In *Zippo Manufacturing Co* v *Zippo Dot Com Inc* 952 F Supp 1119 (WD Pa 1997), the claimant made cigarette lighters and sued the defendant which operated a web-based subscription news service on the ground of trade mark dilution by its use of zippo.com and other domain names. The claimant sued in the state of Pennsylvania, where its company was based. The defendant argued that the courts there did not have jurisdiction as its principal place of business was in California and it had no physical presence in Pennsylvania. The court in Pennsylvania rejected that argument as the defendant had several thousand subscribers in that state and actively sought business there. The use of the zippo name was targeted there by the use of the domain name. In deciding this preliminary issue, the court developed a useful test, called the 'Zippo sliding scale'.

At one end of the scale, a defendant has an interactive website and makes contracts with residents within the particular jurisdiction. This involves the knowing and repeated transmission of files over the internet. In such a case, the defendant is clearly doing business and is using the trade mark for trade mark purposes within that jurisdiction. At the other end of the scale, the website is passive in nature. This is where the person responsible for the site has done no more than to post information on it which, although accessible by persons within the jurisdiction concerned, is not associated with commercial activity. The trade mark is not used in a trade mark sense. There is a middle ground, however, where the website is interactive and where the user can exchange information with the host computer. In such cases, it is a question of looking at the level of interactivity and the commercial nature of the website to decide whether the trade mark is used in a particular jurisdiction.

The first UK case to look at this issue was *800-FLOWERS Trade Mark* [2000] FSR 697 in which an American company applied to register '800-FLOWERS' as a trade mark in respect of receiving orders for flowers and transferring them to florists. The application was opposed. At first instance, it was submitted that simply placing a sign on a website could infringe trade marks anywhere in the world. This was because the sign was used in an 'omnipresent cyberspace' and was 'putting a tentacle' into the computer of every person who visited the website. In rejecting that argument, Mr Justice Jacob gave the example of a fishmonger from Bootle, Lancashire who advertised on his own website for local delivery. This could not be seen as aimed at persons all over the world and anyone using a search engine who accessed the site would quickly realise it was not intended for him or her unless they lived in a reasonable proximity of the fishmonger's shop. It is a fact of the internet that using a search engine will inevitably retrieve irrelevant hits.

Later, in *Euromarket Designs Inc v Peters and Crate & Barrel* [2001] FSR 288, Jacob J had a further opportunity to consider the matter. In that case, the American claimant company had a chain of stores in the US operating under the name 'Crate and Barrel'. It had registrations of the name as a trade mark in the UK and as a Community trade mark. The defendant owned a shop in Dublin which sold furniture and household items and used the name Crate and Barrel for the shop and advertised in a magazine and on its website using the Crate and Barrel name. There was no evidence to show that the defendant had actively sought business in the UK. The claimant sought summary judgment for infringement of its trade mark, even though it did not have any real trade in the UK.

Section 9(1) of the Trade Marks Act 1994 states that the exclusive rights in a trade mark are infringed 'by use of the trade mark in the United Kingdom without [the proprietor's] consent'. The claimant argued that this suggested that mere use without consent in the UK infringed. However, Jacob J rejected this saying that section 9(1) simply adds a gloss to the infringing acts in section 10 to the effect that the acts within section 10 must be without the proprietor's consent. This means that section 9 does not stand on its own and provides for infringement on the basis of use, *per se*, without consent. This would run contrary to the trade marks Directive which has no equivalent to section 9(1).

Jacob J looked at the practical reality of websites and the fact that many are visited following a search which usually results in lots of irrelevant hits. If the defendant was using Crate & Barrel in the UK in the course of trade, bearing in mind there was no evidence of actual trade or an intention to trade in the UK, potentially it was using the name in every country in the world. However, there must be a distinction between active and passive use on a website and the terminology of the internet supports this. When a person gains access to a website, he is said to go to the site or to visit the site. At this stage use of any trade mark on a website is passive only. Jacob J approved of the submission that using the internet to visit a website was like the user focusing a super-powerful telescope on the site concerned. Without evidence of commercial activity in the UK, the defendant could not seriously be said to be using the Crate & Barrel trade mark in the course of trade in the UK. Of course, this would be different if the defendant had built into the website a facility for visitors to place orders, especially if prices in pounds sterling were displayed and it was clear that delivery to the UK was possible.

This approach was followed in Scotland in *Bonnier Media Ltd v Greg Lloyd Smith and Kestrel Trading Corp* [2002] SCLR 977. The defender registered domain names which were variations of the names used by the pursuer. Although the judge accepted that operating a website has the potential for infringement all over the world, it does not follow that infringement occurs in every country in the world. It is a question of considering the content of the website and the commercial or other context in which it operates. On the facts, the defenders had announced an intention to offer online services of interest in Scotland and similar to those offered by the pursuer. The defenders' planned activities would have their main impact in Scotland and that impact would be commercially significant. Therefore, the Scots courts had jurisdiction.

The *800-FLOWERS* case, discussed earlier, went to the Court of Appeal (*800 FLOWERS Inc v Phonenames Ltd* [2002] FSR 12) where the approach of Jacob J was accepted as correct in general terms. Lord Justice Buxton said:

> There is something inherently unrealistic in saying that A 'uses' his mark in the United Kingdom when all that he does is to place the mark on the internet, from a location outside the United Kingdom, and simply wait in the hope that someone from the United Kingdom will download it and thereby create use on the part of A . . . the very idea of 'use' within a certain area would seem

to require some active step in that area on the part of the user that goes beyond providing facilities that enable others to bring the mark into the area. Of course, if persons in the United Kingdom seek the mark on the Internet in response to direct encouragement or advertisement by the owner of the mark, the position may be different; but in such a case the advertisement or encouragement in itself is likely to suffice to establish the necessary use.

To infringe a trade mark in a particular jurisdiction, an identical or similar sign must be placed on a website by someone who is actively pursuing a commercial activity in that jurisdiction.

PASSING OFF

In many ways, the law of passing off is a common law version of trade mark law although of older pedigree. Passing off protects business goodwill and safeguards the public from deception by giving a right of action against anyone who tries to pass off his goods or services as those of someone else. One trader might try to 'cash in' on the goodwill and reputation of another trader by dressing up his goods in such a way that they resemble those of that other trader. There is a large overlap between trade marks and passing off and it is not unusual for a legal action to involve both passing off and trade marks. The law of passing off is particularly useful if there is no registered mark to be infringed; perhaps a trader or manufacturer has used a mark for several years without registering it as a trade mark. The mark may fail to qualify for registration or the act complained of might fall outside the scope of trade marks – for example, if it relates to the format of an advertising campaign.

The following example shows the application of passing off. A computer retailer has been operating for three years under the name of 'Computer Equipment Sales' and has a chain of stores in the south of England. The retailer has acquired a reputation for low prices and efficient service. Recently, another retailer has opened a store in the south of England and uses the name of 'Computer Equipment Sales and Service'. Neither name is registered as a trade mark; in fact the names would be refused registration as word trade marks because they are too descriptive of computer retailing generally and would make it difficult for other traders to describe their business activities. As there is a danger that people will be confused and might buy from the second retailer thinking that they are buying from the first, if he has built up sufficient goodwill, the first should be able to obtain an injunction preventing the second retailer from continuing to use the name he has chosen. If the first retailer has only been in business a short time before the second retailer opens his store then it is unlikely that anything can be done. This is because there has not been sufficient time to build up goodwill connected with the name and, hence, there is little danger that the public will be confused. Similarly, if the second trader's store was situated in North Wales, it would be unlikely that the first trader's business would be affected, unless his goodwill extends to that location, for example, because he advertises nationally.

Basic requirements for a passing-off action

Before the claimant can suffer the type of damage caused by passing off, he must have a reputation associated with goodwill. He must be able to show that his name, mark, get-up or something else which is distinctive about his business will be associated with his goods by the public. If a trader has just started in business he will not succeed in a passing-off action but a newly registered trade mark has immediate protection. However, the necessary reputation could be obtained relatively quickly by an intensive advertising campaign on a national scale.

The ingredients necessary to a successful passing-off action were described in *Erven Warnink Besloten Vennootschap* v *J Townend & Sons (Hull) Ltd* [1979] AC 731. The claimants made a liqueur called advocaat which came to be well known. It was made from brandewijn, egg yolks and sugar. The defendants decided to enter this market and they made a drink called 'Keeling's Old English Advocaat' which was made from Cyprus sherry and dried egg powder, an inferior but cheaper drink. This captured a large part of the claimants' market in the UK. It was held that, because of the reputation the claimants' product had gained, it should be protected from deceptive use of its name by competitors even though the goodwill was shared by several traders. There was a misrepresentation made by the defendant calculated to injure the claimants' business or goodwill and an injunction was granted in favour of the claimants. Lord Diplock laid down the essentials for a passing-off action as:

- a misrepresentation;

- by a trader in the course of trade;

- to prospective customers of his or ultimate consumers of goods or services supplied by him;

- which is calculated to injure the business or goodwill of another trader; and

- which causes actual damage to a business or goodwill of the trader by whom the action is brought.

Lord Oliver, in *Reckitt & Colman Products Ltd* v *Borden Inc* [1990] 1 All ER 873 (which involved the Jif Lemon and a competing lemon-shaped container for lemon juice), usefully condensed the test for passing off into the presence of the claimant's goodwill, a misrepresentation as to the goods or services offered by the defendant and damage or likely damage to the claimant's goodwill.

Normally, one would expect damage in the form of lost sales as a result of the defendant's misrepresentation. However, it also extends to damage to the claimant's goodwill itself such as where its unique character is eroded. This happened in *Taittinger SA* v *Allbev Ltd* [1993] FSR 641, in which the defendant produced a sparkling non-alcoholic drink which he called 'Elderflower Champagne'. It was sold for £3.50 in green bottles which resembled champagne bottles. It was held that this was passing off. Although it was unlikely that many would be deceived, the use of the name champagne in this way would reduce its distinctiveness and, hence, injure the champagne manufacturer's goodwill.

The misrepresentation

The misrepresentation is not necessarily limited to an exact copy of the name or get-up. It may be sufficient if it unfairly imputes a quality into some product or service, such as where a new trader uses another, established, trader's name or mark. An important factor is whether the buying public will be deceived by this unauthorised use of another's name. In deciding this it is not necessary to consider whether members of the public who are knowledgeable about the product are deceived; it may be sufficient if members of the public who have very little knowledge of the product concerned are likely to be deceived (see *J Bollinger* v *Costa Bravo Wine Co Ltd (No. 2)* [1961] 1 All ER 561, where an injunction was granted to prevent the use of the name 'Spanish Champagne').

As mentioned earlier, a misrepresentation does not have to be confined to a name or mark. The tort of passing off is wide enough to encompass other descriptive material such as slogans and visual images associated with an advertising campaign if this material has become part of the goodwill of the claimant's product. The test is whether the claimant has acquired an intangible property right for his product deriving from the distinctive nature of this material which is recognised by the market. In applying the test, the courts have to bear in mind the balance between the claimant's investment in the product and the protection of free competition.

In one respect, Lord Diplock's judgment is misleading. He spoke of the misrepresentation being calculated to injure. This suggests that passing off must be deliberate. However, this is not necessary and innocence is not an absolute defence although it may influence the remedies granted.

The misrepresentation may come about by modifying an image of a famous person to suggest that the person concerned is endorsing or recommending a particular product or service. In *Irvine* v *Talksport Ltd* [2003] FSR 619, Eddie Irvine, the well-known Formula 1 racing driver complained about the defendant's promotional campaign which included a photograph of Eddie Irvine. The defendant had permission to copy the photograph but had doctored it. Originally, the photograph showed Eddie Irvine holding a mobile telephone but it had been replaced by an image of a portable radio on which the words 'Talk Radio' could be seen. At first instance, Mr Justice Laddie confirmed that Eddie Irvine had goodwill which could be protected against a false claim that he endorsed the defendant's products. The Court of Appeal upheld the judge's finding as to passing off but increased the award of damages from £2000 to £25,000. Doctoring images on webpages so as to suggest someone endorses a particular product will undoubtedly be passing off. What is not clear, however, is the position where the famous person is deceased, although there may be issues of copyright in the original photograph or film used in the marketing.

Common fields of activity

If the traders in a passing-off action operate in different fields of activity, it will usually be assumed that there is less danger of confusion and thus less danger of damage to the claimant. For example, in *Granada Group Ltd* v *Ford Motor Company Ltd* [1973] RPC 49, the Granada television group could not prevent the Ford Motor Company calling one of their cars a Ford Granada; the court held that there was no danger of confusion because of the different fields of activity – namely television and cars. However, in *Lego UK Ltd* v *Lego M Lemelstrich Ltd* [1983] FSR 155, the Lego company, which makes children's construction kits comprising coloured plastic bricks, was granted an injunction against the manufacturers of coloured plastic irrigation material preventing them from using the name 'Lego' as part of the description of the material. The claimant was able to show that there was a real danger of confusion and damage to its goodwill.

The claimant in *Silicon Graphics Inc* v *Indigo Graphic Systems (UK) Ltd* [1994] FSR 403 supplied computer work-stations for computer-aided design under the 'Indigo' mark and had 3 to 5 per cent of the top end of the pre-press market, that is the market for all stages in the printing process prior to actual printing. The defendant made printing equipment under the Indigo name and although the claimant did not make printers it sued for trade mark infringement and passing off and applied for an interlocutory injunction. As far as passing off was concerned, the claimant based its claim on a natural future extension of its business into the manufacture of printers. The judge accepted that there was a triable issue on passing off, but on the balance of convenience, refused the injunction requested.

There is no copyright in a fictitious name and an action in passing off is unlikely to be of much help if the defendant uses that name in relation to different goods or services. The test, as always, is whether the public is likely to be deceived by the use of the name, and in applying this test it is important to consider the fields of activity involved: do the two parties operate in the same or different fields? In the past, judges have not assumed that the public has a detailed knowledge of character merchandising. An example is provided by the case of *Wombles Ltd* v

Wombles Skips Ltd [1977] RPC 99. Wombles were fictitious animals from a TV series noted for their cleanliness, and for cleaning up litter and putting it to good use. The claimant company owned the copyright in the books and drawings of the Wombles, and their main business was granting licences so that manufacturers, in return for a fee, could use the Womble characters to promote their goods. They granted one such licence for waste-paper baskets. The defendant formed a company to lease builders' skips for rubbish. After considerable thought, and remembering the Wombles' clean habits, he decided to call his company Wombles Skips Ltd. In finding for the defendant, the court held that there was no common field of activity and, therefore, no danger of confusion. However, some judges do seem prepared to accept that the public are now more aware of character merchandising and there may be a change in this aspect of passing off before too long.

As technology moves on, sometimes two distinct fields of activity may converge. In *Nad Electronics Inc* v *Nad Computer Systems Ltd* [1997] FSR 380, the claimant sold high quality hi-fi systems and the defendant sold computers. Developments in computer technology have resulted in modern personal computers being equipped with compact disc drives capable of playing music CDs. As the fields of audio entertainment and computers are converging, the judge held that the defendant was liable in passing off. An important factor was that the parties' respective goods were similarly advertised and were sold alongside each other in retail outlets.

In *Teleworks Ltd* v *Telework Group plc* [2002] RPC 535, both companies operated in the field of computer telecommunications market. The claimant's main business was the design, supply and setting up of equipment used in computer networks and internet related services. It was a relatively small company. The defendant specialised in computer telephony and labour management software through two subsidiary companies. The claimant argued that the law of passing off protected its present goodwill and also any goodwill it might acquire in the future. The claimant's action for passing off failed as it failed to show that it had adequate goodwill at the time the defendant commenced the activities complained of. The court held that, although passing off could protect the development of a growing business. If a trader's goodwill was strong enough to induce the relevant belief in purchasers in the circumstances of the trade in question, the goodwill could be protected in fields the trader had not yet entered and had no present intention to do so. This case, which followed the Lego case in this respect, shows that there is no longer such a rigid division into fields of activity.

Internet domain names

Every internet domain name must be different to every other one. However, computers can distinguish the smallest changes, so inserting another character such as a hyphen will result in two potentially usable and distinct domain names: for example, **smithjones.com** and **smith-jones.com**. Another distinct domain is **smithandjones.com**. If closely resembling names are registered by different traders, it is highly likely there may be confusion on the part of persons accessing their websites using the relevant internet addresses. There is a distinct possibility of passing off where traders are using similar domain names.

It has been the practice of domain name registries to accept applications to register domain names on a first-come, first-served basis without any consideration as to whether the applicant had the right to register the name. Individuals have registered names such as '**mcdonalds.com**', '**mtv.com**' and '**harrods.com**'. Such registrations may have been made in order to sell the addresses to the relevant organisations but, in the UK, the law of passing off has proved valuable in respect of such practices.

In *Pitman Training Ltd* v *Nominet UK* [1997] FSR 797, two companies, at the time of the case distinct from each but sharing a common origin, had similar names: Pitman Training Ltd and

Pitman Publishing. The case concerned the right to the domain name 'pitman.co.uk'. Pitman Publishing, which was the second defendant, successfully applied to register that name but did not make use of it for a period of time. Due to an error, the name was re-allocated to Pitman Training Ltd. Pitman Publishing complained when it found out and the name was re-allocated to Pitman Publishing. Pitman Training Ltd commenced proceedings, wanting the name transferred back to it, claiming, *inter alia*, that its use by Pitman Publishing was passing off. However, this failed to impress the judge who thought it highly unlikely that the public would associate the domain name with Pitman Training Ltd. Rather, it was more likely to think it belonged to Pitman Publishing as it had been trading under that name for nearly 150 years. An additional factor was that, when the Pitman companies were sold off in 1985, there was an express agreement that Pitman Training Ltd would not use the word Pitman without the word 'Training'.

Cybersquatting

The *Pitman* case above was not really an example of cybersquatting. This occurs where a person registers a company name, trade mark or the name of a celebrity in the hope of selling on the name to the relevant company or celebrity. There have been many examples of this. The majority have been settled by dispute resolution processes, discussed later. There have been a number which have resulted in litigation which now has an almost inevitable conclusion finding passing off and requiring the transfer of the domain name to the 'rightful owner'.

A company with no connection to Harrods (the famous store in Knightsbridge) registered 'harrods.com' as a domain name. Use of the name was suspended pending the outcome of the dispute resolution procedure provided by the registration body in the US but, in the meantime, Harrods launched an action in England for passing off and trade mark infringement: *Harrods Ltd* v *UK Network Services Ltd* [1997] EIPR D-106. Summary judgment was granted and the defendant was ordered to release the domain name to the claimant.

In a subsequent case, *Marks & Spencer plc* v *One in a Million Ltd* [1998] FSR 265, five actions were brought by well-known organisations, each of which had substantial goodwill, against the defendant which was a dealer in internet domain names. It had registered names such as 'bt.org', 'sainsbury.com' and 'marksandspencer.co.uk'. The defendant wrote to the organisations offering to sell the domain names. The judge considered that threats of passing off and trade mark infringement were made out and he granted injunctions ordering the defendant to transfer the domain names to the claimants. Even though the domain names had not been used, the judge thought the defendant was guilty of passing off by being in possession of instruments of fraud.

The defendant's appeal to the Court of Appeal was dismissed; *British Telecommunications plc* v *One in a Million Ltd* [1999] FSR 1. It was confirmed that the court had jurisdiction to grant relief where a defendant had or was intending to transfer an instrument of fraud to another. It was said that the registrations, described as blocking registrations, were made for the purposes of obtaining money from the owners of the goodwill attached to the names and that the domain names were instruments of fraud as the only realistic use of the names, other than by the owners of the goodwill attaching to them, would result in passing off. Similar activities in relation to company names in another case were described by the judge as a 'scam'.

A manager of a civil engineering company registered easyRealestate.co.uk to use as a cut-price web-based estate agency. He approached the founder of the easyJet airline and associated companies such as easyRentacar hoping to induce him into entering a partnership and providing capital to help get the web-based estate agency up and running. In *easyJet Airline Co Ltd* v *Dainty (t/a easyRealestate)* [2002] FSR 6, summary judgment was granted to the claimants. The defendant was ordered to transfer the domain name to the claimants as it was accepted that he had intended to take advantage of the goodwill of the claimants by choosing a name and design of website that was similar to that of the claimants. Although it was accepted that the claimants had no rights in the word 'easy', *per se*, coupling it with a word describing the service offered, using it in lower case as a prefix with a word starting with an uppercase letter and using the same livery colours as the claimants all suggested that the defendant had copied the claimants' get-up when he commissioned the design of his website. Again the judge accepted that the domain name, in the hands of the defendant was an instrument of fraud and the order requiring its transfer to the claimants was appropriate. However, as the defendant had only done minimal, if any, business through the website, there would be no award of damages as such an award, in favour of a very large organisation, could be seen as oppressive. An interesting aspect of the judgment is that the judge did not consider the use of the domain name alone, without taking the other factors into account, was such as to inherently lead to a conclusion of passing off. It was by looking at the circumstances and the perceived intention of the defendant that convinced the judge that the domain name was a 'vehicle of fraud'.

Where someone registers a company name as a domain name for reasons other than for cybersquatting, hoping to sell it at a premium to the company, different factors may apply. However, usually, the circumstances will be such that the only sensible outcome will be for a court to order that the domain name is transferred to the company. In *Global Projects Management Ltd* v *Citigroup Inc* [2006] FSR 721, Citigroup Inc, one of the world's foremost financial groups, was formed in 1998 from the merger of two large US financial organisations. This attracted a lot of publicity. The claimant, 'GPM' was a one-man company owned and controlled by Mr Davies. In 1998 Mr Davies registered **citigroup.co.uk**. He applied later on the same day that the merger had first been publicised. He also applied on the same day to register **citigroup.com** but it was already taken. In 2003 Citigroup became aware of the domain name and its solicitors wrote to GPM threatening legal action for passing off and trade mark infringement. GPM brought proceedings under section 21 of the Trade Marks Act 1994 for groundless threats of infringement proceedings. Citigroup counterclaimed for passing off seeking an order that the domain name be assigned to it.

Any person accessing **citigroup.co.uk** would be taken to the claimant's website but all that appeared was the message 'an error has occurred'. If an e-mail was sent to an employee at Citigroup Inc, but using the **.co.uk** suffix by mistake, it would be delivered to the claimant's website. This resulted in a return message pointing out that the e-mail had been incorrectly addressed. GPM received over 4,000 e-mails intended for Citigroup employees in this way. Some of the e-mails contained sensitive and confidential information.

GPM never used the domain name for its own business (its own website was at **gpm.co.uk**) and had never attempted to sell it to Citigroup Inc. In fact, Mr Davies refused to sell it to Citigroup Inc, saying it enabled him to look out for improprieties which he could draw to the attention of the authorities. He claimed he was not a cybersquatter.

Summary judgment was given to Citigroup Inc on its counterclaim for trade mark infringement. It was held that it was no defence to a passing off claim that the domain name had not been used to make fraudulent representations that any goods or services supplied through the domain name were those of another company. Mere registration and maintenance in force of the domain name which led or might lead people to believe the holder of the domain name was linked with someone else was enough for it to be a potential instrument of fraud. It appeared that the reason GPM registered and maintained the domain name was not genuine or *bona fide* but was for the purpose of snooping on misdirected e-mails. As the counterclaim succeeded, GPM's groundless threats action was dismissed.

It is clear that the courts will not look sympathetically at persons who register famous names as domain names with the intention of selling them for large sums of money or for carrying out some other use that is not *bona fide*. The law of passing off is appropriate, though at the time there may not have been any actual use of the name. The threat of passing off if the intended

11

Trade marks, passing off and malicious falsehood

buyer does not accede is very real where someone registers a name in bad faith. However, real difficulties still may arise, for example, because of the international nature of the internet. What if an American company, having a website in the United States accessible from the United Kingdom, has a very similar name for its internet address to that of an English company having an established goodwill? Furthermore, what if a sole trader whose name happens to be John Sainsbury wishes to register **john-sainsbury.com** as his domain name?

Dispute resolution

There are now effective dispute resolution systems in place to deal with disputes as to the right to own a domain name. The Internet Corporation for Assigned Names and Numbers (ICANN) developed a Uniform Domain Name Disputer Resolution Policy (UDRP Policy) to settle disputes by a registrant and a third party claiming the registration is abusive in relation to the gTLDs (generic Top Level Domains) **.com**, **.net**, **.org**, **.biz**, **.info** and **.name** and in respect of ccTLDs (country code Top Level Domains) in respect of those countries which have adopted the policy on a voluntary basis. The World Intellectual Property Organisation operates the ICANN UDRP.

The UK is not one of those countries that has adopted the UDRP Policy in respect of the .uk ccTLD but Nominet UK has a dispute resolution policy and procedure for dealing with complaints by third parties against registration of domain names. In other countries that have not adopted the UDRP Policy in respect of ccTLDs, complaints have to be directed to the relevant domain name registry. The general rule is that dispute resolution procedures can only be implemented by a person objecting to registration of a domain name and not, for example, by a person who, having registered a domain name, has been threatened with legal action if he fails to hand over the domain. Nor can the system be used to submit complaints against the registrar. Making a complaint or responding to a compliant does not prevent the commencement of legal proceedings.

There may be good reasons for going to litigation in the courts rather than submitting to dispute resolution systems. The courts can grant injunctions, including interim injunctions, award damages or an account of profits and make orders for payment of costs and even make an order for security of costs if, for example, it appears that a person defending a hopeless case has no funds, being a 'man of straw'. Other orders are available to the courts such as a freezing order, being an order freezing a party removing his assets from the jurisdiction of the courts.

Remedies for passing off

The available remedies are injunctions, including interim injunctions, and damages. An account of profits may be available as an alternative to damages. The damages are assessed by considering the harm done to the claimant's goodwill and the lost sales of the claimant's goods as a result of the passing off. The most desirable remedy is an injunction, preventing the other person or business from continuing to use the claimant's established name, get-up or style.

MALICIOUS FALSEHOOD

An action related to passing off is malicious falsehood, sometimes known as trade libel. This is the commercial equivalent of defamation and an example is where a person publishes untrue information concerning the quality of a trader's goods. In terms of computer technology, malicious falsehood would occur if someone, acting maliciously, falsely claimed that a particular software dealer was trading in pirated software or was in financial difficulties or that a software house's products were defective or would not operate on a particular make of computer. Of course, the information must be false and must be published or stated maliciously. This means made without good cause or excuse and could extend to a reckless statement. In *Compaq Computer Corp* v *Dell Computer Corp Ltd* [1992] FSR 93, discussed earlier in this chapter, it was held that there was an arguable case of trade libel because the computer systems compared were materially different and the representations as to price were misleading and not justified. However, the requirement to prove malice reduces the frequency with which malicious falsehood actions are successful.

Embarking upon a comparative advertising campaign can precipitate an action for malicious falsehood, if malice can be shown and if the information used is palpably false. In *DSG Retail Ltd* v *Comet Group plc* [2002] FSR 58, the defendant ran an advertising campaign claiming that it had a price guarantee and would always undercut competitors' price-cutting promotions. This campaign was held to be an attempt to denigrate competitors' goods or services and contained clear references to the claimant. Further, the defendant's claims were deceptive in that its stores were instructed to lower marked prices only if challenged by customers. Thus, the statements were false and the defendant knew this. The tort of malicious falsehood requires that the statement is made with knowledge of its falsity or recklessness as to its truth. The judge accepted that the defendant knew full well that the statements were false and confirmed the injunction previously granted.

In *International Business Machines Corp* v *Web-Sphere Ltd* [2004] EWHC 529 (Ch), discussed earlier, there was also a claim for malicious falsehood as the defendant had published a leaflet claiming that IBM had threatened trade mark infringement proceedings and had acted in an arrogant manner. There was also an allegation that proper opposition procedures had not been followed and, consequently, IBM's WEBSPHERE trade mark had not been duly and lawfully registered. The essential elements for an action in malicious falsehood are:

- publication of a falsity concerning the claimant;
- the fact that the publication was made maliciously; and
- special damage suffered by the claimant or, alternatively, that the words published were calculated to cause pecuniary damage to the claimant.

Malice may be inferred if the words published were calculated to cause damage and the defendant knew that the words were false or was reckless as to whether they were false, at the time he published the words. The judge accepted that the words in the leaflets were false. Although the defendant believed the truth of some of the statements made in the leaflets, the judge thought that the distribution of them was motivated by ill will and they were, in that sense, made maliciously. The statements were designed to sting IBM into action and the sting would have been useless had it not been motivated by a desire to injure IBM. However, the last requirement had not been established. IBM had not pleaded any special damage and there was no evidence of any likelihood of damage, for example, by any possibility that IBM's customers would have been diverted to the defendants.

SUMMARY

- Trade mark law and the law of passing off can usefully protect signs and marks used with hardware and software and on websites.
- For registration as a UK trade mark or a Community trade mark the mark must be:
  - capable of being represented graphically;

- capable of distinguishing goods or services from one undertaking from those of other undertakings;
- not caught by the absolute or relative grounds for refusal.

■ The absolute grounds for refusal cover a number of grounds, for example:
- where the basic requirement is not satisfied or the mark is devoid of distinctive character;
- where the mark is descriptive or laudatory or in common usage;
- where the mark is a particular type of shape, such as a shape dictated by technical function;
- where the mark is contrary to public policy or morality.

■ The relative grounds for refusal depend on the relationship with the mark and earlier trade marks or marks protected by other means, such as by passing off.

■ Forms of infringement are equivalent to the relative grounds applicable to earlier trade marks.

■ There are a number of issues relating to the internet:
- domain names may be registered if they are perceived as trade marks and otherwise comply with the requirements for registration;
- in some cases, it may be arguable whether a trade mark on a webpage is used as a trade mark;
- where a likelihood of confusion is required for infringement, it is debatable whether websites are different to bricks and mortar stores;
- it is questionable whether keyword meta-tags can infringe trade marks;
- to infringe within a particular jurisdiction it must be targeted by the advertising.

■ The law of passing off can protect unregistered trade marks, names, signs and get-up.

■ Three things are required for an action in passing off:
- the existence of goodwill belonging to the claimant;
- a misrepresentation made by the defendant;
- actual or potential damage to the goodwill.

■ Manipulating images of famous people to give false endorsements is passing off.

■ Passing off is useful to deal with cyber-squatting and other domain name abuses.

■ Having a domain name which should rightly belong to someone else is being in possession of an instrument of fraud.

■ Malicious falsehood is useful where:
- someone denigrates another's business, goods or services;
- however, it is difficult to prove malice; and
- there must be proof of damage.

SELF-TEST QUESTIONS

Note: there is only one correct answer to each multiple choice question.

1   **Which one of the following trade marks CANNOT be registered as a trade mark in the UK?**

(a) A new and distinctive computer icon for computer software.

(b) 'MEDCORPS' (a made up word) for a website carrying health information.

(c) The domain name 'tesco.com' for a variety of foodstuffs and goods found in a typical super-market.

(d) The smell of mountain dew applied to a laptop computer.

2   Harvey retails computer software from his online store which is called VIZSOFT which is a registered trade mark for applications software, games software, operating system software and other software products. The trade mark is very well-known. Tony, a market trader has just started selling pornographic magazines from his market stall under the name VIZSOFT TRADERS. Which one of the following statements is most likely to be CORRECT?

(a) Tony has not infringed the trade mark as he is using it for goods which are different to those for which the mark is registered.

(b) Tony has infringed Harvey's trade mark as the use of his sign is not in accordance with honest practices and takes unfair advantage of, or is detrimental to, the repute of the trade mark.

(c) Tony has infringed the trade mark because he is using a sign identical to the trade mark for non-similar goods, providing it can be shown that there is a likelihood of confusion which includes a likelihood of association.

(d) Tony has not infringed the trade mark because the addition of the word 'TRADERS' means that Tony's sign is not identical which is required for infringement by taking unfair advantage of, or being detrimental to, the repute of a trade mark.

3   Lindridge Telecommunications Ltd has a website where it advertises its telecommunications services. On the website there is a table comparing its services with those of TeleSouth plc, another telecommunications company. The table comprises three columns. The first lists the features being compared, for example, 'bandwidth' and 'cost per minute'. The second column contains data relating to Lindridge's services and the third column, those of TeleSouth. This last column is headed 'TeleSouth' which is a registered trade mark for telecommunications services belonging to TeleSouth plc. The features chosen tend to be those which show Lindridge's services to be better and cheaper. Underneath the table is the following text 'Switch to Lindridge and you can save up to £15 each month'. A survey carried out by TeleSouth indicates that the average saving would only be around £11 per month. Which one of the following statements is CORRECT?

(a) There is no infringement of the TeleSouth trade mark as the advertising falls within section 10(6) of the Trade Marks Act 1994.

(b) The TeleSouth trade mark has been infringed because it is not in accordance with honest practices to selectively choose features to show the advertiser's services are better or cheaper.

(c) The TeleSouth trade mark has been infringed because it is not in accordance with honest practices to make a statement about a likely saving which must differ for different customers and no amount of hyperbole is allowed under section 10(6) of the Trade Marks Act 1994.

(d) There is no infringement of the TeleSouth trade mark because there is no likelihood of confusion among persons who might visit the Lindridge website.

4   Martino is a solicitor. One day he read in the newspaper that two English companies in the weapons industry, Gilbert and Smith Ltd and Kandela Ltd, were going to merge. He immediately applied successfully to register 'gilbertsmithkandela.co.uk', 'gilbertsmithkandela.com', 'gsk.co.uk' and 'gsk.com' as domain names. A few days later, there was a press announcement that the name of the newly merged company was to be GilbertSmithKandela Ltd. When the new company attempted to register its name and the abbreviation 'GSK' as domain names for its new business, it discovered Martino's domain name registrations. The company brought a passing-off action against Martino who claims he had no intention of

using the domain names. However, some e-mails had been sent to employees at the company by persons who thought the e-mail address might be at one of Martino's domains. These were read by Martino before he forwarded them on to the company. Martino, who is opposed to armed conflict, said that this was his way of checking the company was not selling arms to unstable governments contrary to the new Foreign Office ethical policy. He explained that being able to monitor the company's business was the sole reason he registered the domain names. Which one of the following statements is CORRECT?

(a) As domain names are issued on a first-come, first-served basis and Martino is not cybersquatting, he will successfully defend a passing-off action.

(b) The court will not intervene because issues as to entitlement to domain names should be resolved amicably by using an appropriate domain name dispute resolution process.

(c) The court will not grant an order requiring Martino to transfer the domain names to the company as he is using them for the purpose of monitoring compliance with Foreign Office policy and, by doing so, is providing a service for the public good.

(d) The court will order Martino to transfer the domain names to the company, as they are instruments of fraud, even though he did not register them for the purpose of selling them to the company at an inflated price.

5   The use of trade marks on the internet raises a number of issues in respect of which the law on trade marks should be modified to fully address these issues. What are those issues and in what ways should trade mark law be modified?

For further resources and updates please go to the Companion Website accompanying this book at **www.mylawchamber.co.uk/bainbridgeIT**

12 Criminal offences and intellectual property

INTRODUCTION

Some time ago, the criminal law had little impact in the field of intellectual property. This is no longer the case and a study of criminal offences relating to intellectual property is now a subject in its own right. At one time, most offences applied only to matters such as making or causing to be made a false entry on the register of patents or failing to comply with a secrecy direction made in respect of a patent application. The criminal penalty for copyright infringement was a fine of 40 shillings (£2.00) under the Copyright Act 1956 before the penalties were raised to include imprisonment in response to the growing threat of copyright piracy in the 1980s. Falsely claiming an article was subject to a patent under the Patents Act 1949 could attract a maximum penalty of £50.

The areas of intellectual property law where criminal offences carrying severe penalties have been brought in are copyright, rights in performances and trade marks. There were two main reasons for this. First, the scale of piracy and counterfeiting reached such proportions that the owner's economic rights were being seriously prejudiced. Secondly, it appeared that organised criminal gangs were becoming heavily involved in piracy and counterfeiting. Intellectual property crime is now taken very seriously and comes within the remit of the recently established Serious Organised Crime Agency and certain offences under copyright, rights in performances and trade marks law are among the offences to which certain provisions of the Serious Organised Crime and Police Act 2005 apply. Although it is impossible to obtain accurate figures, the Home Office estimates that the market for counterfeit goods is at least £1 bn per annum in the UK. Most of this relates to digital media, particularly software and film.[1] Counterfeit luxury goods and even pharmaceuticals and spare parts for vehicles and aeroplanes are also involved in criminal operations. It is believed that many of the criminal gangs involved in intellectual property crime are also involved with other criminal activities such as drug trafficking and people smuggling.

Piracy of copyright and performances together with counterfeiting of goods to which trade marks have been applied are the main areas of concern. The same problems do not arise in relation to patents and designs. This is probably because it can be expensive to manufacture articles subject to patent rights, particularly in a complex technology. In any case, and the same applies to articles and products subject to design rights, infringing trade marks are likely to have been applied to them also.

There are still a number of offences such as falsifying registers of patents, registered designs and trade marks and falsely claiming that an article is subject to a patent, registered design or

---

[1] Serious Organised Crime Agency, *The United Kingdom Threat Assessment of Serious Organised Crime 2006/7*, 2006, p. 38.

registered trade mark. For some of these the penalties are relatively low. For example, falsely representing that a trade mark is registered is triable only in the magistrates' courts and only carries a financial penalty. These offences are outside the scope of this book and this chapter looks at the offences related to piracy and counterfeiting in the two main areas of copyright and trade marks only. There are related offences which apply in respect of recordings of live performances but these are not dealt with here.

COPYRIGHT LAW

We have already seen that infringement of copyright can give rise to a wide range of civil law remedies such as injunctions, damages and accounts of profits. Piracy of copyright works has been described as an offence of dishonesty. It also involves deception in many cases. Although it is true to say that the majority of copyright infringements will be dealt with in a satisfactory manner by the civil law, for example, where the parties are legitimate companies, the offences may be more appropriate in cases of out and out piracy.

The maximum penalty for some of the copyright offences is 10 years' imprisonment and/or a fine if convicted in the Crown Court. Because of this, there is a concern that the mental element which has to be proved to secure a conviction is set at a relatively low standard. Proof of dishonesty is not required and, in practice, all the prosecution has to show is that a reasonable person having knowledge of the facts known to the accused, would have reason to believe that he was dealing with infringing copies. This is a carry-over from the time when the penalties for criminal offences under copyright law were relatively minor. Similar concerns apply to trade mark law, where the offences are almost of strict liability subject to the defendant proving that he believed on reasonable grounds that his use of the sign did not infringe a registered trade mark.

Some of the criminal offences are equivalent to some of the civil infringements of copyright known collectively as secondary infringement. The same activity can result in both criminal and civil liability. For example, if a person distributes in the course of a business an article which he knows or has reason to believe is an infringing copy of a copyright work, he is liable for civil infringement under section 23 of the Copyright, Designs and Patents Act 1988 and also commits a criminal offence under section 107. It is not unheard of for someone who has been convicted of an offence to be sued later for civil infringement. The conviction can be put in as evidence in the civil trial raising a presumption that the defendant committed the offence: see, for example, *Microsoft Corporation* v *Alibhai* [2004] EWHC 3282 (Ch), discussed in Chapter 3.

Provisions also apply enabling search and seizure and forfeiture of infringing copies, devices, products or components as the case may be. There are other offences in relation to the fraudulent reception of broadcasts and in respect of unauthorised decoders. A decoder is apparatus designed or adapted to enable an encrypted transmission to be decoded, whether on its own or with other apparatus.

Corporate bodies, such as a limited company, can commit many offences and offences under copyright law are no exception. Where an offence under section 107 is committed by a corporate body, with the consent, connivance of a director, manager, secretary or other similar officer of the body, or any person purporting to act in such a capacity, that person as well as the corporate body if guilty of the offence and may be liable to prosecution for it: section 110. It is possible for a single offence to result in the prosecution of a company, the person in the company who actually carries out the act and any senior officer who consented or connived in the commission of the offence. For example, if Jack, an employee of a Buccaneer Trading Ltd, offers infringing copies music CDs for sale and Jill, a director of the company has consented to the offer for sale, Jack, Buccaneer and Jill are all potentially liable. Jack will be liable under section 107(1)(d)(ii) if

Table 12.1 Criminal offences under copyright law

Offence (Copyright, Designs and Patents Act 1988)	Maximum term of imprisonment (see below)
Section 107(1) With respect to an article which the person concerned knows or has reason to believe is an infringing copy of a copyright work, and without the licence of the copyright owner:	
(a) making for sale or hire;	10 years
(b) importing into the UK other than for his private and domestic use;	10 years
(c) possessing in the course of business with a view to committing any act infringing the copyright;	6 months*
(d) in the course of a business:	
(i) selling or letting for hire;	6 months*
(ii) offering or exposing for sale or hire;	6 months*
(iii) exhibiting in public;	6 months*
(iv) distributing;	10 years
(e) distributing otherwise than in the course of a business to such an extent as to affect prejudicially the owner of the copyright.	10 years
Section 107(2) With respect to an article specifically designed or adapted for making copies of a particular copyright work where the person concerned knows or has reason to believe that it is to be used to make infringing copies for sale or hire or for use in the course of a business:	
(a) making such an article;	6 months*
(b) being in possession of such an article.	6 months*
Section 107(2A) Infringing copyright by communicating a work to the public, knowing or having reason to believe that he is infringing copyright, either:	
(a) in the course of a business;	2 years
(b) otherwise than in the course of a business to such an extent as to affect prejudicially the owner of the copyright.	2 years
Section 107(3) Causing a work to be performed, played or shown where copyright is infringed (other than by communicating to the public) by a public performance of a literary, dramatic or musical work or by the playing or showing in public of a sound recording or film where the person concerned knows or has reason to believe that copyright would be infringed.	6 months*
Section 296ZB(1) With respect to any device, product or component primarily designed, produced or adapted for the purpose of enabling or facilitating the circumvention of effective technological measures:	
(a) manufacturing for sale or hire;	
(b) importing otherwise than for his private and domestic use;	All these offences carry a maximum of 2 years
(c) in the course of a business:	
(i) selling or letting for hire;	
(ii) offering or exposing for sale or hire;	
(iii) advertising for sale or hire;	
(iv) possessing;	
(v) distributing;	
(d) distributing otherwise than in the course of a business to such an extent as to affect prejudicially the copyright owner.	

12

Criminal offences and intellectual property

Table 12.1 continued

Offence (Copyright, Designs and Patents Act 1988)	Maximum term of imprisonment (see below)
Section 296ZB(2) Providing, promoting, advertising or marketing a service the purpose of which is to enable or facilitate the circumvention of effective technological measures:	
(a) in the course of a business;	2 years
(b) otherwise than in the course of a business to such an extent as to affect prejudicially the copyright owner.	2 years
Defence to section 296ZB(1) and (2) It is defence for the defendant to prove that he did not know and had no reasonable ground for believing that the device, product or component or service enabled or facilitated the circumvention of effective technological measures. The offences in section 296ZB(1) and (2) do not apply in relation to certain things done by or on behalf of the law enforcement agencies or intelligence services.	

Technological measures are any technology, device or component designed in the normal course of its operation to protect a copyright work other than a computer program. Such measures are 'effective' if the use of the work in question is controlled by the copyright owner through:
(a) an access control or protection process such as encryption, scrambling or other transformation of the work; or
(b) a copy control mechanism;
which achieves the intended protection.
All the offences are triable either in the Crown Court or a magistrates' court with the exception of those marked with an asterisk (*) which are triable only in a magistrates' court. All the offences may be punished with a fine instead or in addition to a custodial sentence. Fines in the Crown Court are unlimited. For magistrates' courts there is a standard scale of maximum fines and a statutory maximum fine.

he personally had reason to believe the CDs were infringing copies, the company will be liable under section 107(1)(d)(ii) if a senior officer had reason so to believe (which might be Jill). Jill will also be liable under section 110 because she consented to the offer for sale. Where the offence requires a mental element, such as under section 107, it is usual to impute to a corporate body the mental element of a senior officer such as a director or company secretary.

The scope of the criminal offences is fairly wide and will cover most forms of commercial exploitation as well as offences connected with circumventing technological measures applied to copyright works to prohibit or restrict unauthorised acts. These latter offences were brought in by the Copyright and Related Rights Regulations 2003.

Making an article designed to make copies is a criminal offence, as is being in possession of such a device if the person knows or has reason to believe that the article will be used to make infringing copies for sale or hire or for use in the course of business. This would cover a piece of equipment specifically designed for this purpose but not a computer with DVD or CD writer drive or a floppy disk drive. Although these optical or magnetic devices can be used for making infringing copies, they are not designed for infringing copyright; they are designed for legitimate uses. The word 'article' is used in section 107(2) but is not defined in the Act in this context. In terms of older technology it would cover, for example, a master for making vinyl records or plate for making prints.

Distributing a work of copyright otherwise than in the course of a business to such extent as to affect prejudicially the owner of the copyright could apply where a person places music or video files on his computer so that others may download copies using peer-to-peer sharing software. The copy so made available would have to be an infringing copy and it would have to be shown that the person responsible had reason to believe that it was an infringing copy. This is an objective test as discussed below. However, where a young person, say in their early teens, is responsible, it is not clear whether the test should be based on the reasonable adult of reasonable young person.

Knows or has reason to believe

The formula used for the mental state necessary to impose criminal liability for the copyright offences under section 107 is that the person concerned 'knows or has reason to believe'. The meaning of this phrase was considered in *LA Gear Inc* v *Hi-Tec Sports plc* [1992] FSR 121, where the Court of Appeal said that the test to apply was an objective one – that is, whether the reasonable person, having the defendant's knowledge of the facts, would have believed that the copy was an infringing copy. Previously, at first instance, the High Court had gone further, saying that the phrase connoted the allowance of a period of time to allow the reasonable man to evaluate the facts and so form a reasonable belief. Although the Court of Appeal said the test was objective, it is not truly so if it takes into account the facts known to the defendant. What if the defendant fails to make enquiries that a reasonable person might make, for example, where the copies had been obtained from a stranger without a permanent place of business at prices greatly below the normal price? It would seem sensible to think such circumstances would cause a reasonable person to be suspicious and make further enquiries to satisfy himself or herself as to whether the copies were legitimate. Failing to make enquiries where a reasonable person would make enquiries should be the same as having reason to believe. This would make the offence broadly equivalent to the trade mark offences as regards the mental state for a conviction, although with the trade mark offences, as with the offences under section 296ZB, the mental state operates as a defence rather than being something to be proved by the prosecution.

The criminal offences under section 107 certainly cover copyright piracy but they are not restricted to cases of blatant piracy and can apply to legitimate businesses and even to honest businessmen in the right circumstances. In *Thames & Hudson Ltd* v *Design and Artists Copyright Society Ltd* [1995] FSR 153 the Design and Artists Copyright Society Ltd commenced private prosecutions against Thames & Hudson Ltd, a publisher of books on art and other illustrated books, and its directors for offences under sections 107 and 110 of the Copyright, Designs and Patents Act 1988 on the basis that Thames & Hudson was selling and distributing a book knowing, or having reason to believe, that it contained material infringing copyright. (Section 110 imposes liability on directors and other officers of corporate bodies for offences under section 107.) An application by Thames & Hudson for a stay of proceedings until after the civil case had been heard was rejected by the judge who confirmed that section 107 does not differentiate between a reputable company and a pirate. The mental element for the offences is made out if the accused had reason to believe that the copies were infringing copies.

Defence for offences under section 296ZB

The offences under section 296ZB do not require the prosecution to prove any mental element on the part of a person accused of one of the offences. It is sufficient that the person was responsible for the relevant acts, for example, by offering for sale in the course of a business a device primarily designed to enable to circumvention of effective technological measures (the meaning of 'effective technological measures' is given in Chapter 7 and under Table 12.1 above). To temper the potential unfairness of this where, for example, the accused had no knowledge that he was offering a device with the appropriate qualities, a defence is provided in section 296ZB(5). The accused has a defence if he proves that he did not know, and had no reasonable ground for believing, that the device, product, component or the service enabled or facilitated the circumvention of effective technological measures.

Thus far, there have been no reported cases on the meaning of the phrase '... did not know, and had no reasonable ground for believing' in the context of section 296ZB. Having no reasonable ground for believing must be determined objectively. Would a reasonable person having knowledge of the facts known to the accused have the relevant belief? Again, it is likely that this would extend to the duty to make enquiries if the circumstances were such to raise a suspicion.

As the defendant has to prove that he did not know and had no reasonable ground for believing that the device, etc. enabled or facilitated the circumvention of effective technological measures, the standard of proof will be on a balance of probabilities. In criminal offences, the prosecution normally has to proof the ingredients of the offence including the requisite mental element beyond reasonable doubt. However, if the accused carries the burden of proof, that is usually discharged by proof on a balance of probabilities, the normal standard of proof in civil proceedings.

There is no equivalent provision imposing criminal liability on directors, etc. of corporate bodies where the offence has been committed by the body with the consent or connivance of the director, etc. as there is under section 107.

TRADE MARK OFFENCES

Where a counterfeiter or copyright pirate includes a sign which resembles a registered trade mark on the infringing copies, apart from infringing copyright, designs rights and trade marks, he also runs the risk of a prosecution under section 92 of the Trade Marks Act 1994. The offences in section 92 carry a maximum penalty on conviction in the Crown Court of 10 years' imprisonment and/or a fine. Section 92(1) to (3) sets out the forms of offences, being in relation to a sign identical to or likely to be mistaken for a registered trade mark:

■ applying to goods, selling or letting for hire, offering or exposing for sale or hire or distributing goods bearing the sign or having in possession, custody or control in the course of business such goods with a view to selling or letting for hire, etc., either by himself or another;

■ applying to material intended to be used for labelling or packaging goods, as a business paper in relation to goods or for advertising goods or using such material in the course of a business for such purposes or having in possession, custody or control such material with a view to such uses, either by himself or another;

■ making an article specifically designed or adapted for making copies of the sign or having such an article in possession, custody or control in the course of a business knowing or having reason to believe that it has been or is to be used to produce goods, or material for labelling or packaging goods, as a business paper in relation to goods or for advertising goods.

For all the offences, the accused must be doing whatever it is with a view to gain for himself or another or with intent to cause loss to another and it must be without the consent of the proprietor of the trade mark.

The goods in question must be goods in respect of which the trade mark is registered or the trade mark has a reputation in the UK and the use of the sign takes or would take unfair advantage of, and is or would be detrimental to, the distinctive character or repute of the trade mark.

Apart from one case, the only mental element that the prosecution has to provide, assuming it is denied, is the view to gain or intent to cause loss. This is not usually going to be an issue as it almost goes without saying that the accused will have such a view or intent. In that sense, the offences are almost of strict liability. However, it is a defence for the accused to show he believed on reasonable grounds that the use of the sign and the manner in which it was used was not an infringement of the registered trade mark. The standard of proof as is usual with defences to criminal offences is the balance of probabilities.

This defence requires what has been described as a 'reverse persuasive burden of proof'. It was challenged as being contrary to the presumption of innocence in a criminal trial under Article 6(2) of the Convention on Human Rights[2] but this was rejected by the House of Lords in *R v Johnstone* [2003] FSR 748. In that case, Johnstone had been convicted under section 92 of the Trade Marks Act 1994 in respect of bootleg recordings of performances by famous singers and pop groups and had been sentenced to six months' imprisonment and a confiscation order was made of just over £130,000. The Court of Appeal had quashed the conviction on the basis, *inter alia*, that an offence under section 92 presupposed a civil infringement of the trade mark.

In respect of the defence itself, the House of Lords held that it applied where the accused did not believe on reasonable grounds that he did not infringe a trade mark of which he was aware and also applied where the reason he believed he did not infringe a registered trade mark was because he reasonably believed that no relevant trade mark had been registered. Furthermore, the offence could only apply where the use of the sign was as an indication of origin. The offences may not be made out, for example, where the trade mark is the name of a pop group and it is applied to a counterfeit CD to denote the identity of the performers rather than being used in a trade mark sense.

Ignorance of trade mark law appears to deprive a defendant of the defence under section 92(5) as the second case – reasonable belief that no relevant trade mark existed – cannot apply where the defendant admits to knowing nothing about trade mark law and registration of trade marks. The Court of Appeal confirmed this is *R v McCrudden* [2005] EWCA Crim 466 where a market trader had been prosecuted for selling, exposing for sale and being in possession with a view to selling counterfeit goods (clothing and accessories) bearing famous trade marks. In *R v Kahraman* [2006] EWHC 1703 (Admin) the Divisional Court of the High Court confirmed that a trader who bought goods bearing famous trade marks at very low prices from an unknown person with no evidence of trade reputation was not sufficient to show that he believed on reasonable grounds that the use of the trade marks was not an infringement. Nor was it sufficient to say that other traders were buying goods from that person or that the defendant was inexperienced as a market trader.

OTHER OFFENCES

Apart from specific offences under intellectual property laws, other offences may be relevant, depending on the circumstances. They are:

- Forgery by making a false instrument (an 'instrument' includes any disc, tape, sound track or devices on which information is stored by mechanical, electronic or other means) under section 1 of the Forgery and Counterfeiting Act 1981. There must be an intention that it will be used to induce someone to accept it as genuine. An example is where someone is selling counterfeit Microsoft certificates of authenticity.

- Offences in relation to trade descriptions, for example, in the course of a trade or business, applying a false trade description to goods or supplying or offering to supply goods to which a false trade description has been applied under section 1 of the Trade Descriptions Act 1968.

---

[2] Council of Europe Convention for the Protection of Human Rights and Fundamental Freedoms 1950.

This could apply where a person makes unauthorised copies of a film on DVD and applies a label suggesting they are genuine.

■ Deception offences under the Fraud Act 2006, include making a false representation, failing to disclose information or abuse of position.

Some of the above offences proved useful in the fight against piracy and counterfeiting before the copyright and trade mark offences were strengthened. Another possible offence is common law conspiracy to defraud (except in Scotland). This could apply, for example, where two or more persons conspire to sell infringing copies of music or video files online.

SUMMARY

■ Some of the offences under copyright law carry a maximum penalty of 10 years' imprisonment and/or a fine.

■ Some copyright offences relate to commercial activity, such as importing or selling.

■ Senior officers who consent or connive in these offences committed by their corporate bodies are also liable.

■ Copyright offences are not restricted to 'pirates'.

■ Having reason to believe is an objective test:
  – would a reasonable person, knowing the facts known to the accused have reason to believe?

■ There are some offences in relation to the circumvention of effective technological measures applied to copyright works other than computer programs.

■ Trade mark offences are of almost strict liability.

■ Trade mark offences carry a maximum penalty of 10 years' imprisonment and/or a fine.

■ It is a defence to believe on reasonable grounds that a registered trade mark was not infringed.

■ The House of Lords interpreted the defence as applying in two cases:
  – belief that a trade mark is not infringed, being aware of the registration;
  – the reason for the belief is a reasonable belief that no relevant registration exists.

■ Other offences may be committed by piracy and counterfeiting operations.

SELF-TEST QUESTIONS

Note: there is only one correct answer to each multiple choice question.

1 **Which one of the following is NOT an offence under section 107 of the Copyright, Designs and Patents Act 1988?**

(a) Making an article for sale or hire knowing or having reason to believe that it is an infringing copy of a copyright work.

(b) Possessing an article, knowing or having reason to believe that it is an infringing copy of a copyright work, otherwise than in the course of a business, with a view to committing any act infringing the copyright.

(c) Distributing an article, knowing or having reason to believe that it is an infringing copy of a copyright work, otherwise than in the course of a business to such an extent as to affect prejudicially the owner of the copyright.

(d) Infringing copyright by communicating a work of copyright to the public in the course of a business, knowing or having reason to believe that, by doing so, he is infringing copyright in that work.

2   **Which on the following statements CORRECTLY describes the state of mind required for the offence of selling in the course of a business a device, product or component primarily designed, produced or adapted for the purpose of enabling or facilitating the circumvention of effective technological measures applied to a copyright work other than a computer program?**

(a) The prosecution has to prove that the defendant knew or had reason to believe that the device, product or component was designed, produced or adapted for the purpose of enabling or facilitating the circumvention of effective technological measures.

(b) The prosecution does not have to prove anything about the defendant's state of mind but he has a defence if he can prove that he did not know and had no reasonable ground for believing that the device, product or component enabled or facilitated the circumvention of effective technological measures.

(c) The prosecution has to prove that the defendant knew or had no reasonable ground for believing that the device, product or component was designed, produced or adapted for the purpose of enabling or facilitating the circumvention of effective technological measures.

(d) The offence is one of strict liability subject only to a defence of lack of technical knowledge concerning the circumvention of effective technological measures.

3   **Directors, managers and other similar officers of corporate bodies convicted of an offence under section 107 of the Copyright, Designs and Patents Act 1988 are also treated as committing the offence in question in certain circumstances under section 110. Which one of the following statements DESCRIBES those circumstances?**

(a) Where they have consented or connived in the offence.

(b) Where they have consented or connived in the offence or if it is attributable to their neglect.

(c) Where they have turned a blind eye to the commission of the offence by the corporate body.

(d) Where they knew or had reason to believe that the article in question was an infringing copy of a copyright work.

4   **Which one of the following statements is NOT CORRECT in relation to the offence of selling goods bearing a sign identical to or likely to be mistaken for a registered trade mark?**

(a) The goods must be those for which the trade mark is registered or the trade mark has a reputation in the UK and the use of the sign takes or would take unfair advantage of, or would be detrimental to, the distinctive character or the repute of the trade mark.

(b) Section 92(5) provides a defence where the defendant believes on reasonable grounds that his use of the sign does not infringe a registered trade mark of whose existence he is aware.

(c) Section 92(5) provides a defence where the reason the defendant believes his use of the sign does not infringe a registered trade mark is that he reasonably believes no relevant trade mark is registered.

(d) For the offence to be made out, it is not necessary to show that the defendant's use of the sign is as an indication of origin. Simply using a trade mark to identify the nature of the goods, such as in the case of placing the name of a pop group on a counterfeit music CD will suffice if the name is a trade mark.

12

Criminal offences and intellectual property

5   What is the justification for the trade mark offences to be of almost strict liability subject to the defendant having the persuasive burden to prove his defence (you may find it useful to refer to the judgment of Lord Nicholls in the House of Lords in *R* v *Johnstone* at paras 44-54)? (The judgment is available for free access at http://www.bailii.org/)

For further resources and updates please go to the Companion Website accompanying this book at **www.mylawchamber.co.uk/bainbridgeIT**

Part 2

Information technology contracts

Contracts for the acquisition and use of computer hardware and software and related contracts are dealt with in this part of the book. Many 'computer contracts' are not sale contracts as such but are contracts for services and often also involve licence agreements; this is particularly so with respect to computer software where the owner of the rights subsisting in the software grants licences to customers, giving them permission to use the software in return for a licence fee. For these agreements, the existence and scope of intellectual property rights is of primary importance. Permission to perform certain acts restricted by copyright may be fundamental to a licence but agreements to write software often contain numerous other terms, for example, to deal with liability for defects, time for completion, the scope of use, maintenance, payment and termination. Computer contracts are subject to numerous legal controls which may make some terms of the contract void and unenforceable. A statutory example is the Unfair Contract Terms Act 1977 which controls attempts to exclude or restrict liability for negligence and faulty performance of the contract.

In this part of the book, first the fundamental principles of contract law as it applies to computer contracts is examined. This includes a discussion of the nature of software contracts which is still not absolutely clear. Following this, liability issues related to defective hardware and software and the defective performance of computer contracts is explored including the liability for negligence and negligent misstatement (neither of which are dependant upon the existence of a contract). Product liability is also discussed as is the employer's liability for RSI (repetitive strain injury) caused by long periods of work at a keyboard. In subsequent chapters, particular types of computer contracts are described: contracts for the writing of computer software, ready-made software licences (which used to be referred to as 'off-the-shelf' software licences), open source software licences, website development contracts, IT outsourcing contracts and contracts for the acquisition of computer hardware.

13 Fundamentals of information technology contracts

INTRODUCTION

It is important to know precisely what the contract is. This may sound simple enough but there may be problems where the contract is partly in writing and partly oral. What are the terms of the contract? Also, the law, either by legislation or by common law, may imply terms into a contract. We also need to be able to classify the contract. For example, is it a contract for services – such as the service of writing new software or modifying existing software – or is it a contract for the sale of goods? The distinction is not always an easy one to make but it can be important, particularly as the terms implied into the contract may be different depending on its classification.

Once we have determined what sort of contract it is and what the express and implied terms of the contract are, we need to consider the consequences of a breach of the contract, for example, where one of the parties fails to fulfil his obligations under the contract, as imposed by the contract. In some cases, it may enable the other party to bring the contract to an end and also seek damages (monetary compensation for the breach). In other circumstances, it may only leave the aggrieved party with a remedy sounding in damages only.

Even if we know precisely what the terms of the contract are, there may be an issue concerning a misrepresentation made by one party to induce the other party to enter into the contract. This may be a particular problem where the contract says on its face that it represents the entire agreement between the parties and nothing else counts. Obviously, the law has to provide remedies for misrepresentations in appropriate circumstances.

These are the fundamental questions considered in this chapter which provides a basic toolkit for the following chapters in this part of the book.

TERMS OF THE CONTRACT

Sometimes, it may be difficult to determine whether a contract exists, particularly where there have been long and protracted negotiations. This aspect is discussed in Chapter 15 with some examples where a court has had to determine this in the context of computer contracts. Assuming there is a contract, it is important to know precisely what the terms of the contract are. *Vogon International Ltd* v *Serious Fraud Office* [2004] EWCA Civ 104 concerned a data recovery contract with the Serious Fraud Office. The meaning of 'database' for the purposes of the contract was not clear. This was serious as the work had been quoted at a price per database. Vogon thought it included all the individual personal store files, giving a total bill for the work of £314,375 whereas the SFO thought it only covered Microsoft Exchange databases, which made the total payable £22,500. The court confirmed the latter, after deciding what a database meant in the context of that contract.

In many situations where the whole contract is in writing (by deed or otherwise), this might appear to be an easy matter, providing one is skilled in 'legalese', the technical legal jargon still commonly found in legal documents and notwithstanding that many words used in the computer industry are lacking precision (such as database in *Vogon* above). But even where the contract is wholly in writing, things are not necessarily that straightforward and the law may insert additional terms (implied terms) into the contract or strike out some of the terms apparently agreed upon by the parties to the contract. This is notwithstanding the English tradition of freedom of contract – to the effect that the parties should be free to agree precisely what terms they want in their contract, though this old principle has been somewhat compromised by legislation and implied terms in the interests of fairness and protecting consumers and other parties to contracts who may be in a weak bargaining position.

A particular problem is where the contract is not in writing or is only partly in writing. An example of the latter is where a signed note or memorandum indicates that a contract exists but clearly does not contain all the terms on the face of it. For example, the note may state that Ace Software Ltd agrees to write process control software for Boris Boring and Drilling Co Ltd for the sum of £45,000. On its own such a note would be unenforceable because it lacks certainty. Apart from other missing information, there is no specification or other description of what is required of the software nor is there mention of any time for completion. In relation to oral contracts and contracts partly in writing, it will be a matter of submitting evidence of the other terms to give the contract sufficient certainty. To overcome some of these difficulties, the law may imply terms into the contract.

The first task is to look at what has been expressly agreed by the parties. The *express terms*, whether oral or in writing, may be the only terms of the contract, although this would be rare. In many cases, the law will imply terms into the contract, particularly as a result of legislation. These *implied terms*, such as those implied into certain contracts by the Sale of Goods Act 1979 or the Supply of Goods or Services Act 1982[1] are particularly important and are discussed later in this and subsequent chapters. Sometimes, the courts may imply terms into a contract on the basis of common law. However, this will only be done in limited circumstances as indicated by Lord Pearson in *Trollope & Colls Ltd* v *North West Metropolitan Regional Hospital Board* [1973] 1 WLR 602 where he said (at 609):

> An unexpressed term can be implied if and only if the court finds that the parties must have intended that the term form part of their contract: it is not enough for the court to find that such a term would have been adopted by the parties as reasonable men if it had been suggested to them: it must have been a term that went without saying, a term necessary to give business efficacy to the contract, a term which although tacit, formed part of the contract which the parties made for themselves.

In other words, the term must be such as is necessary to make the contract effective and must be a term which the parties would clearly have agreed to have included had it been mentioned to them at the time. It is not enough for the term to be one which would be reasonable to include. The above sentiment was agreed with in the Court of Appeal by Sir Iain Glidewell in *St Albans City & District Council* v *International Computers Ltd* [1997] FSR 251 where he held that, in a contract for writing computer software without involving the transfer of property in tangible items such as optical or magnetic discs, the court could imply a term to the effect that the software was reasonably fit for its purpose.

---

[1] Some of the implied terms under the Sale of Goods Act 1979 and the Supply of Goods and Services Act 1979 do not apply, or apply with modification, to Scotland.

Often, the successful development and installation of software will be possible only if the software developer and client cooperate fully with each other. The case of *Anglo Group plc* v *Winther Browne & Co Ltd* (2000) 72 Con LR 118 gives an example of a duty to cooperate being implied by the court. The client did not want a bespoke system and a standard package was delivered but this meant inevitably that the client's other software systems would have to be modified to fit with the standard system. This required full cooperation between the parties and this was particularly important, as the client did not have the full technical knowledge of a computer professional. The judge said that, in relation to a contract for the supply of a standard computer system, it was an implied term that:

- the purchaser communicates clearly any special needs to the supplier;
- the purchaser takes reasonable steps to ensure that the supplier understands those needs;
- the supplier communicates to the purchaser whether or not those precise needs can be met and if so how they can be met. If they cannot be met precisely the appropriate options should be set out by the supplier;
- the supplier takes reasonable steps to ensure that the purchaser is trained in how to use the system;
- the purchaser devotes reasonable time and patience to understanding how to operate the system;
- the purchaser and supplier work together to resolve the problems which will almost certainly occur. This requires active cooperation from both parties. If such cooperation is not present it is likely that the purchaser will not achieve the desired results from the system.

Controls over express terms

As well as implying terms into a contract, the law may impact upon the express terms. It may make a term, agreed by the parties, void and unenforceable. Normally, this will be the result of a statutory provision. For example, a term in a software licence which prohibits or restricts the making of a necessary back-up copy of a computer program by a person having the right to use it under an agreement is declared void and unenforceable by section 296A(1) of the Copyright, Designs and Patents Act 1988. The Unfair Contract Terms Act 1977 is important in controlling the use of terms which try to exclude or limit liability for negligence and breach of contract, among other things. Another way the courts will control contract terms is by using the common law: for example, by declining to enforce a term which is in restraint of trade such as where a computer programmer's contract of employment prevents him working for a competitor of his employer for a period of five years without any geographical limitation. A common ploy in some contracts is where the party in the stronger bargaining position inserts some draconian terms and, knowing that the courts may interfere with them, seeks to save as many of them as he can. A 'saving' clause, sometimes referred to as a 'blue pencil' clause, may be worded as follows:

> **In the event that any provision of this agreement is unenforceable but would be enforceable if part of the wording of the provision were to be deleted, it shall apply with the minimum of such deletions being made as required to make the provision enforceable.**

Such terms are unlikely to be met with judicial favour. Judges will not write the contract for the parties and draconian contracts in restraint of trade may be consigned to the court's waste bin rather than the judge striking out the offending parts. The general rule, however, is that if a term is severable, that is, the contract can stand without it, the term will be deleted, leaving the rest of the contract in force. If the term in question is of fundamental importance to the contract, then the entire contract will be in jeopardy. Of course, the ploy of having draconian terms which may be unenforceable is that they may be accepted at face value by the other party and not tested in the courts. Nevertheless, great care must be taken not to attempt to take away certain statutory rights as to do so may result in criminal prosecution.

Inconsistent terms

BCT Software Solutions Ltd v *Arnold Laver & Co Ltd* [2002] EWHC 1298 (Ch) concerned a contract to purchase software. The quotations submitted by the software developer made reference to the developer's new and revised standard terms and conditions which were inconsistent with the terms expressly agreed by the parties. The terms expressly agreed treated the grant of the software licence and ongoing maintenance as two separate issues and failure to continue to take and pay for support would not bring the licence to an end. The new standard terms and conditions made the licence to use the software conditional upon the client continuing to pay for support services. The software developer went into receivership and the claimant acquired the intellectual property rights of the software developer and the client informed the claimant it no longer wanted support. The claimant sought damages for the continued use of the software by the client. The court held that, in a case where any of the terms imported into a contract conflicted with those expressly agreed between the parties, the latter would prevail. Therefore, the client could continue to use the software and the claimant was not entitled to damages.

ENTIRE AGREEMENT

In negotiations leading up to the formation of a contract, it is easy to make exaggerated claims as to the performance and specification of computers and software and the carrying out of obligations under the contract. Such representations, which may be in writing or oral or both, can prove troublesome later especially if one party's understanding of the representations differs from the others or if they conflict with the formal contractual documents. In some cases, it may be difficult to know whether a letter of intent or a letter setting out the client's requirements or the software developer's recommendations is part of the contract between the parties. To overcome such difficulties (and, in some cases, to prevent being bound by an exaggerated or false claim made earlier) it is common for the formal written contract to include a term to the effect that it represents the entire agreement between the parties. (In terms of the effect of false statements, see the section on misrepresentation later in this chapter.)

In *Watford Electronics Ltd* v *Sanderson CFL Ltd* [2002] FSR 19, a computer software contract was on standard written terms and included an entire agreement clause which added that no statement or representations made by either party have been relied upon by the other in agreeing to enter into the contract. At first instance, the judge considered that the second part of the clause was, in effect, an exclusion clause, excluding liability for misrepresentation and, that being so, subject to the test of reasonableness under section 3 of the Misrepresentation Act 1967 (as amended by the Unfair Contract Terms Act 1977). The Court of Appeal rejected that interpretation saying that section 3 applies only where a party has relied on the representation. Lord Justice Chadwick said that in a case where the parties have acknowledged in the contract itself that they have not relied on any pre-contractual representation:

> . . . it would be bizarre . . . to attribute to them an intention to exclude a liability which they must have thought could never arise.

Counsel for both parties in *Sam Business Systems Ltd* v *Hedley and Co* [2002] EWHC 2733

(TCC) considered that this part of the judgment in *Watford Electronics* was wrongly decided but did not advance any real argument as to why that was so. In that case, the contract also contained an entire agreement clause but added that it superseded all prior representations, negotiations, etc. (apart from fraudulent misrepresentation). However, by virtue of subsequent conversations and letters between the parties, the judge held that the software developer had waived the entire agreement clause.

The question as to whether an entire agreement clause also serves to exclude liability for false pre-contractual statements is not wholly clear. Obviously, the precise wording of the clause will be important. If it purports to exclude or limit liability for misrepresentation, then it will be enforceable only to the extent that it meets the requirement of reasonableness. If, as in the *Watford Electronics* case, it states that the parties have not relied on any prior representation, perhaps the better view is that it does seek to exclude liability for misrepresentation and is not subject to the requirement of reasonableness. This will, however, need a reversal of that part of the Court of Appeal's judgment in *Watford Electronics*.

NATURE OF THE CONTRACT

It is not always easy to separate hardware and software and this fact has been demonstrated on several occasions in the courts. For example, in *Dyason* v *Autodesk Inc* [1992] RPC 575, there was much confusion as to whether a 'dongle', a device required to be inserted into a computer before a program would operate, contained a computer program and in *Gale's Application* [1991] RPC 305, the judge at first instance, overturned on this point by the Court of Appeal, drew a distinction between a program on disk and one hard-wired into a ROM chip. Such confusion is largely a result of the difficulty many lawyers have when dealing with a highly technical field such as computer science but it does not stop there. Even if the technological aspects are fully understood, the application of the law to them may still perplex.

Although there is some common ground and some similarity in other provisions, contracts for hardware and software are governed by different legal rules. Computer hardware, if it is sold, will be subject to the Sale of Goods Act 1979 and related consumer protection legislation, whereas an agreement to write software ('bespoke' software) will be within the scope of the Supply of Goods and Services Act 1982. There are other differences, for example, as regards the statutory controls over exclusion clauses. This simple distinction is not always easy to apply in practice because hardware equipment often incorporates software and the contractual position of ready-made ('off-the-shelf') software is far from clear. Nevertheless, the classification in terms of the legal nature of the transaction is important and the author's suggested approach is to look at the predominant purpose of the transaction. In other words, did the person acquiring the subject matter think that he was obtaining hardware or software?

Consider a person purchasing a new motor car. Motor cars are goods and the transaction is clearly subject to the Sale of Goods Act 1979, section 2(1), which states:

> . . . a contract of sale of goods is a contract by which the seller transfers or agrees to transfer the property in goods to the buyer for a money consideration called the price.

The whole purpose of the transaction is to transfer ownership in the car. Suppose the car is faulty, however, and that fault is traced to a computer program installed in the electronic ignition system. The purchaser would still expect, rightly, to be able to obtain a remedy from the seller under the Sale of Goods Act even though he has not obtained ownership of the copyright subsisting in the computer program. After all, the buyer wanted to acquire a car not a computer program. Therefore, a contract to purchase a computer is a sale of goods contract notwithstanding

13

Fundamentals of information technology contracts

the inclusion of computer software embodied within the computer. If other software is provided (often referred to as 'bundled') that will usually be subject to a separate, collateral licence agreement. A basic rule is that a licence is required to use computer software, otherwise the copyright (and any other intellectual property rights) subsisting in it would be infringed.

Software contracts

Contracts for the acquisition of software alone cannot be sale of goods contracts; the title to the copyright and other intellectual property rights is not normally transferred and, in any case, computer programs or databases are not 'goods'. Under section 61(1) of the Sale of Goods Act 1979, 'goods' are defined as '... including all personal chattels other than things in action and money ...'. A copyright, for example, is a 'thing in action', like a company share.

The only proviso to this is that, as far as paper manuals, optical or magnetic discs and packaging are concerned, we might have a collateral sale of goods contract. However, the predominant nature of the contract is the provision of a service, the function of the software being the service in question. This is so even if the copyright ownership is transferred, that is, if the agreement is an assignment and not simply a licence.

The nature of software contracts has long puzzled judges and legal writers. Certainly, in the case of software which is specifically written for a client, it must be a service contract as opposed to a sale of goods contract. Although some writers have focused on the fact that tangible items such as optical or magnetic discs may be provided, suggesting a sale of goods contract, where software is delivered online or by loading it onto the client's computer, the nature of the arrangement becomes clearer. The delivery of tangible items in addition to the software has only served to cloud the reality of the transaction.

A case which involved a book gave an indication of the approach preferred by the author of this book. In *Ashley* v *Sutton London Borough Council* (1994) 159 JP 631, the appellant, Ashley, brought an appeal against his conviction for an offence under section 14 of the Trade Descriptions Act 1968. The charge was that he had made a statement which he knew to be false as to the nature of services he provided in the course of a trade or business.

Ashley had supplied books by mail order which described a winning strategy to be used with fixed odds gambling and he guaranteed to refund the purchase price if customers were not satisfied. It was argued on his behalf that he had supplied books, not services, and, consequently, could not be guilty under section 14 which only concerns services not goods. The Divisional Court of the Queen's Bench Division held that, although goods were supplied (that is, the books), the essential nature of the contract was the provision of a service – the service of providing information. The book was merely the medium through which the information was imparted and the contract was, therefore, predominantly a contract for services and the appeal against conviction was dismissed. The same can be said in terms of software even more forcefully. It is a copy of the programs and/or data that the customer wants. As in the *Ashley* case, the high price of the information relative to the tangible items delivered confirms this. The fact that software can be transmitted without the need for a tangible carrier reinforces the view that software contracts are service contracts. At best, any tangible items delivered with the software give rise to a collateral sale of goods contract in respect of those items only. To return to the analogy with a book, sale of goods law will give a remedy if the book is physically defective: for example, if it falls apart or has pages missing. It will not give a remedy simply because the plot is not very good or if there are grammatical errors. Such defects relate to the information not the good itself.

Two software cases have reinforced the deceptive simplicity of that approach. In *St Albans City & District Council* v *International Computers Ltd* [1997] FSR 251, Sir Iain Glidewell said that computer programs are clearly not within the meaning of 'goods' for the purposes of the

Sale of Goods Act 1979 and the Supply of Goods and Services Act 1982. However, at first instance, Mr Justice Scott-Baker accepted that software was goods within the Sale of Goods Act 1979 (although he did not have to decide the point) because '... it is difficult to see what it can be other than something to which no statutory rules apply ...'. Not a very convincing argument!

As has often been the case, it was a Scots judge who most ably defined the nature of a software contract in the context of a licence for ready-made software. In **Beta Computers (Europe) Ltd** v **Adobe Systems (Europe) Ltd** [1996] FSR 367, Lord Penrose in the Outer House of the Court of Session in Edinburgh had to determine the nature of an agreement to acquire ready-made software. He decided that the supply of such software for a price is a *sui generis* (unique) contract rather than a sale of goods contract or a hybrid contract. He considered the Copyright, Designs and Patents Act 1988 and concluded that the supply of the medium on which the program is stored must be accompanied by an appropriate licence conferred directly or by implication from the acquisition of the software. An essential feature of the arrangement was that the supplier undertook to make available to the purchaser both the medium and the right of access and use of the software.

There are some differences between English and Scots contract law and, at that time under Scots law, it was possible to grant third parties rights under a contract. Nevertheless, the judgment is an excellent analysis of the nature of a software contract and an important feature of the case was that the predominant purpose of the contract – that is, to acquire the right to use the software – would be subjugated if it were classed as a sale of goods contract. Subsequently, in England and Wales and Northern Ireland, the Contracts (Rights of Third Parties) Act 1999 gives third parties a right to enforce a contract if the contract expressly provides that he may or the relevant term of the contract in question purports to confer a benefit on him and the contract does not provide that the third party cannot enforce it. Certain types of contract are excluded such as an employment contract where, otherwise, a third party could enforce the contract against an employee. The third party may be identified in the contract by name or as a member of a class of persons or by answering a particular description. These provisions will facilitate the enforceability of software licences by the copyright owners in the case of ready-made software.

The European Court of Justice considered the nature of a software contract in Case C-41/04 **Levob Verzekeringen BV** v **Staatssecretaris van Financien** [2005] ECR I-9433, which involved a liability to pay VAT on software. The software in question was a standard software package which was then modified so that it could be used by Dutch speakers. The modification work was substantial. There were two separate contracts, both similar in value. The first was for the purchase of the standard package and the second contract was for the modifications. It was held that the contracts had to be viewed as a single transaction being a contract for the provision of a service. The modification was the dominant part of the whole as the software was of no use to the client without it. Looking at a transaction which includes delivery of pre-existing software (including perhaps also hardware) and subsequent substantial modification to the software from the perspective of the predominant purpose is a pragmatic approach. However, it still leaves a grey area, for example, where the amount of software development or modification is more finely balanced with the value and utility of the pre-existing software. The court did not examine this type of situation. It might be more logical in such a case to look at the contract as comprising two separate transactions.

SOFTWARE ACQUISITION

The most common method of acquiring computer software is by way of a licence which is granted by the copyright owner to the person or company acquiring a copy of the software, giving permission to use the software in return for the licence fee – the 'price'. The licence may be for a fixed, perhaps renewable, period of time or there may be no mention of duration, in which case it can be assumed that the licence will last as long as the software is subject to copyright protection. (After expiry of the copyright, a licence is not longer required to perform the acts restricted by the copyright.) The copyright owner will prefer to grant a licence because he will want to retain the copyright in the software and be free to grant licences to others. The licence may be exclusive, however, which means that the copyright owner cannot grant licences to others in respect of that software. More usually, the licence will be non-exclusive so that the copyright owner will be free to grant licences to anyone else he wishes to. An exclusive licence might be appropriate in connection with bespoke software written for a client in accordance with the client's requirements, as described in Chapter 15. Sometimes, ownership of copyright will be transferred instead and this form of transaction is called an assignment of copyright but apart from transferring ownership of copyright an assignment, as with a licence agreement, will contain numerous other terms dealing with aspects such as warranties, liability for defects, permitted uses, termination, applicable law, etc.

The special nature of computer software and the fact that a copy of software is usually acquired by means of a licence have several legal implications. To begin with, the Sale of Goods Act 1979 does not apply to computer software as such. This Act is very important in the commercial world; in addition to being a very comprehensive regulator of contracts of sale it implies important terms into contracts such as requirements that the goods must match their description, be of satisfactory quality and that the seller has the right to sell the goods. However, as noted earlier, 'goods' are defined by section 61(1) of the Act as including:

> . . . all personal chattels other than things in action and money.

It seems unlikely, even if the copyright is transferred with the computer programs, that an intangible computer program resident on a magnetic or optical disc or installed on a computer chip is a personal chattel (as opposed to the disc or chip), because copyright is a 'thing in action' like company shares or a money order, to be contrasted with the more tangible 'things in possession' such as motor cars or computers. Copyright is thus excluded from the definition of goods. In any case, a licence cannot be a sale of goods contract as there is no transfer of property. The result of all this is that the terms contained in the Sale of Goods Act which are implied into a contract for the sale of goods will not apply to a computer software contract, at least as far as the software is concerned. Any tangible items such as optical or magnetic discs transferred with the software may be subject to a collateral contract (a subsidiary or parallel contract). This may seem unfortunate as these implied terms are a very useful weapon for the buyer and, in the case of consumer sales, the implied terms cannot be excluded or modified at all. In non-consumer sales the implied terms can only be so excluded or modified if the terms purporting to do this are reasonable in accordance with the Unfair Contract Terms Act 1977, sections 6–7. However, service contracts are also subject to statutory implied terms and, as a last resort, the courts would be likely to imply terms on the basis of common law and which, for practical purposes, would be likely to have a broadly similar effect.

Supply of Goods and Services Act 1982: implied terms

The Supply of Goods and Services Act 1982 implies terms into contracts under which the property (ownership) in goods passes, and also into contracts for the hire of goods and contracts for services (Scotland continues to rely on common law rights). Some of the terms implied by the Supply of Goods and Services Act 1982 are similar to those implied by the Sale of Goods Act 1979. Examples of contracts governed by the Supply of Goods and Services Act 1982 are hybrid contracts: that is, those which involve part services and part goods such as a contract for the painting of a portrait. In this particular instance the service is the actual act of painting; the goods are the canvas, frame and paint. The Act also governs a contract purely for services, such as a contract for a haircut. Has the Supply of Goods and Services Act any relevance for computer software contracts? As far as 'goods' are concerned, the situation is the same as with a sale of goods contract because the definition of goods excludes things in action of which copyright is an example. The 1982 Act will be particularly relevant, however, if an independent computer firm or a programmer is engaged to write a computer program as this should come within the meaning of 'service'. The draftsmen of the Supply of Goods and Services Act elected not to attempt to define 'service', probably in deference to the very wide variety of services offered both to consumers and to businesses.[2] A contract for writing a computer program will fall within that part of the Act dealing with the supply of services: sections 12–16. The fact that goods such as paper manuals and optical or magnetic discs may also be transferred does not prevent the contract from being a contract for the supply of services: section 12(3).

Expert systems, also known as knowledge-based systems, and other types of software, including databases, which provide information or advice could, arguably, be construed as supplying a service and thus fall within the ambit of the Supply of Goods and Services Act 1982. If this view is taken by the courts, bearing in mind that 'service' is not defined in the Act, it will result in the appropriate terms from the Act being implied into a contract for the supply of such computer software systems. The dealer who supplies an expert system may be deemed to be supplying a service (that is, providing the advice available from the system) even though others, such as the experts who provided the knowledge used in the system and the makers of the system, are responsible (in a non-legal sense) for how the system operates. This is because section 12(1) of the Supply of Goods and Services Act 1982 states that a 'contract for the supply of a service means':

> . . . a contract under which a person (the supplier) agrees to carry out a service.

It may sometimes be difficult to determine the identity of the supplier where computer software is obtained ready-made. For example, if an expert system or knowledge-based system is obtained from a dealer, is he the supplier or is it the company which made the expert system? In other words, who is the contracting party? Two possibilities exist:

- either the contract is between the person acquiring a copy of the system (the 'acquirer') and the dealer;

- or it is between the acquirer and the software company, in which case the dealer acts as the company's agent.

The answer to this is of crucial importance because of the doctrine of privity of contract: only the parties to a contract can sue on it, except where covered by the Contracts (Rights of Third Parties) Act 1999 or the equivalent rule in Scotland. If the expert system turns out to be

---

[2] Certain specific services have been excluded by statutory instrument. These include services in relation to advocacy, services of company directors and services rendered to a building society by a director of the society.

defective the acquirer will need to know who is liable. Apart from contract law there may be liability in negligence which does not depend on a contractual relationship and may even extend to others involved in the development of the system such as the experts who provided the knowledge contained in the system.

If a dealer has been asked to supply a suitable expert system it is possible that, by doing so, he carried out a service. By supplying expert systems, the dealer has enabled the advice-giving service to be performed and in some respects it is similar to the position where a supplier sub-contracts all or part of the work. The customer relies on the dealer to provide a suitable and effective system and, consequently, there is a duty on the dealer to select and recommend an adequate system (see *Stewart* v *Reavell's Garage* [1952] 2 QB 545). Therefore, dealers marketing expert systems and any software which provides advice or information intended to be taken seriously and acted upon should satisfy themselves as to the veracity and reliability of these systems and their suitability for particular customers. Dealers may also wish to consider including appropriate and reasonable exemption clauses in their supply contracts with respect to advice-giving computer systems.

The dealer as agent for the software company is a more likely interpretation if the acquirer specifies the system he wants. Of course, the fact that there will, invariably, be a licence agreement with the software company reinforces the view that the dealer acts as an agent to bring about the contract between the software company and the acquirer. The legal position is far from clear, however, and there is a lack of authority on this point. The situation is much simpler where software is written for and at the request of a client. This is a straightforward service contract between the client and the software developer and is covered by the Supply of Goods and Services Act 1982. This has been confirmed in *The Salvage Association* v *CAP Financial Services Ltd* [1995] FSR 654 in which the Official Referee in the High Court confirmed that a contract to develop new accounting software for a client was a service contract. He went on to imply into that contract section 13 of the Supply of Goods and Services Act 1982.

Reasonable care and skill

Section 13 implies a term that the supplier, if acting in the course of business, will carry out the service with reasonable care and skill. This restates the previous position at common law, that a person who holds himself out as being prepared to carry out a service is expected to exercise a level of skill that could be expected of a reasonably competent member of the relevant trade or profession. Therefore, if a firm engaged to write a computer program fails to measure up to the standards that would normally be expected from able computer programmers and the program is defective as a consequence then, *prima facie*, the firm will be liable in contract. It does not matter that the firm's employees tried their best; the question is whether the program meets this objective standard.

In the *Salvage Association* case it was held that there was a breach of section 13 and also a breach of an express term in the contract that the software developer would assign suitably qualified staff to perform the work. The staff originally assigned to write the software were insufficiently experienced in the use of ORACLE, the language in which the software was to be written.

Time for performance

Another term implied by the Supply of Goods and Services Act 1982 concerns the time for performance. Again, this only applies to suppliers acting in the course of business, although a similar term would have been implied at common law. Section 14 states that, in the absence of an agreed time for performance or an agreed formula to determine the time for performance, the supplier will carry out the service in a reasonable time. The Act also says that what is reasonable is a question of fact; that is, it depends on the facts of the case. The case of *Charnock* v *Liverpool Corporation* [1968] 1 WLR 1498 gives an example of an unreasonable time. The defendant garage was liable in damages because it took eight weeks to repair a motor vehicle when a normally competent garage would have taken about five weeks. A contract for the writing of computer programs should have detailed provisions about completion times and all section 14 does is to provide a safety net to catch those instances where there has been an oversight or when some additional or unforeseen work is required. What is a reasonable time will depend on the nature of the programs and their complexity, taking into account the time required for testing and acceptance. How long would a reasonably competent software developer take?

Payment

Section 15 of the Act states that, unless the contract fixes the payment or a method of calculating payment, the supplier will be paid a reasonable amount. Usually, the contract will mention the fee, but this provision might be useful if the supplier takes on additional work at the request of the other party and no mention is made at the time of agreement of the charge for this extra work. It means that the supplier cannot, much as he might like to, charge an unreasonably high price. Comparative fees and prices for writing similar software would provide a good indicator of what is reasonable, although it would be sensible to include a mechanism for working out payment for additional work, such as by including a schedule of rates.

HARDWARE ACQUISITION

As far as computer equipment (hardware) is concerned, this may be purchased outright or hired. If purchased then the Sale of Goods Act 1979 will apply and terms as to quality, complying with description, satisfactory quality, etc. will be implied into the contract, subject to any valid exemption clauses. There have been some important changes to this Act. The Sale and Supply of Goods Act 1994 replaced the old section 14(2) of the Sale of Goods Act 1979 (which required that goods were of merchantable quality) with a requirement that goods must be of *satisfactory quality*. This is stated by section 14(2A) to apply if the goods meet the standard that a reasonable person would regard as satisfactory. Account is to be taken of the description of the goods, the price (if relevant) and all other relevant circumstances. In a welcome tightening of the implied term, section 14(2B) defines the aspects of quality to be taken into account, being:

- fitness for all the purposes for which goods of the kind in question are commonly supplied (this is simply a restatement of the previous law);
- appearance and finish;
- freedom from minor defects;
- safety; and
- durability.

This implied term is a condition in England, Wales and Northern Ireland in consumer sales and applies where goods are sold in the course of business. In terms of sales to non-consumers, it is a warranty rather than a condition if the breach is so slight that it would be unreasonable for the goods to be rejected. In Scotland, it is simply a term, the remedies depending on whether the breach is a material one. For a breach of condition (or a material breach in Scotland), the buyer may reject the goods without prejudice to any claim for damages.

The old requirement that goods must be of merchantable quality caused injustice in a number of cases. It did not appear that the goods had to be durable and the presence of minor defects did not necessarily render goods unmerchantable. For example, in *Millars of Falkirk Ltd* v *Turpie*, 1987 SLT 66, it was held that an oil leak from the power-steering unit of a new car did not make the car unmerchantable and, in *Bernstein* v *Pamson Motors* [1987] 2 All ER 220, an engine seizure in a three-week-old car that had covered only 140 miles did not render the car unmerchantable. Only occasionally did the courts seem to take a sympathetic view of the buyer's position: for example, in *Rogers* v *Parish (Scarborough) Ltd* [1987] QB 933 the Court of Appeal recognised that the buyer of a luxury car such as a Range Rover had a right to expect a vehicle that did not continually break down and suffer from rust.

In the context of computers, the courts also took a fairly narrow view of what was not of merchantable quality and in *Micron Computer Systems Ltd* v *Wang (UK) Ltd* (unreported) 9 May 1990, the High Court considered that the failure of a computer's hard disk was a perfectly normal teething problem and did not give the buyer the right to reject the computer. Of course, the buyer may still have a claim to damages in respect of such a defect. Now, because of the test of satisfactory quality, it is more likely that the buyer of a computer with a faulty hard disk would be able to reject the computer and insist on a refund of the purchase price. The same should apply if the computer has an intermittent but troublesome fault. In any case, the technology has moved on somewhat and there are generally higher expectations of what would meet the requirement of satisfactory quality.

If the supplier goes beyond the mere supply of the equipment and carries out some work such as assembling and installing the equipment, the Supply of Goods and Services Act 1982 will apply, as discussed above. If the contract is for the hire of the equipment, then the Supply of Goods and Services Act 1982 will apply, whether or not installation or other services are also provided by the supplier. An agreement which is described as a lease or a rental is essentially a contract of hire, and a hire agreement is one under which the possession of the goods passes to the other party but the property in the goods (the ownership) remains with the supplier. 'Hire' does not include hire-purchase agreements, which are covered by the Supply of Goods (Implied Terms) Act 1973 – this Act implies similar terms into the contract as under the Sale of Goods Act 1979. The relevant provisions in the Supply of Goods and Services Act 1982 (sections 6–11) regarding hire agreements include implied terms about the right of the supplier to transfer possession of the goods, that the goods must correspond with their description and implied terms about quality and fitness for purpose (sections 7–10). These terms are equivalent to those in the Sale of Goods Act 1979. Similar provisions for hire contracts in Scotland are in the Supply of Goods and Services Act 1982, sections 11G–11L.

BREACH OF CONTRACT

If a party to a contract is in breach of one or more of its terms, the remedy depends on the status of the particular term or terms which have been broken. The aggrieved party may want to repudiate the contract, treat the contract as discharged by reason of the other party's breach and recover any money he has paid out as well as any other expenses and losses suffered. In the *Salvage Association* case it was held that the client was entitled to repudiate the contract when it became clear that the software developer would fail to meet the extended deadline for delivery of the software. The client was entitled to £662,926 in damages being made up of:

- £291,388 paid under the contract;
- £231,866 wasted expenditure; and
- £139,672 wasted management time.

Alternatively, the injured party might prefer to hold the other party to the contract but would like some compensation for the breach and if the breach concerns a minor term this is usually the better solution. However, the injured party does not always have a free choice as the law lays down rules determining and limiting the scope of remedies.

Conditions and warranties

Traditionally there are two types of terms in contracts: 'conditions' and 'warranties'. The distinction is important because breach of a condition gives the other party the right to repudiate the contract and claim damages. For example, consider a contract to deliver a computer by '1 June at the latest'. If the machine has not been delivered by that date, the buyer can treat the failure to deliver as a breach of a condition and he can cancel the contract as time for delivery is usually construed as being a condition (see *Hartley* v *Hyams* [1920] 3 KB 475). Furthermore, the buyer can claim damages that would be equivalent to the difference in cost of buying another similar computer elsewhere and any other expenses and losses he has been put to as a direct consequence of the breach, with the proviso that he mitigates his losses – that is, he keeps them to a minimum. The buyer may have wanted the computer to expand his business and he will be able to claim the resulting loss in profits, provided the seller knew or should have known of this – that is, it was in the reasonable contemplation of the parties.

On the other hand, a breach of warranty allows the aggrieved party to claim damages only. The contract is still in force and must be completed by both parties. They must both perform the remainder of their agreed duties under the contract. For example, if a supplier has agreed to deliver a computer system and the contract states that the terminals are to be a deep yellow colour but, instead, he delivers a computer with lemon coloured terminals, this will amount to a breach of warranty unless there is some special reason why the deep yellow colour was specified. The buyer will be entitled to damages only and he will still have to pay the purchase price of the computer, although he may be able to set off a sum representing the damages. Damages are assessed on the basis of the damage naturally arising from the breach and in the contemplation of the parties. In the example given, the damages would be likely to be nominal only.

In *Koufos* v *C Czarnikow Ltd* [1969] 1 AC 350, a ship was chartered by sugar merchants to transport a cargo of sugar. The ship owners knew that there was a sugar market at the port of destination but did not know that the merchants wanted to sell the sugar immediately on its arrival. The ship deviated from the agreed voyage and arrived about ten days late; in the meantime the price of sugar had fallen and the merchants lost over £4,000. It was held that this loss should be recoverable from the ship owners because they should reasonably have contemplated that the delay would have resulted in a loss. The ship owners knew there was a commodity market at the destination and that prices would be liable to fluctuate, so that any delay could lead to a diminution of the value of the cargo. Unfortunately, this does not appear to work the other way – the ship owners would not be entitled to any share in a windfall profit if the market value of the cargo increased dramatically and was sold for much more than it would have done had it arrived on time.

How does the basic principle that damages are based on the losses that were within the contemplation of the parties when the contract was made to work in the context of computers? Suppose that you run a computer bureau and carry out ordinary data processing work. You decide to expand the business and buy a more powerful computer to be delivered by a certain date. You tell the supplier that you need the computer to carry out some additional data processing but neglect to inform him that you are negotiating a very lucrative top secret government contract on the basis of having the new computer. If the computer is delivered late, then you would be entitled to damages based on the loss in profits in the normal course of business but you would not be entitled to anything should you lose the government contract. This is simply because the supplier did not know, and could not reasonably be expected to know, of this potential contract. A buyer should therefore consider informing a supplier of all the uses to which the equipment or programs will be put, especially if they are unusual.

Innominate terms

The distinction between conditions and warranties is not always clear. Sometimes a contractual term lies in a grey area between the two. If the term is broken, then it will be classified in the light of the facts surrounding the breach and it will depend on the facts as to whether the breach goes to the root of the contract. If it does, then the term will be effectively promoted to the rank of condition with all that that entails; otherwise it will be classed as a warranty. These intermediate terms are called innominate terms and their nature is determined retrospectively, after a breach. The case which paved the way for this approach was *Hong Kong Fir Shipping Co Ltd* v *Kawasaki Kisen Kaisha* [1962] QB 26, in which it was held that a term implied in a hire contract for a ship that it must be seaworthy was such an innominate term. The nature of the breach determined the nature of the contractual term. For example, if the ship had a five-degree list and was badly leaking, it would be totally unseaworthy and this would be a breach of a condition enabling the hirer to repudiate the contract. However, if the breach concerned some trifling defect, perhaps a mere technicality, which could be put right very quickly and easily, the term would be classed as a warranty. For example, if a word processing program is acquired which is claimed by the supplier to be a 'professional package' and it does not have a built-in thesaurus, this might be considered to be a breach of warranty. It cannot be truly said that the breach goes to the root of the contract if the program has all the other usual features normally found in powerful word processing systems. However, if the package does not include features such as fully-functional paragraph formatting, a spelling and grammar checker, tables and frames this would be more serious and could make the system virtually useless in a business environment. Such a breach would go to the root of the contract and would be a breach of a condition, giving the person acquiring the program the right to cancel the contract and recover the cost of the system plus any direct losses.

This way of looking at terms and not deciding their status until there has been a breach is very useful as it gives a welcome degree of flexibility to contracts, although it could be criticised for introducing uncertainty. There may be some terms, however, which are obviously conditions: for example, if the contract is for the delivery of a particular make of computer, and the seller attempts to deliver a different make altogether, this would clearly be a breach of condition.

What sort of terms in computer contracts could be described as innominate terms? Suppose that a contract is made for the provision of hardware and software for a company's intranet. If the transmission of e-mails is slightly slower than provided for in the contract, that could be regarded as a breach of warranty, something the supplier would be expected to improve. However, if e-mails are continually being lost or corrupted and documents and other material placed on the server cannot be retrieved properly or the portal to the internet does not function at all, these defects might be treated as breaches of condition, unless they can be overcome within a reasonable time by the supplier of the hardware and software involved.

Sometimes a term can start as a condition, become a warranty and then revert to a condition. In *Rickards* v *Oppenheim* [1950] 1 KB 616, the defendant wanted a body built on his Rolls-Royce chassis and he agreed that the claimant (from whom he had purchased the chassis) could use a sub-contractor to do this specialised work, which should have been completed in March 1948. The work was not complete by that time and, although time for delivery is usually a condition, the defendant did not cancel the contract as he was entitled to do, but continued to press for delivery, thereby waiving his right to cancel. In the end the defendant gave an ultimatum. He said that the car must be ready by 25 July 1948 and that he would refuse to take delivery after that date. The car was not ready by that date, so the defendant bought another car elsewhere and claimed back the price he had paid for the chassis. It was held that when time for delivery is of the essence of a contract for the sale of goods (that is, a condition) and, after the stipulated time has elapsed, the buyer waives his right to cancel by pressing for delivery, converting the term into a warranty, he may later give notice setting a reasonable deadline, once again making the time for delivery a condition of the contract.

Late delivery and late payment

It is not unusual for new software to be delivered late. In this case, the client must be careful when granting extensions of time and should bear in mind that he will hope to avoid fudging the issue of the date at which he can repudiate the contract on the grounds of the software developer's late delivery. It is essential that any extensions be agreed in writing with the new date being firmly stated as a condition. If this is not done, the client must allow a reasonable time when delivering an ultimatum to the software developer. It is not satisfactory to allow work to drag on for months and then to suddenly state that the contract will be repudiated if the software is not completed 'by the end of this week'.

It is common to find provisions for late delivery and late payment included in contracts. The contract might state that the supplier will pay £150 per week if he delivers late, or that the buyer will pay interest at 0.75 per cent above the current base bank rate, should he be late in making payment. Predetermined and agreed damages, known as liquidated damages, are frequently found in contracts. 'Liquidated' simply means that the damages or the method of calculating them are fixed and agreed. Liquidated damages are to be distinguished from a penalty. Liquidated damages are a genuine pre-estimate of the loss resulting from the breach, whereas a penalty, which might be out of all proportion to the loss suffered, will not be enforced by the courts. The stipulation of liquidated damages for breach of a particular term contradicts the possibility of that term being a condition. Terms backed by liquidated damages will usually not be regarded as conditions, therefore, unless the scale of the breach is considerable.

Other terms and breaches

In practice, many terms will be innominate terms, in which case it will only be possible to determine whether breach of the term allows a party to repudiate the contract in the light of the actual facts of the breach. A similar approach applies in respect of the terms implied by sections 13–15 of the Sale of Goods Act 1979, as amended by the Sale and Supply of Goods Act 1994, in relation to the sale of goods to non-consumers. Under section 15A of the Sale of Goods Act 1979, in England, Wales and Northern Ireland, if the breach is so slight that it would be unreasonable to reject the goods, it will be treated as a breach of warranty. In Scotland, it depends on whether the breach is deemed to be a material breach.

Provisions concerning the performance of a computer system, how fast the programs work in practice and the degree of compatibility with other equipment are likely to be innominate terms. Terms probably classifiable as conditions from the outset deal with aspects such as the time for delivery and the description of the actual computer concerned. Time for payment is usually treated as being a warranty unless the contract states otherwise or the circumstances suggest a different interpretation (see, for example, section 10(1) of the Sale of Goods Act 1979).

By its very nature, when delivered, bespoke software often contains errors and it may be some time before they can all be traced and corrected. It is a brave software producer who claims that his software is error-free. The contractual position was considered in *Saphena Computing* v

13

Fundamentals of information technology contracts

Allied Collection Agencies [1995] FSR 616. A contract for writing a number of programs was terminated while there were still errors in the programs. The Court of Appeal accepted that software was not a commodity that was handed over once and for all and that it would usually require testing and further modification. It would not, therefore, be a breach of contract to deliver software that might, initially, have a defect in it. Usually, the supplier would have a right and a duty to correct the errors within a reasonable time. In this particular case the client, who had a copy of the source code, could carry out error correction himself but, because he had brought the contract to an end, the supplier would cease to be liable for the remaining errors.

MISREPRESENTATION

If you are negotiating with a salesperson with a view to acquiring computer software, he or she may make statements regarding the software and its performance. It is not unknown for a salesperson to describe the product in glowing terms and you would expect him to highlight the best features. Sometimes, he can go too far; he may be anxious to make a sale and may make statements which are simply untrue in an effort to try to induce you to buy the product. Some statements are so wild that no one is expected to take them seriously; these are sometimes referred to as advertising 'puff'. Examples abound from the second-hand motor trade: for example, an ageing car may be described as being 'immaculate'. Such statements are not to be taken seriously and the courts would not support a case brought on them. Less extravagant statements, however, if untrue, may give rise to remedies. The standing of the statement needs initially to be determined and it may be elevated to the rank of contractual term if the courts consider on the facts that this was the intention of the parties. If this happens then normal contractual remedies are available to the aggrieved party if the statement turns out to be untrue.

If the statement does not become incorporated into the contract, it is said to be a representation – something said in the course of the negotiations leading up to the contract itself. It may well induce the other party to conclude the contract, in which case a remedy may be available on the basis of misrepresentation if the statement turns out to be untrue. Obviously, if the party, to whom the representation is made, knows that the statement is untrue he will not have any remedy. He has entered into the contract with his eyes open to the true facts; the statement itself will not have influenced him.

There are three forms of misrepresentation:

■ fraudulent;

■ negligent; and

■ innocent.

If the representation has been made fraudulently (or recklessly, not caring whether or not it is true), then at common law the remedy of rescission is available (setting the contract aside as if it had never been made at all), together with a right to recover any money laid out. Fraud may be difficult to prove; the person making the statement may simply say that he honestly believed, at the time he made it, that it was true. The Misrepresentation Act 1967, as amended by the Unfair Contract Terms Act 1977, made the situation more satisfactory. Rescission is the standard remedy for misrepresentation but this may cause hardship in some circumstances. Therefore, in the case of negligent or innocent misrepresentation, a court may award damages in lieu of rescission by section 2 of the Misrepresentation Act. This is important because rescission is an equitable remedy and as such will only be ordered by the courts if the aggrieved party has acted promptly. Formerly, if the aggrieved party had already accepted the goods, the very fact of acceptance would mean that rescission would not be available.

Imagine that a company buys a computer. It is important that this computer is directly compatible with its existing equipment and the supplier confirms in good faith, before the contract is made, that the computer is compatible although the contract itself is silent on the matter. Some weeks after accepting delivery and paying for the computer, it is found that, although the computer works well in every other respect, it is not compatible with the company's other machines and cannot reasonably be made so. Before the 1967 Act, the company acquiring the computer would have no remedy for this innocent misrepresentation, unless it was deemed to be a contractual term, as it would be too late to have the contract set aside. Now the courts would be likely to award damages instead, which might be considerable in our example. The better approach would have been for the company to insist that an express term was inserted into the contract to the effect that the computer to be acquired must be compatible with the existing equipment.

An actionable misrepresentation may be compromised by a subsequent agreement between the parties. In *I-Way Ltd* v *World Online Telecom Ltd* [2004] EWHC 244 (Comm), an internet service provider (the claimant) made a contract with the defendant offering telephony services through the claimant's server. The agreement was based upon projections of the numbers of customers, proportions of customers using the service during peak and other times (the call profile) and the average duration of calls. Although the call profile was not supportable on reasonable grounds, there had been a subsequent meeting at which revised figures were allegedly agreed and the rebate due to the defendant on the agreed prices reduced accordingly. This could be seen as a compromise of potential claims for misrepresentation. Accordingly, a claim for misrepresentation failed. However, the defendant was in breach of the agreement by taking steps to divert (the defendant used the word 'migrate') actual and potential customers to the defendant's own server.

SUMMARY

- Terms of a contract may be:
  - written or oral or a combination of both;
  - express or implied.
- Terms may be implied by legislation or by the courts (common law).
- Terms will be implied by the courts only if necessary to give business efficacy to the contract.
- Particular terms may be implied in contracts for the supply of computer systems.
- Express terms may be controlled by:
  - legislation – for example, exclusion clauses may be struck out;
  - the courts, where the term is in restraint of trade.
- Terms may be implied to set quality standards.
- Entire agreement clauses are common but:
  - may be seen as exclusion clauses where they exclude liability for pre-contractual representations.
- Contracts for writing software are contracts for services controlled by the Supply of Goods and Services Act 1982, which implies terms into such contracts, for example:
  - requiring that the services are performed using reasonable care and skill.
- Contracts for the acquisition of hardware are sale of goods contracts for which:
  - terms are implied by the Sale of Goods Act 1979 including that the goods must be of satisfactory quality.

13

Fundamentals of information technology contracts

■ The consequences of a breach of contract depend on the classification of the term in question:
  – for conditions, the aggrieved party may repudiate the contract and/or seek damages;
  – for warranties, the aggrieved party may seek damages only;
  – in the case of innominate terms, it depends on the seriousness of the breach.

■ Late delivery is normally a breach of condition, but:
  – in a contract for writing software, it is more likely to be a warranty, especially:
  – if the contract has a term for liquidated damages for late delivery.

■ It is accepted that software usually contains errors and delivering software with errors:
  – is not necessarily a breach of condition;
  – or even a breach of contract if the contract provides that the developer will fix errors.

■ The normal remedy for misrepresentation is rescission, however:
  – if the misrepresentation is negligent or innocent, a court may award damages instead.

SELF-TEST QUESTIONS

Note: there is only one correct answer to each multiple choice question.

1 **In relation to terms implied into contract by the courts, which one of the following statements is CORRECT?**
   (a) Terms will be implied by the courts only if reasonable in the circumstances.
   (b) Terms will be implied by the courts only if necessary to give the contract business efficacy.
   (c) Terms will be implied by the courts only when the contract is void for uncertainty.
   (d) Terms will never be implied by the courts because of the doctrine of freedom of contract.

2 **Express terms in contract may be made void under certain circumstances. Which one of the following is NOT one of those circumstances?**
   (a) Where the term is an unreasonable exclusion clause.
   (b) Where the term is an unreasonable restraint of trade.
   (c) Where the term provides for liquidated damages.
   (d) Where the term attempts to prohibit the making of back-up copies of computer programs which are necessary to the lawful use of the computer program.

3 **A contract between a computer dealer and a company provides that the company is to purchase 20 new computers to be delivered during the last week of March but certainly no later than the end of Friday of that week. Two weeks later, despite a number of phone calls urging delivery, the dealer failed to deliver the computers. In the last phone call, the construction company said it would only accept delivery of the computers if they arrived within the following week. When they failed to arrive by the end of that week, the construction company sent a letter to the dealer cancelling the contract. The dealer responded by saying he would sue the construction company for breach of contract. Which one the following statements is CORRECT?**
   (a) The construction company was entitled to cancel the contract and failure to deliver on time would be seen as a breach of condition, without prejudice to any claim for damages it might have for the breach of contract.

(b) The computer dealer will be entitled to damages for unlawful repudiation of the contract as it is reasonable to expect delivery to be late by a few weeks.

(c) By making phone calls urging delivery, the construction company waived its right to repudiate the contract and such a waiver cannot subsequently be withdrawn. Therefore, the computer dealer is entitled to damages.

(d) Both the construction company and the computer dealer are in breach of contract and the court would refuse to make any award to either party as both are at fault.

4 **In a contract for the writing of new computer software, there is an implied term to the effect that the work must be carried out using reasonable care and skill. In respect of that implied term, which one of the following statements is NOT CORRECT?**

(a) The standard is an objective one and is satisfied if the software is written to the standard that a reasonably competent software developer would reach.

(b) It is accepted that software may contain errors and still reach the required standard.

(c) The standard requires that the software developer assigns suitable qualified staff to write the software.

(d) Software which contains errors is not written using reasonable care and skill even if the software developer had tried his hardest.

5 **Distinguish between the following forms of contract for the purposes of determining the nature of the contract (note: this is not a multiple choice question).**

(a) A contract to develop, install and test new software for a client.

(b) A contract to supply a computer system including a server with modem link to the internet, computers linked to the server, printers, scanners and copiers and all necessary operating systems software.

(c) A contract to supply a computer together with operating system software and applications software, such as MS Office.

For further resources and updates please go to the Companion Website accompanying this book at **www.mylawchamber.co.uk/bainbridgeIT**

13

Fundamentals of information technology contracts

14 Liability for defective hardware or software

INTRODUCTION

There have been occasions when defects in software have had very serious consequences. The term 'safety-critical' is applied to software (and hardware) which is used in situations involving risk to life and limb. For example, in 1992 it was discovered that around 1,000 patients at a North Staffordshire hospital had received incorrect dosages of radiation therapy because of an alleged fault in a computer program. Later that same year the London Ambulance's new computer system failed dramatically throwing the ambulance service into chaos and, possibly, resulting in a number of deaths caused by the consequential delays in getting ambulances to their call-out destinations. A flaw in Microsoft's Windows 2000 operating system allowed hackers to penetrate a computer server belonging to the United States Military (*BBC News*, 18 March 2003) and there were rumours that a software bug could cause Patriot missiles to lock onto the wrong target (*InfoWorld News*, 27 March 2003). A software bug was claimed to have caused a radioactive spill at a uranium processing plant in Australia in 2001. The bug was detected and corrected (*ZD Net UK News*, 30 January 2002).

Defects in computer equipment and software can cause all manner of damage. The failure of flight control systems, nuclear power station systems and defence systems could result in major loss of life. The same could be true of software used to design buildings and vehicles. Defects in other systems might result in financial loss only where an expert system is used to provide financial advice or information. The fact that organisations developing or supplying software or manufacturing and distributing hardware could be liable for the consequences of failure requires them to consider means of reducing or limiting liability and, while practical measures such as quality control and testing are of vital importance, regard must be had to the legal position regarding defects.

The 'Millennium Bug' focused minds in 1999 as regards the potential for disaster caused by 'computer error'. That particular problem was caused by the old (and now clearly perceived to be foolish) convention of only using two digits to store the year of a date. Thus, the date 4 August 1999 would be stored in a form equivalent to 04/08/99. Where a calculation is performed which involves dates, such as in determining the duration of some computer-controlled process or operation, it is obvious that things can quickly go wrong on or after 1 January 2000. The convention of using two digits for the year was a result of a desire to save what was then very expensive computer storage. Additionally, most programmers working in the 1960s and 1970s thought the programs they were writing would become redundant long before the millennium. In those days, in terms of the pace of development of computer technology, the turn of the century seemed a very long way off. In the event, nothing serious seems to have resulted from the Millennium Bug, apart from the considerable expense and work in checking and modifying older software systems.

If a person suffers loss or damage as a result of defective hardware or software, one or more of the following areas of law might provide a remedy:

- contract;
- law of negligence;
- negligent misstatement; or
- product liability.

The basic principles of contractual liability have already been discussed in Chapter 13 and often can provide the simplest route to a satisfactory remedy. If the aggrieved person is not in a contractual relationship with the person responsible for the loss or damage, or does not have the right to enforce the contract as a third party, other areas of law must be looked to for a remedy.

Once the risks and liabilities have been identified, the contract should provide a suitable mechanism for apportioning liability between the parties. As Judge Bowsher QC said in *Stent Foundations Ltd* v *M J Gleeson Group plc* [2001] BLR 134:

> In all projects, the allocation of the risks of negligence and the duty to insure against those risks is a matter to be considered. Clear allocation of risk may reduce the likelihood of litigation or arbitration ... the parties should be clear and explicit in their contracts so that parties start a project with clear knowledge as to where the risks lie rather than disputing the allocation of risk when the project goes awry.

Once risk has been allocated, insurance can then be obtained to cover the potential losses resulting from defects and from issues relating to the performance of the contract. This is important as case law has amply demonstrated that reliance on contract terms, limiting liability to a relatively small sum, is misplaced.

In this chapter, forms of liability for defects, other than contractual, are examined. The focus is upon the law of negligence, negligent misstatement and product liability. These areas are of particular concern because they impose liability in respect of loss or damage sustained by third parties. Finally, the legal control of exemption clauses and notices, which attempt to exclude or limit liability, is considered.

14

Liability for defective hardware or software

NEGLIGENCE

Negligence is part of an area of law known as tort. Basically, a tort is a civil wrong, independent of contract. It imposes legal liabilities on a person who has acted carelessly or unreasonably omits to do something. Under certain circumstances a person will be liable to another for failing to exercise a required duty of care. In the case of consumer goods, such as a chair or television set, if the negligence of the manufacturer causes them to be defective, a person injured as a result will be entitled to damages. A claim in negligence does not depend on the presence of a contract, so if the person injured is someone other than the buyer, that person can still sue. The buyer also should be able to sue, but on the basis of breach of contract if the item is defective and fails to comply with implied terms such as those concerning satisfactory quality and fitness for purpose. To be able to sue in negligence, three essential ingredients must be present:

- a duty of care owed to the injured party;
- a breach of that duty of care; and
- consequential loss – that is, loss which is a direct and natural result of the breach of duty of care.

The landmark case on negligence is *Donoghue* v *Stevenson* [1932] AC 562, in which the claimant had been bought a bottle of ginger beer by a friend in a café. The bottle was made of opaque glass and so the contents could not be seen. The café owner poured part of the contents into a glass which the claimant drank. The claimant's friend then poured out the rest of the contents and the decomposed remains of a snail came out of the bottle. The claimant suffered shock and severe gastroenteritis as a result of the revolting sight and the fact that she had already swallowed some of the ginger beer. The claimant could not sue in contract because she was not a party to the contract – it had been her friend who had bought the drink. Nevertheless, the House of Lords held that a manufacturer, who sold food or medicine or the like in containers of a nature that the distributor or ultimate purchasers or consumers could not discover the defect by inspection, is under a legal duty to the ultimate purchaser or consumer to take reasonable care that the article is free from any defect likely to cause injury to health. This duty of care is owed to any person who might be contemplated to be injured by the act or omission of the manufacturer (the 'neighbour' or proximity test). Negligence can be thought of as an early form of product liability and has developed over the years to its present wide scope, although this is tempered to some extent by the growth of insurance. It is also limited, to some extent, by policy considerations. This is particularly so where the loss is purely economic or the claim is in respect of nervous shock or if a professional would be exposed to an unlimited number of claims from persons other than those for whom he performed his duties.

Negligence and computers

What is the significance of the tort of negligence as far as computers and software are concerned? Although it is unlikely that decomposing snails will be found within the workings of computers, it is possible to come across computer 'bugs' and there may still be some further nasty surprises. At first sight it may seem unlikely that computers and computer software could kill or cause serious injury; however, negligent liability does not stop at personal injury but extends to damage to property. Computer equipment runs on electricity so there is always the danger of electrical shock and, if this results from negligence, there is a strong possibility of an action in negligence. But computer software also has the potential to cause serious loss of life as well as causing economic losses. Consider a large passenger aircraft being re-fuelled ready for flight. A computer program is used to calculate the amount of fuel required. This is based on information such as the number of passengers, the weight of baggage, the flight distance and prevailing winds, etc. Then, because of a hitherto undiscovered bug in the computer program, less fuel is loaded than required, with the result that the aircraft runs out of fuel over the sea. A 'fly-by-wire' system in an aircraft may have a bug which, under a particular set of circumstances, makes it difficult for the pilot to override it. It is possible that the software developer was negligent in writing and testing of the software.

Other nightmare scenarios include where an air traffic control system contains a software error which incorrectly records the location of an aircraft or where a railway signalling system contains a fault or where guidance software directs a missile with a warhead to the wrong location. Fortunately, most software errors do not have catastrophic effects but they can have very costly consequences if they are not detected and fixed. A simple error in software to assist self-employed persons to calculate their tax liability for the purposes of self-assessment of tax resulted in many people underestimating their tax liability bringing the possibility of fines from the Inland Revenue (*The Times*, 13 August 1997, p. 5). The error was a mistake where pounds and pence were confused. In this case, most of the persons affected would have contractual remedies had they been charged interest on the underpayment on the basis of the licence agreement with the software developer (subject to any valid exclusion or limitation clauses).

The fact that an action in negligence lies without the need for a contract is important both for computer program writers and manufacturers of computer equipment. If a program is licensed by a publisher, the program author could be liable in negligence even though he is not a party to the licence agreement. In the case of computer hardware, a person suffering loss or injury as a result of the negligence of the manufacturer will have a claim in negligence against the manufacturer regardless of the fact that the equipment was bought from a dealer.

There are limitations, however, to the scope of the law of negligence and, as mentioned above, certain ingredients must be present. A person writing a computer program, or a company manufacturing computer equipment, will not necessarily be potentially liable to the world at large in negligence. The person/company will be liable, however, to those whom they could contemplate being adversely affected by any negligent act or omission by them. A further limiting factor is that the claimant bears the burden of proof; he has to show that the defendant was negligent and this is not always easy to do. There may be an exception if the event causing the injury or damage could only be reasonably explained by assuming there had been negligence. This is known as *res ipsa loquitur*, that is, 'the thing speaks for itself'. If you are hit on the head by a pot of paint while walking under a ladder you would not be asked to show the precise act of negligence that caused the paint to fall; it goes without saying that someone had been negligent. This is the exception, however, and normally the claimant must prove the negligent act or omission.

Even if negligence is proved, the amount of damages awarded may be reduced if the claimant has contributed in a causal sense to the negligence. If a computer has been badly made and is an electrical hazard then, if the person who has been electrocuted had tampered with the machine, the damages awarded may be reduced in proportion to the extent of his contribution to the accident. Fortunately, death or personal injury resulting from the use of a computer has been a rare occurrence, but other forms of loss or damage might be more common: for example, in a business context where a computer may be used to assist with decision making, there is a strong probability that a financial loss will be blamed on the computer. However, an action based solely on economic loss is unlikely to succeed under the normal law of negligence due to policy considerations. It may be possible in such a case to base an action on negligent misstatement instead, as described later.

NEGLIGENCE AND RSI

Many office workers spend long periods of time at a keyboard. By doing so, they may risk acquiring some form of cramp or painful condition in their wrists and fingers which is often described as repetitive strain injury (RSI). RSI is not, however, a medical term of precision, but for some time the Department of Health has recognised a condition known simply as PDA4 which is on a list of prescribed diseases for the purposes of industrial injury benefit. It is defined as cramp of the hand or forearm due to repetitive movements, such as writer's cramp. The types of occupations where it can occur are those which involve prolonged periods of handwriting, typing or other repetitive movements of the fingers, hand or arm.

The most important case to date on RSI (or PDA4) in the context of a word processor operator was *Pickford* v *Imperial Chemical Industries Ltd* [1998] 3 All ER 462. The claimant worked for the defendant for a number of years as a secretary and spent around 50 per cent of her time using a word processor. She claimed that, at times, that went up to 75 per cent. Eventually, she complained of pain in both hands and, after consulting a number of doctors and specialists, she commenced proceedings against her employer alleging negligence. She claimed that it was reasonably foreseeable that operating the word processor for long periods without breaks or rest periods would cause the condition and that the employer was negligent in failing to warn her of it and the need to take rest breaks. At the trial, the judge found that the claimant failed to establish the case against her employer but the Court of Appeal overturned that decision by a 2:1 majority. The employer appealed to the House of Lords which allowed the appeal by a 4:1 majority.

The majority in the House of Lords considered that the Court of Appeal was wrong to overturn the decision of the trial judge. All the relevant issues related to findings of fact and an appeal court will interfere with such a finding only in exceptional circumstances as it is the trial judge who has the benefit of seeing and hearing the witnesses including, in this case, a number of expert and lay witnesses. Lord Hope of Craighead made a number of observations as follows:

- PDA4 has two possible causes: one is organic and the other is that its basis is psychogenic (that is, 'it is all in the mind'), the product of conversion hysteria whereby the mind uses the body to escape from an objectionable working situation.
- Medical opinion is divided as to the cause.
- The trial judge rightly decided that the claimant failed to prove that the cause was organic and the defendant did not have to prove that the cause was psychogenic (the burden of proof lay on the claimant).
- The judge was right to hold that PDA4 resulting from typing work was not reasonably foreseeable, in the light of the state of knowledge at the time the claimant developed the condition (that is, in 1988–89).
- The nature of the work meant that the claimant had ample non-typing work to intersperse with her word processing and, consequently, there was no duty on the employer to prescribe rest periods.
- There was no duty on the employer to warn of the dangers of PDA4 – this was particularly so as issuing such a warning might bring about the condition, given that one possible cause was psychogenic.

Although the claimant failed in her claim, that does not mean to say that word processor operators and others who, as part of their work, spend long periods at a keyboard would also fail. In the present case, the claimant failed to prove causation – that is, that her injury was caused by the negligence of the employer. Indeed, the dissenting judge, Lord Steyn, said that among the 'tangled words and imperfect scientific insights' the central proved facts established that the claimant's work caused her disability and this could, had the employer exercised reasonable care, have avoided the occurrence of the disability.

One point to make is that it appears that an action might lie only if the court accepts that the cause is an organic one. If the court finds that it is a result of the mind (psychogenic), any claim is bound to fail. That is somewhat controversial, as to the sufferer the pain and discomfort will probably feel just as real and it might have been brought on by having to work at a keyboard at high speed for intolerable periods. In terms of causation, the injury will be the result of the work.

The case raises the question of what advice an employer should give to an employee about the dangers of working at a keyboard for long periods of time without breaks. To warn specifically of PDA4 might induce it in persons of a nervous disposition. The best approach, as was suggested in the above case, is to tell employees simply to go and see a doctor if unusual pain or discomfort is experienced. To warn word processor operators and the like that if they developed pain they would never work again was, in the words of one expert witness, 'disgraceful'. The defendant had an excellent record with respect to health and safety and gave advice to persons using computers with respect to eye-strain, ensuring that work stations were suitably designed and sited.

In the past, there were concerns about the safety of cathode ray tubes used for televisions and personal computers. There have been worries about the safety of persons living near to masts used for mobile phone communications. The latest 'scare' is that wireless networks could be unsafe or cause headaches or other health problems. If an association is found, there may be implications under the law of negligence and also under the Health and Safety at Work etc. Act 1974. As far as computer screens are concerned, there is specific legislation dealing with their use and safety, extending to the ergonomic features of the computer equipment and the desk at which the computer operator sits (Health and Safety (Display Screen Equipment) Regulations 1992). These Regulations came into force on 1 January 1993. Nowadays, the technology used for visual displays for computers and other items of equipment with visual displays has moved on and there do not appear to be any particular health issues associated with the technology itself. Even so, employers, schools and other bodies should ensure that the use of computer equipment is designed to avoid health problems, such as eye-strain or wrist injuries.

NEGLIGENT MISSTATEMENT

It is in terms of expert systems or other items of computer software designed to provide advice or information intended to be taken seriously and acted upon that the potential for liability for negligence takes on special significance. If the system is used to derive advice for a professional to use in the execution of his duties, the ultimate recipient of the advice may find that he has a right of action against the professional or the system developer (or even the independent experts and knowledge engineers engaged by the system developer). The leading case on tortious liability for negligent advice, referred to as negligent misstatement, is *Hedley Byrne & Co Ltd* v *Heller & Partners Ltd* [1964] AC 465. In that case, the House of Lords concluded that a bank, giving information as to the liquidity of one of its own customers to another bank so that the latter could show the information to one of its customers, could be liable to that customer, even though the first bank did not know the identity of the second bank's customer – the ultimate recipient of the information. The fact was that the bank giving the reference must have appreciated that the information would be shown to a customer of the other bank and this was sufficient to satisfy the 'neighbour test'. Therefore, the required relationship exists where one person holds himself out as an expert and gives advice which is intended to be taken seriously and acted upon even though no contractual relationship exists.

This could have the effect of making the persons and organisations responsible for the creation of expert systems and decision-support systems liable to the ultimate consumers of the advice generated. The experts who provided the rules and facts used by the system, the knowledge engineers who formalised the knowledge, the programmers and analysts responsible for designing the inferencing and interface programs could all find themselves liable if the advice generated by use of the system is incorrect. There are, however, two factors which might negate or reduce liability. The first is whether a duty of care will be imposed and the second is the status of any disclaimer. Although the people involved in the development of the system are directly responsible for the performance and accuracy of the system, they have little control over the way the system will be used or interpreted. Unlike a simple bank reference where the significance and use of the information provided is fairly obvious, the advice obtained from an expert system or decision-support system depends on the interaction between the system and its user. As expert systems are designed for use by persons who have some general understanding of the knowledge domain, it is reasonable to assume that the user will take at least some of the responsibility for the output obtained. However, a professional such as a general medical practitioner who has to seek the advice of a specialist consultant will find it difficult to verify and validate the advice of the specialist and this is true also of expert systems and decision-support systems which contain knowledge beyond that of the user of the system. Lack of control over the use to which the information will be put does not in itself negate liability. The central issue is whether a duty of care will be imposed by law.

In *Caparo Industries plc* v *Dickman* [1990] 2 AC 605, it was held that there are three criteria for imposing a duty of care:

- foreseeability of damage;
- proximity of relationship; and
- the reasonableness or otherwise of imposing a duty of care.

In that case, a company bought additional shares in another company following receipt of audited accounts prepared by the defendant. The House of Lords said that liability for statements, put into general circulation in such circumstances that they might foreseeably be relied on by strangers, would only be imposed when the maker of the statement knew it would be communicated to the person relying on it either as an individual or member of a class and that it would be likely to be relied on for a known purpose. In the present case it was held that an auditor owed no duty of care to the general public nor to individual shareholders who relied on the accounts to buy shares because of a lack of proximity. To hold otherwise would give rise to unlimited liability on the part of the auditor. However, in allowing a claim by the intended beneficiaries of a will which should, but for the negligence of the solicitor acting for the person making the will (the testator), have been prepared before the testator died, the House of Lords, in *White* v *Jones* [1995] 2 AC 207, raised the spectre of widening the scope of persons to whom a duty of care was owed. Two of the five Law Lords dissented on the basis that this could lead to the recognition of an extensive new area of potential liability.

Since *White* v *Jones*, the House of Lords has confirmed that this area of law has not 'ossified' but the law should develop incrementally by analogy with established categories: *Commissioners of Customs and Excise* v *Barclays Bank* [2006] 2 Lloyd's Rep 327. Although many cases of negligent misstatement involved a voluntary assumption of responsibility (not necessarily towards to person suffering the loss), that was not a prerequisite for an action for negligent misstatement. However, an assumption of responsibility is likely to be present in most cases involving advice derived from running computer software.

Advice produced using expert systems or other decision-support systems is nearer to the *Hedley Byrne* facts than those of *Caparo* v *Dickman* in which the primary purpose of the information was to comply with a statutory requirement; that is, having the company's accounts audited. Advice flowing from expert systems is intended to be taken seriously and acted upon. If the system is designed to produce advice as to trading in stocks and shares that is precisely the use to which it will be put. Therefore, the law of negligent misstatement ought to apply to such systems.

On the other hand, factual software such as a database of vehicles performance lies nearer to the *Caparo* v *Dickman* case. The maker of the database has no clear idea as to the particular uses to which the data will be used, unless it has been sold for a specific purpose. Thus, the maker of the database should not be liable to a third party in respect of a mistake contained within it. He may be contractually liable, however, to the purchaser of a copy of the database. Of course, many computer systems lie between these two extremes.

In the *Hedley Byrne* case, the bank providing the advice was able to escape liability because it had printed a clear disclaimer on the information excluding legal responsibility for the advice. Since the *Hedley Byrne* case, the Unfair Contract Terms Act 1977 was enacted to con-

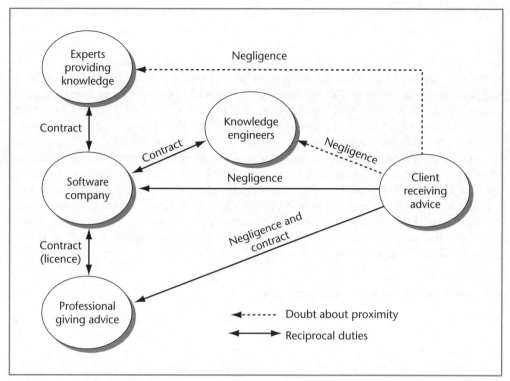

Figure 14.1   Liability for defective advice from an expert system
Note: For a duty to arise in negligence, owed to the client by anyone other than the person giving advice, it would have to be shown that the client relied on that person's statement rather than on the statement of the person giving advice.

trol, *inter alia*, exclusion or limitation of liability for negligence, whether under contract or tort. As far as business liability for death or personal injury is concerned, it cannot be excluded or limited by a notice or term in a contract. In other cases, the notice or term must satisfy the requirement of reasonableness. Furthermore, the use of a disclaimer will be effective only if it is clear and unambiguous and drawn to the attention of the person relying on the advice. Figure 14.1 shows the potential liability (tortious and contractual) with respect to incorrect advice derived from a defective expert system. It assumes that the experts and knowledge engineers are consultants to the software company and not its employees (this will be a common arrangement in practice).

The person using an expert system to advise a client will be potentially liable under the laws of contract and negligence. Liability will not be avoided simply because the system has a fault and the same principles apply here as in the case of conventional computer software. It might be important to consider whether it would be reasonable for the person using the system for the purpose of advising others to rely on the system's output. In relation to the exercise of a profession such as medicine, the fact that a person has acted in accordance with practice which is recognised as proper by a responsible body of persons skilled in that profession means that there has been no negligence. In *De Freitas* v *O'Brien* [1995] 6 Med LR 108, however, the Court of Appeal stressed that a responsible body of expert opinion does not have to be a substantial body. A small number of specialists could constitute a 'responsible body'.

Consider an expert system designed to recommend financial investments which is used by a responsible body of financial advisers. If a particular financial adviser uses the system to recommend an investment to a client, the adviser will not be negligent if the system was used in a reasonable and satisfactory manner, even if the advice turns out to be bad retrospectively. The problem is that, until such time as a particular expert system is used by a sufficient number of skilled practitioners (sufficient to be classed as a responsible body), anyone using an expert system is taking a chance should the advice turn out to be wrong, although it must be stressed that the fact that advice is wrong does not inevitably and conclusively mean that there has been negligence. In *Whitehouse* v *Jordan* [1981] 1 All ER 267, the House of Lords confirmed that an error of judgment does not automatically indicate negligence; it depends whether the error would have been made by a reasonably competent professional man professing to have the standard and type of skill that the defendant held himself out to have. If the person using the expert system does not have the degree of skill and knowledge contained in the system he should make this clear to the client and obtain his agreement prior to using the system. The advantage of negligent misstatement over normal negligence claims is that it can be used where the loss has been economic only, although it is not restricted to this.

Liability for indirect statements

Where the original maker of the statement does not directly communicate it to the person relying on it, it appears that for a duty of care to arise, the latter must realise who is the source of the statement. In *Abbott* v *Strong* [1998] 2 BCLC 420, a firm of accountants made statements as to a profits forecast, which were included in a circular sent to shareholders inviting them to subscribe for new shares in a rights issue. It was held that the accountants were not potentially liable for any misstatement to shareholders who subscribed as they had not relied on the accountants' statement. Where a person makes a statement to another person who uses it to advise another but that other does not know of the first person's participation in the advice, then the recipient cannot be said to have relied on the first person. Thus, where a person uses computer software in order to advise a client who believes that the advice comes from the person using the software alone, then any person who has been involved in the development of the software cannot be liable to the client in tort. Of course, this will be different if the client knows that the advice derived from using the software emanates from a person or persons involved in the development of the software, such as in the case of an expert system which contains rules and advice set forward by a particular person.

This approach is based on the concept of reliance. The person originally giving the advice cannot be liable if the ultimate recipient is shown not to have relied on that person but on advice given by another (even if originally given by that person) and can be contrasted with *Hedley Byrne* where it was clear that the recipient of the advice did indeed rely upon the first bank. The recipient's bank was merely the messenger. Thus, if a patient, Tom Cobb, consults a general practitioner, Dr Akerman, in respect of an illness and the doctor uses diagnostic software which includes diagnostic rules and suggested treatment devised by a specialist, Mr Rudge, he will not have a claim against Mr Rudge as he does not rely on him. It is Dr Akerman on whom Tom Cobb relies. It would be different if Dr Akerman first told Tom Cobb that he was going to use a computer system which contained advice from Mr Rudge, a specialist in the field.

The need for reliance does not necessarily require that the recipient of the statement knows the precise identity of the person from whom the advice originated providing that he knew it came from some other person. Reliance as an essential ingredient in an action for negligent misstatement was confirmed by the House of Lords in *Williams* v *Natural Health Foods Ltd* [1998] 2 All ER 577. In that case it was held that a director of a franchisor company (the franchise was in respect of health food shops) was not liable to the franchisees for loss resulting from negligent advice *given by the franchisor company* as there was no evidence that the franchisees believed that the director was undertaking a personal responsibility to them. In the example given in Fig. 14.1, if liability for negligent misstatement is to be imposed on anyone other than the professional giving the advice directly to the client, it would be necessary to show that the client relied on any statement made by that person.

Negligent provision of a service and concurrent liability

At first, it was thought that *Hedley Byrne* was limited to negligent statements but it is now apparent that it also applies to the negligent provision of a service. In *Henderson* v *Merrett Syndicates Ltd* [1995] 2 AC 145, discussed later, Lord Goff said that there was no reason why a person should not be liable under the *Hedley Byrne* principle for economic loss which flows from the negligent performance of a service, and this sentiment was approved in *Williams* v *Natural Health Foods Ltd* [1998] 2 All ER 577. The provision of the service must be coupled with a concomitant reliance and will often be set in the context of a contract. This brings into question whether there can be concurrent liability under contract and tort where, for example, a service is provided under a contract.

At one time it was thought that where there was a contract between the parties, that contract would provide the sole basis for the injured party seeking a remedy. At least liability in negligence could not be imposed if it contradicted the express terms of a contract. However, the position was clarified in *Henderson* v *Merrett Syndicates Ltd* [1995] 2 AC 145, where the main issue was whether the defendants (managers of syndicates at Lloyd's) could be liable concurrently in contract and tort to Lloyd's underwriters for the negligent management of syndicates to which the underwriters belonged.

The House of Lords held that such concurrent liability can exist unless the contract itself precludes it. This means that in many cases, the injured party may choose whether to sue on the contract or in tort. Although in many cases the outcome will be the same in practical terms, in some the contractual and tortious duties may be different and the limitation periods may be different. The limitation period is the time within which an action must be commenced, otherwise it will be time-barred. For contract it is six years from the breach (Limitation Act 1980, section 5), while for negligence (and negligent misstatement) generally it is six years from the date the damage occurred (Limitation Act 1980, section 2); although for personal injury cases, the period is three years.

As an example of the above principles, consider a situation whereby Conway Computer Systems Ltd has agreed to maintain for one year the computer system of Willett & Co Ltd, a company with a parcel delivery operation. The contract states that Conway will remedy any defects within 24 hours of being informed by Willett and there is a clause in the contract providing for the payment of £500 per day in liquidated damages by Conway for every 24-hour period in excess of the first such period during which the computer system remains out of action because of a defect. One day, Willett informed Conway of a fault on its computer system. Due to the negligence of its programmers, Conway took 72 hours to remedy the defect. Under the contract Conway is liable to pay £1,000 to Willett. However, under the circumstances, Willett's operations were badly disrupted and its total loss was in the order of £15,000. It was reasonably foreseeable that Willett would be so affected by its computer system being inoperable for such a period of time. That being so, the damages arising out of negligence ought to be in the order of £15,000, whereas, under contract, they are only £1,000. Although, theoretically, there are concurrent liabilities in contract and tort, it would be highly unlikely that a court would allow Willett to pursue a remedy in tort as the contract has an express limitation on the measure of damages for failure to repair the defect in time. If the limiting clause did not exist, however, it would seem that Willett could be free to chose which route to pursue. This might be advantageous, particularly if the duty of care under the contract is of a lesser standard than that under the tort of negligence.

PRODUCT LIABILITY

Related to negligence are the product liability provisions contained in the Consumer Protection Act 1987. Under the Act, an ultimate consumer can claim against the producer of a defective product regardless of the lack of a contractual relationship between the consumer and the producer and without having to show the basic requirements for an action in negligence. Part I of the Act deals with product liability and stems from the product liability Directive.[1] A 'product' is defined by the Consumer Protection Act as being any goods including electricity and includes a product comprised in another product whether a component part or a raw material or otherwise. A computer would therefore come within the meaning of product but computer software, *per se*, will be outside the scope of this part of the Act.

Although product liability does not appear to apply to software it will apply to a defective product which incorporates software which most electronic products now seem to do. There would seem to be no reason why liability on the basis of product liability should be avoided even if the defect which causes the damage lies within the software. A defect in software controlling a microwave oven or any other product will result in the microwave oven itself being defective.

There is an argument for extending product liability to software directly. For example, defective software could corrupt files, compromise privacy, leave a computer system vulnerable to viruses, spyware, hackers and fraudsters. The advantage of product liability is that, compared to the law of negligence generally, it is almost a form of strict liability. The person suffering the damage or loss does not have to show fault on the part of the producer. On the other hand, imposing product liability to software could prejudice the distribution of freeware and open source software. Nevertheless, there is a feeling that software developers get off lightly compared with manufacturers of tangible products (*BBC News*, 30 September 2005).

Liability

The producer of a defective product is liable for damage resulting wholly or partly from that defect. Distributors and retailers selling 'own brand' goods can be liable if they can be said to be holding themselves out to be the producer. If a person imports a product, in the course of business, into a country belonging to the European Community from outside the Community in order to supply the product to another, then that importer will be regarded as the producer for the purposes of determining liability by section 2 of the Act. This might have implications for the many companies which import computers made outside the European Community, especially importers who affix their own name to the equipment. If one of these machines is defective and someone is injured as a result, then the importer/distributor will be liable under the Act, apart from any remedies available against him under contract. The Consumer Protection Act also makes a supplier liable if he fails to identify the producer within a reasonable time, having been asked to do so by the claimant.

---

[1] Council Directive 85/374/EEC of 25 July 1985 on the approximation of laws, regulations and administrative provisions of Member States concerning liability for defective products, OJ L 210, 07.08.1985, p. 29 (the 'product liability Directive').

A defect is defined by reference to the expectation of safety in the product and this relates to property damage as well as death and personal injury. A computer with an exposed unearthed metal chassis would fall short of the expectation of safety.

'State of the art' defence

An important defence is the 'state of the art' defence contained in section 4(1) of the Consumer Protection Act 1987. This provides that it is a defence in any civil proceedings to show that 'the state of scientific and technical knowledge at the relevant time was not such that a producer of products of the same description as the product in question might be expected to have discovered the defect if it had existed in his products while they were under his control'. This defence would apply, for example, where a product failed suddenly as a result of a form of material fatigue hitherto not generally known amongst producers of such products. The defence as set out in the Act has been criticised as introducing a subjective element as it is a question of whether the producer might be expected to discover the fault, not whether a reasonable producer would be expected to discover the defect. The product liability Directive seems to imply a more objective test as it requires the state of scientific and technical knowledge to be such as to enable the existence of the defect to be discovered. However, in Case C-300/95 *Commission of the European Communities* v *United Kingdom* [1997] ECR I–2649, the European Court of Justice concluded that the Act validly implemented that part of the Directive and rejected the Commission's argument that the UK had widened the defence so that the strict liability imposed by the Directive had been turned into mere liability for negligence. As Part I of the Consumer Protection Act 1987 is stated to be intended to comply with the Directive and shall be construed accordingly, it would appear that the courts in the UK are likely to interpret the 'state of the art' defence on an objective basis.

A possible application of the defence is in the aeronautical industry, for example, where software companies develop sophisticated software for 'fly-by-wire' aeroplanes. Imagine there are two such companies: one is a very large company, Goliath plc, with enormous resources at its disposal whereas the other company, David Software Ltd, is much smaller, being a new entrant into this field, and having proportionally less resources. As a result of considerable research and testing, Goliath is aware of an inherent danger in such software in that it takes a short period of time for the pilot to override the computer software. Consequently, Goliath has incorporated an emergency override command in its software. David Software is not aware of this problem because it has not been published by Goliath and David Software has not carried out sufficient research to detect the problem. If the test in section 4 of the Consumer Protection Act 1987 is subjective, David Software might be able to avail itself of the defence but is less likely to if, as it appears it should be, the test is objective.

The defence is most likely to be relevant in leading-edge technology where new types of products are being developed. This is particularly so where computer technology is being used in process control, traffic control, guidance systems and the like. Consider, for example, the implications of a car with a computer software designed to apply the brakes in an emergency, say if the traffic in front comes to an abrupt standstill. One day a cat runs across the road in front of the car. The software interprets the image of the cat as a stationary object immediately ahead and brings the car to an emergency stop, even though the cat would have safely made it to the other side of the road anyway. A lorry following the car runs into the back of it injuring the occupants. Who is liable? The company making the braking system could be potentially liable subject to the state of the art defence (a product includes a product comprised in another product as a component part). The lorry driver, and his employer, may also be liable in negligence.

Extent of liability

Under section 5 of the 1987 Act, the liability covered by Part I of the Act extends to:

- death or personal injury;
- damage to or destruction of any item of property (including land) other than the defective product itself (there is a lower threshold of £275 before a claim can be made) provided that the property:
  - is the type normally intended for private use and consumption; and
  - it is used mainly for the private use or consumption of the person claiming.

Therefore, in dealings between businesses, the product liability part of the Act will only apply to defective products causing death or personal injury. As far as property damage is concerned, the provisions are really aimed at the consumer market, so, if you buy a computer as a present for your aunt and, because of a fault it catches fire and causes £1,500 of damage to her house, your aunt will have a claim under the 1987 Act against the manufacturer of the computer for the damage to the house and furniture. Personally, you may have a separate claim against the retail outlet because the computer was not of satisfactory quality under the Sale of Goods Act 1979.

CRIMINAL LIABILITY FOR DEFECTIVE PRODUCTS

Part I of the Consumer Protection Act 1987 imposes civil liability on producers. However, if a person is killed as a result of a defective product and the defect is attributable to the negligence of any person, that person could be exposed to a prosecution for manslaughter. This could even expose a company to prosecution if the negligence of a senior officer of the company is the root cause of the negligence and this is imputed to the company on the basis that the acts of its senior officers are the acts of the company.

Apart from liability for manslaughter resulting from defects in safety critical systems, there are numerous statutes which impose criminal liability and which may be triggered by a computer defect. Examples include the Health and Safety at Work, etc. Act 1974, the Food Safety Act 1990 and the Environmental Protection Act 1990, all as amended. An offence might be committed under the Food Safety Act where a computer is used to calculate cooking times for food sold to the public and underestimates safe times because of a defect. A pollution control system run by a computer may result in an offence under the Environmental Protection Act 1990 if toxic substances are released into a stream without treatment because of a software error. The areas where civil and criminal liability may result from the use of defective computer technology are immense and, with the growth of safety legislation and environmental protection law, these areas are increasing rapidly.

The General Product Safety Regulations 2005 (replacing the previous 1994 Regulations) impose criminal liability on producers and distributors in respect of products that are not safe. A 'product' means 'a product which is intended for consumers or likely, under reasonably foreseeable conditions, to be used by consumers even if not intended for them and which is supplied or made available, whether for consideration or not, in the course of a commercial activity and whether it is new, used or reconditioned and includes a product that is supplied or made available to consumers for their own use in the context of providing a service'. It does not include equipment used by service providers themselves to supply a service to consumers, in particular equipment on which consumers ride or travel which is operated by a service provider. A 'safe product' is one which, under normal or reasonably foreseeable conditions of use, including duration, does not present any risk or only the minimum risks compatible with the product's use considered as acceptable and consistent with a high level of protection for the safety and health of persons. Amongst other things, account is to be taken of the product's characteristics, presentation (including information given) and categories of consumers at serious risk (for example, children). There is a defence of due diligence.

These Regulations are highly relevant in terms of second-hand computer equipment and any electrical equipment sold to children. In terms of software the same difficulty will apply as identified above – that is, that it is unlikely that software will be deemed to be a product although it is possible that the disks and other tangible items supplied with the software may be so classed.

EXEMPTION CLAUSES

An exemption clause is one which excludes or restricts the liability of a party who is in breach of contract. Exemption clauses can be sub-divided into exclusion clauses and limitation clauses. An exclusion clause gives the party relying on it total exemption for the breach whereas a limitation clause limits liability to a specified amount. An example of an exclusion clause is where a supplier totally excludes his liability under the contract for late delivery if this is caused by circumstances beyond his control such as industrial action. An example of a limitation clause is where a supplier of computer software limits his liability for faulty software to the licence fee he has received for that software.

When people draft contracts they are usually keen to limit or exclude their liabilities and yet wish to ensure that the other party is absolutely bound to perform his part of the contract. Such one-sided contracts were fairly common in the past (they are by no means extinct now), particularly in circumstances where there was an inequality of bargaining power. An ordinary individual buying a product from a supplier who had a monopoly in the product had little choice but to accept the terms imposed on him or manage without it. A golden principle in contract was 'freedom of contract' meaning that the parties should be free to agree whatever terms they wished. This doctrine was acceptable where two powerful companies were negotiating a contract in a free market, but contractually weaker persons suffered. Over the years, however, Parliament and the courts have intervened to mitigate the harshness of the situation and certain terms are now implied into sale of goods and similar contracts, while exclusion clauses have been disapproved of by the courts, especially if such clauses are demonstrably unfair.

The courts developed techniques to limit the effects of exclusion clauses, including the interpretation of an ambiguous clause to the disadvantage of the party seeking to rely on it. For example, in *Andrews Brothers (Bournemouth) Ltd* v *Singer & Co Ltd* [1934] 1 KB 17, the claimant ordered a new Singer car from the defendants. When the car was delivered it was found to have done some 550 miles. The defendants sought to rely on an exclusion clause which stated that liability for terms implied by statute was excluded; one of these terms was that goods must comply with their description. The contract, however, repeatedly described the car as a 'new Singer car'. It was held that, because the car was referred to in the contract as a new car, this was an express term and since the exclusion clause sought to exclude liability for implied terms only, the defendants were liable. The exclusion clause was of no effect for this breach of an express term. The claimant was awarded £50 in damages.

The Unfair Contract Terms Act 1977

Importantly nowadays, exemption clauses are also controlled by statute. The Unfair Contract Terms Act 1977 limits the extent to which liability can be excluded or limited for breach of contract, or for negligence, or under the terms implied by the Sale of Goods Act 1979 and other legislation containing similar provisions, such as the Supply of Goods and Services Act 1982. Sections 2–4 of the Unfair Contract Terms Act apply to contractual terms or notices which attempt to exclude or restrict liability for negligence and breach of contract. (The equivalent provisions for Scotland are sections 16–18 of the Unfair Contract Terms Act 1977.)

A person may seek to exclude or limit his liability for negligence by means of a notice or a term in a contract. Whether the liability arises in tort or contract, the legal controls are the same and mainly result from section 2 of the Unfair Contract Terms Act 1977. This applies to business liability for negligence whether a breach of a contractual obligation to exercise reasonable care and skill in the performance of a contract or a breach of an equivalent common law duty. Section 2 of the Act prohibits the exclusion or limitation of liability for death or personal injury resulting from negligence, while liability for other loss or damage may only be excluded or restricted in so far as the term or notice satisfies the requirement of reasonableness. Section 11 of the Act provides that a term in a contract is reasonable if it is fair and reasonable to have been included in a contract having regard to the circumstances which were, or ought reasonably to have been, known to or in the contemplation of the parties when the contract was made. In relation to a notice, the test is whether it is fair and reasonable to allow reliance on it having regard to the circumstances. By section 11(4), where the term or notice seeks to limit liability to a specified sum of money, regard must be had to the resources available to the person who would have to meet the liability and how far it was open to that person to take out insurance cover. The burden of proof is on the person claiming that the term or notice is reasonable.

In terms of defective hardware, the basic provisions of the Unfair Contract Terms Act work reasonably predictably but it is in respect of software that doubts were expressed as to the reach of the Act, and this has been the source of some speculation. This is because, as regards England, Wales and Northern Ireland, Schedule 1, para. 1 to the Act states that:

Sections 2 to 4 of this Act do not extend to – . . .
(c) any contract so far as it relates to the creation or transfer of a right or interest in any patent, trade mark, copyright or design right, registered design, technical or commercial information or other intellectual property . . .

One view was that the important provisions in section 2 (liability for negligence), section 3 (contractual liability for breach or in relation to performance) and section 4 (unreasonable indemnity clauses) were inapplicable to software contracts because the essence of most software contracts is the granting of a licence to use the software – the creation of a right under copyright law. A number of software companies considered that they could largely ignore the effects of the Unfair Contract Terms Act 1977 and exclude or strictly limit their liability for defects. The courts have taken a more restrictive approach, however, to the scope of para. 1 of Schedule 1.

In *The Salvage Association* v *Cap Financial Services Ltd* [1995] FSR 654, the claimant invited tenders for the computerisation of its accounts system. The defendant submitted a successful bid for a feasibility study (strategy study and definition stage) and was awarded the contract in the sum of £30,000. Following this, a second contract was awarded to the defendant to develop and implement the software specified in the feasibility study. The date for completion of the second contract was 18 July 1988 and the contract price was £291,654. The system was to be implemented using ORACLE, a fourth-generation language operating as a relational database management system. In July 1988, the software was declared to be ready for user-training but almost immediately it became apparent that it was unusable and contained a large number of errors that would require substantial work to correct. Many of the errors could be attributed to the fact that the defendant's project team was not sufficiently experienced in the use of ORACLE. Nevertheless, the claimant persevered and allowed additional time for the defendant to complete the work satisfactorily. Several new dates for delivery were agreed but, eventually, it became clear to the claimant that the work was likely never to be completed satisfactorily and, on 13 July 1989, the claimant terminated the contract because of the serious breaches of contract on the part of the defendant.

The claimant argued that it was entitled to reject the system and terminate the second contract and claimed damages of £855,550 (being the sum of £291,388 already paid under both contracts and £564,162 for wasted expenditure resulting from the defendant's breaches of contract). The defendant sought to rely on limitation clauses in its standard form contract which formed the basis of the first contract and, in relation to the second contract, terms which purported to exclude liability except as provided for by the contract and, in any case, to limit liability under that contract to £25,000. The limit in the first contract was £250,000 in respect of physical damage and £25,000 for other loss or damage (except for liability for death or physical injury where there was no limit).

Both contracts contained terms to the effect that the defendant would assign appropriately qualified staff to perform the work and the judge in the High Court held that there was a breach of these terms. Furthermore, the judge implied a term under section 13 of the Supply of Goods and Services Act 1982 to the effect that the defendant would exercise reasonable care and skill and held that the defendant was also in breach of this term. The time for completion of the second contract was extended on a number of occasions but the judge held that time was of the essence and the extensions agreed by the claimant did not alter that simple fact. The claimant's patience had been stretched to the limit and it was entitled to repudiate the contract at the time it did.

If sections 2 and 3 of the Unfair Contract Terms Act 1977 applied to the limitation clauses, they would be upheld only in as much as they met the requirement of reasonableness – otherwise the defendant would probably be able to rely on them. The judge decided that para. 1 in Schedule 1 only concerned those provisions in a contract that dealt with the creation or transfer of a right or interest in the relevant intellectual property and did not extend to all the other terms of a service contract simply because the service will result in a 'product' that is subject to intellectual property rights. Thus, terms concerned with aspects of the contract other than those relating to the creation or transfer of an intellectual property right are still subject to sections 2–4 of the Unfair Contract Terms Act 1977. In other words, para. 1(c) does not create a blanket exception for software contracts.

Test of reasonableness

As mentioned above, the reasonableness test is expressed in section 11 of the Act. Schedule 2 provides guidelines for the application of the reasonableness test and, though expressed as being applicable only to sections 6 and 7 of the Act, the judge accepted the suggestion of Potter J in *Flamar Interocean Ltd* v *Denmac Ltd (The Flamar Pride)* [1990] 1 Lloyd's Rep 434 that it would be sensible to take the guidelines into account in such cases. He referred also to the judgment of Lord Griffiths in *Smith* v *Eric S Bush* [1990] 1 AC 831 where his lordship identified four matters that should always be considered:

- the relative bargaining power of the parties;
- whether it was reasonably practicable to obtain advice from an alternative source;
- the difficulty and dangerousness of the task to be undertaken – that is, the risk; and
- the practical consequences of the court's decision, the ability of the parties to bear the losses involved and the availability of insurance.

In *The Salvage Association* v *CAP Financial Services*, the parties were of equal bargaining power but it would have been almost impossible for the claimant to insure to cover the liability excluded by the defendant. The insurance factor was crucial to this case as the defendant itself had recognised the inadequacy of the £25,000 figure in its standard form contracts and it had been raised to £1 m at around the time of the first contract. Unfortunately for the defendant, it had not been able to explain convincingly why the higher figure had not been used in its contracts with the claimant. The judge, therefore, held that the terms limiting liability to £25,000 were unreasonable and awarded a total of £662,926 in damages comprising £291,388 (already paid by the claimant), £231,866 for items of wasted expenditure (computer time, wasted computer stationery, payments to consultants and for testing) and £139,672 for wasted management time.

Community charge bug

In another important case, *St Albans City & District Council* v *International Computers Ltd* [1995] FSR 686, the judge had to consider the effectiveness of clauses limiting liability in the context of a software 'bug' which caused financial loss to the client. It concerned software used to administer the community charge (poll tax) and has far-reaching implications for software developers, who should look carefully at their standard term contracts and level of insurance cover.

The claimant, a local authority, was responsible for setting the level of and collecting the community charge and invited tenders for the supply of suitable hardware and software to keep a register of charge payers and to carry out additional functions such as raising the necessary bills. The contract was awarded to the defendant in 1988. Perhaps exacerbated and compounded by unbelievably tight deadlines, an error in the software resulted in the population being over-estimated by some 2,966 persons and the community charge was set at too low a level as a consequence. This had a knock-on effect in terms of money flows to and from central government and the total financial loss to the claimant was £1,314,846. The contract was made on the defendant's standard written terms.

Mr Justice Scott Baker accepted that the defendant was under an obligation to provide software that would maintain a reliable database of names entered on to the community charge register, accurately count those names and accurately retrieve and display the population count. Furthermore, the software had to be reasonably fit for its purpose of maintaining and retrieving a reliable register. There was a plain breach of contract because of the erroneous figures produced by the software. Additionally, an assurance made by the defendant's project manager that the figures could be relied upon was a breach of the project manager's contract of service which was part of the overall agreement. This was a negligent misrepresentation and the project manager's obligations were not, as required, exercised with due diligence. A term in the contract that errors had to be notified to the defendant within three months was of no effect because the claimant was unaware of the error and had no way of discovering it.

The judge, in awarding the claimant the full amount claimed, said that the claimant was not at fault in failing to discover the error nor in failing to take different action when it became apparent that there was a problem with the software. He was of the opinion that the defendant had failed to establish that the limitation clauses in the main agreement and the service agreement incorporated in it were reasonable in the circumstances. By section 3 of the Unfair Contract Terms Act 1977, where one party deals as consumer or on the other's written standard terms of business, the other cannot, by reference to any contract term, exclude or restrict any liability for his own breach of contract except in so far as the term satisfies the requirement of reasonableness. The claimant was not dealing as consumer but the judge held that the contract was based on the written standard terms of the defendant even though there had been some negotiation between the parties. He said that it was not necessary for all the terms to have been fixed in advance by the supplier for the contract to be deemed to be on the basis of written standard terms. Some terms, such as those dealing with quality or price, would often be the result of negotiation but that did not necessarily take the contract out of the reach of section 3. In any case, the judge held that either section 6 or section 7 of the Unfair Contract Terms Act 1977 also applied.

Sections 6 and 7 deal with implied terms in contracts of sale or hire purchase of goods and other contracts under which the title to goods pass and also require that the reasonableness test be satisfied in relation to terms excluding or restricting liability. Scott Baker J followed the approach of Judge Thayne Forbes in *The Salvage Association* v *CAP Financial Services Ltd* and considered that it would be better for the loss to fall on a large international computer company (which was well able to insure itself against such claims) rather than falling on a local authority. Other factors of particular note were the resources of the defendant and its total insurance cover which was claimed to amount to £50 m. The judge decided that the claimant was in a slightly weaker bargaining position than the defendant and, although the claimant knew of the term (indeed, it had complained about its presence in the contract), had received no inducement, and was unable to enter into a similar contract with another without such a term, the defendant had failed to discharge its burden of establishing that the term was fair and reasonable in the circumstances.

The Court of Appeal confirmed that the limitation clause was unenforceable in *St Albans City & District Council* v *International Computers Ltd* [1997] FSR 251. However, the defendant's appeal was allowed in part in that the award of damages was reduced to £685,000. The claim in relation to payments by charge payers was held not to be recoverable as they were under an obligation to pay (otherwise they would get a bonus) and the claimant could simply increase the charge the following year to recoup that loss. This was notwithstanding the fact that some persons would have left the district and some would have moved into the district in the meantime. The Court of Appeal confirmed that the claimant could recover for the increased precept payments made to the County Council which it was unable to recover.

The *St Albans* case is very instructive and shows the difficulty that a software company may have in convincing a judge that any term excluding or limiting liability for defective software is reasonable. Here, the defendant's term was deemed to be unreasonable even though the claimant was aware of the term, other software companies had comparable terms and the software was in use while still under development. However, the judge's view that the claimant was in a weaker bargaining position can be criticised. It was a local authority responsible for a population in excess of 100,000 persons, employing professional staff and making use of a respected firm of management consultants to advise on the tender process. The claimant would certainly be in a stronger bargaining position than most small and medium-sized commercial enterprises dealing with a major computer company. Nevertheless, there are important lessons for computer software companies contained within the judgment.

Further developments on exclusion clauses

The *Salvage Association* and *St Albans* cases were important in that they recognised the general applicability of the Unfair Contract Terms Act 1977 to computer contracts including software contracts. In both cases, a fairly robust approach was taken to the question of whether exclusion clauses satisfied the requirement of reasonableness. Both cases indicated that insurance was an important factor and stressed that the Act places the burden of proof to show that an exclusion clause is reasonable in the party seeking to rely on it.

There have been a number of cases subsequently were the reasonableness of exclusion clauses has been under scrutiny. Of course, in contracts that include exclusion clauses, the validity or otherwise of those clauses is a very important issue. If they are valid, they can rob the client to whom software is supplied of a very substantial claim if the software turns out to be defective. If an exclusion clause is invalid, the financial implications can be such as to put the software company out of business or at least put it into serious financial difficulties, especially if it is not insured or is inadequately insured. Apart from the first, the following cases seem to indicate that the courts are taking a more generous view of exclusion clauses, particularly where there is equality of bargaining power and the parties can be said to enter into the contract with their eyes wide open, knowing the implications of what they are agreeing. Surprisingly, it also seems that a failure to have appropriate insurance is fatal to a software supplier seeking to rely on an exclusion clause. After all, insurance can prove expensive, particularly in relation to software development (most if not all insurance companies refused to insure against the Millennium Bug) and this will be passed on to the client by way of increased prices. This could jeopardise the competitiveness of a software developer who takes out a high level of insurance cover as compared to one who takes out no cover or minimal insurance cover.

In *Pegler Ltd* v *Wang (UK) Ltd* (unreported) 25 February 2000, Pegler decided to replace its existing computer systems with a new integrated system. It eventually contracted with Wang to carry out the work for over £1 m. Wang's performance was described by the judge as disastrous and, eventually, Wang ceased to carry out further work, abandoning the contract. Pegler terminated the contract and claimed over £22 m in damages. The clause in the contract allowing Pegler to terminate did not appear to be subject to Wang's exclusion clauses and Wang sought rectification of the contract so that the exclusion clauses would apply. In such cases, rectification is only possible if it could be shown that the parties were in complete agreement as to the terms but had failed to write them down correctly. Wang failed to adduce convincing evidence that this was the case and the claim for rectification failed and the exclusion clauses were of no effect. However, the judge went on to consider the reasonableness of the exclusion clauses in case of an appeal against his decision.

One of the exclusion clauses excluded liability for indirect, special or consequential loss and the other excluded liability (except in the case of death or personal injury) in respect of actions brought by either party more than two years after the cause of action occurred. Pegler claimed that the contract was on Wang's written standard terms and, therefore, the exclusion clauses were subject to section 3 of the Unfair Contract Terms Act 1977. Wang disagreed, arguing that the contract was the result of a process of negotiation, some important terms of the contract coming from Pegler's own standard terms and conditions. The latter were stated to have precedence over the other terms in case of conflict. The judge said the phrase 'written standard terms' was not confined to written contracts in which both parties use standard forms and he accepted that Pegler was dealing on 'the other's written standard terms' at least as far as the exclusion clauses were concerned, saying that it was not necessary for the whole contract to be on the other's written standard terms of business. That being so, the Unfair Contract Terms Act 1977 applied to the contract and the judge considered the reasonableness of the clauses. The judge analysed the facts in relation to the guidelines in Schedule 2 to the Act, as follows:

- strength of bargaining position – although Pegler was a substantial company it had burnt its boats by accepting the arrangement in principle and allowing work to proceed before the precise terms of the contract were agreed;

- whether the customer had an opportunity of entering into a similar contract with others without having to accept such a term – on the evidence, the judge accepted that all computer companies contract on similar terms as to the exclusion of liability;

- whether the customer knew or ought reasonably to have known of the existence and extent of the term – Pegler was advised by solicitors throughout the negotiation and was aware of the terms on which it was contracting with Wang;

- where a term excludes or restricts liability if some condition was not complied with, whether it was reasonable to expect compliance – to Wang's knowledge, Pegler had been oversold the system: Pegler had every reason to be confident that the system was suitable for its purposes and had been let down disastrously;

■ whether goods were manufactured, processed or adapted to the special order of the customer – the overselling included substantial misrepresentations as to the 'fit' of Wang's standard package to Pegler's requirements and Wang represented its solution as being 'low risk'.

In these circumstances, the judge decided that Wang could not rely on the exclusion clauses. Whilst it might be acceptable to exclude liability for some lapse that was not readily foreseeable, it was quite another thing to exclude liability when, because it had blatantly misrepresented what it was selling, breaches of contract were very likely. In the event, the judge made a total award of damages of £9,047,113.

Overcomplicated contracts

Sometimes, those responsible for drafting computer contracts write contracts so complex they are bound to contain ambiguities or contradictions. The case of *Kwik-Fit Insurance Services Ltd v Bull Information Systems Ltd* [2000] EWHC 88 (TCC) provides an example. Kwik-Fit wanted a new computer system and Bull carried out the work but the contract ran into problems and the system was not delivered on time. Kwik-Fit gave notice requiring the breaches of contract to be remedied within 30 days, but just before the end of that period, Bull withdrew from the project. Soon after, Kwik-Fit wrote to Bull accepting the latter's repudiation of the contract or, alternatively, terminating the agreement. Kwik-Fit claimed damages in excess of £17 m, including indirect and consequential losses of over £6 m. Bull counterclaimed for over £8 m in damages alleging, *inter alia*, that Kwik-Fit failed to state precisely what functionality it required, failed to agree a proper baseline against which the development of the software could be controlled, made changes to the functionality required without going through proper procedures and failed to provide information.

The case involved a number of preliminary issues and the judge had to make some difficult decisions regarding the contract which was very complex, difficult to construe and which conflicted in places. One clause on the contract stated that Bull would not be able to rely on any default of Kwik-Fit in completing agreed tasks or providing information or materials if Bull did not give prompt notice of such failures or breaches by Kwik-Fit. This required consideration of section 7 of the Unfair Contract Terms Act 1977 which applies to miscellaneous contracts under which goods pass and which states:

(1) Where the possession or ownership of goods passes under or in pursuance of a contract not governed by the law of sale of goods or hire-purchase, subsections (2) to (4) below apply as regards the effect (if any) to be given to contract terms excluding or restricting liability for breach of obligation arising by implication of law from the nature of the contract.

(2) As against a person dealing as consumer, liability in respect of the goods' correspondence with description or sample, or their quality or fitness for any particular purpose, cannot be excluded or restricted by reference to any such term.

(3) As against a person dealing otherwise than as consumer, that liability can be excluded or restricted by reference to such a term, but only in so far as the term satisfies the requirement of reasonableness.

The key issue was whether the phrase 'that liability' as used in sub-section (3) referred to the specific liability under sub-section (2) or the general liability for breach of an implied term under sub-section (1). If the latter applied, the test of reasonableness would be available under much wider circumstances. The judge held that the liability in section 7(3) referred back to subsection 2 and was, therefore, not wider and only applied to correspondence with description or sample or quality or fitness for purpose of goods. That being so, the test of reasonableness did not apply to the clause in question which excluded liability subsequent to a failure to report defaults in performance. The judge said that, consistently with the scheme found elsewhere in the Act, the draftsman of the Act had intended to provide limited protection rather than total prohibition of exclusions in non-consumer cases.

One reason for that sentiment is that businesses and other organisations are expected to be circumspect, to inform themselves and take appropriate advice before committing themselves to important contracts which can seriously affect their operations if they go wrong or fail to deliver the advantages sought. In some cases, the client will have a duty to fully cooperate with the software developer to ensure its satisfactory installation, modification and operation. Failure to cooperate might be a factor in deciding whether an exclusion clause is reasonable.

Reasonable exclusion clauses

At one time, it seemed that the courts were only too willing to hold that exclusion clauses were unreasonable even in contracts between business organisations that might be expected to have taken legal advice in relation to the contract. However, there appears to have been a move to a more balanced view of what is reasonable between businesses. In *Anglo Group plc* v *Winther Browne & Co Ltd* (2000) 72 Con LR 118, the defendant wanted to replace its outdated computer system and obtained a quote for new hardware and a standard software package from BML Office Computers. The defendant and BML entered a written agreement for the supply of the hardware and software for £64,133 and to pay for this, the defendant entered a lease agreement with the claimant. The contract was one for the transfer of goods (notwithstanding software also was supplied) other than under a sale of goods contract or a hire-purchase agreement and, as such, was subject to section 7 of the Unfair Contract Terms Act 1977 which, *inter alia*, makes any terms excluding or limiting liability in a non-consumer contract in respect of correspondence with description or sample, quality or fitness for any particular purpose subject to the test of reasonableness.

After delivery of the equipment and software a number of problems arose, some of which were probably the fault of BML, but others were probably the result of the defendant's reluctance to adapt its working practices. Eventually, the defendant instructed its bank to stop payment of an instalment due to the claimant which then claimed the whole amount of the loan outstanding. The judge held that BML were not in breach of contract and the defendant did not have the right to terminate. The claimant's exclusion clause extended to losses arising from a failure of the equipment to function properly.

The judge held that the exclusion clauses were reasonable. The defendant could have obtained finance elsewhere and was fully aware of the terms and conditions. Although the system was a standard one, its successful implementation would require considerable input from the defendant, and the claimant had not been involved in the negotiations between the defendant and the software supplier. The contractual arrangements were such that the defendant had recourse against the software supplier and financing the acquisition from a finance company rather than buying it direct from the supplier was not a trap (that is, a way of avoiding liability for defects by means of a leasing arrangement).

Another case showing that exclusion clauses may be reasonable where the parties are fully aware of the risks and the allocation of those risks is *Watford Electronics Ltd* v *Sanderson CFL Ltd* [2002] FSR 19 in which the claimant, Watford, sold computers, mainly by mail order. The defendant, Sanderson, supplied software products. Its key product was 'Mailbrain', a marketing package used for mail order operations and which could be used in conjunction with another of its products, 'Genasys' for marketing sales, purchase and nominal ledgers and other accounting operations. A number of contracts were made for the supply of equipment, licences and maintenance agreements in respect of Mailbrain and Genasys and for bespoke modifications to the software and training. Later, after complaints from Watford about performance, further contracts were made for the supply of a Bull minicomputer and a further software licence. All the contracts were subject to similar terms and conditions. After Watford had paid a total of £104,596, it decided to replace the entire system with a new computer system from a third party and claimed damages from Sanderson on the basis of misrepresentation and breaches of implied terms. Sanderson relied on the exclusion clauses in the contracts and an entire agreement clause (discussed earlier in this chapter). The exclusion clauses were of two types. One excluded liability for indirect or consequential losses, whether arising in negligence or otherwise. The second limited liability to the price paid for the equipment or software connected with any claim.

Although Sanderson's written standard contracts had been modified by an addendum which had been negotiated between the parties, it was held that the Unfair Contract Terms Act 1977 applied to the contracts (the Court of Appeal did not even consider this as an issue). At first instance, the judge held that the exclusion clauses were unreasonable in their entirety.

The Court of Appeal disagreed, holding that both forms of exclusion were reasonable. As regards the exclusion of liability for indirect or consequential losses, the court made a number of points. As the parties were of equal bargaining power, the court should be very cautious before concluding that the agreement reached between the parties was not fair and reasonable. In such a case, the parties themselves were often the best to judge this. As a starting point in determining whether exclusion clauses were reasonable in such cases, regard should be had to:

- the significant risk that a customised product might not perform to the customer's satisfaction (there had been some bespoke modification of the software delivered);
- in such a case, there was a significant risk that the customer will not make the profits or savings that it hoped to make and could incur consequential losses;
- those risks which were or ought reasonably to be known or in the contemplation of the parties when the contract was made;
- the software supplier was in a better position to assess the risk that the product would fail to perform to the customer's satisfaction;
- the risk was likely to be capable of being covered by insurance, though at a cost;
- both parties would have known or ought reasonably to have known when the contract was made the identity of the party bearing the risk and that the identity of the party bearing the risk would affect the price the supplier would want or the customer would be prepared to pay.

On the basis of these factors, it was entirely reasonable that the contract should provide that one party only bears the risk of indirect or consequential losses. On the facts of the case, the parties did negotiate as to price and Watford obtained significant concessions. There was also some negotiation as to risk but Watford only obtained a concession that Sanderson would use its best endeavours to allocate appropriate resources to ensure that the product conformed to the specification. A further factor was that the product had been, to some extent, modified to meet the special needs of Watford. Therefore, it was impossible to say that Sanderson took unfair advantage of Watford or that Watford did not properly understand and consider the effect of the clause excluding liability for indirect and consequential losses.

On the issue of the clause limiting liability to the price paid, the Court of Appeal considered that this was also reasonable. An important factor was that section 53(3) of the Sale of Goods Act 1979 sets the damages for breach of a warranty of quality, *prima facie*, at the difference between the value of the goods as delivered and their value had they complied with the warranty.

14

Liability for defective hardware or software

Failure to acquire appropriate software can sound the death-knell for a business. The fears generated by the Millennium Bug gave an example of the dangers – in that case, of failing to be Year 2000 compliant. The following case shows that failing to take prompt and timely action to replace outmoded equipment and software can result in serious consequences and can put a client out of business, though fortunately it did not do so in the event. In *Sam Business Systems Ltd* v *Hedley and Co* [2002] EWHC 2733 (TCC), the defendant, Hedley, used old DOS-based software for its stockbroking business and was concerned that it was not Year 2000 compliant. In any case, it was about time for Hedley to upgrade its software. The claimant, Sam, specialised in ready-made software, comprising a number of packages, for stockbrokers and banks dealing in stocks and shares and in administering their back-office systems. Sam supplied a new computer software system to Hedley. Problems arose with the software and, eventually, Hedley outsourced its back-office systems to a third party and withheld further payment to Sam which sued for the amount it considered to be outstanding, amounting to over £300,000. (In pre-contractual nego-tiations, Sam had told Hedley, the whole system would cost no more than £180,000 and Hedley had already paid over this figure.)

Hedley counterclaimed on the basis of misrepresentation and breaches of the licence and maintenance agreements, asking for damages of nearly £800,000 which included money already paid, increased cost of working, additional costs and loss of profit. The licence agreement con-tained an entire agreement clause (discussed earlier in the chapter) and a clause limiting liability to the fees paid by the client should the software prove to be unacceptable in accordance with the agreement. There was also a deemed acceptance clause and a sweeping exclusion of warranties and implied terms.

The agreements were on Sam's written standard terms, therefore, section 3 of the Unfair Contract Terms Act 1977 applied. Therefore, the exclusion and limitation clauses must meet the requirement of reasonableness and HH Judge Bowsher QC first looked at insurance as a factor. Neither party had insurance to cover the risk. It may have been that Sam thought it did not need insurance cover because of its exclusions clauses and there was no reason for Hedley to have insured against risk of Sam failing to perform properly. Because there was no evidence about the ability of either party to obtain insurance or the cost of such insurance, as a factor it was neutral.

The judge quoted from *The Salvage Association* v *CAP Financial Services* [1995] FSR 654 where HH Judge Thayne Forbes QC said:

> Generally speaking where a party well able to look after itself enters into a commercial contract, and with full knowledge of all relevant circumstances willingly accepts the terms of the contract which provide for apportionment of the financial risks in the transaction, I think that it is very likely that those terms will be held to be fair and reasonable. [This was approved by Peter Gibson LJ in the *Watford Electronics* case in the Court of Appeal.]

Although this is a sensible approach, in the context of the present case, it was questionable whether Hedley was well able to look after itself. At the time, there was a lot of panic about Year 2000 compliance. Also, no one at Hedley knew about computers, unlike Sam as its business was computers.

The judge then turned to the guidelines in Schedule 2 to the Act, accepting that they were of general application to the question of reasonableness although only expressed in the Act as being relevant to sections 6 and 7. It seemed that, in the relevant field, it was standard practice to exclude liability, one reason being that the few software suppliers capable of supplying equival-ent software knew their client's services intimately. In terms of bargaining power, both Sam and Hedley were small businesses. Hedley had no option but to acquire Year 2000 compliant software very quickly but that was a problem of its own making and it should have woken up to the dan-gers sooner, as others did. Furthermore, Hedley did not attempt to negotiate the terms of the agreements. Had they done so, Sam might have responded on a take-it-or-leave-it basis. However, they might not have done so and might have been prepared to negotiate the terms of the agreements.

There were enormous potential liabilities. If Hedley had not acquired Year 2000 compliant software, it would have been in serious trouble with the regulator and would have gone out of business. Had Sam not excluded liability for warranties, it too could have gone out of business. As it was, Sam had provided that Hedley could get its money back had the system not been acceptable, if Hedley went through the contractual machinery to reject the software. That being so, the judge thought the exclusion clauses in the licence agreement reasonable and, as Hedley had not gone through the proper procedures to reject, it was not entitled to its money back. However, with respect to the maintenance agreement, the judge thought it would be unreasonable for Sam to be paid for putting right a defect for which it had excluded liability under the licence agreement. The judge said:

> Of course, any product, whether it be a motor car, or a washing machine, or computer software, may, after working well to start with, then develop faults and faults arising in that way, provided they did not exist in a hidden form on delivery, would be the proper subject of a maintenance agreement. But no consumer would or should accept liability to pay for rectification of defects existing in goods on delivery even if there was no contractual liability on the part of the supplier to pay damages arising out of those defects.

This is quite surprising and suggests that a software company, having supplied software, cannot charge for corrected defects that were not known about at the point of delivery. This sits uncomfortably with the Court of Appeal's decision in *Saphena Computing Ltd* v *Allied Collection Agencies Ltd* [1995] FSR 616 where the court accepted that it is not necessarily a breach of contract to deliver software which contained a defect. If HH Judge Bowsher QC is correct, this throws into doubt the role and validity of maintenance contracts, unless they go further than correcting latent defects and provide other services, such as enhancements.

Having found the exclusion clauses reasonable (except in respect of the maintenance agreement to the extent that, in effect, it permitted charging the client for inherent defects for which liability was excluded by the licence agreement), Hedley's counterclaim failed. The judge also dismissed Sam's claims for additional work because of the existence of the maintenance agreement and did not allow the claim for a final instalment for the licence of £29,000 payable on completion because completion never took place. The final award to Sam was £7,467 plus interest.

The courts' approach to exclusion clauses in relation to computer contracts has changed from its initial position, where it seemed as if it would be extremely rare for such a clause to be seen to be fair, especially as the burden of proof lies on the party seeking to rely on the clause and the feeling that it was the software developer's responsibility to take out an appropriate level of insurance. Now, there seems to be a much more *laissez-faire* attitude, especially as between businesses of broadly equal bargaining power. It also now seems to be recognised that insurance is no longer the key factor and it may be acceptable for a software developer not to insure against the risks of certain losses, such as indirect or consequential losses. The contract is once again seen as a reflection of the allocation of risk between the parties and it should be the one on whom the risk is placed who should insure against it or take the chance that the contract will run smoothly and be performed satisfactorily. The interaction between the amount of insurance cover taken out by a software developer and the price paid by the client is an important factor as is the practice amongst software developers in the same or similar line of business as regards their exclusion clauses.

Fundamental breach

Before the Unfair Contract Terms Act 1977 came into force, the courts developed, somewhat erratically, the doctrine of 'fundamental breach' as a way of curbing the worst excesses of exclusion clauses. *Pinnock Bros* v *Lewis & Peat Ltd* [1923] 1 KB 690 concerned a contract for the purchase of copra cake. When delivered, it was discovered to be poisonous because it had been contaminated with castor oil. It was held that it was not copra cake at all but a substance quite different to that contracted for and, because of this, the sellers could not rely on an exclusion clause purporting to exempt them from liability. Later, it was said that where there had been a fundamental breach of contract – that is, if one party fails to carry out his part of the bargain at all or attempts to render a performance totally different from that contemplated – then the party in breach could not rely on an exclusion clause (see *Karsales (Harrow) Ltd* v *Wallis* [1956] 2 All ER 61). However, the courts later took a more *laissez-faire* attitude to exclusion clauses and fundamental breach on the basis that the parties should be free to agree that there should be no liability under the contract even for a fundamental breach, if that was their desire: see *Photo Production Ltd* v *Securicor Transport Ltd* [1980] AC 827. This case concerned the law before the implementation of the Unfair Contract Terms Act 1977, but the impact of this Act on exclusion clauses was in the minds of their lordships.

Nevertheless, the doctrine of fundamental breach may still have some utility when it comes to controlling exclusion clauses in contracts which do not come within the scope of the Unfair Contract Terms Act – for example, where the breach concerns the grant of the licence itself such as where the licensor turns out not to be entitled to grant the licence or in the context of liability arising outside the course of business. Of course, where a purported licence for the use of software fails because the licensor does not have the right to grant the licence (for example, if he does not own the copyright and does not have the copyright owner's permission to grant licences) then it could be said that the contract will be void on the basis of a total failure of consideration.

Exclusion of liability for misrepresentation

Section 3 of the Misrepresentation Act 1967 provides that a clause in a contract which purports to exclude or restrict liability for misrepresentation will only be effective if it satisfies the requirement of reasonableness. The burden of proof is on the person seeking to rely on the clause. If a computer salesperson claims that the computer she is selling will run a particular software package and this claim turns out to be untrue, it will be for the company selling the computer to show that any exemption clause it hopes to rely on passes the test of reasonableness. The test is laid out in section 11 of the Unfair Contract Terms Act 1977 which requires that the term be:

> ... fair and reasonable ... having regard to the circumstances which were, or ought reasonably to have been, known to or in the contemplation of the parties when the contract was made ...

This is a nebulous requirement which also applies to some of the other provisions in the Act. It gives the courts scope to be flexible and to take the facts of a particular case into account. Some indication of the court's approach was given by the decision in *George Mitchell (Chesterhall) Ltd* v *Finney Lock Seeds Ltd* [1983] 2 All ER 737. The claimant bought cabbage seed from the defendant for £192. The seed was defective and the resulting crop was little better than useless. The loss to the claimant, a farmer, was in the order of £61,000. When sued, the defendant claimed to be liable only for the cost of the seed because of a clause in their contract to that effect. Lord Denning (it was his last case) said that the term was not fair and reasonable in the circumstances, although he did say that this was a borderline case. The following were important factors:

- Farmers had no way of knowing or discovering that the seed was defective.

- The defendant seed merchant could have insured against the risk of defective seed but it was unlikely that an individual farmer could so insure.

- The defendants had not relied on the clause but had reached a negotiated settlement in similar prior cases.

- It was likely that the seed merchant or their Dutch suppliers had been negligent.

In a subsequent appeal to the House of Lords, the Court of Appeal's decision was affirmed. It should be noted that, by section 7 of the Unfair Contract Terms Act 1977, liability for defective products under Part I of the Consumer Protection Act 1987 cannot be excluded or limited by any contract term.

Unfair terms in consumer contracts

Individual consumers making contracts for non-business purposes are given greater protection in relation to standard form contracts by the Unfair Terms in Consumer Contracts Regulations 1999 (replacing the 1994 Regulations). These Regulations control terms which are unfair and, being contrary to the requirement of good faith, cause a significant imbalance in the parties' rights and obligations under the contract to the detriment of the consumer. To some extent, the Regulations overlap the Unfair Contracts Terms Act 1977 but in some respects, in terms of consumer contracts, they supplement the Act. The nature of the goods or services must be taken into account in assessing the unfair nature of the term in question.

Schedule 2 contains a list of terms that are likely to be regarded as unfair. Some of these would be of dubious enforceability in any case under English law. The provisions do not apply to terms which have been individually negotiated (unless an overall assessment of the contract indicates it is a pre-formulated contract) or, if written in plain intelligible language, which define the main subject matter of the contract or are concerned with the adequacy of the price or remuneration. For example, in *Bankers Insurance Company Ltd* v *South* [2003] EWHC 380 (QB), a clause in an insurance contract contained an exclusion clause in relation to claims arising from the use of 'motorised waterborne craft'. Whilst riding a jet-ski, the insured collided with another jet-ski, the rider of which suffered injuries. The court rejected an argument that the exclusion clause was not written in plain intelligible language and, therefore, no assessment of fairness was to be made although the judge did not consider the clause unfair in any case. Where negotiation is in issue, the seller or supplier has the burden of proof in showing that a term was individually negotiated. Where there is any doubt as to the meaning of a term, the meaning most favourable to the consumer will be taken. If a contract contains an unfair term, it will not be binding on the consumer but the contract will continue in existence if it is capable of so doing without the unfair term.

SUMMARY

- The law of negligence requires:
  - a duty of care (neighbour test);
  - breach of that duty of care; and
  - consequential loss.

- The law of negligence can apply to defective hardware and software and RSI.

- Where loss is purely economic resulting from defective advice or information, the law of negligent misstatement may give a remedy if:

14

Liability for defective hardware or software

- the loss is foreseeable;
- the relationship of the parties is sufficiently proximate; and
- it is reasonable to impose a duty of care.

■ For negligent misstatement, an assumption of responsibility is usual.

■ Product liability applies to defective products though not software.

■ Exemption clauses are primarily controlled by the Unfair Contract Terms Act 1977.

■ Liability for death or personal injury arising in the course of a business cannot be excluded or limited.

■ Other liability can only be excluded or limited subject to the test of reasonableness:
- where the liability arises from negligence;
- in a contract on standard written terms;
- where a party to a contract is in breach of the contract; or
- in some other circumstances, for example, where there has been a misrepresentation.

■ Whether a term is reasonable depends on a number of factors, including:
- the relative bargaining strength of the parties;
- whether it was possible for the party in question to have taken out insurance.

SELF-TEST QUESTIONS

Note: there is only one correct answer to each multiple choice question.

1   **e-harbour plc is an English company operating an e-commerce website. It is listed on the London Stock Exchange. Percy is an accountant who prepared e-harbour's annual accounts for submission to Companies House as required under company legislation. The accounts were placed on e-harbour's website. Anna saw the accounts on the website and was so impressed by them that she bought 50,000 shares in e-harbour. Unfortunately, due to some serious (though not deliberate) errors in Percy's calculations, the annual accounts gave a grossly misleading picture of the financial position of e-harbour. A few weeks later, e-harbour went into voluntary liquidation as it was no longer able to pay its debts. The shares are likely to be little more than worthless. Anna has decided to sue Percy on the grounds that he was negligent. Which one of the following statements is CORRECT in relation to Percy's liability to Anna?**

(a) Percy will not be liable for negligent misstatement.

(b) Percy will be liable for negligent misstatement.

(c) Percy will not be liable under the law of tort as the loss is an economic loss only.

(d) Percy will be liable under the rule in *Donoghue* v *Stevenson* but any damages awarded to Anna will be reduced because of her contributory negligence.

2   **Which one of the following statements in relation to Part I of the Consumer Protection Act 1987 is NOT CORRECT?**

(a) Computer software, *per se*, falls within the meaning of 'product'.

(b) There is a 'state of the art' defence which the European Court of Justice has held is compatible with the product liability Directive.

(c) The definition of 'product' includes electricity.

(d) As regards damage to or destruction of property (other than the product itself), there is a lower threshold of £275 for a claim to be successful.

3   Section 2 of the Unfair Contract Terms Act 1977 controls clauses excluding or limited liability for negligence. Which one of the following statements is NOT CORRECT?

(a) Section 2 only applies to business liability.

(b) Section 2 only applies to contractual terms.

(c) Section 2 applies to terms in contract and to notices excluding or limiting liability for negligence.

(d) Under section 2, liability for death or personal injury arising from negligence cannot be excluded or limited.

4   Which one of the following statements is CORRECT?

(a) Repetitive strain injury allegedly caused by long periods entering data using a computer keyboard is not actionable at law.

(b) Contractual terms excluding liability for negligent performance of a contract for writing software are never valid under any circumstances.

(c) Contractual terms excluding liability for negligent performance of a contract for writing software are valid but only where the contract is between business organisations.

(d) A party to a contract, who has been negligent in performing his obligations under the contract, may have concurrent liability both under the contract and the law of tort.

5   The use of exclusion clauses in contracts for writing software can be seen as a sensible way of allocating risk between the parties. Legal control over such clauses unnecessarily distorts the relationship between parties to such contracts. Discuss.

For further resources and updates please go to the Companion Website accompanying this book at **www.mylawchamber.co.uk/bainbridgeIT**

14

Liability for defective hardware or software

15 Contracts for writing software

INTRODUCTION

If an organisation wishes to obtain some new computer software, there may be several options open to it. Appropriate software may be available as a ready-made ('off-the-shelf') package or the organisation may employ its own computer staff who can develop the software. In other circumstances, it may be advantageous to have the software written or adapted by a software development company – a firm specialising in particular types of computer software. In some cases, the organisation may wish to obtain a standard software package and have it modified for its own particular requirements. This is likely to be less expensive than having a wholly 'bespoke' package written. The following example is typical of instances when software will be developed under a contractual agreement.

A company has a network of computers. It requires software to automate its accounting and invoicing systems. After reviewing software available ready-made, the company comes to the conclusion that none is ideally suited to its methods of operation and it is neither appropriate nor satisfactory for it to change its methods to suit the available software. Although the company employs a number of analysts and programmers, it decides against asking them to write the software, as they are not sufficiently experienced in the development software that is likely to be used as a platform to deliver the applications software. The company selects an experienced software company to carry out a comprehensive feasibility study which includes development and strategy studies. The software company produces a detailed plan and specification for the work and is awarded the contract to carry out the work following the submission of bids by it and a number of other experienced software companies.

Sometimes, software development contracts may be entered into hastily before a formal fully binding contact is drawn up and agreed by both parties. This may be a result of the urgency of starting work. If a dispute later arises, the courts may be faced with the difficult task of deciding whether there is a binding contract in place or, if not, whether the software development company is entitled to any payment for work done. The question of whether there is a contract is examined first, followed by a consideration of the terms and provisions commonly found in a contract for writing computer software and other implication of contract for writing software. The company commissioning the development of the software will be referred to as the 'client' and the company writing the software will be called the 'software development company'.

IS THERE A CONTRACT?

It is not unusual for work to begin on a contract for the development of software before the precise details of the contract have been properly agreed and formalised. The modern pressures of business life may make it tempting to commence work before the 'legal stuff' has been sorted out but it is a temptation that should be avoided if at all possible. After committing resources or carrying out work, the other party may claim that there is not a contract. Even if it is accepted that there is a binding contract, there may be some uncertainty as to the precise terms of the contract and there is a limit to how much the courts may be willing to imply. Uncertainty itself can be a factor in making a purported contract void and unenforceable.

The case of *Prudential Holborn Ltd* v *Fraser Williams (Southern) Ltd* (unreported) 14 May 1993 provides an example of the dangers and difficulties which might ensue if work begins before a contract is properly in place. Fraser Williams submitted a proposal to Prudential to develop software. It was dated 3 March 1989 and was expressed as being 'subject to contract'. Two telephone calls from Prudential on 7 and 9 March 1989 confirmed that the claimant had got the job and a letter was sent on 10 March 1989 confirming this, though the letter showed that there were still some things to be resolved, in particular how responsibilities would be shared between Fraser Williams and an independent consultant engaged by Prudential in respect of the software. On 13 March 1989, at the invitation of Prudential, Fraser Williams commenced work and on 5 April it sent its standard form contract to Prudential. Subsequently, Fraser Williams raised three invoices which were paid by Prudential, but on 5 May 1989 Prudential informed Fraser Willams that it was terminating the relationship and requested that Fraser Williams vacate the defendant's premises immediately. Fraser Williams complained in writing about the alleged breach of contract by Prudential but the correspondence remained unanswered until, on 27 November 1989, Prudential's solicitor wrote to Fraser Williams asserting that there was no contract between them. It was argued that the letter of 10 March 1989 was merely a letter of intent and, even if it were an acceptance, there was still no contract as Fraser Williams' 'offer' was expressed to be subject to contract.

At first instance the judge held that there was a binding contract but the Court of Appeal overturned this on a majority decision. The phrase 'subject to contract' when used by experienced business persons meant more than simply requiring acceptance to be in writing. The standard form contract had not been agreed by Prudential and there remained important matters to be decided such as the boundary between the work to be done by Fraser Williams and the independent consultant. Lord Justice Kennedy considered that the letter of 10 March 1989 was no more than an acceptance that, in the light of Fraser Williams proposals, the parties should go a stage further.

It had also been argued that a contract could be implied on the basis of the parties' conduct as in *Brogden* v *Metropolitan Railway Co* (1877) 2 App Cas 666 where the conduct of the parties in supplying and paying for coal over a period of time in accordance with a draft contract could only be explained on the basis that they approved of the contract. The present case differed. Although the work commenced at the invitation of Prudential this could be explained by concluding that the parties expected a formal contract would be agreed. Of course, Fraser Williams was entitled to payment for the goods and services supplied at the invitation of Prudential until 5 May 1989 (on the basis of a *quantum meruit*, see below).

The dangers inherent in embarking on work without a formal contract in place are fairly obvious. In the above case, if the court had held otherwise, the software developer would have found it difficult to obtain any recompense for the work it carried out. One possibility is under a *quantum meruit*. Another difficulty is determining the precise nature and scope of the contractual terms. If, eventually, in the above case, an administrative decision was taken assigning responsibility between the software developer and the independent consultant, it could have been detrimental to the software developer. It could, for example, reduce the total job value for the software developer or increase the amount of work to be completed in an already tight timescale. However, where there is some uncertainty as to the precise terms of the contract, the terms implied by the Supply of Goods and Services Act 1982 or common law may save the contract. Otherwise, if there is a previous course of dealing between the parties, that may provide some clue as to the precise scope of the parties' rights and obligations under the contract. The courts will not, however, write the contract for the parties and, as HH Judge Richard Seymour QC said in *Co-operative Group (CWS) Ltd* v *International Computers Ltd* [2003] EWHC 1 (TCC):

> If satisfied that parties did indeed intend to enter into a binding agreement and sought to do so, it is no part of the function of the court to seek to frustrate that intention. At the same time it is no part of the function of the court to impose upon the parties a contract which they did not, objectively, make for themselves.

In *DMA Financial Solutions Ltd* v *BaaN UK Ltd* (unreported) 28 March 2000, BaaN originally provided training to customers of its accounting software. BaaN decided to outsource its training and wanted DMA to take over this role, as BaaN's authorised training provider. Negotiations began between BaaN and DMA for this purpose. Negotiations went well and both sides seemed confident that there would be final agreement. Eventually, BaaN started closing down its training facilities and DMA began recruiting staff to provide training. BaaN passed on training enquiries to DMA but there was still no formal written contract, as BaaN's lawyers were preoccupied with other matters. Eventually, BaaN's lawyers starting raising objections about what had been agreed by the negotiators and eventually sent DMA its standard form contract which differed in many respects from what had been agreed. After a number of exchanges, DMA's position was that a binding contract existed whilst BaaN, which had changed its mind about outsourcing its training, argued that there was not a binding contract.

As to whether the negotiations resulted in a binding contract before a formal written agreement had been executed, Mr Justice Park thought that three possibilities existed:

1 The negotiations were not intended to result in a contract even if fully concluded until such time as a written contract had been drawn up and executed by both sides. This was equivalent to the usual practice when negotiating to buy a house where the phrase 'subject to contract' was commonly used.

2 The negotiations were such that a contract could exist before the execution of a formal written contract – the negotiations resulted in complete agreement.

3 As 2 above but the negotiations did not get far enough for there to be sufficient agreement for a contract to exist.

The judge said that there was no evidence to satisfy him that, in the computer software industry, it was the generally understood usage that agreements are never binding until they have been drawn up by the lawyers and signed. In this particular case, the phrase 'subject to contract' had not been used during negotiations. All the main terms were agreed including the price of $250,000, payable in six quarterly instalments. If some point was not raised in negotiations but was not an essential point, that would not prevent a contract coming into existence. An example was the applicable law for the contract. The fact that this had not been raised did not matter as, although it was certain that BaaN's lawyers would insert such a term in the formal written contract, it was highly unlikely that DMA would have complained about it on the basis it had not been previously agreed. Therefore, the judge held that a valid binding agreement existed between the parties.

The fact that there have been extensive negotiations does not, of course, automatically mean that a contract exists. It depends on whether all the terms considered to be important by the parties have been agreed. In *Co-operative Group (CWS) Ltd v International Computers Ltd* [2003] EWHC 1 (TCC), the claimant alleged that there was a contract between it and the defendant (ICL). It was true that there had been extensive negotiations between the parties and that both expected that agreement would be reached. However, no agreement as to liquidated damages for late delivery had been agreed, amongst other things. CWS had insisted that liquidated damages were included in the contract but ICL was unwilling to accede. The inclusion of liquidated damages in a contract to write software is usually a very important term and failure to agree this was clearly fatal to the argument that there was a valid binding contract between the parties. Some of the negotiators for CWS had been unhappy about ICL's performance on other projects and the judge said that a malevolent influence hung over the negotiations. As the judge held that there was no binding contract, CWS's claim for repudiatory breach of contract was doomed. CWS had claimed no less than £11 m. However, CWS appealed to the Court of Appeal in *Co-operative Group (CWS) Ltd v International Computers Ltd* [2003] EWCA Civ 1955. A re-trial was ordered as a result of the apparent bias of the judge at first instance. He had made findings of bad faith and false evidence against CWS and its principal witness when no bad faith had been pleaded or suggested. This may have distorted his findings of fact and prejudiced his objectivity. There is no record of any re-trial taking place.

As negotiations for a contract to write a substantial software system can proceed over a long period of time, it is sensible for the parties to make it absolutely clear what their position is. The use of a suspensive phrase such as 'subject to contract' on documents created during negotiations should be considered. As parties to drawn out negotiations can run up considerable expenses, this seems the safest approach so that both know exactly where they stand. In some cases, the negotiations could run alongside a feasibility study or the development of prototype systems, which could be subject to a separate contract. Where the phrase 'subject to contract' is used, the parties should ensure that a formal contract is drawn up and signed by both of them before work proceeds. Simply sending a written acceptance is not necessarily enough as shown in *Prudential Holborn v Fraser Williams*, above.

Quantum meruit

Where it turns out that there is no valid contract – for example, through a lack of certainty as to the terms of the contract – the software developer may be entitled to payment on the basis of the work he has done in pursuance of what he believed was a valid contract. The law will require that the defendant pays the claimant for the 'fruit of his labour'. This is what is termed a *quantum meruit* (roughly translated – as much as he deserves). Of course, the defendant must have agreed to or at the very least acquiesced in the claimant carrying out the work. For example, if a software development company is appointed to write some software for a client but the purported contract between them is so vague and uncertain that it is ruled void, then if the software company has done satisfactory work for the client, it ought to be entitled to payment on the basis of a *quantum meruit*. Nevertheless, it is clearly preferable to have a valid and detailed contract containing all the necessary terms in writing and signed by both parties before the work commences. Writing computer software is sufficiently difficult and unpredictable without adding to the problems by having unsatisfactory legal provision for the work.

An example of a software development company being entitled to a *quantum meruit* is the case of *Prudential Holborn Ltd v Fraser Williams (Southern) Ltd*, above.

DEFINITIONS

The very first clause in the contract is likely to deal with a description of the parties to the contract and appropriate definitions relating to the software and the equipment on which the software will be installed. Apart from being a word-saving provision in that the client's full business name can be abbreviated throughout to CLIENT or CUSTOMER, the definitions clause can usefully describe terms such as software and hardware and thus assist with the interpretation and construction of the agreement. Consequently, any expressions defined here should be defined precisely and comprehensively as they will be the key to understanding the remainder of the contract and the scope of the parties' obligations and liabilities under it. The case of *Cyprotex Discovery Limited* v *University of Sheffield* [2004] RPC 887 gives an example of the difficulties that may ensue from failing to use precise definitions. That case concerned the development of software for the mathematical modelling the effects of drugs on the human body. The relevant agreement attempted to distinguish between software written made by the members or agents of the University, whether or not jointly with others including the sponsors of the project and software developed solely by employees of the sponsors. The ensuing dispute as to ownership of intellectual property rights in the software was almost inevitable.

LICENCE AGREEMENT

What will the software development company deliver to the client in return for the payment? On the face of it a set of programs, data files, databases and associated documentation is what will be provided, but will the software development company really hand over ownership of the programs and other software? This will be unlikely and an important term usually states that the software is being licensed; the contract is, first and foremost, a licence agreement. A licence is a permission to do something; in terms of computer software, a licence is a permission to use the software and, without this permission, using the software would be an infringement of the copyright subsisting in it. This is because loading programs and data into a computer's memory is making a copy and copyright can be infringed even if the copy is transient by section 17(6) of the Copyright, Designs and Patents Act 1988.

The software development company will undoubtedly want to retain the ownership of the intellectual property rights in the programs and the documentation, for its business is licensing software and it will want to grant licences in respect of the software, or variants of it or modules contained within it, to others. If it is especially important for the company acquiring the software that it is not made available to others, it should insist on an exclusive licence, which is likely to be much more expensive. Alternatively, ownership of the copyright subsisting in the software could be transferred to the client under an assignment of copyright. In practical terms, there is little difference between an exclusive licence and an assignment of copyright. Where an exclusive licence or assignment of copyright is granted, however, the software development company would be wise to reserve the right to reuse modules in other software or even in the writing of new software to perform similar functions. The drafting of an appropriate and workable clause to allow for this will require a great deal of care and the implications must be thoroughly considered. On the one hand, the client may not want its competitor obtaining similar software from the software development company whilst, on the other hand, the latter will not want to unduly constrain its future software development activities. In *SCI Games Ltd* v *Argonaut Games plc* [2005] EWHC 1403 (Pat), a contract for writing a computer game contained an assignment of intellectual property rights except in relation to some sub-routines for which the client was granted a royalty free licence.

Important points to check in the licence agreement will include the duration of the licence and its scope (sometimes the licence will be silent on the matter of duration). Because a licence is a permission to do something which would otherwise be unlawful, it does not give any proprietary interest in the software. The implications of this are twofold.

1 The licence should be for a fixed duration or there should be some provisions for termination of the licence. If the licence appears, on the face of it, to be perpetual, this contradicts the nature of a licence and it might even be implied that the agreement is not a licence but an assignment of the copyright and other rights in the software, especially if the rights granted appear to be exclusive. It is more likely, however, in the absence of any express reference to duration, that the licence will endure as long as the copyright subsists in the software. The wording of the agreement as a whole should give a clue as to which interpretation is correct.

2 The licence agreement should state whether the software can subsequently be transferred to a third party. In the absence of any provision covering this aspect, it would appear that the benefit of the licence is transferable, depending on the circumstances (see the following section).

The scope of the licence is very important. Is it permissible to run the software on a network of computers or just one particular computer? Can it be installed on a server? If the acquiring company is part of a group of companies, can the programs be used throughout the group or just within the one company? Is the licence a single-user licence (if so, can it be used on any computer by the user)? Is it a site licence, a company licence or group licence? Can the software be transferred to another company? Is transfer subject to approval? All these questions should be considered and discussed with the software development company in the light of the contract and the intended uses to which the software is to be put. The possibility of expanding computing facilities and usage in the future must not be overlooked. In this respect, the client should carry out regular audits to make sure that its licensed software is not being used in excess of the licence agreements and to identify whether existing licences are adequate.

ASSIGNMENT AND NOVATION

It is common for contracts to contain a term dealing with the assignment of the benefit of the contract. That is, the transfer of the right to use the software. For example, in an agreement for the writing of new software by a software development company for a client, there may be a term stating that neither party shall assign the agreement. Sometimes, assignment is permitted providing the other party consents. Note that in this context, we are talking about the assignment of the benefit of a contract rather than the assignment of the ownership of copyright. Terms dealing with assignment are particularly relevant where the performance of the contract will be carried out over a period of time, such as a building contract or a contract for writing new software.

Both parties to a contract enjoy benefits and suffer burdens emanating from the contract. For example, a client for whom software is to be written under a contract may have the benefits and burdens listed in Table 15.1.

Unless prohibited, a party to a contract may assign (that is, transfer) the benefit of the contract but not the burden. The original parties remain liable for their obligations under the contract. In *Linden Gardens Trust Ltd* v *Lenesta Sludge Disposals Ltd* [1993] 3 WLR 408, a building contract contained a term which stated: 'The employer [the client] shall not without the written consent of the contractor assign this contract.' There was a purported assignment of the contract but the House of Lords held that this was void. There was some criticism of the drafting of the above term. Lord Browne-Wilkinson said:

> On any basis, clause 17 is unhappily drafted in that it refers to an assignment of 'the contract'. It is trite law that it is, in any event, impossible to assign 'the contract' as a whole, i.e. including both burden and benefit. The burden of a contract can never be assigned without the consent of the other party to the contract in which event such consent will give rise to a novation.

(A novation is where a new contract is substituted for an old one.) Lord Browne-Wilkinson also said, later:

> ... lawyers frequently use those words ['assign this contract'] inaccurately to describe an assignment of the benefit of a contract since every lawyer knows that the burden of a contract can never be assigned.

The House of Lords confirmed that a party to a contract might have good commercial reasons for refusing to grant consent to an assignment. For example, if a software company is providing continuing maintenance of software it might not want to maintain it if the client transfers the software to a third party. As the burden cannot be assigned, the original party remains liable to fulfil his obligations under the contract. For example, if a client transfers the benefit of a software licence to a third party, that original client remains liable for any outstanding payments. Where there is an assignment, the original party, the assignor, might want to consider an indemnity clause to protect himself against any legal action brought by the other party in respect of his obligations under the contract.

It is common for a licence agreement (and the same applies to other forms of agreement such as a maintenance agreement) to state that the benefit of the agreement shall not be assigned without the prior written permission of the other party.

In *Circuit Systems Ltd & Basten* v *Zuken-Redac (UK) Ltd* (1995) 11 Const LJ 201, the defendant rented computer equipment to the first claimant (Circuit Systems) and also entered into a maintenance agreement with it. Both agreements prohibited assignment though, in the case of the maintenance agreement, assignment with written consent was possible. The same day that the first claimant issued a writ against the defendant alleging, *inter alia*, breach of contract and economic duress, the first claimant went into liquidation. The second claimant, Mr Basten (who owned at least 98 per cent of the shares in Circuit Systems) took an assignment of Circuit Systems' rights of action for £1 and was granted legal aid to pursue the claim. It was held that the assignments were not valid and the action was an abuse of process. However, the House of Lords allowed Mr Basten to pursue his claim and, eventually, the case was restarted in the Technology and Construction Court. However, the judge made orders with time limits requiring the claimant to put the statement of case in order (it was very poorly pleaded and unsatisfactory). When the claimant failed to comply the judge struck out the claim, effectively bringing the litigation, which had started in 1988, to an end. The Court of Appeal refused permission to appeal in *Circuit Systems Ltd and Another* v *Zuken-Redac (UK) Ltd* [2001] Build LR 235.

Table 15.1 Benefits and burdens in software contract (client)

Benefits	Burdens
1 The services of the software development company in writing the software	1 The obligation to pay the software development company
2 A copyright licence allowing use of the software	2 Providing facilities and information to the software development company
3 The grant of ownership of the property in tangible items such as discs, manuals, etc.	3 Accepting the software after attending testing
4 The services of the software development company in maintaining the software, correcting errors and delivering enhancements	4 The obligation to pay for ongoing maintenance and enhancements

In *Orion Finance Ltd v Crown Financial Management Ltd* [1994] 2 BCLC 607, the assignment was subject to consent but the party whose consent was required, Crown, knew that the assignment had been made without consent but failed to draw the other party's attention to this before a lease of computer equipment was registered as a charge under the Companies Act 1985. Crown was estopped from relying on the lack of consent. Crown's lack of activity was, in effect, a representation that it accepted the assignment as valid.

Where the contract requires the consent of one party to the assignment of the benefit of the contract to the other party and that consent is not obtained, the courts may imply a contract between the assignor and assignee to overcome the lack of nexus between the client and the assignee of the developer. In *SCI Games Ltd v Argonaut Games plc* [2005] EWHC 1403 (Pat), the defendant had agreed to write a computer game for the SCI Games Ltd. The contract required consent to the assignment of the benefit of the contract by Argonaut Games plc, the defendant. It also contained a terms to the effect that, in the event of the defendant ceasing to trade, it would deliver the source code to the claimant. It transpired that a subsidiary company of the defendant, Argonaut Software Ltd, had done all the work of writing the software but it went into administration before the work was completed. The administrators initially refused to hand over the source code to SCI Games Ltd. After some compromises, the source code was handed over but the claimant suspected that not all of it had been delivered. The judge held that there was a real prospect that the claimant would show, at a full trial, that there was an implied contract between Argonaut Games plc and Argonaut Software Ltd that the latter would comply with the terms of the contract between SCI Games Ltd and Argonaut Games plc. He also went on to accept that it was possible that the failure of Argonaut Software to hand over all the materials constituted the tort of unlawful interference with contract in relation to the contract between SCI Games Ltd and Argonaut Games plc.

Under what circumstances might an assignment of the benefit of a contract be appropriate? Consider a client, Acme Manufacturing Ltd, which is a member of a group of companies and which makes an agreement with Grotsoft Ltd, a software development company, for the development, installation and maintenance of stock control software. After a while, because of changes in Acme's manufacturing methods, the software is no longer useful but another company in the group, Zenith Fabrications Ltd, would like to use the software. After seeking Grotsoft's permission as required in the contract, Acme assigns the benefit of the agreement to Zenith and Grotsoft will continue to maintain the software at Zenith's offices for the remainder

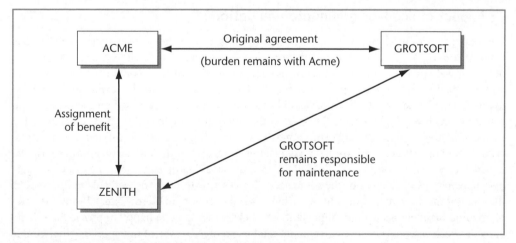

Figure 15.1 Assignment of benefit of agreement

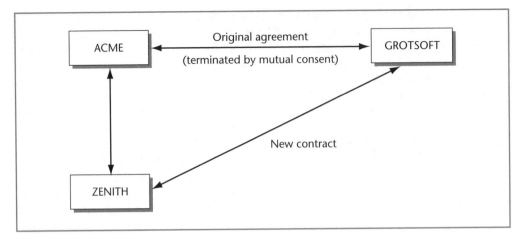

Figure 15.2 Novation

of the maintenance period. Assuming that Grotsoft will be entitled to a final payment at the end of the maintenance period, this will be payable by Acme which remains responsible for this. In the separate agreement between Acme and Zenith in which the benefit of the agreement with Grotsoft is transferred to Zenith, there is provision for Zenith to refund Acme after it has made the final payment. Figure 15.1 shows the effect of the assignment to Zenith.

If, on the other hand, Acme had wished to hand over the entire contract to Zenith, this would result in a novation (providing Grotsoft agreed to this). The original agreement would be set aside and a new contract between Zenith and Grotsoft would come into existence. If Grotsoft refused to agree to this, however, and Acme indicated that it no longer wanted to proceed with the contract, Grotsoft could sue for wrongful repudiation of contract or anticipatory breach. A novation is shown in Fig. 15.2.

In *Cyprotex Discovery Limited* v *University of Sheffield* [2004] RPC 887, the claimant company was formed after a significant amount of work had already been carried out on a software development project by a person who was employed by the company when it came into existence was dealt with by way of a novation of the contract for the project.

Impact of licensor going into liquidation

When a software developer, who has granted licences to use the software but, as usual, has retained copyright, goes into liquidation, provision should be made to allow the continuing use of the software by the licensees. It may be possible to sell the software company as a going concern, in which case, a new company may simply step into the shoes of the former and continue to provide maintenance. If this is not possible, the liquidator will seek to sell off the assets of the company which will include its major asset of the copyright and any other intellectual property rights subsisting in the software. The money received will go towards satisfying the creditors' claims. (It may be that a creditor has a fixed charge in respect of the intellectual property rights, in which case, the sale of those rights will go towards satisfying that charge.) The original developer may have placed copies of the source code into escrow to be made available to licensees in the event of the developer going out of business (see the section on escrow later). If not, the issue of ongoing maintenance will be important. The new owner may be happy to provide maintenance, in which case, new licence agreements can be executed by way of novation or otherwise. If not, the liquidator may grant new licences which provide for copies of the source code to be given to the licensees. But this is by no means a foregone conclusion and it is sensible to consider the impact of a software developer going into liquidation when negotiating software licences in the first place.

In *Profile Software Ltd* v *Becogent Ltd* [2005] CSOH 28, in the Court of Session, Outer House, Scotland, the software developer, Coranta, went into liquidation. Companies, including the defender, had licences to use the Coranta's software and the liquidator granted the licences allowing them to continue to use the software. The licences were more extensive than before and provided for delivery of the source code so that the licensees could arrange maintenance of the software. The new licences did not transfer any intellectual property rights to the licensees and provided that the copyright could be assigned without the consent of the licensees.

The liquidator then assigned the copyright in the software to the pursuer, Profile Software. The assignment was expressed as being with or without the rights under the licence. This and the fact that the assignee had no commitment to maintain the software for the licensees and the new licences were granted on a royalty-free, non-exclusive, non-transferable basis indicated that there was no contractual nexus between the copyright owner and the licensees. When the pursuer wanted to sue the defender for infringing copyright and breach of the licence agreement, the defender argued that the pursuer did not have title to sue. Rather, it was the liquidator who retained title to sue. The judge held that the assignment was sufficiently wide to include the title to sue although he did describe the relevant part of the assignment as 'not perhaps the finest flowering of the draftsman's art'. Had the judge found the other way, it would have meant that the liquidator had title to sue but no interest in doing so and the new copyright owner, who had an interest in suing, had not title to do so.

SUB-CONTRACTORS

It is common for a software development company to engage sub-contractors to perform some of the company's obligations under the contract. The sub-contractor may be a company, a firm or may be a self-employed consultant. Normally, contracts contain provisions dealing with sub-contractors. There may be a term stating that none of the software development company's obligations may be sub-contracted without the express written permission of the client. In other cases, the contract may identify those parts of the work which will be sub-contracted out. Where part of the work is sub-contracted out, the normal rule is that the main contractor remains responsible for the work carried out by sub-contractors and liable for any defective work or other breach of contract attributable to the sub-contractor. Sometimes, a client may require that a particular sub-contractor be used for part of the work. This may be appropriate where the client has identified a company which has a particular specialisation relevant to the contract. For example, in a contact to write software for marketing purposes, the client may want, as a sub-contractor, a company with particular expertise in profiling for targeted advertising campaigns to work on developing algorithms used in the software. Such sub-contractors are known as nominated sub-contractors and particular care must be taken to deal with issues that could arise, such as where a nominated sub-contractor fails to perform his obligations satisfactorily or on time. Quite often, a client may already have obtained quotations from nominated sub-contractors and these will be built into the overall contract price, usually with an uplift for the main contractor.

15

Contracts for writing software

THE CONTRACT PRICE

As the agreement will be almost certainly in the nature of a licence, the sum payable should be termed a licence fee. This fee is often described as the price, however, and may include other things such as installation and testing, an initial period of maintenance and error correction, training and tangible items such as discs and documentation. The word 'price' will be used, therefore, bearing in mind that this will include a once and for all licence fee which will usually make up the largest portion of the overall price. In some cases, the agreement will not be a licence but, instead, will provide for the assignment of the copyright subsisting in the completed software to the client. Nevertheless, similar considerations will apply as regards the price and many other aspects of the contract.

Wherever possible, the question of price should be tied down precisely. If it comprises a licence fee, maintenance fee, price for any hardware supplied, etc., there should be a breakdown of the constituent costs (in many cases, maintenance will be provided under a separate contract on an annual basis). Apart from anything else, this could be important for tax reasons. In addition, the contract should provide some machinery for calculating the cost of any extra work or services provided other than those which the software development company has agreed to provide as its consideration for the contract. There may be unanticipated problems with the computer equipment, for example, or the client may change his mind halfway through the work and require modifications to be made to the specification. Therefore, the contract should include a list of hourly rates for programmers, analysts and others.

If a fixed price is agreed, it should be clear from the contract exactly what this includes: whether maintenance and training are included, whether the price includes the documentation and, if so, how many copies. What about the cost of the media such as optical and magnetic discs? If the payment is to be made in instalments, when are they due? If they become due following the performance of certain stages of the work (often referred to as 'milestones'), can these stages be clearly identified? For example, the contract might provide for payment of two-thirds of the total price when certain specified programs are operational, usable in practice and acceptable to the client, apart from the fact that further work may need to be carried out. If the client is late in paying, does the contract include provision for charging interest? What if the client shows no intention of paying? It is in the interests of both parties that there should be no ambiguity as far as time for payment is concerned.

An example of ambiguity was *Peregrine Systems Ltd* v *Steria Ltd* [2005] EWCA Civ 239 where there was some doubt as to what the contract required of the software developer. The defendant terminated the contract alleging late performance by the claimant which brought an action for wrongful termination. The contract was not a fixed price contract but on a time and materials basis. A number of tasks were set out in the contract for which £200,000 was payable. The defendant argued that the entire implementation required completion within a reasonable time. However, the court accepted that the correct construction of the contract was that, once £200,000 worth of work had been done, the defendant could obtain further services to complete implementation from the claimant or from a third party.

It may be that the software development company feels unable to quote a firm price from the start. Perhaps the client's computer equipment is unusual or unfamiliar in some respect. A software development company may refuse point blank to be tied down to a fixed price, particularly if the work involves modifying existing software to run on unfamiliar equipment. If the software development company refuses to quote a fixed price the reason should be ascertained. Is it because the software development company is tackling something beyond its capabilities or are there more acceptable reasons? Is it genuinely difficult even for an experienced company to forecast the amount of work and the timescale because of the complexity of the work? One way round this problem is to ask the software development company or, preferably, a competent and independent consultant, to carry out a feasibility study. This will enable the viability of the project to be determined before the parties are committed, and the actual amount of work involved and the price can be more accurately predicted. If carried through to the writing of a detailed specification, it can form the basis for inviting tenders or quotations from a number of software development companies to carry out the work. The cost of the feasibility study, however, can be a considerable addition to the overall cost of implementing the software though it may prove money well spent in the long run.

Failure to have a feasibility study carried out before the development contract can prove disastrous to any subsequent claim that the software is unsuitable. In *Comyn Ching Ltd* v *Radius plc* (unreported) 17 March 1997, the claimant group of companies wanted to integrate its computer systems and appointed the defendant to carry out the work. There was a misunderstanding as to exactly what was required. During negotiations before the contract was entered into, the defendant twice offered to carry out a feasibility study to assess the claimant's precise requirements. The fee for carrying out the study was only £6,930. The claimant refused on both occasions and when it was not satisfied with the system, sued the defendant for damages in excess of £3 m. The claimant had little knowledge of computers but decided not to employ a consultant but argued that the defendant owed it a duty of care which extended to investigating the claimant's requirements beforehand without payment. This submission was rejected by the judge who considered the claimant's requirements to be very fluid. He described them as a 'moveable feast'.

If the work involved in writing the software is substantial, the possibility of obtaining quotations by competitive tender should be considered but, if this course is chosen, specialist advice should be sought as to the specification and other aspects of the tender documentation. The company inviting tenders is taking upon itself the responsibility for the feasibility of the project and the quality of the documentation provided to the tenderers. If the specification is inadequate, any software development company awarded the contract will be able to point to this in its defence should the programs fail to be satisfactory, or use the deficiencies as a basis for claiming additional payment. Therefore, this approach can only be recommended for companies who have access to the necessary professional expertise. A major problem with comparing quotations and tenders is that it is unlikely that all those submitting will have put their bids together on the same basis. The chances are that some or all will have modified the specification in some way or another in spite of a request not to diverge from the specification. Some of those quoting may be unable to obtain a particular piece of equipment or software tool and will offer an alternative or they may offer an alternative simply because it is cheaper and they hope this will make their quotation appear more attractive. Although it could be argued that initiative should be rewarded, in fairness to the others quoting, all should be asked to reconsider their quotes in the light of the alternative should it appear to be worthwhile considering. The legal position regarding tenders is discussed in Chapter 20 in relation to hardware and the same principles apply to software.

SPECIFICATION

Whether the company acquiring the software, an independent consultant or the software development company writes the specification, there are several important points to be made in respect of it. The specification is the main provision in the contract which concerns the performance and capabilities of the software. It should be a detailed description of what the software is, what it will do and how quickly it will do it. The specification may well be contained in a separate document or be an appendix to the contract, but it must be noted that it is of crucial importance, being the yardstick by which the software will be measured in the case of a dispute about the character and performance of the software.

Ideally, the specification will be clear, comprehensive and exactly mirror the client's requirements. Alas, this is not always the case and one of the most common problems is that the client moves the goalposts part way through the work, typically asking for changes to be made to the specification. The client may decide that he requires different or additional reports to be generated, links to other software not envisaged at the outset or the inclusion of additional routines, none of which are mentioned in the specification. Alternatively, some parts of the specification may have to be compromised because of operational and other difficulties not envisaged at the time the specification was written and agreed on by the parties to the contract. For example, the client may want to take advantage of a newly available upgrade to his operating system software which will require changes to the application software being written under the agreement. While changes made to the specification during the performance of the contract may result in the completed software being of a higher standard, more powerful or of increased functionality, the contractual implications of such changes must be catered for in the original agreement.

While the law will imply terms, based on reasonableness, dealing with additional payment and extensions to the time for completion, for example, under the Supply of Goods and Services Act 1982, it is better to build mechanisms into the contract for this purpose. A schedule of rates is a useful addition to a contract to be used for the determination of the additional price to be paid for extra work not included in the original contract because of changes to the specification made part-way through the work. Another term dealing with extensions to the time for completion would also be useful, as discussed later. If the changes are required because of unforeseen problems, then it would be useful to provide a term allowing additional payment if, and only if, a reasonably competent software company would not have anticipated the problem. The use of an independent professional contract supervisor, as advocated at the end of this chapter, will be very useful in dealing with the contractual implications of changes to the specification.

It is useful to include a mechanism for variation orders in the agreement. A basic method is for any variation to the specification or work required to be set out in writing and signed by both parties before the changes are implemented or incorporated in the work programme. The additional cost (or reduction to the overall price) should be agreed by the parties, as should the impact on the overall time for completion. It is far better to have agreement before any additional work is done or any other changes made to the planned programme of work implemented and for the consequences of any changes to be thoroughly considered and agreed. Trying to agree additional costs and extensions to the time for completion after the event can often result in acrimonious disputes although it has to be admitted that time pressures sometimes force retrospective action on the parties. At least a schedule of rates provides a safety curtain and a wise software development company will ensure that all the additional or modified work is carefully noted in terms of resources and duration.

If the changes made to the specification are considerable, the contracting parties ought to contemplate whether it would be better to terminate the existing contract and substitute it with another after negotiating a new contract and any settlement under the old contract. This is an example of novation. If the changes made are substantial this is probably the best route. Of course, the costs and liabilities under the original contract which had already been incurred must be dealt with by mutual agreement (otherwise there could be an action for breach of contract). An experienced software development company should not get into a situation such that the original contract has to be substituted by a new one. Where the work to be carried out is particularly difficult or covers new ground, it may be better to make an agreement to build a prototype system first backed by a broad specification, with a view to a subsequent contract to build the finished system backed by a much more detailed and explicit specification, written with the benefit of the experience gained in building the prototype.

The specification will have to address all the technical issues associated with the performance of the software. In particular, the three most important items which the specification should discuss are:

- a detailed description of the tasks the software will perform;

- the equipment on which the software will run and other software with which it will interface; and

- how quickly the software will carry out the operations involved, bearing in mind any networking and concurrent use requirements.

The client may have little knowledge of the mysteries of computer science and will hope to receive some guidance on these matters from the experts writing the programs. Here, as elsewhere, however, the client should contemplate seeking independent advice unless he has his own computer professionals to consult. There are real dangers at this stage of over-optimism by both parties, plain misunderstanding or just a difference in emphasis of priorities. A great number of retrospectively ill-founded assumptions can be made about performance; computer programmers and analysts cannot be expected to know all the intricacies of the client's business, the nature of which may call for very fast information processing.

If the client does rely on the software development company to supply a system that will do a particular job, he can expect that it will bring a certain degree of expertise to bear upon the work and will perform its part of the contract in a workmanlike manner, using reasonable care and skill. Companies in the business of writing computer systems are implicitly holding themselves out to possess a minimum level of skill and experience when it comes to writing their particular type of system, and the courts have long been prepared to imply an appropriate duty in contracts for supplying services, such as in the case of hairdressers, garages and the like. A contract to write or modify computer software is analogous to such contracts; indeed it is a service contract. In *Stewart* v *Reavell's Garage* [1952] 2 QB 545, a customer relied on a garage to reline the brakes on his 1929 Bentley. The garage obtained a quotation from a sub-contractor; the quotation was recommended to the customer who agreed to it. The work by the sub-contractor was carried out in a way unsuitable for Bentley cars and because of this the customer crashed the car, causing £362 worth of damage. It was held that, because the customer had relied on the garage to repair the brakes in a suitable and efficient manner and because the garage owed a duty to provide good workmanship and materials of good quality so that the braking system would be reasonably fit for its purpose, the garage was liable for the faulty work, even though the work itself was carried out by a sub-contractor. The garage had a duty to select and recommend a suitable sub-contractor. The implications of this are very appropriate in the field of software development, given that it is very common for sub-contractors and freelance programmers to be used by the main contractor.

An equivalent duty of care and skill is implied into service contracts, where the supplier of the service is acting in the course of business, by section 13 of the Supply of Goods and Services Act 1982 or equivalent common law terms in Scotland. We have already seen in Chapter 14 that the courts are willing to imply these terms into contracts for writing software and, indeed, into contracts for feasibility studies for software. Liability for loss resulting from failure to exercise reasonable care and skill can be excluded or limited subject to the controls in the Unfair Contract Terms Act 1977. However, the inclusion of exclusion or limitation clauses would be unlikely to add to the client's confidence in the software development company and, in any case, the courts have shown some reluctance to enforce such terms. The fact that the burden of proof in respect of the reasonableness of an exclusion clause lies with the party seeking to rely on it is another point to bear in mind. Generally, it will be better (and safer) business practice for the software development company to provide a reasonable level of insurance cover against its own negligence and to use that as a basis of any limitation of liability clause. Nonetheless, the expense of arranging insurance is an overhead which will be reflected in the price of the software. A high level of insurance cover could significantly reduce a software company's competitiveness. It should be noted that, by section 2(1) of the Unfair Contract Terms Act 1977, business liability for death or personal injury cannot be excluded or restricted at all.

In terms of computers, if you have a particular computer and approach a company to write software for that computer, the company has a duty to bring a reasonable amount of skill to the task and to supply software that will be fit for its purpose. If your computer is heavily committed to other processing tasks and has little spare processing capacity, you can expect the software development company to use its skill in taking this into account. If it sub-lets part of the work, it is under a duty also to select a sub-contractor capable of carrying out the work in a like manner. The software development company cannot avoid liability for defective software merely because it has asked you to agree to the particular sub-contractor recommended by it. An example of a sub-contract is where a software development company, contracted to write an accounts package, uses another specialist firm or, perhaps, freelance programmers to carry out part of the work. The software development company owes a duty to the client to choose the specialist firm and the freelance programmers carefully.

Other matters to which the specification should address itself include details of any data files and information to be entered to be used by the programs and how they will be entered. Will entry be by keyboard, scanner, from optical or magnetic disc or through a modem? Will the entry be of an interactive nature and can the programs operate quickly enough? What results and reports are expected from the system and is there any likelihood of further reports being required once the programs have become established in use? What files, temporary and permanent, will be created? Is access to be controlled by passwords and, if so, is a hierarchical system of passwords required? What other security aspects are addressed by the specification to ensure that the software is not vulnerable to hacking, spyware and viruses, etc.? With what other software must the new software interact or be interoperable?

The feature of computer systems which lies at the root of many disputes is the speed of operation. Computers work at fantastic speeds, measured in microseconds, but they have a great disadvantage in that the vast majority are designed to process information in serial fashion, a piece at a time. The human brain, because of its massive parallel processing capabilities, can easily outperform a computer and, when given real work to do, computers are anything but fast. Therefore, it is essential that the specification contains information about the speed of the programs in use – for example, response times at the keyboard (two seconds can seem an eternity), the time taken to sort items into ascending or descending order, the time taken to compile and print reports. These timings should indicate the effect of multiple concurrent use of the same files and the fact that the equipment might be carrying out other demanding work at the same time. The specification should also describe the portability of the software – that is, can it be run on other equipment with little effort or will a major 'refit' be needed? The client should ask questions about the effect of a future change of or a modification to his computer equipment or operating system software. Another problem might concern the compatibility of the software with other systems run by the client; can data be easily transferred from the new system to the client's existing computer systems and vice versa?

TIME FOR COMPLETION

A contract for writing computer programs and preparing associated documentation is fundamentally different in character from a contract for the sale of goods but is, however, analogous to a building contract. The performance of the contract is not a single event but rather extends over a period of time. This fact alone brings some doubt to any assumption that time is of the essence of the contract. We have already seen that, although time for payment is not usually a condition in a commercial sale of goods contract, time for delivery is. If we enter into a contract with a builder for the construction of a house, however, we would not expect that we could lawfully repudiate the contract if the house was completed a day late and the position is similar with contracts for writing computer software. A delay of a few days might give rise to a claim for damages but would be unlikely to give the client the right to cancel the contract altogether, although if completion is very late the client may be entitled to terminate the contract.

Writing computer software carries with it a degree of unpredictability and the client should be aware of this, especially if he is planning his business operations around a particular completion date. Unexpected problems frequently arise which can add considerably to the overall time for performance, just as construction projects are often delayed because of unanticipated problems with the sub-soil which has to support a new building, requiring extensive changes to be made to the design of the foundations. In *The Salvage Association* v *CAP Financial Services Ltd* [1995] FSR 654, however, the judge held that time is of the essence in a contract for writing software, though, in that case, the delay was inordinately long. It is submitted that, if the delivery of the software is late by only a few days, this would not amount to a breach of condition (or a material breach in Scotland) giving the client the option of cancelling the contract. An exception would be where the delivery date was particularly important such as where the software was to be written for some special event such as the launch of a new product at an international exhibition or the launch of a new e-commerce website.

In the absence of specific provision for the time for completion in the contract, section 14 of the Supply of Goods and Services Act 1982 implies a terms that the service will be carried out in a reasonable time. In *Peregrine Systems Ltd* v *Steria Ltd* [2005] EWCA Civ 239, the Court of Appeal rejected an argument that an obligation to perform within a reasonable time meant that time was of the essence. Even if there had been a breach of an obligation to perform in a reasonable time that would not necessarily mean that the breach was repudiatory. In the Court of Appeal, Maurice Kay LJ cited with approval Judge Richard Seymour QC in *Astea (UK) Ltd* v *Time Group Ltd* [2003] EWHC 725 (TCC) where he suggested whether a reasonable time had been exceeded required a broad consideration with the benefit of hindsight, taking account of factors such as any estimate given by the performing party, whether the other party needed to participate by collaborating or being in a position to receive performance, whether third parties had to collaborate and what the cause or causes of the delay were.

Liquidated damages

In case the software is completed late, it would be sensible to have some contractual provisions to cover this situation rather than arguing about the level of compensation. The usual method of dealing with late completion is to include a term which gives the client a right to liquidated damages. These damages may be quantified as a certain sum of money for every week completion is late – for example, £1,500 per week. The sum must be a genuine pre-estimate of the financial losses which the client will suffer as a result of the delay and it must not be in the nature of a penalty. The courts will not enforce a penalty. An example of acceptable liquidated damages would be a pre-estimate of the loss of profits arising from the late completion. Sometimes, it may be in the client's interests to offer a bonus for early completion.

It is not always easy to determine when completion has taken place. The software might have been installed on the client's computer and be working in a fashion, but it requires some further work to be carried out. Alternatively, the programs may be finished but the documentation is only available in draft form. It is clear that problems might arise in determining when completion takes place and it is advisable to define completion in the contract. Does it include testing and documentation? What, if anything, does the client have to do to signify his acceptance of the software? What is the effect of completion on payment? Do all outstanding moneys become due? The concept of substantial completion could be used whereby upon substantial completion a large percentage of the agreed price becomes due with the moiety retained by the client until the remaining work has been completed. Of course, substantial completion must be defined if this approach is used.

If completion is late, this will not necessarily be the fault of the software development company. The completion of the work could be late as a result of the inaction of the client in providing information necessary to the continuation of the work or the client might fail to provide on time the facilities required by the software development company. The contract should clearly state what information and facilities the client must provide and when he must provide them. The contract should also contain machinery dealing with extensions to the time for completion as a result of the client's default in his duties under the contract and compensation for the additional expenses incurred. Ideally, the contract should include rates or formulae to help determine such additional costs.

MAINTENANCE OF AND ENHANCEMENTS TO THE SOFTWARE

No matter how much skill and care have been put into the writing of the software or how much testing has been carried out, the odds are overwhelmingly in favour of it containing errors or, colloquially, 'bugs'. Some of these bugs might not appear for a considerable period of time and they may be discoverable only under a very rare combination of factors. If a bug does appear this will normally be a breach of warranty and the client can expect that the software development company will correct the error. Naturally, the latter will wish to limit responsibility to correct such errors to a specified period of time. It is therefore important that the contract takes account of the maintenance of the software. A compromise might have to be struck: perhaps the software development company will be happy to rectify errors in the programs and manuals free of charge for a period of time and thereafter they will be prepared to offer this service for a fee. The Court of Appeal in *Saphena Computing Ltd* v *Allied Collection Agencies Ltd* [1995] FSR 616 has recognised that even when software is delivered there will still be some work to be done. The software will almost certainly contain errors and the software development company will normally be expected to test the software to locate errors and make the necessary modifications. This duty will endure for a period of time though it is difficult to predict how long.

A software development company will usually offer an ancillary contract for maintenance for which the client will have to pay. It would be reckless to eschew a maintenance agreement and the cost of it should be allowed for in the overall budget for the work. However, care needs to be taken to ensure that a maintenance agreement does not simply result in the client paying the software development company for correcting errors that are breaches of quality warranties under the development contract. A maintenance agreement should also provide for enhancements and updates to be made available to the client, which can be very useful because software is continually being developed and having new features added to it. There is likely to be a long-term relationship between the client and the software development company if the software is complex or likely to require ongoing development and enhancement.

Section 50C of the Copyright, Designs and Patents Act 1988 allows the lawful user to copy or adapt a computer program for error correction purposes. Terms in a licence agreement prohibiting this are not automatically void under copyright law though they may be subject to other legal controls such as the principle of non-derogation from grant or competition law. Without a copy of the source code (and preparatory materials), however, maintenance of a computer program is, to all intents and purposes, a practical impossibility.

In many cases, the software development company will be unwilling to allow third parties, or even the client himself, to modify the software. The person carrying out the work might do so badly and the software could acquire a bad reputation as a result and this would reflect on the software development company. If the client considers it very important to be allowed to modify the software himself or use the services of a third party providing software maintenance, this should be discussed before the contract is made and a suitable term incorporated. It is highly desirable that the client receives a copy of the source code to facilitate the making of modifications should this be permitted and the contract must clearly provide for this. The contract should also cover questions of copyright ownership in the modifications, the assignment of modifications and whether the software development company has any other rights in respect of them.

In extreme cases, a court may be prepared to order the software company to hand over a copy of the source code. In *Psychometric Services Ltd* v *Merant International Ltd* [2002] FSR 8, the claimant created and marketed tests to assess job candidates and decided to carry on its business on the internet. It engaged the defendant to design the websites. The original price was said to be capped at £195,000. The work turned out to be much more complex than originally envisaged and the cap was lifted by the claimant. Eventually, the claimant paid over £700,000 but the defendant claimed a further £960,000 was outstanding. Eventually a software audit was carried out by a third party which indicated that there were serious problems with the software and that it had been written in a substandard fashion. The claimant had lost confidence in the defendant's ability to correct the software effectively and quickly enough and was worried that if the websites did not function properly very soon, the claimant would go out of business. The claimant therefore sought a mandatory injunction requiring the defendant to deliver up the source code to it so that a third party could correct the software. Mr Justice Laddie granted the injunction. This was an interim hearing and the judge had to consider the effects of a wrong decision. He accepted that the claimant would probably go into liquidation if it did not get a copy of the source code and this would mean that the defendant would not get the money it alleged was outstanding. This favoured granting the order to hand over a copy of the source code.

ESCROW

Possession of a copy of the source code is vital to the ongoing maintenance of computer software. Even if the client is in possession of copies of the source code, it is important to make sure there are sufficient copies at different locations (perhaps using the services of a 'disaster recovery' company holding back-up copies) and to check that any insurance policy covers any eventuality. In *Tektrol Ltd* v *International Insurance Company of Hanover Ltd* [2005] EWCA Civ 845, two unfortunate and unrelated incidents caused the loss of all copies of the source code. One was a hacking incident which infected a number of copies with a virus and the other was a burglary where computers were stolen together with the only printout of the source code. Even though the company had a back-up copy held by a third party, that too became infected with the virus.

The insurance company refused to pay on an 'all-risks' policy pointing to what the court described as a formidable array of exclusions. The Court of Appeal held, however, that the insurance company could not rely on the exclusion clauses but only by a 2:1 majority.

When a copy of the source code is not delivered to the client, it is worthwhile considering what happens if the software development company goes out of business. Will the client be able to maintain and modify the software or find another company to do this for him? If the software development company has only supplied the object code this will be very difficult, if not impossible. A company receiver or liquidator or a company taking over the software development company's business may obtain the source code and design materials and expect to be paid by the client for a copy. If the software development company is taken over, the new parent company might refuse to support the software yet not be willing to make the source code available. Many licence agreements include an escrow clause which is invaluable in such situations – that is, where the client is not given a copy of the source code and other design materials.

Source code escrow describes a situation where the software development company deposits, with an independent person, a source code copy of the programs together with copies of all the documentation and design and preparatory materials essential to the continuing maintenance of the software – in short, all the materials that will enable the client or a third party to take over the maintenance and further development of the software. The independent person, may be a trusted third party (such as a solicitor or bank) but it is more usual to use the services of an escrow agent. The escrow or trusted third party will hold the source code and other materials and will not divulge them to anyone and keep them generally secure. If a specified event occurs, such as the software development company going out of business or being unable to continue to support the software, then the stakeholder will release all the materials to the client who will then have all the information he needs to arrange for the software to be supported. Escrow works in the form of a guarantee or as insurance should something unfortunate happen to the software development company or if it fails to maintain the software properly or at all. The stakeholder must obviously be someone who can be absolutely trusted in the performance of his duties under the escrow arrangement and the details of the agreement need to be carefully thought out. It should include terms dealing with the following matters:

- definitions of the source code and other materials subject to the escrow;
- confidentiality of the source code imposed on the escrow organisation and the client should the source code be released under the agreement;
- delivery of updates to the escrow organisation;
- payment details and provisions in respect of late payment;
- a detailed description of the eventualities which will bring about the client's right to obtain the source code;
- an indemnity that the software development company owns the rights in the source code or otherwise has the right to deposit the source code and eventually, if the right to obtain the source code comes to fruition, that the client will be able to use the source code without hindrance ('quiet enjoyment');
- a system of formal notices requiring the software development company to carry out maintenance by a given deadline subject to the release of the source code;
- termination of the agreement, for example, because of the failure of the client to pay an outstanding fee after receipt of a written demand; and
- the liability of the escrow organisation for loss of or damage to the source code and other materials.

An organisation which provides guidance about escrow is the National Computing Centre at Oxford House, Oxford Road, Manchester M1 7ED (www.ncc.co.uk). A spin-off company, NCC Group plc offers an escrow service (NCC started offering escrow services in 1983).

The typical mechanism is that an agreement is signed by the client, the software development company and the organisation offering the escrow service. This is a strange tripartite arrangement as shown in Fig. 15.3. A basic rule of English contract law is that there can only be two parties to a contract although, in some circumstances, a third party may be able to enforce a term in a contract. An escrow agreement can be seen as two separate contracts: one between the software development company and the escrow organisation, the other between the escrow organisation and the client. The way the service will be paid for reinforces this analysis. Usually, the software development company will pay a fee upon depositing the materials with the escrow organisation and the client will then pay the periodic fees to the escrow organisation and, if it becomes necessary, a release fee.

The implications of mergers and takeovers will need to be carefully dealt with: the new company might want to carry on business as usual, keeping the source code from the client, for reasons connected with confidentiality. The basic test determining whether to pass on the source code and other materials subject to an escrow agreement should be the permanent inability, for whatever reason, of the software development company to continue to support the software.

Where there is a requirement on the software development company to place a copy of the source code into escrow, there should be some arrangement for notification when this has happened and some way of verifying that it has happened and that the materials are what they are meant to be. In *SCI Games Ltd* v *Argonaut Games plc* [2005] EWHC 1403 (Pat) the developer failed to deliver anything to the escrow agent (although the claimant eventually obtained a court order requiring that the source code be handed over). One problem which should be given consideration is that the source code itself will be under development and, at the beginning of the contract, may not exist at all or only in part. During the performance of the contract it will be expanded and modified and it may be sensible to require that the latest versions of the source code are deposited with the escrow agent at regular intervals. In this way, if the software development company goes out of business part way through the contract, the source code should be in a reasonably contemporary state to enable another developer to complete the work of writing the software.

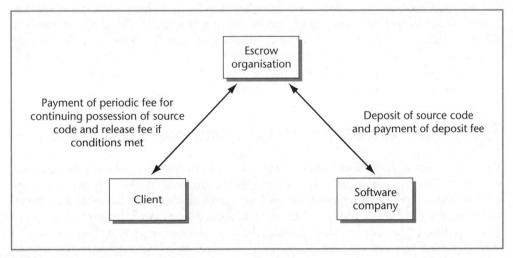

Figure 15.3 Escrow arrangemnt

Once the contract has been completed the final version of the source code should be delivered to the escrow agent to be released if the software developer is no longer willing or able to continue to support the software. Source code for any subsequent enhancements and modifications should also be deposited.

Once the event that triggers release of the source code and other materials occurs, the client should act within a reasonable time to seek release. In *CardBASE Technologies Ltd* v *ValuCard Nigeria plc* [2002] EWHC 991 (Ch), the claimant, a supplier of software, granted a non-exclusive licence to the defendant which provided services to banks in Nigeria in respect of smart card computer software. The escrow agreement (with the National Computing Centre as escrow agent) provided for release of the source code under certain conditions including if the software company entered into liquidation or had a receiver appointed or entered into any composition in satisfaction of its debts, or a scheme of arrangement of its affairs, with its creditors. On 18 December 2001, the claimant entered into a scheme of arrangement with its members and creditors. Two days later, the defendant asked for confirmation that the latest version of the source code had been deposited with the escrow agent and, on 10 January 2002, the defendant asked the escrow agent to verify that the newly deposited material was capable of being used to generate the latest version of the software. The verification was carried out on 17 January 2002 and, on 29 January 2002, the defendant served the escrow agent with a declaration of release as required by the agreement.

The claimant sought an order restraining the escrow agent from releasing the source code on the basis of two arguments. First, by exercising the right to have the verification process carried out, the defendant had elected not to exercise its right to release under the escrow agreement. This argument was rejected as it was not inconsistent with release to seek confirmation that the latest version of the source code was suitable for its purpose. It was reasonable for the defendant to exercise this right as a precursor to exercising its right to seek release of the source code. Furthermore, verification after the trigger event was a result of the claimant's tardiness in depositing the latest version of the source code. The second argument was that there was an implied term to the effect that the defendant had to exercise its right to seek release of the source code within a reasonable time of the trigger event and the defendant had failed to do this. The judge accepted that such a term could be implied but the defendant had sought release within a reasonable time of the trigger event. The defendant was entitled to consider its position once the release event occurred and was entitled to satisfy itself that the latest version of the source code had been deposited and was satisfactory. Other factors were that Christmas and the New Year intervened and the defendant had to get certain documents together, including a statutory or notarised declaration. Finally, the claimant could not prove that the delay, such as it was, was prejudicial to it or anyone else. This seems an entirely reasonable decision but it does indicate that a client should act expediently to apply for release once the client becomes aware that an event triggering release has occurred.

COPYRIGHT AND OTHER INTELLECTUAL PROPERTY RIGHTS

The contract may impose duties on both parties associated with intellectual property rights. The software development company will be anxious to prevent unauthorised copying of the programs and will want its techniques kept secret. The client will want to be able to use the software with impunity, without interfering with the rights of some third party who might seek an injunction preventing continued use of the software. The client will also be worried about the fact that some of the software development company's staff will have gained a detailed insight into his business. The law of copyright and, to some extent, the law of confidence will give some protection to the software development company should the programs or the ideas contained therein be copied or plagiarised, but problems of proof and evidence make it desirable to place a contractual duty on the client to prevent copying or unauthorised disclosure of methods. This duty will run in parallel to any duties imposed by intellectual property law, but the contractual approach will be useful because it will draw the client's attention to the existence of these rights and the importance of making his employees aware of them and the consequences of infringement.

The client's employees may make, surreptitiously, copies of the programs and pass these on to others. If the software development company discovers these copies, it has remedies available under copyright law to prevent the use of these copies by the recipients and their further transmission to others, but it might be difficult to prove that the copies originated from the client. A unique serial or code number could be embedded in the programs identifying the software as being that given to the client and if the client is made aware of this and the consequences he may be more careful. The contract may state that the licence is to be terminated forthwith should copies of the programs find their way into the hands of third parties without the permission of the software development company. This will not preclude the software development company from seeking remedies for infringement of copyright – a fact which is often expressly stated in software licences.

On the subject of confidentiality, the client will want a term included strengthening and extending the common law duty of confidence. He will want to prevent the software development company's employees divulging details of his business methods and techniques and other confidential information such as client accounts, debtors and creditors. It is inevitable, if the contract is for a substantial amount of work, that the employees of the software development company and any freelance staff they use will be exposed to confidential information. Without such a term in the contract, the client may be lacking legal recourse, especially if the confidential nature of materials involved is not otherwise made clear. The software development company, too, may have worries about confidentiality: it may have developed special techniques for writing and testing software which the client's staff might see when the software is installed and tested. A contractual term imposing a two-way duty in respect of confidentiality should be included in the contract. There may also be data protection issues and the software development company may be required to be under obligations in relation to the security of personal data which must be in writing or evidenced in writing (see Part 5 of this book).

WARRANTIES AND INDEMNITIES

It is usual for a licence agreement to contain a section headed 'Warranties and Indemnities'. Warranties normally found include those relating to the fact that the software development company warrants that it has the right to grant the rights to the client provided for by the agreement and that the client will have 'quiet enjoyment' of the software and the client's use of it will be unaffected by any third party rights. Where, instead of licensing the right to use the software, the agreement is one under which the title to the copyright (ownership) is transferred (that is, an assignment of copyright), the Law of Property Act 1925 used to contain a form of words which would automatically include such warranties in the agreement (although that Act was primarily concerned with rights in or over land, it also had some impact on other forms of property transactions). The person granting the rights would use the term 'As beneficial owner'. This term has not disappeared from use but now, as a result of the Law of Property (Miscellaneous Provisions) Act 1994, the phrase to use is 'With full title guarantee'. This automatically implies covenants to the effect that the person making the assignment has the right to do so and that the property right transferred is free from all charges and encumbrances and all other rights exercisable by third parties: sections 2 and 3. Other warranties may be given which relate to the performance of the software and its freedom from major defects. These may find their full expression in the specification.

Another aspect of intellectual property rights concerns the possibility that the software might infringe a third party's copyright or other right such as a patent or trade mark. Whether or not the infringement is deliberate will not usually be relevant. The client could have been using the software quite happily for a number of years when the software development company is successfully sued for infringement of copyright by some third party. That third party may then decide to pursue all the clients of the software development company who are using the infringing software and seek injunctions to prevent them continuing to use the software. Even if the client is not troubled in this way by the third party, the software development company will be prevented from continuing to support the software. It may be that the third party will be happy to allow the client to continue to use the software in return for a licence fee. In any case, the client should satisfy himself that there is a term in the agreement with the software development company covering the infringement of intellectual property rights belonging to others. The term should give the client an indemnity against the event of legal action being taken against him as a result of the software infringing third-party rights. The term should be widely drafted so as to include all forms of intellectual property rights such as copyright, patents, designs and trade marks. The costs and implications of suddenly being unable to use an item of software might be quite enormous and it is likely that the software development company will hope to limit its liability under this head, perhaps to the amount of the licence fee. Any term dealing with an indemnity against third-party claims should allow the software development company a reasonable time to modify the software so that it no longer infringes the third-party right, if that is a possibility without jeopardising the software's functionality.

LIABILITY

Computer software is widely used to assist in the decision-making processes in business. A decision to engage upon a particular line of action may be based upon an interpretation of the results of running a computer program. For example, a construction company might submit a bid for a motorway contract worth many millions of pounds; the bid total will have been calculated by estimators using computer software. If there is an error in the software, the total might be miscalculated by, say, £1 m. This could mean that the company fails to secure the contract because their bid is too high or, worse still, they win the contract by too great a margin and make a substantial loss.

The software development company will be very keen to limit its liability if the software proves to be defective. The software development company will attempt to limit or exclude its liability for defects by the insertion of a suitably drafted exemption clause – for example, limiting its liability to the cost of replacing the software or remedying the defect. This is unsatisfactory from the client's point of view. This way of dealing with liability was very common but now must be reviewed in the light of recent court decisions such as those discussed in the previous chapter. It is now beyond doubt that the controls over exclusion clauses in the Unfair Contract Terms Act 1977 will apply to most terms in software licences, the only major exception, in England, Wales and Northern Ireland, being those terms dealing exclusively with the transfer or creation of intellectual property rights. Thus, section 2 of the Act applies to liability for negligence and section 3 controls attempts to exclude liability arising from the performance of the contract. In some cases, liability cannot be excluded or limited at all – for example, in the case of death or personal injury resulting from negligence. In most other cases, the exclusion or limitation of business liability depends upon the reasonableness of the appropriate term.

A software development company should consider taking out professional liability insurance to a reasonable and affordable level and limit its liability accordingly. Alternatively, the software development company could offer a minimum level of insurance and offer to increase this if the client is prepared to pay the additional premium. How successful this approach will be is difficult to predict but, above all, the software development company must make sure that its liability under the licence and its insurance are matched as far as it is possible to do this and that the client is fully aware of any limitation of liability and agrees to it.

It should be noted that a defect in software does not necessarily and inexorably lead to the conclusion that the software development company has been negligent or has failed to exercise reasonable care and skill. The problem may result from the client's use of the software and the question of how much control the software development company has over the use by the client may be a factor. For example, in the case of a spreadsheet, a mistake may be the result of an incorrect formula entered by the client or the client may be using the spreadsheet software to make calculations requiring extreme mathematical precision. If the software development company has exercised the level of care and skill to be expected from responsible software development companies writing equivalent software, there should be no liability. If a financial loss arises because the software development company and the client have both been negligent, the amount of damages awarded will be reduced on the basis of contributory negligence.

ARBITRATION

It is prudent to include provision in the agreement for arbitration whereby a dispute between the parties will be referred to an arbitrator, an independent expert, who will rule on the dispute. Arbitration is a commonly used method of resolving disputes without having to go to the courts. The parties to the contract appoint an independent third party who will listen to both sides and then make a ruling. Arbitration is less formal than a court hearing, although the basic rules of evidence and procedure are adhered to, and it has the advantage that the arbitrator, unlike a judge, will be an expert in the technical matters involved. In a dispute involving computer software, the arbitrator would be expected to have considerable knowledge of software engineering and be a leading member of the computer profession. Another advantage of arbitration over a normal court hearing is that arbitration should be, in principle, quicker and cheaper, although this is not always so. Arbitration hearings can be fairly formal involving the calling of expert witnesses.

It is common for arbitration clauses to state that the arbitrator's decision shall be final and binding on the parties, and the courts will not interfere with an arbitrator's decision unless he has erred on a point of law. A court will usually accept the arbitrator's evaluation of the facts of the case as being conclusive. If the contract provides for arbitration, neither party will be able to take a short cut to the courts because a judge will insist that the arbitration procedure is adhered to in the first instance. It must be stressed that the decision of an arbitrator, and any award(s) he makes, is binding upon the parties.

A disadvantage of arbitration is that the arbitrator might not have the depth of legal knowledge of a High Court judge and an arbitrator could be more likely to err on a point of law or procedure. Although a judge will not usually have the technical expertise of an arbitrator, judges by their training and experience have the knack of getting to the kernel of a dispute and are able to concentrate on the important issues without being sidetracked. It must be said, however, that, in practice, arbitration works extremely well and the standard of arbitrators, who belong to the

Chartered Institute of Arbitrators, is very high. If an arbitration clause is included in the agreement, the machinery for selecting an arbitrator should also be dealt with, the usual practice being to appoint an arbitrator agreed upon by the parties or, failing such agreement, a person to be nominated by the President, for the time being, of the British Computer Society which holds a register of suitably qualified arbitrators.

ALTERNATIVE DISPUTE RESOLUTION

Taking a dispute to the courts or submitting it to arbitration will plunge the parties into the adversarial contest fundamental to the English legal system. The outcome often will be total success or failure with no half measures even though the decision of the court may be based on the most slender weight in favour of one party on a balance of probabilities. Occasionally, a more attractive route may be that offered by alternative dispute resolution (ADR) where a mediator is appointed to assist and encourage the parties in the negotiation of a settlement to their mutual satisfaction.

The mediator can take an active role and make suggestions for resolving the conflict. However, there is no legally binding obligation on the parties to continue with the process and they may abandon it at any time. The process itself is based on informality and consent. It is said to be a highly successful means of settling disputes with an estimated settlement rate of 75 per cent or better.[1] One technique which may be used is for both sides to make a presentation before senior members of the organisations who will then attempt to negotiate a settlement with the assistance of the mediator. It would be better if the negotiators were not directly involved in the matters leading to the dispute as they are likely to be more objective and more willing to compromise. The following example shows how ADR might present the best course of action.

Imagine that Pickwick Trading has asked Bardell Software to develop and deliver new accounting software. An appropriate contract was made and a detailed specification annexed to it. When the software was delivered it was found to be slightly slower than allowed by the benchmark tests in the specification. Additionally, one particular feature was missing in that the software would not produce annual VAT summary reports as detailed in the specification. The total price is £85,000, 10 per cent of which was payable upon commencement of the work. The time for delivery is three months.

Pickwick has refused to accept the program and has withheld the final payment of £76,500. Bardell presses for more time to add the VAT report and argues that the speed of the software is so close to that specified as to be of no consequence. The possible outcomes of resolving the dispute by litigation and ADR are discussed below.

Litigation

Bardell sues Pickwick for wrongful repudiation of the contract and seeks damages equivalent to the outstanding sum plus interest and other direct costs. Pickwick submits a defence and counterclaim based on the shortcomings of the program. Pickwick claims the return of the £8,500 already paid plus £12,500 in wasted management time, etc. At the court action, the judge holds that Bardell is guilty of a breach of condition and that Pickwick's repudiation was lawful. He awards Pickwick £21,000 plus costs, leaving Bardell to pick up the bill for £31,000 in legal costs also.

This result is unsatisfactory from the point of view of both parties. At the end of it all, Pickwick does not have the program it wanted and will now have to engage another software

---

[1] See the Centre for Effective Dispute Resolution at its website at **www.cedr.co.uk**.

development company. It may be another six months or so before the program is ready. This could seriously handicap Pickwick's business. Bardell is even less happy as three months' work has been wasted and it has a bill for £52,000. Bardell now thinks that it would have been better had it never heard of Pickwick – a view that is reciprocated by the latter.

Alternative dispute resolution

The contract between Pickwick and Bardell contains a term providing for ADR and a mediator is appointed. After only two days of negotiation the following settlement is reached:

- Bardell will be given two more weeks to complete the software so that it will be capable of producing the VAT report. (Bardell has also agreed to alter a particular screen display because Pickwick has had second thoughts about it for a fee of £3,000.)
- Pickwick will be given a 5 per cent discount on the total price which it will put towards some additional memory for its computer which should increase its speed of operation.
- Pickwick and Bardell will share the mediator's fee of £2,500. It is left to the reader to reflect on which is the best solution.

Other ADR techniques are adjudication in which a neutral third party gives a non-binding ruling on the case or certain aspects of the case and expert appraisal in which a technical expert assesses each of the parties' cases for the purpose of assisting negotiations.

ADR is not always appropriate; indeed, it may only be a minority of disputes for which it represents a satisfactory method. There are some drawbacks. It is inappropriate where a point of law is involved, where the issues are very complex or where one party seeks interim relief such as an interim injunction or interim payment or a permanent injunction or court declaration. Although any negotiations will have taken place without prejudice to either party's legal rights, there is danger that subsequent litigation could be influenced by what has been said in abortive negotiations. ADR allows the parties to gauge the strengths and weaknesses of each other's case and could even be used, cynically, as a prelude to litigation. It should be noted, however, that the court will not, under normal circumstances, allow evidence to be given of what has been admitted in negotiations which have been conducted 'without prejudice'. Another factor is that getting involved with ADR could compromise any insurance policy that might be relied upon to pay damages and costs awarded in any court action.

Any ADR clause in a contract must make it clear that anything admitted, said or done in connection with ADR is without prejudice to the legal rights of the parties. The clause should make provision for the appointment of a mediator (who should be skilled in resolving disputes by negotiation), payment of his fees (usually these will be borne equally by the parties) and procedures to be adopted. The Centre for Effective Dispute Resolution (**www.cedr.co.uk**), provides information and advice about ADR and the procedures to be adopted.

The courts are becoming increasingly keen to encourage parties to consider ADR and, indeed Rule 1.4(2)(e) of the Civil Procedure Rules 1998 states that the courts should encourage the parties to use an alternative dispute resolution procedure if the court considers it appropriate. Practice Directions have been issued to deal with the impact this may have on legal proceedings and directions given by the judge. See, for example, *Practice Note* [1995] 1 All ER 385 (Queen's Bench Division and Chancery Division); *Practice Note* [1998] 1 Lloyd's Rep 126 (Commercial Court) and *Practice Note* [1999] 2 All ER 490 (Court of Appeal). Further guidance notes send a clear message that parties in dispute really ought to attempt ADR before going to court. In *IDA Ltd* v *University of Southampton* [2006] RPC 567, Lord Justice Jacob in the Court of Appeal said (at para. 44), in relation to a dispute about entitlement to a patent for a cockroach trap:

15

Contracts for writing software

Parties to these disputes should realise, that if fully fought, they can be protracted, very very expensive and emotionally draining. On top of that, very often development or exploitation of the invention under dispute will be stultified by the dead hand of unresolved litigation. That may be the case here: there has not yet been any exploitation by either side, some 8 years after the original [patent] application. It will often be better to settle early for a smaller share than you think you are entitled to – a small share of large exploitation is better than a large share of none or little.

This sort of dispute is particularly apt for early mediation. Such mediation could well go beyond conventional mediation (where the mediator facilitates a consensual agreement). I have in mind the process called 'medarb' where a 'mediator' trusted by both sides is given the authority to decide the terms of a *binding* settlement agreement.

Pulling out of an agreement to submit to ADR may have serious implications in costs if the dispute comes before the courts. In *Leicester Circuits Ltd* v *Coates Brothers plc* [2003] EWCA Civ 290, a dispute arose about the quality of ink supplied by the defendant to the claimant for the manufacture of printed circuit boards. The claimant sought damages of over £600,000 but the parties agreed to mediation. However, just before it was about to start in earnest, the defendant withdrew from mediation, leaving the claimant no option but to commence legal proceedings. The trial lasted for 18 days and judgment was given in favour of the claimant. However, the defendant successfully appealed to the Court of Appeal. Normally, costs follow the result. In other words, the losing party pays the legal costs of the winning party. However, in this case, the Court of Appeal made no costs order for the period between just before the time the defendant withdrew from mediation until the appeal, leaving the defendant to pay its own costs during that period which included the very expensive trial at first instance. The claimant was ordered to pay the defendant's cost before that time and subsequently in relation to the Court of Appeal proceedings.

OTHER TERMS

A contract for the writing or modification of software will undoubtedly contain other terms dealing with matters such as the training of the client's staff, termination of the licence and misrepresentation. These will be dealt with in Chapter 16 which covers ready-made software. It is also usual to include a term stating which is the applicable law; this is essential where there is any doubt – for example, where a Scottish and English company are entering into a contract. Entire agreement clauses are common which attempt to limit the terms of the contract to those expressly contained within the formal agreement, thereby attempting to exclude any representations that may have been made in preliminary negotiations. Notwithstanding this, there may still be a remedy for misrepresentation should one party have entered into the contract on the basis of a promise by the other party which turns out to be untrue. Finally, the question of staff poaching is often addressed. This is where one party offers employment to an employee of the other party. The employees of each party will probably be in close contact for some time – for example, because the software is being developed at the client's premises – and this gives each party the opportunity to spot a 'star'. The client may have a vested interest in employing a key member of the software development company's staff who has intimate knowledge of the software written under the contract. Over a period of time, a software development company could find that it has a high turnover of staff. The usual means of countering this threat is for a clause stating that neither party will offer employment (or canvass with a view to offering employment) members of the other party's staff for a period of time, normally six months. In practical terms, there is little to be done beyond this, especially as such terms could be deemed to be in restraint of trade.

Consideration could be given to the use of standard form contracts such as those published by the Chartered Institute of Purchasing and Supply (**www.cips.org**). These contract forms have been developed to provide a fair balance between the parties' interests and incorporate a great deal of experience in this field. Standard form agreements exist for a variety of hardware and software contracts and can be adapted, if necessary, for a specific contract.

INDEPENDENT PROFESSIONAL SUPERVISION

In the case of large important contracts for writing software it may be advisable that the performance of the contract is overseen by a chartered engineer who is a member or fellow of the British Computer Society. This person would be responsible for the following aspects:

- ensuring compliance with the specification;
- general supervision;
- determining whether the software is acceptable;
- certifying payments and completion;
- fixing rates for delays or extra work;
- authorising extensions of time for unavoidable delays or additional work; and
- acting as a first-stop informal mediator.

Although it is normal for such a person to be paid by the client, the contract should give certain powers to him as regards determination of the reciprocal rights and duties of the client and software development company. A chartered engineer will remain neutral as between the parties and will help the parties to resolve difficulties amicably and fairly, being particularly good at dealing with the day-to-day minor problems that are bound to occur. This will prevent small problems turning into full-blown disputes with the parties breathing fire at each other. This form of contract supervision has been used to great effect for well over 100 years in the construction industry. Should the engineer be unable to bring the parties to agreement concerning a serious difference, the parties could still have recourse to an independent arbitrator or ADR.

SUMMARY

- Care must be taken to ensure a formal contract is in place with all terms agreed.
- Use of the phrase 'subject to contract' suggests a formal contract must be executed.
- Where there is no contract:
    - a software developer who has been invited to carry out work may be entitled to payment under a *quantum meruit*.
- The benefit of an agreement may be assigned:
    - unless where the agreement states otherwise, or
    - may be subject to the consent of the other party.
- Substantial changes to a contract may result in a new contract (*novation*).
- Sub-contracting is common but may be subject to the consent of the other party.
- The contract price should be:
    - precisely fixed or there should be provision for calculating it precisely;

15

Contracts for writing software

- there should be a mechanism for pricing variations and extra work.
- The specification is a very important document:
  - it should provide the benchmark by which acceptance can be measured.
- Time for completion should be express:
  - if not express, it will be implied on the basis of a reasonable time for performance;
  - the contract should provide for liquidated damages for late delivery.
- Satisfactory provision should be made for maintenance and enhancement of the software.
- The contract should specify whether the source code will be delivered to the client.
- If the client does not obtain the source code, a copy must be placed in escrow.
- Warranties and indemnities are usual.
- There are legal controls over clauses excluding or restricting liability for defects:
  - business liability for death or personal injury arising out of negligence cannot be excluded or restricted,
  - a reasonable level of insurance cover should be obtained by the software developer.
- Contracts should include arbitration or alternative dispute resolution (ADR) clauses:
  - even if there is no such provision, the parties should still consider ADR;
  - the courts may encourage the parties to try ADR first to try to settle the dispute.
- Large complex software contracts should be supervised by an independent professional.

SELF-TEST QUESTIONS

Note: there is only one correct answer to each multiple choice question.

1   Reckless Software Ltd sent Hasty Consumables plc a proposal for writing software for Hasty's new online selling venture. The proposal was headed 'subject to contract'. A few days later, Mr Flash, the managing director of Hasty phoned Reckless to inform Reckless that it 'had got the job' and asking Reckless to start work forthwith, which Reckless did. A day later Mr Flash wrote to Reckless confirming his phone call. Two months later, Mr Flash told Reckless to stop work as he decided to terminate the contract because Reckless was not getting on with the work fast enough. The proposal originally sent by Reckless envisaged that it would be paid on a time and materials basis but it failed to specify the work to be carried out with any precision and much would have remained to be finalised and agreed. Which one of the following statements is most likely to be CORRECT?

(a)   There is a binding contract, implied by the conduct of the parties and Hasty will be liable for wrongful repudiation of the contract.

(b)   There is a binding contract, implied by the conduct of the parties but Reckless is in breach of condition by performing the contract too slowly and this means that Hasty's repudiation is lawful.

(c)   There is no contract but Reckless will be entitled to payment on the basis of a *quantum meruit* for the work it carried out at Hasty's request.

(d)   There is no contract but Mr Flash will be personally liable for misrepresentation.

2   In terms of the assignment of an agreement to write software, which one of the following statements is NOT CORRECT?

(a) It is not possible to assign the burden of an agreement, for example, where a software developer purports to assign his obligation to write the software to a third party.

(b) As the benefits of an agreement are personal to the parties and part of their mutual obligations, they can only be assigned if one of the parties goes into liquidation.

(c) It is possible to assign the benefit of an agreement providing the agreement does not prohibit this or, where the consent of the other party is required, it is forthcoming.

(d) Where consent of the other party is required to the assignment of the benefit of an agreement and that party knows about an assignment made without his consent but takes no action, he may later be estopped from relying on his lack of consent.

3   Which one of the following is CORRECT in relation to liquidated damages?

(a) They are a performance bond to pay for completion of a contract should the contractor go out of business.

(b) They are a genuine pre-estimate of the damages likely to arise from a breach of the contract.

(c) They are damages to be assessed by the court for a breach of warranty.

(d) They are a penalty to encourage the other party to perform his obligations under the contract.

4   Which one of the following statements CORRECTLY describes source code escrow?

(a) It is an arrangement whereby the software company deposits a copy of the source code with an independent party who will release this to the client only in the case of certain events occurring such as the developer going out of business or refusing to maintain the software.

(b) It is an arrangement whereby the software developer deposits the source code with a trusted third party, such as a bank, so that if the developer goes out of business before a software development contract is completed, the bank will sell the source code and release the money obtained for it (less the bank's fee) to the client to enable the client to appoint another software developer to complete the software.

(c) It is an arrangement whereby the software developer undertakes to maintain the software by correcting errors in the source code on an annual basis to include the delivery of the source code of enhancements as and when they are available.

(d) It is an agreement between the parties, in a dispute as to delivery of the source code to the client, to submit to alternative dispute resolution and, failing resolution under alternative dispute resolution, to submit to arbitration.

5   In what ways is alternative dispute resolution better than litigation and under what circumstances is alternative dispute resolution most appropriate? (In answering this question, to supplement the text of this chapter, you may find it useful to consult the website of the Centre for Effective Dispute Resolution at www.cedr.co.uk.)

For further resources and updates please go to the Companion Website accompanying this book at **www.mylawchamber.co.uk/bainbridgeIT**

15

Contracts for writing software

16 Licence agreements for ready-made software

Ready-made software (sometimes described as 'off-the-shelf software') is that which is acquired as a completed package ready to install. It includes mass-produced software which may be obtained from a dealer or online and includes familiar packages such as word processing systems, spreadsheets and databases. It can be described as 'general purpose software'. It may be applications software (word processing, etc.), operating system software (for example, Windows, MS-DOS or Linux) or utility software such as disk management software, software for archiving files, firewall or anti-virus software. In some cases, ready-made software comes with some peripheral device such as a printer or some other piece of equipment such as a digital camera. It must also be remembered that when we speak of software, this includes materials other than computer programs, such as databases, literary, dramatic and audio-visual works.

The contractual nature of transactions involving ready-made software is still not absolutely clear. Four possibilities exist (in the first and last, there may or may not be tangible items handed over):

- a licence agreement with the software publisher;
- a sale of goods contract with a dealer (only where tangible items are included);
- a hybrid licence agreement/sale of goods contract with the software publisher (again where tangible items are part of the overall package and where the dealer can be seen as acting as the software publisher's agent in respect of the licence); or
- a *sui generis* (unique) form of contract.

Before looking further at these possibilities, it must be noted that it is the intangible rights which are dominant in the transaction – for example, the right to use the software. This right requires that the licence of the copyright owner, otherwise the copyright and other rights, such as the database right, subsisting in the software (there are likely to be a number of distinct rights in the software), will be infringed. This is confirmed by section 16(2) of the Copyright, Designs and Patents Act 1988 which states that the copyright in a work is infringed by a person who without the licence of the copyright owner does, or authorises another to do, any of the acts restricted by the copyright. As copying a work of copyright extends to making copies which are transient, it is quite clear that simply operating or running software involves making copies, whether transient or not, and this must have the licence of the copyright owner. Of course, in many cases, the software will be copied from the media on which it was supplied to the hard disk of the computer of the person acquiring the software. Alternatively, it may be downloaded from a website. Subsequent copies will be made when the software is used as it will be loaded into the volatile memory (RAM) of the computer. Where the software is or includes a database subject to the database right, a licence will be required to permit the extraction and/or reutilisation of a sub-stantial part of the contents of the database. This will include a repeated and systematic extraction and/or reutilisation of insubstantial parts of the contents if these collectively are equivalent to a substantial part of the contents.

The fact that a licence is required to use software appears to have been overlooked in the past by some who have considered the nature of a contract for ready-made software. Another key fact is the method of delivery of the software. It may be handed over in a box which contains optical or magnetic discs together with printed documentation such as a manual and licence agreement.

METHOD OF DELIVERY

Increasingly, these days, software may be delivered online, with no tangible items being delivered to the person acquiring a copy of the software. In the past, where software was supplied on physi-cal media, it was common for the licence agreement to be exposed on the outside of the package. This was the so-called 'shrink-wrap' licence. The idea was that it enabled the person acquiring the software to inspect the terms of the licence before opening the package. This was usually backed by a statement to the effect that, if the person acquiring the software did not agree with the terms of the licence, he could return the package unopened to the dealer and recover his pay-ment. Another technique was to have the media carrying the software in a sealed package carry-ing a statement to the effect that breaking the seal signified acceptance of the terms of the licence agreement, again, usually backed by a promise that the software could be returned and any pay-ment refunded providing the seal was intact. These forms of licence are referred to in this chap-ter as 'rip-seal licences'.

In the case of software delivered online, the person acquiring it will usually be required to sig-nify his acceptance of the terms of the licence before the software can be 'downloaded', usually by clicking a check-box before being allowed to proceed. This form of licence has been described as a 'click-wrap' or 'web-wrap' licence. They are referred to in this chapter as 'click licences'. The advantage of these forms of licences is that it is much easier to confirm their legal existence as the person downloading the software usually has to positively confirm his or her acceptance of the terms of the licence (which is normally available for inspection) before assenting to the transac-tion.

The word 'download' has come in for judicial scrutiny and in *R v City of London Magistrates Court, ex parte Green* [1997] 3 All ER 551, it was held that it meant 'transfer from one storage device or system to another', as in the *Concise Oxford Dictionary* which also suggests it applies especially in relation to it being done remotely.

WHAT TYPE OF CONTRACT?

Deciding how to classify the contract is important so we can decide what terms will be implied into the contract and what legal controls there are over those terms. If the Sale of Goods Act 1979 applies there are certain implied conditions and warranties. An implied condition usually gives the buyer the right to reject the goods. If the contract is a contract for services, the Supply of Goods and Services Act 1982 implies other terms. If neither applies, the common law will imply terms to deal with standards to be achieved, such as fitness for purpose. Some commentators have had a fixation in the past that contracts for ready-made software are sale of goods contracts. They have been influenced by the fact that tangible materials have been handed over in the past. Now that software is available for downloading online, with nothing tangible being delivered to the person acquiring the software surely no one can still subscribe to the view that the contract is a sale of goods contract, which is a contract under which the seller transfers or agrees to transfer the property in goods to the buyer for a money consideration, called the price (section 2(1) of the Sale of Goods Act 1979). 'Goods' are defined as including all personal chattels other than things in action and money (in Scotland all corporeal moveables except money). These technical legal definitions certainly do not apply to contracts under which rights in or under intellectual property rights pass. The grant of a licence to use software is the grant of a right under copyright and any other intellectual property rights subsisting in the software.

The only time the nature of the contract becomes clouded is where hardware is delivered which includes software. A contract to buy a computer is a sale of goods contract. But what about the software also supplied, either pre-loaded or on media for the buyer to install? There is only one possible approach to this. It is a sale of goods contract for the physical equipment coupled with the necessary licence agreements for the software. Using software, whatever form of work it is, requires a licence if the use of the software involves acts that are restricted by copyright and other relevant intellectual property rights. If the licences are not express (most are) then a licence must be implied otherwise using the software infringes copyright and may also infringe other rights, such as the database right.

What about goods that do not at first sight appear to have anything to do with computers? Take a motor car or washing machine, for example. A great deal of modern goods incorporate computer technology. Again the answer must be the same. The contract is a sale of goods contract (assuming it is a sale and not a hire or lease contract) coupled with the appropriate licences if the use of the goods involves the performance of any act which would otherwise infringe any intellectual property right.

Having made these points, the four possibilities identified earlier are now considered in greater detail.

Licence agreement

Where no tangible items are transferred to the person acquiring the software – for example, where the software is downloaded from the internet – the contract can only be in the form of a licence agreement. Where software is specially written for a client and installed on the client's computer, the contract for writing the software is a service contract governed by Part II of the Supply of Goods and Services Act 1982. The fact that the client may be provided also with copies of the software on tangible media does not change this. Under section 12(3) of that Act, the fact that goods may also be transferred does not prevent the contract being one for the supply of a service. However, the client must be given a licence to use the software. Usually, the contract for supplying the service of writing the software will include the necessary licence rather than having a separate licence agreement.

If the software is obtained remotely, it is likely that an opportunity will be given to read the licence agreement before the person wishing to obtain a copy of the software is committed to the transaction. Some software is available without cost over the internet but it must be stressed that its copying and subsequent use must still be licensed by the copyright owner. This may be under a standard licence used for 'open-source software' such as under a general public licence.[1] (Open source software is discussed in the following chapter.) Whether the software is open source or other 'free' software, there is likely to be a licence agreement (even if implied). Such licences may

---

[1] Open-source software is software where the source code is made available to others who may use it, modify it, re-distribute it freely. More information and examples of licences for such software can be seen at the OSI website at **www.opensource.org**.

impose terms governing its use and copying and even requiring the licensee to further distribute it or a modified or improved version freely under the same licence agreement. There may also be other rights in relation to the software such as the author's moral rights to be identified as such and to object to a derogatory treatment of the work. (These rights do not apply to computer programs but can apply to other items of software such as a database or document or image in digital form.)

The licence agreement is likely to state what the applicable law is and, in many cases, it will be that of one of the states of the US such as California, New York or Florida. Where this is so, it should be noted that the copyright owner can still enforce his rights in the UK. The Copyright and Performances (Application to Other Countries) Order 2006 extends the qualification provisions for UK copyright in the original works, *inter alia*, to persons and incorporated bodies from a considerable number of other countries. This is to give effect to the international conventions on copyright, in particular, the Berne Copyright Convention. Thus, an American company or citizen of the US having a US copyright can bring an action for copyright infringement occurring within the jurisdiction of the UK on the basis of a UK copyright.

As far as the licence agreement itself, this may be enforced subject to the rules of jurisdiction. The licence may state that not only is the licence subject to the law of a particular country or Federal state but that it is also subject to the sole jurisdiction of that country or state. The rules on jurisdiction are complex and, in relation to bringing an action outside the European Economic Area, leave of the court is required before proceedings can be commenced. Within Europe, the Brussels and Lugano Conventions and the Brussels Regulation on jurisdiction and enforcement of judgments in civil matters apply (see Chapter 23 on torts related to electronic information for more on these Conventions and Regulation).

The licence will often be of indefinite duration, with no fixed period being stated, although there may be some provision for termination, such as if the person acquiring it, the customer, contravenes some term in the licence agreement which is stated to terminate it. A term requiring the customer not to transfer the software to a third party could be an example. Strictly speaking, the licence cannot endure longer than the copyright in the software because, when the copyright expires, the software effectively falls into the public domain and can be used freely without requiring permission. Some licence agreements allow the customer to terminate unilaterally simply by destroying all the copies of the programs and documentation, although why he should want to do this is hard to understand. If he no longer requires the software, he may be able to transfer both it and the licence to a third party in return for a payment unless the licence agreement provides otherwise. If the software and licence are transferred, all copies must be transferred and any copies retained will be treated as infringing copies for the purposes of copyright law under section 56 of the Copyright, Designs and Patents Act 1988.

Sale of goods contract

We have already seen in Chapter 13 that a contract for the acquisition of computer software is unlikely to be regarded as a sale of goods contract, especially where the predominant purpose of the transaction is the acquisition of the software. It has also been noted that where the software is incorporated into goods such as motor cars and the predominant purpose is the acquisition of the goods rather than the software, then it will be a sale of goods contract. If the normal use of the goods involves acts controlled by intellectual property rights, then necessary licences would be implied. Where ready-made software is obtained, it cannot be a sale of goods contract because to so classify the contract is to trivialise the main purpose of the contract, being the right to use the software. To say it is a sale of goods contract on the basis that some tangible items are handed over is to defy logic and to completely ignore the fact that the use of software requires the licence of the copyright owner. Even so, some writers (and some judges) seemed unconvinced and preferred to rely on a familiar and tried and tested area of law to discuss or resolve actual or potential disputes. The convenience of this is that the Sale of Goods Act 1979 implies important terms into sale of goods contracts which give the person acquiring the software some useful rights if it turns out to be defective in some way.

The perceived problem of taking a contract to acquire ready-made software out of the sale of goods arena is not serious as the common law has long since been capable of implying appropriate terms into contracts – indeed, many of the terms implied by the Sale of Goods Act 1979 and the Supply of Goods and Services Act 1982 are derived from terms which were implied under common law. This was recognised by Sir Iain Glidewell in the Court of Appeal in *St Albans City & District Council v International Computers Ltd* [1997] FSR 251 where he implied a term into a contract for the transfer of a computer program that the program would be reasonably fit for its purpose, that is, for achieving its intended purpose.

Hybrid contract

This is a possible scenario where the property in tangible items also passes to the person acquiring the software in addition to the right to use it, typically where a person goes into a retail computer shop and buys a software package. There may be two separate contracts: one between the person and the shop owner, being a sale of goods contract; and a licence between the person and the owner of the copyright subsisting in the software.

Consider a situation where George, who wishes to obtain a copy of the ABC spreadsheet software, goes to a computer software dealer, Acme Computers, and asks for a copy of the ABC spreadsheet software. He pays £200 and is given a sealed box. Inside the box is an optical disc on which the software is recorded, a manual and a licence agreement. There must be a contract between George and Acme Computers on the basis of normal sale of goods law. This will relate to the tangible items. Thus, if the optical disc is physically damaged and the software cannot be loaded onto George's computer because of this, he will have a remedy under section 14(2A) of the Sale of Goods Act 1979 as the disc is not of satisfactory quality. He will be able to obtain a replacement from Acme Computers or he may return the whole package and obtain a refund of the price he paid.

As between George and the owners of the copyright subsisting in ABC, Lemming Software plc, George must have Lemming's licence to use the software. The problem relates to what the terms of that licence are. It could be that they are those printed on the licence agreement which came with the software but there may be some problems with this as George may not have seen the licence until after he bought the software. A basic rule of English contract law (and most other jurisdictions) is that it is not possible to unilaterally introduce new terms into a contract after it has been made, that is, without the agreement of the other party. If the contract is made at the time George hands over the money in return for the box containing the software, then he will not have seen the licence until it is too late.

Software publishers have tried various methods to ensure that their licence agreements have the force of law. One technique used is to have the licence exposed on the outside of the package, the whole being wrapped in clear plastic, so that the licence may be inspected before the package is opened. This is the 'shrink-wrap' licence. Another technique used is for the software to be contained in a sealed packet or case which is accompanied by the licence agreement with a notice saying that breaking the seal signifies acceptance of the terms of the licence. This is usually coupled with a promise that the customer can obtain a refund if he returns the software with the seal unbroken in the event of the customer being unwilling to accept the terms. This was the arrangement in *Beta Computer* v *Adobe Systems*, discussed below in the section on *sui generis* contracts.

Sui generis contracts

One way to look at a contract for the acquisition of ready-made software is to consider it a unique (*sui generis*) form of contract, unlike any traditional form of contract. This has a lot to commend it providing it is remembered that the contract must include a licence to use the software. Two forms of these contracts can be identified. The first is the modern version of the shrink-wrap licence, referred to below as 'rip-seal licences', where the person acquiring the software has to do some act assenting to the licence, such as breaking the seal on a case containing the software on media), with the opportunity of returning the software with seal intact, in which case no contract is made. The contract is made only if and when the seal is broken.

The other form of these contracts is where software is downloaded from the internet. The mechanism for bringing the contract into existence is different and, arguably, more satisfactory. The same principles apply whether the software includes computer programs, databases or other works protected by copyright and other rights. Downloading music, films and even documents requires a licence in respect of copyright and, where appropriate, other rights such as rights in performances. These forms of licences are referred to below as 'click licences'.

Rip-seal licences

A Scots judge suggested that contracts for the acquisition of ready-made software with a rip-seal licence in *Beta Computers (Europe) Ltd* v *Adobe Systems (Europe) Ltd* [1996] FSR 367 were *sui generis*. Beta, the pursuers, supplied Adobe, the defenders,[2] with computer software produced by Informix Software Inc, a third party. It was accepted that Informix owned the copyright subsisting in the software. It had been ordered by Adobe by telephone and was a standard upgrade package suitable for Adobe's computer. The software was delivered with a rip-seal licence and the package bore the words 'Opening the Informix S.I. Software package indicates your acceptance of these terms and conditions'.

Adobe claimed that it had the right to return the software without using it and that it had the right to reject it until such time as the package was opened, which it had not been. Beta sued for the price of the software.

Lord Penrose, in the Outer House of the Court of Session, in Edinburgh, reflected upon the legislative framework of the Copyright, Designs and Patents Act 1988 in the context of computer programs. He concluded that the supply of the medium on which the program is stored must be accompanied by an appropriate licence conferred directly or by implication from the acquisition of the software. An essential feature of the supply of ready-made software is that the supplier undertakes to make available to the purchaser both the medium and the right of access and use of the software. (Of course, nowadays, the software may be obtained without any physical medium.) In effect, the supplier undertakes that he has the right to communicate the benefit of the use of the software: in other words, that he transfers the benefit of the copyright owner's licence. Lord Penrose said:

> The supply of proprietary software for a price is a contract *sui generis* . . . [it is] unacceptable to analyse the transaction in this case as if it were two separate transactions relating to the same subject matter. There is but one contract . . .

---

[2] Pursuer and defender are the Scots equivalent of claimant and defendant respectively.

The time such a contract is made is when the conditions imposed by the owner of the copyright were tendered to the purchaser of the software and accepted by the purchaser. Otherwise, there could be no *consensus ad idem* (agreement of the same thing), essential for a contract to exist. That being so, the purchaser can reject the software at any time before acceptance by performing the stated act – in this case, opening the sealed package.

Lord Penrose said that if the contract was considered to be a sale of goods contract this would produce the odd result that the dominant characteristic of interest to the parties (the right to use the software) was subordinated to the medium by which it was transmitted to the users.

There is one problem with the Lord Penrose's analysis. Scots law is based on Roman law, not common law, and it was held that the contract gave rights to the copyright owner as a third party. This is possible under the Scots law of contract but was not at that time under English law. However, an alternative way of looking at the transaction is that it does not give rights to the copyright owner. Conversely, it is the copyright owner who gives rights to the purchaser of the software. Where there are restrictions in the licence agreement, they simply constrain the rights given to the purchaser rather than giving rights to the copyright owner. In any case, the Contracts (Rights of Third Parties) Act 1999 provides that a third party may enforce a term in a contract under certain circumstances and this would be apt to allow the copyright owner to bring an action for breach of the licence agreement in England, Wales and Northern Ireland.

In the US, there has been less difficulty with shrink-wrap licences. In the 7th Circuit Court of Appeals, shrink-wrap licences were held to be enforceable; terms did not have to be exposed on the outside of the package containing the software. It was sufficient if there was a notice to the effect that there was a licence agreement inside. Furthermore, the purchaser was entitled to a full refund if, after reading the licence, he did not agree with the terms and conditions (*The Times*, 'Interface Supplement', 10 July 1996, p. 6).

Click licences

Computer software and other works protected by intellectual property rights, such as music and visual works, may be acquired online. For the owner of the rights in the software or other works, this has the advantage that the person acquiring it can be presented with the terms of the licence before agreeing to download a copy. This means that question of enforceability, as discussed above in the context of rip-seal licences though now largely resolved, should not be an issue. The person acquiring the software is presented with the licence (or the opportunity to read it) and usually has to click a box (more often a small circle now) to indicate agreement with the licence before being able to proceed to download the software. This should be effective to incorporate the terms into the contract, whether or not the person concerned actually takes the trouble to read the terms of the agreement (most probably do not). This method of incorporating terms into contracts is not restricted to software and other intangible things subject to intellectual property rights and is also commonly used in the contracts for the supply of goods and services made online.

By incorporating the terms of the licence agreement into the contract is not an end to the matter however. Other information available on the relevant website could give rise to misrepresentation if it conflicts with the terms of the licence and the terms themselves may be subject to legal controls. The fact the licence may be subject to the law of another jurisdiction may not prejudice consumer rights provided for by European Community law, such as those relating to distance selling and electronic contracting (as discussed in more detail in Part 3 of this book).

Although, on the face of it, there is no real problem with click licences, a number of points can be made.

1   Unless legally recognised electronic signatures are used, they may be some doubt as to whether they are suitable to assign intellectual property rights or to grant exclusive licences in respect

of them as there is a general requirement for such agreements to be in writing and be signed by the assignor or owner as the case may be. In the case of some forms of contract, such as a contract for the supply of a service, such as a construction contract. However, the law has taken a fairly pragmatic approach to what constitutes a signature and has even held that a typed name on a telex could constitute a signature for the purposes of the Limitation Act 1980 in *Good Challenger Navegante SA* v *Metalexportimport SA* [2004] 1 Lloyd's Rep 67. However, a person's e-mail address, which included his name, in the header of an e-mail did not count as that person's signature in *Mehta* v *J Pereira Fernandes SA* [2006] 2 Lloyd's Rep 244.

2 The identity of the person agreeing to the licence. It may be, for example, that a person purporting to acquire software for another person, as an agent, does not have the authority to bind that person. There was a recent case where a three-year-old boy bought a £9,000 Nissan Figaro car on eBay using his mother's computer (*BBC News*, 25 September 2006).

3 There may be difficulties in relation to legal disputes where questions of proof of the agreed terms, the time the contract was made and the fact of assent of both parties may be at issue.

4 Applicable law and jurisdiction may be in issue.

TYPICAL TERMS IN LICENCES FOR READY-MADE SOFTWARE

The owner of the intellectual property rights in the software, who will usually be the licensor (it may be that an exclusive licensee is the licensor), will want to set out the conditions of use of the software and confirm the fact of copyright subsistence and the grant of a licence to the purchaser. The licence may include some warranties and will have to address the impact of the applicable law on the licence. It may also deal with upgrades, user support and termination. Typically, the use may be limited to a single computer or a stated number of computers or users. A term dealing with whether the software and licence can be transferred to another person is also common.

It has been noted in Part 1 of this book that the Copyright, Designs and Patents Act 1988 makes void and unenforceable some terms in licence agreements which try to prohibit or restrict the permitted acts of decompilation of computer programs and making necessary back-up copies of computer programs. There are some other controls which relate to databases. A form of words which might be used in a licence agreement to restrict decompilation (of any computer program included in the software) to that permitted under the Act is: 'You may not reverse engineer, decompile, disassemble or otherwise modify or alter the software except as provided for by section 50B of the Copyright, Designs and Patents Act 1988.'

The inclusion of warranties is not universal by any means and where they are given by the copyright owner, they are usually very limited. It may be that they are restricted to the return of the price paid for the software if it fails to perform substantially as stated in the documentation. We have seen that terms excluding or restricting liability for defective software are fairly strictly controlled by the Unfair Contract Terms Act 1977 in the context of bespoke software. However, it is possible that much greater restriction or even exclusion is possible with ready-made software, bearing in mind, of course, that liability for death or personal injury caused by negligence cannot be excluded or restricted by a term in a contract or notice by virtue of section 2 of the Unfair Contract Terms Act 1977. In respect of other types of liability, it would seem reasonable that liability can be restricted or excluded. The main reason is that the software is 'general purpose' and has not been written for a particular client's requirements. Furthermore, the company producing the software has no knowledge of the uses to which end users will put the software. If a person using spreadsheet software to perform some complex financial calculation makes a mistake, that is hardly the software company's fault. However, if there is an inherent defect in the software which is not obvious to a reasonable user, it is a moot point as to whether a clause excluding liability completely would be effective. Until such time as exclusion clauses in ready-made software licences come under judicial scrutiny, it is likely that no warranties will be given or, where they are, compensation for breach of warranty will be limited to the price paid for the software.

If there are no warranties (whether the licence expressly states this or is silent on the point), would the courts be likely to imply any warranties? We have seen in the *St Albans* v *International Computers* case that one judge thought an implied term of fitness for purpose would be appropriate. This would seem a sensible approach with ready-made software, the purpose being that for which such software is usually obtained.

Finally, the licence is almost certain to contain an applicable law clause and, possibly, a term stating which courts are to have jurisdiction. A typical formula might be: 'This licence agreement is governed by the laws of England and Wales and any dispute under it is subject to the sole and exclusive jurisdiction of the courts of England and Wales.' However, the effectiveness of such an attempt to restrict jurisdiction is not beyond doubt.

MISREPRESENTATION AND ENTIRE AGREEMENT

If software is bought from a dealer, he may have made representations about the software which turn out to be false. Statements on a website may contain false or misleading claims about the software. In such cases, there may be a remedy for misrepresentation as discussed in Chapter 13. It is common for licences to contain a term to the effect that the software company will not be bound by statement made in pre-contractual negotiations or in advertising or marketing material and that the licence itself contains the entire agreement between the parties to the exclusion of anything else. Entire agreement terms are subject to the reasonableness test as stated in section 11(1) of the Unfair Contract Terms Act 1977 by virtue of section 3 of the Misrepresentation Act 1967. In *Mackenzie Patten & Co* v *British Olivetti Ltd* (unreported) 11 January 1984, discussed in more detail in Chapter 20, the buyer of computer hardware claimed, *inter alia*, that he had been induced into entering into the contract on the basis of a salesman's misrepresentation. However, the judge did not need to rule on whether an entire agreement clause in the contract was effective to remove any liability resulting from the misrepresentation as he found for the buyer on the basis of a collateral warranty (a term in a subsidiary contract inducing the party to enter into the main contract).

BACK-UP COPIES OF PROGRAMS

Making a back-up copy of a computer program infringes copyright unless its making is:

- permitted by the copyright owner;
- within the scope of an implied term; or
- necessary to the licensed use of the program.

Notwithstanding that there may be some doubt as to the contractual status of the licence agreement, as discussed above, it is sensible to check any provisions concerning back-up copies. If making a back-up copy is necessary to the licensed use of the program as provided for by section 50A of the Copyright, Designs and Patents Act 1988, then section 296A of that Act states that any term in a licence agreement which attempts to take this right away is void and unenforceable at law. Where back-up copies have been lawfully made, there should be no problem in depositing a back-up copy with a company providing disaster recovery services. However, if the software and licence is subsequently transferred to a third party, assuming the licence does not prevent this, all back-up copies must also be given to the third party otherwise they become infringing copies under section 56 of the Copyright, Designs and Patents Act 1988.

In practical terms, a sensible approach to back-up copies is required by both sides. Licensees should guard against the danger of proliferation of back-up copies which can soon become working copies, exceeding the licensed use. Organisations using software should carry out software audits regularly to check and monitor the number of copies in use. There are a number of other benefits. Regular auditing is part of good practice and quality management and will encourage a responsible attitude towards the use of software. During an audit, some employees might be found to be using old or defective versions of software and any pirated software brought into work by an employee may be discovered and dealt with. The implementation and enforcement of effective software audits also prevents the embarrassment of being raided by software copyright owners who have obtained a search order, giving them powers, accompanied by a solicitor, to enter and inspect the computer equipment and remove unauthorised copies of software to be used as evidence in copyright infringement actions.

INTEGRATION AND UPGRADES

A person acquiring software should always check how well, if at all, the software will integrate with other software and whether data can be easily transferred to and from the software. Will the software run satisfactorily on the customer's hardware? What is the position if the customer decides to upgrade his equipment or operating system software: will the software still be usable? What if a better version of the software is made available in due course: can the customer trade in his old software or will he have to pay the full licence fee for the new version? These are the type of questions someone contemplating acquiring ready-made software should consider. Even though some of the events described might seem unlikely at the time, they have a nasty habit of becoming relevant later and if a customer is in doubt it is better to err on the side of flexibility. The pace of development in the computer industry shows no signs of slowing down and, as more powerful hardware becomes available, existing software packages will be enhanced in a like fashion and new software applications which were hitherto impossible or impracticable will appear on the market.

TRAINING AND SUPPORT

Training is an aspect which is often overlooked. A computer dealer may offer services such as installation, training and support under a separate contract between himself and the customer. The quality of the training will obviously be important as will the provision of refresher courses. Most software publishers provide help and support, online and/or by telephone, and it is worth checking with existing users as to the effectiveness of the service. Many such support services leave much to be desired and there seems to be a general inability to deal with anything but the most obvious problems. A typically hard nut to crack is whether the fault is caused by a hardware defect or software fault. A computer dealer may be able to help but, in many cases, a user group may be of more assistance.

A final point concerns 'hotline' support. Will the dealer be prepared to provide an emergency call-out service if there is a problem related to the use of the software, such as trying to interface the software with other equipment? A dealer will charge for this type of support and the rate he requires will depend, amongst other things, on the speed of call-out expected by the customer.

SUMMARY

- Four possibilities exist for the nature of a contract for ready-made software.
- A clue to the nature of the contract is given by the fact that software can be downloaded from a website without any tangible items being involved.
- Using ready-made software requires a licence from the owner of the copyright and any other intellectual property rights in the software.
- A contract to buy a computer is a sale of goods contract but licences are still required for the software delivered with the computer.
- Contracts for the acquisition of ready-made software are likely to be *sui generis*, being:
  - 'rip-seal' licences; or
  - 'click' licences.
- Issues with click licences are:
  - where a signature is required (for example, where copyright is being assigned);
  - the identity of the licensee;
  - the time and place the contract is made;
  - applicable law and jurisdiction.
- Licences for ready-made software remain subject to legal controls, such as:
  - the right to make necessary back-up copies of computer programs;
  - the right to decompile computer programs for 'interoperability';
  - controls over exclusion clauses.
- There may be remedies for false or misleading statements about the software.
- Other issues are:
  - whether the software will integrate with existing software;
  - the availability of upgrades;
  - support and training.

SELF-TEST QUESTIONS

Note: there is only one correct answer to each multiple choice question.

1   In *Beta* v *Adobe,* Lord Penrose made a number of findings in relation to a rip-seal licence. Which one of the following statements was NOT one of his findings?

(a)   It is a *sui generis* contract which must be accompanied by an appropriate licence.

(b)   The contract is suspensory and is not made until the act signifying acceptance of the terms is carried out.

(c)   The software may be returned and the price reimbursed providing the act signifying acceptance of the terms has not been carried out.

(d)   There are two contracts, one for the tangible items and another which is a licence agreement, permitting use of the software.

2   Julia has bought a new laptop computer from LAPWORLD plc. It came with Microsoft Windows XP preloaded. Which one of the following statements CORRECTLY identifies the contractual nature of Julia's purchase?

   (a) It is a *sui generis* contract with LAPWORLD plc for the computer and a contract governed by the Supply of Goods and Services Act 1982 in respect of the copy of Windows XP.

   (b) It is a sale of goods contract with LAPWORLD plc in respect of the computer and a licence agreement with Microsoft for the copy of Windows XP.

   (c) It is simply a sale of goods contract as pre-loaded software is considered to be goods as defined in the Sale of Goods Act 1979.

   (d) It is a sale of goods contract with LAPWORLD plc in respect of the computer and a contract of hire with Microsoft for the copy of Windows XP.

3   Jeremy bought a copy of software which included a computer program and a database online. He downloaded it onto the hard disk of his computer. There was a licence agreement available to read on the website from which the software was downloaded and Jeremy had to click a box to confirm his acceptance of the terms of the licence. Jeremy did not bother to read the licence but simply clicked the box enabling him to proceed to download the software after giving his payment details. There is a term in the licence which states that the licensee may not make back-up copies of the software. Which one of the following statements is CORRECT?

   (a) The term is void and unenforceable to the extent that it purports to take away the right to make a back-up copy of the computer program and database if necessary to the licensee's lawful use of them.

   (b) The term is void and unenforceable to the extent that it purports to take away the right to make a back-up copy of the computer program if necessary to the licensee's lawful use of it.

   (c) The term is void and unenforceable in this particular case as Jeremy did not read the terms of the licence agreement.

   (d) The term is enforceable as it was clearly stated in the licence agreement and Jeremy will be bound by it even though he did not read it as he signified his acceptance of the licence agreement by clicking on the box in question.

4   Petra bought computer software which she ordered online from a trader, zambesi.com. Zambesi.com's website stated that the software in question was compatible with Petra's make and model of computer and its operating system. When the software arrived by post, she found that the licence agreement contained a term stating that the licence represented the entire agreement between the parties and no liability could be accepted for any other statements or representations by whomsoever made. Petra discovered that the software would not work on her computer. It turned out to be incompatible. Which one of the following statements is CORRECT?

   (a) The 'entire agreement' term is an acceptable business term and this is an example of the principle *caveat emptor* (let the buyer beware). It was up to Petra to ensure that the software was compatible.

   (b) 'Entire agreement' terms are void and unenforceable, *per se*.

   (c) The 'entire agreement' term is subject to the reasonableness test in the Unfair Contract Terms Act 1977 as a result of section 3 of the Misrepresentation Act 1967.

   (d) Zambesi.com is guilty of making a fraudulent misrepresentation.

5   What are the terms that you would expect to find in a licence agreement, subject to the law of England and Wales, for software obtained by downloading from a website. Comment on their enforceability.

For further resources and updates please go to the Companion Website accompanying this book at **www.mylawchamber.co.uk/bainbridgeIT**

17   Open source software licences

17

INTRODUCTION

A person may write some software such as a computer program and be quite happy to allow others to use, modify, copy and distribute it free of charge. A significant amount of 'free' software (often referred to as 'freeware') is available. There also exists software called 'shareware' which is often freely available but on a trial basis with a request that the user pays a licence fee if he wishes to continue to use it. However, as is often the case with computer terminology, the term 'shareware' is imprecise and can mean several things. It could mean software simply distributed free and which may be copied and given freely to others or a cut-down version of licensed software, distributed in the hope that the user will be so impressed that he will pay for the full version. Another model is software which is distributed freely but which may only be used a number of times before it ceases to function. Again the idea is that the user will pay a licence fee to obtain a fully functioning version.

Open Source Software is the term used for software distributed freely under the Open Source Initiative's requirements for licensing arrangements. A number of organisations, individuals and software companies distribute software in this way under licences controlling the distribution and use of open source software and many such licences are available. One example is the GNU General Public Licence which operates a 'Copyleft' system enabling the distribution of free software and ensuring all modified and extended versions of the software are also available free of charge. Copyleft operates by using a licence to control the use and further distribution of free software. Another popular licence is the Mozilla Public Licence.

The fact that software is made freely available does not mean that it is not subject to copyright or other intellectual property rights, if applicable. The normal rules apply as to subsistence of copyright and the identity of the author and owner of the copyright. Furthermore, in some jurisdictions such as the UK and many European countries the author may enjoy the moral rights to be identified as the author and to object to a derogatory treatment of the software. In the UK, this does not apply to computer programs but can apply to other forms of software such as copyright databases and other works, such as audio-visual works and documents, included in the software. Distributing software to others with permission to carry out certain acts in relation to it gives rise to a licence, assuming the person distributing the software has the right to give such permission. The licence may be express or implied.

If a person, being the owner of copyright in software, wishes to allow others to use it free of charge, to modify it and redistribute it, a number of technical and legal issues arise. First, the rationale behind open source software is that it should be freely available to others who may use it, modify it and/or include it in an overall software package containing other items of software (whether free or otherwise) and freely distribute it in its original or modified form without charging end users. For this to work effectively, the source code should also be readily available free of charge (or for a small charge reflecting the cost of distributing it). One of the aims is to encourage the evolution, development and spread of good software. A danger is that someone who has obtained a copy of open source software modifies it and then claims proprietary rights in it and then distributes the modified version only in return for a substantial licence fee. Another concern is that liability might attach to the originator or persons subsequently modifying the software if it proves defective or if it interferes with a third party's intellectual property rights. It is usual, therefore, to include a written licence with the software to deal with such matters. Some of the issues for open source software are discussed below.

CONTRACT LAW

A valid, binding contract requires that there is an offer, an unequivocal acceptance of that offer and consideration, for example, the price or the item delivered as the case may be as each party's part of the bargain. There are some other aspects but they need not concern us here. Consideration is a key element and the only time it is not required is where the contract is made by deed. When one obtains a typical software package conventionally, a price is paid in return for the software. The buyer's consideration is the payment and the software company's consideration is to give the buyer a copy of the software and permission to use it, in circumstances set out in the licence agreement.

With open source software, usually no payment is made by the person obtaining a copy of the software unless it includes proprietary software not subject to the open software initiative. Does this mean that there is no valid contract? Judges have in the past shown some imagination in finding the existence of consideration and it might be argued the consideration is the fact that the person will use that software rather than someone else's and modify it and further distribute it. It may be that a small charge made to cover the cost of distributing the software, allowed by some open software licences, will suffice. Alternatively, a nominal £1 or $1 fee can be charged which will put the contractual nature of the licence beyond doubt. Consideration must be sufficient but need not be adequate and a nominal fee will be deemed to be sufficient. Nevertheless, whether there is or is not consideration is not that important. With a copyright work, certain acts fall within the owner's exclusive rights. Anyone doing any of these acts in respect of a substantial part of the work without the permission of the owner infringes the copyright. Therefore, in terms of open source software, the copyright owner is, in effect, giving the person acquiring a copy of the software permission to use it. If there is consideration, there is a contractual licence but, if not, there is at least a bare licence.

A bare licence can generally be revoked at any time. A contractual licence usually can be terminated only in accordance with the licence agreement itself. With a bare licence, one concern might be that it will be terminated without warning. Hence, it is desirable that it contains terms to the effect that it will not be terminated, except under specified circumstances. Although not contractually binding, if the copyright owner later attempts to terminate the licence unjustly, the doctrine of estoppel would probably apply. This would mean that a court would prevent the termination of the contract.

As with any licence, it is preferable that it is in writing and communicated to the persons who acquire the software. By having a written licence, this can overcome some of the possible pitfalls that could otherwise be associated with open source software.

If the arrangement is contractual, there is a possibility that the implied term under section 13 of the Supply of Goods and Services Act 1982 will apply. This requires that the service is carried out using reasonable skill and care. However, there is some doubt as to whether writing software and then subsequently distributing it could be viewed as a service under that Act, although 'service' is not defined in the Act. The better view is that it is not a service but it is still possible that the courts would imply a similar term on the basis of common law.

COPYRIGHT

It is always advisable to include a copyright notice on the software (preferably also displayed on screen when the software is operated) with the familiar copyright symbol ©, the name of the owner of the copyright and the year of first publication. If there are any moral rights (which there might be in relation to elements of the software that are not computer programs) these should also be spelt out, for example, by a notice stating that: [Name of author] hereby asserts his moral right to be identified as author of [name of relevant works].

The licence should spell out precisely what rights are being granted and, if it is desired that the software can be modified and redistributed, that relevant copyright notices are placed on such copies. It may be sensible to include all such information and, indeed, the licence itself within the software.

In many countries, anyone removing or modifying such information without permission will be liable as if they had infringed the copyright. Section 296ZG of the Copyright, Designs and Patents Act 1988 (inserted by the Copyright and Related Rights Regulations 2003) provides that persons knowingly and without authority removing or altering electronic rights management information are liable as if they had infringed the copyright (or database right, rights in performances or publication right, as appropriate). This also applies to persons who distribute, import for distribution or communicate to the public copies in respect of which the information has been removed or altered if they know or have reason to believe that, by doing so, they are inducing, enabling, facilitating or concealing an infringement of copyright. Liability is owed to the copyright owner, exclusive licensee or person issuing copies to the public or communicating it to the public. Liability is concurrent to such persons where applicable. It is important, therefore, to ensure that the electronic rights management information is associated with the software, usually by including it in the software itself. The licence agreement should also cover the position where someone further distributes the software to ensure that a copy of the electronic rights information is included, together with any additions to it where the software has been modified before further distribution. Normally, open software licences are quite explicit about what may and may not be done with the software and include the names of the original developer and those who have modified it. Without such information, a recipient may think he can redistribute the software and charge a licence fee, for example.

If the software is modified by subsequent users, they should be required to indicate on the software that this has happened, when it happened and that they have copyright in the modification. If possible, some indication of the nature of the modifications should also be given. The originator of the software may require being informed of modifications and want a copy of the software as modified made available to him.

DELIVERY AND DISTRIBUTION

The software should be made available in both object code and source code form. The source code should be accompanied with any preparatory materials and details of development and testing. In other words, it should have a good and comprehensive provenance. Even though the basic principle is that the software should be free, it is usually acceptable to expect payment for such ancillary materials and information though this should not exceed the cost of copying it and distributing it. Of course, most if not all of the software and associated materials may be delivered online nowadays. But, without such associated materials, further development and modification of the software may prove difficult and unpredictable.

The general rule is that the software can be distributed freely and this applies also to modified versions of it. Some licence agreements permit the distributor to charge a fee but usually the distributor is bound nevertheless to give everything that he has had the advantage of, including a copy of the source code. Some licences allow onward distribution to commercial organisations though others do not permit this. In the spirit of open source software, it should be available to all irrespective of identity or technological platform. One restriction that might apply, particularly in some countries, notably the US, is that there may be government restrictions on the distribution of software to certain countries.

PATENTS

Software patents are relatively easy to obtain in the US and there are also large numbers of software patents in Europe, despite the apparent difficulty in obtaining patents for software caused by the exclusion of computer programs and business methods, such as under Article 52 of the European Patent Convention and section 1(2) of the Patents Act 1977. A danger is that a person may modify open source software and then obtain a patent in respect of it. It will not be possible for such a person to prevent predecessors of the software continuing to use it (either on the basis that the earlier versions are in the public domain or by taking advantage of section 64 of the Patents Act 1977 – right to continue use begun before the priority date of the patent). However, the patent could interfere with other later versions that could be deemed to be variants. One solution is to include a term in the licence prohibiting the patenting of modified or extended versions of the software though this could be fairly complex as it might be reasonable to allow a person to incorporate the software as part of an overall package and to obtain a patent on the whole. Another way might be to require that free and non-exclusive licences are granted in relation to the modified software itself, thus keeping in tune with the spirit of open source software.

WARRANTIES AND LIABILITY FOR DEFECTS

As a general rule, all software contains errors. In some circumstances, these may result in serious loss or damage to the user of the software or a third party. The approach usually used for open source software is to exclude all warranties as to fitness for purpose, quality, performance, freedom from defects, etc. subject to the applicable law. In the UK, exclusion clauses, whether contractual or not, are governed by the Unfair Contracts Terms Act 1977. Section 2 of this Act prevents the exclusion or limitation of business liability for death or personal injury caused by negligence. The exclusion or limitation of business liability for other forms of loss or damage caused by negligence is possible but only if the term or notice seeking to do this is reasonable in the circumstances. Whether insurance can be obtained is a factor. What is customary in a particular context may also be a factor. In the case of open source software it would be almost impossible to obtain insurance at a reasonable cost, if at all. A major reason is that the person distributing the software has no control of how it will be used, and how it may be modified in the future and in what software it may be incorporated in the future. In any case, bearing in mind that no profit is being made by the person distributing the software it would seem unreasonable to expect insurance to be taken out. It may be that the courts will find it reasonable to exclude liability for negligence causing loss or damage other than death or personal injury. However, liability for death or personal injury cannot be excluded or limited at all. A person originating or modifying open source software ought to consider this carefully.

The inclusion of a term in an open source software licence agreement to the effect that the licensee must indemnify the licensor, the originator and others who have previously modified the software may be of doubtful enforceability. The safest way to proceed is to make sure as best one can that the software being distributed has been written and modified using reasonable care and skill. One danger area however, is where software that has been used for normal business activities and transactions is later incorporated into software used in safety critical applications.

It would seem reasonable to require the licensee who further distributes the software to include a term in the licence stating that the originator and others who previously modified the software make no warranties about the software and accept no liability in respect of it apart from liability for death and personal injury caused by negligence. The inclusion of a statement requiring the licensee to satisfy himself that the software is appropriate for his intended uses and to fully test the software should also help.

There is one last point to be made in respect of liability for negligence. It is a possibility (one can put it no higher than that) that the courts would hold that persons writing or modifying open source software do not owe a duty of care to subsequent users of it. This could be a further development of the law on proximity for imposing a duty of care as set out in *Caparo Industries Ltd v Dickman* [1990] 2 AC 605. Lack of control over subsequent use and not knowing all the potential uses and users of the software are factors that suggest such a possibility. However, it would probably depend on the circumstances of a particular case. Proximity might be found to exist in respect of donors of the software and their immediate recipients but no further. Perhaps it is a tribute to the quality of open source software that there is, as yet, no case law on this in the UK.

THIRD-PARTY RIGHTS

There is always a danger that software infringes a third-party right such as a copyright, trade mark, registered design or patent. Provision should be made for this eventuality. It may be that the person who wrote or modified the software can write out the offending part. If not, the further distribution of the software can only exaggerate the problem and lead to even larger awards of damages, apart from the embarrassment of injunctions being granted against the originator, intermediaries and end users of the software or modifications of it.

A term can be included to the effect that no warranty is given to the effect that the software does not infringe third-party rights. However, this does not send out a positive message and can be combined with a 'best endeavours' term along the lines that every effort has been taken to avoid infringing third-party rights. It may also be prudent to build into the licence provisions for informing persons supplying the software and recipients of any allegations of intellectual property infringements.

As far as infringement of copyright and database right are concerned infringement requires an act done in respect of the work alleged to have been infringed. The obvious example is copying. Liability for copyright infringement is, therefore, fairly easy to avoid – do not copy existing software. Likewise with trade marks and signs protected by passing off. Make sure that any images or logos used with the software are not the same as or similar to registered and unregistered trade marks. Unfortunately, the same is not true of patents and registered design rights. These are monopoly rights and do not depend on copying. Infringement can be completely innocent and with no knowledge of the subject matter of these rights. Furthermore, patent infringement actions are notoriously expensive.

Indemnities may be used to protect the originator of the software and intermediaries from claims from end users (although the originator and intermediaries may also be sued). A term should also be inserted prohibiting the further distribution of software if it is believed to infringe third-party rights, until such time as the allegation is defeated or retracted or a compromise reached if any of those outcomes occur.

A further term could be considered requiring persons acquiring the software and modifying it to make every effort to avoid infringing third-party rights. It is clear that in such a situation, asking for an indemnity is perfectly reasonable.

SUMMARY

- Open source software is software which:
  - may be freely used and modified;
  - includes delivery of source code;
  - may be redistributed on the same terms.
- Free software is still subject to copyright and may also be subject to other intellectual property rights.
- A licence is required even for free software.
- The contractual nature of open source software licences is uncertain.
- Copyright notices and other electronic rights management information should be included.
- There may be restrictions on recipients of open source software.
- There may be patent rights obtained by the originator or persons modifying the software.
- It is usual to include exclusions of all warranties and liabilities for defects, but:
  - liability for death or personal injury resulting from negligence cannot be excluded or limited in the UK and some other countries;
  - other liability for negligence can only be excluded or limited subject to the test of reasonableness.
- There should be provisions to cover the possibility that the software infringes a third party's intellectual property rights.

SELF-TEST QUESTIONS

Note: there is only one correct answer to each multiple choice question.

1 **Which one of the following statements CORRECTLY describes open source software?**
   (a) Software which is made freely available and which may be modified and/or further distributed on the same or similar terms and which includes a copy of the object code only.
   (b) Software which is made freely available and which may be modified and/or further distributed on the same or similar terms and which includes a copy of the source code.
   (c) Proprietary licensed software subject to royalty payments which includes the delivery of source code.
   (d) Free software which may be used, modified and further distributed which includes an arrangement for source code escrow.

2   Which one of the following statements in respect of open source software is INCORRECT?

   (a) Open source software is subject to copyright and may be subject to other intellectual property rights such as the database right.

   (b) Open source software requires a licence which covers its use, modification and further distribution.

   (c) Open source software is likely to have electronic rights management information included or associated with it.

   (d) Open source software may be distributed freely to any person or organisation but may only be used for non-commercial purposes.

3   Which one of the following statements in respect of open source software is CORRECT?

   (a) As open source software is made freely available it is acceptable to exclude all warranties (for example, fitness for purpose) and liabilities for negligence.

   (b) As the contractual nature of open source software is doubtful, the Unfair Contract Terms Act 1977 does not apply to it.

   (c) A person who originates open source software is not negligent if he or she objectively meets the standard to be expected of reasonably competent software writers.

   (d) The law of negligence does not apply to open source software as the persons writing or modifying it have no control over how it will be used by others.

4   To what extent does the law in the UK hinder the widespread distribution of open source software?

For further resources and updates please go to the Companion Website accompanying this book at **www.mylawchamber.co.uk/bainbridgeIT**

17

Open source software licences

18 Website development contracts

INTRODUCTION

Website development contracts share many features with contracts for the writing of software to a client's specific requirements though there are some additional factors to be taken into account. A great deal of ready-made software is used only within an organisation and, generally, is unseen by the public at large. There are, of course, exceptions to this, for example, where a person goes to a travel agent to book a holiday and sees screen displays and printed reports. A website, however, gives the owner an immediate presence in cyberspace. All manner of things about the owner and his business are laid bare and exposed to the world. As the World Wide Web is such a powerful marketing tool, it is essential that the design of a website is very carefully thought out and this applies also to the content on the website and its performance. It is not just commercial organisations that have websites, all manner of other organisations have websites, such as government departments, local authorities, not-for-profit organisations and professional bodies. Many private individuals also have their own websites. It is vital that websites are attractively designed, easy-to-use, informative and up-to-date, especially if they are for commercial, governmental or charitable organisations. It is also important to make sure that the website content is not offensive, defamatory or otherwise illegal and does not link to websites having such material.

Some organisations and a great many individuals design their own websites. They acquire a suitable domain name and obtain hosting facilities from an internet service provider (ISP). They use a suitable hypertext mark up language ('HTML') editor to format the content of their webpages, building in links between pages and, possibly, links to other websites, before uploading the files to the host computer. This might be satisfactory if there is sufficient expertise in-house but there are now numerous companies which specialise in website design who can create and maintain very effective websites. Whilst what has been said in the previous chapters in terms of software contracts is still highly relevant, there are a number of particular issues that relate to website design that should be addressed by both the client and the website design company. The purpose of this chapter is to examine those issues and make suggestions as to how they should be dealt with in contractual terms. The first thing to note, however, is that the scope of website development contracts can vary enormously, from the developer simply providing technical support to the complete design, including creating content, registering domain names, uploading and hosting the website, monitoring its use and providing ongoing maintenance and upgrading.

SPECIFICATION

During initial negotiations, the scope of the work should become apparent. It may be that the website development company takes the responsibility for the technical aspects but the client provides all the content for the webpages and updates of the content, perhaps with the developer formatting the content and adding links, meta-tags and the like, uploading it and testing to ensure that the website works properly. After deciding the scope of the developer's obligations under the contract, the next thing to consider is the specification. It is likely that the website development company has a standard specification but even then, it will probably need some modification to account for the client's particular needs.

The specification will describe the general functionality of the website and the content but will also set out other details such as those set out below.

1 *Browser compatibility* – different browsers (for example, Netscape Navigator and Internet Explorer) may display webpages differently and some may ignore certain HTML tags or formatting. Whilst it may be tempting to take advantage of the most sophisticated and up-to-date browser, care must be taken as persons accessing the website with a different browser or an older version may lose some of the functionality of the website which might detract from its overall attractiveness.

2 *Hosting and bandwidth* – the question of where the website will be hosted and who will be responsible for this must be dealt with. It may be that the website developer provides a dedicated server or a shared server to host the website or arranges hosting by a third-party service provider. A further alternative is that the site is hosted by the client using the client's server. Clearly hosting on dedicated servers will optimise performance. The specification also ought to address bandwidth, as this too will affect the speed of transfer of the webpages to the person accessing them.

3 *Back-office systems* – the developer may also write software to link the website to the client's back-office systems, such as its orders, accounts, marketing and other systems. This work will have to be fully specified and may require some preliminary work to allow the developer to become familiar with the back-office systems and how they can be linked with the website.

4 *Search engines* – the developer will probably be expected to register the website with appropriate search engines and the client may also want to pay to have certain terms reserved to increase the likelihood of appearing high up on a list of search results or to have sponsored links. There may also be the possibility of having an advertising banner or logo displayed when the result of a search is displayed.

5 *Security* – where orders are placed with the client via the website, personal data will be collected from the customer and passed through to the client's back-office systems for further processing. The specification should deal with security measures taken and the encryption of data transferred to appropriate standards, for example, by using public key/private key cryptography.

6 *Content* – the specification will describe the content and state the overall size, structure, image standards and other features such as program code used on the website. It should be made clear who is responsible for providing the content and for formatting it. If the client is to deliver content to the developer, clear delivery times should be set out. Responsibility for other features, such as the meta-tags to be used on the website, should be set out.

7 The specification must contain a *schedule of dates* for certain milestones to be reached. It is difficult to generalise, but it is likely that the following milestones will be set out:

18

Website development contracts

- delivery of a prototype and acceptance thereof;
- delivery of content of other data or information if provided by the client;
- development of the website proper;
- testing (including checking that all the links work properly and all text and images are displayed properly);
- acceptance and the date for the site to 'go live'.

8 *Maintenance* – this is a very important area and may be subject to a separate agreement. It should cover improvements, enhancements, modification and further development to keep pace with changes to browser and search engine technology. Error correction is likely to be an issue (strictly speaking this should not be subject to any separate obligation to pay where the errors are such that they would be seen as a breach of the original development contract). In the first few days and weeks after the website has gone live, it is imperative that the developer responds very quickly to deal with any problems – a typical problem is that the website and the links to the back-office systems cannot cope with the demand. A poorly performing commercial website can result in serious loss of business. A simple error, for example, in the price payable for goods, can have serious repercussions. There have been a number of examples of incorrect prices, for example where a price was shown as £1.00 and not £100. The difficulty with this sort of error is that placing an order is often followed immediately and automatically by an acceptance notice. Amongst other things the specification should deal with the techniques and systems used for placing and accepting orders. Most e-commerce websites now make it clear that the contract does not come into existence immediately and only happens at some later event such as sending an e-mail later to confirm acceptance of the order.

9 If the client's staff will be responsible for uploading new or modified content in the future, they will probably need *training* and the detail of the training should also be set out in the specification.

10 *Data protection* – the specification will set out what sort of personal and other data are to be collected and processed. As regards data protection law, the website development company is likely to be acting as the client's data processor and, as such, is required to be under security obligations as required by the Data Protection Act 1998 and these obligations are required to be in, or evidenced in, writing. The specification is an appropriate place to include such obligations, although they may be expressed in the main body of the contract or reference to the obligations in the specification may be made in the main body of the contract.

11 The specification may contain the *mechanisms for dealing with legal changes* that may affect the website, such as changes in consumer protection law.

TERMS

The website development contract will contain many express terms and there will be schedules and annexes, including a fully detailed specification. The express terms will set out the obligations and duties of each party, hopefully in precise details, and also contain terms to deal with difficulties that might arise during the performance of the contract or otherwise, for example, late delivery, breach of warranty and variations. Apart from terms dealing with ownership of the intellectual property rights in the content (formatted and unformatted) and associated works such as computer programs, there are likely to be terms dealing with performance levels and delivery terms, warranties, liability for defects and other breaches of contract and the usual terms concerning arbitration or alternative dispute resolution, applicable law and jurisdiction and entire agreement clauses. There may also be a schedule of rates and prices to be used to determine the price payable for any additional work asked for by the client.

Terms will also be implied by law. A website development contract is a contract for services and, as such, terms under the Supply of Goods and Services Act 1982 will be implied. Section 13, the requirement to carry out the service using reasonable care and skill, is particularly important. In some cases this duty may be extended or more clearly defined by express terms, for example, by a term requiring the website development company to assign suitably qualified staff to the performance of the contract. As is the case with software development contracts, and in the absence of an appropriate express term, it is likely that there will be implied into the contract a term imposing a duty on the website development company to correct errors appearing after the website and its content have been accepted by the client; see for example *Saphena Computing Ltd* v *Allied Collection Agencies Ltd* [1995] FSR 616, discussed in earlier chapters. This duty will exist whether or not there is a contractual obligation to maintain the website, though it is difficult to say for how long the duty will endure beyond the client's acceptance of the website. It is not likely to endure for very long if the client takes responsibility for maintenance and further development of the website.

The rights, duties and obligations under the terms implied by the Supply of Goods and Services Act 1982 into contracts for services may be excluded, subject to the Unfair Contract Terms Act 1977, providing the terms seeking to exclude or restrict liability are not inconsistent with the implied term in question. However, it is unlikely that a term excluding liability for breach of the implied term to carry out the service using reasonable care and skill would ever meet the requirement of reasonableness in the 1977 Act. Incidentally, if hardware is also supplied by the website development company, that does not prevent the contract being a contract for services as confirmed by section 12 of the Supply of Goods and Services Act 1982.

In software development contracts generally, there are usually express warranties to the effect that the developer will not use or incorporate material that infringes third-party intellectual property rights. In the absence of an express term, such a term will be implied. In *Antiquesportfolio.com plc* v *Rodney Fitch & Co Ltd* [2001] FSR 23 the client wanted to start advertising and selling antiques over the internet. It engaged the services of a design consultancy to design the website and carry out other work such as designing business cards. The website was delivered to the client which complained that the content and watermarks used on the website infringed third-party rights and the client commenced proceedings claiming the return of the price already paid of around £37,000 (invoices for a further £31,000 had been submitted by the design consultancy) or, alternatively, £8,000 damages assessed at what the client had claimed it had paid another designer to modify the website to overcome the problem.

Mr Justice Neuberger held that there was an implied obligation to carry out the work with reasonable care and skill and there was also an implied obligation to provide the website fit for the purpose for which it had been commissioned. The supply of material that potentially infringed third-party rights was a breach of that obligation. There was a risk that photographs of furniture used in the design of the website infringed copyright. Although, if that was so and was a breach of the implied term, it did not go to the root of the contract and did not entitle the client to treat the contract as repudiated. The judge went on to say that the client still had an obligation to pay money outstanding under the contract subject to a set-off. That is, the client would be allowed to set off the cost of modifying the website to remove the offending material but the client would have to prove the amount of the set-off. The judge accepted that photographs of single antique items could be the subject of copyright, although he thought the degree of originality was small. He did, however, reject the argument that an outline watermark or logo made by tracing the outline of a photograph of an antique item could be a work of copyright.

Another common term is that the content, if provided by the developer in whole or in part, will not contain any statement which is defamatory or that could otherwise result in the client being faced with legal action or even criminal prosecution, for example, if the material incited the commission of a criminal offence. Liability for information that is inaccurate and could give rise to liability, for example, for negligent misstatement should also be considered. Other forms of liability could be in the form of trade mark infringement and passing off. Care must be taken to ensure that keyword meta-tags do not infringe trade marks belonging to others, especially as it now seems likely that this can infringe even though the keyword meta-tags are not normally seen by persons visiting a website. This is because some forms of infringement of trade marks do not require the presence of a likelihood of confusion on the part of the public.

There should be a term requiring that the website complies with relevant laws, for example, laws relating to misleading advertising, consumer protection and electronic commerce legislation. In the case of a website targeted at more than one country, this should include a reference to the equivalent laws in all the countries affected.

A common phenomenon in software development generally which also applies to website development contracts is 'feature-creep'. That is, where partway through the performance of the contract, the client decides that it wants more features or different or enhanced functionality in respect of the website. There should be a term in the contract to cover variations to the contract so that the impact of additional or modified work can be allowed for before the work is carried out. The additional or altered work must be clearly defined and the difference in the price payable under the contract agreed together with any changes to the time for delivery and acceptance of the website. The ideal of having full and informed agreement as to the impact of additional or altered work on the contract before the work in question is started is not always achieved due to factors such as the urgency of getting on with the work or the persons who are in a position to agree such things being tied up with other matters at the time. Trying to reach agreement retrospectively is always more difficult but keeping records of the work in progress and having a mechanism in the contract for pricing additional work should help. The use of an independent professional to supervise the performance of the contract and certify payments due can be extremely helpful in resolving what could prove to be a potential source of conflict.

Feature-creep or failing to agree clearly and precisely what the work will entail at the outset can prove disastrous. In *Psychometric Services Ltd* v *Merant International Ltd* [2002] FSR 8, the claimant was in the business of designing and marketing tests, including multiple-choice tests for job applicants and a number of companies used these when recruiting new staff. The claimant decided to carry on its business on the internet and paid a company to carry out a preliminary study and design. Following this, the claimant awarded the contract to design fully three variants of the website to the defendant for a price which was initially capped at £195,000. Soon after, the defendant was asked by the claimant to design a further website outside the scope of the original agreement. This was done quickly by the defendant for the price of £20,000. Because of the speed with which it had been written, the software could not be re-used for the main contract. The commercial prospects for the claimant if its websites were fully operational and running properly appeared to be immense but problems arose. It was not clear to the judge whether this was the result of additional requirements asked for by the claimant or because the defendant had underestimated the work involved or because the defendant had not carried out the work properly. The defendant decided that the amount of work it was required to do was far in excess of what had originally been anticipated by the parties and a Variation Letter was signed by the parties lifting the £195,000 cap.

The defendant put in a great deal of effort in further developing the websites and the claimant paid out substantial sums, in the end paying over £700,000 with the defendant charging at an agreed hourly rate of £90 per person-hour. The defendant claimed that it was still owed

£960,000. The relationship between the parties broke down and the claimant sought delivery of the source code for the software used for the website which was granted by the court. Mr Justice Laddie thought that, if the source code was not made available to the claimant, it would be likely to go into liquidation and this would cause immense injustice to the claimant if proved right at the full trial. On the other hand, if the order was not granted, the defendant would be unlikely to recover the money it claimed was outstanding and, if the order was granted, the defendant would suffer no loss (all it would have to do was to hand over a copy of the source code) and it would be more likely to recover the outstanding money if it was proved to be right at full trial. It was noted that, if the websites were perfected, the claimant would be in a market-leading and highly profitable business.

MAINTENANCE

It is virtually inevitable that the website will contain errors, whether in the content, HTML code, links, underlying software or in the interaction between the website and the client's back-office systems. It is also a fact of life that the website will require changes over time, whether in the overall look and feel to improve its overall appearance or in the content details, for example, where prices or taxes change. In some cases, the client may take over complete responsibility for future changes and enhancements but it is usual for there to be a maintenance agreement with the website developer. In some cases, it may be a combination of the two, for example, where the client retains responsibility for changing the content with the developer being responsible for the underlying software and more significant design changes.

Without a maintenance agreement, the developer will be under an implied obligation (unless this is express) to correct errors in the software and content if and to the extent that the developer was responsible for creating this. However, if only subject to an implied term, the speed of response might not be as quick as the client might wish for, as the implied term would only require the error to be corrected with a reasonable time. It is certainly better to use express terms to deal with error correction.

Where there is a maintenance agreement it should cover work such as upgrading the website and underlying software, redesigning the website to increase its attractiveness, maintaining links and modifying the content (or converting content provided by the client into HTML format). The agreement should also set out response times and an obligation to make modifications necessary as a result of legislative and tax changes in a timely fashion. For example, if there is a change in value added tax which affects goods or services sold on the website, the appropriate changes to the website must take effect at the same time the tax change comes into effect. As is usual, the date the site was last updated should be shown.

The maintenance agreement should contain appropriate benchmarks to assess the developer's compliance with the obligations in the agreement and relevant warranties. For a commercial website, downtime is very serious and there are likely to be terms dealing with this and the developer's liability if it exceeds a stated period of time. There are also likely to be obligations on the client to inform the developer immediately an error is suspected or in relation to a pending change in prices, legislation or tax. The developer will probably want a term included in the maintenance agreement to cover wasted time and costs, such as where the developer has been asked to deal with a suspected problem which turns out not to exist.

Payment under a maintenance agreement is likely to be on the basis of an agreed annual fee, perhaps payable in instalments with additional payment for upgrades, enhancements and the supply of new content. There may be a formula to work out such additional costs, such as an hourly rate per person engaged on the work with any items of hardware or additional software licences for third-party software being supplied at cost plus a percentage uplift. Provision is likely also to be included for the payment of the developer's expenses. However, where the additional work is substantial, it will usually be better to agree the amount of work and payment in advance.

The client may need to consider whether it wants to be able to engage a different developer in the future to maintain and carry out other work on the website design and content. Apart from having clear provisions dealing with termination of the agreement, allowing another developer to take over, perhaps at the end of an annual maintenance period, the original agreement and maintenance agreement should address matters such as delivery of the source code and ownership of copyright and other rights subsisting in the materials.

DOMAIN NAME, ETC.

If the developer registers the domain names for the website, the client may want to ensure that the contract deals with renewal of the domain names as failure to renew in time could result in loss of the domain name. Probably the best solution is for the client itself to register its domain names, if it has not already done so. Alternatively, if the developer registered domain names, it could transfer the name to the client and inform the domain name registry accordingly.

Great care needs to be taken in choosing a domain name that will not lead to legal conflicts in the future. Consideration should be given to future expansion and diversification. In *World Wide Fund for Nature* v *World Wrestling Entertainment Federation Inc* [2002] EWCA Civ 196, an agreement was reached between the parties to severely restrict the defendant's use of the letters WWF outside the US. If the defendant wanted to develop a world wide trade using **www.wwf.com** as its domain name for its website was a very risky thing to do and it should have been aware of that fact when it developed its website. The substantial costs of 'rebranding' were entirely attributable to its own decision to take that risk.

The developer may be responsible for registering the site with search engines and organising pop-up banners to be displayed with a list of search results to enhance the retrieval rates of the site and generally raise its profile. The costs of all this will, of course, be passed on to the client and it may be better if arrangements are made for the client to take over responsibility for recurring fees and costs associated with such things, particularly if the client wants to make it easier to switch to another developer for subsequent maintenance.

Statistics will be generated by the website relating to matters such as number of hits, the 'close rate' (rate of orders compared with number of hits), the 'click rate' (number of clicks on, for example, a web advertisement, compared to the number of visits to the page containing it) and the 'clickstream' (the path used by visitors). These can all provide useful market research information. The website developer should be responsible for producing periodic reports of these statistics and in a form intelligible to the client.

OTHER ISSUES

The precise nature and content of a website development contract will depend, of course, on the requirements of the client, the obligations imposed on the developer and the allocation of risk between them. From what has been discussed in this chapter, it is clear that there are many variables. For example, the client may decide to provide all the content for the developer to format and structure and to provide all the underlying software. Whilst website development contracts have many points in common with contracts for writing software generally, there are some particular issues that are relevant. Unlike back-office computer systems, a website is a window through which the world can see the company, contact it and do business with it. A website is a supreme marketing tool but a slow, unwieldy, badly structured and unattractive website can send out all the wrong messages and be very detrimental to the company's future prospects. It is, therefore, vitally important to bear this in mind when writing the specification and the contract for the design and development of the website. Feature-creep seems to be a particular danger with website development contracts and is likely to be a reflection of the inability of both parties to fully appreciate what the other expects.

It is usual for a website to contain both a privacy policy and a set of terms and conditions. The chances are that these will be written by the client or by the client's legal advisers to be incorporated into the overall design by the developer. Where this is so, and the same goes for any other content provided to the developer by or on behalf of the client, it is important for the client to check that it has been transposed accurately and that the style is appropriate. It is also usual to ensure that anyone placing an order has had an opportunity to read the terms and conditions and privacy policy and has had an opportunity to download them. Obtaining positive assent to the terms and conditions is also important, even though the person placing an order has not bothered to read them. Other issues affecting the design of the website will be how personal data is to be collected, processed and stored. This will be discussed in more depth in Part 5, on data protection law.

SUMMARY

- The specification is a key document and should address, *inter alia*:
  - browser compatibility;
  - where and how the website will be hosted and the bandwidth used;
  - in the case of an e-commerce website, how it will integrate with back-office systems;
  - domain name registration and renewal;
  - registration with search engines and using sponsored links with logos;
  - security against fraud and data protection issues;
  - form and nature of content and its delivery;
  - external links;
  - milestones;
  - testing and acceptance;
  - maintenance.
- Important terms in a website development contract include:
  - the obligations of the parties;
  - performance issues;
  - intellectual property rights in the website and third-party rights;
  - variations to the contract and pricing them;
  - termination of the contract;
  - dispute resolution, applicable law and jurisdiction.
- A term that the service will be carried out using reasonable care and skill will be implied.
- Exclusion clauses are controlled by the Unfair Contract Terms Act 1977.
- Feature-creep is a common problem and a mechanism to deal with it should be included in the contract.

18

Website development contracts

SELF-TEST QUESTION

1   Electricals Ltd sells consumer electrical products and, although it has had a web presence at www.electricals.co.uk for a number of years, its website was not an e-commerce website, it simply provided information about the company and its goods for sale. It decided to upgrade its website to a fully-functioning e-commerce website which would be hosted by its internet service provider GBOL plc. Electricals Ltd made a contract with Webwise & Co, a firm of web-site designers to carry out the necessary work. Discuss what terms should be included in the contract and explain their importance.

For further resources and updates please go to the Companion Website accompanying this book at **www.mylawchamber.co.uk/bainbridgeIT**

19 Outsourcing contracts

INTRODUCTION

A situation whereby a contractor provides services to a client in respect of information technology may be described as outsourcing or facilities management. It is different to a straightforward contract for services in that the client usually retains some management control, shared with the contractor. 'Outsourcing' occurs where an outside contractor takes over the operation, maintenance and future development of a particular business function, not usually being a core function of the client's business, such as the information technology function. There are a number of issues related to outsourcing and we have all experienced the degradation in quality that is sometimes associated with outsourcing of 'call centres', particularly to overseas organisatons.

It is has become common for organisations to outsource certain of their functions and processes by engaging specialist contractors. A typical area for outsourcing is information technology and there are numerous specialist companies, including IBM, that specialise in taking over and running an organisation's information technology facilities and related functions. Outsourcing contracts may range from simply running the client's computer ('platform operations') to full applications operations where the contractor takes complete responsibility for all the client's information technology operations up to and including call centre facilities.

Advantages obtained by engaging a specialist information technology outsourcing contractor include:

- *the access to knowledge capital* – the outsourcing company will have specialist technology, knowledge and skills;
- *cost savings* – there may be efficiency gains, for example, the outsourcing company may have a number of clients which share its equipment and expertise;
- *reduction in staffing* – the client's information technology staff may be transferred to the outsourcing company which then takes on the responsibilities of employer;
- *added value* – the knowledge, skills and experience of the staff of the outsourcing company may result in new and the improved uses of the client's information technology functions;
- *responsiveness and flexibility* – the outsourcing company is more likely to be able to respond to technological change;
- *savings in capital expenditure* – the client is likely to see a significant reduction in capital expenditure, for example, for new hardware and software;
- *maintenance* – the client may be released from responsibilities to maintain and upgrade hardware and software;

- *strategic issues* – the outsourcing company may take over responsibilities for developing and suggesting future strategies in relation to the information technology function.

Outsourcing information technology facilities will not be appropriate in all cases and many organisations may prefer to keep their information technology function in-house, for example, for reasons of confidentiality or privacy.

An outsourcing management contract is likely to be considered primarily as a contract for the supply of a service subject to the implied terms under the Supply of Goods and Services Act 1982. Section 13 of that Act requires that the service is performed using reasonable care and skill. The outsourcing contract is likely to also have express terms which go beyond that.

The contractual framework for outsourcing is usually through a service level agreement which has to provide for:

- the overall control and management of the outsourcing operation and decision-making processes;
- transfers of staff, equipment and software (including necessary licences) and employment responsibilities where staff are transferred;
- the level and nature of the service provided;
- supervision, performance and performance targets and milestones and remedial action to be taken if targets are not met;
- payment mechanisms and methods of calculating payment for additional or modified obligations;
- variations and impacts of unforeseen circumstances such as strikes and lock-outs;
- third-party rights, including intellectual property rights, and third-party software licences;
- warranties, liabilities, insurances and indemnities;
- renewal and termination and the impact of termination including intellectual property rights and the transferability back to the client or to another outsourcing company;
- systems to deal with dispute resolution.

The form and content of a particular agreement will be constrained by the circumstances and should be tailored to those circumstances. It is not possible to predict every aspect that should be covered in the agreement. There follows a discussion of some of the terms commonly found in outsourcing contracts.

DEFINITIONS

As with most forms of agreement it is useful to start with important definitions. This is particularly important in terms of outsourcing contracts due to the great number of issues involved, for example where existing equipment or software is being transferred to the outsourcing company. The definitions must be precise, setting out the services provided, staffing levels, experience and qualifications, location of service, telecommunications and data transfers, equipment and software to be used, acquired or transferred. In most cases, the service will be provided remotely but, where it is provided wholly or partly on the client's premises the extent of the premises and other facilities being made available should also be spelt out. The definitions are likely to refer to the specifications, schedules of equipment and software.

OUTSOURCING COMPANY'S OBLIGATIONS

The services provided by the outsourcing company will be of prime concern. A schedule to the agreement will usually set out the services provided in detail. In addition to the ongoing service provision, there may be an obligation to provide training to the client's staff who will be the direct recipients of the services provided. For example, if part of the service is the provision of a look-up database, some of the client's staff will need training in the access to and use of the database. Other services may include advising future developments and strategic issues, new potential uses and functionality. The client is likely to want guidance on the acquisition of additional software (which may be written by the outsourcing company for the client). The outsourcing company may also carry out periodic reviews of the client's information technology requirements, making recommendations for future action as appropriate.

In some cases, the outsourcing company may use its own staff, equipment and software for the benefit of the client. It may even use another client's hardware and software on a shared basis to provide the services to the client. Again, this must be spelt out and provision included to deal with upgrades, new applications and other changes.

CLIENT'S OBLIGATIONS

A client outsourcing its information technology function for the first time may transfer its existing hardware and software to the outsourcing company. Hardware may be sold or hired or, where it is leased by the client, the lease may be transferred to the outsourcing company (providing the leasing agreement allows this). There may be copyright and database assignments or licences in relation to the client's own software and transfers of any licences in third-party software, if the licences can be transferred. If not, the outsourcing company will have to acquire its own licences from the copyright owner. Where the client owns rights in software to be transferred to the outsourcing company, it is sensible to grant licences to the outsourcing company for the duration of the contract. If the rights are assigned instead, there should be provision for an assignment back to the client on termination.

Where the outsourcing company provides the services at the client's premises, in whole or in part, the implications of this must be catered for, such as health and safety issues, occupier's liability and insurances. It may be that the agreement grants a licence or lease of the relevant office space to the outsourcing company until termination. This should provide for a period of time after termination to allow the outsourcing company to remove its equipment. It may seem unnecessary to licence or even lease premises to the outsourcing company (which will only build the cost of this into the overall fee) but it could prove useful in the calculation of any changes to the payments due should it later be decided to move the information technology function offsite, reduce the extent of the office space provided to the outsourcing company or where an extension to the time for performance of the service is granted. This could happen where there is a delay caused by the client.

It is highly probable that the client has a number of subsisting contracts and licences with third parties which may be affected by the change to outsourcing the information technology function. Apart from licences, the client may have current hardware or software maintenance agreements with third parties. The benefit of these agreements will have to be assigned to the outsourcing company if possible. Alternatively, novation may be possible. The assignability of the benefits of current contracts and licences must be determined before the outsourcing contract is made so that provision can be made for this. If it is not possible to assign, transfer or novate existing contracts and licences, they may have to be terminated and provision in the out-sourcing contract made for the acquisition of new contracts and licences. In cases of doubt, the outsourcing contract may include a best endeavours clause to the effect that the client will use its best endeavours to secure the necessary assignments or transfers or, failing that, to obtain equiv-alent equipment or software by alternate means. The cost implications must also be addressed by the outsourcing contract.

EMPLOYMENT OBLIGATIONS

Where a client outsources his information technology function for the first time, there will usually be a transfer of staff to the outsourcing company. Where this is so, the effect of the Transfer of Undertakings (Protection of Employment) Regulations 2006[1] must be borne in mind. These Regulations, which replaced the earlier 1981 Regulations of the same name, apply to secure the contractual and statutory employment rights of transferred employees. Under Regulation 3, the Regulations apply, *inter alia*, to service provision changes, such as:

- a transfer of activities from a client (A) to a contractor (C);
- a transfer of the activities from such a contractor or (C) to another contractor (C1) and so on;
- a transfer of the activities from a contractor (C, C1, etc. as the case may be) back to the client (A).

A contractor includes a sub-contractor. An example of the possibilities is shown in Fig. 19.1. This shows a service provision change from a client (A) to a contractor (C1). Later, the service activi-ties are transferred to a second contractor (C2) which sub-contracts out part of the activities to a sub-contractor (SC). Later still, contractor (C2) then transfers the activities to a third contrac-tor (C3) (this will bring the sub-contract to an end, if it still exists at that time). Finally, contrac-tor (C3) transfers the activities back to the client which once again carries out those activities itself.

All these transfers are within the Regulations where there is an organised grouping of employees in Great Britain[2] which has as its principle purpose the performance of those activi-ties on behalf of the client (though not where the activities consist wholly or mainly in the supply of goods for the client's use). The Regulations apply to private and public undertakings engaged in economic activities whether or not they are operating for gain.

Generally, employees' employment rights are protected and their contracts of employment are not terminated but transferred to the contractor. These rights include unfair dismissal rights and redundancy rights. Normally, a variation to the contract of employment is not permitted although may be possible where the employee agrees if the sole or principal reason connected with the transfer is economic, technical or organisational, entailing changes in the workforce or a reason unconnected with the transfer. If an employee is dismissed where the sole or principal reason for the dismissal is the transfer itself or a reason connected with the transfer that is not an economic, technical or organisational reason entailing a change in the workforce, the dis-missal will be treated as unfair. The transferor must provide the transferee with 'employee liab-ility information'. This includes the identity and age of the employee, information required to be given to employees under the Employment Rights Act 1996, information as to disciplinary and grievance procedures taken against or by the employee, court or tribunal cases, claims or actions

---

[1] TUPE Regulations 2006.
[2] The Regulations are modified for Northern Ireland.

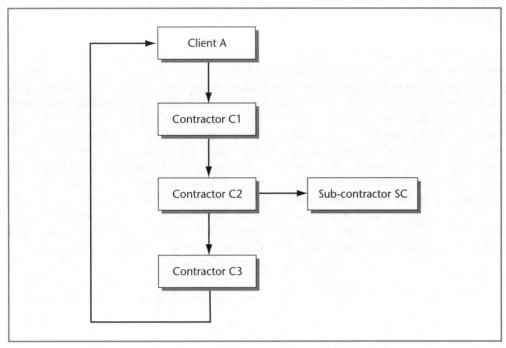

Figure 19.1 Service change provisions under TUPE Regulations 2006

in the previous two years. Further information about collective agreements is required to be given. The outsourcing contract should contain a reference to the relevant obligations under the TUPE Regulations 2006 if employees are to be transferred. There are further provisions in the Regulations dealing with pension rights.

DURATION OF CONTRACT

A fixed period of time should be set for the provision of the service. It may be for one year, renewable by agreement or for a number of years, subject to termination provisions, including no-fault termination. Often a fixed period is used with automatic renewal subject to agreement as to changes to services and payment to reflect planned changes to the information technology function which, by its very nature, are likely to be fairly frequent. Changing outsourcing contractor or reverting the activities back to the client will probably take some time, for example, in obtaining quotations, going through a tendering process or where the client needs to prepare to take over the activities itself. There should be sufficient time allowed for these eventualities and a deadline for renewal to be agreed is usual. If the existing contract is not renewed, the client will have a reasonable time to engage another contractor or make the necessary arrangements to carry out the activities in house once more. The process of renewal can be seen as a major and important exercise requiring considerable evaluation, planning and negotiation between the parties. Of course, the ideal outcome in an outsourcing contract is for the parties to establish and maintain a workable and mutually beneficial long-term relationship. This desiradatum is, however, difficult to achieve and sustain so the contract should make switching contractors or reverting to performing the activities in-house is made as trouble-free as possible.

PAYMENT

Some of the most disputed terms in contracts are those relating to payment. This is particularly so in the context of the provision of a service over long periods of time. It is even more likely if the specification of the services to be provided, descriptions of targets and milestones is insufficiently precise or is ambiguous. It is essential that the contractor knows exactly what is to be provided and what activities are to be carried out together with relevant dates and deadlines. It is also important to make sure that the contract has a precise mechanism for calculating payments due and their timing and any retention monies kept back. There should also be the means of calculating additional payments for equipment used or activities undertaken not included in the original contract. The nature of any outsourcing activity means that variations and addition to the services provided are common. This is even more so in the field of information technology.

For a lengthy outsourcing contract, it is likely that the outsourcing company will want prices to be index linked in some way to allow for inflationary costs, such as changes in equipment and labour costs, including changes in costs such as employer's national insurance contributions.

Including a mechanism for adjustment in payment due in the case of late or defective provision of services, for example, in the form of liquidated damages for late delivery, is also sensible. The client will expect a reduction in payments due to the outsourcing company in respect of any downtime or lack of availability to service. This will entail an examination of the potential impacts of such occurrences and an agreement as to what the financial implications will be to insert appropriate provisions into the contract.

SERVICE CHANGE

Given the complexity of many outsourcing contracts it is almost inevitable that changes will be required to the nature and level of service. For example, once the service provision has been underway for a period of time, the client may decide that it would be beneficial to enhance the level of service or include additional functions and activities in the service agreement. Alternatively, there may be new developments in hardware or software which can add value to the services provided. A decision may be made to move the service provision wholly or partly off-site or on-site as the case may be. Given the nature of information technology and its fast rate of change, it is difficult to predict all the changes that may occur even over a relatively short period of time, and some of the changes may be substantial. If a major change now looks attractive and which could not reasonably be envisaged and provided for in the initial agreement, the parties may find that they have to engage in some significant negotiation, perhaps with the outsourcing company submitting costed proposals and alternatives to form the basis of negotiation. Of course, change does not necessarily mean increased costs, in many cases as information technology becomes more sophisticated and powerful, there might be significant reductions in costs coupled with improvement in the service provided.

In some cases, the changes may be implemented by means of a variation to the contract. In other cases, the changes may be so fundamental and radical that the parties might want to consider a novation of the contract with a new agreement drawn up to reflect the radical changes in the service provided. In other cases it may be a matter of modifying the service level agreement by mutual agreement the next time the contract is renewed.

WARRANTIES

Both parties will be expected to provide warranties. The outsourcing company is likely to be subject to the following warranties:

- to use reasonable care and skill in the performance of the services (this will be implied anyway under section 13 of the Supply of Goods and Services Act 1982);
- to assign competent staff to the service provision who are adequately trained (such training to be updated and enhanced as appropriate) and, where appropriate, engage competent subcontractors or consultants;
- that the outsourcing company has the right to use the software it provides or acquires for the purposes of providing the services;
- that any software provided by or used by the company in the provision of the services will be 'fit for purpose', free from serious errors and viruses and other harmful code.

The client may be subject to the following warranties:

- that the client owns the rights in any software it will transfer (by assignment or licensing) to the outsourcing company or, if not, it has the benefit of appropriate licences which are transferable;
- where licences and third-party contracts (such as equipment leases) are transferred to the outsourcing company, there are no subsisting or unresolved breaches and provision is made for payment of any unpaid fees or other payments;
- that there are no outstanding claims by employees to be transferred with respect to salaries, wages or other benefits nor any outstanding disciplinary or grievance procedures and no unfair dismissal or wrongful dismissal claims (such matters, within the previous two years, are among the information that must be provided under the TUPE Regulations 2006);
- that any equipment transferred has been appropriately upgraded and is free from defects and any software transferred to the outsourcing company is the current version, 'fit for purpose', free from serious errors and viruses and other harmful code.

The general rule is that all software contains errors, most of which may be quite minor and insignificant. It may be that the software does not contain an error as such but fails to interact with other software as well as it should. It is unreasonable to expect a warranty that software is completely error free and the presence of minor errors does not necessarily mean that the software concerned is not fit for its purpose, as confirmed in the Court of Appeal in *Saphena Computing v Allied Collection Agencies* [1995] FSR 605. Of course, the detection of errors may trigger an obligation on the part of the supplier of the software to correct them expediently and software licences and maintenance agreements should be checked to make sure the provisions dealing with error correction are satisfactory. This may not be possible with ready-made software but even then, it should be checked to see if there is suitable provision, for example, for downloading upgrades.

In terms of errors, one approach is to limit the warranty to serious errors and have some form of liquidated damages associated with them if they cause the software to be inoperable for a significant amount of time. A serious error may be defined in the agreement in terms of its consequences, for example, where it interferes with the service provision so as to prevent it or degrade it for more than a set period of time.

Of course, there are likely to be further warranties, depending on the nature of the functions outsourced, the equipment and software used. Where equipment is included, there may be a warranty that it does not infringe third-party rights, such as patent rights.

PERFORMANCE MONITORING

The performance of the outsourcing contract should be subject to continuing assessment and quality control. Performance against agreed targets must be checked and any deficiencies in this respect can inform requests for improvement or change. Both the client and outsourcing company should allocate individuals to this role with a system of regular meetings where unsatisfactory performance can be considered and plans for improvements agreed. The same applies to changes to modify or enhance the nature and level of service provided. The cost implications, if any, should also be agreed at such meetings. Consequently, the meetings should be attended by persons from both sides who have the authority to bind their respective organisations. In some circumstances, the client may need access to the outsourcing company's premises and equipment for the purposes of monitoring and assessing performance. Provision should be made for such access to be available, usually by giving formal notice.

Sometimes, unsatisfactory performance may be a result of the acts or omissions of the client or of a third party. Where the cause is a sub-contractor or consultant engaged by the outsourcing company, it will be liable for that. If, however, a sub-contractor is used which has been nominated by the client, liability for any performance-related issues resulting from failures attributable to the nominated sub-contractor must be addressed by the contract. It is not unusual for a nominated sub-contractor which has particular specialisations to be imposed on an outsourcing company who takes over full responsibility for the sub-contractor's work. An example, where a nominated sub-contractor may be used is where the service provision requires access to a particular database owned and operated by the sub-contractor, with no reasonable alternative available. For the sake of expediency, the client may have entered into negotiations and obtained prices from the sub-contractor as a preliminary to awarding the outsourcing contract which will include the nominated sub-contract.

SPECIALLY WRITTEN SOFTWARE

The outsourcing company may write software specifically to meet the client's service provision requirements. The ownership of copyright and other intellectual property rights, such as the database right, should be addressed. Usually, the client will think ahead and want some continuing right to use the software after termination of the outsourcing contract. This may entail an assignment of rights, an exclusive licence or a non-exclusive licence. One possible arrangement would be for the client to have an exclusive licence during the currency of the outsourcing contract and a royalty-free non-exclusive licence thereafter. It is impossible to be prescriptive and it all depends on the circumstances. Both parties will need to think this through and make appropriate provision in the contract. Sometimes, the writing of such software may be subject to a separate contract preliminary to the outsourcing contract but in some cases it may not exist at the time the outsourcing contract is entered into. Where this is so, there is no problem with assignment or licensing as the Copyright, Designs and Patents Act 1988 provides for the prospective ownership of copyright and the granting of licences in software not yet in existence. For example, under section 91 of the Act, where the agreement to assign the future copyright is signed by or on behalf of the prospective owner of the copyright then when the copyright comes into existence, it will automatically vest in the assignee. For existing software, the equivalent requirement is a written assignment signed by or on behalf of the present owner of the copyright. Assignments are normally made with 'full title guarantee'.

The contract should describe 'future copyright and other rights' as copyright, database right and all other intellectual property rights which will or may come into existence in respect of software specifically written for the client during the provision of the service by the outsourcing company or any third party engaged by the outsourcing company. If third parties are likely to be engaged to write software, there should be a term requiring the outsourcing company to use its best endeavours to acquire such rights or licences and to do everything necessary to make such rights and licences effective, to assign the rights or the benefit of licences to the client, to execute any necessary documents and register any registrable transactions. This last aspect will only apply where the software is likely to be the subject of a patent, trade mark or registered design.

Of course, where software is specially written for the client by the outsourcing company, provision should be made for an escrow agreement if the source code and other preparatory materials are not made available to the client. This will enable the client to take possession of the source code should the outsourcing company go out of business or terminates the agreement prematurely. The position of the source code should also be considered following completion of the outsourcing contract, for example, where the function is transferred to another outsourcing company or where it reverts to the client.

PRIVACY AND DATA PROTECTION LAW

Inevitably, an outsourcing contract will include the processing or personal data, some of which may be sensitive personal data. Data protection law will almost certainly be relevant to the processing activities. Apart from data protection law, there may be issues relating to individuals' right to respect for private and family life and the right of freedom of expression, under Articles 8 and 10 respectively of the Council of Europe Convention for the Protection of Human Rights and Fundamental Freedoms. The outsourcing contract must address these. Although data protection law and the impact of the Convention are covered in depth in Part 5 of this Book, a few points can be made at this stage in relation to outsourcing contracts.

Basic provisions

A data controller is defined as '... a person who (either alone or jointly or in common with other persons) determines the purposes for which and the manner in which any personal data are, or are to be, processed': section 1(1) of the Data Protection Act 1998. A data processor is defined as '... a person, other than an employee of the data controller who processes data on behalf of the data controller'. Data controllers have to comply with the Data Protection Act 1998 and, unless exempt, have to notify their processing activities. Data processors are only required to comply with the 'security requirements' in the seventh data protection principle. This requires that:

> Appropriate technical and organisational measures shall be taken against unauthorised or unlawful processing of personal data and against accidental loss or destruction of, or damage to, personal data.

There are also requirements that a data controller chooses a data processor who offers sufficient guarantees in relation to security measures and takes reasonable steps to ensure compliance with those measures. Furthermore, where a data processor is used, the processing must be carried out under a contract, made or evidenced in writing and which requires the data processor to comply with the obligations imposed by the seventh data protection principle.

Data controller or data processor?

The question that immediately arises is whether an outsourcing company is a data controller or a data processor. If the former, it will be subject to the full range of obligations under the Data Protection Act 1998 and, unless the processing activities involved are exempt, it will have to notify its processing activities. If the latter, the client will be subject to the Act and, unless exempt, will have to notify the processing activities. In practice, the client is already likely to have notified the processing activities (especially if this is the first time they have been outsourced). Importantly for the outsourcing contract there must be terms imposing the security measures on the outsourcing company.

Terms dealing with data protection

Of course, no definitive answer can be given to the question 'controller or processor?'. It will depend on the circumstances. In some cases, both the client and outsourcing company may be deemed to be joint data controllers. Whatever the position is, it must be addressed by the contract and appropriate provision made for compliance with data protection law by both parties as appropriate. For example, if the outsourcing company is the data processor, there should be an express reference to the security measures imposed by the seventh principle and other terms dealing with, for example, data flows between the parties, permitted disclosures, informing data subjects and dealing with data subject access requests. There should also be a term requiring the outsourcing company to take reasonable steps to ensure the reliability of any employees having access to the data. Some form of indemnity may be usefully included in the agreement to cover a failure of the outsourcing company to ensure the required level of security of the data and claims for compensation made by data subjects.

FURTHER TERMS IN OUTSOURCING CONTRACTS

An outsourcing contract will have other terms dealing with matters such as liability for defective performance, liquidated damages, insurances, staff poaching, whether the benefit of the agreement can be assigned, confidentiality, alternative dispute resolution (most important in an outsourcing contract) and/or arbitration, termination and *force majeure* (a serious and unanticipated event which makes it impossible to complete the contract as originally envisaged), applicable law and jurisdiction.

There may be a requirement that the outsourcing company arranges a performance bond to deal with the situation where the outsourcing company is no longer able to complete the performance of the contract, perhaps because of its insolvency. This releases a sum of money which can be used to engage another company to complete the contract. There should also be terms dealing with security arrangements including back-up facilities, disaster recovery, access protocols, encryption, password systems and their maintenance.

SUMMARY

- An outsourcing contract is primarily one for the provision of services.
- It is important to have precise definitions and specifications of the services to be performed.
- Both parties obligations should be spelt out in detail.
- Where employees are transferred with the function being outsourced:
  - the TUPE Regulations 2006 apply to protect their employment rights;
  - the transferor must supply the transferee with employment liability information.
- The outsourcing contract must make provision for:
  - the duration, renewal and termination of the contract;
  - payment and methods of calculating payment for additional or varied services;
  - mechanisms for dealing with change and variations to service levels and activities.
- Typical warranties include those covering:
  - performance of the services;
  - fitness for purpose of equipment and software;
  - ownership of intellectual property rights;
  - freedom from interference with third-party rights;
  - where employees are being transferred, that there are no outstanding claims or other issues.
- Ongoing and effective performance monitoring should be provided for.
- Where the outsourcing company writes software for the purpose of providing the services, copyright ownership and licensing should be addressed.
- Where personal data is being processed by the outsourcing company:
  - data protection law (and privacy laws) will apply;
  - including compliance with the Data Protection Act 1998;
  - especially important are security measures and the need to deal with these in the contract.

19

Outsourcing contracts

SELF-TEST QUESTIONS

Note: there is only one correct answer to each multiple choice question.

1   **Which one of the following statements is CORRECT in relation to a contract to outsource a client's information technology function and activities?**

   (a) It is a contract for services subject to the implied terms under the Supply of Goods and Services Act 1982.

   (b) It is a contract of service governed by the Employment Rights Act 1996.

   (c) It is a contract *sui generis* without any statutory implied terms.

   (d) It is a sub-contract under which the client becomes the main contractor.

2   **Which one of the following statements is CORRECT in relation to a service provision change involving a transfer of employees to the company now taking responsibility for the service provision (the transferee)?**

(a) The previous contracts of employment are terminated and new contracts of employment are made as between the employees and the transferee, such that there is an effective break in service by the employees.

(b) The TUPE Regulations 2006 apply also to sub-contracts.

(c) The transferee may dismiss any of the employees transferred for any reason whatever.

(d) The TUPE Regulations 2006 only apply to private undertakings engaged in an economic activity for gain.

3   **In relation to copyright in software written by the contractor (CO) under an outsourcing contract for the purposes of providing the relevant service to the client (CL), which one of the following statements is CORRECT?**

(a) CL is the first owner of the copyright simply because it was written for the purposes of providing the relevant service.

(b) The ownership of the copyright is 'at large' and automatically transfers to subsequent outsourcing companies until such time as the function reverts to CL, when it becomes the owner of the copyright.

(c) CO is the first owner of the copyright unless there is a term in the contract assigning copyright to CL (the contract being signed by or on behalf of CO) or there is some other written assignment of the copyright to CL signed by or on behalf of CO which pre-dates the writing of the software.

(d) It is an implied term that the copyright will be jointly owned by CO and CL unless the contract makes provision to the contrary.

4   **In a case where an outsourcing company is deemed to be a data processor and the client is the data controller for the purposes of the Data Protection Act 1998, which one of the following statements is NOT CORRECT?**

(a) The processing must be carried out under a contract made or evidenced in writing.

(b) The contract must require the outsourcing company to comply with the obligations imposed by the seventh data protection principle.

(c) The outsourcing contractor must take reasonable steps to ensure the reliability of employees of his who have access to the data.

(d) The outsourcing company must notify the processing activity unless exempt.

5   **Discuss the advantages and disadvantages of outsourcing contracts for the provision of information technology services and suggest situations where outsourcing is appropriate.**

20 Hardware contracts

INTRODUCTION

Computer hardware may be purchased outright, hired or leased. Much of what has already been discussed in relation to computer software contracts, in particular contracts for the writing or modification of software, will apply to contracts for the acquisition of hardware. Very often, the purchase of or hire of computer equipment will include software, such as operating system software, computer programming languages, utility programs or applications programs. These items of software will be subject to collateral licence agreements.

Computer software is important; the choice of the software best suited to the client's requirements is critical and this can determine the hardware requirements. Other issues are also important such as the suitability of the hardware for networking, internet access and telecommunications functions. Data storage and transmission and data security are also significant factors in the choice of hardware as is its compatibility with existing systems and equipment. In many cases, the suitability of computer equipment and software for carrying out e-commerce operations will be a major consideration.

This chapter looks at some of the terms and issues of particular relevance to hardware contracts. First, the question of who bears the risk, for example, if computers on their way to the buyer or lessee are stolen, damaged or lost.

PASSING OF PROPERTY IN HARDWARE AND RISK

It is all too common for computer equipment to be stolen. This varies from the casual thief who walks in off the street and takes a laptop computer left in an unlocked office to large-scale organised theft. In the case of the latter, it may be that a consignment of computers or computer chips on route to the buyer is stolen. The total value can be very high. In a contract to acquire computer equipment, it is important to deal with this risk and insurance to cover the loss. As between seller and buyer, where goods are in transit, there are certain rules to decide when the property in the goods (that is, ownership) passes and which party bears the risk. The Sale of Goods Act 1979 provides these basic rules. Section 18 of the Act states, *inter alia*, that where the contract is for specific goods in a deliverable state, property passes when the contract is made. If something has to be done to the goods by the seller to put them into a deliverable state, property passes when the seller has done that thing and the buyer has notice that it has been done. This could be the case where the seller has to install an optical drive, a computer chip or motherboard or even install software. Different rules apply in other cases, such as where the seller has first to acquire the goods subject to the contract. In this case, the property passes when the goods are unconditionally appropriated to the contract by the seller with the assent of the buyer or by the buyer with the assent of the seller. The latter possibility, goods being appropriated to the contract by the buyer, could apply where the goods are growing crops and the buyer harvests them.

Section 20 of the Act contains the basic rule that the risk remains with the seller until such time as the property in the goods passes to the buyer. This is so, whether or not the goods have been delivered at that time. Where delivery is delayed through the fault of either party, that party bears the risk in relation to any loss which might not have occurred but for the fault. The rule as to the passing of risk in a consumer contract is different and, in such a contract, the risk stays with the seller until the goods are delivered to the consumer.

Rather than rely on the rules in the Sale of Goods Act 1979, it is usual for the parties to a sale or lease contract for computer equipment to provide for the passing of property and risk expressly in the contract. If not, there is a possibility that the party which bears the risk of loss or damage during transit does not realise this and fails to take out appropriate insurance.

In *Computer 2000 Distribution Ltd* v *ICM Computer Solutions plc* [2004] EWCA Civ 1634, a fraudster, purportedly acting on behalf of a reputable company, AMEC plc, placed three orders with ICM for laptop computers. The value of the orders was over £130,000. ICM, in turn, placed three orders with the claimant computer suppliers asking for delivery to a named person (the name used by the fraudster) at a business address. When they were delivered, a security guard signed for them (there was no suggestion that the security guard was implicated in the fraud). AMEC had never carried on business at the delivery address and the fraudster later collected the computers. Neither he nor the computers were ever seen again. It was confirmed in the Court of Appeal that the computers had been delivered in accordance with the purchase orders to the person (the fraudster) named in those orders. ICM's standard terms and conditions stated that ownership would pass to ICM after delivery in accordance with the purchase order. Consequently, ICM was liable to the claimants for the price of the computers they delivered. ICM had earlier been the victim of a similar fraud and failed in an action for the price of computers to be delivered under a lease agreement. Rather than delivering the computers to the agreed delivery address, ICM allowed the fraudster, purporting to be from a reputable company, to collect the computers in person: *ICM Computer Solutions plc* v *Black Horse Finance Ltd* (unreported) 24 November 2000.

PERFORMANCE

The performance of software is directly related to the computer's performance. The speed of operation of the computer will be very important and a contract for the purchase or hire of computer equipment should make reference to this. Information about processing speeds, storage capacities, data transfer and networking capabilities will be paramount. The purchaser must satisfy himself as to the performance of the equipment, bearing in mind the environment in which the equipment will be working.

Simple benchmark speed tests may not provide a very good picture of the computer's performance if it will be used to carry out many different tasks at the same time, with multiple concurrent access to data files. The client should think about the operating system and whether it is a common one able to run a large variety of applications programs. Similar considerations apply to networking hardware and software. Another point which might be relevant is whether there are any limitations on the number of data files the computer will permit to be in use at the same time and whether programs and databases will be installed on a central server or on individual PCs or workstations.

REPRESENTATIONS AND ENTIRE AGREEMENT CLAUSES

A salesperson will usually extol the virtues of the equipment he is trying to sell and he will try to convince the would-be purchaser that it is everything he needs. If the equipment turns out to be totally unsuited to the client's needs, the supplier will probably point to a term in the contract of sale which states that the printed agreement represents the entire agreement between the parties and nothing said or done in preliminary negotiations is part of the contract. This ploy may not always work, as the case below demonstrates.

In *Mackenzie Patten & Co* v *British Olivetti Ltd* (unreported) 11 January 1984, the claimant was a firm of solicitors which wanted a computer to handle its accounts and the defendant company was approached by the claimant with this in mind. Following negotiations with the defendant's salesman, the claimant agreed to obtain one of the defendant's computers under a leasing agreement with a third party. The computer proved totally unsuitable for the claimant's needs and the claimant's staff was incapable of using the computer effectively even following training by the defendant. After hearing expert evidence, the judge decided that the computer was obsolete and not suitable for the claimant's requirements. Indeed, as the claimant firm was a small one, it was questionable whether a computer was needed at all. (Things are much different now; even the smallest firm needs computer technology, electronic mail and access to the internet.)

The judge held that the claimant relied on the salesman's statements when entering the leasing agreement. The statements operated as a collateral warranty and, as they were not true, there was a breach of this warranty. There was an entire agreement clause in the contract but this was held to be ineffective as it was stated in terms of a contract of sale and, in fact, the contract entered into by the claimant was a leasing contract. No sale to the claimant took place or was contemplated (the claimant could not afford to buy the computer outright). The contract contained an exclusion clause but the judge held that the defendant had failed to prove that it was reasonable, applying the test in section 11 of the Unfair Contract Terms Act 1977. The judge awarded the claimant the sum of £16,204 which comprised £2,661 for payments made under the lease agreement, £12,692 for payments owing under the agreement and £851 interest. A further claim for wasted time in meetings and the like in the sum of £1,200 was dismissed by the judge as being both too vague and too remote.

If the entire agreement clause had been found to be effective to exclude the salesman's statements, the claimant would probably have had a remedy under section 2 of the Misrepresentation Act 1967, any attempt to exclude liability being subject to the reasonableness test in the Unfair Contract Terms Act 1977. Hence, suppliers of computer equipment should make every effort to ensure that the would-be purchaser is fully aware of the equipment's capabilities and limitations. The purchaser would be wise to seek independent advice and the supplier, if there is any doubt about the suitability of a particular piece of equipment, would be wise to suggest that such independent advice is sought. In particular, it is unwise to attempt to sell obsolete or unsuitable equipment to a solicitor, although, in the above case, it appears that the solicitor signed the agreement without first reading it thoroughly!

In the context of parties to a contract of equal bargaining power who are assumed to desire commercial certainty and on the assumption that the price paid reflects the risk based on the warranties that have been given, an entire agreement clause which goes on to say that one party did not rely upon any pre-contractual representation of the other will, almost certainly, deprive the first party to succeed in a claim for misrepresentation (*Watford Electronics Ltd* v *Sanderson CFL Ltd* [2002] FSR 19). Such an agreement of non-reliance will not be subject to section 3 of the Misrepresentation Act 1967. Furthermore, an entire agreement clause will deprive any collateral warranty previously given of any legal effect (*Inntrepreneur Pub Co Ltd* v *East Crown Ltd* [2000] 41 EG 209).

For a misrepresentation to have legal effect in the light of an entire agreement clause, according to the Court of Appeal in *Lowe* v *Lombank Ltd* [1960] 1 All ER 611, the statement must be:

- clear and unambiguous;
- such that a reasonable person would expect the other party to understand that he was meant to act on the basis of the representation; and
- the other party had entered into the agreement on the basis that the representation was true.

Businesses and other organisations having the advantage of professional advisers are unlikely to fall within what can only be described as an exception to the basic rule. As Mr Justice Lightman said in the *Inntrepreneur* case:

> The purpose of an entire agreement clause is to preclude a party to a written agreement from threshing through the undergrowth and finding, in the course of negotiations, some (chance) remark or statement (often long-forgotten or difficult to recall or explain) upon which to found a claim . . .

MAINTENANCE AND UPGRADES

The contract should state exactly who does what in terms of installation and initial testing. Once the equipment is installed, how well will the supplier support it? Maintenance will probably be provided for by a separate contract, renewable annually, and the client should check this contract to see what it has to say on the point of speed of response to a breakdown. If repairs have to be made to the computer equipment, does the client have to pay for parts or labour or both and is there a minimum call-out charge? The maintenance contract may provide for the loan of alternative equipment while repairs are carried out and, if it does not so provide, it could be worth asking why not. The client should also check whether third party maintenance is a possibility.

Sooner or later the computer equipment will become obsolete as faster, more powerful equipment is continually being developed. This can have one of two consequences. First, the new equipment is better in so many respects and so different that there is no possibility of upgrading the old equipment to the new standards. It is then a matter of making do, standing by the existing equipment, consolidating it and adding improvements when they become available with a view to reviewing the situation in a year or two, when the quality and performance of the new equipment has been fully tested by others. The general acceptance of equipment amongst the computer world is very important. Sometimes, a new computer or processor will catch on and sell in volume and this will then encourage the leading software companies to produce appropriate software for the new machine, making it an even more attractive proposition. Once a new computer attracts the attention of the software companies it is well on its way to becoming established. It is very tempting to stay with the market leaders when buying computer equipment. As the old adage used to go, 'no one was ever fired for buying IBM!'

A second consequence of the announcement of new, improved equipment is that it may be possible to upgrade the existing equipment to those standards, and the new equipment may be in the form of an upgrade. When buying computer equipment, it is worthwhile finding out what the manufacturer's attitude is to existing customers regarding upgrades or new equipment. Will the improved equipment be sympathetically priced as far as existing customers are concerned? Will a generous trade-in be allowed on the old equipment or is there a good second-hand market for the manufacturer's equipment? Does the manufacturer have a history of upwardly compatible machines or does he bring out new equipment that is totally unlike the old equipment? Does he change operating systems frequently?

Ideally, the manufacturer should have a policy of building on his past products. It must be borne in mind that there is a dichotomy here for manufacturers. A manufacturer will want to attract new customers and, to do this, the equipment must be up to date and make use of the latest technological developments. On the other hand, the manufacturer will owe a moral duty to his loyal customers to maintain some degree of compatibility. The history of computing is one of change and abandoning out-of-date equipment and the person or company considering purchasing a computer or other computer equipment would do well to bear this in mind. There is little that can be done contractually, apart from insisting that the supplier (it will be the supplier and not the manufacturer who will be a party to the contract unless the supplier and manufacturer are one and the same) will continue to support the equipment for a reasonable period of time, regardless of whether it is later withdrawn from the market place.

To provide flexibility, a client may buy computers or other items of hardware on the basis of a contract which includes a buy-back option. If exercised this requires the hardware supplier to buy back the old hardware. The client may then put the payment towards buying new, up-to-date equipment from the hardware supplier or from a third party. Like any other provision in a contract, buy-back options must be clear in their effect. In *Boots the Chemists Ltd* v *Amdahl (UK) Ltd* (unreported) 3 November 2000, Amdahl had supplied Boots with computer processors and upgrades to their existing processors under a contract which contained a buy-back option. Boots could require Amdahl to buy-back two processors, each for over £1 m.

Following negotiations, Amdahl wrote to Boots extending the deadline for exercising the buy-back option until mid-August 1995 but the buy-back values quoted were as at August 1996. During August 1995, Boots exercised its option in respect of one of the processors and this was accepted by Amdahl and Boots bought a replacement processor from IBM. In June 1996, Boots purported to exercise its option in respect of the second processor but this was not accepted by Amdahl which withdrew its offer to buy-back the processor. Boots sold the processor elsewhere and sued Amdahl for the difference between the sale price and the buy-back value quoted by Amdahl.

The Court of Appeal accepted that Amdahl's letter was either an offer from Amdahl or confirmation of an agreement already reached orally for variation of the original agreement between the parties. This was not dependent upon Boots either upgrading one processor or retaining the other processor, as had been argued by Amdahl. A further argument that the agreement lacked consideration was unsuccessful. The Court of Appeal said that the requirement for consideration was satisfied because the variation to the original contract was capable of benefiting either party. From Amdahl's perspective, a delay in the decision of Boots to exercise its option for a buy-back of the second processor meant that Amdahl did not have to buy both back in 1995 and, if exercised in 1996, Amdahl would pay a lesser price. Amdahl also had the benefit of a further opportunity of persuading Boots to allow Amdahl back as its hardware supplier in 1996. From Boots' point of view, the benefit was the ability to postpone the decision until 1996 and there was also a detriment in as much as Boots would receive a lower price if it postponed the exercise of the option.

Computer equipment may be hired or leased. Strictly speaking the word 'lease' is used in relation to land but the term is used increasingly to describe contracts under which goods are made available for a period of time, which may be subject to renewal, for a price. 'Hire' in this context means the same but should be distinguished from a hire purchase contract. If the equipment is hired, problems of obsolescence are less important providing the hirer is not committing himself to an unduly long period. The duration of the agreement will be important as will be the presence of any term in the agreement concerning termination and the relevant circumstances.

If a much better piece of equipment is suddenly available, the hirer may wish to terminate the agreement quickly so that he can avail himself of the new equipment. The company hiring out the equipment will obviously want some form of compensation should the hirer want to return the computer equipment before the normal time and this requires a sensible compromise.

LEGAL CONTROLS

Statutory safeguards are more in evidence when it comes to hardware contracts. For example, the Sale of Goods Act 1979 will apply because computers or other related equipment come within the meaning of 'goods'; a computer is a personal chattel. This means that the important terms such as compliance with description and meeting the requirement of satisfactory quality will be implied into a contract to purchase a computer. Certain terms implied by the Sale of Goods Act 1979 are implied into all contracts of sale while others only apply where the seller sells in the course of business. Compliance with description is an example of the former while satisfactory quality is an example of the latter. Most of the contracts under consideration in this book will be in the course of business. Similar terms will be implied into hire contracts by the Supply of Goods and Services Act 1982. Some of these implied terms can be excluded or limited in the case of a non-consumer sale but only in so far as the exemption clauses purporting to do this meet the requirement of reasonableness as provided for by the Unfair Contract Terms Act 1977, sections 6 and 7 (in Scotland, sections 21 and 22 of the Unfair Contract Terms Act 1977 apply and there the test is whether the term was fair and reasonable to incorporate into the contract).

The fact that the hardware is sold complete with software does not prevent the contract from being a sale of goods contract. For example, in the Australian case of *Toby Constructions Products Pty Ltd v Computer Bar Sales Pty Ltd* (1983) 50 ALR 684, the Supreme Court of New South Wales held that the sale of a computer system, comprising both hardware and software, was a sale of goods contract. The contract was primarily one for equipment as the hardware cost was A$12,230 and the software cost was A$2,160. This logic was approved of by Scott Baker J in *St Albans City & District Council v International Computers Ltd* [1995] FSR 686. Looking at the primary objective of the contract is a sensible approach. After all, the purchaser of a washing machine which turns out to be defective would be surprised to find that the Sale of Goods Act did not apply, even if the defect was traced to the program controlling the washing cycle. Where the balance between hardware and software is more even, however, it may be better to make two separate contracts so that the application of statutory controls is predictable. In any event, using computer software must be licensed by the owner of the copyright and any other rights subsisting in it. Even if the predominant purpose is the acquisition of hardware, any accompanying software must be subject to a licence agreement.

In a distributorship agreement, a retailer may sell to the public substantial numbers of computers that are supplied by a large computer manufacturer. If the computers turn out to have some inherent defect, that can be very damaging to the distributor's business as he will have to refund the price paid or pay for repairs to be carried out. By the time the defect comes to light, many thousands of computers with the defect may have been sold. The case of *Time Group Ltd v Computer 2000 Distribution Ltd and IBM United Kingdom Ltd* [2002] EWHC 126 (TCC) illustrates the difficulties. During 1994, the second defendant, IBM, sold 20,160 Blue Lightning PCs to the first defendant, as IBM's exclusive distributor of Blue Lightning PCs in the UK. Later that year, the first and second defendants agreed that the claimant, Time, should take over as exclusive distributor in the UK. IBM sold over 20,000 Blue Lightning PCs to Time who also bought Computer 2000's surplus stock of over 4,000 Blue Lightning PCs. The Blue Lightning PCs were alleged to have two defects, one in a chip on the motherboard, the other was a hard disk fault.

During 1994 and 1995, both Time and Computer 2000 received complaints from customers about the computers and both Time and Computer 2000 sought compensation from IBM. In 1996, IBM and Computer 2000 agreed to settle the latter's claim for £240,394 and the settlement included a term to the effect that Computer 2000 would not pursue any other claims, nor assist any third party in any such claims. Time failed to settle at that stage. Actions were commenced in the UK against the second defendant but before trial a settlement was reached by which IBM agreed to pay £6 m to Time on the basis that it was a final settlement of the claim. The payment was received by Time on Friday 21 July 2000. On Monday 24 July 2000, Time sent Computer 2000 a letter before action and, on 14 August 2000, Time commenced proceedings in England against Computer 2000 for £2.2 m. On 16 August 2000, Time brought an action in the US against IBM's American parent company claiming US$54 m. This was dismissed by the court in New York on the basis of *forum non conveniens* (not the appropriate forum, that is, in the interests of justice, the action should take place somewhere else, that is, the UK). The settlement Time came to with IBM only referred to the English subsidiary company.

Computer 2000 joined IBM in the action as Part 20 defendants (this is where a person sued as defendant joins another party as defendant on the basis that the other should indemnify the first or make a contribution in respect of any award in damages). The purpose of Time suing Computer 2000 appeared to be so that Time could get a second bite at IBM. This was held to be an abuse of process and the claim and the Part 20 claim were dismissed. Generally, the courts will not allow bringing a second action on issues related to issues in the first action that could properly have been brought up in the first action. HH Judge Bowsher QC said that it was a very serious matter to stop any litigation but he considered it right in this case. He described the actions of the managing director of the claimant as having been 'tricky and devious . . . seeking to engineer court procedures as to pressure IBM into making further payment by way of settlement when IBM thought they had achieved finality of settlement on payment of large sums of money'. He ordered the claimant to pay both the defendant's costs and those of the Part 20 defendant.

THIRD-PARTY INTELLECTUAL PROPERTY RIGHTS

A final point to consider is that there is a possibility that the computer hardware or the software sold with it infringes some intellectual property right. The hardware itself could infringe a patent, design or trade mark while the software might infringe a copyright or trade mark. The client should make sure that the contract contains a term indemnifying him in case this should happen. If the contract is governed by the Sale of Goods Act 1979, however, there will be remedies available to the buyer if he is prevented from using or is hindered in his use of the equipment because it infringes another person's rights. Under section 12(1), there is an implied term that the seller has the right to sell the goods and, under section 12(2), there is an implied term that the buyer will enjoy quiet possession of the goods. In England and Wales and Northern Ireland, the implied terms under section 12(1) is a condition (breach of which gives the other party the right to repudiate the contract and/or seek damages). The implied term under section 12(2) is a warranty, breach of which only gives a right to damages. However, in a sale to a non-consumer, in England and Wales, a breach of condition may be treated as a breach of warranty only if the breach is so slight such that it would be unreasonable for the buyer to reject them, under section 15A of the Sale of Goods Act 1979.

Section 6 of the Unfair Contract Terms Act 1977 (section 21 in Scotland) provides that section 12 of the Sale of Goods Act 1979 cannot be excluded or restricted by reference to any contractual term. If a company buys a computer and, at the time of the sale, the computer infringes a trade mark or patent, then the seller is in breach of section 12(1) of the Sale of Goods Act 1979. Because this is a condition, subject to section 15A, the buyer can repudiate the contract and claim back the purchase price, plus damages for any consequential losses he has suffered (provided they are not too remote).

In *Niblett Ltd* v *Confectioners' Materials Co Ltd* [1921] 3 KB 387, it was held that because goods, when sold, infringed a trade mark, this entitled the buyer to repudiate the contract. In Scotland the question is whether the breach is a material one.

It may happen that equipment does not infringe a patent when it is sold but does infringe a patent soon afterwards, perhaps because at the time of sale a patent application, made by a third party, was being processed. When the patent is granted, the third party may commence an infringement action against the buyer of the equipment. This occurred in a case involving road marking machines, *Microbeads AC* v *Vinhurst Road Markings* [1975] 1 WLR 218, where it was held that:

- there was not a breach of section 12(1) because, at the time of the sale, the seller had every right to sell (the patent could not be enforced at that time); but
- the seller was in breach of section 12(2), the implied warranty as to quiet possession, and was liable to the buyer in damages.

There is always a danger that computer equipment or software will infringe a third party's rights (even if it is inadvertent) because of the rapid development of new hardware and software. This is a particular concern with software patents in the US. The remedies in section 12 of the Sale of Goods Act 1979 are useful but it is advisable to make specific contractual provision for the eventuality. For example, in a situation like that in the *Microbeads* case, the buyer may prefer to repudiate the contract rather than being limited to damages only. However, there is a defence to a patent infringement action if a person, in good faith, does the act or makes effective and serious preparations to do the act before the patent's priority date (see Patents Act 1977, section 64).

TENDERS

An organisation wishing to obtain computer equipment (the client) may ask a number of suppliers or manufacturers to submit tenders. Each of the companies submitting tenders will be asked for their price to supply the equipment described in a detailed specification. In this way, the bids can be compared on a like-for-like basis and, usually, the one submitting the lowest bid will be awarded the contract to supply equipment complying with the specification. Letting contracts by means of a tendering process is very common and public authorities and many large private organisations make use of this process. In some cases, the organisation will have no other option as it will be laid down in the constitution or articles of association. In other cases, it may be imposed from elsewhere – for example, where the contract value exceeds a particular value, it will have to be open to tenders because of government or European Community Regulations.

The contractual status of a tender is that a company submitting a tender is making an offer which can be rejected or accepted by the client as he thinks fit. Indeed, the client can choose not to accept any unless, for example, he has bound himself to accept the lowest. Consequently, the company submitting a tender bears the cost involved in its preparation such as determining which equipment is suitable and calculating the total price. If the hardware is complex, this cost can be considerable. The use of tendering as a means of letting contracts is very common in the construction industry. The convention that the person submitting the tender bears the costs of preparation of the tender is deeply ingrained; that it also applies in the context of computer contracts was emphatically stated in *Comyn Ching Ltd* v *Radius plc* (unreported) 17 March 1997, which concerned a tender for the supply of computer equipment and software. The judge cited a passage from *Keating on Building Contracts*, 6th edn (a leading practitioner text), to the effect that the contractor preparing a tender may incur considerable cost in doing so but there is no implication that he will be paid for this work. Indeed, '. . . he undertakes this work as a gamble, and its cost . . . he hopes will be met out of the profits of such contracts as are made as a result of tenders which prove to be successful!' The judge went on to say, 'I see no difference in principle between a building contract and a computer contract'.

Tenders can be requested from a selected list of companies or open tendering can be used – that is, where anyone who wishes to may submit a bid. Select list tendering is more usual nowadays and has the advantage that only those companies perceived as being competent are invited to submit bids. However, this may again be subject to rules imposed by government or through the European Community. Sometimes, the rules applicable to the tendering process may differ depending on the classification of the contract. In *Jobsin Co UK Ltd (t/a Internet Recruitment Solutions)* v *Department of Health* [2001] EWCA Civ 1241, the claimant submitted a tender for the development and management of a website for online recruitment to the Department of Health. The claimant was informed that it would not be included in the final shortlist. The issue was whether the services covered by the contract were computer and related services or personnel placement and supply services. The Regulations covering the contract differed depending on which it was. The Court of Appeal held that it was the former, which meant that the tender process was defective according to the applicable regulations (the Public Services Contracts Regulations 1993).

The tender process

The tender process is broadly as follows:

1 A detailed specification is drawn up detailing the functional and performance requirements.

2 If it is to be a select list tender, that list is drawn up and those on it are asked if they are interested in submitting tenders. If open tendering is to be used, an advertisement will be placed in an appropriate newspaper or journal or other publication (for example, the *Official Journal of the European Communities*).

3 To each tenderer, a set of tender documents will be sent comprising the specification (including any drawings and schedules), a form of agreement (so that the tenderer can see what the contractual obligations will be) and, in some cases, a bill of quantities in which the tendering company can write prices or a schedule of rates to be completed or a simple form on which the overall price can be written. The bill, schedule or form will contain a reference to the other documents.

4 A period of time will be allowed and a deadline will be stated for return of the tenders in sealed envelopes – for example, 'no later than noon on 6 September 2007'. Tenders received after this deadline must be rejected (to prevent the possibility of corruption). Of course, nowadays, tenders may be invited and submitted electronically, in which case, care must be taken to ensure confidentiality of the bids before the deadline and that they are opened and compared in circumstances reducing the possibility of corrupt practices.

5 The sealed tenders will be opened after the deadline. This may be before a senior officer and chairman of the appropriate committee in the case of a public authority. Any arithmetic will be checked carefully. (Mistakes can cause all sorts of problems if not picked up and dealt with. If there is a mistake it is usual practice to ask the company submitting that particular tender whether it wishes to stand by its mistake or withdraw the tender.)

6 A letter of acceptance will be sent to the successful company (usually that submitting the lowest bid) and a contract will be executed, typically under seal, as per the original form of agreement.

Tenders can be seen as a very fair means of letting contracts and the system has evolved as a way of reducing the possibility of bribery and corruption. However, tendering is not without difficulties. The client has to make sure that the tender documents are of a high quality, accurately describe the desired equipment and its performance and provide fully for any eventuality. If there are any shortcomings, the successful company may use these as a basis of additional payments and extensions to the time for delivery. A major headache for the client is that the companies submitting tenders, or at least some of them, will wish to make changes to the specification or time for delivery, etc. If this is permitted, it makes comparison of the tenders more difficult. A usual means of trying to maintain some comparability is to ask any company which has expressed a wish to submit on a different basis to submit two tenders, one as per the original tender documents, the other on its preferred specification.

PERFORMANCE BOND

Where hardware is delivered and installed over a period of time, for example, where the hardware has to be built up from numerous components and pieces of equipment and software specifically written for the hardware, it may be wise for the client to insist on a performance bond. This operates to provide a sum of money to the client if the supplier fails to complete the work, typically where the supplier goes into receivership part-way through performing the contract. In such circumstances, it will be more costly to engage a second supplier/developer to complete the work. Of course, the agreement must make specific provision dealing with the ownership of the hardware and when title to it passes to the client, otherwise the receiver may have a claim over it and may seek repossession in order to go towards satisfying the creditors of the supplier.

Performance bonds are usually set at a percentage of the total price agreed for the contract, 10 per cent being a common figure. The bond will usually be arranged with a bank, insurance company or other financial institution. The contract will have to be very precise as to the event when the right to claim the bond is triggered. Standard precedents use a form of words commonly used by lawyers in situations where the supplier goes into receivership, bankruptcy, becomes insolvent or enters an arrangement with its creditors. However, in this context, provision must also be made for the possibility that the supplier simply fails to perform its obligations satisfactorily or effectively or simply abandons the work. This is likely to require formal notice being given to the supplier specifying the alleged breaches of contract and, where remedial, requiring the supplier to remedy the situation within a reasonable time (without prejudice to any remedy the client may seek for damages). Continued failure will trigger release of the bond but usually only after a sworn statement from the client.

CONSUMER PROTECTION – ADDITIONAL SAFEGUARDS

Some further safeguards apply to sales to consumers, following modifications made to the Sale of Goods Act 1979, the Supply of Goods and Services Act 1982 and the Unfair Contract Terms Act 1977 by the Sale and Supply of Goods to Consumers Regulations 2002. These Regulations, which came into force on 31 March 2003, implement the Directive on the sale of consumer goods and associated guarantees.[1]

Satisfactory quality and relevant circumstances

Section 14(2A) of the Sale of Goods Act 1979 states that goods are of satisfactory quality if:

> ... they meet the standard that a reasonable person would regard as satisfactory, taking account of any description of the goods, the price (if relevant) and all other *relevant circumstances* (emphasis added).

The Regulations insert new section 14(2D) to (2F) into the Act and include in the meaning of 'relevant circumstances' public statements as to specific characteristics of goods made by the seller, the producer or his representative, particularly in advertising or labelling. Thus, any claims made in advertising by a manufacturer of a computer will be included in the relevant circumstances even though a consumer might buy a computer from a retailer, rather than directly from the manufacturer. Therefore, a consumer who buys a computer which fails to perform as stated by a manufacturer may be able to reject the computer and claim a refund of the price even though the retailer did not personally make that statement concerned. This additional implied term also applies, of course, to advertising made by the seller as well. A 'producer' is defined as the manufacturer of goods, the importer of goods into the European Economic Area or any person purporting to be the producer by placing his name, trade mark or other distinctive sign on the goods.

There are some exceptions to this additional implied term and it does not apply if:

- at the time the contract was made, the *seller* can show that he was not and could not reasonably have been aware of the statement – this protects a seller unaware of the statement who is not held responsible for statements made by the producer of the goods that he could not reasonably have been expected to have known about;
- the statement had been withdrawn in public before the contract was made or anything in it that was incorrect or misleading had been corrected in public;
- the decision to buy the goods had not been influenced by the statement.

In all these cases, the burden of proof lies with the seller to show that the exception relied on applies.

These provisions do not prevent other public statements, whether or not the buyer is a consumer (or, in Scotland, whether or not it is a consumer contract) from being relevant circumstances. In other words, the meaning of public statements considered to be relevant circumstances are not limited to the basic definition and exceptions. For example, a statement as to the performance of a computer made in advertising directed at business sales may be a relevant circumstance. This could apply where a consumer sees such advertising and buys the computer from a retailer on the strength of that statement.

If goods fail to meet the requirement of being of satisfactory quality, this will give a buyer who is buying as a consumer the right to reject the goods as it is a breach of condition or, in Scotland, a material breach. This absolute right was modified by the Regulations and sections 48A–48F were inserted into the Sale of Goods Act 1979. Depending on the circumstances, the buyer can require that the goods be repaired or replaced or that there is a reduction in the price. Only if neither of these remedies is appropriate can the buyer reject the goods. The modified rights apply

---

[1] Directive 1999/44/EC of the European Parliament and of the Council of 25 May 1999 on certain aspects of the sale of consumer goods and associated guarantees, OJ L 171, 7.7.1999, p. 12.

20

Hardware contracts

if the goods do not conform to the contract of sale at the time of delivery. This is defined as a breach of any express term in the contract or any breach of the terms implied by sections 13, 14 or 15 of the Sale of Goods Act 1979. (Section 13 requires that goods conform to their description, section 14 requires that goods are of satisfactory quality and fit for their purpose and section 15 applies where sale is by sample and requires that the bulk corresponds with the sample.) Thus, a breach of the condition in section 12(1) that the seller has the right to sell the goods is unaffected by the changes made by the Regulations and the buyer still has an absolute right to reject goods for breach of this condition.

Additional remedies in consumer contracts

An important change is that, if the goods do not conform to the contract of sale at any time within a period of six months from the date the goods were delivered to the buyer, they are treated as not so conforming at the delivery date, giving the buyer these additional remedies. There are two exceptions to this and it does not apply if it is established that the goods did conform at the date they were delivered to the buyer or if the application of that provision is incompatible with the nature of the goods or the nature of the lack of conformity, for example, if the goods are perishable or certain items of clothing or if they are foodstuffs with a 'use by' date that expires within the six-month period.

The Regulations are not clear as to whether the buyer can elect for either repair or replacement but the Directive makes it clear that, if this remedy is available, it is the buyer who can choose whether to have the goods repaired or replaced. Repair or replacement must occur within a reasonable time without causing significant inconvenience to the buyer and the seller must bear any necessary costs including the costs of labour, materials or postage. However, this remedy is not available if repair or replacement is impossible (for example, if the defect is such that repair is not possible or there are no more of those goods available) or if it is disproportionate to the other remedies available, including repair where the buyer has elected for repair rather than replacement or vice versa. Disproportionality is defined in terms of the costs imposed on the seller which, compared to the other remedy (whether repair or replacement), are unreasonable taking into account the value of the goods had they conformed to the contract of sale, the significance of the lack of conformity and whether the other remedy could be effected without significant inconvenience to the buyer. What is a reasonable time or what is a significant inconvenience to the buyer are to be determined by reference to the nature of the goods and the purpose for which they were acquired. Therefore, if a consumer buys a computer that breaks down a short time after delivery, it might be unreasonable to expect the buyer to wait several weeks for repairs when a replacement can be offered.

The alternative remedies, reduction in price or the right to reject the goods (a right to rescind the contract) are available if the buyer is not entitled to require repair or replacement (for example, if it would be impossible or disproportionate) or if the buyer has elected for repair or replacement and the seller has not done so within a reasonable time and without significant inconvenience to the seller. If a buyer does rescind the contract, he will be entitled to the return of any money paid to the seller. However, if the buyer has used the goods since they were delivered to him, the seller may reduce the reimbursement to take account of such use. Setting off any repayment on account of the use made of goods by the consumer and agreeing the amount by which the price of goods should be reduced if that remedy is chosen could prove to be difficult. In terms of the latter, the Regulations state that the buyer can require the seller to reduce the purchase price of the goods by an appropriate amount. One possibility seems to be that the buyer can leave the seller with the option of either agreeing to the reduction asked for by the buyer or having the buyer rescind the contract and having to reimburse the purchase price.

In terms of conformity with the contract of sale, the Directive states that the buyer may not rescind the contract if the breach is minor but this does not appear in the Regulations. The Sale of Goods Act 1979 has a provision such that, in a non-consumer sale, a breach of condition (under sections 13–15 of the Act) is turned into a breach of warranty (giving a remedy in damages only) if the breach is so slight that it would be unreasonable to allow the buyer to reject the goods. This does not apply, however, to consumer sales.

Risk and delivery

The Sale of Goods Act 1979 contains provisions dealing with who bears the risk of goods being lost, damaged or destroyed, as discussed earlier, where it was pointed out that the basic rule as to the passing of risk is different in a consumer contract where the risk stays with the seller until such time as the goods are delivered to the buyer.

Where a seller is authorised or required by the buyer to deliver to a carrier, under section 32 of the Sale of Goods Act 1979, this is deemed to be delivery to the buyer with the necessary implications as to the passing of risk. Again, does not apply in the case of sales to consumers and delivery to a carrier in such circumstances is not deemed to be delivery to the buyer.

Meaning of 'consumer' for purposes of the Unfair Contract Terms Act 1977

Some of the controls over clauses excluding or limiting liability differ depending on whether the party to the contract under consideration is dealing as a consumer or not. For example, in the case of a person dealing as a consumer, under section 4 of that Act indemnity clauses must be reasonable in the circumstances to be enforceable and liability for breach of sections 13–15 of the Sale of Goods Act 1979 cannot be excluded or restricted by any contract term (in other cases, the term must satisfy the requirement of reasonableness).

The meaning of 'dealing as a consumer' is defined in section 12 of the Unfair Contract Terms Act 1977 which requires that the person is dealing as a consumer if he does not make the contract in the course of a business (nor holds himself out as so doing), the other party does make the contract in the course of a business and, in the case of a contract governed by the law of sale of goods or hire-purchase or other contracts under which ownership of goods passes as set out in section 7 of the Unfair Contract Terms Act 1977, the goods are of a type ordinarily supplied for private use or consumption. The Regulations modified this and the limitation that the goods should be of the type ordinarily supplied for private use or consumption no longer applies where the first party is an individual. Therefore, the greater protection afforded to consumers in respect of unfair contract terms applies to consumers buying goods from a business even if the goods are not of the type ordinarily bought for private use or consumption.

There is a *caveat* to this and a person is not taken to be dealing as a consumer if the goods are second-hand goods sold at a public auction at which individuals have the opportunity of attending the sale in person or if the buyer is not an individual and the goods are sold by auction or by competitive tender.

Equivalent changes were made to section 25 of the Unfair Contract Terms Act in respect of Scotland.

Consumer guarantees

The status of guarantees given by manufacturers of goods has been something of a grey area where the contract for the sale or supply of goods is not with the manufacturer directly but with, for example, a retailer. As there is no contractual link between the consumer and the manufacturer, it was generally assumed that the guarantee operated as a form of collateral warranty. To some extent, this was alleviated by the Contracts (Rights of Third Parties) Act 1999 but, in line with the Directive, the Regulations put this beyond doubt and state that such guarantees take effect as collateral obligations under the conditions set out in the guarantee and any associated advertising.

The contents of the guarantee and the necessary particulars for making claims must be set out in plain intelligible language and the consumer may apply to have the guarantee made available to him in writing or other durable medium within a reasonable time. Where the goods in question are offered with a consumer guarantee within the territory of the UK, the guarantee must be written in English. The guarantee must state that the consumer has certain legal rights under applicable law and that these are unaffected by the guarantee (this is in the Directive though not mentioned in the Regulations as law in the UK already provided for this). Any failure of the guarantee to comply with these conditions does not invalidate it and failure of the guarantor to comply with the terms of the guarantee may result in an enforcement order by injunction or, in Scotland, a compliance order.

SUMMARY

- The Sale of Goods Act 1979 contains rules to determine when the property and risk in goods passes to the buyer.
- Parties to a sale of goods contract may prefer to make express provision for the passing of property and risk.
- Where the buyer is a consumer, the risk does not pass until the goods are delivered to him.
- Performance standards for hardware should be provided for in the contract.
- Entire agreement clauses are common:
  - they will normally be valid in contracts between businesses of similar bargaining power;
  - nevertheless, there may be remedies for misrepresentation.
- Maintenance and the provision of upgrades should be considered and dealt with in the contract or be subject to a separate contract.
- The sale of computer hardware will be a sale of goods contract even if software is also supplied.
- The Sale of Goods Act 1979 implies important terms into contracts for the sale of goods, including that:
  - the seller has the right to sell;
  - the buyer will have quiet possession;
  - the goods will be of satisfactory quality and fit for their purpose.
- The effect of a breach of a term implied under the Sale of Goods Act 1979 depends, *inter alia*:
  - on the contractual status of the term;
  - on whether the buyer is a consumer;
  - in the case of a sale to a non-consumer, whether any exclusion clauses satisfy the requirement of reasonableness.
- Inviting tenders for the supply of computer equipment is a common practice where:
  - the contract value is likely to be high;

- the equipment is complex; or
- the equipment is for a public authority.

■ Normally, those submitting tenders bear the cost of preparing the tender.

■ A performance bond may be required in complex and lengthy contracts.

■ There are special provisions where the buyer is a consumer, giving the buyer additional protection.

SELF-TEST QUESTIONS

Note: there is only one correct answer to each multiple choice question.

1 Which one of the following statements is CORRECT in relation to a contract for the sale of goods to a buyer who deals as a consumer (or, in Scotland, a consumer sale in which the buyer is a consumer)?

(a) The risk passes to the buyer as soon as the contract is made.

(b) The risk is with the buyer unless an extended guarantee has been paid for.

(c) The risk does not pass to the buyer until they are delivered to him.

(d) The risk remains with the seller until the payment has cleared when the risk passes to the buyer.

2 According to the Court of Appeal, for a misrepresentation to have legal effect in the light of an entire agreement clause, the statement must have three qualities or effects. Which one of the following is NOT one of those qualities or effects?

(a) It must be clear and unambiguous.

(b) It must be backed by a warranty as to its truth.

(c) It must be such that a reasonable person would expect the other to understand that he was meant to act on the basis of the representation.

(d) The other party must have entered into the agreement on the basis that the representation was true.

3 EeeZee Manufacturing Ltd bought computer equipment to control its widget manufacturing production line from Process Controls plc during January. Later that year, during September, EeeZee received a letter from Trolls Inc claiming that the equipment infringed its UK patent which was granted in March. Which one of the following statements is CORRECT (the contract under which EeeZee obtained the equipment from Process Controls had no provisions covering such eventualities although it appears that the equipment does indeed fall within the claims of the patent and infringes it)?

(a) EeeZee can continue to use the equipment as it started using the equipment before the patent was granted.

(b) EeeZee can repudiate the contract with Process Controls and claim damages for a breach of the condition that the latter had the right to sell the equipment in January.

(c) EeeZee must cease using the equipment if it does not want to be sued by Trolls for infringement of the patent but has no remedy against Process Controls.

(d) EeeZee can bring a claim for damages against Process Controls for a breach of the implied term of quiet possession.

20

Hardware contracts

4   In relation to the preparation of a tender by a computer company hoping to win a massive contract to supply and install complex computer equipment for a major petro-chemical company, which one of the following statements is CORRECT?

(a) The computer company must bear all the costs associated with the submission of its tender unless the petro-chemical company has agreed otherwise.

(b) It is a rule of tendering that the lowest bid must be accepted even if the company calling for tenders has stated the contrary.

(c) It is a rule of tendering that the highest bid must be accepted even if the company calling for tenders has stated the contrary.

(d) The computer company must provide a performance bond as a condition of submitting a tender, whether or not expressly called for by the petro-chemical company.

5   Discuss the circumstances under which consumers can elect to have goods repaired or replaced or accept a reduction in price rather than rejecting the goods outright. Give examples in relation to computer equipment bought by a consumer.

For further resources and updates please go to the Companion Website accompanying this book at www.mylawchamber.co.uk/bainbridgeIT

Part 3

Electronic contracts and torts

The laws of contract and torts are often grouped together under the description of the law of obligations. Obligations may be contractual, for example, the duties set out in a contract to be performed by the parties to the contract. On the other hand, obligations are imposed outside the context of a contract, such as those imposed by the law of negligence, where the imposition of the obligation is imposed on persons satisfying the 'neighbour' test, as mentioned in Chapter 14. Issues relating to contract and the tort of negligence have been discussed in the previous part of this book as they apply to computer contracts, such as contracts for writing software, and defective software. This part of the book looks at contract and tort in relation to electronic commerce (e-commerce). Much of what is discussed is relevant to the use of the internet by public bodies and authorities as well as commercial enterprises.

The initial hysteria surrounding e-commerce subsided but it has now become widespread and ubiquitous. It is now a preferred way of buying goods for many. It can be a more satisfactory experience than going to a store to buy for a number of reasons. One is the cooling-off period that applies to most online purchases and, in many cases, discounts are offered. Another advantage is that buying online frees the purchaser from high-pressure salespersons trying to talk him or her into buying expensive extended warranties. Legislators quickly noticed the importance of e-commerce and it has attracted a substantial legal response. Largely, this has been to facilitate e-commerce, for example, by promoting consumer protection. It is clear that e-commerce must be regulated, but it must be done in such a way so as not to discourage the use of the internet as an appropriate arena within which to carry out commercial activity and other forms of transactions, for example, e-government. There is a growing use of the internet for central and local government activities and it is now possible to pay for road fund tax for vehicles and television licences online.

It is important to have legal certainty for transactions carried out electronically. When a contract is made online, we need to know that it is enforceable, what the terms are, what law applies and in which country any legal action can be commenced in case of a breach of the contract. Will a document produced by computer signed using an electronic signature be admitted in court as evidence of the status of the document and the facts and statements contained therein? We also need reassurance that any the transaction we enter into is secure and we will be protected from the consequences of fraud.

Liability for online torts is another important aspect of electronic information. For example, if a person publishes information on a website which is potentially defamatory of another person, in what countries can legal action be brought? What if a company publishes information on its website which disparages a competitor? What if information on a website is incorrect and someone acts in reliance and is injured or suffers financial loss as a result? What is the position of internet service providers for illegal material available on their computer systems or transmitted through them? These and other issues are looked at in this part of the book.

The first chapter in this part discusses the nature, content and formation of electronic contracts. It will be seen that the law has gone a long way to providing mechanisms for e-commerce. The following chapter looks at the performance and breach of electronic contracts and includes a discussion of particular consumer protection legislation related to distance selling. The next chapter covers electronic torts, such as defamation, malicious falsehood and negligent misstatement. The final chapter in this part of the book examines the potential liability of information society service providers for illegal material made available through their services and how that liability is eliminated in 'no-fault' situations.

21 Nature, content and formation of electronic contracts

INTRODUCTION

Information technology allows and encourages the conduct of many aspects of commercial or business activity by electronic means. Forms of agreement and other contractual documents are likely to be created using a computer and may be transmitted in electronic form anywhere in the world. Standard forms and precedents used by solicitors to draw up agreements, such as a software licence or a will, are now published electronically. Typically, a solicitor acting for a party to a contract will open an appropriate form of agreement using his word processor software, make any required modifications and additions, and then either print it out or transmit it to the other party's solicitor. A contractual offer may be made in this way and may be accepted electronically by the other party transmitting his acceptance of the terms of the agreement.

Many transactions are now effected electronically. For example, by the use of automated teller machines (ATMs or cash point dispensers outside banks) and electronic fund transfers (EFTs) transactions are made between financial institutions and at the point of sale. Most organisations now exchange data electronically. For example, a large manufacturing company may order components automatically and electronically from its suppliers when stock levels reach a predetermined lower limit. Electronic data interchange (EDI) has the potential to maximise efficiency by reducing repetition and delays, increasing accuracy and permitting the maintenance of minimum stock levels by placing orders for 'just-in-time' delivery. A large proportion of the information flowing between organisations may be handled electronically, including quoting or submitting tenders for work, ordering, scheduling, invoicing and accounting. Land can be bought and sold electronically and the Land Registration Act 2002 includes provisions for e-conveyancing (in force from 13 October 2003).

All of this sounds very good apart, perhaps, from concerns about security but as expected, there are a number of legal consequences associated with electronic trading.

- The law requires that some contracts are in a particular form – for example, by deed or in writing.
- There may be doubts as to when the contract was made and, if the parties are in different countries, which country's law will apply to the contract.
- The evidential weight of electronic documents must be considered and assessed. For example, will a court admit an electronic signature as proof of a person's consent to a transaction?

To take an example, imagine that Karen, who has a large footwear store in London, wishes to buy 1,000 pairs of shoes from Luigi in Milan. Both Karen and Luigi have computers and both use electronic mail. Luigi has a website advertising his shoes. After seeing this, Karen submits an enquiry to Luigi via the website. Further negotiations are carried out using electronic mail.

Eventually, Karen transmits a contract for Luigi's approval on Monday at 10.00 am GMT. Later that day, at 2.00 pm GMT, Luigi sends a message to say that he accepts Karen's offer. However, Karen does not read that message until Wednesday as she has to make a trip to Scotland in the meantime. There is a term in the contract to the effect that Karen can terminate the contract if she fails to sell more than 50 pairs of shoes in any one week, returning the remaining stock to Luigi and paying only for those that she has sold. After four weeks, Karen has sold 250 pairs of shoes but 175 pairs were sold in the first week following an intensive advertising campaign. Sales have plummeted since and in the fourth week only 12 pairs were sold. Karen wishes to exercise her right to terminate the contract but the only evidence she has of the numbers sold each week is the record of sales on her computer, entered by her various shop assistants as and when they sold shoes.

The questions that arise in the above scenario related to the use of electronic contracting are:

- Is the contract valid – that is, did the electronically transmitted offer and acceptance create a binding contract? (If so, what would the position have been if Luigi, who did not receive confirmation until Wednesday, had sold the shoes to a third party on Tuesday?) If Karen and Luigi attached or associated their electronic signatures to the contract would this be admissible in a court of law as to the existence of a valid contract?

- If there is a valid contract, when was it made and is it subject to English or Italian law?

- Can a printout of the computer record of sales be used as evidence to prove that Karen sold insufficient numbers of shoes so allowing her to invoke the termination clause?

The main issues relating to electronic contracting concern the legal formalities, the admissibility of electronic signatures, the time that the contract was made, the applicable law and the admissibility of computer evidence in civil proceedings. These are considered below. At the end of the chapter, we will return to Karen and Luigi and advise them accordingly.

LEGAL REQUIREMENT AS TO FORM

A contract may be made in a number of different forms. For example, a contract may be made by deed, made in writing, evidenced in writing or it may be oral, or it may be a combination of all these. For example, section 4 of the Sale of Goods Act 1979 states that a contract of sale:

> . . . may be made in writing (either with or without seal), or by word of mouth, or partly in writing and partly by word of mouth, or may be implied from the conduct of the parties.

An example of a contract implied from the conduct of the parties is given by the case of ***Brogden v Metropolitan Railway Co*** (1877) 2 App Cas 666 concerning a contract to supply coal. It was held that the conduct of the parties by dealing with each other in accordance with a draft contract could only be explained on the basis that they approved the draft contract and a binding contract came into existence, at the latest, when the claimant supplied the first order of coal placed by the defendant.

Although for some contracts the form used does not matter (as in a sale of goods contract above), occasionally the law requires that a particular form be used. Some contracts must be by deed, an example being a lease of real property (land) for more than three years (sections 52 and 54(2) of the Law of Property Act 1925). A deed is a written document that is signed, sealed and delivered and a contract made by deed is referred to as a contract under seal. This requirement can be traced back to the Statute of Frauds 1677, and was intended to prevent lack of documentation being used as a means of fraud. The formality associated with a deed demonstrates a clear intention to be bound and, therefore, in terms of a contract, there is no requirement for consideration (for example, payment or goods), normally a prerequisite of legally binding contracts.

In recognition of the fact that some flexibility is now required and the traditional form of deed – originally written in beautiful cursive script on vellum with a wax seal attached (or more recently a red adhesive wafer) – is no longer relevant in today's society, the Law of Property (Miscellaneous Provisions) Act 1989 abolished some of the old rules that applied to some deeds. For example, under section 1 of that Act, the requirement for a seal was abolished as was any requirement as to the substance the deed was written on. Now, to qualify as a deed, the instrument must make it clear on its face that it is intended to be a deed (for example, by using a form of words making it clear that it is a deed) and it must be validly executed – for example, signed in the presence of witnesses and delivered (section 1(2) and (3)). The meaning of 'sign' includes making one's mark. It is possible that this could extend to a digital electronic representation of a signature and, because of the other relaxations in the rules, there seems to be no reason why an electronic deed cannot be valid. Nevertheless, because there is still a degree of uncertainty, it would be wise to print out the deed on paper before it is signed before witnesses, although this would then require physical delivery, losing one of the advantages of using information technology. As noted below, this uncertainty probably no longer applies to documents required to be in writing other than deeds.

Relatively few legal documents are required to be by deed. However, some must be in writing. For example, an assignment of a copyright must be in writing and signed by or on behalf of the assignor (section 90(3) of the Copyright, Designs and Patents Act 1988), and regulated consumer credit agreements must be in documentary form and signed (section 61 of the Consumer Credit Act 1974). The same applies to contracts for marine insurance, by section 22 of the Marine Insurance Act 1906, and contracts for the sale or other disposition of an interest in land, which must also incorporate all the terms expressly agreed by the parties (section 2(1) of the Law of Property (Miscellaneous Provisions) Act 1989). Yet other contracts must be evidenced in writing, an example being a contract of guarantee by section 4 of the Statute of Frauds 1677, which is still in force.

For contracts where writing is a requirement it is important to determine whether documents stored magnetically in digital form comply. Fortunately, Schedule 1 to the Interpretation Act 1978 contains the following definition:

> **'Writing' includes typing, printing, lithography, photography and other modes of representing or reproducing words in a visible form, and expressions referring to writing are construed accordingly.**

This would appear to include computer storage. Words stored in a computer may be reproduced on screen or printed on paper. In any case, it is unlikely that a judge would take a restrictive view of this, although the preceding words are somewhat narrow.

Signatures

The essential attributes of a signature are that it indicates recognition and approval of the contents of a document. A person's name printed on a telex, fax or computer document should suffice providing it bears the hallmark of that person's assent to the contents of the document. At one time, a good proportion of the population was illiterate and used a mark instead of writing their name in a stylised manner. Most of us now have one or more PIN numbers so that we can draw cash from the 'hole in the wall' without the need for any signature. However, use of such facilities is founded on a printed contract signed in the usual way!

The courts have tended to take a very pragmatic approach when it comes to deciding whether a printed name is a signature. For example, in *Good Challenger Navegante SA* v *Metalexportimport SA* [2004] 1 Lloyd's Rep 67, it was accepted by the Court of Appeal that a typed name on a telex was a signature for the purposes of section 30 of the Limitation Act 1980 which requires an acknowledgement of a claim must be in writing and signed by the person making it. The Court held that '. . . as a matter of general principle, a document was signed by the maker of it when his name or mark was attached to it in a manner which indicated, objectively, his approval of the contents; in the case of a telex, the typed name of the sender at the end of the telex not only identified the maker but led to the inference that he had approved the contents'. However, this will not necessarily apply to every type and format of document. It would be unlikely to apply, for example, to a formal contract with the names of the parties printed on it together with a space under each name for the parties to write their respective names. Conversely, with a telex, where there is no such facility, the typed name of the sender at the end of the telex not only identifies the maker but leads to the inference that he has approved the contents. Therefore, the typed name on a telex can be a signature. There is no reason why this analysis should not also apply to other documents transmitted electronically.

The signature must be such as to show, objectively, that the signatory understood that by printing or typing his name on a document that he intended to approve of the contents of the documents and be bound by them. As with any legal document, unless the contents have been misrepresented by the other party or someone acting on his behalf, it does not matter whether the contents have been read in detail or at all by the person signing. However, we must be able to infer from the circumstances that the person whose name appears in any form other than in handwriting intended to be bound legally. The appearance of a person's name as part of an e-mail address in the header of an e-mail does not do this. It may be explained in other ways, for example, it may be a pre-contractual enquiry or proposal or part of the preliminary negotiations for a contract. In *Mehta* v *J Pereira Fernandes SA* [2006] 2 Lloyd's Rep 244 it was confirmed that a name as part of an e-mail address in the header of an e-mail was not a signature for the purposes of section 4 of the Statute of Frauds Act 1677. The automatic insertion of an e-mail address could not count as a signature.

If the formalities required by law are not complied with then, at law, the contract will be unenforceable. However, equity may still be available. For example, the party denying that there is a legally binding contract may be estopped from denying its existence and may have to perform his obligations nonetheless. This would be appropriate where that person had behaved in some dishonourable way in the knowledge that the other person was acting to his detriment in the belief that the contract would be binding.

Electronic signatures and electronic communication

Section 7 of the Electronic Communications Act 2000 deals with electronic signatures and related certificates. This provision came into force on 25 July 2000. An electronic signature is so much of anything in electronic form which:

- is *incorporated* into or otherwise *logically associated* with any electronic communication or electronic data, and
- purports to be so incorporated or associated for the purpose of being used in establishing the *authenticity* of the communication or data, the *integrity* of the communication or data, or both.

Certification of an electronic signature requires that the person whose signature it is has made a statement (whether before or after making the communication) confirming that the signature, a means of producing, communicating or verifying the signature, or a procedure applied to the signature (either alone in combination with other factors) is a valid means of establishing the authenticity or the integrity of the communication or data or both.

Section 7 makes admissible in evidence electronic signatures incorporated or logically associated with a particular electronic communication or particular electronic data and the certification by any person of such a signature. The admissibility relates to the *authenticity* or *integrity* of the communication or data. Authenticity is defined in section 15(2) in terms of the source of the communication or data, the accuracy of time and date, and whether it is intended to have legal effect. Integrity relates to whether there has been any tampering or other modification of the communication or data.

Section 8 of the Act allows the Secretary of State to modify enactments or subordinate legislation or schemes, licences, authorisations or approvals for the purpose of facilitating electronic communications or electronic storage for one or more of a number of specified purposes. These include things required to (or that may) be done or evidenced in writing or otherwise using a document, notice or instrument; things required to (or may) be done by post or other specified means of delivery; things required to (or may) be authorised by a person's signature or seal or is required to be delivered as a deed or witnessed.

These provisions allow the Secretary of State the power to overcome specific requirements in respect of legal formalities to allow for electronic communications or electronic storage to satisfy the requirements. However, this must not compromise the records of things done for their relevant purpose. Changes have been made in a number of cases to facilitate electronic communication in particular including in terms of patents, housing, health, public records and in relation to unsolicited goods or services. The Secretary of State also has the power to make provisions as to the electronic form of electronic communications or storage and conditions for authorisation, manner of proof, provision of criminal offences for making false or misleading statements and other matters.

Part I of the Electronic Communications Act 2000 provides for a register of approved cryptography service providers and regulation of them. However, the government preferred to keep the present voluntary scheme in place and Part I of the Act has not been brought into force. It was automatically be repealed on 25 May 2005.

The Electronic Signatures Regulations 2002 deal with the liability of certification service providers in the context of electronic signatures and with certain data protection issues. Members of the public who rely on a certificate and who suffer loss are entitled to damages for any loss as a result of that reliance unless the certification service provider can prove that he was not negligent. This is a useful reversal of the normal burden of proof. There are also data protection issues relating to such certificates and personal data may only be obtained for the purpose of issuing or maintaining the certificate either directly from the data subject or with his express consent. The Secretary of State also has some supervisory powers over certification service providers.

WHEN IS THE CONTRACT MADE?

The ability to point to the exact time that a contract is made may be important in a number of cases. For example, a contract for the writing of a new item of software may require that the work is completed no later than three months from the date of creation of the contract. A contractual offer for the sale of computer equipment may be expressed as being open for acceptance for seven days only (though such an offer will be binding only if supported by consideration – for example, where the person to whom the offer has been made has paid a fee for the benefit of the 'option').

The normal way that a contract is made is when an offer made by one party is accepted, unconditionally and on identical terms, by the other party. The contract is made the instant that the person to whom the offer is made (the offeree) communicates his acceptance to the person making the offer (the offeror). The first time this rule ran into difficulties was in relation to the use of the postal system, which, as a means of communication, inevitably results in a time lag between making the offer or the acceptance and its receipt by the other party. Typically, problems can arise where the person making an offer revokes that offer before receiving the other's acceptance. A revocation of an offer is effective when communicated to the offeree – that is, when it is actually received by him. If, in the meantime, he posts an acceptance of that offer there is likely to be a conflict.

In *Adams* v *Lindsell* (1818) 1 B & Ald 681, the claimant was a manufacturer of woollen items located in Bromsgrove. The defendant was a wool merchant in St Ives, now in Cambridgeshire, some distance away. The defendant wrote to the claimant making an offer to sell wool to the claimant requiring an answer in the course of the post. Due to the defendant's negligence, the letter was delayed by three days but almost immediately upon receiving it, the claimant wrote back accepting the offer. In the meantime, not having received a reply by the date he expected, the defendant sold the wool to a third party. The claimant successfully sued for breach of contract as the court decided that the contract was made when the letter of acceptance was posted.

This exception to the general rule applies only where it is reasonable to expect communication of acceptance through the post – for example, where the offer is made through the post and there is no stipulation for a different form of communication (see *Byrne* v *Van Tienhoven* (1880) 5 CPD 344). The rule would not apply if the offeror required communication of acceptance by some other method – for example, by telephone, facsimile transmission or by electronic mail.

The postal rule is an exception and where the means of communication being used by the prospective parties is almost instantaneous, the general rule will prevail. Thus, in *Entores Ltd* v *Miles Far East Corp* [1955] 2 QB 327, where offer and acceptance were communicated by telex, it was held that the acceptance took effect not when it was transmitted from Amsterdam but when it was received in London and, accordingly, the contract was subject to English law rather than Dutch law (this manner of determining which law applies has been substantially modified by the Rome Convention, discussed later). The House of Lords approved of this decision in *Brinkibon Ltd* v *Stahag Stahl und Stahlwarenhandelsgesellschaft mbH* [1983] 2 AC 34. In that case, the claimant, an English company, wished to buy a quantity of steel from the defendant, an Austrian company. The claimant sent a telex from London to Vienna, accepting the defendant's offer but the steel was not delivered and the claimant sought damages for breach of contract in England. The House of Lords confirmed that the contract was made in Austria and, therefore, outside the jurisdiction of the English courts. Where the method of communication of acceptance is instantaneous a contract is made when the acceptance is received by the offeror.

The House of Lords went on to stress that this is not a universal rule and the circumstances of a particular case might result in a different outcome. There may be all sorts of variations – for example, where the transmission will be received outside office hours and it is expected that it will be read later or where it is sent to a third party's telex machine or to the agent of the offeror. Lord Wilberforce said:

> No universal rule can cover all such cases; they must be resolved by reference to the intention of the parties, by sound business practice and in some cases by a judgment where the risks should lie.

Brinkibon remains useful in providing a rule of thumb for determining when a contract is made. Some of the other parts of the judgments are, however, of less relevance today because of

Conventions and Regulations on jurisdiction, discussed in the following chapter and the Rome Convention, which governs the question of applicable law.

Where an offer and acceptance are to be communicated by electronic mail, the basic rule should prevail, that is, that the acceptance is effective when it is received. It is sensible to request confirmation of receipt. Difficulties may arise where the message accepting the offer is not read immediately upon receipt, perhaps because it is received during the night (for example, where one party is in Hong Kong and the other is in England) or the person to whom the receipt is addressed is out of the office for some time. It makes sense in such situations for the parties to stipulate their own rules – for example, that the acceptance is not effective until such time as it is read by the offeror or acknowledged by him.

Bearing in mind the trans-national nature of the internet, issues of applicable law and jurisdictions should be agreed expressly by the parties to the contract. Although there are Conventions and Regulations that apply in this context, it makes sense to tie things down properly at the outset. Even then, however, there may be some interference, for example, some rules on jurisdiction in consumer contracts cannot be ignored and consumer protection legislation cannot be comprised in Europe by a choice of law clause.

Care must be taken by any person who has made offers to a number of other persons in respect of the same subject matter. However, where a person wishing to sell an item of computer equipment, for example, places details on a website, this will not generally be deemed to be an offer as such (unless entered into an online auction). It is more akin to placing an advertisement in a magazine, which is an invitation to treat – in other words, an invitation to others to make offers to buy the equipment. In *Partridge* v *Crittenden* [1968] 2 All ER 421, Partridge placed an advertisement in the *Cage and Aviary Birds* magazine for the sale of Bramblefinches at £1 5s each. He was prosecuted under section 6(1) of the Protection of Birds Act 1954 for offering for sale a wild bird. His conviction was quashed – he had not offered the birds for sale because the placing of the advertisement was not an offer, merely an invitation to treat.

Online 'auction' sites, such as eBay, have their own agreements setting out the act that brings a binding contract into existence. It may be that this happens when at the end of the 'auction' if the highest bid has met the minimum and any reserve price. However, the relevant terms in these agreements can be vague. For an auction style listing on eBay, the user agreement states that the bid has to be accepted by the seller. For a traditional auction, the contract is made 'when the hammer falls'.

APPLICABLE LAW

Most contracts contain a term, often at the end of the agreement, stating under which country's law the contract is to have effect. For example, the agreement may state that 'this agreement is subject to the laws of England and Wales'. In Europe, the 1980 Rome Convention on the law applicable to contractual obligations,[1] given effect in the UK by the Contracts (Applicable Law) Act 1990, contains rules governing applicable law that apply in all the Member States of the European Community. The Convention applies to contracts but there are exceptions, for example, contracts of insurance. The basic rule is in Article 3 and is that the parties are free to choose the law governing their contract, whether in whole or in part. The choice must be expressed with reasonable certainty and they may choose a foreign law or even to vary the choice of law, providing third parties are not prejudiced.

---

[1] OJ C 27, 26.01.1998, p. 34, consolidated version.

In the absence of choice, Article 4 states that the contract shall be governed by the law of the country with which the contract is most closely connected. There are further rules to determine which this country is. The basic rule is that it is the country where the party who is to effect performance, which is characteristic of the contract, is based. In the case of a contract for the carriage of goods the country whose law applies is generally the country where the carrier has his principal place of business. If the contract involves immovable property (for example, land) it is the country where the land is situated. These rules are just presumptions and do not apply if, in the circumstances, the contract is more closely connected to another country. In some circumstances, consumer contracts are governed by the law of the country in which the consumer has his habitual residence in the absence of any choice of law clause and even if such a clause exists, the consumer cannot be deprived of the consumer protection laws applicable in the country in which he has his habitual residence.

Determining the place where the party is established whose performance is characteristic of the contract in a sale of goods contract should be based on the country where the party responsible for delivering the goods is established, rather than the country of the party who is to pay for the goods. Payment of money is not considered to be the characteristic performance for the purpose of deciding which country's law applies. This was suggested by Professors Giuliano and Lagarde in a Report on the Rome Convention.[2] By virtue of section 3(3) of the Contracts (Applicable Law) Act 1990, this Report is to be taken into account in ascertaining the meaning or effect of any provision in the Rome Convention.

In terms of contracts for the supply of goods or services to consumers, a choice of law clause cannot deprive the consumer of mandatory rules of consumer protection in the country where the consumer has his habitual residence:

- if in that country the conclusion of the contract was preceded by a specific invitation addressed to him or by advertising, and he had taken in that country all the steps necessary on his part for the conclusion of the contract; or
- if the other party or his agent received the consumer's order in that country; or
- if the contract is for the sale of goods and the consumer travelled from that country to another country and there gave his order, provided that the consumer's journey was arranged by the seller for the purpose of inducing the consumer to buy.

Otherwise, in a contract for the supply of goods or services to a consumer, in the absence of a choice of applicable law, the law governing the contract is the law of the country where the consumer has his habitual place of residence.

ELECTRONIC COMMERCE (EC DIRECTIVE) REGULATIONS 2002

The Directive on electronic commerce[3] was implemented on 21 August 2002 by the Electronic Commerce (EC Directive) Regulations 2002 (apart from one provision relating to 'Stop Now Orders', court orders to prevent activities by traders that contravene European Community consumer protection legislation). As the Regulations closely follow the Directive, references in this section are to the above Directive unless stated otherwise. The part of the Directive concerned with the liability of intermediary service providers in this context is discussed in Chapter 24.

---

[2] Published in the *Official Journal of the European Communities*, OJ C 282, 31.10.1980, p. 1.

[3] Directive 2000/31/EC of the European Parliament and of the Council of 8 June 2000 on certain legal aspects of information society services, in particular electronic commerce, in the Internal Market, OJ L 178, 17.07.2000, p. 1 (the 'Directive on electronic commerce').

The aims of the Directive are to:

■ eliminate the extent to which a Member State can control information society services emanating from another Member State by coordination of certain national laws and by clarification of certain legal concepts;

■ lay down a clear and general framework covering certain legal aspects of electronic commerce thus ensuring legal certainty and consumer confidence;

■ secure the freedom of movement of information society services;

■ secure effective and speedy access to dispute resolution, including by electronic means and injunctive relief.

Scope

The Directive on electronic commerce applies in relation to information society services. These are services normally provided for remuneration, at a distance, by means of electronic equipment for processing and storage of data. Processing includes digital compression. Information services within the meaning in the Directive cover a wide range of activities, including:

■ online contracting including selling goods online;

■ remuneration other than by those who receive the service such as online information or commercial communications or the provision of search facilities for access to and retrieval of data (for example, Google or as in sponsored links retrieved during a search);

■ transmissions point to point such as video on demand or provision of commercial communications by electronic mail (but not individual communications by natural persons outside their trade, business or profession including their use for the conclusion of contracts).

The contractual relationship between an employer and employee is not an information society service nor are activities which cannot, by their very nature, be carried out at a distance and by electronic means, such as the auditing of company accounts or medical advice requiring a physical examination of the patient. The definition of information society services refers to Article 1(2) of Directive 98/34/EC,[4] amended by Directive 98/48/EC.[5] Annex V to the latter Directive gives an indicative list of services which are not provided at a distance, not provided by electronic means, offline services (for example, distribution of CDs) and services not provided via electronic processing/inventory systems (for example, certain telephony, telex, fax, telephone and telefax services and consultations). Other exclusions include television and radio broadcasting services.

The Directive on electronic commerce does not apply to taxation, aspects relating to the data protection Directive and the privacy in telecommunications Directive (discussed in detail in Part 5 of this book), or agreements or practices governed by cartel law. Nor does it apply in respect of certain activities of information society services, being:

■ activities of notaries or equivalent professions to the extent that they involve a direct and specific connection with the exercise of public authority;

---

[4] Directive 98/34/EC of the European Parliament and of the Council of 22 June 1998 laying down a procedure for the provision of information in the field of technical standards and regulations, OJ L 204, 21.07.1998, p. 37.

[5] Directive 98/48/EC of the European Parliament and of the Council of 20 July 1998 amending Directive 98/34/EC laying down a procedure for the provision of information in the field of technical standards and regulations, OJ L 217, 05.08.1998, p. 18.

21

Nature, content and formation of electronic contracts

- the representation of a client and defence of his interests before the courts;

- gambling activities involving wagering a stake with monetary value in games of chance, including lotteries and betting transactions.

The Directive on electronic commerce is also without prejudice to the level of protection already available, in particular, in terms of public health and consumer interests, as established in a number of other Directives. For example, in relation to unfair terms in consumer contracts, distance contracts, misleading advertising, the advertising of medicinal products and advertising and sponsorship of tobacco products.

The internal market and law governing service providers

By virtue of Article 3 of the Directive on electronic commerce, the requirements for taking up the activity of an information society service provider and pursuing such activities, as laid down in Member States' legal systems, are not to be used to restrict the freedom to provide information society services from another Member State. Derogation is allowed on the basis of public policy (including the prevention and detection of criminal offences, the protection of minors and the fight against incitement to hatred and violations of human dignity), public health, public security and the protection of consumers including investors. The UK has taken advantage of all these derogations.

Information service providers established in a Member State must comply with the relevant national provisions related to the 'coordinated field'. This includes online information, advertising, online shopping and online contracting, without prejudice to future harmonisation in these areas. The scope of the coordinated field does not extend to national requirements as to safety and labelling of goods, liability for goods, delivery or transportation of goods or rights of pre-emption concerning goods such as works of art. These provisions do not apply in some circumstances, set out in the Annex to the Directive on electronic commerce, including in relation to copyright and industrial property rights and the freedom of parties to choose applicable law.

The recitals make it clear that the concept of establishment is to be determined in accordance with the case law of the Court of Justice. It is not the place where the organisation's website is located (that is, the technology supporting the website) nor where the website is accessible. Rather it is the place where the organisation pursues its economic activity. Where a service provider has several places of establishment it may be difficult to determine which is the place where the service is provided from. In such cases, it will be the place where the provider has its centre of activities for the relevant activities relating to the service in question. This could be relevant where a service provider is a company with a number of subsidiary companies established in other Member States.

Services provided by undertakings established in a third country (outside the European Union) are not affected by this Directive but, in view of the global nature of electronic commerce and the desirability of Community rules being consistent with equivalent rules on a broader international stage, the Directive is without prejudice to the results of discussions within international organisations such as the WTO (World Trade Organisation), OECD (Organisation for Economic Cooperation and Development) and UNCITRAL (United Nations Commission on International Trade Law) on legal issues.

Article 4 of the Directive on electronic commerce requires that Member States do not make the taking up and pursuit of information society services subject to prior authorisation, except in the context of licensing schemes for telecommunications services not being specifically and exclusively targeted at information society services.

▪ Provision of information by service providers

A key aim of the Directive on electronic commerce is to improve transparency so that, for example, a person accessing information offering goods for sale is fully aware of matters such as the identity of the service provider, price and discounts, etc. or, in the case of an unsolicited communication such as a marketing special offer, the recipient can see it for what it is. Whilst the concept of a provider of an information society service is straightforward, the meaning of 'recipient' is any natural or legal person who, for professional ends or otherwise, uses an information society service, in particular for the purposes of seeking information or making it accessible. This can mean either the provider of information on open networks such as the internet or a person who seeks information on the internet for private or professional reasons.

There is a requirement for information society service providers to supply specified information to recipients of the service and to the competent authorities in Member States. This requirement is in addition to other information requirements under Community law, for example, the requirement to provide information to individuals if personal data relating to them are being obtained. The minimum information to be given is set out in Article 5 and is:

- the name of the service provider and the geographic address at which the provider is established;
- details of the service provider to enable him to be contacted rapidly and communicated with in a direct and effective manner, including his electronic mail address;
- in cases where the service provider is registered in a trade or similar public register, the trade register and his registration number or equivalent means of identification;
- where the activity is subject to an authorisation scheme, particulars of the relevant supervisory authority;
- VAT number, if applicable;
- in the context of a regulated profession, there is also a duty to provide information about the body or similar institution with which the service provider is registered, the professional title and Member State where it has been granted and a reference to the applicable professional rules in the Member State of establishment and the means of access to them.

There is a further requirement that where the services refer to prices, they must be indicated clearly and unambiguously and, in particular, indicate whether they are inclusive of tax and delivery costs.

Article 6 requires information to be provided in the case of commercial communications which are defined as those which are directly or indirectly promotional of the goods, services or image of a company, organisation or person carrying on a commercial, industrial or craft activity or exercising a regulated profession. However, this does not extend to information allowing direct access to the activity, such as a domain name or e-mail address, nor to communications relating to goods, services or image compiled in an independent manner, particularly when this is without financial consideration.

The information to be provided in the case of commercial communications must comply with the following conditions:

- the communication must be clearly identifiable as a commercial communication and the person on whose behalf it is made must be clearly identifiable;

21

Nature, content and formation of electronic contracts

- promotional offers (such as discounts, premiums and gifts) and promotional competition and games, where permitted by the Member State in which the service provider is established, must be clearly identifiable as such and the qualifying conditions or conditions for participation must be easily accessible and presented clearly and unambiguously.

In cases where Member States allow unsolicited commercial communications by electronic mail, as is the case in the UK, and in addition to any other requirements under Community law, they must be clearly and unambiguously identifiable as such as soon as received by the recipient; Article 7. Furthermore, service providers must regularly consult opt-out registers in respect of natural persons. This is without prejudice to the Directive on the protection of consumers in respect of distance contracts (see the following chapter) which deals, *inter alia*, with the issue of consent to unsolicited communications and the Directive on privacy in telecommunications (see Part 5 of this book).

Commercial communications which are part of, or constitute, an information society service provided by a member of a regulated profession are permitted, subject to compliance with the appropriate professional rules regarding, in particular, the independence, dignity and honour of the profession, professional secrecy and fairness towards clients and other members of the profession. This is in addition to Community Directives relating to the access to, and the exercise of, activities of the regulated professions. Member states and the Commission are to encourage the development of codes of conduct in terms of the information to be provided in accordance with professional rules.

Contracts concluded by electronic means

Article 9 of the Directive on electronic commerce requires that Member States ensure that their legal systems allow contracts to be concluded by electronic means and relevant legal requirements do not create obstacles for the use of electronic contracts or deprive such contracts of their effectiveness and validity. The UK by way of the Electronic Communications Act 2000 seeks to facilitate the use of electronic communications and data storage by encouraging a system of approved cryptography service providers and, in particular, by providing that electronic signatures are admissible in evidence.

Some forms of contract may be excepted from the general principle that there should be no legal obstacles to electronic contracting, should Member States wish to do so. These are contracts:

- that create or transfer rights in real estate, except for rental rights;
- that require by law the involvement of courts, public authorities or professions exercising public authority;
- of suretyship;
- governed by family law or the law of succession.

In terms of electronic contracting, Article 10 requires certain information to be provided, in addition to other information requirements under Community law. The information must be given by the service provider clearly, comprehensively and unambiguously and prior to the order being placed by the recipient. This does not apply where the parties, not being consumers, agree otherwise. The information to be provided is:

- the different technical steps to follow to conclude the contract;
- whether or not the concluded contract will be filed by the service provider and whether it will be accessible;

- the technical means for identifying and correcting input errors prior to placing the order;
- the languages offered for the conclusion of the contract.

Unless the parties, not being consumers, agree otherwise, the service provider must also indicate any relevant codes of conduct to which he subscribes and how these codes can be consulted electronically. However, the above provisions do not apply to contracts concluded exclusively by the exchange of electronic mail or by equivalent individual communication. Contract terms and general conditions provided to the recipient must be made available in a way which allows him to store and reproduce them.

By Article 11, where the recipient of a service places his order through technological means, the service provider must acknowledge receipt of the order without undue delay and by electronic means. Where the order is for the online service itself, the acknowledgement may take the form of the provision of the service itself. The order and acknowledgement are deemed to be received when the parties to whom they are addressed are able to access them. The language of the Article tends to suggest that this does not require that the party actually does access the communication. It seems enough that it is available for the party to access, that is, it is accessible rather than accessed.

There is a requirement that appropriate, effective and accessible technical means are provided to all the recipients to identify and correct input errors prior to placing the order. The above provisions of Article 11 do not apply where the parties, not being consumers, otherwise agree. With the exception of the deemed receipt of order and acknowledgement, these provisions do not apply to contracts concluded exclusively by the exchange of electronic mail or by equivalent individual communication.

However, recital 39 curiously states that this should not enable, as a result, the bypassing of these provisions by providers of information society services in relation to the provision of information and the placing of orders. Reading this with the Article would appear to mean that, in relation to contracts concluded exclusively by the exchange of electronic mail and the like, there is still a duty to provide contract terms and conditions in a manner such that the recipient can store and reproduce them (for example, by recording them in a data file or by printing them out) and the deemed provisions on placing the order and acknowledgement still apply to such contracts.

MODEL LAWS

The United Nations Commission on International Trade Law (UNCITRAL) brought out a model law on electronic commerce in 1996, amended in 1998 and adopted by the United Nations in 2001. This has been instrumental in informing the debate as to how legislation should be framed to deal with some of the issues relating to electronic commerce and has certainly been influential in European responses to electronic commerce though not as yet adopted by the European Community. An important definition in the model law is that of a 'data message' being information generated, sent or received or stored by electronic, optical or similar means including, but not limited to, electronic data interchange (EDI), electronic mail, telegram, telex or telecopy. By 2006, legislation based on the UNCITRAL model law on electronic commerce had been adopted in many countries, States of the United States and Provinces of Canada.

Some of the main provisions of the model law are as follows.

- Information should not be denied legal effect, validity or enforceability on the grounds that it is contained in a data message. This also extends to information not contained in a data message but referred to in a data message.

21

Nature, content and formation of electronic contracts

- Where there are requirements for writing, these are satisfied by a data message providing the information is accessible so as to be usable for subsequent reference.

- Where there are requirements for signatures, these are satisfied by a data message if the method used to identify the person who sent it and to indicate approval are contained in the data message and that method is as reliable as is appropriate for the purposes, in the light of all the circumstances, including any agreement between the parties.

- Where there are requirements for originality, these are satisfied by a data message if there is a reliable assurance as to the integrity of the information from the time it was first generated in its final form, whether as a data message or otherwise. Further the information must be capable of being displayed when it is required to be presented.

- Formation of the contract – offer and acceptance – may be by data messages unless the parties otherwise agree. There are also rules as to acknowledgement of receipt. If not asked for, this can be by any communications (automatic or otherwise) or by conduct. Any offer may be conditional on the receipt of acknowledgement but otherwise, if acknowledgement is requested within a specified or agreed time (or failing that a reasonable time), a notice may be sent requesting acknowledgement within a reasonable time. If stated conditional upon receipt of acknowledgement it is to be treated as never sent unless acknowledged.

- Despatch of a data message takes place when it enters an information system outside the sender's control (unless otherwise agreed).

- Receipt takes place (unless otherwise agreed) at the time the data message enters the information system designated by the recipient (if sent to an information system other than the one designated, it is deemed to be received when retrieved). If the recipient has not designated an information system, receipt takes place when it enters his information system. It does not matter if, where the party concerned has more than one place of business, the location of the information system is different to that at which the data message is deemed to be received.

The intention is that the model law provides essential procedures and principles to facilitate the use of up-to-date techniques used to record and communicate information in various types of circumstances. It does not, however, set out all the rules and regulations necessary to implement those techniques and is not intended to cover every aspect of the use of electronic commerce. An enacting Member State may wish to provide specific laws to build in comprehensive procedures. Other legal issues may be raised, for example, in relation to applicable administrative, contract, criminal and judicial-procedure law.

REVIEW

The law has developed to take account of the use of information technology in commercial activity and, on a number of occasions, judges have had to deal with modern modes of information transmission such as telex, facsimile machines and computers. As has been shown, there are still some grey areas and those wishing to make full use of new technology to conduct their business must be aware of these areas and make appropriate provision. The strictness of the old rules relating to deeds and written documents was relaxed some time ago and in *Hastie and Jenkerson* v *McMahon* [1990] 1 WLR 1575, the Court of Appeal accepted that some documents could be validly served by fax. In this case a list of documents was required to be identified by court order and served by the claimant on the defendant. All that was required was a legible copy of the document in question placed in the possession of the party on whom it was served and the fax machine achieved this. Now, under Rule 6.2 of the Civil Procedure Rules 1998, documents may be served by a number of methods including by fax or other means of electronic communication providing the appropriate practice direction permits this. Furthermore, where the Rules or a practice direction require a document to be signed, this can be effected by printing the signature by computer or other mechanical means: Rule 5.3.

To conclude this chapter, it will be useful if we return to consider the position of Karen and Luigi and their contract for shoes. First, is there a valid contract? Karen appears to have made a clear offer by sending a copy of the contract for approval and Luigi has indicated his acceptance of its terms. If the transmission of the contract and Luigi's acceptance have been accurate, there should be a legally binding contract providing all the other requirements are met (for example, that the offer and acceptance were unconditional and that there was *consensus ad idem*, that is, clear mutual agreement).

The next question to determine is the time that the contract was made. It would seem reasonable to expect that the acceptance became effective when it was first read by Karen on Wednesday, on the basis of the *Brinkibon* case – that is, when it was first communicated to Karen. The Directive on electronic commerce uses the concept of deemed receipt for orders and acknowledgement of orders, being the time the parties are able to access them. Non-consumers can agree otherwise and they are also free to determine how and under what circumstances a binding contract will come into existence. In the absence of any express agreement between Karen and Luigi, it would seem that the latest the contract came into existence was when Karen first read the acceptance on Wednesday. In any case, it is clear that a contract did come into existence because the parties performed their obligations as if the contract existed, as in *Brogden* v *Metropolitan Railway*. On the basis of *Brinkibon* the contract would have been subject to English law in the absence of any choice of applicable law by Karen and Luigi. However, this has been overtaken by the Rome Convention and the question is answered by looking at the country where the party whose performance is characteristic of the contract is based. In a sale of goods contract the characteristic performance is the supply of the goods, therefore, it is the law of Luigi's country, Italy, that will be the applicable law. Had a consumer, Mary (who has her habitual residence in England), ordered a pair of shoes direct from Luigi, in the absence of any choice of law clause, the contract would have been subject to English law.

Karen appears to be in a position to reject the remaining shoes on the basis of the contract, providing the relevant term is enforceable under Italian law. Other aspects, such as which country's courts have jurisdiction to hear a legal action, for example, if Luigi wishes to sue for wrongful repudiation of the contract and whether the computer print out is admissible as evidence of the contents of the print out are discussed in the following chapter.

SUMMARY

- Some contracts must be made by deed:
    - deeds must be signed by both parties and witnessed;
    - a deed may be a computer document;
    - there remains an element of doubt as to whether a printed name will suffice as a signature.
- Some contracts are required to be in writing.
- The legal meaning of writing is wide enough to cover computer documents.
- The purpose of a signature on a contract is that it indicates approval of the contents and a willingness to be legally bound.
- Signatures generally do not need to be handwritten and may be a printed or typed name.

- A name as part of an e-mail address printed in the header of an e-mail is not deemed to be a signature.
- An electronic signature is one which is incorporated into or otherwise logically associated with a communication or electronic data.
- The purpose of an electronic signature is to establish the authenticity and integrity of a communication or data.
- Where the form of communication is instantaneous, the contract is made when the acceptance is received and the postal rule does not apply.
- In Europe, the rules to determine applicable law are set out in the Rome Convention:
  - the basis rule is that the parties are free to choose which law applies to the contract;
  - however, consumers cannot be deprived of consumer protection laws;
  - where there is no choice of law clause, the applicable law is that of the country most closely connected with the contract.
- Electronic Commerce Directive applies to providers of information society services (ISS):
  - certain forms of services provided at a distance;
  - established a single European market with no barriers to providing ISS;
  - providers of ISS required to give certain information to recipients and competent authorities;
  - commercial communications must be clearly identifiable as must be the identity of the provider;
  - promotional offers must be clearly identifiable as such;
  - providers of ISS must consult opt-out registers;
  - Member States must facilitate the making of contracts by electronic means;
  - further information must be provided clearly and unambiguously.
- The UNCITRAL model laws on electronic commerce has been widely adopted.

SELF-TEST QUESTIONS

Note: there is only one correct answer to each multiple choice question.

1   Gracie is the major shareholder of Bits & Pieces Ltd, a company which runs a number of retail shops selling small items of furniture and items such as lamps and framed prints. She bought large quantities of goods to sell in the shops from George who imports goods from the Far East. Bits & Pieces Ltd still owes George £12,500 for goods delivered in the past. When he said he would not supply any more goods until the debt was paid, Gracie sent him an e-mail stating 'I will personally guarantee the amount of £12,500 owed to you by Bits & Pieces Ltd if you continue to supply goods to Bits & Pieces Ltd'. Below this statement, Gracie typed her name. George supplied further goods but still has not been paid and he now seeks to call in Gracie's guarantee. Which one of the following statements is CORRECT?

   (a) Only a handwritten signature will suffice to make the guarantee enforceable under section 4 of the Statute of Frauds 1677.

   (b) Gracie's typed name will not be considered to be a signature for the purposes of section 4 of the Statute of Frauds 1677.

   (c) Gracie's typed name will be considered to be a signature for the purposes of section 4 of the Statute of Frauds 1677.

(d) Gracie's e-mail is not legally enforceable as section 4 of the Statute of Frauds requires that a guarantee must be in writing and an e-mail is not considered to be in writing.

2   **Which one of the following statements CORRECTLY describes the purpose of an electronic signature under the Electronic Communications Act 2000?**

   (a) To signify that the person to whom it belongs intends to be legally bound by the contents of the document to which it is associated.

   (b) To establish the authenticity or integrity of a communication or electronic data.

   (c) To establish that the document into which it is incorporated or to logically associated is not intended to have legal consequences.

   (d) To verify that the contents of the document are true.

3   **According to the general working rule in Brinkibon, WHEN is a contract made when the form of communication used by the parties is virtually instantaneous (assuming the offer and acceptance are otherwise legally binding and the other requirements for a valid contract are present)?**

   (a) When the acceptance has been received and the recipient has responded by acknowledging it and his agreement to it.

   (b) When the offer has been received.

   (c) When the acceptance is transmitted.

   (d) When the acceptance is received.

4   **Which one of the following statements is NOT CORRECT in relation to the Rome Convention on applicable law?**

   (a) The parties are free to choose which country's law applies to the contract.

   (b) Where one of the parties to a contract is based in Europe, the applicable law must be that of a Member State of the European Community.

   (c) In Europe, consumers cannot be deprived of their own country's consumer protection laws by the choice of applicable law.

   (d) In the absence of a choice of law by the parties, the law will be that of the country most closely connected with the contract.

5   **Providers of information society services are required to provide information in a number of circumstances. Describe those circumstances and the nature of the information to be provided.**

For further resources and updates please go to the Companion Website accompanying this book at **www.mylawchamber.co.uk/bainbridgeIT**

21

Nature, content and formation of electronic contracts

22 Performance of electronic contracts and evidential aspects

INTRODUCTION

The performance of a contract made electronically has a number of implications that do not generally apply to conventional contracts, although generally, the basic rules of contract apply. We saw in the previous chapter that there are certain requirements placed on information society service providers, particularly in relation to the provision of information prior to the making of the contract and mechanisms to determine the applicable law and when the contract is made. There are further requirements in respect of the provision of information both before and after making the contract in consumer contracts made at a distance as well as the availability of a cooling-off period. These provisions, introduced into the UK by the Consumer Protection (Distance Selling) Regulations 2000, as amended, are explained in this chapter.

If there is a breach of contract that has been made electronically, notwithstanding the applicable law, there are issues relating to jurisdiction and enforcement of judgments obtained in other countries. In the example used in the previous chapter involving Karen and Luigi, say that the shoes turned out to be defective and fell apart after a few days wear. Can Karen sue in the English courts or does she have no option but to commence legal proceedings in Italy? There are Conventions and a European Community Regulation dealing with such issues and other legislation in the UK providing for jurisdiction on a wider scale.

Where a contract has been made electronically, most, if not all of the contractual documents and other evidence of performance and breach may be in electronic form. A further issue is whether this affects the admissibility of such evidence in court proceedings. In the UK, stringent and complex rules were developed in relation to the admissibility of evidence in civil and criminal proceedings. Fortunately, this has been alleviated in the UK by the Civil Evidence Act 1995, as will be discussed later.

Other issues, outside the scope of this book, relate to tax liabilities and, particularly, value added tax and customs duties, for example, where goods are ordered online from a country outside the UK.

DISTANCE SELLING

Because of dangers such as impulse buying on the internet and credit card fraud, there was a possibility that some Member States of the European Community could be tempted to impose restrictive legislation whilst others would wish to encourage electronic contracting by leaving it largely unregulated. Harmonisation to avoid such disparities was the driving force behind the

Directive on the protection of consumers in respect of distance contracts.[1] The Directive has a number of implications for contracting over the internet and was implemented by the Consumer Protection (Distance Selling) Regulations 2000 which came into force on 31 October 2000.

Definitions and exemptions

A 'distance contract' is, under Regulation 3(1), one concerning goods or services between a supplier and a consumer under an organised distance sales or service provision scheme run by the supplier who, for the purposes of the contract, makes exclusive use of one or more means of distance communication up to and including the moment the contract is concluded. Thus, right up to and including the time the contract is made, all negotiations and contacts must be by distance communication which includes electronic mail, videotext, videophone, television, radio, videophone and fax as well as more traditional forms of distance selling such as by post (whether or not addressed), telephone (whether with or without human intervention), catalogue and advertising in the press with an order form. The list is contained in Schedule 1 to the Regulations and is not exhaustive, being intended to be indicative only.

A consumer is an individual ('any natural person') who is acting for a purpose outside his business and a supplier is a person (an individual or legal person such as a company) who makes the contract in a commercial or professional capacity. An operator of a means of communication is a public or private person whose business involves making one or more means of distance communication available to suppliers. This will include, for example, internet service providers, telecommunications companies, commercial television and radio bodies and postal authorities and bodies.

Certain types of contracts are excluded and the Regulations do not apply to contracts relating to financial services, automatic vending machines, automated commercial premises, in relation to land (whether or not including the construction of a building) but not rental, concluded with a telecommunications operator through the use of a public pay-phone and contracts concluded at an auction. There is an equivalent Directive concerning the distance marketing of financial services[2] which was implemented by the Financial Services (Distance Marketing) Regulations 2004. The right of cancellation for such services is longer than that generally available for goods or other services governed by the 2000 Regulations.

The provisions in the Regulations that apply to the giving of information, the right of cancellation and the obligation to execute an order within 30 days do not apply to certain contracts for the supply of perishables and for the provision of accommodation, transport, catering or leisure. In Case C-336/03 *easyCar (UK) Ltd* v *Office of Fair Trading* [2005] ECR I-1947, the European Court of Justice ruled that a contract for self-drive car hire was a transport service and, consequently, the right of cancellation did not apply to the contract. A number of complaints had been made about easyCar's terms and condition which only allowed cancellation under 'unusual and unforeseeable events beyond [the customer's control]' such as serious illness of the driver. The Court of Justice accepted that transport services including making a means of transport available to a customer, such as in a car hire agreement. If there was a right of cancellation, without reason, that would place a disproportionate burden on the hirer. Bookings could otherwise be cancelled at the last minute.

---

[1] Directive 97/7/EC of the Parliament and of the Council of 20 May 1997 on the protection of consumers in respect of distance contracts, OJ L 144, 04.06.1997, p. 19 (the 'Directive on the protection of consumers in respect of distance contracts').

[2] Directive 2002/65/EC of the European Parliament and of the Council of 23 September 2002 concerning the distance marketing of consumer financial services, OJ L 271, 09.10.2002, p. 16.

22

Performance of electronic contracts and evidential aspects

Timeshare agreements are exempt from most of the provisions but the Timeshare Act 1992 applies to such contracts and package holidays are exempted from the provisions relating to performance but the Package Travel, Package Holidays and Package Tours Regulations 1992 apply to these.

Provision of information

Certain information must be provided to the consumer before the contract is concluded. This is set out in Regulation 7 of the Consumer Protection (Distance Selling) Regulations 2000 and includes information about the identity of the supplier, the main characteristics of the goods or services, the price including all taxes, delivery costs where appropriate, arrangements for payment, delivery and performance, existence of the right of cancellation where applicable, the cost of using distance communication where other than calculated at a basic rate, the period for which the offer and price remain valid and the minimum duration of the contract in the case of contracts for the supply of goods or services to be performed permanently or recurrently. If the supplier proposes to provide substitute goods or services of equivalent quality or price in the event of those ordered being unavailable, he must also state this and inform the consumer that the cost of returning any such substitute goods will be met by the supplier. The information must be provided in a clear and comprehensible manner, having regard to the principles of good faith in commercial transactions and the principles protecting the interests of those unable to give their consent such as minors. The supplier must make his commercial purpose clear when providing the above information and, where the telephone is used, the supplier must make his identity known at the beginning of any telephone conversation with the consumer.

Regulation 8 requires that written confirmation must be provided (or confirmation in another durable medium which is available and accessible to the consumer). This must be provided in good time, either before conclusion of the contract or in good time thereafter and, in any event, not later than during the performance of the contract in the case of services or at the latest at the time for delivery where goods not for delivery to third parties are concerned. The consumer has a right to cancel the contract in some cases, discussed below, and where this is so, the consumer must be informed of the conditions and procedures for exercising this right, including who will be responsible for returning the goods and the costs of doing so. There is a separate requirement to inform the consumer of the conditions for exercising the right of cancellation where the contract is of unspecified duration or of a duration exceeding one year. Where a service is provided the consumer must be informed about how the right to cancel will be affected where the consumer agrees to the performance of the service beginning before the end of the seven working day cancellation period.

The consumer must also be informed of the geographical address of the supplier to which the consumer may address complaints. Further information, such as that relating to after-sales service guarantees, must also be given. These provisions for providing further additional information do not apply, however, to services performed through the use of distance communication where supplied on only one occasion and invoiced by the operator of the means of distance communication although the geographical address must be divulged nonetheless and the place of business to which the consumer may address complaints.

Right of cancellation

The consumer has a right to cancel the contract under Regulation 10. This is often referred to as the 'cooling-off period'. This period starts the date the contract is concluded (when the contract is made and comes into being) whether it is a contract for the supply of goods or the supply of

Table 22.1 The cancellation period for distance contracts

Case	Contracts for the supply of goods (Regulation 11)	Contracts for the supply of services (Regulation 12)
Supplier complies with Regulation 8	7 working days beginning the day after the day the consumer receives the goods	(If Regulation 8 complied with on or before the day the contract is concluded) 7 working days beginning the day after the day the contract is concluded
Supplier fails to comply with Regulation 8 but provides the information required by Regulation 8 within 3 months beginning the day after the day the consumer receives the goods or, in the case of a contract for the supply of services, the day after the day the contract is concluded	7 working days after the day the consumer receives the information	7 working days beginning with the day after the day the contract is concluded
Supplier fails to comply with Regulation 8 and fails to supply information within 3 months as above	3 months plus 7 working days after the day the consumer receives the goods	3 months plus 7 working days beginning the day after the day the contract is concluded
Contract provides for goods to be delivered to a third party	Determined as if delivery to third party was delivery to consumer	N/A

services. The rules about when the cooling-off period ends are more complex and differ in the case of contracts for the supply of goods or services. They are set out in Table 22.1.

It would be inappropriate to provide for a cooling-off period in respect of everything that can be supplied through a distance contract. For example, if computer software is delivered online, the consumer might be tempted to make a copy of the software and then attempt to exercise a right of cancellation. Consequently, Regulation 13 contains a number of exceptions to the consumer's right to cancel, being where the contract is for:

- the supply of services where the supplier has informed the consumer that he does not have the right to cancel once the performance of the services has commenced with the consumer's agreement during the seven-day period mentioned in Table 22.1;
- the supply of goods or services the price of which is dependent on fluctuations in the financial market which cannot be controlled by the supplier;
- the supply of goods made to the consumer's specifications or clearly personalised or which by reason of their nature cannot be returned or are liable to deteriorate or expire rapidly;
- for the supply of audio or video recordings or computer software if they are unsealed by the consumer;
- for the supply of newspapers, periodicals or magazines; or
- for gaming, betting or lottery services.

Regulation 14 provides for the speedy reimbursement of sums paid by or on behalf of the consumer. In some cases, the supplier may make a charge but not, for example, where the consumer has a right to reject under implied terms or where a term requiring the consumer to return the goods is deemed to be an unfair term under the Unfair Terms in Consumer Contracts Regulations 1999. Any related consumer credit agreement is automatically cancelled when the consumer exercises his right of cancellation under Regulation 15. A duty is imposed on the consumer to retain possession of the goods and to take reasonable care of them until they are restored to the supplier.

For distance marketing of financial services, the right to cancel is generally 14 calendar days except in the case of life insurance and personal pensions where the period is 30 calendar days: Regulation 10 of the Financial Services (Distance Marketing) Regulations 2004. Again, when the cancellation period starts depends on whether the consumer has been provided with the requisite information (subject again to a three month maximum starting period if the information is not provided) and there are exceptions, such as where credit is given secured on land by way of legal mortgage.

Performance of a distance selling contract

The basic rule is that, unless the parties agree otherwise, orders must be executed within 30 days beginning the day after the day the consumer sent his order to the supplier under Regulation 19. If the supplier is unable to deliver within that time because of the unavailability of goods and services, the consumer must be informed and any sum paid by or on behalf of the consumer must be reimbursed. Substitute goods or services of equivalent quality and price may be supplied if the contract provides for such a possibility and prior to the conclusion of the contract the consumer was provided with information in a durable form to that effect.

Other provisions

Credit card fraud is a major problem and there are particular risks in relation to distance selling contracts. Under Regulation 21, a consumer is entitled to cancel a payment where fraudulent use has been made of his card (including credit cards, charge cards, debit cards and store cards) in connection with a contract governed by the regulation by another person not acting, or to be treated as acting, as his agent. Furthermore, a consumer is entitled to be recredited, or to have all sums returned by the card issuer, in the event of fraudulent use of his card by another person not acting, or to be treated as acting, as the consumer's agent. Where a consumer alleges that any use made of the payment card was not authorised by him the burden of proving that the use was authorised lies with the card issuer, being the owner of the card. These provisions do not apply, however, to an agreement within section 83(1) of the Consumer Credit Act 1974, which confers equivalent protection in relation to regulated consumer credit agreements.

Inertia selling is controlled and the general rule, subject to some exceptions, is that a consumer may treat unsolicited goods as an unconditional gift, the rights of the sender to the goods are extinguished. If, in the course of a business, a person making a demand for payment, or threatening legal proceedings, not having reasonable cause to believe there is a right to payment, knowing the goods or services are unsolicited, commits a criminal offence under Regulation 24. Any contractual term inconsistent with the regulations is void if and to the extent that it is inconsistent.

EVIDENTIAL STATUS OF ELECTRONIC DOCUMENTS IN CIVIL TRIALS

Article 9 of the UNCITRAL Model Law on Electronic Commerce 1996, amended 1998, states that nothing in the application of the rules of evidence shall apply to prevent the admissibility of a data message in evidence on the sole ground that it is a data message or, if it is the best evidence the person adducing it could reasonably be expected to obtain, on the grounds that it is not in its original form. (A 'data message' means information generated, sent, received or stored by electronic, optical or similar means including, but not limited to, electronic data interchange (EDI), electronic mail, telegram, telex or telecopy.)

Putting barriers up to the admissibility of computer documents as evidence of the facts stated therein could seriously prejudice the growth of electronic commerce, for example, making it difficult if not impossible to prove the existence of a contract or the terms of the contract or details of the performance of the contract or determining whether there has been a breach of the contract. Although the rules on the admissibility of computer evidence in civil proceedings were unduly complex, fortunately the civil law has moved on and adopted a far more sensible and realistic approach.

Originally, the best evidence rule insisted that only an original document could be admitted as evidence and copies were not allowed. This could cause significant hardship if the original had been lost or destroyed. The best evidence rule has all but disappeared but remnants of it still remain. The courts have recognised that a rigid adherence to the best evidence rule is inappropriate in the context of the accuracy with which copies of originals may now be made. Lord Justice Lloyd said in *R v Governor of Pentonville Prison, ex parte Osman* [1989] 3 All ER 701:

> We accept that it [the best evidence rule] served an important purpose in the days of parchment and quill pens. But, since the invention of carbon paper and, still more, the photocopier and telefacsimile machine, that purpose has largely gone.

A general exclusion on copies of original documents is no longer fitting. Indeed, in some cases, a document may be unintelligible in its original form without its being converted and displayed on a screen or printed out – for example, in the case of a document stored digitally on a magnetic disk. However, the original must still be produced if it is available. This would not apply where the original had been destroyed or lost.

A long tradition in English law has been the importance of a person giving evidence of what he personally knows or has witnessed with his own eyes. The fact that a witness is confined to matters of which he has personal knowledge and can be examined and cross-examined on those matters is a central plank of the English law of evidence. Second-hand or third-hand evidence is by its nature very unreliable, so much so that it was not allowed to be given in court.

There was a rule against admitting hearsay evidence in civil trials (the rule still exists subject to exceptions in a different form relation to criminal trials). Hearsay evidence is secondary evidence such as where a witness relates something that was told to him by another person but not directly seen or heard by the witness – for example, where Bill states that Jenny told him that she saw Paul trying to erase a computer program. The rule was quite strict and such evidence would not be admitted at all except in specific circumstances, some of which applied to information stored on a computer. Section 5 of the Civil Evidence Act 1968 (now repealed by the Civil Evidence Act 1995) allowed statements contained in documents produced by a computer to be admitted in civil trials as evidence of any fact stated therein if the evidence would have been admissible as direct oral evidence, but only subject to certain conditions.

Fortunately, the Civil Evidence Act 1995 has effectively swept aside the old rule against hearsay evidence in civil cases. The relevant provisions came into force on 31 January 1997 but the Act does not extend to Scotland which has its own rules. Hearsay evidence is admissible under section 1 of the Civil Evidence Act 1995 and is defined as a statement made otherwise than by a person giving oral evidence in the proceedings and includes hearsay evidence of whatever degree. There are certain safeguards as regards notice to be given to other parties.

Although hearsay evidence is now admissible, it may not be given much weight. For example, if it is a document stored on computer which has undergone many alterations that have not been properly recorded or logged, it may carry little weight. Under section 4 of the Act, the weight, if any, to be given to hearsay evidence depends on the circumstances and regard shall be had to whether:

- it would be reasonable and practicable to call the original maker of the statement as a witness;
- the original statement was made at the same time as the occurrence or existence of the matters stated;
- the evidence involves multiple hearsay;
- any person involved has any motive to conceal or misrepresent matters;
- the original statement was an edited account or made in collaboration with another for a particular purpose; and
- the circumstances in which the evidence is adduced as hearsay are such as to suggest an attempt to prevent proper evaluation of its weight.

Hearsay may carry little weight unless it would have been admissible under Part I of the Civil Evidence Act 1968, now repealed. Factors included:

- *regularity* – whether the computer was regularly used to store or process information, for the purposes of any activities regularly carried out, over a period which includes the time when the document was made;
- *consistency* – during the relevant period information of the kind contained in the document (or of a kind from which such information is derived) was regularly supplied to the computer in the ordinary course of those activities;
- *reliability* – the computer was operating properly during the material part of that period (or, if not, any malfunction or breakdown that occurred would not have affected the accuracy of the material contained in the document);
- *orthodoxy* – the information contained in the document reproduces or is derived from information supplied to the computer in the ordinary course of the activities regularly carried out over the period in question.

Where a number of computers had been used – for example, successively or in a network – all the computers involved were treated as a single computer in determining the purpose of the activities. A person wishing to proffer a computer statement as evidence had to provide a certificate identifying the relevant document and the manner in which it was produced and giving other particulars. The certificate was required to be signed by a person occupying a responsible position in relation to the operation of the relevant device or the management of the relevant activities. It did not matter if the information was supplied or produced without any human intervention by means of appropriate equipment. This covered the situation where a computer was set up to record information and produce documents automatically.

Although the hearsay rule has been relaxed, if not altogether scrapped, the fact that a number of factors determine the weight to be given to such evidence means that it may not always be very influential, if at all. The main advantage flowing from the 1995 Act is that the formal rules under the 1968 Act have gone to be replaced by a welcome degree of flexibility. It will still be important, however, to show that the computer was operating reliably at the time and there is nothing to indicate that the evidence is unreliable. Adherence to the relevant standards applying to security and good computer practice will help in this respect.

SUMMARY

- Consumers are protected by the Consumer Protection (Distance Selling) Regulations 2000 which apply to:
  - contracts for goods or services between a supplier and consumer;
  - where exclusive use is made of one or more means of distance communication up to and including when the contract is concluded.
- Some forms of contract are excluded, for example:
  - financial services (separately provided for);
  - contracts concerning land; and
  - auction sales.
- The Regulations give rights to consumers to:
  - specified types of information before the contract is concluded;
  - cancel the contract in some cases;
  - written confirmation and further information once the contract is concluded.
- The right of cancellation, where available, is based on a period of seven working days:
  - the commencement is based on the time the consumer receives goods; or
  - the contract is concluded, in the case of a service contract;
  - the start of the seven days will be postponed if the supplier delays in providing the further information.
- Orders must be executed within 30 days unless the parties agree otherwise.
- Consumers are protected against credit card fraud.
- The best evidence rule has all but been swept aside.
- Hearsay evidence is now admissible in civil proceedings:
  - however, the weight to be given to hearsay evidence will depend on the circumstances.

SELF-TEST QUESTION

1   Describe the extent to which consumers are protected in relation to distance selling. Look at a typical e-commerce website and note how well it conforms to the requirement to provide information before a contract is concluded under Regulation 7 of the Consumer Protection (Distance Selling) Regulations 2000, the relevant parts of which are set out below.

7 – Information required prior to the conclusion of the contract

(1) ... in good time prior to the conclusion of the contract the supplier shall –

　(a) provide to the consumer the following information –
　　(i)　the identity of the supplier and, where the contract requires payment in advance, the supplier's address;
　　(ii)　a description of the main characteristics of the goods or services;
　　(iii)　the price of the goods or services including all taxes;
　　(iv)　delivery costs where appropriate;
　　(v)　the arrangements for payment, delivery or performance;

22

Performance of electronic contracts and evidential aspects

        (vi)   the existence of a right of cancellation except in the cases referred to in Regulation 13;

        (vii) the cost of using the means of distance communication where it is calculated other than at the basic rate;

        (viii) the period for which the offer or the price remains valid; and

        (ix) where appropriate, the minimum duration of the contract, in the case of contracts for the supply of goods or services to be performed permanently or recurrently;

    (b) inform the consumer if he proposes, in the event of the goods or services ordered by the consumer being unavailable, to provide substitute goods or services (as the case may be) of equivalent quality and price; and

    (c) inform the consumer that the cost of returning any such substitute goods to the supplier in the event of cancellation by the consumer would be met by the supplier.

(2) The supplier shall ensure that the information required by paragraph (1) is provided in a clear and comprehensible manner appropriate to the means of distance communication used, with due regard in particular to the principles of good faith in commercial transactions and the principles governing the protection of those who are unable to give their consent such as minors.

(3) ... the supplier shall ensure that his commercial purpose is made clear when providing the information required by paragraph (1).

For further resources and updates please go to the Companion Website accompanying this book at www.mylawchamber.co.uk/bainbridgeIT

23 Torts related to electronic information

INTRODUCTION

Tort is an area of law in which civil liability may attach to a person independently of the existence of a contract. Areas covered by the law of tort include negligence (including negligent misstatement), defamation, malicious falsehood and nuisance. Tort is a wide-ranging area of law and other torts relate to assault (as opposed to criminal offences relating to assault), trespass to the person, trespass to goods, unlawful interference with contract, passing off, breach of statutory duty and malicious prosecution.

Some torts are outside the scope of this book and some have already been dealt with in appropriate places in the book, for example, in Chapters 11 and 14. This chapter concentrates on torts particularly relevant to the internet and information placed on websites or transmitted through internet service providers (ISPs). Negligent misstatement has already been dealt with in Chapter 14 in the context of computer contracts but further mention is made in this chapter as appropriate. Defamation is also covered here, including the tort of malicious falsehood and the liability of ISPs and the like as publishers of defamatory information in the context of the publisher's defence. The next chapter looks specifically at the provisions removing liability from information society service providers including ISPs generally for illegal material passing through or stored on their systems. A defence is provided where the provider acts as a mere conduit and in connection with caching and hosting activities under the Electronic Commerce (EC Directive) Regulations 2002.

NEGLIGENT MISSTATEMENT

The fundamentals of an action in negligent misstatement are set out in Chapter 14. To recap, on the basis of *Hedley Byrne & Co Ltd* v *Heller & Partners Ltd* [1964] AC 465, liability can ensue where a statement which proves to be incorrect is made negligently by a person holding himself out as being an expert in the relevant field who intends that statement to be taken seriously. Typically, any person giving advice, whether or not in the course of performing a contract, would attempt to minimise their potential liability by adding a notice or term excluding or limiting his or her liability should the statement turn out to be incorrect. In the UK, we have seen that the Unfair Contract Terms Act 1977 controls such notices or terms and they will be ineffective in the case of death or personal injury and, in other cases, will only be effective if and to the extent that they meet the requirement of reasonableness as set out in that Act.

Potentially, any information placed on a website which purports to give advice could be actionable under the law of negligent misstatement if it turns out to be incorrect, subject to any valid exclusion or limitation clauses. However, a number of factors may be relevant. If, for example, someone gives advice specifically directed to a particular person or class of persons by e-mail which is intended to be taken seriously and acted upon by that person or persons, then there is no reason why liability in principle cannot ensue should the advice turn out to be wrong and given negligently. The normal rules of negligent misstatement should apply.

Things might be different where information containing advice, whether or not intended to be taken seriously and acted upon, is placed on a website, bulletin board or in a blog. Cases on negligent misstatement have in the past concentrated on the importance of a special relationship between the giver of the statement and a person who suffers loss as a result of relying on it. Was the advice or information compiled for and directed for the person who relied on it? In other words, is there sufficient proximity between the maker of the statement and the person relying on it; *Caparo Industries plc v Dickman* [1990] 2 AC 605? The importance of proximity and a contemplation that the advice would be relied upon by the claimant has been reinforced in numerous cases after *Caparo*. For example, in *Barings plc v Coopers and Lybrand (No 1)* [2002] 2 BCLC 364, the court stressed the importance of reliance and the question of whether the statement maker had in his contemplation that his advice would be relied upon by the claimant for a particular transaction or class of transactions. Furthermore, the claimant must have, in fact, relied upon the advice before embarking upon the transaction, which resulted in the loss for which compensation is claimed.

This calls into question whether simply posting information on websites or bulletin boards could result in liability for negligent misstatement. Two situations are possible. The first is where the information is placed there for a general audience. In such a case, it is highly unlikely that liability could result no matter how negligently the advice was compiled. Persons accessing the internet have become accustomed to the fact that there is a phenomenal amount of information available, some of which is of little or no merit. Most of us have become wary and sceptical of claims made on webpages. The amount of questionable material available has made visitors to websites cautious.

On the other hand, if the advice or information is directed towards individuals or classes of individuals, the situation is less clear. For example, if the information is aimed at potential clients, there is a possibility of finding the necessary proximity. For example, a firm of solicitors may operate a website that provides advice and updates intended to impress existing clients and attract new business. In such a case, it is arguable that the necessary proximity applies not just with the existing clients but also with the potential clients. The firm of solicitors might be well advised to place a disclaimer on the website. In terms of loss or damage other than death or personal injury, it would seem reasonable to do so, provided it was made clear that the information was in a general form and visitors to the site were warned that they should seek professional advice rather than act on the information in what might prove to be an inappropriate context.

Another factor is that negligence is an area of law in which the courts are often influenced by policy considerations. In extending liability for negligence, including negligent misstatement, the courts have been wary of opening the floodgates and imposing liability too widely. This was an important factor in *Caparo Industries plc v Dickman*. A further issue is whether it is feasible to take out insurance to cover a particular form of liability. By too readily making owners of websites liable for negligent misstatement, that could leave them facing an enormous number of claims against which they could find it hard if not impossible to insure.

Owners of websites must also take account of variations in the scope and extent of liability for statements in different jurisdictions. Again, the use of a suitably worded disclaimer could be important.

DEFAMATION

Lord Bingham of Cornhill in his foreword to Collins, M., *The Law of Defamation and the Internet*, Oxford University Press, 2005, said the law of defamation in the context of the internet would require '. . . almost every concept and rule in the field . . . to be reconsidered in the light of this unique medium of instant worldwide communication'. The issues that arise relate partly from the nature of defamation as a cause of action, differences in national laws on defamation and jurisdictional issues. In terms of traditional forms of publishing, a publisher exerted a great deal of control over where copies of his publications were made available. Publication on the internet is different in that it is, potentially, publication to the entire world. Factors relevant to intellectual property rights such as where a particular advertisement on a website is targeted seem less relevant for defamatory statements. For trade mark infringement, it is a question of where the website owner actively seeks to attract business; see *Zippo Manufacturing Co v Zippo Dot Com Inc* 952 F Supp 1119 (WD Pa 1997), discussed in Chapter 11. For defamation, the key is more likely to focus on the place where the claimant has a reputation to be harmed by the defamatory statement.

There have been a number of cases of defamation on the internet. Some of the early cases give a flavour of dangers of being careless or too forthright in making statements available over the internet. For example, in *Rindos* v *Hardwick* (unreported) 31 March 1994, the Supreme Court of Western Australia found that a statement made by an academic which seriously denigrated another academic's competence and which also imputed misconduct on his part was defamatory and an award of A$40,000 in damages was made. (However, judgment was given in default as the defendant did not put in an appearance.) In *Stratton Oakmont Inc v Prodigy Services Co*, 1995 NY Misc. LEXIS 229, the Supreme Court of the State of New York held that the defendant, a service provider, was the publisher of statements on its bulletin board and granted summary judgment against it in respect of libellous statements made on the bulletin board. The statements made claims that the claimant had committed fraudulent acts in relation to a public offering of company stocks. In the United Kingdom, a lecturer accepted undisclosed damages in an out-of-court settlement for online statements that were potentially defamatory (Calow, D. (1995) 'Defamation on the Internet', *Computer Law and Security Report*, 11(4), p. 199). More recently a college lecturer had to pay £10,000 in damages together with costs of £7,200 after posting a blog describing a UKIP candidate a 'lard brain', 'Nazi', 'racist bigot' and a 'nonce' (*The Guardian*, 23 March 2006).

Following the *Stratton* v *Prodigy* case, which seemed to impose liability against ISPs who actively checked and screened the content available through its service (deemed to be original publishers) as opposed to those that did nothing (deemed to be distributors subject to a lower 'knowledge' standard), the US enacted the Communications Decency Act 1996 47 USC §230 which states that 'no provider or user of an interactive computer service shall be treated as the publisher or speaker of any information provided by another information content provider'.

Defamation is something of a rarity in that it is a civil action in which a jury may be sworn in and, if this is the case, it is the jury which decides whether defamation has been made out and, if so, the jury also decides the award. Under section 8 of the Defamation Act 1996, however, the judge may deal with the case summarily where it appears that the case is very clear cut – for example, where the claimant has no real chance of success. Juries have been known to award very substantial damages in defamation actions but there is an argument that damages for injury to reputation should not exceed damages awarded for serious or even catastrophic personal injury arising out of negligence. However, it is not really proper to equate damage to reputation with personal injury. The former has an element of deterrence absent in personal injury cases and, often, defamation is an intentional wrongdoing whereas actionable personal injury is usually the result of negligence. The deterrent effect in defamation should not, however, be so high as to inhibit responsible journalism; *Gleaner Company Ltd* v *Abrahams* [2003] UKHL 55 (Privy Council).

There are two branches of defamation: libel and slander. Generally, libel relates to written statements whereas slander relates to the spoken word. The distinction is important because libel is actionable *per se* – that is, without proof of damage. Except in some cases, slander requires proof of damage. It appears that a defamatory image will be classed as libel rather than slander. In *Yousopouff* v *MGM Pictures Ltd* (1934) 50 TLR 581, the defendant made a film which suggested that the claimant was a Russian princess who had been 'ravished' or seduced by Rasputin. This was held to be libel, not slander.

An image taken from a computer game resulted in a libel action in the House of Lords. In *Charleston* v *News Group Newspapers* [1995] 2 AC 65, a Sunday newspaper carried a photograph which had been taken from a pornographic computer game. It depicted a man and woman who appeared to be engaged in sexual intercourse or other sexual activity. Superimposed on the photographs were images of the heads of the claimants, actors who played Harold and Madge Bishop in the television 'soap' *Neighbours*. The captions ran 'Strewth! What's Harold up to with our Madge?' and 'Porn Shocker for Neighbours Stars'. However, because the text underneath made it clear that the image had been produced as part of a pornographic computer game which had used the images of the claimants without their permission, it was held not to be libellous. The law does not take account of 'a moron in a hurry' – that is, a careless reader, who would not read such a 'disclaimer' and might not realise the true nature of the image, is ignored in determining whether it is libellous. Since that case, the data protection law would almost certainly provide a remedy in that such processing of personal data (and an image from which a living individual can be identified is personal data) has caused substantial distress to the actors concerned.

Before looking further at defamation in the context of the internet, including considering recent cases in the UK and elsewhere, the basic nature of defamation is described below.

Basics of defamation

A defamatory statement is one which, when published, tends to lower a person in the esteem of right-thinking members of society generally; or which tends to make them shun or avoid that person. The statement does not have to allege some moral turpitude or wrongdoing on the part of the claimant and it can be defamation to allege insanity or being the victim of a crime such as rape.

It is common to see disclaimers as to the characters portrayed in a film. It is dangerous to publish something containing, for example, a fictional character with a name that might be the same as a real person. In *Hulton & Co* v *Jones* [1910] AC 20, an article was published by the defendant which was alleged by the defendant to be fictitious. It contained defamatory statements about one 'Artemus Jones', a churchwarden from Peckham. However, and unfortunately for the defendant, by coincidence there was a person with that name who happened to be a barrister living in North Wales. He successfully sued for libel. It was thought that some of his friends and acquaintances might think the article referred to him.

Hulton v *Jones* was distinguished in *Kerry O'Shea* v *MGN Ltd* (unreported) 4 May 2001 in relation to images. In that case, the first defendant, the Sunday Mirror published advertisements for the second defendant's internet service which carried the headline, 'Free Internet access for adults only. The world's first free adult ISP.' The advertisements included photographs of females, one of which looked incredibly like the claimant, and was inviting readers to 'see me now' at the website in question. The woman whose photograph it actually was had consented to its publication. The claimant, who was a respectable 24-year-old woman sued for defamation on the basis that persons who knew her would believe it was her photograph in the advertisement. The defamatory meaning alleged was that the claimant was appearing on a pornographic website.

In cases like *Hulton* v *Jones* where a name was used, it would be possible to discover the existence of the claimant. However, in respect of a photograph, it would be impossible to discover the identity of everyone who was a look-alike or doppelganger of a person whose photograph was to be published or, indeed, whether there was a look-alike. The judge considered the fact that a publisher is subject to strict liability and, subject to the offer of amends procedure in section 2(4) of the Defamation Act 1996, will be liable even if blameless. This could interfere with freedom of expression. Article 10(2) of the European Convention on Human Rights allows restrictions on freedom of expression 'necessary in a democratic society, in the interests of national security, territorial integrity or public safety, for the prevention of disorder or crime, for the protection of health or morals, for *the protection of the reputation or rights of others*' (emphasis added). Mr Justice Moreland concluded that the principle of strict liability should not be extended to look-alike situations as this would unjustifiably interfere with freedom of expression and this would be disproportionate with the legitimate aim of protecting the reputations of others.

For defamation to be actionable, publication is required and it must be to at least one person other than the claimant. It may be by means of words, pictures, visual images, gestures or any other method of signifying meaning. The defendant must either publish the material himself or be responsible for publication. Every repetition of a defamatory publication is a fresh publication and actionable. Thus, if defamatory material is placed on the internet, every time it is accessed and read by someone, this constitutes a separate defamation. This is certainly the case in some jurisdictions such as England and Australia (though in some states of the United States of America, there is a single publication rule such that only the first publication counts to give rise to a cause of action).

The potential of the multiple publication rule is that thousands or even millions of causes of action could accrue in respect of placing defamatory material on a webpage or a bulletin board. Also, a reasonably foreseeable repetition of a publication by a third party will also bring liability. In *Slipper* v *British Broadcasting Corp* [1991] 1 QB 283, which concerned a film broadcast by the defendant, the claims made by the claimant included damages for reviews of the film in the press. The Court of Appeal refused to strike out these additional claims. In respect of republication it was held that this could be a *novus actus interveniens* (a new act breaking the chain of causation) if it was unauthorised. However, where reasonably foreseeable, the chain of causation was not broken.

There are a number of defences to a defamation action including fair comment, justification (that is, that the statement is true), an offer to make amends and privilege (absolute and qualified).

DEFAMATION ON THE INTERNET – SPECIAL ISSUES

The placing of defamatory material on a website or bulletin board or in a blog, or sending such material in or attached to e-mails, gives rise to a number of issues that relate to the nature of the internet. One is the multiple publication rule which applies in the UK and some other places where every time a libel is published a new cause of action accrues. Another area of concern has to do with the global nature of the internet and may cause courts to question whether they have jurisdiction to hear a defamation claim. There is also the danger that posting a defamatory statement on a website or in a blog may give rise to concurrent liability in a number of jurisdictions, exposing the person responsible (and, possibly also the service provider) to multiple claims in different countries. The position of publishers, as opposed to the author of the defamatory state-ment is also an issue. A European Directive attempted to deal with this (and other liabilities of service providers in respect of illegal material) and is discussed in the following chapter. However, in this chapter, specific reference is made to the 'publishers' defence' under section 1 of the Defamation Act 1996. The Directive on electronic commerce[1] and legislation made to imple-ment it is of wider significance though may supplement the protection afforded ISPs in respect of defamation.

Multiple publication rule

In the UK and some other jurisdictions, defamation occurs each and every time the offending statement is published, the 'multiple publication rule'. In others, most notably in many of the states of the United States of America, there is a 'single publication rule' and only the first pub-lication gives rise to a cause of action, although subsequent publications may be taken into account when assessing damages. This is an important distinction as the limitation period for defamation (the time within which legal proceedings must be commenced) is comparatively low. Under section 4A of the Limitation Act 1980, the period is one year from the date that the cause of action accrued (although this period may be increased in special circumstances at the court's discretion, for example, where the claimant did not become aware of the facts giving rise to the cause of action until after expiry of the limitation period and he acted expediently once he did become aware). Until 4 September 1996, the limitation period in England and Wales and Northern Ireland in relation to defamation (and slander of title, slander of goods and other mali-cious falsehoods) was three years (six years before 1985) and it remains at three years in Scotland (section 18A Prescription and Limitation Act (Scotland) 1973).

To take an example of the two rules, say that A writes an article which contains a defamatory statement and it is published in a daily newspaper. Two years later the article is included in a web archive containing interesting articles published in the newspaper. Say also that the person defamed, B, was aware of the first publication but took no action at that time. It was only on seeing the second publication in the web archive that she decided to commence legal proceedings against A. If the single publication rule applied, B would be time-barred in England and Wales but if the multiple publication rule applied, she will be able to commence proceedings in respect of the second publication. Alternatively, B might be able to bring separate proceedings in Scotland in respect of both publications as the limitation period for defamation is three years in Scotland.

The multiple publication rule was considered by the Court of Appeal in *Loutchansky* v *Times Newspapers Ltd* [2002] QB 783. In that case, the defendant published, on 8 September 1999 and 14 October 1999, in its newspaper articles alleging that the claimant, who had dual Russian and Israeli nationality, was a Russian mafia boss and involved in international criminal activities. The claimant commenced proceedings in respect of the articles on 6 December 1999. The articles where placed on the defendant's website and were available after 21 February 2000 and the claimant commenced a second action in respect of that publication on 6 December 2000. The defendant claimed qualified privilege, which applies, *inter alia*, where the publisher has a duty to publish and the public had a right to know of the allegations. The judge at first instance rejected that defence in the first hearing and, in respect of the second proceedings relating to the website publication, the defendant argued that this was time-barred as the second proceedings were commenced more than one year after the first publication of the articles in the newspapers.

---

[1] Directive 2000/31/EC of the European Parliament and of the Council of 8 June 2000 on certain legal aspects of infor-mation society services, in particular electronic commerce, in the Internal Market, OJ L 178, 17.07.2000, p. 1.

As regards the qualified privilege point, the Court of Appeal held that the judge had applied the wrong test in deciding that, as the defendant would not be subject to legitimate criticism had it failed to publish, the defence did not apply and this matter was remitted back to the judge for reconsideration (who confirmed that the defendant could not rely on qualified privilege). Rather, the test should have been whether there was a duty to publish the material to the intended recipients who had an interest in receiving it. The interest being (*per* Lord Philips of Worth Matravers at para. 36):

> ... that of the public in a modern democracy in free expression and, more particularly, in the promotion of a free and vigorous press to keep the public informed ... [the] corresponding duty on the journalist (and equally his editor) is to play his proper role in discharging that function. His task is to behave as a responsible journalist.

The single publication argument was rejected by the Court of Appeal which confirmed that each and every publication causes a fresh right of action to accrue. The basis of this rule is firmly entrenched in English law and goes back to the striking old case, *Duke of Brunswick* v *Harmer* (1849) 14 QB 185, where back issues of a newspaper containing an article libelling the Duke of Brunswick were bought some 17 years after first publication and which were considered to be a separate publication on which the Duke could bring a libel action (the limitation period for libel was six years at that time). Although in the present case, there was some importance in maintaining and publishing archives, that was not as important as contemporary publication. That the multiple publication rule imposed restrictions on giving access to archive material, this was justified as being necessary and proportionate in a democratic society to protect the reputation of others and, consequently, the rule was not in conflict with the right of freedom of expression provided for by Article 10 of the European Convention on Human Rights. In any case, publishing archive material should be possible, even if the content was hotly contested, by adding an appropriate statement or qualification. This had not been done and the Court of Appeal confirmed that qualified privilege could not apply to the internet publication which had been done after the defendant was aware that allegations of defamation had been made in respect of the articles by the claimant.

Jurisdiction

The 'Brussels' Regulation on jurisdiction, etc.[2] contain a set of rules to determine which courts in the European Community have jurisdiction in civil matters.[3] The basic rule under Article 2 is that defendants domiciled in a Member State are sued in that Member State (whatever their nationality). In relation to torts, a further possibility is that a defendant may be sued in the Member State where the place where the harmful event occurred under Article 5(3) and, for defamation, that is the place where the publication took place. Where there are two or more defendants jointly responsible for the tort who are domiciled in different Member States, the claimant may elect which one of those states to commence legal proceedings. A further rule is that, where proceedings have been brought in the courts of more than one jurisdiction, the courts other than the court first seised (that is, the court where proceedings were brought first) must stay their actions until the jurisdiction of the first court is established. If it is so established, the other courts must then decline jurisdiction in favour of the first; Article 27. Some examples

---

[2] Council Regulation (EC) No 44/2001 of 22 December 2000 on jurisdiction and the recognition and enforcement of judgments in civil and commercial matters, OJ L 12, 16.01.2001, p. 1.

[3] The Lugano Convention is similar and with the Brussels Regulation extends the rules to the European Economic Area.

23

Torts related to electronic information

may help (assume in all cases that the person defamed has a reputation in the country or countries of publication, unless otherwise stated).

- F, domiciled in France, publishes in England an article defamatory of G, domiciled in Germany. G may sue F in France (on the basis of the defendant's domicile) or England as that is where the tort occurred.

- F, domiciled in France, and S, domiciled in Spain, jointly write an article defamatory of E, domiciled in England. The article is published in England. E may sue in England (where the tort occurred), France or Spain (based on the co-defendants' domicile).

- D, domiciled in Denmark, E, domiciled in England, and F, domiciled in France, each individually contributed to a blog about G, domiciled in Germany. G is well known in Germany and Austria only but the material added to the blog by D, E and F individually is defamatory of G. G can sue D in Denmark, E in England and F in France separately on the basis of Article 2 of the Brussels Regulation. G can sue all three in Germany and Austria on the basis of Article 5(3), as he has a reputation in those countries. Technically, there will be three separate actions in each country as the torts are separate though these may be consolidated into a single action in each country.

- X is a European Commissioner who is well known throughout Europe. E, domiciled in England, posted a blog on the internet which falsely accused X of being involved in large-scale corruption. As every time the blog is accessed counts as a separate publication, potentially, X can bring proceedings in all the countries where there is evidence that this has happened. The rule about courts other than that first seised does not apply as each publication is a separate tort.

In case of defamatory material published on the internet, if a person has a reputation in a number of jurisdictions and the material is downloaded in at least some of those jurisdictions, it would seem that a cause of action arises in each of them. Four points can be made about that possibility. First, where a libel is disseminated via the internet does this give rise to a separate cause of action in each country (as in the above examples) or is there such a thing as a global tort of defamation which can be heard and dealt with by the courts in one country only? Secondly, is there a *de minimis* principle such that if only a few persons in one jurisdiction access the material, the courts will decline jurisdiction on the basis that no tort has been committed? The third point is whether there is any place for the doctrine *forum non conveniens* by which courts decline jurisdiction on the basis that the courts in another country are better suited to hear the case? Finally, can the courts in one country hear concurrent cases of defamation occurring in more than one jurisdiction?

Global tort theory

The global tort theory, convenient as it might be resulting in a single court hearing to resolve the issue of defamation in its entirety, has no place in English law, or for that matter the law in many other countries. It was narrowly rejected by a 3:2 majority in the House of Lords in *Berezovsky* v *Michaels* [2000] 2 All ER 986, in which a magazine published in the US contained an article alleging that the claimants, who were Russian citizens, were involved in organised crime in Russia. The magazine had a circulation of 785,000 in the US, 13 in Russia and around 2,000 in England. It was also placed on the defendant's website which was accessed by a number of persons in England and it was accepted that, altogether, around 6,000 people had read the article in England. Both claimants had significant connections in England and decided to bring an action for defamation in England.

Counsel for the defendants argued that, on the basis of the US single publication rule, in a multi-jurisdiction case on defamation, the correct approach was to treat it as giving a single cause of action and then to decide in which jurisdiction that single cause of action arose. In most cases, of course, that would be the country in which the publisher is established as that would be likely to be the place where the largest amount of publication takes place. That approach was rejected. Whilst it may make sense in the US because of its federal constitution, it conflicts with the English multiple publication rule, that each publication is a separate tort. In the present case, the claimants had a reputation in England and there had been a significant distribution of the defamatory material in England. Therefore, England was an appropriate place to hear the action and allow service on the US defendant.

The global theory also conflicts with the decision of the European Court of Justice in Case C-68/93 *Shevill* v *Presse Alliance SA* [1995] ECR I-415. In that case, the court considered the Brussels Regulation on jurisdiction, etc.[4] The European Court of Justice held that a victim libelled in a newspaper article which had been distributed in several Member States may bring an action for defamation either:

- before the courts of the Member State where the publisher was established; or
- before the courts of each Member State in which the article had been distributed and where the victim claimed to have suffered damage.

The criteria for assessing whether the event was harmful and the evidence required of the existence and extent of the harm alleged were to be determined by the substantive law determined by the national conflict of laws rules of the court concerned.

The decision is particularly important in England and Wales as libel is actionable *per se*, that is, without proof of damage. Nor is it required that the victim is well known. If the victim is named in the defamatory statement, that is sufficient to found an action in defamation. The global tort theory has no place in the UK or in most other jurisdictions. In terms of the US, the single publication rule makes sense as between the different states but not between different countries.

The Australian High Court has taken a similar stance to the House of Lords and rejected the single publication rule and the consequences of it for jurisdiction. In *Dow Jones & Co Inc* v *Gutnick* [2002] HCA 56, Dow Jones printed the *Wall Street Journal* and *Barron's Online* (available on WSJ.com). On 28 October 2000, an article 'Unholy Gains' appeared on the website which was claimed by Mr Gutnick to be defamatory of him and he sued in the Supreme Court of Victoria, Australia. The article had suggested that he was a money launderer. WSJ.com was on a server in New Jersey in the United States. Although Mr Gutnick conducted his business outside Australia, it could fairly be said that much of his social and business life was in Victoria. Dow Jones claimed that the publication complained of took place in New Jersey but, at first instance, this was rejected by the judge who considered that the publication also took place in Victoria because it was accessible there. He refused the defendant's application to stay proceedings.

Dow Jones had strongly argued that a distinction should be drawn between internet publishing and traditional publishing. The former was passive as material was made available for would-be readers to actively seek out using web browsers and to download. In relation to traditional publishing such as in a printed newspaper or a broadcast, this was more active as the publisher had to circulate and distribute the information or arrange to have it broadcast.

The High Court of Australia held that it was important that publishers can act with certainty. However, this does not necessarily require singularity in that publishers can act in accordance with a single legal system where the material they publish has an international flavour. Publishing

---

[4] Actually, it was its forerunner, the 1968 Brussels Convention on Jurisdiction and the Enforcement of Judgments in Civil and Commercial Matters (consolidated version), OJ C 27, 26.01.1998, p. 1.

23

Torts related to electronic information

activities that have effects in a number of jurisdictions may properly be said to be the concern of each legal system in which they have such effects. As the tort of defamation is located at the place where the damage to reputation occurs, the claimant must have a reputation in that place and the offending material must be available in a comprehensible form in that place. This could be the case where a person downloads the material in the place where the claimant has a reputation.

The reference to having a reputation is somewhat misleading. A person does not have to be well-known to be defamed and may carry on a very private existence. He may even be a hermit. It is submitted that the requirement to give rise to an action in defamation to a person in a particular country is that the defamatory material is, in fact, made available and is seen by someone who is physically in that country and that the person defamed is either domiciled in that country or has some real and significant connection with it, for example, by having business interests there, family, relatives or others who know him who are domiciled there or that he enjoys a reputation there in that he is well-known and respected in that country.

An argument that this approach would inhibit publishing because a publisher would have to consider the laws of defamation in every country was described by the court as unreal in *Dow Jones* v *Gutnick* because identifying the person about whom the material was going to be published would, in most cases, identify the defamation law to which the claimant would be likely to resort, usually being the law of the country in which that person was domiciled. However, an important factor in that case was that the claimant said that he would only seek redress in Victoria and not bring other actions elsewhere. This may be a useful tactic in encouraging a court to accept jurisdiction.

De minimis rule

The *de minimis* rule (in full: *de minimis non curat lex* – the law does not concern itself with trifles) applies in some cases to deprive a claimant of a cause of action. For example, in tort of negligence it is accepted that an action does not arise until damage which is more than *de minimis* is suffered. However, in some areas of law, the rule does not apply and a cause of action might exist no matter how trivial the act or omission concerned. The fact that it is trivial may, of course, be reflected in any remedy granted. For example, an award of damages may be nominal only.

In defamation, if the attack on a person's character is trivial, this may mean that the basic test is not fulfilled and the standing of the person may not be damaged in the minds of right thinking members of society. However, if that test is satisfied, then publication to a single person is sufficient to give rise to a claim in defamation. There is no *de minimis* rule in terms of the number of persons to whom the defamatory statement is published. As Lord Esher MR said in *Whittaker* v *Scarborough Post Newspaper Company* [1896] 2 QB 148:

> The amount of the damages in [an action concerning the publication of an article in a newspaper] would not, in my opinion, generally speaking, depend on the number of copies of the newspaper that were published. If a *libel* were a serious one, a jury would give heavy damages, though it were only *published once*. On the other hand, if a *libel* were a trivial or ridiculous one, in respect of which the jury thought that an action ought not to have been brought, they would only give contemptuous damages, though many copies of the libel had been circulated.

It is further acknowledged that there is no need for the act of publication to be a positive act. It is sufficient if a person leaves the offending material in a place where others are liable to see it. As was stated in Milmo, P. and Rogers, W. V. H., *Gatley on Libel and Slander*, 9th edition, Sweet and Maxwell, 2001 (at p. 134):

> If the claimant proves facts from which it can be inferred that the words were brought to the attention of some third person, he will establish a prima facie case. This is particularly obviously

so where the matter is . . . distributed . . . on the Internet, where in practice it would be impossible to rebut the inference . . .

This sentiment was approved by the New South Wales Supreme Court in *Macquarie Bank Ltd* v *Berg* [2002] NSWSC 1110, in which the claimant alleged that the defendants had placed material on the internet on a website established in the US. Solicitors acting for the claimant downloaded the material in New South Wales and this appeared to be sufficient to give rise to a cause of action. However, the case was fraught with procedural difficulties and leave to proceed with the action was given subject to an application to amend the statement of claim and that application itself being granted. The court acknowledged that getting material on a server from outside Australia into New South Wales requires 'pull technology' whereby the operator of a local computer chooses to visit the website to bring the material into jurisdiction. The person who places the material on the server does not choose the destination or the identity of the recipient.

Although a single publication is sufficient to bring a defamation action, a single publication in a particular jurisdiction may, if there exist significantly greater incidences of publications in other jurisdictions, be a reason why a particular court may decline jurisdiction on the basis of *forum non conveniens*, discussed below. However, this doctrine no longer applies where the Brussels Regulation on jurisdiction, etc. applies and has been engaged.

Forum non conveniens

Forum non conveniens is a doctrine by which a court will refuse jurisdiction on the basis that, in the interests of justice and of the parties, the case would be better heard in another jurisdiction. It has been described as a form of self-denial and the court applying the doctrine will stay the action before it (the doctrine also applies to an application to serve proceedings on a defendant outside jurisdiction). The doctrine was not properly set out until the case of *Spiliada Maritime Corp* v *Cansulex Ltd (The Spiliada)* [1987] 1 AC 460. However, the doctrine has all but been swept aside in relation to Europe and even in respect of cases with a foreign (outside Europe) element where proceedings have first been commenced in Europe on the basis of the Brussels Regulation.

In Case C-281/02 *Owusu* v *Jackson (t/a 'Villa Holidays Bal-Inn Villas') & Ors* [2005] ECR I-1383, the claimant, Mr Andrew Owusu, lived in England and was on holiday in Jamaica staying at a villa at Mammee Bay which was owned by the first defendant, Mr Jackson, who was domiciled in England. Mr Owusu walked into the sea up to his waist and then dived in. He struck his head on a submerged sandbank and was rendered tetraplegic. Two years earlier another English holidaymaker suffered a similar accident and was also rendered tetraplegic.

Mr Owusu commenced proceedings in England against Mr Jackson for breach of contract and the other defendants, Jamaican companies involved in one way or another with the beach at Mammee Bay for the tort of negligence. The claim against Mr Jackson was based on an implied term to the effect that the beach would be reasonably safe and free from hidden dangers. The tort claims were based on a contention that the other defendants failed to warn swimmers of the hazard of the submerged sandbank and that they failed to heed the earlier accident.

The Court of Appeal referred questions to the European Court of Justice for a preliminary ruling under Article 234 of the EC Treaty. The main point was whether Article 2 of the Brussels Convention (now Brussels Regulation) was mandatory or whether it was subject to the *forum non conveniens* rule in cases where there was a connection between a contracting state and a non-contracting state (in this case Jamaica).

The Court of Justice noted that one of the main purposes of the Convention was to bring about certainty and predictability so that persons who were likely to be sued could predict in which state they might be sued. Article 2 clearly has an international flavour and determines jurisdiction (subject to other provisions of the Convention) where relationships between different contracting states are involved. However, it still applies where the issue is international involving a contracting state and a non-contracting state. This does not displace the general rule in Article 2. The rules of jurisdiction in the Convention are not intended to apply only to situations where there is a real and significant link with the working of the internal market in Europe.

It was argued that the Convention cannot impose obligations on states which have not agreed to be bound by it. The Court of Justice countered this by saying that designating a contracting state in which a defendant has a domicile, even where the proceedings are at least partly connected with a non-contracting state is not such as to impose an obligation on that latter state. Consequently, the Court of Justice held that Article 2 applies to circumstances involving relationships between the courts of a single contracting state and those of a non-contracting state.

Article 2 is mandatory in nature and there can be no derogation from it except as laid down in the Convention itself. Therefore, national rules such as the doctrine of *forum non conveniens* provide no exception. The principle of legal certainty would be undermined otherwise as would the legal protection of persons domiciled within the European Community. The fact that there may be practical difficulties, such as logistical difficulties, enforceability of a default judgment in Jamaica and cross-claims against other defendants was of no consequence and cannot affect the mandatory nature of Article 2 of the Convention.

In *Thomas Tracy* v *Niall O'Dowd* (unreported) 28 January 2002, the High Court of Northern Ireland granted a stay in a defamation action on the basis of *forum non conveniens*. The defendants wrote and published an article which was alleged to be defamatory of the claimant. Publication took place in a New York newspaper entitled *Irish Voice* and, *inter alia*, described the claimant's appointment as American Ambassador to Ireland as being ludicrous, a disaster and would 'turn the Bush White house into a laughing stock with Irish Americans'. The newspaper circulation in America was in the order of 45,000 copies per week but there was no circulation in Northern Ireland. The article appeared also on the newspaper's website where it was available only during the week of publication, no archiving system being used for the website. There was evidence that it was accessed just over 2,000 times but only 14 times from the UK. The judge ran through factors in favour of the US and the UK respectively, applying the guidelines from *The Spiliada*, and came to the conclusion that the courts in New York were the most appropriate forum. This case has been overtaken by *Owusu* v *Jackson* and must now been seen as wrongly decided in retrospect.

The only application of the *forum non conveniens* rule is in proceedings brought in Europe which are not covered by the Brussels Regulation (or Lugano Convention), for example, in a claim for beneficial ownership of copyright, or in proceedings first started outside Europe, for example, in a case between an Australian and an American. The Court of Justice in *Owusu* v *Jackson* did not address the situation where proceedings were first commenced outside Europe but a parallel action was started in Europe for the same matter. What would the position have been if the defendants had commenced an action in Jamaica for a declaration that no breach of contract or tort had been committed but, subsequently, Mr Owusu brought his action for breach of contract and tort in England?

Concurrent actions

Another point of interest is that defamatory publications outside England may be actionable in England also. Take, for example, a situation where a person is domiciled in England but is also well-known in a number of other countries, say, Eire, Sweden, Australia. A statement which is defamatory of that person is placed on a website located in Brazil. The person defamed will be able to sue in England on the basis of any third party who accessed the statement in England and on the basis of any persons who access the statement in Eire, Sweden and Australia. In respect of these latter publications, there is an old rule, known as the rule in *Phillips* v *Eyre* (1870) LR 6 QB 1, to the effect that the publications must be actionable as a tort under English law and there is an equivalent civil liability in the other countries where publication took place. This rule was abolished in 1996 for all torts except those relating to defamation to which it still applies (including in Scotland); see section 13 of the Private International Law (Miscellaneous Provisions) Act 1995. Clearly, it is more expedient to the claimant to be able to recover in respect of all the publications in the courts of one country rather than bring several different actions before the courts in different countries.

E-MAILS, DEFAMATION AND MALICIOUS FALSEHOOD

As a libellous statement is actionable if published to a single person (other than the person who is the subject of the statement), there is potentially great scope for defamation by e-mail, especially as many of us send e-mails without carefully checking what is contained in them. It can be said that a great many people ought to have a delay on their e-mails, to give them an opportunity to read them through a little later before sending them. The immediacy of this method of sending messages and attached documents, images and the like is one of its strengths but also one of the dangers of the medium.

The use of e-mail to work out a grudge is very foolish, even if the e-mail is sent to only one person or a small number of persons. In *Takenaka (UK) Ltd* v *Frankl* (unreported) 11 October 2000, defamatory e-mail messages were sent via Hotmail to the claimants. It was accepted that the messages were defamatory and the central issue was whether the defendant had been responsible for sending them. At the time, he was employed by Thames Water and working in Turkey. He had access to the computer from which the e-mails were sent. When informed of the messages, Thames Water agreed to help to trace the culprit but the investigation was described by the judge as ill-conceived and incompetent. The difficulty, of course, is finding whose fingers had been on the keyboard at the relevant times. A lot of forensic work was carried out involving checking access logs of Compuserve and Hotmail and temporary internet files. The judge was of the opinion, on a balance of probabilities that it all pointed to the defendant being responsible for the messages. The alternative explanation was that a third party was in Turkey at the relevant times, had access to the computer which was in the defendant's possession, had a grudge against the defendant and wanted to incriminate him, had a grudge against the claimants, had access to the defendant's password and had the necessary expertise and foresight to carry out the plan. The judge thought that to be highly unlikely. Although the e-mails were not published to many people, in relation to the second claimant they were described as salacious and the judge approved counsel's description that a 'defamatory statement can seep into the crevasses of the subconscious and lurk there ever ready to spring forth its cancerous evil'. He awarded £1,000 damages to the first claimant and £25,000 damages to the second claimant. There would be an enquiry into the considerable costs resulting from the extensive and costly litigation needed to track down the defendant.

Malicious falsehood is a tort related to defamation and applies where someone makes a false statement maliciously about, in particular, a person's business. In 1995, rumours started to spread that a competitor, Western Provident Association, was being investigated by the Department of Trade and Industry and that the Association was close to insolvency. The statements had been made by employees of Norwich Union on its internal e-mail system. Western Provident brought an action for malicious falsehood and Norwich Union eventually settled out of court for £450,000.

23

Torts related to electronic information

E-MAILS AND TRESPASS TO GOODS

Another action that might be available in respect of unwelcome e-mails might be that of trespass. There are a number of forms of trespass, which is an ancient form of action deriving from the writ of trespass circa 1215. In the famous old case of *Entick* v *Carrington* (1765) 19 Stat Tr 1029, Lord Camden CJ distinguished between taking away a person's papers and simply reading them saying that '. . . the eye cannot by the laws of England be guilty of trespass'. Also around that time the importance of trespass as an action was summed up by the phrase 'An Englishman's home is his castle', William Pitt, Earl of Chatham (1708–78) said:

> The poorest man may in his cottage bid defiance to all the forces of the Crown. It may be frail – its roof may shake – the wind may blow through it – the storm may enter – the rain may enter – but the King of England cannot enter – all his force dares not cross the threshold of the ruined tenement.

Whether the concept of trespass, which has since been supplemented by statute, applies in relation to electronic information is an important question and could have significant implications in relation to unwanted transmissions of e-mails and electronic advertising materials that are no worse than being of nuisance value, let alone containing defamatory statements.

In terms of the sending of unwelcome e-mails, is this trespass to goods? This action is included in section 1 of the Torts (Interference with Goods) Act 1977 under wrongful interference with goods. It must be a direct interference with goods and it has been said that this would include, for example, moving a chattel or throwing something at it or writing with a finger in the dust on the surface of a car. It could be argued that sending an unwanted e-mail could fall within this tort, whether or not it contains defamatory material. The main questions are whether this would be seen as a *direct* interference, which is an essential ingredient of the tort, and whether sending unwanted e-mails and 'spam' (unsolicited e-mails or junk e-mails) interferes with *goods*, defined in the Act as chattels personal other than things in action and money. The latter would depend on whether the inference was deemed to be in relation to the computer (hardware) or the data (software). However, an analogy may be made to cases on criminal damage to computer data prior to the coming into force of the Computer Misuse Act 1990, where it was accepted that the damage did not have to be tangible, the main point was that tangible goods had been damaged, for example, by being rendered less useful as a result; see, for example, *R* v *Whiteley* (1991) 93 Cr App R 381, discussed in Chapter 27.

The Financial Law Panel chaired by Lord Donaldson of Lymington, in its discussion paper *e-Commerce – Review of Legal Implications*, December 2001, doubted at pp. 11ff whether the tort of trespass could apply to unwanted e-mails and spam but based its view on the paucity of case law and the definition of goods in the Torts (Interference with Goods) Act 1977. However, this was a timid approach and lack of case law is a neutral factor, especially as the UK approach has been to tackle these and similar problems using the criminal law. It is surely an unlawful interference with a person's computer (hardware) to transmit data or other information (software) to it without consent. This will cause annoyance to the person who has possession of the computer who will have to take action, for example, by erasing the data or information to restore his computer to the state he wants it to be in. Another analogy can be made with sale of goods law. Section 12(2)(b) of the Sale of Goods Act 1979 implies a term into a contract for the sale of goods that the buyer will enjoy quiet enjoyment of the goods. In *Rubicon Computer Systems Ltd* v *United Paints Ltd* (unreported) 12 November 1999, the Court of Appeal accepted that activating a time-lock on a computer subject to a sale contract was a breach of that implied term.

In the US, the courts have been very willing to apply principles of trespass to unwanted e-mails and the like. For example, in *Thrifty-Tel Inc v Bezeneck* (1996) Cal App 4th 1159, the Californian court was happy to accept that electronic signals generated and sent by computer were sufficiently tangible to support a trespass action. In *CompuServe Inc v Cyber Promotions Inc* (SD Ohio 1997) 962 F Supp 1015, a District Court in Ohio used the concept of trespass to chattels to grant a temporary injunction curbing the activities of spammers. A number of other cases were to a similar effect.

More recently, the Supreme Court of California made an important distinction in the case of *Intel Corporation v Hamidi* (unreported) 30 June 2003. The defendant had been an employee of Intel and had been dismissed following a dispute over compensation for work-related injuries. He later sent six e-mails to thousands of employees of Intel claiming that Intel had adopted abusive and discriminatory practices and he was also critical of Intel's employment and personnel policies and practices. It did not appear that the defendant sent further e-mails to any employee who had asked him not to do so. At first instance, the claim for trespass to chattel was accepted and an injunction was granted in favour of Intel. The Californian Court of Appeal upheld that decision but the subsequent appeal to the Californian Supreme Court was successful in a decision that was split 4:3 in favour of the defendant. One of the majority judges, Kennard J said:

> . . . using another's equipment to communicate with a third person who is an authorized user of the equipment and who does not object to the communication is trespass to chattels only if the communications damage the equipment or in some significant way impair its usefulness or availability. . . . Intel has not shown that defendant Hamidi's occasional bulk e-mail messages to Intel's employees have damaged Intel's computer system or impaired its functioning in any significant way, Intel has not established the tort of trespass to chattels. This is not to say that Intel is helpless either practically or legally. As a practical matter, Intel need only instruct its employees to delete messages from Hamidi without reading them and to notify Hamidi to remove their workplace email addresses from his mailing lists. Hamidi's messages promised to remove recipients from the mailing list on request, and there is no evidence that Hamidi has ever failed to do so. From a legal perspective, a tort theory other than trespass to chattels may provide Intel with an effective remedy if Hamidi's messages are defamatory or wrongfully interfere with Intel's economic interests.

Kennard J also alluded to moves to pass laws to deal with such activities which culminated in the Controlling the Assault of Non-Solicited Pornography and Marketing Act 2003 (the 'CAN-SPAM Act, 15 USC Chapter 103). Some States had previously passed their own anti-spam legislation.

The Intel case does not say that sending unwanted e-mails and the like can never be trespass but shows that the activity complained of must be of more than nuisance value. It would be trespass, for example, to clog up a computer system with considerable numbers of e-mails, attachments or 'instant messages' or otherwise disrupt the computer system, for example, by sending a computer virus. It would also seem to be trespass if the sender failed to respond to requests from individuals authorised to use the computers to stop sending e-mails.

In Europe, the Directive on the protection of personal data in the electronics communications sector,[5] implemented in the UK by the Privacy and Electronic Communications (EC Directive) Regulations 2003, controls, *inter alia*, unsolicited marketing by e-mail: see Part 5, Chapter 34.

Finally, one possible action in relation to unwanted e-mails in the UK is to apply for a civil order under section 3 of the Protection from Harassment Act 1997. This can apply where there is a course of conduct which alarms a person or causes distress (clearly more than merely being a nuisance). This was used, in conjunction with a restraining order under section 5 of the Act in

[5] Directive 2002/58/EC of the European Parliament and of the Council of 12 July 2002 on the protection of personal data in the electronic communications sector, OJ L 201, 31.07.2002, p. 37.

a case involving, *inter alia*, offensive messages placed on a website and e-mails sent to staff at a hospital by a person who tried to get the treatment regime for her daughter reinstated; *Chelsea and Westminster Healthcare NHS Trust v Redmond* [2003] All ER (D) 87. The Protection from Harassment Act 1997 provides for criminal offences but contains civil remedies also.

INTERNET SERVICE PROVIDERS (ISPs) AND DEFAMATION

Organisations providing internet access or providing website space or otherwise publishing online material created by other persons are potentially liable in a number of ways for the content of the material so made available. Information placed on the internet (or other electronic publishing medium) may infringe copyright, include a defamatory or negligent misstatement, breach a confidence, be pornographic or be illegal in a number of other ways. This section is concerned with defamatory statements and is written from the perspective of ISPs but much the same principles apply to others deemed to be publishers of the information. The following chapter looks at the position in relation to illegal information generally and, to some extent supplements this section which is concerned primarily with defamation and the specific 'publisher's defence' in section 1 of the Defamation Act 1996.

Traditional publishers usually include in the formal contract with an author a warranty from the author that the material concerned is not defamatory in any way (a similar warranty will apply in respect of third parties rights such as copyright). In the agreement, the author will be required to indemnify the publisher should the publisher be sued for libel or malicious falsehood and have to pay damages.

Publishing information on the internet can be done in a number of ways, some of which differ considerably to publishing in paper form under a formal agreement between a publisher and author. For example, an ISP may act as a host, providing a subscriber with space to upload webpages or allow a subscriber to post material on a bulletin board or newsgroup or the ISP may simply act as a conduit through which information is passed, such as by e-mail or by instant messaging.

Liability under defamation flows from the act of publishing the defamatory statement. Therefore, prima facie, it is the person publishing the statement who is liable. Generally, the author of the statement will be considered to have published it as will the publisher himself. However, some specific defences have developed to exclude or limit the liability of publishers who were unaware of the defamatory nature of the statement. Certain defences, such as qualified privilege may apply and, under section 4 of the Defamation Act 1952, the publisher of an innocent defamation (such that the words were not defamatory on their face, the publisher was not aware of the circumstances by which the words might be understood to be defamatory and reasonable care was exercised in the publication of the words) may make an offer of amends, requiring the publication of a suitable apology and correction (as commonly seen in newspapers). A further specific publisher's defence is provided for under section 1 of the Defamation Act 1996 as considered below.

Publisher's defence

The Defamation Act 1996 Act has a specific defence in which a person can show that he had no responsibility for the publication. The defence came into force on 4 September 1996. Under section 1, the defence applies if a person shows that:

■ he was not the author, editor or publisher of the statement complained of;

- he took reasonable care in relation to its publication; and
- he did not know, and had no reason to believe, that what he did caused or contributed to the publication of a defamatory statement.

Under section 1(3) of the Defamation Act 1996, a number of persons are not to be considered authors, editors or publishers if only involved:

(a) in printing, producing, distributing or selling material containing the statement;

(b) in processing, making copies of, distributing, exhibiting or selling a film or sound recording containing the statement;

(c) in processing, making copies of, distributing or selling electronic medium in or on which the statement is recorded, or in operating or providing any equipment, system or service by means of which the statement is retrieved, copied, distributed or made available in electronic form;

(d) as the broadcaster of a live programme containing the statement in circumstances in which he has no effective control over the maker of the statement;

(e) as the operator or provider of access to a communications system by means of which the statement is transmitted, or made available, by a person over whom he has no effective control.

It can be seen that (c) above applies in relation to publishers of computer software on disk or CD-ROM and (e) applies particularly to ISPs and, for example, telephone operators. In other cases, the court may use the above provisions by way of analogy in deciding whether a person is considered to be an author, editor or publisher.

Under section 1(4), employees or agents are in the same position as their employer or principal to the extent that they are responsible for the content of the statement or the decision to publish it.

To determine whether a person took reasonable care, under section 1(5), regard is to be had to:

- the extent of his responsibility for the content of the statement or the decision to publish it;
- the nature of the circumstances of the publication; and
- the previous conduct or character of the author, editor or publisher.

Thus, where an author or publisher has been in trouble before for publishing defamatory material, this is a factor in determining whether he took reasonable care. In other words, a previous history of publishing defamatory material requires the person responsible to exercise greater care to prevent it happening again. This could apply, for example, where a publisher of a web-based journal has previously published articles in the journal that included libellous statements.

The section 1 defence seems to be quite fragile and, once an ISP has been warned that material which contains a statement alleged to be defamatory has been placed on the ISP's server, he should consider whether he should remove it, or disable access to it, immediately. In *Godfrey* v *Demon Internet Ltd* [2001] QB 201, a subscriber to an internet service, provided by the defendant, made material available through the service which was alleged by the claimant to be defamatory of him. The claimant brought the present action to strike out part of the defence as disclosing no sustainable defence to a libel action, based on the publication of the material by the defendant. After the claimant informed the defendant of his allegation that the material was defamatory, the defendant did not immediately remove the material (although, eventually, it did so).

23

Torts related to electronic information

It was held that the defence did not apply in this case as, at common law, once the defendant became aware that the material contained defamatory statements it could no longer satisfy two of the requirements in section 1(1) – that is, that reasonable care had been taken in the publication and that the defendant had no knowledge or reason to believe that he caused or contributed to the publication of the defamatory statement. Mr Justice Morland pointed out that section 17 of the Defamation Act 1996 states that 'publication' and 'publish' have the meaning they have generally for the law of defamation but 'publisher' is specially defined in section 1. He did accept, however, that the defendant was not a commercial publisher for the purposes of section 1(2), being a person whose business is issuing material to the public, or a section of the public, who issues material containing the statement in the course of that business. Unfortunately for the defendant, for the section 1(1) defence to apply, all three requirements must be satisfied. The defendant's argument that it had played a passive role was not accepted and the judge thought the situation analogous to that of a bookseller who sold a book containing defamatory material.

The significance of this case is that the special defence may be quite limited in its scope. If a person alleges that defamatory material has been placed on the service provider's server, it may no longer be safe to rely on the defence and the ISP ought to consider removing the material immediately. This is quite important as each time an individual accesses the material, there will be a fresh libel. Whether a service provider has no reason to believe that he causes or contributes to the publication must be an objective test based on the reasonable person having knowledge of the facts known to the service provider and which must be coloured by the allegation of defamation.

Consider a situation where an ISP is informed by someone that a statement defamatory of him has been placed on the service provider's server. If the material is not removed immediately, the issue for the court may become one simply relating to the general law of defamation. If the statement is held by the court to have a defamatory meaning, it is highly unlikely that the section 1 defence can apply. For example, if the matter is being decided by a jury and it finds the statement defamatory, it will almost certainly consider that, after being informed of the allegation of defamation, the service provider did indeed 'have reason to believe'. The same probably applies where there is no jury and the case is heard before a judge alone. On the other hand, if the finding is that the statement is not defamatory, that is an end to the matter. Thus, the section 1 defence is likely to be relevant only up to such time as an ISP has been informed of the allegation. If that is so, ISPs would be well advised to remove the material immediately. However, if they respond in that way, that makes freedom of speech vulnerable to persons who simply do not like what is said about them over the internet without the statements necessarily being defamatory. Given the sensitivity of the issue and the potential of numerous actions for defamation, ISPs are likely to play safe if there is any possibility that the statement complained of may be defamatory. This approach seems to have been the one taken in practice.

There are signs of a swing to the other direction. The High Court took a robust approach to the publishers' defence in **Bunt v Tilley** [2006] EWHC 407 (QB), discussed in more detail in relation to the special defences for ISPs in the next chapter. The court held that, at common law, an ISP could not be deemed to be a publisher. As for the position under the Defamation Act 1996, it was argued that the ISPs fell foul of section 1(1)(c) because, by virtue of his communications with them, they had reason to believe that they were causing or contributing to the postings complained of. The judge did not accept this and considered that there was nothing to undermine the ability of the ISPs to rely on the section 1(1) defence. There was nothing in the communications from the claimant to help locate the information or the e-mail address of the person responsible for the alleged defamatory material. One of the ISPs imposed contractual terms on users of its service to ensure that the service was not used, *inter alia*, to send, receive, upload, download or use defamatory material. The ISP also argued that it was not a publisher for the purposes of section 1(1). The judge accepted that it would be impractical for it to monitor its servers for defamatory material. The judge also accepted that having reason to believe was not a reference to constructive notice but really implied recklessness.

Disclosure of identity of wrongdoer

An ISP, like anyone else, is subject to data protection law and this may restrict disclosures of personal data relating to subscribers to third parties. In many cases, ISPs and website operators will have an express term in their contract with subscribers confirming that their identity will not be disclosed to anyone else, except where required by law: for example, for the purposes of the prevention and detection of crime. The service providers in *Totalise plc* v *Motley Fool Ltd* [2001] 1 WLR 1233 had so provided. In that case, the claimant was an ISP and the defendants operated websites which included discussion boards. The contracts the defendants had with the subscribers contained a term saying that their identity would not be disclosed. An anonymous contributor to the discussion boards, calling himself 'Z Dust', posted material which was alleged to be defamatory of the claimant company, its officers and directors. The judge at first instance thought that the material was plainly defamatory and that Z Dust was waging an intensive campaign of vilification against the claimant.

The claimant sought an order requiring the defendants to disclose the identity of Z Dust. The defendants eventually barred Z Dust access to their sites. However, the identity of Z Dust was not disclosed on the ground that this would be contrary to the Data Protection Act 1998. The judge had no hesitation in granting the order for disclosure on the basis of *Norwich Pharmacal Co* v *Customs and Excise Commissioners* [1974] AC 133 which gives a court jurisdiction to order a third party to disclose the identity of a wrongdoer. However, he awarded costs against the defendants who had taken a fairly neutral stance on the issue of the granting of such an order. The judge, Mr Justice Owen, said:

> I consider that there is considerable force in Mr Maloney's argument that those who operate websites containing discussion boards do so at their own risk. If it transpires that those boards are used for defamatory purposes by individuals hiding behind the cloak of anonymity then in justice a claimant seeking to establish the identity of the individuals making such defamatory contents ought to be entitled to their costs.

The normal rule with costs and *Norwich Pharmacal* orders is that the person applying for the order for disclosure should bear the costs of the application. This was confirmed on appeal to the Court of Appeal which set aside the order for costs, saying that it was legitimate for a party who reasonably agreed to keep information confidential and private to refuse to hand over such information voluntarily.

The United States' position

In contrast, the position of ISPs is more secure in the US as a result of the Communications Decency Act 1996 47 USC §230 which states that 'no provider or user of an interactive computer service shall be treated as the publisher or speaker of any information provided by another information content provider'. This was a response to fears that ISPs would no longer self-regulate the content of material available through their service as the position, following cases such as *Stratton Oakmont Inc* v *Prodigy Services Co*, 1995 NY Misc. LEXIS 229, imposing liability on a service provider which checked the content, thereby providing a disincentive to self-regulation. The position seemed to be that service providers which did not check or monitor the information made available through their service would be less likely to be found liable. Clearly, this situation was untenable, hence the change to the law.

The effects of 47 USC §230 were quickly seen. For example, in *Zeran v America Online Inc* (1997) 129 F 3d 327, the claimant complained of alleged defamatory messages posted by an unidentified third party on AOL. He claimed that 47 USC §230 did not assist AOL once it had notice that the material was defamatory. The messages placed on AOL's bulletin board advertised T-shirts containing offensive messages related to the bombing of a Federal building in Oklahoma City. Anyone wanting to purchase a T-shirt was asked to contact 'Ken' at Zeran's home phone number. Zeran received a large number of angry phone calls and a number of death threats. Eventually, AOL removed the posting from the bulletin board. In confirming that AOL could rely on the defence, Chief Judge Wilkinson said of the rationale for the defence:

> The specter of tort liability in an area of such prolific speech would have an obvious chilling effect. It would be impossible for service providers to screen each of their millions of postings for possible problems. Faced with potential liability for each message republished by their services, interactive computer service providers might choose to severely restrict the number and type of messages posted. Congress considered the weight of the speech interests implicated and chose to immunize service providers to avoid any such restrictive effect.

It was also clear from the wording of the statutory provision that Congress intended that the exclusion of liability from ISPs afforded by 47 USC §230 was not to be compromised by state law or conflicting common law. In *Lunney v Prodigy Services Co* (1998) 250 AD 2d 230, an anonymous prankster used the claimant's name to open accounts with the defendant ISP and posted offensive material and sent offensive e-mails under the claimant's name. When the claimant informed the service provider, the postings were deleted and the fraudulent accounts closed. It was held that the defendant was not liable on the basis of prior common law to the effect that publishers are immune from liability for defamation resulting from material transmitted by them, but over which they merely retained passive editorial control, such as a telephone service. The court considered e-mail services to be like a telephone service. However, this defence can be lost if the publisher is guilty of bad faith or malice. But, even where more active editorial control is exercised, such as in the case of electronic bulletin boards, the court accepted that it would be unreasonable to expect an ISP to monitor the countless messages placed on its bulletin boards. Having said that, the court held that it did not need to consider the effect of 47 USC §230 although it did comment that its decision was in harmony with the provision.

The US acted quickly to protect ISPs against defamation claims when, in practice, they had very little if any editorial control because of the vast amount of information passing through or hosted by the systems. In comparison, the situation in the UK has left ISPs in an invidious position. Once they have been warned that material is potentially defamatory, they have little option but to play safe and remove it. The publisher's defence in section 1 of the Defamation Act 1996 is too influenced by traditional forms of publishing and fails to properly address the reality of the situation which is that ISPs are unable to check everything going through their systems. Even if they could, should we really expect them to become arbiters of what is or is not defamatory? Fortunately, some of the provisions in the Directive on electronic commerce described in the following chapter go some way to alleviating the position.

DEFAMATION AND THE INTERNET - THE WAY FORWARD?

In 2002 the Law Commission commenced a study into defamation law in relation to the internet following a number of concerns raised by online publishers and ISPs by developments such as the *Godfrey* v *Demon Internet* and *Loutchansky* v *Times Newspaper* cases, in particular. The main concerns were:

- the scope of the publishers' defence under section 1 of the Defamation Act 1996;
- the potential liability for a defamation action in relation to archive material made available over the internet;
- the problems of jurisdiction and exposure to claims in foreign jurisdictions and the problem of complying with the laws of every country in which a website could be accessed; and
- the possible exposure to contempt of court resulting from jurors searching the internet to detect whether an accused person had previous convictions.

These issues and responses by interested parties were set out in a 'scoping report', Law Commission, *Defamation and the Internet: A Preliminary Investigation*, Scoping Study No. 2, December 2002. As far as secondary publishers such as ISPs were concerned it was recognised that the present situation in the UK was unsatisfactory and a number of possibilities exist such as exempting ISPs from liability as is currently the situation in the US. Following *Godfrey* v *Demon Internet*, in the United Kingdom service providers were under strong pressure to remove material they have been told was defamatory without considering whether the material was true or whether publication was in the public interest. Another possibility was to extend the innocent publication defence under section 1 of the Defamation Act 1996.

The Law Commission noted that the Electronic Commerce (EC Directive) Regulations 2002, which implemented the Directive on electronic commerce, provided a defence for ISPs and others in relation to acting as a mere conduit, in respect of hosting and caching in respect of 'illegal material' which would include defamatory material but would also cover other forms of illegality, such as obscenity or copyright infringement. This defence (strictly speaking there are three related but slightly difference defences) is discussed in detail in the following chapter. At this stage it can be said that the Law Commission noted that there were two views as to the effect of this defence in the context of defamation. One view was that it simply mirrored the defence under section 1 of the Defamation Act 1996 whilst the other view was that it provided wider protection.

Archives present the spectre of liability arising in years to come, long after initial publication, because of the principle that each publication represents a separate libel. Although the Law Commission had in the past argued that the present one-year limitation period for defamation was possibly too short and could prejudice claimants, the possibility of an action being commenced some years into the future in relation to subsequent accesses to online archives could make it difficult for defendants to prepare an effective defence, for example, because witnesses might no longer be available. Clearly, this was an area which demanded further consideration, otherwise the social utility of making archives available could be compromised.

As regards jurisdiction and applicable law, the Law Commission thought that it would be impossible to come up with a solution in the short or medium terms and that further research was required into how this problem is dealt with in other countries. The only realistic longer-term solution might be by way of international treaties. The Law Commission thought it unlikely that online publishers, for example, of newspaper archives would be exposed to contempt of court actions. The alleged danger was that a juror might search the internet and find archive material carrying reports of previous criminal convictions of a person under trial for a criminal offence. Except in exceptional technical legal circumstances, information about an accused's previous convictions is withheld from a jury. It is only after a guilty verdict is returned that details of previous convictions is made available to the court, where it will be taken into account by the judge when fixing the sentence to impose. The Law Commission thought that most jurors were of good sense and would not engage in searching the internet for previous convictions and, in any case, it thought than internet publishers were already sufficiently protected against 'inappropriate, arbitrary or trivial prosecution'. Consequently, no recommendation was made to make changes to the law in this respect.

There is some disquiet about the exposure to liability resulting from innocent publication by internet publishers and the apparent weakness of the publishers' defence under section 1 of the Defamation Act 1996. It seems apparent that some changes are necessary though it is unlikely that the UK will go as far as the US has where exemption from liability seems available even if the ISP is in no doubt that the material is defamatory and yet takes no action to remove it. It may be that this will be modified or toned down by subsequent developments in the case law or legislation in the US. The difficulty for the UK and other European countries is to strike a balance between protecting the individual whilst maintaining freedom of speech in accordance with the European Convention for the Protection of Human Rights and Fundamental Freedoms, Article 10 of which allows restrictions to be placed on freedom of expression necessary in a democratic society, *inter alia*, for the protection of the reputation or rights of others. It is submitted that the UK's pendulum needs to swing back slightly more in favour of freedom of expression otherwise unscrupulous persons may manipulate the internet to suppress truths or half-truths, the publication of which would be in the public interest.

In terms of the possibility of long-term exposure to defamation actions resulting from material available on archives, perhaps it is time to reconsider the multiple publication rule and, perhaps, replace it with a single publication rule in the context of the internet. However, this would represent a very substantial change to defamation law in the UK and its implications would have to be fully explored before such a change, even a partial change, could be contemplated.

SUMMARY

- Placing misleading or incorrect 'advice' on a website may being liability for negligent misstatement:
  - but only if targeted at specific individuals or groups;
  - otherwise, there is unlikely to be sufficient proximity.
- The law of defamation is important in relation to websites, bulletin boards, e-mails and blogs.
- Placing material, including images, on the internet which tends to lower a person's esteem among right-thinking members of society will be libel rather than slander.
- Libel is actionable without proof of damage.
- The multiple publication rule means that:
  - there is no global tort theory;
  - every time defamatory material is accessed, a fresh libel occurs;
  - causes of action may accrue in numerous jurisdictions.
- In relation to a particular libel, involving a European element, the Brussels Regulation applies to determine which countries courts have jurisdiction.
- There may be a choice of jurisdiction where the defendant is domiciled in one Member State and the defamation occurs in another Member State.
- The *forum non conveniens* rule no longer applies where jurisdiction is determined by the Brussels Regulation.

- An e-mail sent to one person only (other than the victim) can be a libel.
- Unsolicited e-mails may be trespass to goods.
- There is a publishers' defence to defamation that may apply to online publishers and internet service providers, but:
  - the defence may be lost once informed of potentially defamatory material.
- Special defences for information society service providers may be available where the provider acts as a mere conduit or simply caches or hosts illegal material.
- A court may order the disclosure of the identity of a person 'posting' defamatory material.

SELF-TEST QUESTIONS

Note: there is only one correct answer to each multiple choice question.

1 **Fred is a self-employed accountant. He was engaged by Triple Brewing plc to prepare this year's annual company accounts. When they were completed, the company placed the accounts on its website. There was a mistake in the accounts which made the company look in better financial shape than was actually the case. A number of individuals, who accessed the accounts online, bought shares in the company (they had no previous dealings with the company or with Fred). The shares are now worth significantly less. The individuals, who claim that they would have not have bought the shares had they known the true position, are threatening to sue Fred. Which one of the following statements is most likely to be CORRECT?**

   (a) Fred will be liable for negligence under the rule in *Donoghue* v *Stevenson*.

   (b) Fred will not be liable for negligent misstatement as *Caparo* v *Dickman* makes it clear that purely economic loss is not recoverable under this area of law.

   (c) Fred will be liable for negligent misstatement as he was clearly negligent in preparing the accounts.

   (d) Fred will not be liable for negligent misstatement for lack of proximity on the basis of *Caparo* v *Dickman*.

2 **Edna contributed to a blog about Gordon who is a local councillor. The material she included in the blog ('weblog') was to the effect that Gordon had taken bribes to allow developers to obtain planning permission. There is no evidence to suggest that this is the case and it is clear that Edna would have no defence to an action for defamation. Which one of the following statements is CORRECT?**

   (a) Edna's statement is slander rather than libel as material in a blog is not considered to be in writing.

   (b) Edna has libelled Gordon who will have a cause of action irrespective of proof of damage.

   (c) It is implied that material and statements in blogs are not intended to be taken seriously and, therefore, Gordon will have no cause of action against Edna.

   (d) Edna is not guilty of defaming Gordon as it is far comment to criticise a politician.

3 **Pierre, who is domiciled in France, co-wrote an article with Hans, domiciled in Germany. The article was placed on a website by Pierre and Hans and it contained a statement libelling Tommy, a famous actor domiciled in England. The offending statement was written jointly**

by Pierre and Hans. Tommy has proof that the article has been accessed on a number of occasions in England. Which one of the following is CORRECT?

(a) Tommy can commence proceedings in France, Germany or England.

(b) Tommy can commence proceedings in France or Germany only.

(c) Tommy can only commence proceedings in England as 'claimants play at home'.

(d) Tommy must commence proceedings before the European Court of Justice.

4   Which one of the following statements CORRECTLY describes a *Norwich Pharmacal* order?

(a) An order that the defendant pays the claimant's legal costs.

(b) A court order requiring that an internet service provider remove unlawful material.

(c) An order of the court requiring the delivery up of infringing materials.

(d) An order of the court requiring a person to disclose the identity of a wrongdoer.

5   Case law concerning the publishers' defence under section 1 of the Defamation Act 1996 demonstrates that it fails to protect freedom of expression in a satisfactory and balanced manner. Discuss.

For further resources and updates please go to the Companion Website accompanying this book at **www.mylawchamber.co.uk/bainbridgeIT**

24 Liability of information society service providers for illegal material

INTRODUCTION

The Directive on electronic commerce[1] was required to be transposed into national law before 17 January 2002. In the UK, it was implemented on 21 August 2002 by the Electronic Commerce (EC Directive) Regulations 2002. The Directive dealt with a number of issues, such as the obligations of information society service providers to provide information to recipients of their services and competent authorities, in relation to contracts concluded by electronic means and the internal market for information society service providers, as described in Chapter 21. The aspects of the Directive with which this present chapter is concerned are those which give defences for information society service providers in respect of illegal information which has passed through their service to a recipient, where such information has been stored temporarily by information society service providers or in respect of illegal activities or information associated with their storage of information where the service provider is not responsible and, if relevant, acts quickly to remove or disable access to the information and, in terms of storage other than certain forms of temporary storage, does not know of the illegal activity or information.

The recitals to the Directive noted that there were disparities between the laws of Member States in relation to the liability of service providers and this could detract from the smooth functioning of the internal market. The Directive put forward a number of solutions based on:

- limiting liability where the service provider is a mere conduit and in terms of *caching* (automatic, intermediate and temporary storage) and *hosting* (storage at the request of the recipient);

- the courts or administrative authorities in Member States being able to require a service provider to terminate or prevent an infringement or require the removal or disabling of access to information;

- not imposing a proactive duty to look for illegal material (however, Member States could, if they wished, impose a monitoring obligation on service providers in specific cases and, in terms of hosting, Member States were to be free to impose a reasonable duty of care to detect and prevent illegal activities);

- encouraging the drawing up of voluntary codes of practice;

- setting up procedures for removing and disabling access to illegal information, perhaps on a voluntary basis;

[1] Directive 2000/31/EC of the European Parliament and of the Council of 8 June 2000 on certain legal aspects of information society services, in particular electronic commerce, in the Internal Market, OJ L 178, 17.07.2000, p. 1 (the 'Directive on electronic commerce').

- surveillance, where allowed, subject to the data protection Directive and the Directive on privacy in telecommunications.

As was the case in the description of the other aspects of the Directive, references are made to the provisions of the Directive, which are for all intents and purposes the same as in the Regulations, expect in relation to certain evidential and other aspects specifically covered by the Regulations with no equivalent in the Directive.

INFORMATION SOCIETY SERVICES

To remind ourselves, information society services are those normally provided for remuneration, at a distance, by means of electronic equipment for processing and storage of data. Processing includes digital compression. Information services within the meaning of the Directive cover a wide range of activities and include online contracting, online information services such as online newspapers, databases, financial and professional services, access to information through internet service providers (ISPs), search engine providers, online marketing and advertising, video on demand and commercial e-mails. The court confirmed that ISPs were providers of information society services in *Bunt v Tilley* [2006] EWHC 407 (QB), discussed in more detail later. It makes no difference if the remuneration is indirect and not paid for by the recipient of the service, for example, where it results from advertising or sponsorship.

Although the precise scope of services covered by the Directive is far from clear, it does not appear to apply to providers of hyperlinks and location tools or to persons who aggregate information from different sources, selecting and compiling the information for subscribers to access. In terms of hyperlinks and location tools, the omission of such service providers from these defences is potentially serious, especially in the context of defamatory material. In an old case, *Hird v Wood* (1894) Sol J 234, a placard carrying a libellous statement had been placed on the roadside by a person or persons unknown. The defendant sat by the placard, smoking a pipe and repeatedly pointing to it and attracting the attention of passers-by to the statement. It was held by the Court of Appeal that the defendant was a publisher of the statement.

ACTIVITIES RELATED TO ILLEGAL INFORMATION COVERED BY THE DIRECTIVE

The activities covered by the special defences for information society service providers relate to three forms of activities:

- acting as a mere conduit;
- caching; and
- hosting.

The scope and extent of the defences vary according to which activity is concerned. Acting as a mere conduit means that the information in question has simply passed through the service provider's network. This would apply, for example, to information passing through a telecommunications network and certain associated forms of temporary storage do not remove the defence. E-mail is outside this activity as e-mails are stored by ISPs and the same applies to websites.

The act of caching occurs where a service provider places information in temporary storage in order to increase the efficient working of their service. For example, webpages may be placed in temporary store so that they can be re-displayed more quickly than would be the case if they had to be retrieved from their source again.

Hosting is where the service provider stores information for the recipient of the service. This could apply, for example, where the service provider hosts a website for a subscriber to its services. It could also cover e-mail systems where the e-mails are stored, for subsequent access by the subscriber to the service, bulletin boards and newsgroups.

All three defences came under scrutiny in *Bunt v Tilley* [2006] EWHC 407 (QB). The claimant alleged that postings hosted on websites were defamatory of him. In all, there were six defendants, the first three were individuals and the last three were internet service providers (AOL, Tiscali and BT). The ISPs applied to have the claims against them struck out or dismissed summarily. It had not been alleged that the ISPs were responsible for the material complained of or that they had 'hosted' it, except in the case of BT which hosted Usenet newsgroups on its servers where it would normally be stored for a few weeks to enable BT's users to access it. In the case of AOL and Tiscali, the material had merely been made available via their services. The claimant submitted:

> This is not some tuppeny ha'penny storm in a teacup, this is a truly vast case, the like of which English Defamation Law has never before seen, because of both the scope and nature, as well as the medium. It positively screams out for a Trial, and one way or another it will have one.

The findings of the court are discussed below in relation to each of the defences which are now considered in more detail.

MERE CONDUIT

The provider of an information society service consisting of the transmission in a communication network of information provided by the recipient of the service or the provision of access to a communication network is not liable as a result of that transmission where the service provider does not initiate the transmission, did not select the receiver of the transmission and did not select or modify the information contained in it; Article 12 of the Directive.

The transmission or access may include the automatic, intermediate and transient storage of the information transmitted provided this is for the sole purpose of carrying out the transmission in the communication network and it is not stored for any longer than reasonably necessary for the transmission.

This exclusion of liability only applies in limited circumstances and will not apply to information stored for any longer or for any other purpose than intrinsically related to the transmission of the information. Thus, a great deal of the services made available by ISPs, such as e-mail, website hosting and newsgroups, all of which involve deliberate storage for other purposes, are not within this exclusion of liability. Where it might apply, for example, is in relation to facsimile transmission, telex or telephonic transmission.

The Directive is silent on the nature of the liability the service provider is exempt from but Regulation 17 of the Electronic Commerce (EC Directive) Regulations 2002 states that the service provider shall not be liable for damages or other pecuniary remedy or for any criminal sanction as a result of the transmission. Other remedies, such as an injunction may be possible, for example, an injunction requiring the service provider to block transmissions by or received by a particular person. In *Bunt v Tilley*, the court confirmed that an ISP does not have to act as a gatekeeper. Although the claimant argued that this was the case, the judge noted that the Regulations did not require this and to suggest otherwise '... flies in the face of the fundamental policy underlying the regulations'. Article 15 of the Directive on electronic commerce expressly states that an information society service provider does not have a general obligation to monitor the information they transmit or store nor any general obligation to actively seek facts or circumstances indicating illegal activity.

CACHING

Caching is not directly defined in the Directive but it is clear from recital 42 of the Directive that it refers to temporary storage for the sole purpose of making the transmission of information more efficient, being an activity of a mere technical, automatic and passive nature. The very nature of such storage implies that the service provider has neither knowledge nor control over the information that is transmitted or stored: hence the exclusion of liability. There appears to be some overlap between caching and acting as a mere conduit as the latter extends to incidental automatic, intermediate and transient storage. However, the exclusion of liability for caching must be intended to apply to acts of storage that, albeit temporary, go beyond those covered by the mere conduit defence. The reason is that the exclusion of liability is subject to different conditions. Caching may apply, for example, to the transmission of information which involves storage in volatile computer memory which is not automatically deleted on completion of the transmission but left in computer memory until such time as it is automatically overwritten by other information. Another example is the temporary storage by ISPs of commonly requested webpages, enabling them to be more quickly transmitted to subscribers.

Article 13 of the Directive states that the service provider is not liable where the service consists of the transmission in a communications network of information provided by a recipient of the service where the information is the subject of automatic, intermediate and temporary storage for the sole purpose of making more efficient the onward transmission of the information to other recipients of the service upon their request. Again liability for damages or any other pecuniary remedy or for any criminal sanction resulting from the transmission is excluded, under Regulations 18 of the Electronic Commerce (EC Directive) Regulations 2002.

For the defence to apply, there are a number of conditions. First, the service provider must not modify the information transmitted. He must also comply with conditions on access to the information and any rules regarding the updating of the information specified in a manner widely recognised and used by industry. The service provider must not interfere with the lawful use of technology, widely recognised and used in industry, to obtain data on the use of the information. This could apply to access logs and the like. Finally, the service provider must act expeditiously to remove or disable access to the information cached upon obtaining actual knowledge of the fact that the information at the initial source of the transmission has been removed from the network, or access to it has been disabled, or that a court of an administrative authority has ordered such removal or disablement. 'Administrative authority' is defined in neither the Directive nor the Regulations but will include any body having authority to order removal of information or disablement of access. An example is the Office of the Information Commissioner, which has the power to serve enforcement notices requiring, *inter alia*, a data controller to cease certain forms of processing of personal data. This could apply, for example, where a webpage contains sensitive personal data and none of the conditions allowing such processing are present. Another example is where a website contains advertising which is subject to a Stop Now Order imposed by the Office of Fair Trading.

For the purposes of determining whether a service provider has actual knowledge, Regulation 22 states that a court shall take into account all matters which appear to the court relevant in the circumstances and, amongst other things, shall have regard to whether the service provider has received a notice and the extent to which the notice includes the full name and address of the sender of the notice, details of the location of the information in question and details of the unlawful nature of the activity or information. The notice may be sent by e-mail and may be sent by any person, whether a recipient of the service, a person claiming to be libelled by the information or by an enforcement authority, being any authority, other than a court, empowered to take enforcement action. The fact no such notice has been received by the service provider does not necessarily mean that he can avail himself of the defence. It could be the case, for example, that concerns about the information have been published in a widely read newspaper.

In *Bunt* v *Tilley*, the claimant offered no satisfactory evidence to indicate that the ISPs had failed to comply with the caching defence under Article 13 of the Directive.

HOSTING

Hosting applies where the service provider stores information which has been provided by the recipient of the service. This could apply to a website hosted by the service provider, information posted on bulletin boards by subscribers and e-mails sent by recipient which are usually stored until deleted by the subscriber. In *Godfrey* v *Demon Internet*, discussed in the previous chapter, the evidence was that the service provider normally stored information sent to its Usenet service for about two weeks before deleting it. This would certainly fall within the meaning of hosting.

Under Article 14 of the Directive on electronic commerce, a service provider is not liable in respect of storage if the service provider does not have actual knowledge of illegal activity or information and, where a claim for damages is made, is not aware of the facts or circumstances from which the illegal activity or information would have been apparent or, upon obtaining such knowledge or awareness, the service provider acts expeditiously to remove or disable access to the information. The defence does not apply if the recipient of the service (that is, the recipient who provided the information in question) was acting under the authority or control of the service provider. The provisions for determining whether a service provider has actual notice are the same as those that apply to caching, under Regulation 22 of the Electronic Commerce (EC Directive) Regulations 2002.

Again the Regulations define the extent of liability excluded in relation to liability for damages or for any other pecuniary remedy (this could, for example, be an account of profits or compensation) or for any criminal sanction. However, in this case, damages may still be recoverable from the service provider if he has objective knowledge, as opposed to actual knowledge as determined in accordance with Regulation 22, being where he is aware of circumstances from which it would have been apparent to the service provider that the activity or information was unlawful (note that the Regulations use the term 'unlawful' whereas the Directive uses the term 'illegal', though there is no practical distinction between the words). This form of knowledge should be satisfied if the reasonable person, aware of the same circumstances, would have concluded that the activity or information was unlawful. As noted earlier, information society service providers are under no obligation to monitor the information transmitted or stored, under Article 15 of the Directive.

In *Bunt* v *Tilley*, the judge considered whether the requirements for notice had been satisfied. The claimant had sent e-mails to the ISPs. It was accepted, for example, in the case of BT, that it had complied with the requirements of Article 5 of the Directive on electronic commerce (see Regulation 6(1)(c) of the Regulations) which requires an information society service provider, *inter alia*, to provide his details, including e-mail address, which make it possible to contact him rapidly and communicate with him in a direct and effective manner. Mr Bunt was indeed able to send an email to BT. However, his purported notice failed to satisfy all the requirements of

Regulations 22. The e-mail sent to BT was not reproduced in the report of the case though one sent to AOL was (it seems reasonable to assume they were very similar). It stated:

> Hi Guys,
>
> One of your (UK) customers has committed an act of libel against my business on our business forums, the url in question is [url not reproduced here] right at the forum page, and he started a thread entitled 'Be warned about these cheap Batteries! Load of Crap!'
>
> … Chances are the culprit is the scourge of uk.local newsgroups [name and address of the person alleged to be responsible for the statement].
>
> I am emailing you in this instance in order to ask what procedures you need completed by myself before you are able to divulge this individual's name and address to me, so that i can institute legal proceedings against them for libel under UK law as a matter of urgency.

As regards BT, the judge said that there was no evidence that BT was informed of where on its servers the posting was located, of which news group it was posted upon, or of the e-mail address of the person responsible. He added that it would be wholly impractical for BT to monitor its servers for defamatory content about the claimant in any event. Furthermore, the judge said that in order to characterise something as unlawful, a person would need to know something of the strengths or weaknesses of available defences.

In Germany, a court had to consider the hosting defence in connection with the sale of counterfeit watches on an internet auction site hosted by an ISP in Case IZR 304/01 *Rolex Internet Auction* [2005] ETMR 255. The Federal High Court confirmed the following points:

- Providing a platform on the internet on which suppliers can auction goods is not itself a sufficient ground to make the ISP an infringer of a trade mark. Participation in infringement with the supplier requires at least some element of intention.

- An ISP cannot be expected to check every offer placed on the internet (in other words, he is not required to act as a 'gatekeeper').

- However, if the ISP becomes aware of a trade mark infringement, he must not only block the actual offer without delay and also take all measures technically possible and reasonable as a precaution to prevent any further corresponding trade mark infringements.

In respect of the latter, the court made it clear that the further obligation to block other infringements would mean that the ISP should check other offers to sell Rolex watches. Whether it is reasonable to expect an ISP to do this is doubtful and this goes further than is required by Article 15 of the Directive which states, *inter alia*, that there is no general obligation actively to seek facts or circumstances indicating illegal activity. Of course, ISPs are generally keen to prevent their services being used for illegal activities but the extent of the duty suggested by the German court could prove impracticable or unduly onerous. How, for example, would an ISP know that an item offered for sale is counterfeit? The wider use of reporting systems such as eBay's VeRO system for reporting potential infringements of intellectual property rights should be acceptable. After all, one would expect companies such as the manufacturers of Rolex watches and appropriate authorities, such as trading standards in the UK, to police what is being offered on internet auction sites.

IMPLICATIONS

The requirement to remove or disable access is a concern to ISPs and online publishers. ISPs receive numerous requests to remove material, typically by e-mail. Many are not clear or sufficiently specific. The Directive requires Member States to encourage the drawing up of codes of practice (not just in relation to these defences) and this would be of some assistance if a code of practice was developed making it clear under what circumstances the notice requirement for determining whether the provider has actual knowledge would be satisfied. Such a code could also set out 'notice and take down' procedures. This is an area mentioned in the Directive in the provisions to re-examine the application of the Directive with a view to adapting it. The problem for service providers is that, without clear guidance, they may find it difficult to decide whether they have been given notice in an appropriate manner and sufficiently detailed to act upon and to decide whether, indeed, whether the activity or information concerned is unlawful. In terms of defamatory material, it is questionable whether these defences add anything to the publishers' defence under section 1 of the Defamation Act 1996.

For unlawful activities (for example, money laundering) or information (such as obscene material or material infringing copyright or information disclosed in breach of confidence) it may be marginally easier, at least in some cases, for the service provider to come to a conclusion as to whether the activity or information is unlawful. Defamation may still be the most difficult area for the service provider to judge and it is likely that the service provider will simply play safe and remove the information or disable access to it. Old case law shows how easy it is to be liable for a defamatory statement written by someone else. For example, in the Court of Star Chamber (so called because of the star pattern painted on the ceiling of the court) in *Halliwood's Case*, the court noted in (1601) 5 Coke 125b, that it was said that '. . . if one finds a libel, and would keep himself out of danger, if it be composed against a private man, the finder may either burn it or deliver it to a magistrate'. This indicates the danger of inactivity when it comes to defamatory material. (The Court of Star Chamber existed between 1487 and 1641.) In *De Libellis Famosis* (1605) 5 Coke 125a, Lord Coke pointed out the various ways a libel may be published, including fixing some disparaging object at the party's door. In *Byrne v Deane* [1937] 1 KB 818, a verse written by an unknown person had been left on the notice board of a golf club which had a rule that no notice could be posted on club premises without the consent of the club secretary. The verse was:

> You heard the sound of a merry bell
> Those who were rash and those who were not
> Lost and made a spot of cash
> But he who gave the game away
> May he byrnn in hell and rue the day
> Diddleramus.

There were two copies of the verse, the original and a carbon copy underneath. On the original, the word 'byrnn' had been changed to 'burn' and it was accepted that this was a reference to the claimant, who the person writing the verse must have suspected of informing the police that there was a gaming machine in the club which the police had removed. It was accepted that the defendants, proprietors of the club, by allowing the verse to remain, were responsible for publishing it, though the majority of the Court of Appeal did not consider the verse defamatory of the claimant.

Regulation 20 of the Electronic Commerce (EC Directive) Regulations 2002 states that nothing in Regulations 17–19 (the defences) prevents a person agreeing different contractual terms, for example, further limiting or extending the scope of the defences in the context of a contract between a service provider and recipient of the service. Nor are the rights of any person to apply to a court for relief to prevent or stop an infringement of any rights affected. The power of an administrative authority to prevent or stop an infringement continues to apply regardless of Regulations 17–19.

Regulation 21 covers the situation where a service provider is charged with a criminal offence in relation to acts of transmission, provision of access or storage within Regulations 17–19 but seeks to rely on the defences therein. The service provider is placed under an evidential burden in that he is required to adduce evidence sufficient to raise an issue with respect to the defence. Once he has done this, the prosecution has to prove beyond reasonable doubt that the defence is not satisfied otherwise the service provider can rely on the defence.

Although the service provider is under a general duty to remove or disable access to unlawful information or information relating to unlawful activity, he may be placed under a duty to intercept, retain or store the information under a warrant authorising interception granted under the Regulation of Investigatory Powers Act 2000. In terms of removal of information or disabling access to it, there may also be issues under the Computer Misuse Act 1990 and the Data Protection Act 1998 and in relation to the right of freedom of expression under the Council of Europe Convention for the Protection of Human Rights and Fundamental Freedoms. Information society service providers should insert terms in their contracts with recipients of their services making it clear that they may take action to remove information or disable access if they have reason to believe that it contains unlawful information or is associated with illegal activity. This may prevent claims from recipients aggrieved at the removal of their information. Two difficulties remain however. The first is that it is probably not possible to contract out of freedom of expression. The second difficulty is that the contract may not be with the recipient, bearing in mind the Directive extends also to services provided for indirect remuneration.

SUMMARY

- ISPs have defences in relation to unlawful activity or illegal material.
- The defences apply where, in relation to illegal information or unlawful activity (hosting only):
  - the ISP acts as a mere conduit;
  - the ISP simply caches the information;
  - the ISP acts as a host.
- Generally, the ISP does not have to act as a 'gatekeeper'.
- There is no general obligation actively to seek facts and circumstances indicating illegal activity.
- Certain conditions apply, such as the ISP not modifying information and complying with conditions of access, etc.
- The defence gives immunity to an award of damages or other pecuniary remedy.
- Injunctions may still be possible.
- The defences require the ISP to act expeditiously to remove or disable access to information upon receiving actual notice or awareness (hosting).
- The defences overlap with the publisher's defence under defamation law but have much wider application.

SELF-TEST QUESTIONS

Note: there is only one correct answer to each multiple choice question.

1   **With respect to caching, to be immune from damages or any other pecuniary remedy or any criminal sanction, of the following things an information society service provider must do which one is NOT CORRECT?**

  (a) Comply with conditions on access to the information.

  (b) Act expeditiously to remove or disable access to the information he has stored upon obtaining actual knowledge of the fact that the information at the initial source of the transmission has been removed from the network or access to it has been disabled or that a court or administrative authority has ordered such removal or disablement.

  (c) Comply with any rules regarding the updating of the information, specified in a manner widely used and recognised in industry.

  (d) Act expeditiously to remove or disable access to information upon obtaining actual knowledge of unlawful activity or information.

2   **In relation to the sale of counterfeit watches on an internet auction site hosted by an internet service provider in Case IZR 304/01 *Rolex Internet Auction* [2005] ETMR 255, the Federal High Court of Germany made a number of findings. Which one of the following was NOT one of those findings?**

  (a) Internet service providers, in order to comply with the Directive on electronic commerce, have a duty to take reasonable steps to check the information made available through their service is lawful, such as by carrying out random spot checks from time to time.

  (b) The service provider is not required to act as a 'gatekeeper'. He is not to be expected to check every offer made using his service.

  (c) If the service provider becomes aware of a trade mark infringement, he must not only block the actual offer without delay and also take all measures technically possible and reasonable as a precaution to prevent any further corresponding trade mark infringements.

  (d) Providing a platform on the internet on which suppliers can auction goods is not itself a sufficient ground to make the service provider an infringer of a trade mark. Participation in infringement with the supplier requires at least some element of intention.

3   **To what extent do the defences for ISPs provide a reasonable balance between the rights of individuals and holders of, for example, intellectual property rights and the immunity from financial penalties for ISPs?**

For further resources and updates please go to the Companion Website accompanying this book at **www.mylawchamber.co.uk/bainbridgeIT**

24

Liability of information society service providers for illegal material

Part 4

Information and communications technology crime

Information and communications technology impacts on criminal law in two ways. It facilitates the commission of existing crimes, such as fraud and theft, but it has also given birth to a new range of activities such as computer hacking and the development and distribution of computer viruses. The criminal law was perceived to be patchy in its application, both to existing and new forms of crime, and this caused considerable concern to the computer industry and financial institutions. Largely as a result of lobbying and pressure from the industry, the Computer Misuse Act 1990 was enacted, having started life as a private member's Bill. The Act closed the loopholes in the prior law and also dealt with questions of jurisdiction and extradition. In particular, it created a new offence of unauthorised access to computer programs or data (hacking), an ulterior intent offence (hacking with intent to commit a further offence) and an offence of unauthorised modification of computer material. At the time of writing, some changes to the Computer Misuse Act 1990 are in the pipeline and should be brought into force sometime during 2007.

This part of the book concentrates on three areas of criminal activity associated with the use of information and communications technology – fraud, hacking and damage to programs and data. These have all attracted a great deal of media attention and the nature of these offences and the scope of the criminal law in relation to them are discussed. There were problems with deception offences as it was generally considered that it was not possible to deceive a computer and the deception had to operate on the human mind. The Fraud Act 2006 has addressed these problems and brought the law relating to fraud up to date to deal with criminal activities such as 'phishing' and the use of bogus websites to capture data such as a person's bank account details. A further chapter looks at the serious problem of pornography, in particular, child pornography on the internet, threatening e-mails and online incitement. There is also a chapter on the admissibility of computer and digital evidence in criminal proceedings and computer forensics. One point to be remembered when reading the following chapters is that the actions described will sometimes give rise to liabilities under civil law. For example, if a hacker makes a copy of some of the information stored on a computer system, he may be infringing the copyright subsisting in that information and may also be in breach of confidence if he divulges it to others, depending upon the circumstances. Similarly, a fraudster transferring funds will be guilty of the civil law tort of conversion. If the culprit is an employee who has obtained access to parts of a computer system to which he has no authority to access, then internal action such as a reprimand or dismissal may ensue instead of or as well as a criminal prosecution.

▶

Note that although some criminal offences also apply in Scotland, for example offences under the Computer Misuse Act 1990, there are some significant differences between English and Scots criminal law. Furthermore, where offences do apply in Scotland, there may be differences in their application and scope. The Fraud Act 2006 is an example and it does not apply to Scotland where the existing common law offence of fraud continues to be useful in the fight against computer fraud.

25 Information and communications technology fraud

INTRODUCTION

Information and communications technology fraud ('ICT fraud') often makes headline news but it is thought that the number of cases of fraud detected and prosecuted is just the tip of the iceberg. Rumours abound about massive frauds which are not reported by the victims (usually large financial institutions) because of a fear of publicity. It does not help a bank's image of solid dependability to have employees prosecuted for computer fraud at regular intervals. All the major financial institutions throughout the world use networked computers connected to communications systems to carry out their business and vast sums of money are transferred electronically by EFT ('electronic funds transfer').

It used to be the case that the greatest threat to computer systems came from within – that is, from employees. One of the largest reported computer frauds ever attempted, which concerned the transfer of $70 m, involved an employee of the First National Bank of Chicago. Even when such crime is detected and the persons involved are prosecuted and convicted, the penalties imposed seem relatively trivial when compared with other forms of criminal activity. In 1989, a teenage bank cashier who transferred nearly £1 m into his own and a friend's bank account received only one year's youth custody. However, with the growth of networks and the internet, things have changed and new forms of fraud and abuse developed. The 2006 *CSI/FBI Computer Crime and Security Survey*[1] indicated that viruses continued to be the cause of the greatest financial losses for the 616 respondents. For the 313 respondents willing to quantify their financial losses for all forms of computer misuse, the total loss was over $52 m. The average loss was $167,713 (at p. 12). Financial fraud amounted to $2,556,900, telecom fraud £1,262,410 and phishing (obtaining information by sending an e-mail purporting to be from a genuine organisation, such as a bank, asking for confirmation of account and password details) $647,510. In the UK, the Audit Commission figure for the total value of fraud in the public sector was around £83 m though this was not restricted to computer fraud.[2] In the private sector, it is still likely that a significant amount of fraud, as well as other forms of computer misuse, goes unreported. For the 201 firms surveyed in 2003 by the National Hi-Tec Crime Unit, hi-tech crime accounted for £74 m of the total of £195 m for financial crime.[3] Under-reporting was suspected. Another US survey estimated that phishing attacks cost US banks $1.2 billion in 2003 and 57 million Americans had received phishing e-mails.[4] Clearly the problem of computer fraud is very serious and is likely to continue to be so.

---

[1] Conducted by the United States Computer Security Institute with the participation of the San Francisco Federal Bureau of Investigation Computer Intrusion Squad, referred to hereafter as the '*CSI/FBI 2006 Survey*'.

[2] Audit Commission, *ICT Fraud and Abuse 2004 (Public Sector Update 2005)*, p. 22.

[3] Financial Services Authority, *Countering Financial Crime Risks in Information Security*, 2004, p. 10.

[4] Ibid.

This chapter concentrates on the Fraud Act 2006 and how it applies to information and communications technology fraud ('ICT fraud'). The common law offence of conspiracy to defraud proved useful in the past in the fight against computer fraud where two or more persons were involved. This offence remains available for the time being. It may be abolished in due course if it is no longer useful in the light of the Fraud Act 2006. The offence of theft is also covered. This offence may be applicable where the fraud has been completed and the perpetrator has successfully obtained property, including money or financial credit. After briefly looking at how a computer was used as an accomplice, the old deception offences are discussed briefly together with the perceived deficiencies of these offences in relation to information and communications fraud ('ICT fraud'). First, however, some of the basics of English criminal law must be explained.

BASICS OF ENGLISH CRIMINAL LAW

Most criminal offences under English law are creatures of legislation. Most are set out in Acts of Parliament. Examples are the offences under the Theft Act 1968, the Fraud Act 2006 and the Computer Misuse Act 1990. A few common law offences remain such as murder and common law conspiracy.

The elements of a particular offence can be broken down and analysed in terms of the mental element, described by lawyers by the Latin name *mens rea* (roughly equating to a guilty mind), and the prohibited acts or omissions, known as the *actus reus* of the offence. For example, the offence of unauthorised access to computer material under section 1 of the Computer Misuse Act 1990 states:

(1) A person is guilty of an offence if –
    (a) he causes a computer to perform any function with intent to secure access to any program or data held in any computer;
    (b) the access he intends to secure is unauthorised; and
    (c) he knows at the time when he causes the computer to perform the function that that is the case.

The *mens rea* of the offence is an intention to secure access to any program or data and concurrent knowledge that the access is unauthorised. The *actus reus* is causing a computer to perform any function and the fact that the intended access is unauthorised. However, this is not the full picture as will be seen in Chapter 26. For example, whether access is unauthorised has a special meaning.

Some offences are termed strict liability offences for which there is no *mens rea*. For example, driving during the hours of darkness with a faulty rear light is an offence even if the driver did not know the light was faulty. Many strict liability offences are 'regulatory offences' and are not usually too serious in terms of punishment, which is often a fine. There are a number of defences to criminal offences. Some are set out in the statute itself. For example, section 1(3) of the Protection from Harassment Act 1997 provides a defence under specified circumstances: see Chapter 28. Other defences are of a more general nature, such as self-defence, duress, necessity and the prevention of crime. Defences of provocation and diminished responsibility apply only to murder and are not full defences but serve to reduce the conviction to one of manslaughter.

For a person to be convicted of an offence, all the elements must be proved by the prosecution (unless admitted). The standard of proof is beyond reasonable doubt. However, where a defence applies, the accused usually has to prove the facts giving rise to the defence on a balance of probabilities. There are some differences and, in some cases, for example, the accused may be required to raise an issue only after which the prosecution must disprove it.

The prosecution of criminal offences

Before specific offences are examined, it will be useful to describe, very briefly, the procedure for prosecuting offences, the classification of offences and the different modes of trial.

When a criminal offence has been committed, the normal procedure is for the police to be informed (the police detect very little crime themselves but depend on the public bringing incidents of crime to their notice). The police will then investigate the crime and, if they suspect a particular person or persons of having committed the crime, they may charge the person or persons and then pass the case over to the Crown Prosecution Service (Procurator Fiscal in Scotland) which decides whether to prosecute and what charges to bring. The police have the National Hi-Tech Crime Unit, operating within the National Crime Squad.

In coming to its decision to prosecute, the Crown Prosecution Service uses guidelines which include the possibility of securing a conviction and the public interest. If the decision is made to proceed, the accused will appear before a magistrates' court where, depending on the nature of the offence and other matters, either his case will be dealt with, or he will be committed for trial in the Crown Court. It is possible to bring a private prosecution if, for example, the Crown Prosecution Service declines to act. However, the Director of Public Prosecutions has the power to take over a private prosecution. Other bodies may bring prosecutions such as local authority trading standards officers, the Department of Social Security, the Information Commissioner and HM Inland Revenue. Bringing a private prosecution is, in most cases, an extreme action, but it may be relevant to computer crime if the official bodies fail to take an interest in prosecuting certain behaviour, due perhaps to a lack of understanding of the problems involved or a feeling that the civil law offers sufficient remedies. Though this latter point may be true, it does not have the deterrent effect that a successful criminal prosecution can have.

In England and Wales, criminal offences are heard in either the Crown Court or magistrates' courts. The latter tend to deal with the less serious offences which make up the vast majority of criminal cases. Offences are classified according to how they may be tried. Relatively minor offences, such as exceeding the speed limit, may be tried only in magistrates' courts and these offences are described as being *summary* offences. Serious offences such as murder and robbery can only be tried in the Crown Court and these are called *indictable* offences. In between these two types of offence, there are a vast number of intermediate offences which can be tried in either a magistrates' court or the Crown Court; these offences, of which theft and fraud are examples, are called *triable either way* offences. These may be tried summarily in a magistrates' court or, on indictment, in the Crown Court. Many of the offences which will be described in this part of the book fall into this category; they are offences which are triable either way, an example being the unauthorised modification of computer programs or data. On the other hand, computer hacking (unauthorised access to computer material) is triable summarily only.

When an offence is classified as being triable either way, the choice of mode of trial initially rests with the magistrates. They may decide that the nature of the case is such that it should be tried in the Crown Court: for example, if it is a serious example of the offence. If the magistrates decide that the case can be heard in their court, the accused person can then decide whether to proceed in the magistrates' court, or to elect trial in the Crown Court.

The maximum penalties available in magistrates' courts need to be mentioned. Providing the relevant statute does not contain a lower maximum, for a single offence the magistrates may send a person to prison for a term not exceeding six months (which may soon be raised to 12 months) and/or impose a fine not exceeding the statutory maximum, presently £5,000. Other sentencing powers are available to the magistrates such as discharging the offender or imposing a probation order or a community service order. In the context of computer crime, the use of imprisonment and fines are the most likely punishments, although other forms of sentence may be appropriate in some circumstances.

Now we have covered the basic of criminal law and the prosecution of offenders, we can turn to the offences applicable to ICT crime and, in this chapter, ICT fraud in particular.

THE COMPUTER AS AN UNWITTING ACCOMPLICE

A computer system might be used to detect information which assists the criminal in the commission of his crime. For example, in the case of *R v Sunderland* (unreported) 20 June 1983, Court of Appeal, an employee of Barclay's Bank used the bank's computer to discover a dormant account and then forged the holder's signature to withdraw some £2,100. The employee of the bank used the computer in a very simple way to detect an account which had not been used for a long period of time but which had some funds in it, a simple but effective way of stealing money although, eventually, the scheme was discovered when the holder of the dormant account attempted to make a withdrawal and discovered that the account contained less money than it should have done. The employee, who was of previous good character, was sentenced to two years' imprisonment, which was changed on appeal by the Lord Chief Justice who suspended 18 months of the sentence. He said:

> ... other people like bank clerks and bank officials need very little reminding that if they commit this sort of offence they will lose their job and go to prison, albeit for a comparatively short time.

This case illustrates the vulnerability of some computer systems to criminal activities. It also shows that the greatest threat of fraud comes from within an organisation and employees are responsible for a great deal of ICT fraud or attempted ICT fraud, ranging from small amounts of money to very large sums indeed.

THE OLD DECEPTION OFFENCES

These included obtaining property by deception (section 15 Theft Act 1968), obtaining a money transfer by deception (section 15A Theft Act 1968), obtaining a pecuniary advantage by deception (section 16 Theft Act 1968), obtaining services by deception (section 1 Theft Act 1978) and evasion of liability by deception (section 2 Theft Act 1978). All these offences suffered from the defect that it was generally accepted that the deception had to operate on a human mind. If false information was submitted to a computer system and processed by that system automatically, without human intervention, these offences were of no use. If a person had succeeded in obtaining money, for example, by means of a fraud, the offence of theft under section 1 of the Theft Act 1968 could be applicable. However, there was no equivalent offence of theft of a service. These and other deficiencies in relation to fraud were noted by the Law Commission[5] and resulted in section 2 of the Computer Misuse Act 1990 (the ulterior intent offence). This was not restricted to fraud and was intended to deal with situations such as where a more serious offence was attempted by means of computer 'hacking'. It is described in the following chapter. All the above offences under the Theft Acts of 1968 and 1978 have been repealed by the Fraud Act 2006.

---

[5] Law Commission, *Criminal Law: Computer Misuse* (Law Com. No. 186), Cm 819, HMSO, 1989.

The problem with the old deception offences

There was no problem flowing from the intangible nature of money, credits or cheques as section 4(1) of the 1968 Act states that property includes money and things in action. Bankers' cheques, money orders and bills of exchange are all examples of 'things in action'. This definition of property applies to the 1968 Act generally. So far as obtaining property by deception was concerned, section 15(1) of the Theft Act 1968 defined the offence as follows:

> **A person who by any deception dishonestly obtains property belonging to another, with the intention of permanently depriving the other of it, shall on conviction on indictment be liable to imprisonment for a term not exceeding ten years.**

The difficulty with this offence is that it required a deception and this implied that an actual person was deceived, not a machine. In *DPP* v *Ray* [1974] AC 370, Lord Morris said:

> **For a deception to take place there must be some person or persons who will have been deceived.**

Other case law did not help very much and the question was left open in one case involving an automatic car park barrier (*Davies* v *Flackett* [1973] RTR 8). Bearing in mind that *DPP* v *Ray* was decided in the House of Lords, the better view was that the deception must work upon a human mind. In *Re Holmes* [2005] 1 All ER 490, the court noted that the prevailing view was that it was not possible at law to deceive a machine, though the court did not need to rule on this one way or the other.

The notion that a machine could not be deceived was strengthened by the Theft Act 1978 which defines the offences of obtaining services by deception (services such as hiring a car or providing bed and breakfast) and evasion of liability by deception (such as where a debtor tells a lie to his creditor in order to let him off part or the whole of the debt) because the wording used strongly suggested that the deception must operate on the human mind. For example, section 1(1) stated:

> **A person who by any deception dishonestly obtains services from *another* shall be guilty of an offence** [emphasis added].

This interpretation was reinforced by other language used in the statute. There was a requirement for the services to be subject to payment, so the same act with respect to a 'free' service did not involve the offence.

Section 15A was inserted into the Theft Act 1968 as a result of the case of *R* v *Preddy* [1996] AC 815. Charges were brought against the accused persons under section 15 of the Theft Act 1968. They had made over 40 applications for mortgages by making false statements. Their plan was to use the money to buy houses with the intention of reselling them at a profit and redeeming the mortgages. They hoped to make a substantial profit as, at the time, property prices were rising quickly and there was something of a property boom. The lenders said that they would not have lent the money to the accused persons had they known the true motive for obtaining a mortgage. Some of the mortgage advances were made telegraphically or electronically, by electronic funds transfer, while others were made by cheque. The accused were convicted and their appeals to the Court of Appeal were dismissed.

The appeals to the House of Lords were allowed and the convictions were quashed. An account in a bank or building society is classed as a 'chose in action' (thing in action). As regards the telegraphic or electronic fund transfers, it was held that when payment was made from one bank or building society account in credit (the lender's account) to another bank account, the chose in action represented by the credit balance in the lender's account was extinguished or reduced and a new chose in action was created in the borrower's account (or the borrower's solicitor's account). Therefore, the borrower did not get the lender's chose in action. Consequently, the borrower did not obtain 'property belonging to another' as was required by section 15(1) of the Theft Act 1968. The account itself, the chose in action, was not transferred to the borrower.

As regards the cheques, the chose in action represented by the cheque never belonged to the bank or building society as when it came into existence it belonged to the borrower – it was made out to the borrower or his solicitor who would then transfer the payment to the person selling the house. As the chose in action belonged to the borrower right from the start, no property belonging to another was obtained by the borrower. Although the cheque itself was a physical object (that is, the paper as opposed to the chose in action relating to the amount it was made out for) and was property belonging to another, the borrower did not obtain it permanently as it would be returned to be bank or building society after presentation to the borrower's bank (or his solicitor's bank). Therefore, even charging these persons with theft of the piece of paper on which the cheque was written would have been doomed to failure.

Section 15A of the Theft Act 1968 was intended to overcome the shortcomings of section 15 highlighted in *Preddy*. It did so with unnecessary complexity and its repeal by the Fraud Act 2006 is very welcome. In *Re Holmes* [2005] 1 All ER 490, the over-technicality of the offence was criticised. In that case, extradition of Holmes had been sought by Germany. He was accused of dishonestly transferring funds of over $15 m from a bank in Germany for whom he had worked temporarily to an account in a bank in Amsterdam in order to carry out the fraud. For extradition to succeed, the offence in Germany with which he had been charged would also have to be an offence in England. That brought into question whether the section 15A offence was applicable. A submission that the defence did not apply because only a machine had been deceived was rejected. Although the transfer had been made automatically, it was subject to a reservation which was lifted only after he had sent three e-mails of confirmation to the Amsterdam bank. In that way, the recipient of the e-mails had been deceived. Furthermore, it was confirmed that the money transfer was not complete at the time the e-mails were sent as, at that time, the amount credited was conditional.

THE FRAUD ACT 2006

The Fraud Act 2006 fully came into force on 15 January 2007. The Act deals with some of the deficiencies of the Theft Acts 1968 and 1978, especially when it comes to ICT fraud. It is now clear that 'phishing', obtaining information such as a person's bank account details by sending an e-mail purporting to be from that person's bank, is a criminal offence. This remains the case even if nothing further has been done with the information thus obtained or even before the e-mail has been transmitted.

The Act creates three new forms of fraud and an offence of obtaining services dishonestly. None of these require deception to be proved but all are offences of dishonesty. The Act also provides for some offences related to articles for use in fraud. Section 1 sets out the basic statement that a person is guilty of fraud if he is in breach of any of sections 2, 3 or 4. These sections cover:

- fraud by false representation;
- fraud by failing to disclose information; and
- fraud by abuse of position, respectively.

Section 1(3) sets out the penalties for section 1 fraud which are:

- on summary conviction, imprisonment for a term not exceeding 12 months (six months in Northern Ireland) and/or a fine not exceeding the statutory maximum;

- on conviction on indictment, the maximum penalty is imprisonment for a term not exceeding 10 years and/or a fine.

Each of these forms of fraud under section 1 is now examined in detail, followed by the offences relating to articles for use in frauds and then the offence of obtaining services dishonestly.

Fraud by false representation

This fraud is set out in section 2 and occurs where a person dishonestly makes a false representation, intending by making the representation to make a gain for himself or another or to cause loss to another or to expose another to a risk of loss. A 'representation' is any representation as to fact or law, including a representation as to the state of mind of the person making it or any other person. A representation may be express or implied. A representation is 'false' if it is untrue or misleading and the person making it knows that it is, or might be, untrue or misleading.

A representation may be regarded as 'made' if it (or anything implying it) is submitted in any form to any system or device designed to receive, convey or respond to communications (with or without human intervention). This puts it beyond doubt that representations made, for example, by e-mail to a computer or by SMS to a mobile phone, are included. It is not an exhaustive definition. A representation will also be made when it is sent to fully automated equipment or software, for example, where it is sent to an online bank with instructions to pay funds into another account.

Section 5 defines 'gain' and 'loss' as extending only to money or other property but includes a temporary or permanent gain or loss. 'Property' is any property whether real or personal (including things in action and other intangible property). This will include intellectual property though it is difficult to think of situations where intellectual property can be gained or lost. One possibility is were a fraud is perpetrated which results in the assignment of an intellectual property right. Irrespective of the possibility of such an assignment being invalid in equity if not in law, this makes it clear that dishonestly attempting to secure such an assignment by means of a false representation will result in an offence of fraud being committed.

'Gain' includes a gain by keeping what one has as well as a gain by getting what one does not have and 'loss' includes a loss by not getting what one might get as well as a loss by parting with what one has. This definition of gain or loss applies to the other forms of fraud covered by section 1.

Section 2 is wider than the old deception offences, such as sections 15 and 15A of the Theft Act 1968. For example, section 15 of that Act required the offender by any deception dishonestly to 'obtain property belonging to another with the intention of permanently depriving the other of it'. For a breach of section 2 of the Fraud Act 2006, there is no need for the gain or loss to actually happen or, if it does happen, for it to be permanent.

There are three forms of *mens rea* required for the section 2 form of fraud.

- Dishonesty – it is expected that the '*Ghosh* test' (see below) will continue to apply to determine whether a person acted dishonestly.
- The intention, by making the representation, to make a gain or cause a loss.
- Knowledge that the representation is, or might be, untrue or misleading.

In respect of the latter form of *mens rea*, that knowledge that the representation might be untrue should cover the position where the representation is made recklessly though the prosecution would have to show that the accused at least realised that it might be untrue or misleading. Of course, as a matter of fact, the representation must be untrue or misleading. A person who mistakenly believes that the representation is untrue or misleading does not commit the offence.

25

Information and communications technology fraud

The form of fraud by false representation will apply to a wide variety of situations. In particular, it will apply to 'phishing', 'pharming' (diverting traffic to a genuine website to a bogus one), presenting a credit or debit card for payment and even entering a pin number at an ATM (in this case, the 'deception' only works on the machine itself). Section 2 overcomes the difficulty that a machine cannot be deceived.

Section 2 will not cover spyware directly (software surreptitiously installed on a computer used to gather information without the user's knowledge). As such spyware in installed on a computer's hard disk without the owner's or user's knowledge, no representation is made unless it could be argued that there is an implied representation that the site from which it was 'sent' would not install spyware or other malicious software. This seems to be stretching the language of section 2 somewhat. Of course, making use of data collected using spyware subsequently can be the offence of fraud by false representation, for example, where the victim's bank account details are submitted to his bank in order to withdraw funds. The false representation then being made to his bank. Also, writing spyware software or supplying it to another or simply being in possession of it can be an offence under sections 6 or 7 of the Fraud Act 2006; see below.

Fraud by failing to disclose information

This form of the offence of fraud applies, under section 3 of the Fraud Act 2006, where a person dishonestly fails to disclose to another person information which he is under a legal duty to disclose and intends, by failing to disclose the information, to make a gain for himself or another or to cause loss to another or to expose another to a risk of loss.

The duty to disclose information may derive from statute (such as company or tax legislation) or it may be part of the duty of a fiduciary, such as a trustee holding property on behalf of a beneficiary under a trust, such as where a trustee holds the legal title to land on behalf of a person under 18 years of age. It may be a duty imposed by contract law, such as in the case of an insurance contract, where there is a duty to disclose any matter that might influence the insurer in his decision to accept the proposal or accept it at a higher premium. The explanatory memorandum to the Fraud Bill as introduced into Parliament suggested the concept of duty was wide enough to encompass a failure to disclose something that gives the victim a cause of action for damages as well as a right to set aside any change in his or her legal position.

The offence may be relevant in respect of the growing number of transactions between governmental institutions and individuals or corporate bodies that can now be conducted online. Examples are the electronic submission of tax returns, applying for road fund tax and applying for or renewing television licences electronically. It will also be relevant in transactions between businesses ('B2B') and between consumers and businesses ('C2B'), such as applying for motor vehicle insurance online. The offence may also be committed by a politician who dishonestly fails to disclose an interest in a company negotiating or bidding for a government contract.

Fraud by abuse of position

This applies where a person occupies a position in which he is expected to safeguard, or not to act against, the financial interests of another person. Breach of section 4 of the Fraud Act 2006, giving rise to the offence of fraud, occurs where such a person dishonestly abuses that position, intending by that abuse to make a gain for himself or another or to cause loss to another or to expose another to a risk of loss. Abuse of position applies even where the conduct consists of an omission rather than an act, for example, by failing to warn the victim of something that could affect his financial status.

The Law Commission's Report on *Fraud*[6] which set the scene for the Fraud Bill explained the meaning of 'position' in the following terms (at para. 7.38):

> The necessary relationship will be present between trustee and beneficiary, director and company, professional person and client, agent and principal, employee and employer, or between partners. It may arise otherwise, for example within a family, or in the context of voluntary work, or in any context where the parties are not at arm's length. In nearly all cases where it arises, it will be recognised by the civil law as importing fiduciary duties, and any relationship that is so recognised will suffice. We see no reason, however, why the existence of such duties should be essential. This does not of course mean that it would be entirely a matter for the fact-finders whether the necessary relationship exists. The question whether the particular facts alleged can properly be described as giving rise to that relationship will be an issue capable of being ruled upon by the judge and, if the case goes to the jury, of being the subject of directions.

'Abuse' is not defined in the Act because it was intended to cover a wide range of conduct. A typical example of the offence is where a person with an enduring power of attorney misuses that position to draw funds from the donor's bank account. Another suggested possibility is where an employee of a software company uses his position to make unauthorised copies of his employer's software to sell for his own benefit. It could also apply where an employee sends an e-mail containing confidential information belonging to the employer to a rival company, whether for his own personal gain or with the intention of causing his employer a loss.

As the offence can be committed by an omission as well as an act, it could apply where an employee fails to do something he should do to protect his employer's financial interests. An example would be failing to inform the employer of the need to make an official return, in the hope that the employer will suffer a financial penalty. Of course, dishonesty must be present so an employee or trustee or other person in a relevant position who simply forgets to do something will not commit the offence.

Articles for use in fraud

There are two forms of offence involving articles for use in fraud. The first is possession of such an article and the second is making or supplying such articles. The meaning of 'article' is given in section 8 and is the same for both offences. It is defined simply as including any program or data held in electronic form. Of course, it could be much wider and will include a machine for counterfeiting banknotes or credit cards, counterfeit goods and infringing copies of CDs and DVDs. The non-exhaustive definition is added to the meaning of 'prohibited articles' in certain other provisions, such as under section 1(7)(b) of the Police and Criminal Evidence Act 1984. This enables the exercise of stop and search powers in relation to such articles used in the course of or in connection with fraud. Therefore, for example, the police could exercise these powers to stop someone suspected of carrying an optical disc containing a bogus e-mail to be used for phishing.

Possession, etc. of articles for use in frauds

This offence, under section 6 of the Fraud Act 2006, is made out where a person has in his possession or under his control any article for use in the course of or in connection with any fraud. The offence appears to be of strict liability in that there is no requirement that the person intends that the article is to be used for fraud or knows that it is to be, or may be, so used. However, the article must be 'for use in the course of or in connection with any fraud'. This suggests that the

[6] Law Com. No. 276, Cm 5560, 2002.

article must be capable of being used for fraud. This would seem to include articles which also have legitimate uses. This could apply to decryption software which could lawfully be used for the purposes of cryptography research as permitted under section 296ZA(2) of the Copyright, Designs and Patents Act 1988 (circumvention of technological measures). Such software could also be used to decrypt passwords or other access protocols protecting, for example, bank accounts. Because of this, the offence only really makes sense if the accused's intention or knowledge relates to a potential fraud.

It was intended that this offence would attract the case law that built up in relation to section 25 of the Theft Act 1968. This states that 'A person shall be guilty of an offence if, when not at his place of abode, he has with him any article for use in the course of or in connection with any burglary, theft or cheat'. ('Cheat' was removed by the Fraud Act 2006, being the equivalent to the deception offences.) In *R v Ellames* [1974] 1 WLR 1391, Browne LJ, giving the judgment of the Court of Appeal, said (at 1397):

> ... to establish an offence under s 25(1) [of the Theft Act 1968] the prosecution must prove that the defendant was in possession of the article, and intended the article to be used in the course of or in connection with some future burglary, theft or cheat. But it is not necessary to prove that he intended it to be used in the course of or in connection with any specific burglary, theft or cheat; it is enough to prove a general intention to use it for some burglary, theft or cheat; we think that this view is supported by the use of the word 'any' in s 25(1). Nor, in our view, is it necessary to prove that the defendant intended to use it himself; it will be enough to prove that he had it with him with the intention that it should be used by someone else.

As the meaning of 'article' includes any program or data held in electronic form, the offence is of very wide scope. Some examples given in the explanatory memorandum to the Fraud Bill included a computer program used to generate credit card numbers; computer templates used to producing blank utility bills; computer files containing lists of other people's credit card details or draft letters in connection with 'advance fee' frauds. Another example is a HyperText Markup Language ('html') file for a website fraudulently offering escrow services or a letter to be sent to companies asking for their Companies House authentification codes for WebFiling (two current scams Companies House is aware of).

In accordance with *Ellames* and other case law relating to the meaning of possession, the person must know that he has the article in his possession or under his control. However, on the basis of the offence of possession of a controlled drug under section 5 of the Misuse of Drugs Act 1971 and the House of Lords decision in *R v Lambert* [2002] 2 AC 545, providing the accused knows he has an article in his possession, the prosecution does not have to prove that he knew its nature. If this reasoning was applied to section 6 of the Fraud Act 2006, the accused would have the legal burden to prove, on a balance of probabilities, that he did not know and had no reason to believe the article was one caught by section 6. But, there are some difficulties in applying the reasoning in *Lambert* to the section 6 offence.

It is clear that the offence would not apply, for example, where the article in question was spyware which had been placed on a person's hard disk without any knowledge of its presence on his part. Indeed, the use of the phrase 'or under his control' reinforces the need to show knowledge of the article's existence and whereabouts. To give an example, say a person, Alex, uses a computer owned by Brian upon which spyware has been installed without Brian's knowledge, Brian commits no offence even if Alex's personal details have been sent to the person, Cherie, responsible for installing the spyware. Of course, Cherie will be liable for being in control of the spyware and also, possibly, for being in possession of the original and other copies of it as well. Potentially, other offences may have been committed.

The difficulty is where a person knows he has possession or control of software but is not aware that it is an 'article for use on the course of or in connection with any fraud'. According to *Lambert*, he would be guilty but not on the basis of *Ellames*. The only reasonable solution is to accept *Ellames* as being applicable. That case concerned an offence under the Theft Act 1968 and the offences under the Fraud Act 2006 are of the same kind. There are other reasons for the stricter approach in relation to drugs offences, for example, the seriousness of the offences and the difficulty in proving knowledge or reason to believe the true nature of the substance. In terms of computer software, it may be easier to prove the accused's knowledge by the application of computer forensics.

The offence is triable either way and section 6(2) sets out the maximum penalties which are:

- on summary conviction, imprisonment for a term not exceeding 12 months (six months in Northern Ireland) and/or a fine not exceeding the statutory maximum;

- on conviction on indictment, the maximum penalty is imprisonment for a term not exceeding five years and/or a fine.

Making or supplying articles for use in frauds

Under section 7(1) of the Fraud Act 2006, this offence is made out where a person makes, adapts, supplies or offers to supply any article:

(a) knowing that it is designed or adapted for use in the course of or in connection with fraud; or

(b) intending it to be used to commit, or assist in the commission of, fraud.

The meaning of 'article' is as for the section 6 offence, that is, it includes any program or data held in electronic form. The offence could apply where a person writes spyware designed to collect personal data to be used in carrying out a fraud by false representation, prepares an e-mail for phishing or designs a bogus website intended to collect personal data such as identification codes and passwords. The inclusion of 'adapted' would be relevant where, for example, a bogus website is made by copying and pasting elements of the legitimate site it is intended to represent.

Examples of this offence include the making of devices to be attached to electricity meters so as to cause the meter to malfunction and register incorrect usage of electricity. It could also apply where software is written or supplied which can circumvent technological measures applied to copyright works to prevent unauthorised acts in relation to the works. To this extent, the offence overlaps with the equivalent, though wider, offences under section 296ZB of the Copyright, Designs and Patents Act 1988. These offences do not require the prosecution to prove *mens rea* though they are subject to a defence, being where the accused did not know and had no reasonable ground for believing that the device, product, component or service enabled or facilitated the circumvention of effective technological measures.

In terms of knowledge that an article is designed or adapted for use in the course of, or in connection with, fraud, whether the article is actually used for, or in connection with fraud, is irrelevant to the offence. Knowledge that it could be so used should be sufficient. That calls into question the position where the person making or adapting an article which can be used for, or in connection with, fraud but intends to use it for some other reason. For example, say that someone writes spyware to capture personal data but he intends that the data collected will be used not for fraud but for publication contrary to the Data Protection Act 1998. As spyware can be used to commit an offence under the Fraud Act 2006 the person responsible will be guilty of the offence if he knows this is a possibility. The way an offence can be committed by means of spyware is that subsequently using account details captured by the spyware to withdraw funds from the victim's bank account is making a false representation to the bank.

25

Information and communications technology fraud

The maximum penalties for this offence are:

- on summary conviction, imprisonment for a term not exceeding 12 months (six months in Northern Ireland) and/or a fine not exceeding the statutory maximum;
- on conviction on indictment, the maximum penalty is imprisonment for a term not exceeding 10 years and/or a fine.

Obtaining services dishonestly

This offence, under section 11, replaces section 1 of the Theft Act 1978, obtaining services by deception. This suffered from the problem that it might not have applied where the deception did not operate on a human being, such as where a service was obtained by entering a password or other access protocol which was checked automatically by a computer. Furthermore, if the fraudster succeeded in obtaining the services, there was no offence of theft of a service with which he could be charged.

The new offence is committed by a person who obtains services for himself or another by a dishonest act where:

(a) the services are made available on the basis that payment has been, is being or will be made for or in respect of them,

(b) he obtains them without any payment having been made for or in respect of them or without payment being made in full, and

(c) when he obtains them, he knows –
   (i) that they are being made available on the basis described in paragraph (a), or
   (ii) that they might be,

but intends that payment will not be made, or will not be made in full.

The offence would apply, for example, where a person gains access to a database available only to subscribers. The dishonest act would be using a password or access code which the person is not entitled to use, knowing this is the case. Any form of information society service provided for payment could be the target of the dishonest act. Once again, however, the offence is of very wide scope and would apply to a myriad of situations, ranging from pretending to be a senior citizen in order to take advantage of a concessionary travel fare to presenting someone else's debit card to pay for a hotel room to using someone else's bank details to pay for online gambling to climbing over a wall to watch a football match without paying to using an unauthorised decoder to watch cable or satellite television programmes provided for payment only. The removal of the requirement for deception significantly widens the offence compared with the old section 1 of the Theft Act 1978. The offence requires the service actually to have been obtained. However, this should not rule out the possibility of charging a person with an attempt to commit the offence.

It is likely that the *Ghosh* test, below, will be used to determine whether a particular act is or is not dishonest (and will be used for the other fraud offences). Apart from the element of dishonesty, the accused must know that the services are paid for or that they might be paid for and must intend not to pay for them in full or at all. The inclusion of knowing that the services might be made available on the basis that that they are paid for extends the *mens rea* to cover a situation where the accused might not actually know that the services are made available on the basis that they will be paid for, but the circumstances are such that he would realise this is a possibility. It is likely that this will be an objective test, based on what a reasonable and honest person would think in those circumstances.

The way the offence is worded brings the possibility that a person could be convicted for obtaining a free service because he thought that it might be provided for payment only. Many free websites require users to register and log in when visiting the site. Some may allow a limited number of free searches over a period of time. Although it is theoretically possible that a person could commit the offence by accessing such a website, the requirement that the service is obtained by a dishonest act is a safeguard. However, what if a person who understands that payment is required when the number of searches of an online database exceeds, say, 20 in any 24-hour period, logs on twice in the same day, using different usernames and passwords he has set up on different computers and, by doing so, exceeds the limit? (The Royal Mail has such a system for its postcode finder database where free access is limited to 20 searches per day to prevent substantial free use by a business organisation.) Potentially, such a person could be guilty of the offence.

The maximum penalties for the offence of obtaining services dishonestly are:

- on summary conviction, imprisonment for a term not exceeding 12 months (six months in Northern Ireland) and/or a fine not exceeding the statutory maximum;

- on conviction on indictment, the maximum penalty is imprisonment for a term not exceeding five years and/or a fine.

Dishonesty for fraud offences

For all the offences requiring dishonesty, the test in *R v Ghosh* [1982] QB 1053 should apply. The explanatory memorandum to the Fraud Bill recognised this possibility. The *Ghosh* test was set out by Lord Lane CJ as follows (at 1064):

> In determining whether the prosecution has proved that the defendant was acting dishonestly, a jury must first of all decide whether according to the ordinary standards of reasonable and honest people what was done was dishonest. If it was not dishonest by those standards, that is the end of the matter and the prosecution fails.
>
> If it was dishonest by those standards, then the jury must consider whether the defendant himself must have realised that what he was doing was by those standards dishonest.

It would seem highly appropriate for this test to be used to test dishonesty for the fraud offences under the Fraud Act 2006. It is likely to be useful on a wider basis. The House of Lords in *Twinsectra Ltd* v *Yardley* [2002] 2 AC 164 adopted a two-step approach similar to that in *Ghosh*, in a case on liability for acting as an accessory in a breach of trust case. It is even accepted that the *Ghosh* test is useful in determining bad faith for the purposes of trade mark law in *Harrison's Trade Mark Application* [2005] FSR 177. Without the objective element in the two-step test, a person accused of dishonesty or, for that matter bad faith, could end up being judged by his own standards or morality: the 'Robin Hood' test, as it was described by Lord Hutton in *Twinsectra*, following Lord Lane CJ's reference to the famous outlaw in *Ghosh*.

Self-incrimination

An old rule under English law is that a person is excused answering questions in a civil case that may incriminate him or his spouse for an offence. There are a number of exceptions to that rule, for example, in relation to intellectual property. For example, a person may not refuse to submit to a search order for infringing copies of a work of copyright on the basis that to comply would tend to incriminate him for an offence under copyright law. Under section 13 of the Fraud Act 2006, a person is not to be excused from answering any question, or complying with any order, in proceedings relating to property on the ground that by doing so may incriminate him or his spouse or civil partner of an offence under the Fraud Act or any related offence. However, in proceedings for an offence under the Act or a related offence, any such statements or admissions made answering such questions or complying with such orders are not admissible in evidence against him, his spouse or civil partner (providing they did not marry or become civil partners after the making of the statement or admission). Therefore, in such cases, persons will have to cooperate without losing their immunity in respect of anything said or admitted in response to such questions or orders.

Proceedings relating to property means proceedings for the recovery or administration of any property, the execution of any trust or an account of any property or dealings with property. Property is defined as meaning money or other property whether real or personal (including things in action and intellectual property). In some cases, questions about intellectual property could involve fraud, such as where software is used to perpetrate or facilitate fraud or is the subject-matter of the fraud.

A related offence is conspiracy to defraud and any other offence involving any form of fraudulent conduct or purpose.

CONSPIRACY TO DEFRAUD

The Law Commission, in its report on *Fraud*, recommended abolishing the common law offence of conspiracy to defraud. There were serious objections raised by this proposal and it has been decided to retain the offence for the time being. If the Fraud Act 2006 proves to be effective in convicting fraudsters, conspiracy to defraud may well be abolished. However, it has proved useful in the past and, being common law, has the added advantage of flexibility and the ability to adjust to new situations, an important aspect of law applicable to ICT crime.

Generally, a conspiracy is an agreement between two or more persons to carry out an unlawful act. Conspiracy may be statutory or common law. A statutory conspiracy is when a person agrees with another or others to embark upon a course of conduct which will necessarily amount to or involve a criminal offence by section 1 of the Criminal Law Act 1977, as amended. An example is where two persons agree to steal a computer; both will be guilty of a conspiracy to steal the computer even if they do not go on actually to steal it. Statutory conspiracy requires that the proposed act is itself a criminal offence and, in the case of the old offence of obtaining by deception, the difficulties of deceiving a machine remained.

At common law, the offence of conspiracy to defraud proved useful. It appeared that, in this context, 'deceit' is not an essential element of the offence and in *Scott* v *Commissioner of the Police of the Metropolis* [1975] AC 819, Viscount Dilhorne said:

> ... 'to defraud' ordinarily means ... to deprive a person dishonestly of something which is his or of something to which he is or would or might but for the perpetration of the fraud be entitled.

In other words, it is not necessary to show that a person has been deceived. In the *Scott* case, the accused made an agreement with cinema projectionists to make copies of films being shown in the cinemas and to sell those copies for profit. The original films were borrowed overnight, copied and then returned the next day. It was held that it did not matter that no person had been deceived and the appeal against conviction was dismissed.

The common law offence of conspiracy to defraud is separate and distinct from the fraud offences in the Fraud Act 2006. There is certainly a massive if not complete overlap where two or more persons are involved. The maximum penalty for conspiracy to defraud is 10 years' imprisonment and/or a fine under section 12 of the Criminal Justice Act 1987.

The consequence is that if two or more persons agree to dishonestly operate a computer, perhaps entering a password they are not entitled to use, to transfer funds to their own accounts, they will be guilty of a conspiracy to defraud even though no human being has been deceived. Of course, a limitation of the scope of this offence is that it requires an agreement between two or more conspirators and it cannot apply when only one person is involved. In the past, and particularly before the advent of section 2 of the Computer Misuse Act 1990, the track record of conspiracy to defraud in terms of dealing with computer fraud was very good. Indeed, even now, it may be preferable to use this offence because of its inherent flexibility. In one example, a junior bank clerk, in collusions with others, was imprisoned for five years after pleading guilty to conspiracy after trying to transfer £31 m to a bank account in Geneva (*Computing*, 2 March 1995, p. 1).

Conspiring to sell counterfeit computer software and decoder boxes, even on a relatively small scale, resulting in losses hypothetically estimated at £24,000 is almost certain to pass the custody threshold. In *R v Bakker* [2001] EWCA Crim 2354, a computer engineer and serving policeman near retirement set up a business with two others, ostensibly to sell computer systems. The Court of Appeal reduced the sentences imposed at the Crown Court of six months and 12 months to four months and eight months respectively. There were some special factors, for example, there was a long delay between arrest and sentencing and the policemen had lost his job, home and wife and suffered health problems.

At one time it was held that conspiracy to defraud and statutory conspiracy were mutually exclusive – that is, if the carrying out of the agreement would result in some offence being committed, however trivial, then a charge of conspiracy to defraud would be bad for duplicity. Section 12 of the Criminal Justice Act 1987 changed that rule and now it does not matter if carrying out the intended acts involves the commission of some other offence. The activities in the *Scott* case did not entail the commission of another offence. The conspirators were infringing copyright in a film, in those days a civil matter only. Now their activities would be a criminal offence under section 107 of the Copyright, Designs and Patents Act 1988 but this would no longer be fatal to a charge of conspiracy to defraud. Indeed, the conspirators could also be charged with a conspiracy to commit an offence under section 107.

Conspiracy is a useful offence where the planned offence has not been carried out or completed. It has become more useful now as it can apply to planned acts or events outside the UK as a result of the Criminal Justice (Terrorism and Conspiracy) Act 1998. It is a requirement that the act or event would be a criminal offence in the country where it was planned to happen and that the person charged or his agent did anything in the UK in relation to the agreement before its formation, became a party to it in the UK or did or omitted anything in the UK in pursuance of the agreement.

THE LAW OF ATTEMPTS

To be charged with an attempt to commit a criminal offence, the person involved must have done an act which is 'more than merely preparatory to the commission of the offence' (section 1 of the Criminal Attempts Act 1981). The scope of the law of attempts was uncertain when it came to computer fraud. Most of the new offences under the Fraud Act 2006 can be committed without the completion of the relevant gain or loss actually taking place, making the law of attempts redundant for these offences. The only exception is the offence of obtaining services dishonestly. This offence requires that the services in question are obtained. In respect of that offence, the law of attempts retains a residual value in terms of ICT fraud (submitting someone else's credit or debit card details dishonestly to obtain the service should suffice as an attempt). In any case, section 2 of the Computer Misuse Act 1990 will apply. This creates an 'ulterior intent' offence, where someone commits the basic offence of unauthorised access to computer material ('computer hacking') with the intention of committing a further serious offence. Thus, attempting to gain access to computer data in order to carry out a fraud by dishonestly making a false representation will be an offence under section 2 of the Computer Misuse Act 1990 (discussed in the following chapter). If the fraudster gets so far as to actually make the false representation, he will have committed the fraud offence itself, regardless of whether the false representation was successful in meeting its aim.

ICT FRAUD AS THEFT

If a person carries out a fraud which results in that person obtaining property, including money or a bank credit, the offence of theft may have been committed. Theft is defined in sections 1–6 of the Theft Act 1968 and section 1(1) states:

> **A person is guilty of theft if he dishonestly appropriates property belonging to another with the intention of permanently depriving the other of it ...**

The words 'dishonestly', 'appropriates', 'property' and the phrases 'belonging to another' and 'with the intention of permanently depriving the other of it' all have special legal meanings which are set out in sections 2–6 of the Act. As far as ICT fraud is concerned, there is no real difficulty arising from the meanings of these words and phrases although the following points should be noted:

(a) the definition of 'property' is very wide and will cover most things that can be stolen with the aid of a computer or telecommunications equipment, but land does not usually come within the meaning of property nor do wild mushrooms or flowers, fruit or foliage on a wild plant;

(b) property is deemed to 'belong to another' if that person has control of it or has any proprietary right of interest in it;

(c) 'appropriation' is the assumption of the rights of the owner;

(d) the 'thief' must intend to permanently deprive the other of the property; usually a mere 'borrowing' of an article cannot be equated to an intention to permanently deprive but it can be if, for example, it is for a very long period of time or if, when it is returned, there is no 'goodness' or value left in it.

A case involving the borrowing of cinema films adds weight to an argument that a person who uses transfer funds electronically into his own account does not commit the offence of theft. In *R v Lloyd* [1985] 2 All ER 661, a projectionist at a cinema, in association with two others, removed films from the cinema for a few hours so that they could be copied and then returned the films so that no one would know what had occurred. The pirated copies of the films were then sold, making a considerable profit for the pirates. A charge of theft (actually a conspiracy to steal in this case) was held to be inappropriate. As has been seen in the *Scott* case above, where the facts were very similar, a charge of conspiracy to defraud would have been more likely to secure a conviction.

In the *Lloyd* case, it was obvious that there was no intention permanently to deprive the owners of the films, nor was the copyright in the films stolen (it is not altogether clear whether copyright can be stolen). As mentioned earlier, borrowing can be theft if the period and circumstances are equivalent to an outright taking or disposal by section 6(1) of the Theft Act 1968, and this would be when the 'goodness' or 'virtue' in the thing taken had gone from it. Examples would include when a person borrows a radio battery intending to return it when it is exhausted, or borrows a bus pass intending to return it to the rightful owner when it expires. In the case of the films, however, there was still virtue in them when they were returned; they were still capable of being used and shown to paying audiences, so the pirates' convictions were quashed.

SUMMARY

■ Criminal offences may be analysed according to the:

  – *mens rea*, the mental elements (guilty mind);
  – *actus reus*, the prohibited acts or omissions.

■ Most criminal offences are set out in legislation though some common law offences remain.

■ Offences may be classified as:

  – summary, triable in a magistrates court only;
  – indictable, triable only in the Crown Court; and
  – offences triable either way.

■ In terms of tackling ICT fraud, the old deception offences suffered from the probability that it was not possible at law to deceive a machine.

■ The Fraud Act 2006 brought in a number of offences appropriate to tackle ICT fraud, including:

  – dishonestly transferring funds electronically;
  – phishing;
  – using bogus websites to obtain personal details such as bank account details;
  – spyware,
  – dishonest use of telecomms and information society services.

■ Section 1 of the Fraud Act 2006 covers three forms of fraud:

  – fraud by false representation;
  – fraud by failing to disclose information;
  – fraud by abuse of position.

■ There is also an offence of obtaining services dishonestly.

■ There are two offences relating to articles for use with fraud:

  – possession or being in control of an article;
  – making, adapting, supplying or offering to supply an article.

■ The *Ghosh* test is likely to be useful in determining whether the accused was dishonest:

  – would a reasonable and honest person regard what was done dishonest; and
  – if so, did the accused realise this?

■ Conspiracy to defraud remains available for the time being. The offence did not require that a person had been deceived.

■ The law of attempts remains useful in limited cases.

■ If a fraud is completed, a charge of theft may be appropriate.

25

Information and communications technology fraud

SELF-TEST QUESTIONS

Note: there is only one correct answer to each multiple choice question.

1   Tony wrote an e-mail which purported to be from a bank. He sent it to everyone working for a number of companies. The e-mail looked very plausible and informed recipients that there was a suspected fraud on their accounts, asking them to submit details of their accounts so that this could be verified. He intended to steal money from the accounts of any persons who were taken in and sent their details back. Which one of the following offences has NOT been committed by Tony?

(a)   Common law conspiracy to defraud.

(b)   Fraud by false representation.

(c)   Making an article for use in fraud.

(d)   Being in possession of an article for use in fraud.

2   Gordon wrote some software at the request of his friend Hannah to be used by Hannah to install surreptitiously on celebrities' computers as spyware to obtain personal details so that Hannah could sell the details to a newspaper journalist. Which one of the following statements is CORRECT?

(a)   Hannah has committed fraud by false representation.

(b)   Gordon has committed the offence of making an article for use in fraud.

(c)   Gordon and Hannah are guilty of common law conspiracy to defraud.

(d)   Hannah has committed fraud by abuse of position.

3   Which one of the following statements is NOT CORRECT in relation to the offence of obtaining services dishonestly?

(a)   It is not sufficient to prove that the accused knew that the services *might be* made available on the basis that payment has been made, is being made or will be made for them.

(b)   The offence still applies if the accused intends that payment will be paid though not in full.

(c)   The services must be made available on the basis that payment has been made, is being made or will be made for them.

(d)   The offence requires that the services are obtained by a dishonest act.

4   David has been charged with one count of being in possession of an article for use in fraud and one count of fraud by failing to disclose information. He is to be prosecuted in the Crown Court. What potential MAXIMUM periods of imprisonment could David be sentenced to?

(a)   Ten years for possession of an article for use in fraud and 10 years for fraud by failing to disclose information.

(b)   Twelve months for possession of an article for use in fraud and five years for fraud by failing to disclose information.

(c)   Five years for possession of an article for use in fraud and five years for fraud by failing to disclose information.

(d)   Five years for possession of an article for use in fraud and 10 years for fraud by failing to disclose information.

5   In what ways has the Fraud Act 2006 improved the possibilities of securing convictions against persons carrying out ICT fraud?

For further resources and updates please go to the Companion Website accompanying this book at **www.mylawchamber.co.uk/bainbridgeIT**

26 Unauthorised access to computer material

THE PROBLEM IN PERSPECTIVE

Unauthorised access to computer material is sometimes known colloquially as computer hacking. It may be carried out remotely, such as where a person gains access to computer information from a computer connected to a telecommunications network, on by an employee who gains access to programs or information held on his employer's computer for which he does not have the authority to access. It may be that an employee has authorisation to access his employer's programs or computer-held information but uses the programs or information for unauthorised purposes.

At one time, generally, computer security was woefully inadequate and computer networks were very vulnerable to attacks from outside. This threat has not disappeared but it is probably true to say that most unauthorised access now comes from within an organisation. The widespread use of firewall software has helped reduce unauthorised access from outside.

There is no disputing that unauthorised access is very serious. It leaves a computer, network of computers or communications network vulnerable to all manner of threats, such as viruses, fraud, sabotage, denial of service attacks, loss of confidential information and so on. Even if the perpetrator does nothing else but look at the material stored electronically, once the security breach has been discovered, a great deal of time and money may be expended in rectifying security weaknesses and in verifying that the integrity of the information has not been compromised. In the *CSI/FBI Computer Crime and Security Survey 2006*,[1] 32 per cent of those organisations responding to the survey reported incidents of unauthorised access to information (at p. 13). Next to viruses, unauthorised access to information was the most costly form of computer crime, at a total of $10,617,000 for the 313 respondents (at p. 15). There are other concerns. Growing numbers of computer systems concern high-risk activities such as the control of nuclear power stations, defence systems, aircraft flight control and hospital records. The dangers of unauthorised access to programs and information held in these safety-critical systems are self-evident and the potential for terrorism is worrying.

A related area is the unlawful interception of communications. The Regulation of Investigatory Powers Act 2000 makes it an offence to intercept a communication in the course of its transmission in either a public or private telecommunications system. There is a defence in relation to private telecommunications systems allowing the person in control of the system to monitor or record communications, for example, for security purposes. Although in many cases, this legislation is aimed to dealing with unlawful interception of voice messages, it also applies to text messages, e-mails and other forms of electronic information.

[1] Computer Security Institute, 2006.

The House of Lords decision in the case of *R v Gold* [1988] 2 WLR 984 highlighted the problem of unauthorised access to computer material and the ease with which it could be done. After the case, which was taken by many to indicate that computer hacking was not a criminal activity, the computer industry and the financial sector became most dissatisfied with the scope of the criminal law and the perceived lack of haste on the part of Parliament to act. Concern at this position led to the Law Commission Working Paper on Computer Misuse[2] which examined the scope of the law in terms of computer misuse generally and proposed alternatives for legal changes directed at the problem of computer crime.

Emma Nicholson MP, now Baroness Nicholson of Winterbourne, introduced a private member's Bill to combat computer misuse in 1989 but withdrew it after a government promise to legislate in this area. That promise was broken and, in 1990, the late Michael Colvin MP brought in another private member's Bill on computer misuse, which was successfully steered through Parliament and became the Computer Misuse Act 1990. This Act did not restrict itself to unauthorised access but also dealt with some other problems such as the law of attempts, unauthorised modification of computer programs and data, as well as addressing problems of jurisdiction and extradition. This chapter deals specifically with the basic unauthorised access offence, ulterior intent offence and the related area of unlawful interception of communications, following a discussion on the employment law consequences of unauthorised access and the decision in *R v Gold*.

EMPLOYMENT LAW AND UNAUTHORISED ACCESS

This area of law is not criminal law and although employees who gain unauthorised access to programs and information held in their employer's computer systems will usually commit the unauthorised access offence, it is worth mentioning the impact of employment law. A major reason is that many employees who commit the offence using their employer's information and communications technology systems are not prosecuted. Instead, they are subject to disciplinary proceedings which may lead to dismissal.

In *Denco Ltd v Joinson* [1991] IRLR 63, it was held that an employee who used an unauthorised password to gain access to information stored in a computer and which he knew he was not entitled to see was guilty of gross misconduct and could be summarily dismissed from his employment. He argued unsuccessfully that he had been unfairly dismissed. In *Pickersgill v Employment Service* [2002] EWCA Civ 23, the Court of Appeal dismissed an appeal against the Employment Appeal Tribunal's refusal to hear an appeal on extended grounds by an employee who had been dismissed following, *inter alia*, unauthorised access to the employer's computer system on no less than 70 occasions.

There is now legislation to protect employee whistle-blowers. The Employment Rights Act 1996 has provisions protecting employees making certain types of disclosures to his employer or other responsible person. Such types of disclosures are defined as qualifying disclosures under section 43B(1) of the Act and, where the disclosure is made in good faith to an employer or, where applicable, some other person having responsibility, the disclosure is a protected disclosure under section 43A. This means, for example, an employee making a protected disclosure in the reasonable belief that the disclosure is a qualifying disclosure and that he makes the disclosure in good faith is protected from dismissal or other detriment as a result of the disclosure, providing he does not commit a criminal offence by making the disclosure. Indeed, if an employee is dismissed for making the protected disclosure (or that is the principal reason for his or her

---

[2] Law Commission, *Criminal Law: Computer Misuse* (Law Com. No. 186), Cm 819, HMSO, 1989.

dismissal) he or she is to be regarded as being unfairly dismissed. In **Bolton School v Evans** [2006] EWCA Civ 1653, Mr Evans was employed as a technology teacher at Bolton School in the Information and Communications Technology (ICT) Department. He was concerned that a new computer system installed at the school was insecure and was not in compliance with the security requirements imposed on data controllers under the Data Protection Act 1998. To prove his point, with the help of a former pupil of the school, he gained unauthorised access and disabled some user accounts. He was disciplined for his actions and resigned and then brought an action for unfair dismissal on the basis that he had been constructively dismissed. However, the Court of Appeal, agreeing with the Employment Appeal Tribunal accepted that Mr Evans may have been disciplined, not because of his protected disclosure, but because of his illegal act of unauthorised access. The case was remitted back to the same Employment Tribunal, which had found in Mr Evans favour, for reconsideration.

THE CASE OF *R* V *GOLD*

Two journalists gained access into the British Telecom Prestel Gold computer network without permission and altered data. One of them also gained access to the Duke of Edinburgh's personal computer files and left the message:

GOOD AFTERNOON. HRH DUKE OF EDINBURGH

The journalists claimed that they had gained access to the network in order to highlight the deficiencies in its security. They were charged under the Forgery and Counterfeiting Act 1981 on the basis that they had made a false instrument within section 1. This states that a person shall be guilty of forgery if he makes a false instrument, with the intention that he or another shall use it to induce somebody to accept it as genuine, and by reason of so accepting it to do or not to do some act to his own or any other person's prejudice.

It was claimed that the false instrument was the CIN (customer identification number) and password. Section 8(1) of the Act states that a false instrument may be 'recorded or stored on disc, tape, sound track or other device'. However, their lordships suggested that 'recorded' or 'stored' connoted a process of a lasting and continuous nature from which the instrument could be retrieved in the future. In this case, the CIN and password were held only temporarily in the computer system while they were checked for validity and, after the check, they were eradicated totally and irretrievably.

The journalists had been found guilty at the Crown Court – one being fined £750 and the other £600 – but their convictions were quashed by the Court of Appeal and this was confirmed in the House of Lords. In the Court of Appeal, the Lord Chief Justice, Lord Lane, said that the acts of the accused in gaining access to the Telecom Gold files by what amounted to a dishonest trick were not criminal offences. In the House of Lords, Lord Brandon of Oakbrook said:

> The Procrustean attempt to force these facts into the language of an Act not designed to fit them produced grave difficulties for both judge and jury which we would not wish to see repeated. The appellants' conduct amounted in essence, as already stated, to dishonestly gaining access to the relevant Prestel data bank by a trick. That is not a criminal offence. If it is thought desirable to make it so, that is a matter for the legislature rather than the courts. We express no view on the matter.

Had the convictions been upheld, the only rational interpretation of the effect of section 1 in the circumstances was that the defendants had deceived a computer. Bearing in mind the problems this used to cause with the old deception offences, the decision in the *Gold* case was eminently sensible. It did have the effect, however, of making new legislation in this area more urgent.

THE BASIC UNAUTHORISED ACCESS OFFENCE

Section 1 of the Computer Misuse Act 1990 is aimed directly at hackers who gain access to computer programs or data without any further intention to carry out any other act. It says that a person is guilty of an offence if:

- he causes a computer to perform any function with intent to secure access to any program or data held in any computer;
- the access he intends to secure is unauthorised; and
- he knows at the time when he causes the computer to perform the function that this is the case.

The intent does not have to be directed at any particular program or data or at programs or data of a particular kind or at programs or data held in any particular computer. The offence is triable summarily only (that is, in a magistrates' court) and the maximum penalty is imprisonment for a term not exceeding six months or a fine not exceeding level 5 on the standard scale or both.

Section 17 of the Act contains definitions and other aids to interpretation but the Act does not define 'computer', 'program' or 'data'. Securing access is widely defined as causing a computer to perform any function, altering or erasing a program or data, copying or moving it to a different location in the storage medium in which it is held, using it or having it output from the computer in which it is held. References in the act to a program include references to part of a program. Also, programs or data on a removable storage medium which is at the time in the computer are considered to be held in the computer.

Note that the offence is made out if the person involved simply intends to make access regardless of whether he succeeds but he must know, at the time, that the access is unauthorised. Careless or reckless access will not suffice. Because copying is within the meaning of securing access, potentially it can be an offence under section 1 to make an unauthorised copy of a computer program or data or to download an unauthorised copy of a computer program or data.

The language of section 1 is rather strange at first sight as it speaks of access to programs or data in *any* computer, presumably including the computer being used by the person intending to secure access. This has been subject to judicial scrutiny in *Attorney-General's Reference (No. 1 of 1991)* [1992] 3 WLR 432, in which a former employee went to visit his previous employer, a wholesale locksmith, to purchase some articles. While alone (an assistant had temporarily left the room), the ex-employee entered instructions into the computer effecting a 70 per cent discount on the articles he had bought. There was no need for him to use a password. At the trial, the judge said that the wording of section 1 required that a second computer had to be involved. This was rejected on appeal to the Court of Appeal, where it was held that the wording of section 1, given its plain and ordinary meaning, was not limited to the use of one computer with intent to gain access to another computer. The offence was made out even if only one computer was used.

There have been a number of successful prosecutions under section 1 of the Act, the first being in March 1991 when a man was fined £900 for making unauthorised calls to the US using Mercury Communications equipment. Because 'computer' is not defined, it is likely to be given a generous meaning by the courts and can include equipment which has computer technology built into it although it would not normally be described as a computer.

The addicted hacker

A tremendous amount of publicity was generated at the time by the acquittal of Paul Bedworth following his prosecution for conspiracy to commit offences under sections 1 and 3 of the

Computer Misuse Act 1990 (for example, see *The Times*, 18 March 1993, p. 3). Defence counsel argued that Bedworth was addicted to computer hacking and, as a result, he was not capable of forming the necessary intent to commit the offences charged. Although addiction, *per se*, is not a defence to a criminal charge (although it could be a mitigating factor when it comes to sentencing) the jury acquitted him. This raised concerns that the Act was not doing its job and there were calls for it to be strengthened, presumably by watering down the requirement for intention. This is unnecessary and would cause more problems and could result in the imposition of criminal liability on careless, clumsy or inept computer operators who, without meaning to, gained access to material they were not authorised to.

The only sensible explanation of the Bedworth decision is that the jury probably felt some sympathy towards the accused. Perverse jury verdicts are not unknown. Two others who had been charged along with Bedworth pleaded guilty and received six-month prison sentences. Altogether, the activities of these three persons cost the victims hundreds of thousands of pounds.

Employees

It is certainly possible for employees to commit the basic unauthorised access offence when using their own computer terminals at work if they intend to gain access to any program or data in respect of which they know they do not have authority to access. The concept of authority is defined in section 17 in terms of being entitled to control access or having the consent of such a person. If the person is not so entitled and does not have the necessary consent, his intended access is unauthorised. Of course, the accused must know this and the implication is that employers must make it quite clear to employees which programs and data they are entitled to access. This also applies to others such as pupils or students and self-employed consultants. Ideally, a written statement as to access entitlement should be issued.

Authorised access for an unauthorised purpose

An employee may have authorisation to use a computer system as a normal part of his duties to his employer. If the employee subsequently uses the system for an unauthorised use – for example, for his own purposes such as carrying out private work or retrieving information for other purposes unconnected with his employment – does the access become unauthorised for the purposes of the Computer Misuse Act 1990? An example of this form of unauthorised use is given by the Audit Commission in its 1998 report on IT Fraud and Abuse.[3] A nurse at a hospital had authorisation to use the patient administration system but used it to search for medical details relating to friends and relatives. She then discussed these details with other members of her family. The nurse was not prosecuted under the Act but given a written warning for this breach of patient confidentiality.

Where authorised access is used for an unauthorised purpose, is that access authorised? It was held to be so in a surprising judgment in **DPP v Bignell** [1998] 1 Cr App R 1. Two police officers had used the police national computer to gain access to details of motor cars which they wanted for private purposes unconnected with their duties as police officers. They were charged with the unauthorised access to computer material offence under section 1 of the Computer Misuse Act 1990 and convicted at Bow Street Magistrates' Court but their appeals to Southwark Crown Court were allowed and this was confirmed by the Queen's Bench Divisional Court.

---

[3] Audit Commission, *Ghost in the Machine: An Analysis of IT Fraud and Abuse*, Audit Commission Publications, 1998, p. 18.

The sole issue was whether the access was authorised. The divisional court held that it was, even though the purpose of the access was not authorised. Whether access is unauthorised is defined in section 17(5) of the Computer Misuse Act 1990 in the following terms:

> Access of any kind by any person to any program or data held in a computer is unauthorised if –
> (a) he is not himself entitled to control access of the kind in question to the program or data; and
> (b) he does not have consent to access by him of the kind in question to the program or data from any person who is so entitled,
> but this subsection is subject to section 10.

Section 10 is simply a saving in respect of access carried out for purposes associated with any search warrant, etc.

The court decided that as the police officers were, in fact, entitled to control access to the material within section 17(5) they were authorised to access the computer data even if this was for an unauthorised purpose. As part of their normal duties, the police officers were entitled to access such computer information. But being entitled to access computer material is not the same as being entitled to control access to such material. This is an important and crucial distinction which the court failed to make.

This was a worrying decision which left an unsatisfactory gap in the Computer Misuse Act 1990. The judge drew support for his view of the Act from the Law Commission Working Paper on Computer Misuse which suggested that it would be undesirable for the hacking offence to extend to an authorised user who is using the computer for an unauthorised purpose. The Working Paper was far from unambiguous and put forward various options for dealing with computer misuse in all its various forms. It went on to give an example of a situation which should not be criminalised: where a word processor operator uses the office computer to produce private correspondence. That is not the type of behaviour at which section 1 of the Computer Misuse Act 1990 was directed and this is confirmed by the White Paper which preceded the Act.[4] This specifically acknowledged that employees may be liable for the basic hacking offence and stated (at para. 3.35):

> The thrust of the basic hacking offence is aimed at the 'remote' hacker, but the offence is apt to cover the employee or insider as well. For that reason it is particularly important . . . that (in addition to defining 'access' to exclude merely physical access to the computer itself) the mens rea of the offence should catch only the case where the employee consciously and deliberately misbehaves.

Fortunately, this aspect of *DPP* v *Bignell* was soon reversed in the House of Lords. In *R* v *Bow Street Metropolitan Stipendiary Magistrate, ex parte Government of the USA* [2000] 2 AC 216, the House of Lords considered the concept of authorisation in the context of the Computer Misuse Act 1990. In that case, an employee of American Express in Florida, as part of her duties, was authorised to access specific customer accounts. However, she also accessed other accounts without authority and passed on confidential information, enabling counterfeit credit cards to be made, to a number of persons including Mr Allison. Altogether, as a result of these activities, American Express lost around $1 m. Mr Allison was arrested in London in possession of counterfeit credit cards. An application to extradite Mr Allison to the US was made on the basis of three allegations, the first two which involved a conspiracy to commit offences falling within section 2 of the Computer Misuse Act 1990 – the magistrate refused to commit Mr Allison. The third allegation, unauthorised modification of computer material, resulted in a committal. Then, Mr Allison brought *habeus corpus* proceedings on the basis that none of the offences were

[4] Law Com. No. 186, *Criminal Law: Computer Misuse*, 1989.

extradition crimes. Eventually a question of law of general public importance was certified for the House of Lords being:

> Whether, on a true construction of s. 1 (and thereafter s. 2) of the Computer Misuse Act 1990, a person who has authority to access data of the kind in question none the less has unauthorised access if
> (a) the access to the particular data in question was intentional,
> (b) the access in question was unauthorised by a person entitled to authorise access to that particular data,
> (c) knowing that the access to that particular data was unauthorised.

Thus, the main issue was whether the employee of American Express in Florida had the requisite authority under the Computer Misuse Act 1990.

The House of Lords confirmed that the offences were extradition offences, being clearly added to the list of extradition offences by section 15 of the Computer Misuse Act 1990. As regards the issue of authorisation, Lord Hobhouse, with whom the other four Law Lords agreed, criticised *DPP* v *Bignell* in respect of the interpretation of the concept of authorisation. He said that the judge in that case had fallen into error by considering authorisation in relation to programs or data *of a particular kind* (control of the computer at a particular level) when what the Computer Misuse Act required was to consider authorisation in relation to a *particular program or to particular data*. Lord Hobhouse said:

> Nor is s 1 of the Act concerned with authority to access kinds of data. It is concerned with authority to access the actual data involved.

Although the employee had authority to access the kind of data that she accessed, as part of her normal duties, she did not have authority to access the particular data she did access, as such access was made with a view to conspiring with others to commit theft and forgery. This is equivalent to saying that authorisation to access computer material does not extend to accessing computer material for an unauthorised purpose.

Using a logged on computer with permission

Failing to log out of a computer network when leaving the computer is very common. What is the position if someone else comes along later and uses the computer to gain access to material? What if the material accessed could be said to be in the public domain to the extent that it is freely available to anyone with an internet connection? In *Ellis* v *DPP* [2001] EWHC 362 (Admin), Ellis was an ex-student of Newcastle University and a member of the University's Alumni Association. He used non-open access computers at the University to browse websites. The computer had been left logged on by previous users. He had been told by an administrative officer that he did not have permission to use non-open access computers and he said in a tape-recorded interview with a police officer that he had used the computers and that he did not have a password to use them. He also admitted using a computer that had been left logged on to access websites. The Magistrates' Court convicted Ellis on three counts of unauthorised access to computer material under section 1 of the Computer Misuse Act 1990.

A claim that the evidence presented before the magistrates was not sufficient and should, for example, had included direct evidence that the use fell within section 1 and of the lack of authorisation, going beyond the administration officer's and police constable's verbal evidence was rejected by the Divisional Court of the Queen's Bench Division. It was accepted that section 1 of the Computer Misuse Act 1990 was wide enough to encompass the behaviour supported by such evidence as was available. Ellis failed to turn up to the hearing and, consequently, the decision was suspended for 21 days to give him an opportunity to make further submissions. Eventually, he did make further submissions but they were without merit and the decision was confirmed in *Ellis* v *DPP* [2002] EWHC 135 (Admin). A claim that what he had done was analogous to picking up a discarded newspaper and reading it was rejected (unlike unauthorised access to computer material this is not criminalised in any case) and an attempt to rely on the *R* v *Bow Street Stipendiary Magistrate* case above could not help Ellis as it pointed the other way and weakened his case still further.

Changes to the unauthorised access offence

The Police and Justice Act 2006 will make some changes to the section 1 offence when the relevant provisions of that Act are brought into force. Instead of just requiring an intent to secure access and knowledge that access is unauthorised, the offence will also extend to an intention to enable such access to be secured. The offence will become triable either way with the following maximum penalties:

- on summary conviction, a term of imprisonment not exceeding 12 months (six months in Scotland and Northern Ireland) and/or a fine not exceeding the statutory maximum (presently £5,000);

- on conviction on indictment, a term of imprisonment not exceeding two years and/or a fine.

There will also be a new offence, under section 3A of making, supplying or obtaining articles for use in offences under section 1 or 3 of the Computer Misuse Act 1990. 'Article' includes any program or data held in electronic form. The maximum penalties will be as for those under section 1, as amended. This offence is described in more detail in the following chapter.

THE ULTERIOR INTENT OFFENCE

Apart from unauthorised access pure and simple, other problems were identified by the Law Commission in its Working Paper. The law of attempts was of uncertain application to computer fraud and it did not seem that a person who obtained services without permission using a computer committed a significant offence. Of course, if two or more persons were involved a charge of conspiracy to defraud might be apposite but, otherwise, there were problems. Section 2 of the Computer Misuse Act 1990 covers these situations and also provides an alternative and, perhaps, better route to conviction where other offences are intended by the person gaining unauthorised access. The section 2 offence is described in the Act as unauthorised access with intent to commit or facilitate the commission of further offences. It is a preliminary offence, particularly useful where the offence to which the ulterior intent applies is not completed. Another way of looking at it is to say that it is an aggravated form of the basic unauthorised access offence.

The further offence must be one for which the sentence is fixed by law (for example, murder or high treason) or one for which the maximum sentence is not less than five years in the case of an adult not previously convicted. Thus, section 2 applies to theft, blackmail, fraud and a great many other offences, all having maximum punishments of five or more years' imprisonment. If the further offence is completed, then that offence or an equivalent will normally be charged but section 2 is useful where, for one reason or another, this is not the case. An example is where a person attempts to gain access to a computer with the intention of sending a blackmail message to someone but is not able to get beyond the log-on screen. It is unlikely that a charge of attempted blackmail will succeed because he has not done an act which is more than merely preparatory, but a charge under section 2 will be more likely to result in a conviction providing the necessary intentions and knowledge can be proved – that is:

- the intention to secure access;
- the knowledge that the access is unauthorised; and
- the intention to commit blackmail.

Of course, proving the ulterior intent may be very difficult if the accused has only gone part-way to completing the further offence.

The ulterior intent offence is triable either way and carries a maximum penalty of five years' imprisonment and/or a fine if tried in the Crown Court. A person can be found guilty of a section 2 offence even if the commission of the further offence is impossible: for example, where a person intends to erase details of a debt he owes when the person to whom the debt is owed has already written it off or if he is mistaken about owing the debt in the first place.

The section 2 offence applies whether the accused intends to commit the further offence or whether he intends to facilitate the commission of the offence by another person. A custodial sentence is likely. In *R v Delamare* [2003] EWCA Crim 424, the offender, Delamare, worked for Barclays Bank in Poole. He was approached by an old school-friend, X, to whom he owed a favour, to disclose details of certain bank accounts. A cousin of X put pressure on the offender and he eventually gave in. The cousin of X and another person, who impersonated one of the owners of the bank accounts, were later charged and pleaded guilty to obtaining property by deception and were given community punishment orders. Delamare pleaded guilty to two charges of the section 2 offence and was sentenced to eight months' detention in a young offender institution. He appealed against his sentence on the grounds of disparity as the others only received non-custodial sentences. The Court of Appeal was not persuaded by the disparity argument. The trial judge had been fully aware of the other sentences and Delamare had acted in breach of trust. Giving the judgment of the Court of Appeal, Mr Justice Jackson said (at para. 8):

> **Bank customers must be able to open accounts and to carry on their banking affairs in full confidence that their private details will not be disclosed to outsiders. It must be clearly understood that breaches of trust by bank officials of the kind which occurred in this case are likely to attract prison sentences.**

However, taking into account the guilty plea, his previous good character and the relative youth of Delamare, the sentence was reduced to four months' detention in a young offender institution. As in *Delamare*, it matters not if the further offence is to be committed on another occasion to then authorised access offence.

In *Delamare*, the further offence was carried out by others but again this is not a problem as it is sufficient if the intention is to facilitate the commission of the further offence, whether by the person committing the unauthorised access offence or by any other person. This explains why section 2(4) of the Computer Misuse Act 1990 states that a person may be guilty even if the commission of the further offence is impossible.

Probably, the section 2 offence is not used as much as it should be. In *Re Holmes* [2005] 1 All ER 490 the court drew attention to that fact that section 2 of the Computer Misuse Act 1990 might have been more appropriate in relation to a fraud than the old offence of obtaining a money transfer by deception in an extradition case.

JURISDICTION

The international character of some computer crimes caused concern about the possibility of criminals escaping prosecution because of jurisdictional issues. For example, in *R v Tomsett* [1985] Crim LR 369, the accused sent a telex from London intending to divert funds from New York to the accused's account in Geneva. It was held in the Court of Appeal that, had the attempt been successful, the theft would have taken place in New York and the English courts would not have had jurisdiction to try the perpetrator. To prevent this type of problem (making it tempting for fraudsters to set up in England to carry out frauds or other forms of misuse abroad using computers and telecommunications systems), the Computer Misuse Act contains complex provisions relating to jurisdiction and extradition in sections 4–9 (some parts of sections 7 and 8 have been repealed). In essence, all that is required is a link with a home country – England and Wales, Scotland or Northern Ireland, as appropriate. That is, the offender must be in a home country when he does the relevant acts or the computer for which unauthorised access or modification is intended must be in a home country; for example, where a person in England attempts to carry out a computer fraud in Sweden or a person from Italy attempts to hack into a computer located in London.

The provisions for the section 2 offence are more complex as this offence requires a section 1 offence to be carried out. There is no need to show a significant link with a home country for section 1 for an offence in proceedings for a section 2 offence but if there is one, then what the accused intended as the ulterior offence outside the UK is treated as if it took place in the home country, subject to the double criminality rule. Thus, where it was intended that the ulterior offence should be committed outside the UK, for example, if the person operates from within any of the home countries intending to commit the further offence under section 2 in a different country, that offence must be a criminal offence in that other country as well as in the home country. Of course, in most cases this will not present any problems – most countries recognise theft and fraud. It is immaterial how that offence is described in that other jurisdiction. For example, in *Re Holmes* [2005] 1 All ER 490 the offence in Germany alleged to have been committed was breach of trust under section 266(1) of the German Criminal Code which covers an abuse of the power to dispose of another person's assets. The double criminality rule, which is a general rule of jurisdiction in criminal law, meant that the offence in Germany had to be an offence had it happened in the UK. The court confirmed that an offence under section 15A of the Theft Act, obtaining a money transfer by deception was appropriate and the application of the accused for a writ of *habeus corpus* was dismissed.

COMMUNICATIONS OFFENCES

Section 1 of the Regulation of Investigatory Powers Act 2000 makes it an offence to intentionally and without lawful authority intercept in any part of the UK any communication in the course of its transmission by means of a public postal service, public communications system or a private communications system. The interception of a communication in the course of its transmission by means of a private communications system is also actionable under civil law at the suit of the sender or recipient. Interception of a communication during its transmission by means of a telecommunications system is defined in terms of modifying or interfering with the system or its operation, monitoring transmissions made by means of the system or monitoring transmissions made by wireless telegraphy to or from apparatus comprised in the system so as to make all or part of the contents of the communication available, during its transmission, to a person

26

Unauthorised access to computer material

other than the sender or intended recipient of the communication. Presumably the person modifying, interfering or monitoring may also be the person to whom the communication has been made available. These offences only apply to a case where, for example, a person actually intercepts something such as an e-mail being sent through a telecommunications network to its intended recipient. The maximum penalty on conviction on indictment is two years' imprisonment and/or a fine.

Under section 1(6), the offence of intercepting a communication in the course of its transmission in a private communications system does not apply if done by (a) the person having the right to control the operation or the use of the system, or (b) a person with the express or implied consent of such a person to make the interception. The scope of 'control' was considered in *R v Stanford* [2006] 1 WLR 1554. Stanford was convicted of intercepting communications in the course of transmission by means of a private communications system. He had resigned as deputy chairman of Redbus after falling out with the chairman. Later, he was able to arrange the onward transmission of e-mails on the chairman's e-mail account to be automatically copied to his own computer (a process known as 'mirroring'). The mirroring appeared to have been set up by a person referred to as X who had been given an administrator username and password by Y who was authorised to use an administrator username and password. Stanford appealed against his conviction and sentence. As regards the conviction it was argued that he could not be guilty because either:

- X was a person having the right to control the operation or use of the system (section 1(6)(a)), or
- X had the express or implied consent of such a person to make the interception (section 1(6)(b)).

Consequently, if X had no criminal liability then neither could Stanford. At the trial, the judge had referred to Lord Hobhouse in *R v Bow Street Metropolitan Stipendiary Magistrate and Another, ex parte Government of the USA* [2000] 2 AC 216. The relevant passage of Lord Hobhouse's judgment dealt with section 17 of the Computer Misuse Act 1990 which states:

> Access of any kind by any person to any programme or data held in a computer is unauthorised if –
> (a) he is not himself entitled to control access of the kind in question to the programme or data.

Lord Hobhouse said (at 224):

> ... the word 'control' in this context clearly means authorise and forbid ... it is plain that [s 17] is not using the word 'control' in a physical sense of the ability to operate or manipulate the computer.

The judge in *Stanford* applied the same reasoning to section 1(6)(a) of the Regulation of Investigatory Powers Act 2000. That is, 'control' means authorise or forbid. As to section 1(6)(b), the judge said that it applied only if X had the authority to make the specific interceptions which were made. The Court of Appeal agreed.

The defence's interpretation would have meant that control meant the unrestricted ability physically to operate and use the system. Further, Y, by giving X the unrestricted ability physically to operate and use the system without imposing any express restriction on the manner in which he could use that ability, thereby gave X the 'right' to use that ability without restriction. Lord Philips of Worth Matravers, the Lord Chief Justice, in the Court of Appeal said that this would defeat the legislative intention of section 1 of the Regulation of Investigatory Powers Act 2000 which was to protect private telecommunications. The reason for the section was that the European Court of Human Rights, in *Halford* v *UK* (1997) 24 EHRR 523 ruled that the UK failed to protect privacy by intercepting telephone calls made from her office and from her home. Ms Halford was Assistant Chief Constable of Merseyside Police and claimed there had been a campaign against her which included interception of communications. Article 8(1) of the Convention provides a right to respect for private and family life. That is subject to derogation under Article 8(2), *inter alia*, interference by public authority in accordance with the law. However, at the time of the case, the UK did not have provision regulation the interception of calls on private telecommunications systems.

Of course, there are good reasons why a person who has the right to direct how the system should be used, and thus to authorise and forbid particular operations, should be permitted to intercept communications, for example, for internal security and the prevention of fraud or for monitoring phone conversations between telesales staff and customers for training or quality control purposes. Hence the need for section 1(6). The defence submission would mean that if a managing director of a company, who did not himself manage the system or have a password, gave authorisation to intercept communications to an employee, that employee would not have a defence under section 1(6)(b) because the managing director was not a person with unrestricted ability physically to operate and use the system under section 1(6)(a). Lord Philips of Worth Matravers said that would be bizarre.

Section 127 of the Communications Act 2003 makes it a criminal offence to transmit messages or other matter which are grossly offensive, indecent, obscene or menacing by means of a public electronic communications network. This can apply, for example, to sending e-mails of such a description. Similarly, an offence is committed if false messages are sent by a person knowing of their falsity, or persistent use is made of the network for the purpose of causing annoyance, inconvenience or needless anxiety. The Communications Act refers to messages or other matter, so if a pornographic diagram or picture is sent by a person, the offence will be applicable. In some cases, there may also be offences under the various statutes covering obscene publications and pornography, particularly in respect of child pornography, as discussed in Chapter 28.

Menacing messages could be linked to the offence of blackmail where the threat itself is transmitted by such means. The threat could concern the computer system – for example, where someone threatens to destroy information stored on the computer system. Alternatively, the threat may be of a less technical nature – for example, a threat to inform the IT manager's spouse of an adulterous relationship. These offences under the Communications Act 2003 can only be committed where a public electronic communications network is used. It would appear that a person who sends just one false message will commit the offence if he knows that the message is false and transmits it for one of the purposes mentioned – for example, to cause annoyance. The same applies if he persistently makes use of a public electronic communications network for the purpose of causing annoyance, inconvenience or needless anxiety to another. Another possibility is a prosecution under the Protection from Harassment Act 1997, for example, if messages which cause alarm or distress are sent.

OTHER OFFENCES ASSOCIATED WITH HACKING

Unauthorised access to computer material, with or without the intention to commit further serious offences, and causing unauthorised modification of the contents of computers were the forms of abuse the Computer Misuse Act 1990 was designed to deal with. However, other offences may also apply, particularly communications offences and data protection offences, if personal data is involved. If the ulterior intent behind unauthorised access is to carry out fraud, then the Fraud Act 2006 offences are likely to apply. These offences may be easier to proceed with as they lack the technicality (some might say over-technicality) of the Computer Misuse Act. If a person who gains access to information, whether or not that access is authorised, he may commit offences under copyright law, for example, by distributing it on a wide scale without the copyright owner's permission. However, the law of theft is of little use as it appears not to be possible to steal information. Data protection offences may apply where, for example, a person accesses personal data for the purposes of selling it without the permission of the data controller or the person to whom the data relate.

The law of theft

The offence of theft is defined under section 1 of the Theft Act 1968 as a dishonest appropriation of property belonging to another with the intention to permanently deprive the other of it. If a person gains access to a computer system without permission and then makes a printout of some information contained therein, has he committed theft? The fact that the owner of the information has not been deprived of it, because the hacker has only made a copy, is fatal to any charge of theft.

In *Oxford* v *Moss* (1978) 68 Cr App R 183, it was held that confidential information does not come within the definition of property for the purposes of theft. The case concerned the 'borrowing' of an examination paper by a student before the date of the examination. Although the authority of the case is weak, having been decided at first instance only, it is likely that it would be followed because the consequences of the decision are fundamentally sensible. After all, the owner still has the information unless the only copy was taken, but this is different from saying that the information is not property for the purposes of the Theft Act. Property is defined as including 'money and all other property, real or personal, including things in action and other intangible property' and it could fairly be argued that confidential information comes within the meaning of 'other intangible property'. A better construction of *Oxford* v *Moss* is that the taking of the examination paper could not be theft because there was no intention to deprive the owner of it permanently. For this reason a hacker who simply reads or copies information has not committed theft. Similarly, in the Scottish case of *Grant* v *Procurator Fiscal* [1988] RPC 41, an employee who offered copies of his employer's computer printouts to a competitor for £400 was acquitted. It was said that there was no authority for the proposition that the dishonest exploitation of the confidential information was a criminal offence. However, it could be, depending on the circumstances, under copyright law.

If the information concerned is copied on to paper belonging to someone else, such as an employer, there will be an offence of theft committed with respect to the paper. Likewise, if a person copies information from a computer on to a disc which belongs to someone else and takes the disc, this would be theft of the disc if the other elements of the offence of theft are present such as the intention to permanently deprive the owner of the disc.

If a person securing unauthorised access goes further and not only makes a copy of the information but then, immediately after, goes on to erase the original from the computer system, is this more likely to be viewed as theft? An act of deliberate erasure will almost certainly be an offence under section 3 of the Computer Misuse Act 1990, as discussed in the next chapter. In terms of theft, there will be a dishonest appropriation of property belonging to another, but is there an intention to permanently deprive the owner of that information? The difficulty here will be if the person responsible believes that the owner has another copy of that information, for, if he does so believe, there is no intention to permanently deprive. Therefore, it would appear that unauthorised copying, even coupled with the subsequent destruction of the original, is unlikely to be theft.

There is an offence in the Theft Act 1968 which holds out some promise and that is the offence of dishonestly abstracting electricity. The very act of unauthorised access will result in the computer performing work as it retrieves information from its store. If that information is stored on magnetic discs, the disc drive heads will physically move, tracking across the discs, locating and then reading the information which will then be moved into the computer's volatile memory by means of tiny electrical currents. More electricity will be consumed in transmitting the information to the computer display or transmitting the information if the person has secured access remotely. The total amount of electricity used to perform these acts may be tiny but, nevertheless, a definite amount will have been used as a result of the actions of the person securing access.

Section 13 of the Theft Act 1968 describes the offence of abstracting electricity as its dishonest use without due authority, or its dishonest waste or diversion. The offence is committed regardless of the amount of electricity so used and the only difficulty concerns the concept of dishonesty. The test in *R* v *Ghosh* [1982] QB 1053 would undoubtedly apply, as discussed in the previous chapter, but it might be difficult to decide whether the accused would realise that what he was doing was dishonest by the ordinary standards of reasonable and honest persons, the second limb of the *Ghosh* test, as he probably never even gave any thought to the additional consumption of electricity.

Data Protection Act 1998

This Act is described more fully in Part 5. However, there may be some scope for the Act in terms of unauthorised access and intercepting communications and therefore this aspect will be discussed briefly here. The Data Protection Act 1998 regulates the use and storage of personal data – that is, information relating to individuals who can be identified from that information.

A 'data controller' is a person who processes personal data and must notify the Information Commissioner if the processing is carried out by automatic means. Failure to notify is a criminal offence, triable either way, carrying an unlimited fine if tried in the Crown Court, or a fine not exceeding the statutory maximum if tried in a magistrates' court.

If a person secures unauthorised access to a computer system on which personal data is stored and then makes a copy of that data which he stores in his own computer, he is guilty of the offence of processing personal data without having notified the Commissioner. There are a number of other offences under the Act, such as obtaining or disclosing personal data without the consent of the data controller or procuring the disclosure of personal data, for which see Part 5 of this book.

SUMMARY

- Unauthorised access to computer material by employees may result in summary dismissal.
- Unauthorised access to computer material by using passwords, etc. if not an offence of forgery.
- The unauthorised access offence:
  - requires an intention to secure access;
  - knowledge that the access is unauthorised;
  - does not require more than one computer to be used;
  - does not require access actually to be secured.
- Being addicted to 'computer hacking' is not a defence at law.
- Employees may commit the unauthorised access offence.
- The ulterior intent offence requires:

26

Unauthorised access to computer material

- the unauthorised access offence; and
- the intention to commit a further offence which is serious.

■ The ulterior intent offence extends to an intention to facilitate the commission of the further offence.

■ It is not necessary for Computer Misuse Act offences to be committed wholly in the UK:

- providing there is a significant link with a home country.

■ The intentional interception without lawful authority of a communication transmitted by a public or private communications system is an offence.

■ Sending grossly offensive, indecent, obscene or menacing e-mails is an offence under the Communications Act 2003.

■ 'Control' means 'authorise or forbid'.

■ It is not possible to steal information.

SELF-TEST QUESTIONS

Note: there is only one correct answer to each multiple choice question.

1   **In respect of a 'whistle-blower' which one of the following statements is CORRECT?**

(a)   The whistle-blowing legislation is designed to protect an employer from the activities of the whistle-blowing employee.

(b)   The whistle-blowing legislation protects employees who have been dismissed for unauthorised access to their employer's computer material.

(c)   The whistle-blowing legislation is designed to encourage employees to divulge their employer's trade secrets.

(d)   The 'whistle-blowing' legislation does not provide a defence to criminal activity aimed at demonstrating to an employer that he may be in breach of data protection law.

2   **Which one of the following statements in relation to section 1 of the Computer Misuse Act 1990 is NOT CORRECT?**

(a)   There is no need for the intended access to actually have been secured.

(b)   More than one computer is required, being that used by the person seeking unauthorised access and the computer on which the material to which access is sought is stored.

(c)   An employee authorised by his employer to access data of a particular kind can still commit the offence.

(d)   The offence requires the offender to know that the access he intends to secure is unauthorised.

3   **The ulterior intent offence under section 2 of the Computer Misuse Act 1990 requires WHAT of the further offence?**

(a)   It must be an offence for which the sentence is fixed at law or, in the case of a person 21 years old or over, carrying a maximum penalty of five or more years' imprisonment.

(b)   It must be an offence governed by the Theft Acts of 1968 or 1978.

(c)   It must be an offence of dishonesty.

(d)   It must be an offence for which the law of attempts does not apply as the penultimate act prior to the commission of the offence has not been carried out.

4   Mae-Ling maliciously bombarded her ex-employer with unsolicited e-mails which result in the employer's computer system being brought to a virtual standstill. Which ONE of the following offences has she committed?

(a) Under section 1 of the Regulation of Investigatory Powers Act 2000.

(b) Under section 1 of the Computer Misuse Act 1990.

(c) Under section 127 of the Communications Act 2003.

(d) Under section 4(4) of the Data Protection Act 1998.

5   Sections 1 and 2 of the Computer Misuse Act 1990 were a knee-jerk reaction to the then perceived dangers of computer hacking and, in the light of offences relating to communications, data protection and fraud, are no longer of any utility. Discuss.

For further resources and updates please go to the Companion Website accompanying this book at **www.mylawchamber.co.uk/bainbridgeIT**

26

Unauthorised access to computer material

27 Unauthorised modification of computer programs or data

INTRODUCTION

Computer viruses and other forms of malicious code can cause immense and widespread damage to computer and communications systems and cost a considerable amount of time and money to eradicate. The 'I Love You' virus released in 2000 was estimated to have had a world-wide economic impact of $8.75 bn.[1] Virus attacks still represent the greatest source of financial losses in the US.[2] One of the purposes of the Computer Misuse Act 1990 was to criminalise the use of computer viruses. It had already been accepted that this was a form of criminal damage but there were concerns about whether the Criminal Damage Act 1971 was appropriate. Other forms of damage to computer programs and data were also seen as in need of the attention of the criminal law, for example, where someone deliberately and maliciously erased computer programs or data. It was decided to bring in an offence of unauthorised modification of computer material, meaning computer programs or data. This offence, under section 3 of the Computer Misuse Act 1990, is wide enough to catch situations where data is added, for example, in the case of spyware. It may even be relevant in the case of digital rights management tools. Some concern has been shown about these tools being automatically loaded onto a hard disk from music CDs to prevent unauthorised copying. In the Gower Review of Intellectual Property, it was reported that legal action was threatened against one music company for doing this as there was a possibility the hard disk would be damaged as a result.[3]

This chapter briefly examines the position prior to the Computer Misuse Act 1990 and then looks in depth at the section 3 offence of unauthorised modification of computer material and sentencing. Finally, the offence of blackmail is considered. This may be relevant where a person makes a demand for money, threatening to release a virus or 'logic-bomb' if payment is not made. The Police and Justice Act 2006 will make some changes to the Computer Misuse Act 1990, and will insert a new section 3. This change will be discussed after the offence in its present form has been examined. It is not known when the new section 3 will come into effect.

THE LAW BEFORE THE COMPUTER MISUSE ACT 1990

Prior to the Computer Misuse Act 1990, damage or erasure of computer programs or data was an offence under the Criminal Damage Act 1971. By section 1(1) of that Act, a person is guilty of an offence if, without lawful excuse, he destroys or damages any property belonging to

---

[1] According to the *CSI/FBI Computer Crime and Security Survey*, 2002 at p. 16.
[2] *CSI/FBI Computer Crime and Security Survey*, 2006 at p. 13.
[3] *Gowers Review of Intellectual Property*, HMSO, 2006, p. 73.

another. The definition of the offence required that the person intended such consequences to occur or was reckless as to whether property would be so destroyed or damaged. In the case of *R v Caldwell* [1982] AC 341, it was held that whether a person had been reckless was an objective test – that is, whether the course of action undertaken by the accused created what would be an obvious risk of damage in the eyes of the ordinary prudent individual. However, the House of Lords overruled this case in *R v G* [2003] 4 All ER 765 and confirmed that a subjective test was the correct way to determine whether a person had been reckless.

One potential difficulty with the Act is that property must be destroyed or damaged and property is defined by section 10 as meaning tangible property. This creates an immediate problem when programs or data stored on magnetic media such as a disk are erased. Programs or data are not tangible in this form, although the disk itself certainly is. The first case to tackle this apparent difficulty was *Cox v Riley* (1986) 83 Cr App R 54, in which the accused erased programs from a printed circuit card used to control his employer's computerised saw for cutting out timber sections for window frames. He was charged with criminal damage but argued that the programs were not tangible property within the meaning of the Act. Nevertheless, he was found guilty on the basis that the printed circuit card had been damaged and was now useless. It would require some work in reprogramming it before it could be restored to its former condition.

The 'mad hacker'

The Court of Appeal had an opportunity to examine the applicability of criminal damage when it heard the appeal against conviction of the self-styled 'mad hacker'. In *R v Whiteley* (1991) 93 Cr App R 381, the accused gained unauthorised access to the Joint Academic Network (JANET) and gave himself the status of Systems Manager. He deleted and added files, changed passwords and deleted audit files recording his activities. He was very skilled and even deleted a special program inserted to trap him. His activities caused serious disruption and he was convicted of damaging computer disks. The Court of Appeal rejected his appeal confirming that the value of the disks had been impaired. The Lord Chief Justice, Lord Lane, said that the Act required that tangible property had been damaged, not that the damage itself should be tangible.

The appeal in *R v Whiteley* had been heard after the Computer Misuse Act 1990 came into force but had to be decided on the basis of the prior law. The 1990 Act provides that, for the purposes of the Criminal Damage Act 1971, a modification of the contents of a computer is not to be regarded as damaging any computer or computer storage medium, unless its effect on that computer or storage medium impaired its physical condition (Computer Misuse Act 1990, section 3(6)). This is to try and remove any overlap between the unauthorised modification offence under the Computer Misuse Act 1990 and the Criminal Damage Act 1971.

CURRENT POSITION UNDER THE CRIMINAL DAMAGE ACT 1971

It would seem that the 1971 Act no longer applies to damage of programs and data stored in a computer. In *R v Whiteley*, however, the conviction was based on the fact that the state of the magnetic particles on the disks had been altered. These particles, it could be argued, are tangible even if they are not visible. This point may be of academic interest only as it is unlikely that a charge would be brought under the Criminal Damage Act 1971 in respect of damage to programs or data; the 1990 Act would be used instead. There is one occasion, however, when the 1971 Act might have been helpful and that is when the accused denied an intention to cause damage because, under the 1971 Act until recently, objective recklessness sufficed. It goes without saying that a hacker moving around in a strange computer system without training or the appropriate documentation is being objectively reckless.

The Police and Justice Act 2006 will insert section 10(5) into the Criminal Damage Act 1971 to make it clear that modifying the contents of a computer shall not be regarded as damaging any computer or computer storage medium unless the effect is to damage the physical condition of the computer or storage medium.

UNAUTHORISED MODIFICATION UNDER THE COMPUTER MISUSE ACT 1990

One of the reasons for the replacement of criminal damage in relation to computer programs and data stored in a computer or on computer storage media was that there were doubts about the logical validity of the approach adopted in *Cox v Riley*. Section 3 of the Computer Misuse Act 1990 was intended to put the matter beyond doubt and states that a person commits an offence if:

> . . . he does any act which causes an unauthorised modification of the contents of any computer; and at the time when he does the act, he has the requisite intent and the requisite knowledge.

The meaning of 'authority' applies in a way similar to that in relation to the section 1 offence – the modification is unauthorised if the person causing it is not entitled to determine whether the modification should be made and he does not have the consent of any person who is so entitled. Similar considerations in respect of authorisation ought to apply here as in relation to the basic unauthorised access offence, as clarified in *R v Bow Street Metropolitan Stipendiary Magistrate, ex parte Government of the USA* [2000] 2 AC 216. Thus, authorisation to make particular modifications should not extend to a particular modification made in excess of that authorisation, unless it is a natural consequence of making an authorised modification.

'Modification' is extensively defined in section 17, the interpretation section, as the alteration or erasure of any program or data or the addition of any program or data to the contents of a computer. The latter covers situations where someone leaves messages on a computer without authority (a form of computer graffiti perhaps) or the situation where a person introduces a computer virus into the system. It clearly covered the activities of the person who distributed disks claiming to contain advice for the prevention of AIDS; after using one of these disks, data files on the computer were made inaccessible and a message was displayed asking for money in return for a cure. The culprit was arrested in the US and convicted of blackmail.

For the purposes of section 3, the requisite intent is, under section 3(2), an intent to cause a modification to the contents of any computer so as:

(a) to impair the operation of any computer;

(b) to prevent or hinder access to any program or data held in any computer; or

(c) to impair the operation of any program or the reliability of any data.

It is immaterial whether the intent is directed at any particular computer, program or data or programs or data of a particular kind or at any particular modification or any modification of any particular kind. The requisite knowledge is knowledge that the intended modification is unauthorised.

Unsolicited and malicious e-mails

Adding data to a computer is within the definition of modification. If a person adds information to a computer disk or cache (temporary memory store) without authorisation does that mean that the person has the requisite intent? If the information is correct it would seem unlikely as that should not impair the operation of the computer, prevent or hinder access to any program or data held in any computer or impair the operation of any such program or the reliability of any such data. This would apply, for example, where an unsolicited e-mail has been sent. Of course, the situation could be different if large numbers of unwanted e-mails were received from the same person which had the effect of clogging up the computer disk or degrading its performance.

In *Director of Public Prosecutions* v *Lennon* [2006] EWHC 1201 (Admin), Lennon, who was 16 years old at the time, was dismissed from his employment after being employed for only three months. He decided to take revenge on his employer and he bombarded his employer's computer system with e-mails purporting to come from the company's human resources manager. This caused serious disruption to the employer's computer system. Lennon was prosecuted under section 3 of the Computer Misuse Act 1990 for causing an unauthorised modification of the contents of a computer. At first instance, the judge held that there was no case to answer. He said that the e-mails were authorised as the employer's computer system was set up to accept e-mails. He further said that the purpose of section 3 was to deal with the sending of malicious material, for example, computer viruses, which corrupt or modify data. It was not intended to criminalise the sending of e-mails. The Director of Public Prosecutions appealed against that decision.

In the High Court, it was held that the owner of a computer set up to receive e-mails is ordinarily taken to consent to the sending of e-mails to that computer. However, he does not consent to the receipt of e-mails intended not to communicate with him but to disrupt the normal operation of his computer system. Mr Justice Jack said that had Lennon telephoned the human resources manager to ask if he could send an e-mail raising a point about the termination of his employment, no doubt he would have received an answer in the affirmative. However, if instead he asked if he could send the half a million e-mails he did send he would certainly have got a different answer.

If information is added without authorisation and which is factually incorrect to some extent, it appears that it will be easier to find the requisite intent as this will impair the reliability of data held on the computer. In *Zezev and Yarimaka* v *Governor of HM Prison Brixton* [2002] 2 Cr App R 515, the Divisional Court of the Queen's Bench Division rejected an application for *habeus corpus* made by two persons facing extradition to the United States in respect of four charges of blackmail, one offence of conspiracy to commit an offence under section 2 of the Computer Misuse Act 1990 (the ulterior offence being blackmail) and a conspiracy to commit an offence under section 3 of the Computer Misuse Act 1990 in relation to computer material located in New York. Bloomberg LP was a company supplying financial information all over the world and had around 143,000 clients, many of which were financial institutions. Michael Bloomberg founded the company and, at the time of the case, still played an active role as director. In 1999, Bloomberg LP provided database services to a company in Kazakstan, of which one of the applicants for *habeus corpus*, Oleg Zezev, was an employee.

Oleg Zezev and Igor Yarimaka gained unauthorised access to Bloomberg's computer and accessed highly confidential information. E-mails were sent to Michael Bloomberg and the head of security saying that the security of their computer system had been compromised and that they wanted $200,000 or they would inform Bloomberg's clients which would result in a loss of confidence. The e-mails were purported to be from someone named 'Alex'. The US government claimed that Zezev and Yarimaka offered to show Bloomberg how they had compromised the computer system. Eventually, arrangements were made for Michael Bloomberg to meet Zezev and Yarimaka at a London hotel. The room had been fitted with surveillance equipment by the FBI and Scotland Yard. Zezev and Yarimaka were later arrested. Defence counsel raised a specific argument that section 3(2), defining the requisite intent, did not apply. It was said that the purpose of the offence in section 3 was to confine the offence to those who damaged a computer so that it no longer accurately recorded information fed into it. If accurately fed in information was untrue, that does not impair the operation of any computer, nor does it prevent or hinder access to programs or data. The reliability issue was more difficult for defence counsel to argue. She referred to the Law Commission Report on Computer Misuse[4] which distinguished between people who deliberately erased or altered data and those who did so recklessly. At best the information indicated it came from a source other than its true author. The court rejected this last argument. The fact that information was added which indicated it was from someone other than who sent it manifestly did affect the reliability of that data, notwithstanding the Law Commission Report. The language of section 3 made this clear, according to Lord Woolf CJ. In the second judgment, Mr Justice Wright said:

> ... obviously in the case of legitimate e-mails such as are invited by the owner of a computer by the publication of his e-mail address, such modification is not a criminal matter, without more, within the meaning of section 3 of the same Act. But if an individual, by misusing or bypassing any relevant password, places in the files of the computer a bogus e-mail by pretending that the password holder is the author when he is not, then such an addition to such data is plainly unauthorised, as defined in s 17(8); intent to modify the contents of the computer as defined in s 3(2) is self-evident and, by so doing, the reliability of the data in the computer is impaired within the meaning of s 3(2)(c).
>
> Those four elements, modification, lack of authorisation, intent and reliability, are the four elements of an offence under s 3.

Thus, sending accurate data may not affect the reliability of any data held in a computer but it will do so if untrue. If any inaccuracy is the result of an honest error on the part of the sender, then, although the reliability of data might be impaired, the person who sent the data cannot have the requisite intent to affect the reliability of data. Of course, even though reliability of data may be affected, or the operation of a computer impaired, or access to programs or data prevented or hindered, the prosecution still have to prove the requisite intent. It is actual intention that must be proved and carelessness or recklessness will not suffice. Where the modification is in the form of a virus or time-bomb or logic-bomb, it may be easy to infer the requisite intent, providing that it can be shown that the accused placed it in the computer deliberately and not inadvertently, such as in a case where someone innocently forwards an e-mail attachment containing a virus in ignorance of its existence.

Scope of section 3 offence

The section 3 offence is useful in that it deals with the problem of unauthorised modification with precision and is wide enough to cover viruses, time-bombs and logic-bombs as well as dealing with immediate, direct modification. However, the need for the prosecution to prove that the accused possessed both of two states of mind – that is, having the requisite intent and the requisite knowledge – may make conviction less certain, particularly where employees are concerned. There seems to be no justification for narrowing intention in this way and the subjective recklessness approach in criminal damage, as confirmed in *R v G*, is preferable in this respect.

[4] Law Commission, *Criminal Law: Computer Misuse* (Law Com. No. 186), Cm 819, HMSO, 1989.

The offence is triable either way and the maximum penalties in the Crown Court are imprisonment for a term not exceeding five years and/or a fine. The jurisdiction provisions apply to this offence as they do the section 1 offence. The new version of section 3 to be inserted by the Police and Justice Act 2006 will carry a maximum term of imprisonment of 10 years: see below.

Apart from those mentioned in this chapter specifically, there have been a number of successful prosecutions under section 3. For example, in June 1992 a freelance typesetter tampered with a computer owned by a client thereby denying access to the client. He argued that the client owed him £2,000 in fees but was, nevertheless, convicted of an offence under section 3 of the Computer Misuse Act 1990 and given two years' conditional discharge and fined £1,650. The judge said that his crime was not particularly serious even though the client claimed to have lost £36,000 in lost business as a result (*Computing*, 18 June 1992, p. 2). In December 1993, a nurse hacked into the hospital computer and changed patients' drug prescriptions in a way that was potentially lethal. He was found guilty of two offences under section 3 and sentenced to 12 months' imprisonment. It is possible that a charge of attempted murder or manslaughter is appropriate in such circumstances but it might be difficult to prove the required intention. The same applies to the ulterior intent offence in section 2. The section 3 offence is much simpler as the intention only has to be directed towards the computer or programs or data stored in the computer.

If a prosecution is brought under section 3 it is important that there is sound evidence linking the alleged culprit with the unauthorised modification. In *R* v *Vatsal Patel* (unreported) July 1993 (*Computers and Law* (1994) 5(2), p. 4), strange things started to happen on a project to write bespoke software. Database tables started to disappear and eventually development work was halted. The accused was a freelance programmer and was a member of the team writing the software and two 'wrecking programs' were found on his computer. One of the programs was named VAT which was the accused's nickname. A trap was set but nothing further happened – although the wrecking programs had been erased in the meantime. A charge was brought under section 3 of the Computer Misuse Act 1990 but, following a trial lasting six days, the jury acquitted the accused. The total losses to the client were in the order of £90,000 and there was a suspicion that the accused had erased the tables in order to prolong his lucrative contract. However, any number of persons could have been responsible for erasing the data and, in addition, there had been problems with the hardware and the development platform itself had been highly unstable. In other words, there was no real proof that the accused was responsible. It was remarked upon that had he been responsible, he would have been unlikely to use his own nickname for one of the wrecking programs.

A person might modify computer records in order to cover up some other criminal or disreputable activity. In *R* v *Sinha* [1995] Crim LR 68, a doctor at a medical practice in Cardiff was charged with manslaughter and the offence of attempting to pervert the course of justice. A 30-year-old female patient who suffered from asthma consulted the doctor and he prescribed a beta-blocker drug which induced a fatal asthma attack. The doctor later altered the computerised records relating to the patient to remove references to her suffering from asthma. However, although the references were no longer displayed they could still be retrieved from the computer disk. A charge was not brought under section 3 of the Computer Misuse Act 1990. As mentioned previously, because the doctor had authorisation to use the computer and access patient records, there could have been a problem with the issue of whether the modification was unauthorised. The offence of perverting the course of justice is more reliable in this respect and certainly applies to the destruction or concealment of evidence.

27

Unauthorised modification of computer programs or data

■ The new section 3 offence

Section 36 of the Police and Justice Act 2006 will replace the present section 3 with a new section 3 entitled 'unauthorised acts with intent to impair, or with recklessness as to impairing, operation of computer, etc.'. The offence is committed by a person doing any unauthorised act in relation to a computer, knowing at the time that the act is unauthorised and where he intends by doing the act to cause, or is reckless as to whether the act will do, one of the following:

(a) impair the operation of any computer;

(b) to prevent or hinder access to any program or data held in any computer;

(c) to impair the operation of any such program or the reliability of any such data; or

(d) to enable any of the above to be done.

The intention or recklessness need not relate to any particular computer, any particular program or data, or a program or data of any particular kind. A reference to doing an act includes a reference to causing an act to be done and 'act' includes a series of acts. A reference to impairing, preventing or hindering something includes a reference to doing so temporarily.

The penalties will be increased compared with the old section 3 and will be:

- on summary conviction, a term of imprisonment not exceeding 12 months (six months in Scotland and Northern Ireland) and/or a fine not exceeding the statutory maximum;

- on conviction on indictment, a term of imprisonment not exceeding 10 years and/or a fine.

The increases in penalties can be seen as a recognition of the serious damage that can be done by computer viruses and other forms of malicious code. The extension of the *mens rea* to cover recklessness is also welcome, especially now as reckless for criminal damage (and the same ought to apply here) is now based on subjectivity.

No date has been announced as yet to bring the new offence into force but it is likely to be sometime during 2007.

■ SENTENCING FOR SECTION 3 OFFENCES

The courts now take offences under section 3 of the Computer Misuse Act 1990 very seriously and custodial sentences seem to be the norm even for first offenders, particularly if the resulting damage is severe. This is probably a reflection of the concerns that are raised by persons making unauthorised modifications to computer material and it is no longer perceived as a youngster's prank. Some sentencing guidance can be gleaned from Court of Appeal decisions in the two following cases involving appeals against custodial sentences though the facts of the cases are very different.

In the first case, *R v Maxwell-King* [2001] 2 Cr App Rep (S) 136, the accused pleaded guilty to three counts of incitement to commit offences under section 3 of the Computer Misuse Act 1990. He was a co-director (with his wife) of a company, MaxKing Interfaces Ltd, which manufactured and supplied General Instrument devices which, when fitted to General Instrument set-top boxes, made it possible for subscribers to cable television services to access all channels provided by the service provider no matter how many the subscriber had paid for. Therefore, subscribers could pay for a minimum of access and, using Maxwell-King's device, receive all channels, thereby depriving the cable television service provider of an average of £14 per month for each device used. The accused, who first got the idea from an American website advertising such devices which also carried a disclaimer, thought that what he was doing was possibly not illegal provided his website advertising also carried a disclaimer and he did not use the devices himself. The business did not prosper. The accused only sold around 30 devices in the UK and some of the buyers returned the chips. Apparently, the cable television service providers had developed a 'chip-killer' which damaged chips in such unauthorised devices, although this was disputed by the prosecution. The total turnover was about £600, the profit was minimal and the scheme was ended.

Maxwell-King was sentenced to four months' imprisonment and he appealed against the sentence (his company which was also charged pleaded guilty and no punishment was imposed but it was ordered to pay £10,000 towards the prosecution costs). The Court of Appeal noted that he was of previous good character (described by the trial judge as being of exemplary character) and had high-class character references. He had been entirely forthright and open. However, the Court of Appeal thought what he had done was dishonest and was a form of theft choosing not to take seriously his claim that he thought what he was doing was not illegal. However, this was a first offence, the accused had pleaded guilty at the first opportunity and it was thought that the custodial threshold had not quite been reached. The Court of Appeal distinguished an earlier case, *R v Carey* [1999] 1 Cr App Rep (S) 322, where a custodial sentence was imposed on a man who pleaded guilty to a conspiracy to defraud in relation to the production of some 850,000 counterfeit smart cards and had benefited to the tune of many thousands of pounds. In Maxwell-King, the Court of Appeal thought a fine or community service order might be more appropriate and substituted a community service order of 150 hours for the custodial sentence, adding that the court hoped that he could use his undoubted technical skills in computers in the context of the community service order.

It appeared that Maxwell-King was operating on a much larger scale in the US and decoders worth over $1 m were found in Florida. Invoices indicated that they had been exported to the US by Maxwell-King and the US Government sought his extradition in *Maxwell-King v Government of USA* [2006] EWHC 3033 (Admin). He had been charged in the US with conspiracy to import and sell the decoders in the US. He submitted that he should not be extradited on the grounds of double jeopardy. However, this was rejected as the US proceedings were not in respect of the same acts for which he had been previously found guilty under section 3 of the Computer Misuse Act 1990. The US proceedings related to a distinct and discrete activity, the subject matter was substantially different, the earlier prosecution in England did not include all the activities of Maxwell-King, the timescale was different and there was a significant difference in the scale of the activities and the value of the devices involved in the US compared with the UK. Theoretically, it might have been possible to prosecute Maxwell-King in the UK for incitement to commit offences in the US under the Computer Misuse Act 1990. However, the failure to do so did not make the extradition request an abuse of process.

The Court of Appeal decision in *Maxwell-King*, in which his sentence was reduced, is hard to reconcile with a later case before the Court of Appeal where, if anything, the criminal intent seems much less. It does, however, reflect the breathtaking scope of acts that might come within the section 3 offence. In *R v Lindesay* [2002] 1 Cr App R (S) 370, the appellant pleaded guilty to three counts of unauthorised modification of computer material contrary to section 3 of the Computer Misuse Act 1990. Lindesay was a freelance software designer and developer who had considerable experience and repute. He had a short contract with a computer firm but was dismissed on the grounds that the firm was not satisfied with his work. There was a dispute about money said to be owed to Lindesay and, about one month later, after a few drinks and acting under an impulse, he used his own internet account to gain unauthorised access to three clients of the computer firm he was in dispute with. Using passwords he had used when working for the computer firm, he deleted some of the contents of the websites of the clients and modified some of the content (for example, modifying recipes on a supermarket website). He also sent e-mails to customers of the supermarket claiming it was going to increase its prices. The total cost of putting things right was estimated at £9,000. In sentencing Lindesay to nine months' imprisonment, the trial judge took account of the guilty plea, his openness with the police, his remorse and the high esteem he was held in (a university professor provided a character reference for him). But, in Lindesay's case, the trial judge thought the offence so serious that only a custodial sentence was justified. It was an act of pure unmitigated revenge after a slight. The judge equated what he did to a 'glassing' in a public house by a person who took offence at what someone had said.

The Court of Appeal did not think that the trial judge's analogy with a pub glassing was helpful. But the Court of Appeal considered the gravity of the offence. However real the grievance or impulsive the act of revenge and how inevitable that it would be discovered that it was Lindesay's doing, the fact was that he had used his skill and judgment and his knowledge of his former employer's business to cause a great deal of work, inconvenience and worry to clients of the former employer which were completely innocent. In those circumstances, an immediate custodial sentence was proper and the Court of Appeal could not say that the sentence imposed was excessive, let alone manifestly excessive.

The decision of the Court of Appeal in *Lindesay* can be criticised on a number of counts. First, it completely disregards the decision in *Maxwell-King* (which was not cited and not mentioned in the judgment of the court). *Maxwell-King* was a case involving, as the court found, dishonesty. That element was not present in *Lindesay*. Secondly, the maximum penalty for a section 3 offence is five years' imprisonment and/or a fine (though soon to be raised to 10 years' imprisonment and/or a fine). In terms of sentencing practice, it has long been accepted that the maximum penalty should be reserved only for the worst possible conceivable example of the offence. As the section 3 offence covers a whole spectrum of activities, ranging from those that might result in wide disruption to computer systems costing billions of pounds to a silly prank, which can be quickly and easily remedied, nine months in the *Lindesay* case does seem extreme.

In the previous edition of this book, the author suggested that the maximum penalty ought to be reviewed and uplifted, bearing in mind that copyright and trade mark offences, which only damage economic interests, carry a maximum of 10 years' imprisonment. Section 3 offences, on the other hand, can damage economic, security and privacy interests. That is precisely what the Police and Justice Act 2006 will do when the new section 3 offence, inserted by that Act, comes into force.

MAKING, SUPPLYING OR OBTAINING ARTICLES FOR USE IN THE SECTIONS 1 AND 3 OFFENCES

This offence will be inserted into section 3A of the Computer Misuse Act 1990 by section 37 of the Police and Justice Act 2006. There are three forms of the offence, being:

- making, adapting, supplying or offering to supply any article intending it to be used to commit, or to assist in the commission of, an offence under section 1 or section 3;

- supplying or offering to supply any article believing that it is likely to be used to commit, or to assist in the commission of, an offence under section 1 or section 3;

- obtaining any article with a view to its being supplied for use to commit, or assist on the commission of, an offence under section 1 or section 3.

An 'article' includes any program or data held in electronic form. The offence is triable either way and the maximum penalties will be:

- on summary conviction, imprisonment for a term not exceeding 12 months (six months in Scotland and Northern Ireland) and/or a fine not exceeding the statutory maximum;

on conviction on indictment, imprisonment for a term not exceeding two years and/or a fine.

The scope of the offence appears to be quite wide, especially as the second form only requires a belief that the article is likely to be used for an offence under section 1 or section 3. This may be an objective test, based on whether a reasonable person with the same knowledge would have the relevant belief.

In its original form, the Bill made it an offence to made, adapt, supply or offer to supply an article knowing that it is designed or adapted for use in the course of or in connection with an offence under section 1 or section 3. There was no need for the accused to have an intention that it would be so used, this being a separate form of the offence. This was changed due to concerns it would prove unsatisfactory. For example, a person might make such an article for research purposes, having no intention that it should be used to commit an offence under section 1 or section 3. It is likely that this offence will be brought into force during 2007.

DENIAL OF SERVICE ATTACKS

Denial of service attacks are seen as a growing problem. They may come from disgruntled ex-employees, as in *Director of Public Prosecutions* v *Lennon* discussed earlier, or from criminals. A common way to bring down an organisation's computer system is by sending mass e-mails.[5] The unauthorised modification offences in section 3 of the Act cover such a wide spectrum of activities that it could be argued that the time has come to sub-divide them and assign different criminal penalties in respect of them. Activities such as website defacement and denial of service attacks were unthinkable in 1990 but are now of serious concern. Denial of service attacks can seriously damage a business that sells online. It was with such concerns in mind that the Earl of Northesk introduced into the House of Lords a Bill in 2002, entitled the Computer Misuse (Amendment) Bill 2002. The Bill was designed to protect computer systems against denial of service attacks and would have made it an offence to do any act which causes or is intended to cause directly or indirectly a degradation, failure or other impairment of function of a computerised system or part. An objective standard was used so that the prosecution would not have to prove intention providing it could show that a reasonable person could have contemplated that the act would have caused such an effect.

Unfortunately, the Bill did not make it through Parliament and it now looks unlikely that specific provision will be made for denial of service attacks as the opportunity to include this in the Police and Justice Act 2006. However, since the decision in *Director of Public Prosecutions* v *Lennon*, it now seems beyond doubt that denial of service attacks will be viewed as an offence under section 3 of the Computer Misuse Act 1990.

BLACKMAIL

Blackmail is a serious offence and is triable only on indictment: that is, in the Crown Court. The offence is provided for in section 21 of the Theft Act 1968 and carries a maximum penalty of 14 years' imprisonment. Basically, a person is guilty of blackmail if, with a view to gain for himself or another or with intent to cause loss to another, he makes any unwarranted demand with menaces. The menaces are not restricted to threats of violence and include threats of action which is detrimental or unpleasant to the person to whom those threats are directed. An example is where

---

[5] Audit Commission, *ICT Fraud and Abuse, Public Sector Update*, June 2005, p. 34.

a person threatens to reveal someone's previous financial difficulties unless that other person pays him some money. The 'protection racket' provides another example: that is, a shopkeeper's premises will be destroyed unless he makes certain payments.

So far as computers are concerned, a person would be guilty of blackmail who inserted a 'time-bomb' into a computer system and demanded money in return for details of how to disable the time bomb. If the owner of the computer system has already discovered and removed the time bomb when the demand is made, it makes no difference; the offence has still been committed. The offence of blackmail will also have been committed even if the computer owner is not worried about the threat because he has a complete, up-to-date set of back-up copies of everything likely to be affected.

Blackmail may be associated with a virus. The fact a virus is present may focus the victim's mind more wonderfully than would be the case with a time bomb where no harm would be done until a predetermined date. A virus starts its destructive work by immediately spreading throughout a system, corrupting programs and files or filling the computer disk with garbage bringing the system down or seriously degrading performance. If freelance workers feel inclined to leave a virus or time bomb behind to be used to pressurise a client into paying the agreed fee promptly, they should think again. A university lecturer carried out some consultancy work but when he was paid the client deducted part to pay for the telephone bill the lecturer had incurred. The lecturer retaliated by placing a virus in the client's computer with a message to the effect that he was owed money and that files were being modified and that the sooner the matter was settled, the less damage would be done. He was convicted of attempted blackmail and fined £500 (*Computing*, 8 October 1992, p. 2).

The meaning of the word 'unwarranted' can cause problems. A demand is unwarranted unless the person making the demand does so in the belief that he has reasonable grounds for so doing and that the use of menaces is a proper way of reinforcing the demand. In most cases, the demand will plainly be unwarranted on the basis of this test, but there might be circumstances where this was not so. For example, a freelance programmer has carried out a substantial amount of work for a company which, he believes, has substantially and deliberately underpaid him. In order to encourage the company to pay up, the programmer might tell the company that he has entered a computer virus into the computer system and he will not remove it unless the shortfall in his payment is made up. It appears from case law that the accused must be judged by his own standards when it comes to the interpretation of 'unwarranted' and a jury might acquit the programmer if it feels that the programmer genuinely believes that he has reasonable grounds for making the demand and that the means he employs are proper, in his subjective opinion. Although this is somewhat unsatisfactory in that an accused person is being judged by his own moral standards, this is the current state of the law. However, the case discussed above where a university lecturer used a virus as a means of securing payment shows how a jury is likely to react in practice. If the action threatened is of a very serious nature (for example, if it would result in the commission of a serious offence), a jury should be directed that the means cannot be proper.

Bearing in mind the serious nature of blackmail, any victim should not hesitate to inform the police. As with other forms of blackmail, a payment made to a blackmailer in return for not destroying computer data is likely to be followed by further demands in the future. Good security and comprehensive back-up systems are the best defences against this insidious form of crime. At the same time as committing blackmail, the blackmailer may also commit other offences such as unauthorised modification of computer material, basic hacking, abstracting electricity and offences under section 127 of the Communications Act 2003.

SUMMARY

- Damage to programs or data was treated as criminal damage prior to the Computer Misuse Act 1990.

- The offence of unauthorised modification of computer material requires:
  - the modification to be unauthorised;
  - the requisite intent; and
  - the requisite knowledge.

- The requisite intent is, by causing an unauthorised modification, to:
  - impair the operation of any computer;
  - prevent or hinder access to any program or data held in any computer; or
  - to impair the operation of any program or the reliability of any data.

- The requisite knowledge is that the intended modification is unauthorised.

- Apart from the usual forms of committing the section 3 offence, such as by the use of viruses, the following are also likely to be an offence under section 3:
  - sending masses of e-mails to disrupt a computer or communications system;
  - sending bogus e-mails;
  - making a denial of service attack.

- The new version of section 3 is wider than the original as it:
  - also covers enabling the relevant impairment, prevention or hindering access;
  - it extends to recklessness; and
  - the maximum custodial sentence is 10 years.

- Serious examples of section 3 offences are likely to attract custodial sentences.

- There is a new offence of making, supplying or obtaining articles for use in offences under section 1 or section 3.

- 'Article' includes programs and data held in electronic form.

- The offence of blackmail may be associated with viruses or other malicious code.

SELF-TEST QUESTIONS

Note: there is only one correct answer to each multiple choice question.

1 **In respect of an offence under section 3 of the Computer Misuse Act 1990 which one of the following statements is NOT CORRECT?**

   (a) The requisite intent must be directed at a particular computer, program or data.

   (b) The modification need not be permanent.

   (c) The modification is unauthorised if the person causing is not himself entitled to determine whether the modification should be made and he does not have the consent of any person so entitled.

   (d) A modification includes adding a program or data to the contents of any computer.

27

Unauthorised modification of computer programs or data

2   In *Zezev and Yarimaka v Governor of HM Prison Brixton* [2002] 2 Cr App R 515 which one of the following did the court NOT decide in relation to the unauthorised modification offence under section 3 of the Computer Misuse Act 1990?

(a)   It is not required that the computer is damaged so that it no longer accurately records information fed into it.

(b)   If accurately fed in information was true that does not impair the accuracy of the data held in the computer.

(c)   The section 3 offence may be committed if an e-mail contains incorrect information or is bogus.

(d)   There must be some tangible damage to the computer or its components, such as a hard disk, for the offence to have been committed.

3   In *R v Lindesay* [2002] 1 Cr App R (S) 370, the accused pleaded guilty to three offences under section 3 of the Computer Misuse Act 1990. He was a respected freelance software developer. He had undertaken a short contract to write software but was dismissed when his client became dissatisfied with his work and there was a dispute about money he claimed was owed to him. Later, after having had a few drinks and acting under an impulse, he used his own internet account to gain unauthorised access to three clients of the computer firm he was in dispute with, using passwords he had used when working for the computer firm, and he deleted and modified some of the contents of the websites. He also sent e-mails to customers of a client of the computer company claiming the client was going to increase its prices. The total cost of putting things right was estimated at £9,000. He was sentenced to nine months' imprisonment. Which one of the following did the Court of Appeal DECIDE about that sentence?

(a)   An immediate custodial sentence was proper and the length of imprisonment was not unduly excessive.

(b)   The sentence was manifestly excessive because of Lindesay's previous good character and guilty pleas and a sentence of 120 hours of Community Service was substituted for the custodial sentence.

(c)   A fine and order for compensation would be the most appropriate penalty for a first offence and a fine of £3,000 plus £9,000 was substituted.

(d)   On the basis of the sentencing principle of general deterrence a custodial sentence of three years' imprisonment would be appropriate in such a case and the sentence imposed of nine months was unduly lenient.

4   Which one of the following is NOT an offence under section 3A of the Computer Misuse Act 1990?

(a)   Making, adapting, supplying or offering to supply any article intending it to be used to commit, or to assist in the commission of, an offence under section 1 or section 3.

(b)   Supplying or offering to supply any article believing that it is likely to be used to commit, or to assist in the commission of, an offence under section 1 or section 3.

(c)   Obtaining any article with a view to its being supplied for use to commit, or assist on the commission of, an offence under section 1 or section 3.

(d)   Making, adapting, supplying or offering to supply any article knowing that it is designed or adapted for use in the course of, or in connection with, an offence under section 1 or section 3.

5 Making an unauthorised modification to computer material can have very serious consequences, going far beyond a childish prank. Discuss in relation to the increase of the maximum penalty from five years' imprisonment to 10 years' imprisonment.

For further resources and updates please go to the Companion Website accompanying
this book at **www.mylawchamber.co.uk/bainbridgeIT**

28 Computer pornography, harassment and incitement

INTRODUCTION

The ability of computer technology to process, store and make available static and moving images with increasing quality and speed has not all been beneficial. It has also enabled persons with abnormal or perverted sexual drives and desires to gain access to and download phenomenal quantities of pornographic material. Much of the material available goes beyond that which has become acceptable in some societies, even liberal societies, and there are grave dangers that the sheer volume of pornographic material will feed depravity and, this in turn, could lead to increases in sexual crimes, particularly against children, both within the UK and in other countries from which this sort of material originates. Obviously, it is impossible to police the internet on a world-wide basis but the issues are considered so serious that a number of countries, including the UK, have taken measures to criminalise the activities of those who intentionally access such material, whether for their own use or for distribution to others. The maximum penalties available have been increased substantially in relation to child pornography.

Chat-rooms on the internet have been used to groom children for sexual purposes. The same applies to text messages. If a sexual act with a child results, then the full panoply of sexual offences can be used. However, by this time, the harm has already been done. It was considered important to have a preparatory offence of sexual grooming without any act actually having been carried out that would apply even where the offender was on the way to meet the victim.

Another issue covered in this chapter is the position in relation to e-mails and other forms of electronic communications that may cause alarm or distress or which threaten violence or involve racial harassment. The Protection from Harassment Act 1997 is a useful piece of legislation dealing with this problem, though it must be said that the Act was not specifically directed at this problem. However, harassment is not defined in the Act and it now seems clear that, although originally designed to combat stalkers and 'neighbours from hell', it can also be very effective in terms of e-mails and there have been a number of prosecutions in respect of threatening e-mails.

Finally, the law of incitement is examined in the context of information placed on a website or sent electronically in respect of offences generally and child pornography in particular.

PORNOGRAPHY

There has been considerable publicity about the availability of pornographic material on the internet and it is clear that the courts treat this form of computer abuse seriously. The law is reasonably well provided with relevant offences, which has more or less kept pace with technological development. However, there may be difficulties in deciding whether something is obscene. Under section 1 of the Obscene Publications Act 1959, an article shall be deemed to be obscene if its effect is such as to tend to deprave and corrupt persons who are likely, having regard to all relevant circumstances, to read, see or hear the matter contained or embodied in it. By section 2, any person who, whether for gain or not, publishes an obscene article or who has an obscene article for publication for gain (whether gain to himself or another) commits an offence. Publishing an article includes transmitting data stored electronically. Under section 1(2) of the Obscene Publications Act 1964, a person is deemed to have an article for publication for gain if with a view to such publication he has ownership, possession or control of it. This does not apply, for example, if the person in question had not examined the article and had no reasonable cause to suspect that it was such that would lead him to be convicted of the offence.

There may be some difficulty with the requirement for an article but this is defined as any description of article containing or embodying matter to be read or looked at or both, any sound record, and any film or other record of a picture or pictures. There is no reason to doubt that it will include a magnetic or optical disk or other form of electronic storage media.

The maximum penalty for the offence is, on summary conviction, imprisonment for a period not exceeding six months or a fine not exceeding £1000 (there is no reference to both being available as is usually the case). On conviction on indictment, the maximum penalty is imprisonment for a term not exceeding three years and/or a fine.

Obscene material on a website

Publishing obscene material on a website may result in a prosecution under the Obscene Publication Acts. In *R v Perrin* [2002] EWCA Crim 747, the appellant had been convicted of publishing an obscene article, namely a webpage on the internet, contrary to section 2(1) of the Obscene Publications Act 1959. The webpage contained images of people covered in faeces, coprophilia or coprophagia and men engaged in fellatio and it had been accessed by a police officer who recorded the images onto video tape. The webpage could be accessed free of charge by anyone. Other webpages were only accessible on subscription and the one accessed by the police officer acted as a 'trailer'. The appeal was based on a claim that the conviction breached the right of freedom of expression under Article 10(1) of the Council of Europe Convention for the Protection of Human Rights and Fundamental Freedoms (the 'Human Rights Convention'); that the charge was not sufficiently precise to allow the appellant to regulate his behaviour to avoid committing further offences as required under Article 7 of the Convention (no punishment without law); that the trial judge erred in rejecting the argument that the only relevant publication was to the police officer and it was wrong to test obscenity by reference to others who might have access to the material; and, finally, the judge failed to make it clear to the jury that it was necessary for a significant proportion of those visiting the site to be affected by it.

The Court of Appeal rejected the grounds of appeal based on the Human Rights Convention, noting that Article 10(2) allows derogation from the right of freedom of expression where necessary in a democratic society, *inter alia*, for the prevention of disorder or crime or for the protection of health and morals. It also said that the Article 7 point added nothing. As regards publication, the Court of Appeal said that this took place when images are uploaded or downloaded from a website. Section 1(3) of the Obscene Publications Act 1959 provides that a person publishes an article when he distributes, circulates, sells, lets or hire, gives, or lends it, or who offers it for sale or for letting or hire; or '... where the matter is data stored electronically, transmits that data'. Although some types of publishing are based on another person actually having access to the article (for example, 'sells' or 'gives') other forms of publication, such as 'offers it for sale' do not require actual access by another person. The Court of Appeal refined a test to be applied in such cases, being:

First, whether any person or persons were likely to see the article, and if so, whether the effect of the article, taken as a whole, was such as to tend to deprave and corrupt the person or persons who were likely, having regard to all relevant circumstances, to see the matter contained or embodied on it.

That being so, the publication in this case was to any person, including vulnerable young persons, who may choose to access it. The jury was entitled, therefore, to look beyond the police officer who had actually accessed the webpage. The failure to give a direction to the jury that it must consider whether a significant proportion of persons who might access the webpage was also rejected. Such a direction was common in terms of traditional forms of publishing, for example, in the form of books or video tape, but was not necessarily appropriate in terms of publishing on the internet. It would seem, therefore, that there is no need to prove that anyone has accessed pornographic material on a website or that, in fact, anyone who had actually seen it would be likely to be depraved or corrupted. In the present case, it would be implausible that a police officer, working in this area and used to viewing pornographic material would be likely to be depraved or corrupted by what he saw.

Violent pornography

The government intends to introduce an aggravated offence of being in possession of violent and extreme pornography to include, for example, material featuring violence that appears to be life threatening.[1] Although publishing or distributing such material is already illegal under the Obscene Publications Act 1959, the Home Office notes that violent pornography has become increasingly accessible from abroad via the internet. The new proposed law will ensure possession of violent and extreme pornography is illegal both online and offline. A petition had been submitted to Parliament, signed by around 50,000 people, objecting to extreme websites promoting violence against women as sexual gratification, has been presented to Parliament.

At the time of writing, a Bill to cover this proposed offence has not yet been presented to Parliament though one is likely soon. It is proposed the offence will carry a maximum of three years' imprisonment for possession of material depicting serious violence. It is also proposed that the maximum terms of imprisonment for the existing offences of publication, distribution and possession for gain, of pornographic material under the Obscene Publications Acts 1959 and 1964 be increased from the current three years to five years.

Indecent images of children

A major concern is child pornography available on the internet. This is dealt with by section 1 of the Protection of Children Act 1978, as amended, which makes it an offence to take or permit to be taken or to make any indecent photograph or pseudo-photograph of a child or to distribute or show such photographs or pseudo-photographs or to have it in possession with a view to their being distributed or shown by himself to others. It is also an offence to publish or cause to be published an advertisement likely to be understood as conveying that the advertiser distributes or shows such indecent photographs or pseudo-photographs or intends to do so. A person is to be regarded as distributing an indecent photograph or pseudo-photograph if he parts with possession of it to, or exposes or offers it for acquisition by, another person. A person is taken as having been a child at any material time if it appears from the evidence as a whole that he was then under the age of 18: section 2(3).

[1] The Home Office, *Crackdown on Violent Pornography*, 30 August 2006.

Indecent photographs are defined as including data stored on a computer disk or by other electronic means which is capable of conversion to a photograph. Films and video recordings are also covered as are copies and negatives. A pseudo-photograph is an image, whether made by computer graphics or otherwise howsoever, which appears to be a photograph and includes copies of pseudo-photographs and data stored on a computer disk or by other electronic means which is capable of conversion into a pseudo-photograph; section 7 as amended by the Criminal Justice and Public Order Act 1994. If the impression given by a pseudo-photograph is that it is of a child then it is taken to be of a child. This is so even if some of the physical characteristics shown are those of an adult providing the predominant impression is that it is a pseudo-photograph of a child.

It is a defence to a charge under section 1 relating to distribution or showing or being in possession with a view to distributing or showing for the accused to prove that he had a legitimate reason for distributing or showing the photographs or pseudo-photographs or (as the case may be) having them in his possession; or that he had not himself seen the photographs or pseudo-photographs and did not know, nor had any cause to suspect, them to be indecent. There are defences in relation to children who are married, civil partners or in an enduring family relations under section 1A. For example, the offence of making an indecent photograph does not apply where:

- the child is 16 or over,
- the photograph only shows the child or the child and the defendant together,
- sufficient evidence is adduced to raise an issue as to whether the child consented to the photograph being taken or made, or as to whether the defendant reasonably believed that the child so consented, unless it is proved that the child did not so consent and that the defendant did not reasonably believe that the child so consented.

Other defences where there is such a relationship apply to distributing and showing (but not if shown or distributed to anyone other than the child) and being in possession (consent of the child or reasonable belief in consent is an issue here as is whether possession was with a view to showing or distributing the photograph to someone other than the child). These 'relationship' defences only apply to photographs and not pseudo-photographs.

There are further defences relating to making indecent photographs or pseudo-photographs of children if necessary for the purposes of the detection, prevention or investigation of crime or for the purposes of criminal proceedings anywhere in the world. Further exception relate to the Security Services and GCHQ where the making is necessary for carrying out the functions of the Service or GCHQ: section 1B, inserted by the Sexual Offences Act 2003.

Proceedings for offences under the Protection of Children Act 1978 may only be instituted by or with the consent of the Director of Public Prosecutions. The offences are triable either way. The maximum penalty for conviction on indictment is now 10 years' imprisonment or a fine or both (increased in 2001). The maximum penalty on summary conviction is imprisonment for a term not exceeding six months and/or a fine not exceeding £1,000 or such other sum substituted under the Magistrates' Courts Act 1980. Where the offence is committed by a body corporate, such as a limited company, with the consent or connivance of, or through the neglect of, any director, manager, secretary or other officer or a person purporting to act in such a capacity, that person is also guilty of the offence.

In *R* v *Fellows* (1997) 1 Cr App R 244, Fellows was a computer specialist from Birmingham University who used a university computer to store indecent pictures of children and he printed copies. He also made the data available on the internet. The Court of Appeal rejected the accused's argument that the computer data did not comprise a photograph for the purposes of the Protection of Children Act 1978. It was claimed that Parliament could not have envisaged data being stored on computer so as to reproduce photographs which could be transmitted anywhere in the world when the relevant legislation was enacted. However, the Court of Appeal held that the images held in digital form were copies of photographs for the purposes of section 1 of the 1978 Act. The authority of an earlier case was accepted in which the court accepted that a video cassette was an article for the purposes of section 1(2) of the Obscene Publications Act 1959; *Attorney-General's Reference (No. 5 of 1980)* (1980) 72 Cr App R 71. In that case, the court found the accused guilty notwithstanding that it was accepted that Parliament probably had not envisaged that video cassettes would become widely available and provide a means of distributing obscene material.

In *Fellows*, Lord Justice Evans said that a computer disk was not a photograph but was a copy of a photograph which made the original photograph or a copy of it available for viewing by a person with access to the disk. Furthermore, under section 7 of the Protection of Children Act 1978, there was no restriction on the form of the copy of an indecent photograph and later, contemporary copies were included. Fellows' appeal, and that of a person who received material from Fellows' archive, were dismissed. Fellows had been sentenced to three years' imprisonment, demonstrating the seriousness with which the courts regard such activities.

Being in possession

Simply being in possession of an indecent photograph or pseudo-photograph of a child (without any intention to distribute or show it to others) is also a criminal offence under section 160 of the Criminal Justice Act 1988. It is a defence for a person charged with the offence, under section 160(2), to prove:

(a) that he had a legitimate reason for having the photograph or pseudo-photograph in his possession; or

(b) that he had not himself seen the photograph or pseudo-photograph and did not know, nor had any cause to suspect, it to be indecent; or

(c) that the photograph or pseudo-photograph was sent to him without any prior request made by him or on his behalf and that he did not keep it for an unreasonable time.

The maximum penalty for this offence was also increased in 2001 and now stands at five years' imprisonment or a fine or both, if convicted on indictment in the Crown Court.

In Scotland, sections 52 to 52C of the Civic Government (Scotland) Act 1982, as amended, applies to indecent photographs of children in similar fashion to the offences under the Protection of Children Act 1978 and section 160 of the Criminal Justice Act 1988.

◼ Territorial scope of child pornography offences

Under section 72 of the Sexual Offences Act 2003, certain sexual offences committed outside the UK, which constituted an offence under the law of the country or territory in which the offence was committed and would constitute a relevant sexual offence had it been committed in England and Wales or Northern Ireland, is treated as that sexual offence in that part of the UK. It does not matter how the offence is described in the country or territory in which it was committed. Section 72 only applies where the offender was on 1 September 1997, or has since become, a British citizen or resident in the UK. The significance of the date is that it was the date Part 2 of the Sex Offenders Act 1997 came into force. This Act, now repealed by the Sexual Offences Act 2003, had a similar provision.

The sexual offences covered by section 72 are set out in Schedule 2 to the Sexual Offences Act 2003 and include the offences under section 1 of the Protection of Children Act 1978 and section

160 of the Criminal Justice Act 1988 where the photograph or pseudo-photograph shows a child under 16 (17 in Northern Ireland). Inexplicably, the age limit is not 18 years as it now is where the offences have been committed in the UK.

E-mail attachments containing indecent images of children

Section 1 of the Protection of Children Act 1978 applies to opening e-mail attachments containing indecent images of children as it does in the case of downloading such images from webpages. Both acts involve the offence of making indecent photographs. The only exception is where the person in question was not aware that the attachment contained or was likely to contain an indecent photograph or pseudo-photograph of a child. So it was held by the Court of Appeal in *R v Smith and Jayson* [2003] 1 Cr App Rep 212, dismissing the appeals of Smith who received two years' probation and Jayson who was sentenced to 12 months' imprisonment (the sentences were imposed before the increase in maximum penalties). Although the Act is silent on the mental element required for the offence, the Court of Appeal held that the act of making should be a deliberate and intentional act in the knowledge that the image made is, or is likely to be, an indecent photograph or pseudo-photograph of a child.

In *R v Porter* [2006] EWCA Crim 560, Lord Justice Dyson LJ said about e-mail attachments not suspected to contain pornographic material (at para. 18):

> Suppose that a person receives unsolicited images of child pornography as an attachment to an email. He is shocked by what he sees and immediately deletes the attachment and deletes it from the recycle bin. Suppose further that he knows that the images are retrievable from the hard disk drive, but he believes that they can only be retrieved and removed by specialists who have software and equipment which he does not have. It does not occur to him to seek to acquire the software or engage a specialist for this purpose. So far as he is concerned, he has no intention of ever seeking to retrieve the images and he has done all that is reasonably necessary to make them irretrievable. We think that it would be surprising if Parliament had intended that such a person should be guilty of an offence under section 160(1) of the 1988 Act [the possession offence].

This is a sensible approach and it would be unreasonable to expect someone to go to the trouble and expense of getting an expert to permanently remove the file containing the image. However, there is always the danger that the image will be discovered at some later time, for example, if the computer is sold or traded in. The safest thing is not to open any attachment to an e-mail unless the source is known.

SENTENCING FOR CHILD PORNOGRAPHY

Sentencing guidelines based on the increased penalties were laid down by the Court of Appeal in *R v Oliver* [2003] 2 Cr App Rep (S) 64. The Court of Appeal adopted a scale suggested by the Sentencing Advisory Panel, with some modification as follows:

- Level 1 – images depicting erotic posing with no sexual activity.
- Level 2 – sexual activity between children or solo masturbation by a child.
- Level 3 – non-penetrative sexual activity between adults and children.
- Level 4 – penetrative sexual activity between adults and children.
- Level 5 – sadism or bestiality.

Having set out the levels, the Court of Appeal made recommendations (as below), stressing that

28

Computer pornography, harassment and incitement

these were guidelines only and not a straitjacket for sentencers. Regard would also need to be given to the present state of prison overcrowding and to public concerns about child pornography.

■ Possession for own use of small quantities of material not involving exploitation or abuse of children or small quantities of material in level 1, particularly where downloaded from the internet, would suggest a fine might be appropriate. A conditional discharge might be suitable if the offender pleaded guilty and had no previous convictions.

■ A community sentence might be appropriate where the offender had possession of large quantities of material in level 1 or small quantities of level 2 material, provided the material had not been distributed or shown to others. A cooperative and motivated offender might be dealt with by a community rehabilitation order with a sex offender programme. The custody threshold might be passed if the material had been shown to others or where there was a large quantity of level 2 material or a small amount of level 3 or above material. Sentences might vary, depending on the circumstances, from six to 12 months' imprisonment.

■ A sentence of between 12 months' and three years' imprisonment might be appropriate for possession of large quantities on level 3 or 4 material, even if not shown to others or for showing or distributing large quantities of level 3 material or for producing or trading in material at levels 1 to 3.

■ Sentences longer than three years should be reserved for more serious cases, where images in level 4 or 5 had been shown or distributed, where the offender was actively involved in producing material in level 4 or 5, particularly in breach of trust whether or not there was an element of commercial gain or where the offender encouraged or commissioned the production of such images. A higher sentence should be granted if the offender has been involved in more than one of the above activities.

■ Sentences approaching the 10-year maximum would be appropriate in very serious cases where the offender has previous convictions for dealing in child pornography or abusing children sexually or with violence.

Aggravating factors, likely to lead to an increased penalty, include whether the images had been shown to children, if there are a large number of images, how the images have been arranged on a computer (might indicate a sophisticated approach to trading in the images or a higher level of personal interest in the images), whether the images are available on public areas of the internet and whether they are likely to be found by accident by persons not looking for pornographic material, whether the offender was responsible for the production of the images, whether the children were members of his or her own family, or drawn from vulnerable groups or where the offender was in a position of trust such as being a teacher, the age of the children, whether injury to their private parts was likely, and whether they appeared fearful or distressed.

In *Thomson v R* [2004] 2 Cr App R 262, Thompson pleaded guilty to 12 counts of possessing indecent photographs or pseudo-photographs of children. Eleven of the counts relating to specific images but one count covered 3,735 other images. All the images had been downloaded from commercial internet sites but had all been deleted by Thompson. He was sentenced to two years' imprisonment on each count to be served concurrently. The trial judge said that some of the images were of the *Oliver* category 4. There were a number of problems with the indictments, for example, of the 3,735 images, there was no information as to the numbers falling into each of the Oliver categories. The Court of Appeal thought that this placed the judge in a difficult position such that he was not able to properly proceed to sentence according to the Oliver guidelines. The Court of Appeal noted that such lack of precision in charges for child pornography was no uncommon and made some suggestions for improving this. As to the sentence, the Court of Appeal reduced it to nine months' imprisonment. Mr Justice Thomas said (at para. 14):

> Taking into account the unfortunate lack of information before the court, the fact that all the images were deleted from the computer by the appellant, that he was not in any way involved in distribution and that the images were used for his own personal purposes and the personal mitigation to which we have referred, we consider that the sentence passed by the learned trial Judge was too long.

Furthermore, the trial judge could not reasonably have concluded that Thompson had a great deal of category 4 images on the evidence before him.

In *R v Edwards* [2005] EWCA Crim 402, a 47-year old man of previous good character was convicted of 19 charges of making indecent photographs of children by downloading the images from a website based in Texas. Of a total of 1,700 images, around 400 were of category 4 and one was category 5. He was sentenced to a total of 39 months' imprisonment, comprising a custodial term of 15 months and an extended licence period of 24 months. Orders were made for forfeiture and destruction of the images and the appellant was barred from working with children under section 28 of the Criminal Justice and Court Services Act 2000 and he was required to comply with the notification provisions under the Sexual Offences Act 2003. The Court of Appeal considered that this case was rather more serious than that in *Thompson*. But, having regard to that case and the guidance in *Oliver*, the Court of Appeal considered that the offending in the present case was within a lower category. A sentence of nine months' imprisonment as a custodial term and an extension period of licence of twelve months was substituted. The prohibition on working with children remained.

SEXUAL GROOMING OF CHILDREN BY E-MAIL OR IN CHAT-ROOMS

There have been a number of worrying cases where adult men have met young children after contacting them initially by e-mail or through internet chat-rooms. The dangers are apparent, a paedophile could lie about his age and pretend to share similar interests with a child contacted through a chat-room, and arrange to meet the child, intending to engage in sexual activity. The government considered that it was important to introduce a new offence of grooming for sexual activity so that a prosecution could be brought before any sexual activity takes place.

Section 15 of the Sexual Offences Act 2003 makes it an offence to meet a child following sexual grooming. The offence can be committed without the meeting having taken place, if the offender travels to any part of the world with the intention of meeting the child. The offender must be aged 18 years or over and must have met or communicated with the child (being under 16 years of age) on at least two previous occasions. The offender must not reasonably believe that the child is 16 years or over (17 years or over in Northern Ireland). The offence is completed when the offender intentionally meets the child or travels with the intention of meeting the child in any part of the world, though part of the travel must be in England and Wales or Northern Ireland with the intention of doing anything to or in respect of the child which is a relevant offence. Relevant offences include sexual offences under Part 1 of the Act and a number of the sexual offences in Schedule 3 to the Act. Also included are things done outside England and Wales and Northern Ireland which is not an offence under Part 1 of those offences in Schedule 3 but would be if they were carried out in England and Wales or Northern Ireland.

The previous meetings or communications need not be sexually explicit and may appear to be innocuous, such as where the offender offers friendship or help with homework. It may be that the purpose at this stage is to build up a child's trust or confidence.

The maximum penalty for the offence is ten years' imprisonment for conviction on indictment. For summary conviction the maximum penalty is a term of imprisonment not exceeding 6 months and/or a fine not exceeding the statutory maximum. It is clear that the offence is intended to cover communication over the internet. The meeting or communication may be in or from any part of the world and the communication can be by any means. Thus, the offence can be committed if a person sends two e-mails to a child, arranges to meet the child and then travels to meet the child with the intention of doing anything to or in respect of the child that is a relevant offence, such as rape or sexual assault.

In *R v Costi* [2006] All ER (D) 369, the offender, who was 19 to 20 years old at the time of the offences, pleaded guilty to a number of sexual offences against children including taking indecent photographs of a child, meeting a female child under 16 following sexual grooming, sexual acts with a female and causing or inciting a female child under 16 to engage in sexual activity. He had targeted young girls through internet chat-rooms. He groomed one 14-year-old female child for consensual oral and vaginal sex. He encouraged another 14-year-old victim to masturbate for him on a web camera. The police found on his computer 355 logs of his conversations with underage victims, and 43 indecent images. He was sentenced to a total of 10 years' imprisonment and appealed on the basis of, *inter alia*, his guilty plea, previous good character, his age and immaturity and the relatively small age gap between him and his victims. The Court of Appeal considered that the sentence should be reduced to six years' imprisonment. A sexual prevention order was reduced from 15 to 10 years.

In Scotland, the equivalent offence is meeting a child following certain preliminary contact under section 1 of the Protection of Children and Prevention of Sexual Offences (Scotland) Act 2005.

THREATENING E-MAILS

We have seen in Chapter 26 that sending a threatening or malicious message by a public electronic communications network, including by e-mail, can constitute an offence under the Communications Act 2003. A much wider piece of legislation was brought in to deal with the problem of stalking and other antisocial behaviour such as that emanating from 'neighbours from hell'. The Protection from Harassment Act 1997 may apply where threatening messages are sent by e-mail or other forms of communication. It provides for criminal penalties as well as civil remedies. The relevant provisions of the Act came into force on 16 June 1997. Some significant amendments were made by the Serious Organised Crime and Police Act 2005.

Under section 1, a person must not pursue a course of conduct which amounts to harassment of another, and which the person responsible knows or ought to know amounts to harassment of the other. The victim must be an individual, not an artificial legal person such as a company. This applies generally to the Act.

Section 1A provides that a person must not pursue a course of conduct:

(a) which involves harassment of two or more persons, and

(b) which he knows or ought to know involves harassment of those persons, and

(c) by which he intends to persuade any person (whether or not one of those mentioned above) –
   (i) not to do something that he is entitled or required to do, or
   (ii) to do something that he is not under any obligation to do.

Thus, for section 1A sending the same e-mail to two persons counts as a course of conduct whereas, for section 1 at least two e-mails must be sent to the same person, if sending e-mails is the form of conduct involved. As noted below, however, the conduct does not have to be the same on each occasion.

Whether a person 'ought to know' is an objective test based on a reasonable person in possession of the same information. If such a person would think the course of conduct amounted to harassment of the other, that is sufficient. By section 7, references to harassing a person include alarming the person or causing the person distress and a 'course of conduct' must involve conduct on at least two occasions though not necessarily the same conduct for section 1. For the purposes of section 1A, a course of conduct in relation to two or more persons must involve conduct on at least one occasion in relation to each of those persons. 'Conduct' includes speech. Under section 2, it is an offence to pursue a course of conduct in breach of section 1 or section 1A. A person aiding, abetting, counselling or procuring the conduct of another may also be liable for the offence or for the aggravated form if applicable.

It can be seen that the offence can be committed relatively easily. Just sending two e-mails which objectively would cause in a reasonable person alarm or distress should be sufficient. For example, if Rodney sends two messages threatening to harm Wendy that should be an offence. The same applies if Rodney makes unwelcome sexual advances of an unpleasant nature to Wendy by sending her two e-mails. Rodney may also commit the offence by sending one e-mail of such a nature each to Wendy and Patricia provided he has the requisite intention. As the conduct does not have to be the same variety, Rodney could also possibly commit the offence by sending one threatening e-mail and making one telephone call to Wendy.

There are some specific defences to the offence of harassment and it does not apply to a course of conduct if the person who pursued it shows that it was pursued for the purpose of preventing or detecting crime, that it was pursued under any enactment or rule of law or to comply with any condition or requirement imposed by any person under any enactment, or that in the particular circumstances the pursuit of the course of conduct was reasonable: section 1(3). Note that the burden of proof is on the person responsible for the conduct (this will be satisfied on a balance of probabilities – the usual criminal standard of proof, beyond reasonable doubt, does not apply to defences).

The offence is triable in the magistrates' courts only and carries a maximum penalty of imprisonment for a term not exceeding six months and/or a fine not exceeding level 5 on the standard scale. A restraining order may be made under section 5 for the section 2 offence and for the aggravated form under section 4, below.

Although the threshold for the offence under section 2 is relatively low, a software pirate will be unlikely to maintain a claim of harassment in respect of legal and associated action against him by or on behalf of the owners of the copyrights alleged to have been infringed. In *Tuppen* v *Microsoft Corp Ltd, The Times*, 15 November 2000, the claimants alleged that the defendants, Microsoft and their solicitors, had harassed them by suborning the police to raid the home of one of the claimants, by conducting oppressive litigation, by suborning witnesses into lying and by telephoning the claimants late at night. The judge struck out this claim saying that the purpose of the Protection from Harassment Act 1997 was to prevent stalking, anti-social behaviour by neighbours and racial harassment and that, apart perhaps from the telephone call to each of the claimants (an isolated incident), none of the defendants' behaviour came anywhere near falling under the Act. However, the judge was a little too narrow in describing the behaviour sought to be controlled by the Act, as some of the cases mentioned above show. Furthermore, although conducting a course of litigation would not normally amount to harassment, there is no reason why it might not be in extreme cases, for example, where several law suits with no chance of success are made against an individual. In the *Tuppen* case, the allegations that the police and witnesses had been suborned (incited to do something by bribery) were very serious allegations and, as far as the law report indicates, with nothing whatsoever to support such allegations.

28

Computer pornography, harassment and incitement

Harassment and freedom of expression

Notwithstanding the right of freedom of expression under the Human Rights Convention, newspaper articles can amount to harassment under the Act if, for example, they promoted racial hatred of an individual. In *Thomas* v *News Group Newspapers Ltd* [2001] EWCA Civ 1233, two police sergeants had been demoted following a complaint from a black clerk at a police station who was concerned at their treatment of a Somali asylum-seeker and had overheard them make a private remark about the asylum-seeker. *The Sun* newspaper ran a story about it entitled 'Beyond a Joke: Fury as Police Sarges Busted after Refugee Jest'. Several readers wrote in and their letters were published later; a follow-up story was published in *The Sun* which repeated part of the original article. The black clerk, the claimant, was named in the articles. The defendant's appeal against the refusal of a county court judge to strike out the claimant's particulars of claim was rejected by the Court of Appeal which considered that there was an arguable case that the defendant was guilty of harassing the claimant by stirring up racial criticism of her which would cause her distress. It was accepted that the right of freedom of expression did not extend to protect remarks undermining the basic values expressed in the Human Rights Convention.

Cyberstalking

A jilted lover or someone whose advances have been rejected may take to seeking revenge in a variety of ways. Letters or e-mails may be sent discrediting, embarrassing or simply annoying the victim. In *R* v *Debnath* [2006] 2 Cr App R (S) 169, the accused embarked upon an impressive campaign of harassment against the victim with whom she had a 'one-night stand'. The course of conduct, prompted by the belief (mistaken) that she had caught Chlamydia from the victim, included:

- sending e-mails to the victim's fiancée, purporting to be from one of his friends, with information about alleged sexual indiscretions;
- registering the victim on a website '**positive.singles.com**', a database for persons with sexually transmitted diseases seeking sexual liaisons;
- setting up a website '[**victim's name**] **is gay.com**' containing a fake newspaper article alleging homosexual practices by him;
- registering the victim with a gay American prisoner exchange;
- sending an e-mail to the victim's employers purporting to be from him admitting that he was sexually harassing her and trying to frame her for harassing him;
- sabotaging the victim's e-mail account denying him access and diverting his e-mails to one of her accounts, for which she paid $150 to some computer hackers apparently based in Canada;
- at the time when she was bailed on condition she did not access the internet, she engaged another group of hackers which succeeded in hacking into one account and sent an e-mail to the victim's employers suggesting that he had a criminal record (which he did not) and that he had been trying to frame her.

Eventually, Debnath was remanded in custody and the 23 weeks she spent in custody were taken into account by the judge who sentenced her to a two-year community rehabilitation order and a restraining order was made under section 5 of the Protection from Harassment Act 1997 prohibiting her from contacting the victim, his fiancée and other specified persons either directly or indirectly, and from publishing any information concerning the victim or his fiancée, whether true or not, indefinitely. She appealed to the Court of Appeal against the restraining order only. It was submitted by her counsel that the terms of the order were too wide as it impinged upon her fundamental right of freedom of expression under Article 10 of the Human Rights Convention, as it prevented her publishing the truth in almost any circumstances. There was no need to prevent her publishing the truth as this would erode the substance of democracy itself.

The Court of Appeal noted that it is not an offence to do anything prohibited by a restraining order if the defendant has reasonable excuse under section 5(5) of the Act. The appellant had no need to publish anything about the victim and, if a need did arise, she would not commit an offence if she could establish that she had reasonable excuse. The exceptional circumstances of the case made the wide terms of the restraining order necessary to protect the rights of the victims and the prevention of further offences. Creswell J said (at para. 25):

> The appellant has shown that she is incapable of distinguishing between what is true and false. If permitted to publish any information about the complainant and his fiancée, the appellant will go to quite extraordinary lengths to find some new means of harassing the complainants. It is not difficult to envisage examples of how the appellant might further harass the complainant and his fiancée by publishing information which is true, for example, by placing information on a website, such as:
>
> > 'I have harassed Mr A. We had a one-night stand in July 2001. Thereafter he has refused to associate with me. His email address is below.'

Finally, the court confirmed that the terms of the order, exceptional as they were, were justified. The order as drafted was prescribed by law, to further a legitimate aim, necessary in a democratic society and proportionate. In any case, it would always be open to the appellant to apply to the court for a variation to, or discharge of, the order if such variation is justified, as allowed under section 5(4) of the Act.

Aggravated harassment

A more serious form of the offence is covered by section 4 of the Act. This is where the course of conduct causes another to fear violence on at least two occasions. The person pursuing the course of conduct must know or he ought to know that the other person will fear violence. Whether a person ought to know is based on an objective test – whether a reasonable person with knowledge of the same information would think it would put the victim in fear of violence. The offence is triable either way and, on conviction on indictment in the Crown Court, the maximum penalty is imprisonment for a term not exceeding five years and/or a fine.

For the section 4 offence the defences are the same except the last one which is to the effect that the conduct was reasonable for the protection of the person pursuing the conduct or another or for the protection of his or another's property.

Where a person is charged with a section 4 offence and proceeded with in the Crown Court, if the jury find him not guilty, the jury may find him guilty of the section 2 offence, notwithstanding that section 2 is triable in a magistrates' court only.

Newspaper articles can cause distress because others who may know the person to whom remarks in an article are directed see the offending article. However, there is no requirement that the remarks are published to third parties. A person may be distressed by telephone calls, letters or e-mails, even if no one else hears or sees them. The case of *R v Norman* [2003] EWCA Crim 3878 gives an example of how seriously the courts take harassment by e-mail. In that case, a controversial radio broadcaster and journalist received many e-mails from the defendant who had used fictitious names. Eventually, he was traced. A large proportion of the e-mails were racially abusive and referred to the broadcaster's Jewish origin. There were also threats, though not of immediate violence. The defendant was convicted of racially aggravated harassment and sentenced to 18 months' imprisonment. A restraining order under section 5 was also made. He appealed on a number of grounds claiming that the judge failed to take into account that the broadcaster was controversial, he was not a vulnerable person and the threats were made by e-mail and not face to face. The Court of Appeal considered that aggravating factors were the length of time over which the e-mails had been sent and the ferocity of their contents. However, mitigating factors were the defendant's previous good character and the fact that he had apologised to the complainant. The Court of Appeal substituted a sentence of 12 months' imprisonment.

Civil remedies

There is a civil remedy under section 3 for an actual or apprehended breach of section 1. The use of the word 'apprehended' makes it clear that it is the victim's perception which is important. Damages are available and there is provision also for injunctions, for example, prohibiting the person responsible from continuing the conduct.

In respect of an actual or apprehended breach of section 1A, under section 3A an injunction may be granted restraining the person in question from pursuing any conduct which amounts to harassment in relation to any person or persons mentioned or described in the injunction. An application for an injunction may be brought by any person who is or may be a victim of the course of conduct or any person whom the person in breach of section 1A intends to persuade not to do anything he is entitled to do or to do something he is not under an obligation to do.

For breach of an injunction under section 3 or section 3A, the maximum penalty on conviction on indictment is a term of imprisonment not exceeding five years and/or a fine. On summary conviction the maximum penalty is a term of imprisonment not exceeding six months and/or a fine not exceeding the statutory maximum.

There have been a number of cases where civil injunctions have been sought successfully for harassment by e-mail. For example, in *Chelsea and Westminster Healthcare NHS Trust* v *Redmond* [2003] All ER (D) 87, the father of a girl unhappy with the cessation of a particular type of controversial treatment by the hospital published offensive allegations on his website and, *inter alia*, sent numerous e-mails to the claimant's staff. An injunction and restraining order were granted under the Protection from Harassment Act 1997.

In *Chiron Corp Inc* v *Avery* [2004] EWHC 493 (QB), animal rights protestors had engaged in an organised and systematic campaign against organisations involved in research using live animals which extended to employees and contractors. A number of different forms of threats were used and damage to property was also involved. Threatening e-mails sent to employees and others was another tactic adopted. In one case, an employee received over 300 e-mails from the defendants. The court confirmed an injunction granted to prevent a continuation of such behaviour.

Threatening e-mails were sent to an English national resident in Thailand who, it was alleged, owed debts to the sender of the e-mails. They included material referring to the victim as a 'lowlife' and hinted that his life would be made uncomfortable unless he paid up. It was argued that the threatening e-mails, some of which were sent from England, were subject to Thai law and not to English law. This was rejected by the court and a permanent injunction was granted in *Potter* v *Price* [2004] All ER (D) 463. Although the e-mails were sent in an attempt to recover business debts, they went beyond the level of brusque business dealings to call in a debt. It was accepted that the claimant had a real connection with England. That was also where his parents lived.

Employer's vicarious liability for harassment at civil law

An employer may be liable for breaches of section 1 or section 1A of the Protection from Harassment Act 1997 resulting from the acts of employees. In *Majrowski v Guy's and St Thomas's NHS Trust* [2006] 4 All ER 395, Majrowski worked as a clinical auditor co-ordinator for the NHS Trust. He claimed that his departmental manager had bullied him, set unrealistic targets for him and been unduly critical of his time-keeping. The NHS Trust carried out an investigation, finding he had been subject to harassment. He was later dismissed for unrelated reasons. The manager resigned. Nearly four years later, Majrowski commenced proceedings against the Trust for damages under section 3 of the Protection from Harassment Act 1997 for distress, anxiety and consequential loss caused by the harassment. His claim was based solely on the NHS Trust's vicarious liability for the alleged harassment caused by the manager.

At first instance, the judge summarily struck out the claim on the basis that common law already provided adequate protection and it had not been the intention to create another level of liability in employment law. The Court of Appeal allowed Majrowski's appeal by a majority of 2:1 holding that there should be a trial of the action and the NHS Trust appealed to the House of Lords.

In the House of Lords, all five Law Lords agreed that the NHS Trust's appeal must be dismissed. Lord Nicholls of Birkenhead said that, unless a statute expressly or impliedly indicates otherwise, an employer would be vicariously liable for a statutory tort sounding in damages committed by his employee. In relation to the 1997 Act, he said that an employer would be vicariously liable to a customer subjected to harassment by an employee and this must also apply to another employee harassed by an employee.

The provisions of the Act relating to Scotland clearly indicated that it was the intention of Parliament that employers ought to be vicariously liable in Scotland. Section 10 of the Protection from Harassment Act 1997 inserted a new section 18B into the Prescription and Limitation (Scotland) Act 1973 which provides that no action shall be brought more than three years from the date on which the alleged harassment ceased or, if later, the date on which the pursuer:

> ... became, or on which, in the opinion of the court, it would have been reasonably practicable for him in all the circumstances to have become, aware, that the defender was a person responsible for the alleged harassment *or the employer or principal of such a person.* (emphasis added.)

There was nothing to suggest that the intention was that things would be different in England and Wales (however, the limitation period there is six years not the usual three years for personal injury – see section 6). Baroness Hale of Richmond, whilst also dismissing the appeal, pointed out that, had Parliament considered the implications of the Act applying so as to make employers vicariously liable for a course of conduct by one employee against another employee, things may have been different. She also indicated that the threshold might not be very high, saying (at para. 66):

> But conduct might be harassment even if no alarm or distress were in fact caused. A great deal is left to the wisdom of the courts to draw sensible lines between the ordinary banter and badinage of life and genuinely offensive and unacceptable behaviour.

This case raises a serious issue as to the potential liability of employers for the conduct of their employee towards other employees. This is particularly worrying in relation to e-mails for, as mentioned above, employees often send e-mails without properly reflecting on what they say or imply. In many cases, people send e-mails without even reading them through.

The scope of harassment may be quite wide and extends to causing anxiety alone, as suggested by the language of section 3 itself and Baroness Hale. The Act does not attempt to provide an exhaustive definition of harassment, simply saying that it includes causing alarm or distress. Say

28

Computer pornography, harassment and incitement

that a line manager sends a couple of e-mails to a subordinate telling him he needs to improve his performance at work, this could cause anxiety, especially if there is context suggesting that his job is in jeopardy.

As the employer's liability is strict, subject to common law defences only, for example, where there is some doubt as to whether the employee carried out the conduct in the course of employment, it could be argued that an oral warning followed by a written warning as required under employment protection legislation, could certainly cause anxiety, if not distress, and constitute harassment leaving the employee responsible for the warnings criminally and civilly liable and the employer strictly liable at civil law. It will be interesting to see how the courts deal with such a situation. Perhaps amending legislation is urgently needed.

Of course, the employer will be liable only if the employee alleged to have caused the harassment knew or ought to have known that the course of conduct would amount to harassment of the victim. But an employee who puts another employee in fear of losing his or her job whether through incompetence or redundancy would surely know that anxiety and, possibly, alarm and distress would be caused to that other employee.

The fact that an employer has effective disciplinary procedures to deal with harassment, in all its forms, in the workplace does not appear to prevent the employer being vicariously liable. In *Majrowski*, the NHS Trust did have procedures and found that he had indeed been the subject of harassment. Paradoxically, this could make good evidence for a court action for damages based on the Act.

In relation to e-mails, employers should ensure that their employees are fully aware of the dangers of sending e-mails that could be construed as being likely to cause harassment. Appropriate codes of conduct should be drawn up if they do not already exist backed by grievance and disciplinary matters supported by appropriate penalties. If this happens, although it may not prevent the employer remaining potentially liable under the Protection from Harassment Act 1997, it could have a significant impact of the quantum of damages awarded to an employee.

INCITEMENT

Incitement occurs where a person encourages or persuades another to commit a criminal offence. It is largely governed by common law but there are a number of statutory examples, such as inciting a child to become involved in pornography, under section 48 of the Sexual Offences Act 2003. Under section 51 of that Act, a person is involved in pornography if an indecent image of that person is recorded.

Incitement may be carried out by e-mail, by SMS (text message) on a website or in a blog. All sorts of offences could be incited in such a way, ranging from serious offences such as terrorist offences and murder to less serious offences such as minor theft or speeding offences. In *R v A* [2006] EWCA Crim 2103, the accused was found guilty, *inter alia*, of the offence of inciting a child to engage in sexual activity, under section 8 of the Sexual Offences Act 2003, by means of text messaging.

Publishing details of how to write computer viruses could fall within the law of incitement; that is, the person publishing the details could be inciting others to commit a section 3 offence. However, there must be an intention on the part of the inciter to bring about the criminal consequences and this may be difficult to prove, although, in May 1995, an unemployed man who called himself the 'Black Baron' became the first person to be convicted of incitement in respect of computer viruses (*Computing*, 1 June 1995, p. 1). He was also convicted of 11 charges under the Computer Misuse Act 1990.

It is arguably incitement to subscribe to a pornographic website thus encouraging the owners of the business operating the website to continue to operate the pornographic business. So it was held in *R (on application of O)* v *Coventry Justices* [2004] EWHC 905 (Admin) in which the accused visited a website in Texas, entering his personal and financial details to gain access to pornographic material. Although the process of gaining access was purely automated the business was operated by human beings. It was, therefore, irrelevant to claim only the computer had been 'encouraged to commit the crime'. Mr Justice Gage said (at para. 38):

> By subscribing through the means of the computer, the [accused] was, in my judgment, at least for the purposes of a prima facie case, established as inciting someone, namely those lying behind the onus of the company, to commit the offence. Accordingly, in my judgment, it matters not that the process was entirely automated by means of a computer.

This is an interesting view on incitement as one would have thought that those operating the business needed no encouragement to peddle their pornographic materials.

SUMMARY

- An article is obscene if it tends to deprave and corrupt.
- Publishing an obscene article includes transmitting data stored electronically.
- Placing obscene material on a website is an offence under the Obscene Publications Acts.
- A special offence of being in possession of violent pornography is likely to be introduced.
- A number of offences apply in relation to child pornography, including:
  - taking or permitting to be taken an indecent photograph;
  - making an indecent photograph;
  - distributing or showing an indecent photograph or being in possession for such purposes;
  - being in possession of an indecent photograph;
  - advertising the distribution or showing of indecent photographs.
- Indecent photographs include data stored electronically and pseudo-photographs are also covered.
- Opening an e-mail attachment which is an indecent photograph of a child is not an offence if:
  - it was not suspected as such;
  - it was deleted immediately (including from the recycle bin);
  - there is no intention to retrieve it and, if this is the case;
  - there is no need to engage a specialist to ensure it is completely irretrievable.
- The maximum penalty for most child pornography offences is 10 years' imprisonment and/or a fine.
- In *R* v *Oliver*, a scale was set out giving sentencing guidance for child pornography offences.
- It is an offence to meet a child following grooming intending to commit a sexual offence:
  - the act of grooming can include using chat-rooms, sending e-mails or text messages;
  - grooming does not have to be sexually explicit;
  - there is no need for the meeting to actually take place, provided that:
  - the accused travels intending to meet a child to commit a relevant sexual offence.
- Sending e-mails likely to cause alarm or distress is likely to be an offence of harassment.

- Harassment requires a course of conduct, being on:
  - two or more occasions with the same victim; or
  - one occasion with two or more victims.
- Cyberstalking is likely to be harassment.
- Civil injunctions and restraining orders may be available to prevent a continuation of harassment.
- A victim of harassment may be able to obtain damages.
- An aggravated form of harassment is where it causes the victim to fear violence.
- An employer may be vicariously liable for harassment between employees, such as
  - where one employee sends another two or more e-mails which cause:
  - alarm or distress or, perhaps, even just anxiety.
- A person may be guilty of incitement by placing material on a website encouraging others to commit criminal offences.

SELF-TEST QUESTIONS

Note: there is only one correct answer to each multiple choice question.

1 **In respect of obscene publications under the Obscene Publications Acts, which one of the following statements is CORRECT?**

   (a) It is not an offence where the only persons proved to have seen the material are not likely themselves to be depraved and corrupted because they are used to seeing such material.

   (b) Publishing an article includes transmitting data stored electronically.

   (c) The right of freedom of expression means that the offences do not apply where the material in question is placed on a website.

   (d) The offences apply only in respect of pornographic images of children.

2 **Under the Protection of Children Act 1978, as amended, which one of the following is the definition of a PSEUDO-PHOTOGRAPH?**

   (a) It is an image, stored on a photographic negative or plate, from which a black and white or colour print may be produced by electronic or other means.

   (b) It is an image contained in a file format used by and accessible by computer, such as a JPEG, TIFF, WMF or GIF file.

   (c) It is an image stored on digital camera media which can be uploaded to a computer for viewing or replicating at such future date.

   (d) It is an image, whether made by computer graphics or otherwise howsoever, which appears to be a photograph and includes copies of pseudo-photographs and data stored on a computer disk or by other electronic means which is capable of conversion into a pseudo-photograph.

3 Kalifa opened an attachment to an e-mail which contained an image which was an indecent photograph of a child. As soon as he realised what it was, he deleted the attachment and the e-mail. The e-mail was from a source unknown to Kalifa and he had no knowledge about the nature of the image. The subject of the e-mail which was displayed before opening it was

'Artistic image' and there was no text in the e-mail apart from the words: 'Have a look at this'. Which of the following statements is most likely to be TRUE in respect of Kalifa?

(a) Kalifa has committed the offence of making an indecent photograph of a child under section 1 of the Protection of Children Act 1978 and he is likely to be found guilty as there is no defence to this offence as confirmed on the basis of the case of *R* v *Smith & Jayson* [2003] 1 Cr App Rep 212.

(b) Kalifa has committed the offence of making an indecent photograph of a child under section 1 of the Protection of Children Act 1978 and he is likely to be found guilty on the basis that he was reckless to open an attachment to an e-mail when he did not know from whom it had been sent on the basis of the case of *R* v *Smith & Jayson* [2003] 1 Cr App Rep 212.

(c) Kalifa has not committed the offence of making an indecent photograph of a child under section 1 of the Protection of Children Act 1978 as he would not have known that the image was or was likely to be an indecent photograph of a child and he deleted the image soon after opening it on the basis of the case of *R* v *Porter* [2006] EWCA Crim 560.

(d) Kalifa is guilty of being in possession of an indecent photograph of a child under section 160 of the Criminal Justice Act 1988. However, as the duration of his possession was very short, he is unlikely to receive a custodial sentence.

4   Section 2 of the Protection from Harassment Act 1997 makes it an offence to pursue a course of conduct which amounts to harassment of another where the person responsible knows or ought to know that the course of conduct will amount to harassment. Which one of the following statements is INCORRECT in relation to the offence?

(a) Where there is only one victim, a course of conduct requires conduct on at least two occasions which need not be the same type of conduct. Conduct includes speech.

(b) Whether a person 'ought to know' is a subjective test based on the perceptions of the accused and his or her knowledge of the sensitivity, if any, of the intended victim to the nature of the conduct.

(c) A court sentencing a person for the offence of harassment may make a restraining order to protect the victim from further harassment. The victim may also bring civil proceedings in respect of the harassment under section 3 of the Act.

(d) Threatening e-mails may amount to harassment.

5   In the light of the House of Lords decision in *Majrowski* v *Guy's and St Thomas's NHS Trust*, is it reasonable to make employers vicariously liable to harassment caused by their employees, whether to other employees or otherwise?

For further resources and updates please go to the Companion Website accompanying this book at **www.mylawchamber.co.uk/bainbridgeIT**

28

Computer pornography, harassment and incitement

29 Computer evidence and forensics

INTRODUCTION

The admissibility of evidence in criminal proceedings is a complicated subject, littered with rules and exceptions to rules, both common law and statutory. One of the rules governs the admissibility of hearsay evidence, that is, a statement other than by a person giving oral evidence in the proceedings is not normally admissible or any fact or opinion contained in the statement. In relation to civil proceedings, this rule has all but been abolished but it remains firmly in place in criminal cases. The rule against hearsay evidence developed as a way of excluding evidence of which a witness did not have direct knowledge and could not be effectively examined and cross-examined on it. The original maker of a statement is in the best position to give evidence of it.

There are a number of exceptions to the hearsay rule such as statements in public documents, documentary evidence and statements made where the witness who made the statement is not available. This might be the case where that witness has died or is physically or mentally unfit to give evidence or out of the country and it is not reasonably practicable to secure his attendance.

Without these exceptions, the person responsible for the statement in question must attend court and make the statement in person. In the case of computer documents there has to be some exception to the hearsay rule as, in many cases, it will not be possible to identify the person or persons who entered the information in question. The information may have passed through the hands of a chain of employees, a number of whom may have been responsible for its final form into the computer. The law of evidence has to be flexible enough to cope with the realities of the modern business world, otherwise persons committing criminal offences (particularly those involving dishonesty and fraud) would escape conviction all too easily. It must also be recognised, however, that computers are not infallible and some fundamental requirements have to be satisfied before computer documents can be admitted as evidence in criminal proceedings under an exception to the hearsay rule. The law on the admissibility of documents in criminal trial has been clarified by Chapter 2 of Part 11 of the Criminal Justice Act 2003. Previously, the law was contained in section 69 of the Police and Criminal Evidence Act 1984 and sections 23 to 25 of the Criminal Justice Act 1988. The way the rules operated was not altogether satisfactory and resulted in acquittals where, for example, a time clock was incorrectly set on a breathalyser device in one case and, in another, a line of dots on a print out was missing, even though the evidence sought to be admitted in both cases was clear.

The Law Commission investigated the requirement under section 69 of the Police and Criminal Evidence Act 1984 to prove the infallibility of the computer in question in court before computer documents produced by or stored on it could be admitted as evidence of the facts stated therein. In one case cited by the Law Commission, 15 to 20 hours were spent trying to prove that a computer was working properly. It seemed that some lawyers were using section 69 as a device to obstruct the course of justice. The Law Commission recommended, therefore, that section 69 be repealed, as it was during 2000.[1] If there have been problems with the computer in question, or suspicion that this is the case, the defence could put this to the judge who could then rule whether or not the evidence should be admissible and give an appropriate warning to the jury if the evidence was admitted.

In the absence of section 69, a common law rule applies which is to the effect that, in the absence of evidence to the contrary, it is presumed that mechanical instruments were operating properly at the material time. In the past, this rule had been applied to speedometers and traffic lights.

BASIC RULE AS TO ADMISSIBILITY OF HEARSAY EVIDENCE IN CRIMINAL PROCEEDINGS

Under section 114 of the Criminal Justice Act 2003, a statement not made in oral evidence is admissible in criminal proceedings as evidence of any matter stated only if:

(a) any provision of Chapter 2 of Part 11 of the Act (hearsay evidence) or other statutory provision makes it admissible;

(b) any rule of law preserved by section 118 makes it admissible (for example, public documents and records, rules of law where evidence of reputation is admissible and expert evidence);

(c) all parties to the proceedings agree to it being admissible; or

(d) the court is satisfied it is in the interests of justice for it to be admissible.

Note that under (d), the court has a discretion to admit hearsay evidence. However, the court also has a general discretion to refuse to admit prosecution evidence if, having regard to all the circumstances, including the circumstances in which the evidence was obtained, it would have such an adverse effect on the fairness of the proceedings that the court ought not to admit it under section 78 of the Police and Criminal Evidence Act 1984. Also, under section 126 of the Criminal Justice Act 2003, the court may refuse to admit a statement as evidence of any matter stated in it if made otherwise than in oral evidence in the proceedings and the court is satisfied that the case for excluding it, taking account of the danger that to admit it would result in an undue waste of time, substantially outweighs the case for admitting it, taking account of the value of the evidence. In other words, if the evidence is of little or no probative value and/or simply duplicates oral evidence, the court is unlikely to admit it.

Section 117 governs business and other documents and is now the main provision dealing with the admissibility of computer evidence and this is now described below.

BUSINESS AND OTHER DOCUMENTS

The relevant statutory provisions dealing with the admissibility of business and other documents are contained in section 117 of the Criminal Justice Act 2003. This came into force on 4 April 2005. Section 117 can only apply where the document in question is hearsay. In other words, it recorded something said by, or information provided by, a human being. It does not apply to all evidence recorded by computer or other device, some of which is admissible as 'real evidence', for which, see later.

[1] Law Commission, *Evidence in Criminal Proceedings: Hearsay and Related Topics*, LC 245, 1997.

A statement in a document if admissible as evidence of any matter stated if:

(a) oral evidence given in the proceedings would be admissible as evidence of that matter,

(b) the requirements of section 117(2) are satisfied, and

(c) the requirements of section 117(5) are satisfied in a case where section 117(4) requires them to be (see later).

A 'document' is anything in which information of any description is recorded under section 134. A 'matter stated' is one where the purpose of one of the purposes of the maker of the statement is to cause another person to believe the matter or to cause another person to act or a machine to operate on the basis of the matter as stated: section 115(3).

Section 117(2) requires that:

(a) the document (or part containing the statement) was created or received by a person in the course of a trade, business, profession or other occupation, or as the holder of a paid or unpaid office;

(b) the person who supplied the information contained in the statement (the 'relevant person') had or may reasonably be supposed to have had personal knowledge of the matters dealt with; and

(c) each person (if any) through whom the information was supplied from the relevant person to the person mentioned in paragraph (a) received the information in the course of a trade, business, profession or other occupation, or as the holder of a paid or unpaid office.

The persons mentioned in (a) and (b) may be one and the same person.

These provisions could apply, for example, where bank clerk enters details of financial transactions in a computer or a wages clerk in a company enters hours worked by employees submitted on overtime sheets. It can also apply to information entered by a person in a word processed document or into a spreadsheet, sent as an e-mail or text message, providing this was in the course of a trade or business, etc. Apart from the special case under section 117(4) (see later), there is no need for the person who supplied the information to no longer to be expected to have any recollection of the matters dealt with in the statement. Presumably, this means that even if the person supplying the information still can recollect it, he will not be required to give oral evidence and the document can be tendered in evidence instead. However, where this applies, it would be better for the person who originally supplied the information to give oral evidence of it. He can be subjected to cross-examination and, if he performs well under cross-examination, this is likely to increase the credibility of and weight to be given to the evidence.

Documents prepared for criminal proceedings

Additional requirements for documentary evidence to be admissible are imposed by section 117(5) and (5) where the statement in the document was prepared, under section 117(4), for the purposes of pending or contemplated criminal proceedings, or for criminal investigation (this does not apply in relation to certain provisions relating to obtaining evidence overseas).

There are two possibilities. First, the relevant person is unavailable as a witness in accordance with section 116, for example, where he is dead, unfit to give evidence, outside the UK and it is not reasonably practicable to secure his attendance, where he cannot be found or does not give evidence through fear (subject to the leave of the court). The other possibility is where the relevant person cannot be reasonably expected to have any recollection of the matters dealt with in the statement, having regard to the length of time since he supplied the information and all other circumstances.

Court's discretion not to admit business and other documents

The court has a discretion under section 117(6) and (7) of the Criminal Justice Act 2003 to direct that a statement in a business or other document is not admissible if satisfied that the statement's reliability as evidence for the purpose for which it is tendered is doubtful in view of:

(a) its contents,

(b) the source of the information contained in it,

(c) the way in which or the circumstances in which the information was supplied or received, or

(d) the way in which or circumstances in which the document concerned was created or received.

This last point allows, *inter alia*, the court to exclude a computer document on the ground that there is some doubt as to whether the computer was working properly at the time such that the accuracy of the statement is called into question.

STATEMENTS NOT MADE IN ORAL EVIDENCE WHERE THE WITNESS IS UNAVAILABLE

Section 116 of the Criminal Justice Act 2003 is another provision which can allow the submission of documentary evidence and applies where the maker of the statement is not available because:

(a) he is dead;

(b) he is unfit to give evidence because of his bodily or mental condition;

(c) he is outside the UK and it is not reasonable practicable to secure his attendance;

(d) he cannot be found although such steps as it is reasonably practicable to find him have been taken;

(e) that through fear (widely construed including fear of death or injury of another person or of financial loss) he does not give (or does not continue to give) oral evidence in proceedings, either at all or in connection with the subject matter of the statement, and the court gives leave for the statement to be given in evidence.

In such circumstances, a statement not made in oral evidence is admissible as evidence of any matter stated if oral evidence would be so admissible, the person who made the statement is identified to the court's satisfaction and any one of the five conditions above apply.

Leave may be given under (e) above only if the court considers that statement ought to be admitted in the interests of justice, having regard to a number of factors, being: the contents of the statement, any risk that admission or exclusion will result in unfairness (in particular how difficult it will be to challenge the statement if the person making it does not give oral evidence), whether special measures could be granted to young or incapacitated witnesses and any other relevant circumstances.

Any of the conditions in (a) to (e) above is treated as not being satisfied if the circumstances are caused by the person in support of whose case it is sought to give the statement in evidence or by a person acting on his behalf, so as to prevent the person making the statement giving oral evidence. This could apply, for example, where the witness deliberately leaves the UK in the hope of avoiding giving oral evidence.

REAL EVIDENCE

The above provisions making documentary evidence admissible in criminal proceedings apply only where the documentary evidence is hearsay. Where the evidence is automatically recorded by a computer or other device or machine, without further human intervention, it is real evidence and generally admissible. For example, readings of barometric pressure recorded on a barograph, images recorded by CCTV, the time and date stamp on an e-mail, a barcode scanner in a supermarket and so on.

In *R v Spiby* [1990] 91 Cr App R 186, the appellant was charged with two other offences relating to the importation of controlled drugs. Evidence of computer printouts of telephone calls made from a hotel were tendered in evidence by the prosecution. The actual conversations were not recorded but the time date and number of the hotel room from which the calls had been made were recorded. The computer functioned automatically without the intervention of a human being. Defence counsel sought to challenge the admissibility of the evidence, arguing that sections 68 and 69 of the Police and Criminal Evidence Act 1984 applied (both sections now repealed). The Court of Appeal confirmed that the statutory provisions did not apply as the evidence was real evidence.

Later, in *R v Shepherd* [1993] AC 380, the House of Lords overruled *R v Spiby*, and earlier cases to the same effect, and held that section 69 of the Police and Criminal Evidence Act 1984 applied so as to require proof that the computer was operating properly at the material time in accordance with section 69 in all cases involving computer documents. However, since the repeal of section 69, it seems that *R v Spiby* once again represents good law. In *R (on application of O) v Coventry Justices* [2004] EWHC 905 (Admin) the court confirmed that details of the defendant's credit card transactions and other information recorded automatically when he accessed and attempted to access child pornography sites on and from a website based in Texas, was real evidence and admissible. The evidence raised an inference that the accused was responsible.

Even with real evidence which is prima facie admissible, there is no guarantee that it will be admitted. The court always retains a discretion as to whether evidence should be admitted and, at common law, there is a presumption that a machine was operating correctly at the material time, unless the contrary is shown. This is summed up by the Latin phrase *omnia praesumuntur rite esse acta* (all things are presumed to have been done correctly). If there is evidence to indicate that a computer might not have been operating correctly at the material time so as to cast doubt on the accuracy or correctness of the information or data sought to be admitted as evidence, it is likely that the court will refuse to admit it.

THE RULE AGAINST SELF-INCRIMINATION

There is a general rule of law that a person may refuse to answer a question put to him in court proceedings or refuse to comply with an order of the court if to do so would incriminate him for a criminal offence. This is known as the privilege against self-incrimination. It also applies to excuse a person answering questions which would incriminate his or her spouse or civil partner. There are a number of exceptions to the rule. For example, section 72 of the Supreme Court Act 1981 withdrew the privilege in civil proceedings relating to infringement of intellectual property rights and passing off. Thus, where a search order is obtained in relation to an allegation of civil infringement of an intellectual property right, the defendant cannot refuse access to materials that may tend to show that he has committed criminal offences under intellectual property laws.

Another more limited exception is in section 13 of the Fraud Act 2006 which removes the right to answer questions relating to property but retains the privilege by making statements or admissions made in response inadmissible in evidence against the person making it.

It may be important that the privilege is claimed. In *O Ltd* v *Z* [2005] EWHC 238 (Ch), the claimant company obtained a search order in respect of the home of a former employee. He was suspected to have wrongfully retained computer software belonging to the company. When carrying out the order, the expert appointed to engage in the search found an amount of child pornography. The supervising solicitor, carrying out the search order, made no reference to the privilege against self-incrimination and neither did the ex-employee following consultation with his solicitors. Later, the expert asked the court's permission to hand over the pornographic material to the police and it was at that time that the ex-employee sought to rely on the privilege against self-incrimination. The court directed the expert to hand over the material to the police as the ex-employee, by not claiming the privilege earlier, had already lost the privilege and could not now claim it retrospectively.

COMPUTER FORENSICS

We have seen that, whatever the rules on admissibility of documentary hearsay evidence and real evidence consisting of computer print out or other computer data (such as images), the court has a discretion whether or not to admit the evidence. It is important, therefore, to ensure that a computer or any other equipment used in information and communications technologies records information accurately and completely. It is also important that the information or data can be retrieved from the equipment in such a way that its authenticity and veracity cannot be challenged.

Investigatory authorities need to appreciate that a computer may be set up to erase data when switched off or re-booted. A computer switched on should not be turned off until the whole contents can be imaged, if possible. If the computer under suspicion of containing evidence is not switched on, this should only be done after expert advice. It may be desirable, for example, to remove and duplicate the hard disk. Specialist help and software may be needed to recover files which have been 'deleted', including having been deleted from the recycle bin.

It is advisable in most cases where serious offences are suspected to engage an expert who can give appropriate advice and guidance as to how information or data can be retrieved in its entirety without corruption or modification so that challenges to its authenticity and integrity can be countered.

Consideration must be given to the provisions in the Criminal Justice Act 2003. For example, if it is intended to submit business and other documents under section 117 the pedigree of the document should be established. For example, who was the source of the information, how was it supplied or received and what were the circumstances in which it was created or received.

If real evidence is sought to be admitted, and there is any doubt about the operation of the computer at the relevant time, what evidence is there to show that this did not impair the accuracy of the information or data to be given in evidence.

The Association of Chief Police Officers publishes a guide to good practice in relation to computer forensics.[2] Four principles are set out, being:

■ do not change data which may subsequently be relied on in court;

■ exceptionally, where a person finds it necessary to access original data, that person must be

---

[2] Association of Chief Police Officers, *Good Practice Guide for Computer Based Electronic Evidence*. Incredibly, the guide is undated!

competent to do so and able to give evidence explaining the relevance and implications of his actions;

■ create and preserve an audit trail or other record of all processes applied to electronic evidence – an independent third party should be able to examine those processes and achieve the same results;

■ the person in charge of the investigation should have overall responsibility for ensuring the law and these principles are adhered to.

An important aspect is that it should be clear to the court that the evidence submitted is exactly the same as when it was first taken into the custody of the police (or other investigatory authority such as HM Revenue and Customs). The ideal, which may not always be possible or practicable, given the storage capacity of modern electronic or magnetic storage data, is to make an exact duplicate or image of the storage media on the target equipment. It is important that the continuity and integrity of the evidence can be demonstrated to the court. For example, by showing how the evidence was obtained and preserved so that an independent third party could go through technically sound processes to end up with the same results.

SUMMARY

■ Hearsay evidence is evidence given others than the person having first hand knowledge it.

■ Hearsay evidence may be admitted in criminal proceedings only if:
  – Chapter 2 of Part 11 of the Criminal Justice Act 2003 or other statutory provision allows it;
  – rules of law preserved by section 118 of the Criminal Justice Act 2003 allows it;
  – all the parties agree; or
  – the court is satisfied it is in the interests of justice to admit it.

■ The court has a general discretion not to admit prosecution evidence.

■ Computer documents created by human beings are hearsay.

■ Business and other documents may be admissible under section 117 of the Criminal Justice Act 2003 if:
  – they were created or received in the course of a trade or business, etc.;
  – the person supplying the statement could reasonably be supposed to have personal knowledge of the matters dealt with;
  – intermediaries received the statement in the course of a trade or business, etc.

■ Statements may be admissible where the witness is unavailable.

■ Information recorded automatically is not hearsay evidence but is real evidence and admissible.

■ There are exceptions to the rule against self-incrimination.

■ Computer forensics are important to ensure evidence is admissible, for example:
  – that it has not been modified;
  – that its pedigree is fully documented;
  – that an expert can explain how the evidence was obtained and preserved.

SELF-TEST QUESTIONS

Note: there is only one correct answer to each multiple choice question.

1 **Which one of the following is NOT a valid reason for admitting hearsay evidence under the Criminal Justice Act 2003?**

   (a) The court is satisfied that it is in the interests of justice that the evidence should be admitted.

   (b) Chapter 2 of Part 11 of the Criminal Justice Act 2003 or any other statutory provision allows it to be admitted.

   (c) The defendant alone has given his consent to it being admitted.

   (d) Certain rules of law preserved by section 118 of the Criminal Justice Act 2003, such as the rule relating to public information, allow it to be admitted.

2 **Which one of the following descriptions CORRECTLY describes the evidential status of computer data where the computer is set up to record automatically details, such as credit card details, entered in an online form?**

   (a) It is evidence admissible because the witness is unavailable.

   (b) It is hearsay evidence.

   (c) It is inadmissible as it is a business document.

   (d) It is real evidence.

3 **What issues are important in relation to obtaining and preserving computer evidence so that it is likely to be ruled admissible in criminal proceedings if this is challenged by the defence?**

   In answering this question, you may find it useful to look at the Association of Chief Police Officers *Good Practice Guide for Computer Based Electronic Evidence,* **currently available at: http://www.acpo.police.uk/asp/policies/Data/gpg_computer_based_evidence_v3.pdf**

For further resources and updates please go to the Companion Website accompanying this book at **www.mylawchamber.co.uk/bainbridgeIT**

29

Computer evidence and forensics

Part 5

Data protection and freedom of information

Information technology heightens fears about a society of the kind portrayed in George Orwell's *1984*, because of the power of computers in terms of information processing. Even now, there remains a feeling shared by some that computers undermine human skills and that the growth of computer technology heralds the dawn of an austere and coldly logical society. Certainly, the power of computers can be misused and there needs to be a system of checks and balances to prevent abuse of this power. In particular, computers and information processing raise concerns about individuals and their privacy.

Until recently there was no general right to privacy under English law although some legal remedies may have been, and continue to be, available in some circumstances, such as an action for breach of confidence or publishing defamatory material, or the limited protection afforded by the Data Protection Act 1984. Things have changed enormously. The UK finally got round to bringing the European Convention on Human Rights into force on 4 November 2000 (the full title of the Convention is the Convention for the Protection of Human Rights and Fundamental Freedoms, agreed by the Council of Europe at Rome, 4 November 1950). Another Council of Europe Convention is the Convention for the Protection of Individuals with regard to Processing of Personal Data, Strasbourg, 28 January 1981. This latter Convention, which in its Preamble refers to the importance of protecting individuals' rights and freedoms, especially the right of privacy in respect of transborder flows of personal data, can be seen as either supplementary to the Human Rights Convention or as an application of that Convention in a specific context.

The Strasbourg Convention justified and underpinned subsequent developments in data protection law. It was the basis of the UK's Data Protection Act 1984 (now replaced by the Data Protection Act 1998). The European Directive on data protection, from which the 1998 Act derives its force, can be seen as an updating of the Strasbourg Convention in line with the Human Rights Convention. Theoretically, there should be no conflict between the two though, in some cases, litigants may choose the Human Rights Convention on which to base their grievance. For example, Princess Caroline of Monaco brought an action for invasion of privacy by the paparazzi under the Human Rights Convention in *von Hannover* v *Germany* [2005] 40 EHRR 1.

Under section 2 of the Human Rights Act 1998, primary and secondary legislation must, as far as it is possible to do so, be given effect in a way compatible with rights under the Human Rights Convention. This is retrospective. Thus, if a provision of the Data Protection Act 1998 is in conflict with the Human Rights Convention or, for example, a decision of the European

Court of Human Rights, the Act should be interpreted in the light of the Convention. If it cannot be interpreted in accordance with the Convention and there is a clear conflict, a court (in England and Wales, the House of Lords, the High Court or the Court of Appeal) may make a declaration of incompatibility under section 4 of the Human Rights Act 1998. It would then be for Parliament to consider modifying the legislation.

The Data Protection Act 1984, in line with the Strasbourg Convention, only applied to automatically processed personal data. The European Directive on data protection made significant changes to the model of data protection and even extended to certain forms of manual processing, basing its legitimacy on the Human Rights Convention and two of the key features of that Convention, being the right to privacy under Article 8 and the right of freedom of expression under Article 10. Balancing these two, sometime contradictory rights, has not proven easy. Both of the rights contain derogations, for example, both rights can be suppressed in the interests of national security if prescribed by law and necessary in a democratic society.

Data protection law can be truly said to be voluminous with the Data Protection Act 1998, which is a large and complex piece of legislation and numerous statutory instruments made under it. The Act and some of the statutory instruments have been subject to modification and the whole must be interpreted in line with the data protection Directive and the Human Rights Convention, where applicable. There is also a great deal of guidance on data protection law and, taken altogether, it is easy to criticise the breathtaking size and scope of data protection law as taking a sledgehammer to crack a walnut. Most reasonable organisations in the public and private sectors would, as a matter of course, adopt effective and fair systems for their data processing activities, as this is largely a reflection of good practice. However, the dangers posed by the processing of personal data, which may be unfairly processed, inaccurate, out of date or disclosed in a harmful way, are very serious. Furthermore, the reality is that, for the majority of organisations and persons processing personal data, compliance is not onerous and there may be savings available, for example, by destroying or erasing old, irrelevant and inaccurate data and ensuring that good levels of data security are adhered to, including processing by contractors and by sub-contractors.

Readers may be a little confused by some of the terminology which has changed. Originally, the person responsible for data protection was known as the Data Protection Registrar (Eric Howe was the first Registrar). Following the 1998 Act, the position became known as the Data Protection Commissioner (Elizabeth France was in position as this and the following change took place). Following the introduction of the Freedom of Information Act 2000 (being brought into force in stages), the position is now known as the Information Commissioner. He is responsible for data protection law, freedom of information law, privacy in electronic communications and environmental information regulations. The present incumbent is Richard Thomas, the third to be responsible for data protection law in the UK. A tribunal set up originally under the 1984 Act as the Data Protection Tribunal is now known as the Information Tribunal. Other changes in terminology will be noted in relevant places in the following chapters.

Apart from looking at data protection law, this part of the book examines other aspects of the responsibilities falling within the ambit of the Information Commissioner, including freedom of information, environmental information and privacy in electronic communications.

30 Introduction to data protection law

INTRODUCTION

Data protection law affects everybody. Most persons process information about individuals, even if it is simply name, address and telephone number. Many do this by computer, PDA (personal digital assistant) or mobile phone. But data protection law does not stop at personal data processed by electronic means. A great many people have manual filing systems containing information relating to individuals. These may be in the form of a card index system or even a simple address book. Until the 1998 Act, data protection law did not apply to manual processing but it now applies to certain types of manual filing systems. Even if we do not process personal information, it is almost certain that numerous organisations and persons are processing personal information relating to us. Indeed, there can be very few persons who are not affected by data protection law as being the subject of data processed by others. The identities of some of those who process our personal data are easy to guess such as employers, health providers, banks, local authorities, government bodies and creditors. Others who process personal data relating to us are less easy to know specifically in advance, such as organisations involved in direct marketing.

Data protection law has two main influences. First, those who process information concerning individuals are subject to a regulatory framework within which they can process personal data lawfully. Secondly, as individuals we all have rights under data protection law, enhanced by the 1998 Act and, in some cases, supplemented or strengthened by the Human Rights Convention.[1] As this area of law has changed, the rights of individuals are given more prominence and a key phrase is 'transparency of processing'. Individuals should be better informed as to who is processing data relating to them, what the purpose of the processing is and what other processing activities are involved. They also have a right to more information than before in response to a request for access and greater rights to control processing activity. As we shall see, transparency of processing is often compromised, to a greater or lesser extent.

There are many horror stories about people who have had information wrongly attributed to them and stored on computer. For example, a man with an impeccable character and without any convictions at all was arrested and charged with driving whilst disqualified because of incorrect information stored on the Police National Computer. Details about the disqualification had been entered against his name by mistake. He lost his job and had his car impounded. It took him four months to trace the man to whom the previous conviction related and whose name was very similar before he could clear his name (*The Times*, 8 May 1990, p. 4). A more recent example, though of less serious consequences, was the case of *Ogle* v *Chief Constable of Thames Valley Police* [2001] EWCA Civ 598. The claimant had been disqualified from driving for four years following

---

[1] Council of Europe Convention for the Protection of Human Rights and Fundamental Freedoms, 1950, as amended.

drink-driving offences but this was subsequently reduced on appeal to two years. Unfortunately, the reduction of the ban was not recorded on the Police National Computer and, some time after the two years had expired, the claimant was arrested for driving whilst disqualified by a different police authority and he was detained for two and half hours before being released. However, as the claimant had previously accepted a settlement of £950 for wrongful arrest, his later attempt to re-open the case on the basis of a claim for distress under the Data Protection Act 1984 was rejected.

Another problem has been the lack of control of organisations who pass on personal information to others, resulting in many people having been inundated with unsolicited mail, faxes and e-mails. A more sinister aspect of computer-stored information is a direct result of the powerful processing capacity of computers and the ability to use computers to target certain groups of individuals or to build profiles about our preferences and spending habits. There are also serious issues associated with the processing of sensitive personal data stored on computers or in structured manual files and the collection, storage and disclosure of sensitive personal data needs to be subject to special safeguards and should only be processed in limited circumstances.

As information and communications technologies becomes progressively more powerful and more use is made of these technologies, the dangers are set to increase. Numerous concerns have been expressed in the past by the Information Commissioner and others. For example, some data may be very sensitive and may cause considerable harm if its use is not strictly controlled such as data relating to genetic information or illnesses and diseases. Other concerns flow from the use of 'white data' showing that a person has a good credit record and the activities of private investigators has caused concern in the past and continues to do so. Other issues relate to the balance between freedom of speech and individuals' right to privacy, two areas of apparently diametrically opposed interests always very difficult to reconcile. Nor is computer technology the only threat. The Economic League was an organisation which retained details of individuals who had been active trade unionists or members of the Communist Party. All this data was kept on paper. The Data Protection Act 1984 had no effect upon such data processing – it had to be by automatic means. Structured manual files can pose just as many problems as automated processing activities. Other recent concerns relate to identity cards and the disclosure of air traffic passenger data, the latter prompting a European Directive on passenger data.[2]

The Data Protection Act 1984 received the Royal Assent at an appropriate time in Orwellian terms. It was designed to control the storage and use of information about individuals stored and processed by computer. Control of processing was provided for by a system of registration with penalties for failing to register and for acting beyond the scope of the registration. Additionally, the Act introduced a set of *Data Protection Principles*, derived from the Council of Europe's Convention for the protection of individuals with regard to automatic processing of personal data, which must be followed by persons who store or process information, using computers, about living persons. Computer bureaux providing services to those who process such information were also controlled and were required to register under the 1984 Act. Individuals, about whom information was stored on computer, were given rights of access and a right to have inaccurate records corrected or deleted. Under certain circumstances, individuals had a right to compensation.

The history leading up to the 1984 Act was relatively long and there were several Parliamentary Bills, Reports and White Papers concerning privacy and data protection. The Lindop Report[3] was important in respect of moves towards legislation. The final impetus was

---

[2] Council Directive 2004/82/EC of 29 April 2004 on the obligation of carriers to communicate passenger data, OJ L 261, 06.08.2004, p. 24.

[3] *Report of the Committee on Data Protection*, Cmnd 7341, HMSO, 1978.

provided by the Council of Europe's Convention for the Protection of Individuals with Regard to Automatic Processing of Personal Data, signed by the UK in 1981 and ratified in 1987. The Convention included principles for data protection and proposed a common set of standards. In 1982, a White Paper was published, outlining the government's intentions (Cmnd 8539) and following this a Bill was introduced in the House of Lords. However, this failed to become law because of the general election of 1983 and a new Bill was introduced after the election and eventually received the Royal Assent in July 1984. The Data Protection Act 1984 was implemented in stages, the last of which mainly concerned individuals' rights of access and which came into effect on 11 November 1987.

In this chapter, following a brief discussion of the data protection Directive, the catalyst for the current model of data protection law throughout the European Economic Area, the background to the Data Protection Act 1998 is described. Next the data protection principles are stated and there follows a look at the definitions contained in the Act. These are key to determining the scope and reach of data protection law. The work of the Information Commissioner is then considered, followed by material on the Information Tribunal and the Working Party set up under the data protection Directive.

THE DATA PROTECTION DIRECTIVE

In the context of a single European market, it is essential that there should be no barriers to the transfer of information between Member States. The principle of freedom of movement of goods and services has been largely achieved and it would be unthinkable if, in this age of information technology, the same freedom of movement did not apply to computer data. However, not all the Member States complied with the European Convention for the protection of individuals with regard to automatic processing of personal data. Being conscious of the possibility that Member States of the European Community could erect barriers to the flows of computer data on the basis of insufficient protection for individuals in other Member States, the Commission worked towards a Directive laying down a basic framework for the protection of personal data whilst stressing the freedom of movement of personal data. The argument is that, if all Member States adhered to a reasonable standard of protection of personal data, there should be no barriers to the movement of personal data within the Community. The other countries in the European Economic Area (EEA) – Norway, Iceland and Liechtenstein – also agreed to comply with the Directive so, effectively, there are no barriers to the free movement of personal data throughout the EEA.

A proposal for a Directive on the protection of individuals in relation to the processing of personal data was published in 1990[4] and provided a complex system differentiating between the public and private sector as was then the position in some countries such as the Netherlands. A further proposal was published in 1992.[5] The distinction between the public and private sector disappeared but this particular proposal was perceived by data users as being unduly restrictive and extremely onerous to comply with. Particular concerns were directed at the extension of data protection law to manual files, the requirements to inform data subjects and, in some cases, the need to seek data subjects' consent to processing. A survey carried out for the Home Office in the UK indicated that compliance would cost the 625 organisations included in the survey at least £2 bn[6] whilst the Department of Health estimated that it would be necessary to inform every

---

[4] COM(90) 314 final – SYN 287, OJ C 277, 05.11.1990, p. 3.
[5] COM(92) 24 final – SYN 393, OJ C 311, 27.11.1992, p. 38.
[6] *Costs of Implementing the Data Protection Directive: Paper by the United Kingdom,* Home Office, 1994.

member of the population that it held personal data concerning them and that this would cost over £1 bn.[7]

The Commission responded to some of the concerns of data users and changes were made to reduce the financial burden whilst retaining the principle of protecting the individuals' rights of privacy. Furthermore, a survey carried out for the Commission by the author of this book and a number of colleagues at Aston University and the University of Leiden indicated that the above costs were exaggerated. Eventually, the Directive was adopted in July 1995 although the UK abstained in the vote. The full title of the Directive is Directive 95/46/EC of the European Parliament and of the Council on the protection of individuals with regard to the processing of personal data and of the free movement of such data.[8] In December 1999, the Commission decided to take five Member States to the European Court of Justice for failing to implement the Directive, these being France, Ireland, Germany, Luxembourg and the Netherlands. All have since implemented the Directive.

Model of data protection under the Directive

The Directive has, under Article 1, the twin aims of protecting privacy in the context of processing personal data and providing for the freedom of movement of personal data. Article 1 states:

1   In accordance with this Directive Member States shall protect the fundamental rights and free-doms of natural persons, and in particular their right of privacy, with respect to the processing of personal data.
2   Member States shall neither restrict nor prohibit the free flow of personal data between Member States for reasons connected with the protection afforded under paragraph 1.

In other words, providing Member States have complied with the requirements of the Directive there must be freedom of movement of personal data throughout the Community, at least no barriers can be erected on the grounds of privacy concerns.

Although the Directive marks a significant change in data protection law, it has at its heart the data protection principles in Article 6. These derive from the European Convention for the protection of individuals with regard to automatic processing of personal data, supplemented by a Protocol to the Convention. The data protection principles provide a common link between the new law and that under the 1984 Act. Thus, fair and lawful processing must be ensured, personal data must be processed only for specified purposes, the data must be adequate, relevant and not excessive, they must be accurate and up-to-date and not kept in a form which permits identification of the data subject for longer than necessary. Nevertheless, and reflecting the changes to data protection law, the mechanism of protection under the Directive is, it is fair to say, more complex than that under the Data Protection Act 1984. It is shown in Fig. 30.1.

Although the definitions used in the Directive and the Data Protection Act 1998 are described below, for the purposes of understanding the diagram, suffice it to say that the data controller is the person who decides the purposes and manner of processing, the processor is a person who processes personal data on behalf of the data controller, the data subject is the individual to whom the personal data in question relate, a third country is a country outside the EEA. The Information Commissioner is responsible, amongst other things, for supervising compliance with the Act and a third party is any person other than a data controller, processor or employee or agent of either.

---

[7] *Draft EC Proposed Directive on Data Protection: Analysis of Costs,* Department of Health, 1994.
[8] OJ L 281, 23.11.1995, p. 31.

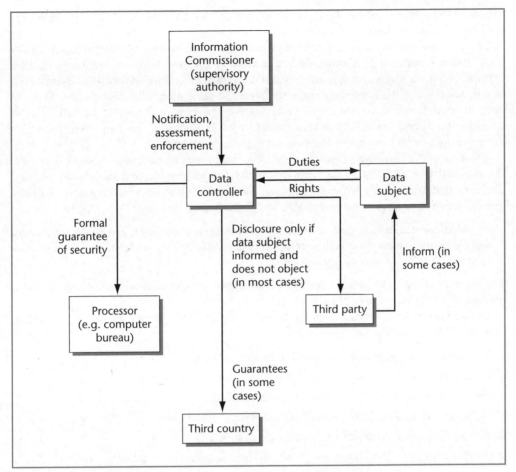

Figure 30.1 Model of data protection under the data protection Directive

Unless exempt, data controllers are required to notify their processing activities to the supervisory authority (the Information Commissioner in the UK). Where the processing in question is likely to pose specific risks to rights and freedoms, the processing operation must be examined before it can commence. The Directive permits exemption from or simplification of notification where the processing is unlikely to affect the rights and freedoms of data subjects or where an 'in-house' data protection official (data protection supervisor) is appointed. Data controllers can only process personal data if they fall within one of a number of conditions. One of a further number of conditions must be satisfied where the personal data are 'sensitive', for example, relating to racial or ethnic origin, health, political or religious beliefs. Further duties are imposed on data controllers to inform data subjects. Data subjects are given rights of access and rights to object to processing and to prevent processing in some cases. They are also given certain additional rights in respect of automated decision taking and rights of rectification, erasure or blocking of data, the processing of which does not comply with the Directive.

Security obligations are imposed on a data controller and, where a data controller engages a processor, such as a computer bureau or a company to provide IT facilities management services, equivalent security obligations must be imposed on the processor. This must be by contractual means or by some other legal act and be in writing or equivalent form. Transfers to countries outside the EEA may be allowed only under certain conditions if the country in question does not have adequate protection for personal data.

The Directive also applies to structured manual files which, because of their structure, make it easy to access personal data belonging to a particular individual. However, there are a number of important derogations and options provided for in the Directive which allow for its impact to be lessened somewhat. Particularly important were the derogations allowing Member States to delay the implementation of the Directive to processing already under way at 24 October 1998 (the date the Directive should have been implemented into domestic law) and to further delay the impact of certain parts of the Directive on manual processing.

A feature of the Directive is that the definitions used are fairly wide. For example, it is clear that personal data can include image data or sound data, providing the data subject can be identified from that data or from that data and other data which the data controller has or may obtain. The definition of processing is breathtakingly wide, including:

> ... collection, recording, organisation, storage, adaptation or alteration, retrieval, consultation, use, disclosure by transmission, dissemination or otherwise making available, alignment or combination, blocking, erasure or destruction.

The presence of the word 'storage' indicates that simply being in possession of personal data is processing for the purposes of the Directive.

To summarise, issues flowing from the Directive which caused particular concern in the lead up to the Data Protection Act 1998 were:

- the extension of data protection law to some manual files;
- the requirement to inform data subjects on collection of data or otherwise;
- the possibility of data subjects objecting to processing;
- having to seek data subjects' consent to processing in some cases;
- the introduction of conditions for processing to proceed;
- possible constraints over transfers of personal data to countries outside the EEA;
- security of processing of personal data; and
- controls over automated decision making.

In the remainder of this chapter and the following two chapters, the provisions of the Data Protection Act 1998 will be examined. Where appropriate, the provisions of the Directive will be discussed though, generally, it must be noted that the 1998 Act appears to be a reasonably faithful implementation of the Directive. The UK took advantage of many (though not all) of the derogations and options available in the Directive. Some of the cases mentioned in this and following two chapters were decided under the 1984 Act. Some are no longer relevant: for example, *R v Brown* [1996] 1 AC 543, an unsatisfactory decision under the 1984 Act by the House of Lords which has been overtaken by the wider definition of processing. But others remain very valuable in determining the scope of the new law: for example, *Innovations (Mail Order) Ltd v Data Protection Registrar* (unreported) 29 September 1993, concerning fair processing. Cases under the 1984 Act will only be discussed where they are still relevant or for comparative purposes only.

THE DATA PROTECTION ACT 1998

The Data Protection Bill was introduced in the House of Lords in January 1998. During its passage through the Lords and, later, through the House of Commons, it underwent many changes.

For example, as first printed, the Bill had no specific provisions for transitional arrangements and the conditions for processing sensitive data were inadequate. The Act finally received the Royal Assent on 16 July 1998. Some provisions came into force immediately, being primarily concerned with the definitions under the Act and the arrangements to make Regulations under the Act. The remaining provisions of the Act came into force on 1 March 2000, apart from section 56 making enforced subject access an offence. This section is dependent upon certain provisions of the Police Act 1997 coming into force but because of subsequent changes, it now looks unlikely that section 56 of the Data Protection Act 1998 will come into force for the time being. There was no express provision in the Directive concerning enforced subject access. Around 30 statutory instruments have been made under the Act and the Act has itself already gone through numerous modifications. The statutory instruments and changes will be mentioned in this and the following two chapters if appropriate.

Before looking at the data protection principles, the definitions and other provisions of the Act, it must be noted that the Act is not the only source of constraints and controls on the collection, processing and use of personal data. Other areas of law may be highly relevant. For example, a person holding personal data may have an obligation of confidence not to disclose the data or a fiduciary duty in relation to them. Disclosure may be allowed only in a limited number of situations as is the case in banking where rules concerning when personal data may be disclosed were laid down in *Tournier* v *National Provincial* [1924] 1 KB 461. In that case, it was held that disclosure of confidential information could proceed where the interests of the bank required disclosure. However, it is an old case and it is arguable whether it would be applied without modification in the present climate of greater respect for individuals' rights and freedoms. Disclosure may otherwise be lawful if the individual consents or where the disclosure is in the public interest or where it is required by law. The laws of copyright and defamation may also restrict the use and disclosure of information relating to individuals.

THE DATA PROTECTION PRINCIPLES

The data protection principles are at the root of data protection law and they are contained in Part I of Schedule 1 to the Act. Part II of the Schedule provides interpretation of the principles. The principles appear much as before although there are some important differences. They are as follows.

1 Personal data shall be processed fairly and lawfully and, in particular, shall not be processed unless –
   (a) at least one of the conditions in Schedule 2 is met, and
   (b) in the case of sensitive personal data, at least one of the conditions in Schedule 3 is also met.
2 Personal data shall be obtained only for one or more specified and lawful purposes and shall not be further processed in any manner incompatible with that purpose or those purposes.
3 Personal data shall be adequate, relevant and not excessive in relation to the purpose or purposes for which they are processed.
4 Personal data shall be accurate and, where necessary, kept up to date.
5 Personal data processed for any purpose or purposes shall not be kept for longer than is necessary for that purpose or those purposes.
6 Personal data shall be processed in accordance with the rights of data subjects under this Act.
7 Appropriate technical and organisational measures shall be taken against unauthorised or unlawful processing of personal data and against accidental loss or destruction of, or damage to, personal data.

30

Introduction to data protection law

8 Personal data shall not be transferred to a country or territory outside the European Economic Area unless that country or territory ensures an adequate level of protection for the rights and freedoms of data subjects in relation to the processing of personal data.

The first principle refers to conditions for processing. It is without a doubt the most important – that processing shall be fair and lawful – and it could be said that the rest of data protection law merely fleshes this out and provides the detail of just what fair and lawful processing is. The second principle concerns the purposes of processing and is, in part, to do with transparency. As, unless exempt, the purposes are noted in a public register, data subjects should know the sorts of data processing activities carried out by a data controller. Compliance with the first principle requires that at least one of the conditions in Schedule 2 applies and, in the case of sensitive personal data, at least one of the conditions in Schedule 3 applies. These conditions for processing are described fully in the following chapter. They include matters such as the data subject's consent and processing for the data controller's legitimate purposes. If none of the conditions apply in Schedule 2 (also Schedule 3 for sensitive personal data) then processing within the scope of the Act may not be carried out at all. Data controllers must be able to point to one condition in Schedule 2 and, if relevant, also Schedule 3.

Principles 3 and 4 relate to data quality and should reflect good processing practices. At the time of the introduction of the Community Charge ('poll tax') a number of local authorities were collecting excessive information about individuals. In *Rhondda BC v Data Protection Registrar* (unreported) 11 October 1991, the tribunal confirmed that asking for individuals' dates of birth was excessive and in *CCRO of Runneymede BC v Data Protection Registrar* (unreported) 1990, the tribunal confirmed that asking for information relating to types of property was excessive.

Principle 5 requires that data controllers do not keep personal data unnecessarily long. How long is 'necessary' will depend on the circumstances. For example, it may be reasonable for an employer to retain data on ex-employees for a few years, for example, for the purposes of providing new potential employers with references. In *R (on application of S)* v *Chief Constable of South Yorkshire* [2004] 4 All ER 193, it was argued that the retention of fingerprints and DNA samples of persons who had not been subsequently convicted of an offence was not contrary to Article 8 of the Human Rights Convention. The fingerprints and samples had been lawfully taken under section 64(1A) of the Police and Criminal Evidence Act 1984. The aim of the underlying policy was the prevention and detection of crime, the investigation of offences, facilitating prosecutions and exculpating the innocent and dealing with miscarriages of justice. Similar considerations ought to apply in respect of data protection law and the interaction between principle 5, other principles and the exemptions under the Data Protection Act 1998, in particular those relating to the prevention and detection of crime.

Data subjects' rights are covered by principle 6. These include rights of access, right to information, rights to have inaccurate data rectified, etc. and are discussed in detail in Chapter 32. The seventh principle is concerned with security. Following a number of thefts of computers from doctors' surgeries, the then Data Protection Registrar warned general practitioners to review their security arrangements otherwise they could be in breach of the security principle (*The Times*, 2 December 1992, at p. 3). Principle 8 reflects concerns about transfers of personal data to countries that do not have adequate protection.

The principles and their interpretation will be discussed in greater depth in the following chapters. It is considered to be useful, however, to let readers have sight of them now and to stress that it is the principles which underpin data protection law.

DEFINITIONS

The definitions are very significant and they set out the scope of the new law. The most important definitions are contained in section 1 of the Act. For the Act to apply, the data must fall within the definition of data and also be personal data as defined. The processing activities involved must be within the meaning of processing. The individual definitions are now considered.

Data

'*data*' means information which –
(a) is being processed by means of equipment operating automatically in response to instructions given for that purpose,
(b) is recorded with the intention that it should be processed by means of such equipment,
(c) is recorded as part of a relevant filing system or with the intention that it should form part of a relevant filing system,
(d) does not fall within paragraph (a), (b) or (c) but forms part of an accessible record as defined by section 68, or
(e) is recorded information held by a public authority and does not fall within any of the paragraphs (a) to (d).

The meaning in (e) was added by the Freedom of Information Act 2000 as from 1 January 2005. This is in relation to a right of access to unstructured personal data held by public authorities. Because access to certain information held by public authorities is now available, the addition of (e) to the meaning of data invokes the protection of any personal data contained in such information, such as constraints over disclosures.

Data within (a) and (b) above are those which are being or are to be processed by automatic means; in other words, computer data. Data within (c) are those in structured manual filing systems ('relevant filing system' is defined below). These are the data to which data protection law has been extended by the Act. The inclusion of such data was seen as one of the most costly provisions in the new law to implement.

Accessible records within (d) above are health records and certain educational and local authority records; these are caught by the new law even if they are processed manually and are not structured within the meaning required for a relevant filing system. The inclusion of such data is to incorporate the effect of the Access to Personal Files Act 1987. This Act gave a right of access to certain local authority files, such as social services files and housing files, and was repealed in full. Access to health records which was covered by the Access to Health Records Act 1990 is also included in the new law. Where local authority files or health records are processed by computer, they are treated in the same way as other data under the 1998 Act.

Automatically processed data are treated somewhat differently than data in relevant filing systems within (c) above and accessible records within (d) above. In particular, only automatic processing need be notified unless specifically exempt (although provision exists for a preliminary assessment to be carried out which could extend to all forms of processing).

Personal data

'*personal data*' means data which relate to a living individual who can be identified –
(a) from those data, or

(b) from those data and other information which is in the possession of, or likely to come into
      the possession of, the data controller,
and includes any expression of opinion about the individual and any indication of the intentions
of the data controller or any other person in respect of the individual.

There was some doubt as to whether the Directive intended to restrict personal data to living individuals but the 1998 Act puts this beyond doubt. The definition confirms that it is not necessary for all the identifying data to be subject to the processing activity. It is enough for there to be further information which the person processing the data has or will obtain and which, together with the data being processed, is sufficient to identify an individual. For example, a computer database may not include names but might, instead, operate on individuals' national insurance numbers. If the person processing the data also has a card index which contains national insurance numbers and the names of the individuals to whom they belong, that is sufficient for the data being processing by computer to be classified as personal data.

The personal data does not have to be in the form of text. It is the fact that a specific individual is identifiable that is important. Thus, a photograph, film and/or a recording of speech could be personal data within the meaning of the Act. It may be that identification requires other data and this is covered by the definition. For example, a data controller may have a set of numbered photographs of individuals and a card index relating the photographs to named persons.

'Personal data' includes expressions of opinion and any indication of intentions. It might be difficult to distinguish between an expression of opinion and a statement of intention. 'The performance of Joe Bloggs as a sale executive indicates that it is unlikely that he will be promoted in the near future' is an example. But as both opinion and intentions are covered, there is no problem. There is an exemption from the subject access and information provisions which applies to management planning. This might grant exemption in relation to intentions though not opinions.

In *Durant* v *Financial Services Authority* [2004] FSR 573, the Court of Appeal gave some guidance as the scope of 'personal data'. The court held that two factors were relevant. First, was the information biographic in a significant sense going beyond the recording of the individual's involvement in a matter or event that has no personal connotations (a life event in respect of which the individual's privacy could not be said to be compromised)? Did the information concern the individual's privacy? The second factor was one of focus: did the information have the individual as its focus rather than someone else with whom that person may have been involved or some event in which he may have had an involvement or interest? The court drew support for this narrow interpretation by the inclusion of expressions of opinion and statements of intention in the definition of personal data. If a wider meaning were to be taken, it would not be necessary to expressly include such expressions or statements.

Relevant filing system

Manually processed personal data can pose dangers if the files containing the data are set up in such a way that it is quick and easy to retrieve specific information about a particular individual. Hence the need to place such filing systems within the ambit of data protection law and this is the purposes of the definition of relevant filing system.

'*relevant filing system*' means any set of information relating to individuals to the extent that, although the information is not processed by means of equipment operating automatically in response to instructions given for that purpose, the set is structured, either by reference to individuals or by reference to criteria relating to individuals, in such a way that specific information relating to a particular individual is readily accessible.

The requirement is that personal data are easily accessible because of the structure, such as in the case of a *pro forma* application form. This is confirmed in the Directive and recital 15 thereto, which emphasises ease of access by virtue of structure. Clearly a card index system where each card bears an individual's name on the top, the cards being stored in name order, will be a relevant filing system. It would appear that a file relating to a specific individual containing, for example, only correspondence to and from that individual will not be deemed to be a relevant filing system. The Home Office view was that some internal structure also is required. However, it is possible that a simple address book set out in alphabetical order is caught by the new law. If this contains name, address, telephone number and e-mail address it is at least arguable that it is a relevant filing system as it enables ease of access to information relating to any particular individual. Furthermore, it probably will have some form of internal structure: for example, it may have two columns, the left-hand column containing a name followed below by an address; the right-hand column might have telephone numbers and the like. Fortunately, if a simple address book is a relevant filing system, as such it does not have to be the subject of formal notification to the Information Commissioner, as we shall see. Note that accessible records in the definition of data are caught by the new law even though they are not processed automatically, nor intended to be processed automatically, and are not structured.

The Court of Appeal considered the meaning of relevant filing system in *Durant v Financial Services Authority* [2004] FSR 573. Manual filing systems were within the meaning of relevant filing system only if broadly equivalent to a computer file or database because their structure permits ready access to information constituting personal data. The fact that a manual file has an individual's name is not sufficient if the data controller has to leaf through documents to see if there are any references to the data subject in a time-consuming and costly manner. As well as being indexed by individual names or unique identifiers the files must have some internal structure giving quick and easy access to specific data relating to a particular individual. The court held that a relevant filing system is one where:

- the constituent files are structured or referenced so as to make it clear at the outset whether personal data relating to an individual is held within the system and, if that is so, in which file or files they are held; and where

- the system has, as part of its own structure or referencing system, a method, sufficiently sophisticated and detailed, to readily indicate whether and where in an individual file or files, specific criteria or information about the data subject can be readily located.

In the present case, the Financial Service Authority's manual filing systems were not relevant filing systems. They were unstructured and did not contain indexing mechanisms to enable location of particular documents and personal data concerning the claimant.

Data controller

Data controllers have to comply with the data protection principles and are required to notify their processing activities under the Act unless exempt. There are a number of exemptions to the principles and certain forms of processing are exempt from the notification requirements. The definition of data controller is as follows.

> '*data controller*' means … a person who (either alone or jointly or in common with other persons) determines the purposes for which and the manner in which any personal data are, or are to be, processed.

There may be two or more data controllers in respect of a single collection of personal data: for example, where an association of builders mutually share and are responsible for a central

30

Introduction to data protection law

database of sub-contractors and suppliers. The significance of the phrase 'jointly or in common with other persons' is that if two or more data controllers agree between themselves as to the purposes and manner of processing, then they determine these matters jointly. However, if two or more data controllers have access to a central database, say a data warehouse, but they each have their own individual purposes and manner of processing, then they determine these matters in common. For example, Company A has a large database of actual and potential customers and uses this to extract information relating to creditworthiness of customers placing orders. Company A also allows Company B to access the database which it uses to identify potential customers for a marketing campaign and to print out addressed envelopes for the campaign.

Where personal data are processed only for purposes for which they are required by or under any enactment to be processed, the person on whom the obligation to process the data is imposed by or under that enactment is for the purposes of the Act considered to be the data controller under section 1(4). Thus, for example, the Chartered Institute of Patent Agents is required, under the Registered Patent Agent Rules 1990 as amended, to keep a register of patent agents and, for the purposes of that register, the Institute is the data controller.

Data subject

A data subject is the person to whom personal data relate or refer to. The use of the term 'individual' shows that data subjects must be human beings and artificial legal persons such as companies are not data subjects. The Directive referred to a data subject as an identified or identifiable natural person. In the Act the definition is simply:

'data subject' means an individual who is the subject of personal data.

Processing

Processing is very widely defined and almost anything that can be done with data falls within the meaning which does not attempt to be completely exhaustive. Processing, in relation to information or data means:

obtaining, recording or holding the information or data or carrying out any operation or set of operations on the information or data, including –
(a) organisation, adaptation or alteration of the information or data,
(b) retrieval, consultation or use of the information or data,
(c) disclosure of the information or data by transmission, dissemination or otherwise making available, or
(d) alignment, combination, blocking, erasure or destruction of the information or data.

Note that processing covers information as well as data. The Directive does not distinguish between the two and it is probably unnecessary to make any distinction between the two and to do so probably reflects the formula under the 1984 Act, as if information was something that was contained in data. This is reinforced by section 1(2) which goes on to say that obtaining, recording, using or disclosing data extends to the information contained within the data. In determining whether information is to be processed by automatic means or form part of a relevant filing system, under section 1(3), it is intended that it should be so processed or form part of such a system after being transferred to a country or territory outside the EEA.

The definition extends to 'holding' personal data (the Directive uses the term 'storage' instead). This means that simply being in possession of personal data will be processing for the purposes of the Act. Even if the data are stored in structured paper files kept as archive material in a dusty basement, the person responsible will be processing those data. Although 'holding' is not defined in the Data Protection Act 1998, one view is that, if the data are in a store and not subject to current processing activity, there must be an intention to process the data in the future. Given the very wide definition of processing, there would be little point in keeping data without having such an intention. This would probably be a breach of the fifth data protection principle.

The definition of processing covers every conceivable use of data and its width is enhanced because the operations referred to are not intended to be exhaustive owing to the insertion of the word 'including'. The House of Lords case of *R v Brown* [1996] 1 AC 543, heard under the 1984 Act, shows the importance of having a wide definition of 'processing'. In that case, a police officer worked in his spare time with a friend in their debt collection agency. The agency was engaged by a third party to recover a debt. The police officer used the police national computer to obtain information concerning the debtor. He denied that he had used the computer for non-police purposes and said that he accessed the data because he had noticed that the debtor's car was without a tax disc. Furthermore, he claimed that he had only accessed the data and had not 'used' it subsequently. He was convicted at first instance for an offence under section 5(2)(b) of the Data Protection Act 1984 which made it an offence to hold or use personal data for a purpose which had not been registered.

The police officer's conviction was quashed by the Court of Appeal and this was confirmed in the House of Lords, which dismissed the appeal by the Crown by a 3:2 majority. The majority confirmed that the word 'use' must be given its ordinary dictionary meaning and simply retrieving the information in computer readable form from the database was not using the information so recorded. The minority judges thought that the word 'use' should be liberally interpreted so as to achieve the purpose of the Act otherwise there would be a serious gap in the law. It is as well that the 1998 Act has consigned this unfortunate decision to history.

Placing information about individuals on a website is processing personal data. The act of placing the material there is clearly processing. Subsequently, it is processing by making available and, if anyone accesses the material it is processing by transmission. If there was ever any doubt about information on a website, the European Court of Justice put an end to this in Case C-101/01 *Bodil Lindqvist* [2003] ECR I-12971. Referring to the equivalent provisions in the Directive, the Court of Justice noted that 'processing' means '… any operation or set of operations which is performed upon personal data, whether or not by automatic means, such as collection, recording, organization, storage, adaptation or alteration, retrieval, consultation, use, *disclosure by transmission, dissemination or otherwise making available*, alignment or combination, blocking, erasure or destruction' (emphasis added). It was clear that loading personal data, such as individuals' names, telephone numbers, jobs and hobbies, onto a webpage fell within that definition. The technical operation of loading the webpages on a computer server together with operations necessary to make the data accessible to people connected to the internet mean that the processing was, at least in part, by automatic means.

Data processor

The definition of 'processing' takes on special significance when we look at the meaning of a 'data processor' which is:

> **any person (other than an employee of the data controller) who processes data on behalf of the data controller.**

A computer bureau or facilities management contractor, processing data on behalf of a data controller, will certainly be a data processor. As the meaning of processing is very wide, it is worth considering the types of persons who will be classed as processors under the present law. There follow some examples (it is assumed that the persons involved are not employees of the data controller – they may be self-employed, freelancers or independent organisations):

- persons collecting data, such as market researchers accosting individuals in a shopping precinct;
- mail order catalogue agents;
- a small IT company providing data entry services;
- a company providing disaster recovery services or other back-up services;
- a company engaged to carry out database quality control by verifying, checking and, where necessary, correcting inaccurate information;
- a person engaged to prepare reports for a client, using the client's database;
- an internet service provider which provides webpages or e-mail services to a client who includes personal data on those webpages or in those e-mails;
- a company providing ICT facilities management services to a client who has outsourced his information and communications technologies functions;
- a company engaged to remove and destroy old computer printout or archived files containing personal data.

The significance of being classified as a processor is that the processor must be subject to security obligations which are at least evidenced in writing. They, and their employees and agents, are also classed as recipients and, unless the data controller is exempt from notifying his processing activities, must be included in the description of recipients or categories of recipients in the notification.

Recipients and third parties

These further definitions are contained in section 70. They are significant in that a description of recipients or categories of recipients must be notified, unless the data controller is exempt from notification and disclosures to third parties may trigger an obligation to inform data subjects of such disclosures.

> '*recipient*', in relation to any personal data, means any person to whom the data are disclosed, including any person (such as an employee or agent of the data controller, a data processor or an employee or agent of a data processor) to whom they are disclosed in the course of processing the data for the data controller, but does not include any person to whom disclosure is or may be made as a result of, or with a view to, a particular inquiry by or on behalf of that person made in the exercise of any power conferred by law.

Note that employees and agents of the data controller and any data processor must be mentioned. The latter part of the definition is intended to excuse the notification of recipients who cannot easily be predicted but to whom personal data may be required to be disclosed by law. A particular example is where a government department makes a particular one-off enquiry to a local authority where the person concerned is based. However, in practice, generic descriptors are used in notifications to the Information Commissioner, obviating the need to expressly identify each recipient specifically.

> '*third party*', in relation to personal data, means any person other than –
> (a) the data subject,
> (b) the data controller, or
> (c) any data processor or other person authorised to process data for the data controller or processor.

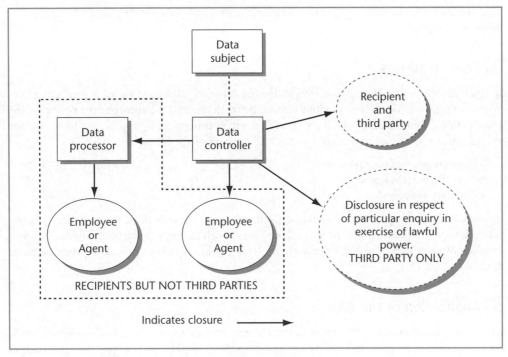

Figure 30.2 Persons involved in processing activity

Where data controller A sells a copy of his customer list to data controller B, a third party, under most circumstances, he should inform all the data subjects concerned unless they are already aware that this would happen.

Now that the main definitions have been introduced, it is useful to reflect on the identity of the various persons involved in data processing and their inter-relationships and this is set out in Fig. 30.2.

Sensitive personal data

This is an important definition as an additional set of conditions for processing apply to sensitive personal data, making the circumstances in which such data may be processed much narrower than in the case of 'normal data'.

Under section 2 of the Act, 'sensitive personal data' means personal data consisting of information as to:

(a) the racial or ethnic origin of the data subject,
(b) his political opinions,
(c) his religious or other beliefs of a similar nature,
(d) whether he is a member of a trade union (within the meaning of the Trade Union and Labour Relations (Consolidation) Act 1972),
(e) his physical or mental health or condition,
(f) his sexual life,
(g) the commission or alleged commission by him of any offence, or
(h) any proceedings for any offence committed or alleged to have been committed by him, the disposal of such proceedings or the sentence of any court in such proceedings.

30

Introduction to data protection law

The conditions for processing normal and sensitive personal data are considered further in the following chapter.

Special purposes

In line with the Human Rights Convention, the Act contains provisions aimed at protecting freedom of expression. There is an obvious tension between this and the enforcement powers of the Information Commissioner which are modified where processing is, or claimed to be, for the special purposes, defined in section 3 as any one or more of the following:

(a) the purposes of journalism,
(b) artistic purposes, and
(c) literary purposes.

Apart from impacting on the Information Commissioner's powers, there is a particular exemption relating to processing for the special purposes which attempts to strike a balance between freedom of expression and individuals' right of privacy in relation to processing their personal data.

Application of the Act

The Data Protection Act 1998 applies to the UK and extends to Northern Ireland. By section 5, except as otherwise provided for by or under section 54 (which concerns the Information Commissioner carrying out designated functions to enable the government to give effect to any international obligations of the UK), the Act applies to a data controller in respect of any data only if:

(a) the data controller is established in the United Kingdom and the data are processed in the context of that establishment, or
(b) the data controller is established neither in the United Kingdom nor in any EEA State but uses equipment in the United Kingdom for processing the data otherwise than for transit through the United Kingdom.

In the last case, the data controller must nominate a representative established in the UK. Thus, an English company processing data in connection with its business operations is subject to the 1998 Act. A Spanish company which engages a French company to process personal data on its behalf will be subject to the Spanish implementation of the data protection Directive under Spanish law. An Australian company using the services of a computer bureau situated in Scotland and using equipment situated there will be subject to the UK Act and must nominate a representative in the UK. In this case, it can be expected that it will be the Scots company which will be the representative. Of course, in the latter case, the Australian company must notify the Information Commissioner of the processing activity carried out in Scotland. If a Brazilian company transfers personal data to Japan via a computer situated in the UK, the UK Act will not apply unless the data are processed in the UK for any purpose other than the purpose of transit to Japan. This latter point is particularly important in terms of transmission via public telecommunications systems including by e-mail and the internet. It obviates the need for the data controller to notify in all the Member States of the EEA if the data is likely to pass through any or all of them (which it is by the nature of transmission over the internet).

ROLE OF THE INFORMATION COMMISSIONER

The Information Commissioner is required to act in an independent manner and is appointed by Her Majesty by Letters Patent. Apart from duties, responsibilities and powers under the Data Protection Act 1998, the Information Commissioner now also has duties and powers in relation to privacy and electronic communications and under the Freedom of Information Act 2000 (together with the Environmental Information Regulations 2004). In terms of the Data Protection Act 1998, the role of the Commissioner can be seen as being concerned with the following major functions:

- consultation and dissemination of information;
- investigation;
- intervention;
- enforcement; and
- cooperation.

Consultation and dissemination of information

As required by Article 28(2) of the data protection Directive, the Information Commissioner (being the UK's supervisory authority), must be consulted as regards administrative measures and regulations relating to the protection of individuals' rights and freedoms with regard to the processing of personal data. Thus, under section 67 of the Data Protection Act 1998, the Secretary of State shall consult the Information Commissioner before making an order under the Act (except for an order bringing parts of the Act into force) or before making any regulations under the Act except for the notification regulations.

The Information Commissioner has a duty to disseminate information, *inter alia*, to promote the following of good practice and the observance of the requirements of the Act by data controllers: section 51. This includes the dissemination of information about other matters within the Information Commissioner's functions under the Act. The Commissioner may give advice to any person as to any of those matters. There is also a duty to lay a report before Parliament annually. Other reports may be placed before Parliament as must be codes of practice ordered to be prepared by the Secretary of State who may direct the Information Commissioner to draw up and disseminate codes of practice after consultation with trade associations, data subjects or persons representing data subjects. The order will describe the personal data or processing to which the code is to relate and may also describe the persons or classes of persons subject to the processing. The Information Commissioner may also draw up codes of practice where he considers it appropriate.

A further function is that the Information Commissioner will disseminate Community findings as regards the adequacy of protection for personal data in third countries (countries or territories outside the EEA) and decisions under Article 31(2) of the Directive made for the purposes of Article 26(3) or (4) as regards measures to be taken in respect of adequacy of protection in third countries and contractual clauses considered to offer sufficient safeguards and such other information relating to processing of personal data outside the EEA. So far, Switzerland, Canada, Argentina, Guernsey and the Isle of Man provide adequate protection which is also afforded by the US Department of Commerce's Safe Harbour Privacy Principles and the transfer of Air Passenger Name Records to the US Bureau of Customs and Border Protection. (See the section on transfers to third countries in the following chapter.)

30

Introduction to data protection law

Investigation

The Information Commissioner has wide-ranging powers of investigation aimed at determining that processing complies with the data protection principles and whether there has been otherwise any contravention of the Act. The powers of investigation are exercised through:

- information notices;
- special information notices; or
- powers of entry and inspection.

Before looking at these individually, it should be noted that any individual who considers that he is directly affected by any processing may, under section 42, apply to the Information Commissioner for an assessment as to whether or not it is likely that the processing has been or is being carried out in compliance with the Act. The Information Commissioner must, upon receipt of such a request, make such assessment, providing he has been furnished with sufficient information to identify the person making the request and the processing in question. The Information Commissioner may take into account the following factors to determine the manner of the assessment:

- the extent to which the request appears to the Information Commissioner to raise a matter of substance;
- any undue delay in making the request; and
- whether the person making the request is entitled to make a subject access request.

The Information Commissioner shall notify the person whether an assessment has been made as a result of the request and any view formed or action to be taken, having regard in particular to any exemption from subject access enjoyed by the data controller. In particular, a request for an assessment may cause the Information Commissioner to serve an information notice. For the year ending 31 March 2006, the Information Commissioner received 22,059 new 'cases' (presumably all requests for assessment under the Act (most in the form of complaints). In over half the cases, advice was given to the individual making the request.[9]

Information notices

An information notice may be served under section 43 as a result of a request for assessment from an individual or if the Information Commissioner has reasonable grounds for suspecting that the data controller has contravened or is contravening any of the principles. The notice requires the data controller to furnish the Information Commissioner with information relating to the request within the specified time and in such form as may be specified. The notice must include a statement that the notice has been served in response to a request from an individual if that is the case or, otherwise, with a statement that the information requested is regarded to be relevant in determining whether the data controller has complied or is complying with the principles, together with reasons why the information is regarded as relevant. The notice must also contain particulars of appeal.

Normally, the time to reply should not be less than the time during which an appeal may be brought, being 28 days, except where the Commissioner considers that the information is required as a matter of urgency where the time limit can be seven days. The Commissioner must state the reasons why the information is required as a matter of urgency. The data controller is

---

[9] Information Commissioner, *Annual Report 2005–2006*, HC1228, 2006, p. 8.

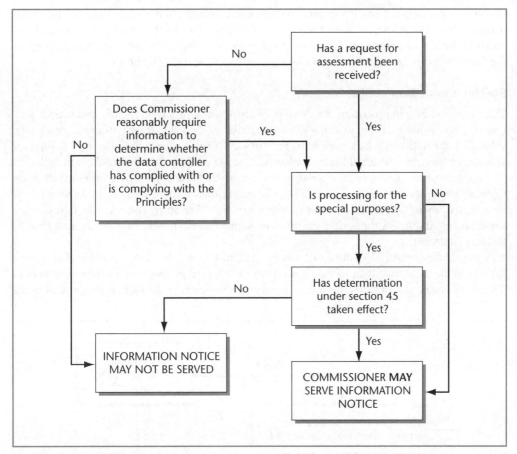

Figure 30.3 Information notice

excused from providing information which is privileged or would reveal evidence of an offence other than an offence under the Act.

Information notices may not be served on a data controller in respect of processing for the special purposes (journalism, artistic or literary expression) unless a determination has been made and has taken effect under section 45 where it appears to the Commissioner that the personal data are not being processed only for the special purposes or are not being processed with a view to publication by any person of any journalistic, literary or artistic material which has not previously been published by the data controller. This provision is intended to prevent undue interference with the right of freedom of expression. Figure 30.3 shows when an information notice may be served by the Commissioner.

Section 45 determinations are important also in respect of special information notices and enforcement notices, as described later. The Information Commissioner must serve on the data controller notice of the determination which must include particulars of the right to appeal and which must not take effect until the end of the period for an appeal or, if an appeal is pending, until the appeal has been determined or withdrawn. Thus, if processing is for the special purposes only or with a view to publication, the Information Commissioner's powers are curtailed until a determination has taken effect. Note that publication can be by any person – presumably this includes the data controller and of any personal data not previously having been published by the data controller. Thus, if the data controller has already published material including the personal data in question, he cannot rely on the restrictions to the Information Commissioner's powers if he is now processing the data with an intention that he should re-publish it. Even so, the Commissioner would still need to make a determination under section 45.

Special information notices

These notices relate to processing for the special purposes (journalism, literary and artistic purposes). These provisions are, in many respects, similar to those for information notices. Under section 44, the notice may be served if the Information Commissioner has received a request for assessment from an individual under section 42 (the Act is silent on whether there must be, on its face, an issue in the request relating to the special purposes) or if the Information Commissioner has reasonable grounds for suspecting that, in a case where proceedings have been stayed under section 32 (exemption for journalism, literature and art), the data are not being processed only for the special purposes or with a view to publication for the first time by the data controller.

A stay under section 32 shall be ordered by the court where the data controller claims, or it appears to the court, that the processing is only for the special purposes and with a view to publication by any person of any journalistic, literary or artistic material which, at the time 24 hours

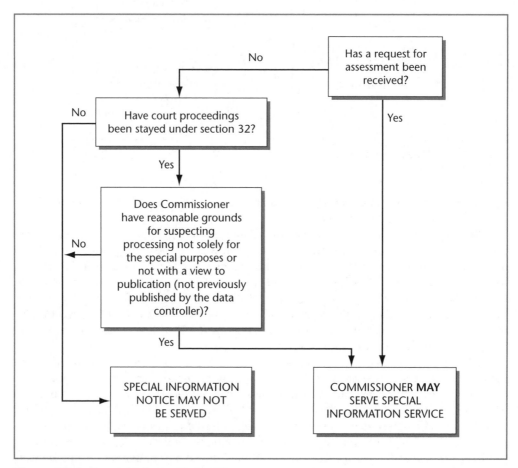

Figure 30.4 Special information notice

immediately before the time of the claim, had not previously been published by the data controller.

The proceedings referred to in section 32 are in relation to subject access, processing likely to cause damage or distress, automated decision taking or rights in relation to inaccurate data. The stay applies until the Information Commissioner makes a determination under section 45 or the data controller withdraws the claim.

Unless the notice is sent after a request for assessment is made, the notice may only be sent where a data controller has used the exemption under section 32 (special purposes – journalism, literature and art) as a shield in any proceedings to obtain a stay. The purpose of the notice is to obtain information to determine whether the exemption for the special purposes does indeed apply. Figure 30.4 shows when a special information notice may be served.

Entry and inspection

The Information Commissioner's powers of entry and inspection are contained in Schedule 9 to the Data Protection Act 1998 and can be exercised by him after obtaining a warrant from a circuit judge who will grant the warrant if he is satisfied by information supplied by the Information Commissioner on oath that there are reasonable grounds for suspecting that a data controller has contravened or is contravening any of the data protection principles or that an offence under the Act has been or is being committed. If the processing is for the special purposes, a warrant must not be issued until a determination under section 45 has taken effect. The warrant must be executed within seven days of the date of its issue.

A judge must not issue a warrant (except if satisfied that the case is urgent as discussed below) unless he is satisfied that the Information Commissioner has given the occupier of the premises in question seven days' notice in writing demanding access and such access was demanded at a reasonable time and was unreasonably refused or although entry was granted the occupier unreasonably refused to comply with a request to permit the Information Commissioner or his officers or staff to do anything within the powers of entry and inspection, and the occupier, after such refusal, has been notified of the intended application for a warrant and has had the opportunity to be heard by the judge concerned. However, where the case is urgent and the judge is also satisfied that to comply with the above provisions would defeat the object of entry, he may issue a warrant without those preconditions being present.

A warrant will permit the Information Commissioner or his officers or staff executing the warrant to use such force as is reasonably necessary to enter and search the premises within seven days, to inspect, examine and operate any test respecting any data processing equipment on the premises and to inspect and seize any documents or other materials (presumably including items such as magnetic disks and tapes) which may be evidence of an offence or contravention of the data protection principles. Warrants are not available in the case of personal data which are exempt from any provisions of the Act under the national security provisions under section 28. In the year to 31 March 2006, 11 search warrants were applied for by the Information Commissioner.

Intervention

The data protection Directive requires that the supervisory authority shall have effective powers of intervention. This requires the Information Commissioner to carry out a preliminary assessment of processing operations likely to pose specific risks to the rights and freedoms of individuals. The types of operations concerned will be specified by the Lord Chancellor and such processing must not proceed until the Commissioner has made the assessment to ensure that the processing will comply with the Act: section 22. In the normal course of events, the

Commissioner should inform the data controller of the results within 28 days of notification by the data controller. The period can be extended for a further period not exceeding 14 days.

It is unlikely that a preliminary assessment will be required in many cases. Indeed, the Directive states in recital 54 that the amount of processing likely to pose specific risks should be very limited. The Home Office indicated that it might apply in the case of genetic data, data matching (that is, where personal data from different sources are matched to find any discrepancies which might indicate that the person concerned is involved in fraudulent applications for credit) and processing by private investigators. The key should be whether the particular description of processing is likely to cause substantial damage or substantial distress to data subjects or to otherwise significantly prejudice the rights and freedoms of data subjects. Processing may not proceed until the 28 days (as extended, if applicable) has expired or the data controller has received a notice from the Information Commissioner permitting processing. At the time of writing, no orders have been made under section 22.

Another form of intervention is that the Information Commissioner may require a data controller to rectify, block, erase or destroy inaccurate data as part of an enforcement notice and the Information Commissioner may also require the data controller to inform third parties to whom the data have been disclosed, having regard, in particular, to the number of persons who would have to be notified.

Enforcement

The Information Commissioner has two ways of enforcing data protection law. One is through enforcement notices, the second is by bringing a prosecution under the Act. In England and Wales and Northern Ireland, prosecutions normally are brought by the Commissioner. Otherwise a prosecution may be brought by or with the consent of the Director of Public Prosecutions (or Director of Public Prosecutions for Northern Ireland). The offences, of which there a several, are set out in the following chapter.

Under section 40, if the Information Commissioner is satisfied that the data controller has contravened or is contravening any of the data protection principles, he may serve a notice requiring the data controller to take or refrain from taking specified steps within a specified time and/or refrain from processing after a specified time:

- any personal data;
- personal data of a specified description; or
- for a specified purpose or purposes or in a specified manner.

As mentioned above, where an enforcement notice relates to a breach of the fourth data protection principle (in that the data are inaccurate), the Information Commissioner may, if reasonably practicable, require the data controller to notify third parties to whom the data have been disclosed. Regard is to be had to the number of persons who would have to be notified. The court also has similar powers in respect of inaccurate data that record accurately information provided by the data subject or a third party.

In deciding whether to serve the notice, the Information Commissioner is to consider whether the contravention has or is likely to cause any person damage or distress. The provisions as to the service of enforcement notices are subject to restrictions as regards processing for the special purposes (journalism, literary and artistic purposes). Here, the provisions envisage that a court must give leave to serve the notice. In particular, the notice shall not be served unless a determination under section 45 has taken effect and the court has granted leave for the notice to be served. Such leave will only be granted if the Information Commissioner has reason to suspect a

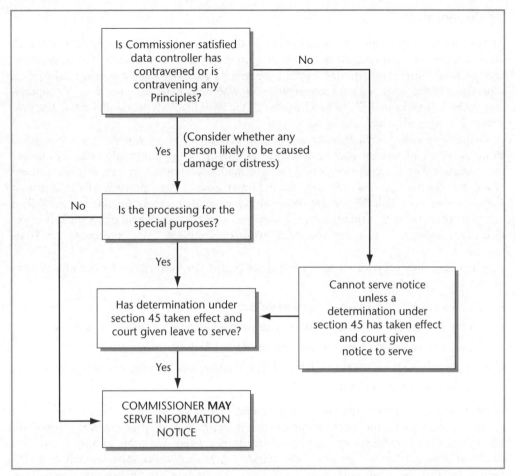

Figure 30.5 Enforcement notice

contravention of substantial public interest and, except in cases of urgency, the data controller has been given notice in accordance with the rules of court for the application to the court for leave to serve the notice. Figure 30.5 shows when an enforcement notice may be served.

Enforcement notices cannot take effect until the period for appeal has expired (28 days) or pending an appeal unless the case is a matter of urgency, in which case the time for compliance is seven days. An enforcement notice may be cancelled or varied by the Information Commissioner. This may be done on the Information Commissioner's own initiative or following a written application by the data controller after the period for appeal has expired where he can show by reason of a change in circumstances that some or all of the provisions of the notice need not be complied with to ensure compliance with the data protection principles: section 41.

Under the 1984 Act, in *British Gas Trading Ltd* v *Data Protection Registrar* (unreported) 24 March 1998, the Data Protection Tribunal, as it was then called, held that the then Data Protection Registrar was right to serve an enforcement notice under the 1984 Act rather than accept an undertaking from British Gas Trading Ltd. Under the 1984 Act, there were other forms of enforcement, by de-registration notices and transfer prohibition notices. These find no direct equivalent under the 1998 Act. The Information Commissioner had developed a preliminary notice with the approval of the Information Tribunal. The preliminary enforcement notice can be seen as a useful 'yellow card' system.

Cooperation

All the data protection supervisory authorities in the EEA are required to cooperate with each other in respect of exchanging all useful information and to the extent necessary for the performance of their duties. Furthermore, each Member State shall designate a representative of its supervisory authority (or a joint representative if the Member State has more than one supervisory authority, unlike the UK) to be a member of the Working Party set up under the data protection Directive, discussed later in this chapter.

Cooperation is also implicit in the drawing up of codes of practice, which may be required by the Secretary of State or may be developed as a result of the Information Commissioner's own initiative. Another provision is that the Information Commissioner can, with the consent of the data controller, assess processing for the observance of good practice. The Information Commissioner may, with the consent of the Secretary of State, charge for this service. This is not to be confused with requests for preliminary assessments which will be required in specified cases posing risks to rights and freedoms of data subjects before processing can commence.

Where an individual is an actual or prospective party to proceedings under one of a number of provisions, including:

- a failure to comply with a subject access request;
- a failure to cease processing likely to cause substantial damage or substantial distress;
- a failure to comply with the provisions on automated decision taking;
- an application to have inaccurate data rectified, erased, blocked or destroyed; or
- the compensation provisions;

that individual can apply to the Information Commissioner for assistance where the processing relates to processing for the special purposes (that is, journalism, artistic or literary expression). The Information Commissioner shall provide assistance where it appears to him to involve a matter of substantial public interest under section 53. The assistance provided may be in the form of legal advice or assistance from a solicitor or counsel or assistance during proceedings. The Information Commissioner has a first charge on any costs or award in respect of the expenses in providing assistance.

The Information Commissioner continues to be the designated authority for the purposes of Article 13 of the Council of Europe Convention for the Protection of Individuals with regard to Processing of Personal Data, Strasbourg, 28 January 1981, and is the supervisory authority for the purposes of the data protection Directive. Orders may be made for the Information Commissioner to cooperate with the European Commission and supervisory authorities in other EEA states and to carry out data functions to enable the government to give effect to international obligations in the UK.

THE INFORMATION TRIBUNAL AND APPEALS

The Information Tribunal (formerly known as the Data Protection Tribunal) is the first line of appeal from notices served by the Commissioner or a determination by the Commissioner under section 45. It also has jurisdiction to hear appeals against notices under the Freedom of Information Act 2000 and the Environmental Information Regulations 2004. The tribunal also has jurisdiction to hear appeals against national security certificates under the Privacy and Electronic Communications (EC Directive) Regulations 2003. The tribunal is made up of:

- a chairman appointed by the Lord Chancellor after consulting the Secretary of State (being a lawyer of at least seven years' standing);

- such number of deputy chairmen as determined by the Lord Chancellor (also being lawyers of at least seven years' standing); and

- such number of other members appointed by the Secretary of State (being persons representing the interests of data subjects and persons making requests for information under the Freedom of Information Act 2000, persons representing the interests of data controllers and persons representing the interests of public authorities).

The functions of the Secretary of State are, as regards Scotland, transferred to the Scottish Ministers. Under section 48, a person may appeal to the tribunal on grounds related to the following:

- enforcement, information or special information notices;

- a refusal by the Information Commissioner to cancel or vary an enforcement notice;

- where a notice contains a statement that the notice must be complied with as a matter of urgency within seven days, the Information Commissioner's decision to include the statement or the effect of the inclusion of the statement as regards any part of the notice; or

- a determination under section 45.

The tribunal may:

- allow the appeal;

- substitute another notice if it considers that the notice is not in accordance with the law;

- where it involved an exercise of discretion by the Information Commissioner, rule that the discretion ought to have been exercised differently;

- cancel or vary a notice;

- rule on a statement made by the Information Commissioner that compliance is required as a matter of urgency;

- cancel a determination of the Information Commissioner.

The tribunal may review any determination of fact on which the notice in question was based. Appeals from the tribunal on a point of law go to the High Court in England or Wales, the Court of Session in Scotland or the High Court of Justice in Northern Ireland, depending on the appellant's address. Detailed procedures before the tribunal are set out in the Information Tribunal (Enforcement Appeals) Rules 2005 and the Information Tribunal (National Security Appeals) Rules 2005. These latter rules apply to appeals against claims to exemption on the basis of a national security certificate under section 29 of the Data Protection Act 1998.

THE WORKING PARTY

A Working Party on the Protection of Individuals with regard to the Processing of Personal Data ('the Working Party') was established under Article 29 of the data protection Directive. It is an independent body with an advisory status. The Working Party is composed of a representative from the supervisory authority of each Member State. Where a Member State has more than one supervisory authority (for example, where one looks after the public sector and another looks after the private sector), a joint representative is nominated. A representative of the authority or authorities established for the Community institutions and bodies and a representative of the

Commission are also members of the Working Party. A chair is elected every two years and decisions are taken by a simple majority of representatives of supervisory authorities. The Working Party considers items placed on its agenda by the chairman, either on his own initiative or at the request of a representative of the supervisory authorities or at the request of the European Commission.

The brief of the Working Party is set out in Article 30 of the Directive and is to:

- examine any questions covering the application of national measures implementing the Directive so as to contribute to the uniform application of such measures;
- give the Commission an opinion on the level of protection afforded in the Community and in third countries;
- advise the Commission on any proposed amendment to the Directive, on any additional or specific measures to safeguard rights and freedoms with regard to the processing of personal data and to advise on any other proposed Community measures affecting such rights and freedoms;
- give opinions on codes of practice drawn up at Community level.

Furthermore, the Working Party must inform the Commission if it finds disparity between the laws of Member States in respect of the protection of individuals with regard to the processing of personal data. It may, on its own initiative, make recommendations on all data protection matters. An annual report, which will be made public, is to be drawn up dealing with the protection of natural persons with regard to the processing of personal data within the Community and in third countries. The Commission must inform the Working Party of the action it takes in response to its opinions and recommendations. This is to be done in a report forwarded to the European Parliament and the Council and will also be made public.

The Working Party has published numerous opinions and press releases, most recently covering issues such as:

- processing of personal data by the Society for Worldwide Interbank Financial Telecommunication (SWIFT);
- on the obligation of carriers to communicate advance passenger data;
- on the review of the regulatory Framework for Electronic Communications and Services, with focus on the ePrivacy Directive;
- privacy issues related to the provision of e-mail screening services;
- on the application of EU data protection rules to internal whistle-blowing schemes in the fields of accounting, internal accounting controls, auditing matters, the fight against bribery, banking and financial crime.

THE EUROPEAN DATA PROTECTION COMMISSIONER

Generally, data protection law applies to the European Community institutions and bodies and there is now a European Data Protection Supervisor, first appointed in 2004. The relevant data protection law is very similar, with necessary modifications, to that under the data protection Directive and is to be found in Regulation (EC) No 45/2001 of the European Parliament and of the Council of 18 December 2000 on the protection of individuals with regard to the processing of personal data by the Community institutions and bodies and on the free movement of such data.[10]

[10] OJ L 8, 12.01.2001, p. 1.

The definition of 'controller' replaces that of 'data controller' under the data protection Directive and relates, for obvious reasons to the Community institutions and bodies.

Each Community institution or body must appoint at least one data protection official whose duties include making controllers and data subjects aware of their rights and obligations; responding to requests from, and cooperating with, the European Data Protection Supervisor; ensuring in an independent manner the internal application of the Regulation; keeping a register of the processing operations carried out by the controller, containing the items of information; and notifying the European Data Protection Supervisor of any processing operations likely to present specific risks such that they require prior checking by the Supervisor.

Apart from the other provisions which are similar or equivalent to those in the data protection Directive, the confidentiality security obligations in the Regulations are noteworthy. Employees of Community institutions and bodies, whether those institutions or bodies act as controllers or processors, are placed under obligations of confidentiality and may only act under the instructions of the controller unless required to do so by virtue of national or Community law. Where personal data are processed by automated means, measures shall be taken as appropriate in view of the risks in particular with the aim of:

(a) preventing any unauthorised person from gaining access to computer systems processing personal data;

(b) preventing any unauthorised reading, copying, alteration or removal of storage media;

(c) preventing any unauthorised memory inputs as well as any unauthorised disclosure, alteration or erasure of stored personal data;

(d) preventing unauthorised persons from using data-processing systems by means of data transmission facilities;

(e) ensuring that authorised users of a data-processing system can access no personal data other than those to which their access right refers;

(f) recording which personal data have been communicated, at what times and to whom;

(g) ensuring that it will subsequently be possible to check which personal data have been processed, at what times and by whom;

(h) ensuring that personal data being processed on behalf of third parties can be processed only in the manner prescribed by the contracting institution or body;

(i) ensuring that, during communication of personal data and during transport of storage media, the data cannot be read, copied or erased without authorisation;

(j) designing the organisational structure within an institution or body in such a way that it will meet the special requirements of data protection.

The position as regards processors is similar to that in the data protection Directive and requires that the processing is carried out under a contract or other legal act. There are particular provisions governing transfers of personal data between Community institutions and bodies and from them to data controllers within the EEA and outside, the latter being equivalent to those under the data protection Directive.

The primary duties of the European Data Protection Supervisor are:

■ to ensure that the fundamental rights and freedoms of natural persons, and in particular their right to privacy, are respected by the Community institutions and bodies;

■ to monitor and ensure the application of the provisions of the Regulation and any other Community act relating to the protection of the fundamental rights and freedoms of natural

30

Introduction to data protection law

persons with regard to the processing of personal data by a Community institution or body; and

■ to advise Community institutions and bodies and data subjects on all matters concerning the processing of personal data.

The European Data Protection Supervisor is appointed for a term of five years and a deputy is also appointed for the same term. A Secretariat is established to assist the European Data Protection Supervisor who shall be chosen from persons whose independence is beyond doubt and who are acknowledged as having the experience and skills required to perform the duties of European Data Protection Supervisor, for example because they belong or have belonged to the supervisory authorities under the data protection Directive.

SUMMARY

■ Data protection law:
  – prevents barriers to the freedom of movement of personal data;
  – by ensuring adequate protection for personal data in the EEA.
■ The eight data protection principles are central to data protection law.
■ The first data protection principle is fundamental, being fair and lawful processing.
■ Data means information:
  – processed or intended to be processed by automatic means;
  – recorded or intended to be recorded as part of a relevant filing system;
  – accessible records not included in the above forms of data (certain health, education and local authority records);
  – public authority information not included in the above types of data.
■ Personal data are data from which:
  – an individual can be identified;
  – from those data; or
  – from those data and other data in, or likely to be in, the possession of the data controller.
■ Personal data can be or include sound and image data.
■ A relevant filing system is one which:
  – permits easy access to specific data relating to a specific individual;
  – because of the manner in which the filing system is arranged or structured.
■ A data controller is the person(s) who decides the purposes and manner of processing.
■ A data subject is the individual who is the subject of personal data.
■ Processing is very widely defined and can include simply being in possession of personal data, erasing or destroying personal data.
■ The meanings of processor, recipient and third party are important:
  – processors must be under security obligations;
  – recipients (including processors, their agents and employees) must be identified;
  – disclosure to third parties may trigger the obligation to inform data subjects.
■ Sensitive personal data are subject to additional conditions allowing processing.
■ The special purposes are the purposes of journalism and artistic and literary purposes.
■ Where processing is for the special purposes, an exemption protects freedom of expression.

- The Information Commissioner has responsibilities, powers and duties under:
  - data protection law;
  - freedom of information law including environmental information; and
  - law concerning privacy and electronic communications.
- The Information Commissioner's powers under data protection law include:
  - investigation, enforcement and prosecuting offences under the Act;
  - powers of entry and inspection.
- Under data protection law, the Information Tribunal hears appeals:
  - in respect of Information Commissioner's notices;
  - statements in notices that compliance is required as a matter of urgency; and
  - determinations in respect of whether processing is covered by the special purposes.
- A Working Party was set up under the data protection Directive.
- A European Data Protection Supervisor oversees data protection law in relation to the Community institutions and bodies.

SELF-TEST QUESTIONS

Note: there is only one correct answer to each multiple choice question.

1   **Which one of the following CORRECTLY describes the first data protection principle?**

   (a)   Personal data must not be transferred to a third country without adequate protection.

   (b)   Personal data must be accurate, not excessive and up to date.

   (c)   Personal data must be processed fairly and lawfully.

   (d)   Personal data may not be processed without the consent of the data subject.

2   **Which one of the following terms is NOT mentioned in the definition of processing in section 1(1) of the Data Protection Act 1998?**

   (a)   Holding.

   (b)   Storage.

   (c)   Adaptation.

   (d)   Blocking.

3   **Aardvark Ltd is a data controller which engages Brownsea Processing Ltd to process personal data on Aardvark's behalf. Clarence is an employee of Brownsea Processing who actually processes the personal data. Aardvark discloses the personal data to Deer Park Marketing plc, another data controller. Which one of the following is NOT CORRECT is respect of the personal data for the purposes of the Data Protection Act 1998?**

   (a)   Brownsea Processing is a recipient but not a third party.

   (b)   Deer Park is a recipient but not a third party.

   (c)   Clarence is a recipient but not a third party.

   (d)   Brownsea is also a data processor.

4   **Which one of the following statements may NOT be included in an enforcement notice issued by the Information Commissioner?**

(a) In the case of a matter of urgency, a statement requiring compliance within seven days.

(b) In the case of, for example, inaccurate personal data in breach of the fourth data protection principle, a statement requiring the data controller to notify third parties to whom the data have been disclosed, if reasonably practicable.

(c) A statement requiring the data controller to take or refrain from taking specified steps within a specified time and/or refrain from processing after a specified time personal data of a specified description.

(d) A statement requiring the data controller to submit an application for a preliminary assessment of processing activity.

5   Read the Information Commissioner's latest annual report. Do you think the work of the Information Commissioner's Office is worthwhile?

A copy of the latest Annual Report and Summary Report (and earlier ones back to 2001) is available from the Information Commissioner's website at: http://www.ico.gov.uk/

For further resources and updates please go to the Companion Website accompanying this book at www.mylawchamber.co.uk/bainbridgeIT

31 | Data controllers and the Data Protection Act 1998

INTRODUCTION

The purpose of this chapter is to explore the model of data protection law under the 1998 Act from the perspective of the data controller. The following chapter looks at the Act from the perspective of data subjects whose rights also impact on data controllers. The discussion will involve further consideration of the data protection principles which, with their interpretative provisions, are very important. Some of these latter provisions contain some of the most important and potentially onerous elements of the Directive. First, the notification requirements will be described. From a data controller's point of view, these are arguably of most immediate impact. This will include a look at the requirements to provide data subjects with information when data are obtained from them and in other cases. Following this, the constraints on processing activity are discussed. These include the conditions for processing which cannot proceed unless one of the conditions applies for normal data and, in the case of sensitive data, a further condition also is satisfied. These conditions were a new departure for the UK except in so far as processing was required to be fair under the 1984 Act.

Following the discussion of the security requirements and their impact also on data processors, the numerous exemptions to certain provisions of the Act are described. Next there is a brief look at enforcement from the data controller's viewpoint. This builds up on the description of the Information Commissioner's functions in the previous chapter. The offences under the Act are then described in summary, as many will have already been covered previously in the chapter. Finally, the transitional provisions are discussed briefly. Some are no longer relevant and some of the transitional provisions came to an end some time ago and others last until 24 October 2007. One 'transitional' provision is of unlimited duration, however, and continues to apply in relation to processing for historical research.

NOTIFICATION

The Data Protection Act 1998 exempts from notification all manual processing of data, for example data that are part of a relevant filing system or accessible record under section 1. Unless exempt, all automated processing must be notified. However, even if required to be notified, processing may still be subject to a preliminary assessment where it poses specific risks and the Secretary of State has made the appropriate order requiring such assessment before processing can commence. Exemption from formal notification to the Information Commissioner is not all good news as the data controller must still furnish information to any person making a written request, as we shall see later. Further exemption from notification is possible by order of the Secretary of State. So far specific exemptions have been made under the Data Protection

(Notification and Notification Fees) Regulations 2000. These apply to staff administration; accounts, marketing and public relations; accounts and records, and in the case of non-profit organisations. The exemptions are not absolute and only relate to specified purposes, data subjects, types of personal data and disclosures. Partnerships are allowed to register under the name of the partnership and the governing body and head teacher of a school may register in the name of the school.

Under section 4(4) a duty is placed on every data controller, unless exempt, to comply with the data protection principles. This applies whether or not he has notified his processing activities. Section 17 states that personal data must not be processed until registered, except in the case of manual processing which is not subject to a preliminary assessment (which will usually be the case) or if the processing is of a particular description to be exempted by notification regulations or if the sole purpose of the processing is the maintenance of a public register – for example, the electoral roll.

Registrable particulars

Unless exempt from the notification requirements, section 18 requires data controllers wishing to be included in the register to notify the 'registrable particulars' together with a general description of security measures. The information to be contained in the registrable particulars is set out in section 16(1), being in relation to a data controller:

(a) his name and address,
(b) if he has nominated a representative, the name and address of the representative,
(c) a description of personal data being or to be processed by or on behalf of the data controller and of the category or categories of data subject to which they relate,
(d) a description of the purpose or purposes for which the data are being or are to be processed,
(e) a description of any recipient or recipients to whom the data controller intends or may wish to disclose the data,
(f) the names, or a description of, any countries or territories outside the European Economic Area to which the data controller directly or indirectly transfers, or intends or may wish directly or indirectly to transfer, the data.

Where the data controller is a public authority (as defined in the Freedom of Information Act 2000), there must also be a statement to that effect. Under Regulation 11 of the Data Protection (Notification and Notification Fees) Regulations 2000, the Information Commissioner may also include other information in the register entry such as the registration number, the date the registration is treated as having been made, the date it falls or may fall to be removed and information to assist individuals communicate with the data controller regarding subject access requests. As regards security measures, data controllers have simply to check a number of boxes indicating, for example, that they have a security policy, train staff and adhere to BS7799, the British Standard on Information Security Management.

Where relevant, a statement must also be included of the fact that the notification does not extend to personal data being processed, or intended to be processed, but not subject to notification. This will apply to manual processing exempt from notification where the data controller has not chosen to notify such processing. For example, if a data controller has a computer database containing personal data, he must notify that. If he also has a card index system processed manually, that will be exempt from the notification requirements. The data controller may choose not to notify his card index system and, if he so chooses, he must include a statement in his notification of his automatic processing that he also processes personal data not subject to notification. This simply flags up the fact that there is other processing being carried on and a person alerted to that fact may wish to obtain further information from the data controller in respect of such processing, as discussed below. Alternatively, the data controller may decide to notify his manual processing also, in which case he need not provide a supplementary statement. The rationale is that of transparency of processing. Individuals should be able to see what processing is being carried out by consulting the register and, if alerted to the fact that there is non-notifiable processing also going on, he can find out what that is also. Notification lasts for 12 months, although the mechanism is included to modify this period.

Under section 19, the Information Commissioner maintains a register of data controllers, available for public inspection free of charge. Certified copies may be obtained for a prescribed fee, currently £2, under the Data Protection (Fees under section 19(7)) Regulations 2000. The general description of security measures is not available to the public. The register is available for public inspection at the Information Commissioner's website at: **http://www.ico.gov.uk/**.

Notification offences

Failure to notify is an offence of strict liability. Even if the person processing personal data had never heard of data protection law, he will be guilty of the offence. There is a further duty on the data controller to notify changes in the registrable particulars by virtue of section 20. However, failure to notify any changes is a criminal offence which is subject to a due diligence defence.

The basis of a due diligence defence is that, generally, liability is strict unless the accused makes out a defence. Such a statutory defence presumes that the fault is the responsibility of another person and that the accused has exercised due diligence to prevent the wrongful act from occurring. One way a data controller may prove that he has exercised due diligence is to show that he had installed systems or procedures aimed at preventing the wrong occurring. This might be by training employees or agents as to the importance of data protection law and providing them with clear information as to what the scope of their duties was. In terms of failing to notify changes, a data controller might escape liability if he can show that clear instructions had been given to an employee responsible for data protection within the data controller's business.

Requirement to provide information to any person on request

Where a data controller has not notified his processing activity because he is not required to do so and has chosen not to do so, he must still be in a position to supply information equivalent to the registrable particulars (as per (a) to (f) above) to any person who submits a written request for such information. The information must be provided within 21 days of the written request otherwise the data controller commits an offence, subject to a due diligence defence under section 24. No charge can be made for providing this information and the person making the request does not have to be a data subject in relation to personal data processed by or on behalf of the data controller. This obligation is justified on the principle of transparency of processing.

The main implication of this provision is that it may suit a data controller to notify processing which he is not required to notify and the Information Commissioner will accept such notifications. A further point is that, if a data controller has not notified all his processing which is within the scope of the Act, he ought to consider implementing a procedure for dealing with such requests although, for many data controllers, they are likely to be quite rare.

Preliminary assessment (prior checking)

In cases, to be specified by the Secretary of State, processing will be subject to a preliminary assessment by the Information Commissioner (known as 'prior checking' in the Directive) and the processing must not proceed until the Commissioner has made a preliminary assessment to ensure that it will comply with the Act: section 22. Such processing is known as 'assessable processing'. Where a preliminary assessment is required, in the normal course of events, the Commissioner should inform the data controller of his assessment within 28 days of notification by the data controller. The period can be extended for a further period not exceeding 14 days. No distinction is made between automatic and manual processing for a preliminary assessment. The Secretary of State will, by order, detail the descriptions of processing for which preliminary assessment is required. It is likely to be required in relatively few cases where it appears to the Secretary of State that a particular description of processing is likely to cause substantial damage or substantial distress to data subjects or to otherwise significantly prejudice the rights and freedoms of data subjects. Processing genetic data, data matching, endangered life databases and other sensitive processing operations are potential candidates for preliminary assessment. Processing may not proceed until the 28 days (as extended, if applicable) has expired or the data controller has received a notice from the Commissioner permitting processing. Otherwise a criminal offence of strict liability is committed. As yet no orders have been made under section 22. On the contrary, it is proposed that data matching will be allowed for anti-fraud purposes under the Serious Crime Bill 2007. Data matching is where sets of data are compared, for example, to detect anomalies in data relating to an individual or to look for patterns which might indicate the presence of or a likelihood of fraud.

The preliminary assessment provisions contain no power for the Commissioner to prohibit processing. The intention is that they enable the Commissioner to give a view on whether the processing is likely to comply. It will then be up to the data controller to decide whether or not to proceed. Of course, if the Commissioner considers the processing unlikely to comply with the Act, he may use his powers of enforcement if the data controller decides to go ahead.

DATA PROTECTION SUPERVISORS

In some Member States, a system of internal data protection supervisors is in place. In-house officials oversee compliance with data protection law. The Directive provided the opportunity for other Member States to adopt such a system which should permit the exemption or simplification of notification and allow internal preliminary assessments to be made, reducing the time delay in introducing new forms of sensitive processing. Under section 23 of the Data Protection Act 1998, the Secretary of State is given the power to make orders providing for personal data supervisors. They are to be responsible in particular for monitoring, in an independent manner, the data controller's compliance with the Act. There are likely to be duties imposed on personal data supervisors owed to the Commissioner who may be given functions in respect of them. No order has been made under section 23 as yet and it may be some time before we see data protection supervisors in the UK. Perhaps when they are brought in, the first place they may be allowed is in the public sector. Of course, most organisations have officials with data protection responsibilities.

INFORMING DATA SUBJECTS ON COLLECTION AND IN OTHER CASES

The provisions on interpretation of the data protection principles require that, for the first principle, the method of obtaining the data and whether the person from whom they were obtained was deceived or misled as to the purpose or purposes of processing are factors in determining whether the processing is fair (although data obtained or supplied under statutory authorisation is automatically deemed to be fairly obtained). Transparency is obviously important here and the individual should know what personal data relating to him are to be used for. This principle of openness is developed further in the interpretative provisions which place further duties on data controllers to provide specific information to an individual on collection of personal data and in other cases, especially where the data are disclosed to a third party.

These obligations to inform data subjects are derived from Articles 10 and 11 of the data protection Directive and have no equivalent under the 1984 Act, except as developed by case law such as in ***Innovations (Mail Order) Ltd*** v ***Data Protection Registrar**, 29 September 1993 before the Data Protection tribunal (now Information Tribunal). In that case, Innovations operated a large mail-order business, advertised through catalogues, newspapers and television. It also had a lucrative business selling its customer lists to other retailers and service providers (an activity known as 'list trading'). Customers ordering goods from Innovations were not told of the list trading activity at the time they placed their orders. It was only when they received a written acknowledgement of their orders that they were informed by way of a notice on the rear of the acknowledgement form. The notice informed customers that they could have their names removed from the lists if they applied formally, sending in details of their name and address.

The Data Protection Registrar (now Information Commissioner) took the view that this was a breach of the first data protection principle, as the data were not being obtained fairly because customers ought to have been informed at the time the data were collected and not later. An enforcement notice was served on Innovations which appealed to the tribunal. The tribunal agreed with the Registrar and said that the question as to whether data had been fairly obtained related to the time of the obtaining and not a later time. If a purpose for which the data are intended to be used is not obvious at the time of obtaining the data, the data subject must be told of that non-obvious purpose at *that* time. If the data user does not inform the data subject at the time of collection of the data, the data subject's express consent must be sought before any non-obvious processing can be commenced.

This approach was adopted again by the tribunal in ***British Gas Trading Ltd*** v ***Data Protection Registrar**, 24 March 1998. British Gas Trading had inherited a large number of its customers from the previous bodies which made and supplied gas. When it wanted to send marketing material to all its customers, British Gas Trading inserted a note to that effect when it sent out gas bills and statements. The note informed customers that they could opt out of receiving such marketing material by writing in. The Tribunal held that this was not fair processing. A number of factors in the case are important and instructive:

- at least some of the marketing material related to services or products that were not directly related to gas or gas appliances (for example, the 'Goldfish' credit card);

- customers should be able to object without having to perform a positive act like writing in – they should be able to signify consent or otherwise at the time data were collected from them, 'there and then';

- new customers could be informed and given an opportunity to object when completing a contract form, for example by ticking the 'opt-out' box.

An argument that the processing was also unlawful, for example, by being in breach of confidence or contract, were rejected by the tribunal. This case was followed by ***Midlands Electricity plc*** v ***Data Protection Registrar**, 7 May 1999. Midlands Electricity had sent a little magazine to domestic customers with their quarterly bills. Some of the material in the magazine had nothing to do with energy such as advertisements for holidays and mobile phones. As with the *British Gas* case, many of Midlands Electricity's customers had been inherited from the previous public utility. An enforcement notice had been served on Midlands Electricity requiring compliance as a matter of urgency. The tribunal agreed that the notice was valid but that the requirement that it be complied with as a matter of urgency in seven days was removed and the tribunal gave Midlands Electricity around 18 months to comply (it had to redesign its database to include a field to record whether individuals objected and to consult its customers as to whether they were happy to receive the booklet). A number of other interesting points arose from the decision:

- it was accepted that processing of personal data was involved as commercial customers received a different magazine;

- no evidence of damage or distress caused to customers was found by the tribunal;

- the tribunal accepted that including information about energy saving was not unfair, nor was advertising gas supplies, but advertising other products and services not related to energy supplies or appliances such as cookers and electric fires was unfair if the positive consent to this had not been obtained;

- obtaining consent in the case of new customers would be easy by use of the ubiquitous 'tick-box' – in terms of existing customers, consent could be sought when the customer returned a document, such as a direct debit mandate.

These cases show that, although there was no specific duty in the 1984 Act to inform individuals of non-obvious uses at the time the data were collected, the duty arose as a direct consequence of the requirement that processing must be fair. The duty under the 1998 Act is much more extensive.

Inform on collection

Part II of Schedule 1 to the Data Protection Act 1998 requires that, where the data are obtained from the data subject, the data controller must ensure, so far as is practicable, that the data subject has or is provided with the 'relevant information' or *has made it readily available to him*. The relevant information to be provided is:

- the identity of the data controller (and representative, if any);

- the purpose or purposes of the processing (but see below on the second data protection principle);

- any further information, having regard to the circumstances in which the data are or are to be processed to enable such processing in respect of the data subject to be fair.

The White Paper, *Data Protection: The Government's Proposals*[1] which preceded the Data Protection Bill suggested that it would be the controller who would decide whether further information was required to be given, though the Act is silent on this point. The second data protection principle requires that data shall be obtained only for one or more specified and lawful purposes and not further processed in an incompatible manner. The interpretation provisions for this principle allows the purpose to be specified either by notification to the Information Commissioner or in a notice given to the data subject for the purpose of informing him, as above. This means that, where the data controller has notified his processing to the Information Commissioner (which he must do in the case of automatic processing, unless exempt), the data controller will not have to separately provide this information to the data subject. As the purposes of processing are amongst the registrable particulars, this information will be publicly

[1] Home Office, Cm 3725, 1997.

available where processing is notified. Thus, the data subject can, by consulting the data protection register, find this information out himself.

Unless further information is deemed to be required to ensure fair processing, all the data controller will have to do is to identify himself to the data subject, unless a non-obvious use is envisaged or disclosure to a third party is possible. *Innovations*, *British Gas Trading* and *Midlands Electricity* remain good law under the 1998 Act. Certainly, if the data are to be used for marketing purposes, this is likely to be a situation where further information must be given. However, it should be noted that the tribunal in *British Gas Trading* accepted that what is or is not obvious may change over time as consumers become more aware of diversification of business activity carried out by a company or group of companies.

Inform in other cases

Other cases will cover the situation where the data have not been obtained directly from the individual concerned. For example, it might be that the data are disclosed by the data controller who obtained the data from the data subject in the first place and now chooses to disclose them to a second data controller. Another example is where a data controller generates for himself data relating to the data subject.

In cases other than where the data are being obtained directly from the data subject, the data controller must ensure so far as practicable that, *before the 'relevant time' or as soon as practicable thereafter*, the data subject has or is provided with the relevant information or *has it made readily available* to him. The requirement to provide information does not apply where its provision would involve a disproportionate effort or where the recording or disclosure is necessary to comply with a legal obligation to which the data controller is subject (other than a contractual obligation) together with such further conditions as may be prescribed by Regulations. Although many data controllers will be tempted to claim 'disproportionate effort' it will probably apply in limited circumstances only. It might apply where a large number of individuals would have to be informed and the processing is non-sensitive. It probably will not apply where the proposed use to be made of the data could trigger one of the rights of data subjects to object to processing – for example, where the purpose is direct marketing or involved automated decision taking.

Some conditions must be satisfied if the data controller seeks to rely on the exclusion of the requirement to inform the data subject. These are stated in the Data Protection (Conditions under Paragraph 3 of Part II of Schedule 1) Order 2000. Articles 4 and 5 of the Order contain the conditions. Where the recording or disclosure is necessary to comply with a legal obligation to which the data controller is subject, where this is not a function conferred on the data controller under any enactment or by court order, Article 4 applies as it does also to the disproportionate effort situation. Article 5 only applies to the disproportionate effort exclusion. Article 4 is to the effect that the requirement to provide information applies in any case if the data subject has informed the data controller by written notice that he requires such information to be given to him. Article 5 requires that the data controller records his reasons for believing that providing the information would involve a disproportionate effort. This could be the case, for example, where there are large numbers of data subjects to inform. However, processing must still be fair and it is submitted that the disproportionate effort excuse would only apply in innocuous situations or in circumstances where it would be reasonable for a data subject to be aware that such a transfer of personal data relating to him and subsequent processing activity was likely. An example where disproportionate effort could apply is where a copy of a customer database is sold to another company to use for marketing purposes, bearing in mind that data subjects have an

31

Data controllers and the Data Protection Act 1998

absolute right to object to direct marketing. The fact that it might be costly to inform data subjects cannot be the sole reason why information should not be provided to data subjects.

It should be noted that the exception to providing information where a disproportionate effort is involved does not apply to the situation where data are being obtained from the data subject. An example of where the recording or disclosure is required by law is in the field of employment law, especially in the context of official returns and disclosures to the Inland Revenue and Department of Social Security or in a case where disclosure of the personal data in question has been ordered by a court.

The information to be provided is exactly as applies in relation to obtaining data from the data subject. The 'relevant time' is when the controller first processes the data or, where disclosure to a third party within a reasonable period is envisaged:

- if it is in fact disclosed to such a person within that period, the time of disclosure;
- if during that period the data controller becomes or ought to become aware that the data are unlikely to be disclosed to such a person within that period, the time he does become or ought to become so aware; or
- in any other case at the end of that period.

Presumably, the disclosure referred to must be envisaged by both the data controller and the data subject. If it is not envisaged by the data subject, the provision of information in the second and third cases would seem fairly pointless.

The need to provide information on first processing could apply where data have been disclosed to a third party and the third party now processes the data (bearing in mind the very wide definition of 'processing'). As in all cases, the data controller is excused where the data subject already has the information or has it made *readily* available to him. It would seem that, in the latter case, it may be permissible to require the data subject to perform some positive task such as making a request for the information though it must be *readily* available. Where data are disclosed to a third party, it may be that the first data controller is in a position to inform the data

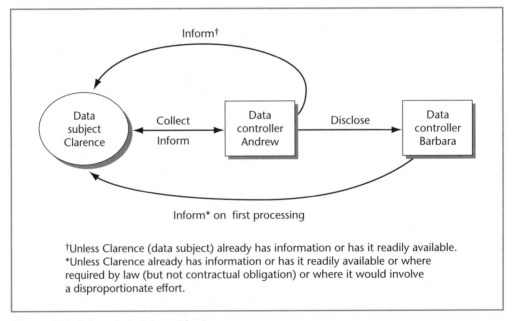

†Unless Clarence (data subject) already has information or has it readily available.
*Unless Clarence already has information or has it readily available or where required by law (but not contractual obligation) or where it would involve a disproportionate effort.

Figure 31.1 Informing data subjects

subject that this will happen. If he does inform the data subject of the identity (at least) of the third party, then the third party may be excused because the data subject already has the requisite information.

For example, consider two data controllers, Andrew and Barbara. Andrew obtained data from Clarence and, at the time, provided information as required. If disclosure to a third party within a reasonable period was envisaged, when Andrew discloses the data to Barbara, Andrew must inform Clarence no later than that time that the data have been disclosed. When Barbara first processes the data, she must inform Clarence of her identity (at least), unless to do so would involve a disproportionate effort or where the recording or disclosure is required by law. However, if Andrew previously informed Clarence that the data would be disclosed to Barbara (or perhaps even if he told him that the data might be disclosed to data controllers of a generic description within which Barbara would fall), then Barbara is excused providing this information and, if required to ensure processing is fair, the further information if Andrew also informed Clarence of it. Figure 31.1 shows the working of these provisions. It assumes that disclosure by Andrew within a reasonable period was envisaged and that the disclosure does in fact take place.

The Secretary of State may by order impose conditions as to the processing of any general identifier (for example, an identity number) should, of course, such an identifier be introduced in the UK. This may include further obligations to inform data subjects.

CONSTRAINTS ON PROCESSING

For processing to comply with the first data protection principle, one of the conditions in Schedule 2 must be met and, in the case of sensitive personal data, one of the conditions in Schedule 3 must also be met. At first sight they can appear restrictive because, if not within the conditions, processing is not allowed at all, unless otherwise exempt or outside the scope of the Data Protection Act 1998. The conditions for processing personal data are central to the controls over processing contained in Articles 7 and 8 of the data protection Directive. As expressed in the Act, the first data protection principle states:

1 Personal data shall be processed fairly and lawfully and, in particular, shall not be processed unless –
   (a) at least one of the conditions in Schedule 2 is met, and
   (b) in the case of sensitive personal data, at least one of the conditions in Schedule 3 is also met.

These conditions are examined further below.

Conditions for processing personal data in Schedule 2

The conditions in Schedule 2 are:

1 The data subject has given his consent to the processing.
2 The processing is necessary –
   (a) for the performance of a contract to which the data subject is a party, or
   (b) for the taking of steps at the request of the data subject with a view to entering into a contract.
3 The processing is necessary for compliance with any legal obligation to which the data controller is subject, other than an obligation imposed by contract.
4 The processing is necessary in order to protect the vital interests of the data subject.

5 The processing is necessary –
   (a) for the administration of justice,
   (aa) for the exercise of any functions of either House of Parliament,
   (b) for the exercise of functions conferred on any person by or under any enactment,
   (c) for the exercise of any function of the Crown, a Minister of the Crown or a government department, or
   (d) for the exercise of any other functions of a public nature exercised in the public interest by any person.

6 (1) The processing is necessary for the purposes of legitimate interests pursued by the data controller or by the third party or parties to whom the data are disclosed, except where the processing is unwarranted in any particular case by reason of prejudice to the rights and freedoms or legitimate interests of the data subject.
   (2) The Secretary of State may by order specify particular circumstances in which this condition is, or is not, to be taken to be satisfied.

Paragraph 5(aa) was inserted by the Freedom of Information Act 2000. The last provision in para. 6(2) sensibly allows for the list of conditions to be modified. However, and this is important, if the data controller cannot fit within one of these conditions, then he may not process personal data unless otherwise exempt.

A number of points can be made about these conditions:

- The data subject's consent is not stated to be express or explicit (unlike the case with the equivalent condition for sensitive personal data) and it would seem reasonable that it may be implied or result from failing to object, having been given the opportunity, for example, by failing to tick a box on a form.

- The word 'necessary' appears in all the conditions apart from the first – this is unlikely to be taken in a strict sense such as it being absolutely essential: it is a question of proportionality and depends on the importance of the goal sought to be achieved as accepted by Lord Woolf CJ in *R (on the application of Ellis)* v *Chief Constable of Essex Police* [2003] 2 FLR 566 adapting the test of Lord Steyn in *R* v *Secretary of State for the Home Department, ex parte Daly* [2001] 2 AC 532 in respect of the right to respect for private and family life under Article 8 of the Council of Europe Convention for the Protection of Human Rights and Fundamental Freedoms. Lord Woolf noted the acceptance of counsel that the effect of Article 8 was the same as the combined effect of section 29 and Schedules 2 and 3 of the Data Protection Act 1998 (section 29 is the exemption that applies to processing for the prevention or detection of crime). In other words, the provision should go no further than necessary to meet the legitimate objective being pursued.

- An example of the vital interests of the data subject could be where his present address is disclosed to an appropriate authority after it has been discovered that he has been in contact with someone with a contagious disease or where he is using a defective and dangerous implement. Perhaps the main reason for this condition is that it is needed to back up an equivalent though inconsistently wider condition in Schedule 3.

- The fifth condition will apply to a great deal of processing in the public sector, including but not restricted to central and local government. The Freedom of Information Act 2000 extended the condition to the exercise of functions of the Houses of Parliament (para. 5(aa)).

- Most commercial organisations will be able to rely on the second or sixth condition (although the data subject's consent may still be required to ensure processing is fair generally). There is, however, a slight difference to the language used in the Directive which speaks of the legitimate interests being 'overridden by the interests for fundamental rights and freedoms of the data subject which require protection under Article 1(1)' (being in particular the right to privacy in relation to processing of personal data) – the Data Protection Act 1998 seems slightly more restrictive; the European Court of Justice gave some guidance in Case C-369/98 *R* **v** *Minister of Agriculture, Fisheries and Food, ex parte Fisher* [2000] ECR I-6751, saying that it requires a balancing of the legitimate interests of the data controller and the data subject. In that case, the Minister refused to disclose details of crops grown in previous years to farmers who had recently purchased a farm. The information was required for an official return and penalties were imposed for errors in making the returns. The farmers could not complete the returns properly without such information.

■ It is a little difficult to say just what 'legitimate interests' are – one view is that they cover any activity that is lawful while another is that, in respect of artificial legal persons, they also cover activities within the organisation's powers. In other words, the organisation is acting *intra vires* and in accordance with the law. Certainly discharging duties imposed by law is included.

■ Some flexibility is introduced by empowering the Secretary of State to specify what is or is not within the 'legitimate interests' form of processing – although this power is not mentioned in the Directive it could prove to be important to cover a situation that could not have been envisaged when the Bill was proceeding through Parliament.

In most cases data controllers should find that they satisfy at least one of the above conditions and, in practice, this requirement has not proved unduly restrictive. It is difficult to think of a form of processing that falls outside all the conditions and would yet be deemed to be fair and lawful. Where the personal data are sensitive, the data controller must satisfy one of the conditions in Schedule 2 above as well as one of the conditions in Schedule 3, discussed below.

Conditions for processing sensitive data in Schedule 3

Sensitive personal data are defined in section 2 of the Data Protection Act 1998 and include data relating to racial or ethnic origin, political opinions, religious or other similar beliefs, trade union membership, physical or mental health or condition, sexual life and data relating to offences (including proceedings, disposal of such proceedings or the sentence of any court). The conditions in Schedule 3 were extended as a result of the Data Protection (Processing of Sensitive Personal Data) Order 2000 and further conditions have been added by the Data Protection (Processing of Sensitive Personal Data) (Elected Representatives) Order 2002 and the Data Protection (Processing of Sensitive Personal Data) Order 2006.

The conditions contained in Schedule 3, as at Royal Assent, were originally as follows (not verbatim).

1 The data subject has given his explicit consent to the processing of the personal data.
2 The processing is necessary for the purposes of exercising or performing any right or obligation which is conferred or imposed by law on the data controller in connection with employment (this is subject to potential modification by the Secretary of State).
3 The processing is necessary –
   (a) in order to protect the vital interests of the data subject or another person, in a case where –
      (i)   consent cannot be given by or on behalf of the data subject, or
      (ii) the data controller cannot reasonably be expected to obtain the consent of the data subject, or
   (b) in order to protect the vital interests of another person, in a case where consent by or on behalf of the data subject has been unreasonably withheld.

31

Data controllers and the Data Protection Act 1998

4   The processing is carried out subject to appropriate safeguards by a non-profit-making body or association which exists for political, philosophical, religious or trade-union purposes – processing must be carried out with appropriate safeguards for the rights and freedoms of data subjects and relate only to individuals who are members or have regular contact in connection with the body's or association's purposes and which does not involve disclosure to a third party without the consent of the data subject.

5   The information contained in the personal data has been made public as a result of steps deliberately taken by the data subject.

6   The processing is necessary in respect of legal proceedings, legal advice and legal rights.

7   The processing is necessary for the administration of justice, the exercise of any functions by either House of Parliament, the exercise of functions conferred by or under any enactment, the exercise of any functions of the Crown, a Minister of the Crown or a government department (the Secretary of State may exclude this condition in specified cases or require further conditions to be satisfied).

8   The processing is necessary for medical purposes (includes preventative medicine, medical diagnosis, medical research, provision of care and treatment and management of healthcare services) and is undertaken by a health professional or a person under a duty of confidentiality equivalent to that owed by a health professional.

9   The processing of sensitive personal data consisting of information as to racial or ethnic origin when it is necessary for the purpose of identifying or keeping under review the existence or absence of equality of opportunity or treatment between persons of different racial or ethnic origins, with a view to enabling such equality to be promoted or maintained, and is carried out with appropriate safeguards for the rights and freedoms of data subjects.

10 The Secretary of State may by order allow sensitive data to be processed in other circumstances.

The last provision allowing the list of conditions to be extended has already proved useful and the Data Protection (Processing of Sensitive Personal Data) Order 2000 added the following conditions to the list:

1   Where processing is in substantial public interest and is necessary for the purposes of prevention or detection of any unlawful act (or failure to act) and must necessarily be carried out without the explicit consent of the data subject being sought so as not to prejudice those purposes.

2   Where processing is in substantial public interest and is necessary for the discharge of any function designed to protect members of the public from dishonesty, malpractice, or other improper conduct by, or unfitness or incompetence of, any person or mismanagement in the administration of, or failures in services provided by, any body or association, and which must necessarily be carried out with the explicit consent of the data subject being sought so as not to prejudice the discharge of that function. These first two conditions also extend to processing for the special purposes with a view to publication where the data controller reasonably believes such publication is in the public interest.

Further conditions cover processing in relation to confidential counselling, in the context of insurance and occupational pensions, equal opportunity monitoring in the context of religious beliefs or physical or mental health, political opinions where processing is by a political party, processing in the substantial public interest for research purposes or where necessary by a constable in the exercise of functions conferred by law.

The Data Protection (Processing of Sensitive Personal Data) (Elected Representatives) Order 2002 allows processing by certain elected representatives in relation to requests made by individuals, whether the data subject or another, to take action on behalf of the data subject or another.

A 'health professional' is defined in section 69 and includes, *inter alia*, registered practitioners such as doctors, dentists, opticians, pharmaceutical chemists, nurses, midwives or health visitors, chiropractors, clinical psychologists, child psychotherapists or speech therapists, music therapists employed by a health service body or a scientist employed as head of department of such a body.

The Data Protection (Processing of Sensitive Personal Data) Order 2006 allows the processing of personal data relating to convictions or cautions for the purposes of administering an account relating to a payment card, or cancelling the card, where it has been used in the commission of an offence concerning indecent images of children. These include offences under section 1 of the Protection of Children Act 1978 and section 160 of the Criminal Justice Act 1988.

These conditions are fairly extensive and the following points can be made in respect of them:

- where the data subject's consent is relied upon it has to be explicit and it should be informed consent – failing to tick a box on a form will not be good enough;
- what has been said above in relation to the word 'necessary' ought also to apply here though the proportionality test will have a higher threshold;
- vital interests in this context will include situations where an individual is unconscious and disclosure of his blood group is required so that he can be given a life-saving blood transfusion;
- certain types of non-profit-making bodies are included as much of the personal data such bodies will be processing will fall within the definition of sensitive data and it is plainly important for them to process such data belonging to their own members or others having regular contact (note that the condition does not necessarily relate only to registered charities): disclosure requires the consent of the data subjects and it is likely that express consent should be obtained;
- conditions relating to legal proceedings and justice, functions of the Houses of Parliament, legally imposed functions and government functions are as expected but note that the Secretary of State has the power to exclude some of these in particular cases or require further conditions;
- processing for equal opportunity monitoring (race, ethnicity, religious belief, physical or mental health or condition) is not specifically mentioned in the Directive but it does allow Member States to include other conditions allowing processing where there is substantial public interest subject to satisfactory safeguards;
- in the Data Protection Act 1998 as enacted, there was no condition allowing processing of personal data relating to criminal offences such that, for example, commercial organisations which grant credit could process such data – hence the additional condition allowing processing for the prevention or detection of crime.

Data controllers who intend to process sensitive data must ensure that they fall within one of the conditions above in addition to one of the conditions in Schedule 2. In some cases, to be specified in the future, the intended processing may fall within the requirement to have a preliminary assessment carried out by the Information Commissioner and, in other cases, where the data controller is unsure, he could consider approaching the Information Commissioner for guidance or consulting a representative body such as a trade association. Guidance notes have been published to further assist the data controller in deciding whether he can process the sensitive data in question. Furthermore, the Information Commissioner may, with the consent of the data controller, individually assess the processing for good practice. A fee can be charged for this service if the Secretary of State so provides.

Suitable safeguards

Article 8(4) of the data protection Directive allows Member States to lay down further conditions for processing sensitive personal data for reasons of substantial public interest, subject suitable safeguards. One such condition in the Data Protection Act 1998 is that in para. 7 of Schedule 3 which includes, *inter alia*, processing necessary for the exercise of any functions conferred on any person by or under any enactment. There is no express mention of 'suitable safeguards'.

In *Stone* v *South East Coast Strategic Health Authority* [2006] EWHC 1668 (Admin), an independent report had been commissioned by the Health Authority, under the National Health Service Act 1977 and other legislation, into the care, treatment and supervision of the claimant prior to his conviction for the murder of Lin and Megan Russell. The Health Authority intended to publish the report to the world at large. The issue under the Data Protection Act 1998 was whether the processing was within one of the conditions for processing sensitive personal data under Schedule 3.

Although the condition in para. 7 did not mention anything about safeguards, the judge accepted that the provision had to be read as being subject to appropriate safeguards. In particular, the use of the word 'necessary', which appears in most of the conditions for processing, carries connotations of the Council of Europe Convention on the Protection of Human Rights and Fundamental Freedoms. This includes the proposition that a pressing social need is involved and that the measure employed is proportionate to the legitimate aim being pursued. The judge, Mr Justice Davis, contrasted para. 7 with para. 9 which explicitly requires appropriate safeguards for the rights and freedoms of data subjects. He also accepted that para. 8 also applied to allow processing (processing necessary for medical purposes).

The principle of proportionality is a basic general principle of European Community law and requires that measures implemented through Community provisions should be appropriate for attaining the objective pursued and must not go beyond what is *necessary* to achieve it.

Patient information

Further provision for processing health data is provided for separately under the Health Service (Control of Patient Information) Regulations 2002, made under section 60(1) of the Health and Social Care Act 2001. Confidential patient information relating to patients referred for the diagnosis or treatment of neoplasia may be processed for medical purposes including the surveillance and analysis of health and disease, monitoring and auditing of health and health related care provision and outcomes, planning and administration of the provision made for health and health related care, medical research approved by research ethics committees, provision of information about individuals who have suffered from a particular disease or condition where the information supports an analysis of the risk of developing that disease or condition and is required for counselling and support of persons concerned about the risk of developing that disease or condition. Processing may only be undertaken by persons approved by the Secretary of State and is authorised by the person who lawfully holds the information. The Regulations do not extend to Scotland.

A person who processes such confidential patient information must inform the Patient Information Advisory Group and make available information required by the Secretary of State to assist in the investigation and audit of that processing. This is because the provisions in the Regulations must be considered annually.

Under section 60(4) of the Health and Social Care Act 2001, the processing concerned must not be inconsistent with provisions made by or under the Data Protection Act 1998. The underlying aims of processing under the Regulations is that it is in the interests of improving patient care or in the public interest.

Other cases

Constraints on processing may be imposed in particular cases. Regulation 5 of the Electronic Signatures Regulations 2002 imposes further constraints of certification-service-providers, being persons who issue certificates or provide other services in respect of electronic signatures. They are not allowed to obtain personal data for the purpose of issuing or maintaining that certificate otherwise than directly from the data subject or after the explicit consent of the data subject, and may not process such personal data to a greater extent than is necessary for the purpose of issuing or maintaining that certificate, or to a greater extent than is necessary for any other purpose to which the data subject has explicitly consented. An exception is made where the processing is necessary for compliance with any legal obligation, to which the certification-service-provider is subject, other than an obligation imposed by contract.

A possible new condition for processing sensitive personal data

The Serious Crime Bill, before Parliament at the time of writing, in its present form will introduce a further condition allowing processing. The Bill has special provision for sharing information between anti-fraud organisations and will allow for data matching by or on behalf of the Audit Commission. In this context, data matching is described as involving a comparison of sets of data to determine how far they match and includes the identification of patterns and trends. The Audit Commission will be able to require, *inter alia*, bodies subject to audit to provide data for data matching purposes. A code of data matching practice must be prepared by the Audit Commission which will also keep it under review.

DATA SUBJECTS AND THEIR EXERCISE OF RIGHTS TO PREVENT PROCESSING

Data subjects have the following rights under the Data Protection Act 1998:

- a right to data subject access;
- a right to prevent processing likely to cause substantial damage or substantial distress;
- a right to prevent processing for purposes of direct marketing;
- rights in relation to automated decision taking;
- a right to compensation available in respect of damage or distress caused by *any* contravention of the Data Protection Act 1998;
- a right of rectification, erasure, blocking and destruction of inaccurate personal data; and
- a right to be informed as required by the first data protection principle (as set out in Part II of Schedule 1 – interpretation of the principles), as discussed above.

There are also rights in relation to 'exempt manual data' which apply only until 24 October 2007, as from that date, manual data in respect of which processing was already underway on 23 October 1998 come fully within the provisions of the Act. Before that date, such data were subject to a transitional provision. The significance of the date is that the Directive should have been implemented by 24 October 1998 at the latest.

Apart from the concerns about the requirement to inform data subjects, data controllers originally expressed some anxiety about the possibility of data subjects objecting to certain forms of processing and being able, in some cases, to require the data controller to stop processing personal data relating to them. The reality is less burdensome. In particular, fair and lawful processing will rarely cause substantial damage or substantial distress. The mail, fax and telephone preference schemes are quite effective at preventing (or at least reducing the amount of unsolicited marketing material or calls an individual receives) and the rights in the context of automated decision taking are considerably reduced in a contractual situation or where authorised or provided for by legislation.

Although the rights of data subjects should not prove too onerous for data controllers, they must ensure that they have systems and procedures in place to recognise and comply with data subjects' requests to the extent they are required to do under the Data Protection Act 1998 and subordinate legislation.

TRANSFERS TO THIRD COUNTRIES

Many data controllers transfer personal data to other countries for processing activities. The Act contains provision that apply where personal data are being transferred to a country outside the European Economic Area (EEA). As mentioned earlier, the rationale behind the data protection Directive is that, by providing a level playing field in terms of effective protection for rights and freedoms of individuals, particularly with respect to their right of privacy in relation to processing personal data, there can be no barriers to freedom of movement of personal data throughout the EEA. However, problems may occur where a data controller wishes, as many do, to have personal data processed elsewhere and the country to which he wants to transfer the personal data for processing has no specific data protection laws or, if such laws exist, they fail to meet the European standards and safeguards. A transfer does not have to be permanent and the language of the Directive suggests that permitting access to personal data, for example, on a website is within these provisions.

The eighth data protection principle requires that personal data must not be transferred to a country or territory outside the EEA unless it ensures an adequate level of protection for the rights and freedoms of data subjects in relation to the processing of personal data. The interpretative provisions in Part II of Schedule 1 state that an adequate level of protection is one which is adequate in all the circumstances of the case, having regard in particular to:

(a)   the nature of the data,
(b)   the country or territory of origin of the information contained in the data,
(c)   the country or territory of final destination of that information,
(d)   the purposes for which and period during which the data are intended to be processed,
(e)   the law in force in the country or territory in question,
(f)   the international obligations of that country or territory,
(g)   any relevant codes of conduct or other rules which are enforceable in that country or territory (whether generally or by arrangement in particular cases), and
(h)   any security measures taken in respect of the data in that country or territory.

Thus, adequacy depends on a number of factors and it will not be possible to say that a particular country does not have an adequate level of protection in all cases. It might be possible to say the opposite, however, where a country embraces a model of data protection law which is, to all intents and purposes, a mirror image of that in Europe. There are no restrictions on such countries and those already declared to have adequate protection include Switzerland, Canada, Argentina, Guernsey and the Isle of Man. Transfers governed by the US Department of Commerce's Safe Harbor Privacy Principles are acceptable as is the transfer of Air Passenger Name Records to the US Bureau of Customs and Border Protection.

Personal data on a webpage

One might think that placing personal data on a website involved transfers to third countries where persons in those countries accessed those data. In Case C-101/01 *Bodil Lindqvist* [2003] ECR I-12971, Mrs Bodil Lindqvist was charged with criminal offences in Sweden under data protection law. She worked as a religious teacher in a parish in Sweden and had set up webpages on her home computer for the purpose of providing access to information useful for parishioners preparing for confirmation. She placed information about her colleagues on the webpages, such as their names, telephone numbers, jobs and hobbies. Mrs Lindqvist failed to obtain her colleagues' consent. She was convicted of a number of data protection offences including transferring personal data to a third country without authorisation. She was fined 4,000 Swedish Kroner and appealed against the convictions. The Swedish appeal court had doubts about the interpretation of certain provisions of the data protection Directive and referred a number of questions for a preliminary ruling under Article 234 of the EC Treaty.

The European Court of Justice ruled that consideration must be given to the activities of Mrs Lindqvist rather than those carried out by the service providers hosting the webpages. Such service providers manage the infrastructure needed to store the personal data and transmit them to any person seeking access to those data. That infrastructure may be located in one or more countries without its clients being aware of that fact. Mrs Lindqvist's webpages did not themselves contain the technical means to send the data automatically to persons who did not deliberately seek access to those pages. A person accessing such data would have to connect to the internet and personally carry out the necessary actions to access those data.

The European Court of Justice noted that the data protection Directive was drawn up at a time when the internet was not fully developed and no express provision was made in relation to the internet. That being so, it could not be presumed that the Community legislature intended that loading personal data on an internet webpage fell within the meaning of transfers of personal data to third countries. If it was otherwise, a finding by the Commission that only one third country did not have adequate protection for personal data would prevent the placing of any personal data in any Member State.

Of course, sending personal data as an e-mail attachment to a person located outside the EEA would be considered to be a transfer to a third country. The *Bodil Lindqvist* case shows that the transfer must involve an act making the transfer rather than placing material passively on a webpage so that others can find and access it. In effect it is that person who initiates the transfer.

Transfers where protection not adequate

Even if a particular country or territory does not have an adequate level of protection in terms of the particular transfer envisaged, it may still be possible to make that transfer. The European Community legislators adopted a sense of reality and accepted that there may be good reasons why a data controller might validly wish to transfer data to such a country. The approach taken is to allow the transfer subject to one of a set of conditions being satisfied, the purpose of which is to overcome danger associated with inadequate protection. Thus, the eighth data protection principle does not apply to data within Schedule 4 (except by order of the Secretary of State), being where any one of the following conditions is present:

1   The data subject has given consent to transfer.
2   The transfer is necessary for the performance of a contract between the data subject and data controller or for taking steps at the request of the data subject with a view to his entering into such a contract.
3   The transfer is necessary for the conclusion of a contract between the data controller and a

third person entered into at the request of the data subject or in his interests, or is necessary for the performance of the contract.

4   The transfer is necessary for reasons of substantial public interest (the Lord Chancellor may specify circumstances in which a transfer is or is not covered by this).

5   The transfer is necessary with respect to legal proceedings, legal rights or obtaining legal advice.

6   The transfer is necessary to protect the vital interests of the data subject.

7   The transfer is part of the personal data on a public register and any conditions subject to which the register is open to inspection are complied with by any person to whom the data are or may be disclosed after the transfer.

8   The transfer is made on terms of a kind approved by the Commissioner as ensuring adequate safeguards for the rights and freedoms of data subjects.

9   The transfer has been authorised by the Commissioner as being made in such a manner as to ensure adequate safeguards for the rights and freedoms of data subjects.

In relation to the eighth condition above, the Information Commissioner may approve terms which ensure adequate safeguards or authorise transfer as being made so as to ensure adequate safeguards. In any proceedings under the new law, questions as to whether the eighth principle has been met are to be determined in accordance with any finding made by the European Commission under Article 31(2) of the Directive as to transfers of the kind in question. In the main, safeguards are likely to come from approved contractual terms. There are obligations to inform the Commission to the European Communities as to authorisations granted and the Commission has agreed standard contractual clauses that are deemed to offer sufficient safeguards.

SECURITY

The seventh data protection principle requires that appropriate technical and organisational measures are taken against unauthorised or unlawful processing of personal data and against accidental loss or destruction of, or damage to, personal data. Security was an important aspect of data protection law under the 1984 Act and is continued under the 1998 Act with additional emphasis on the relationship between the data controller and a processor. Factors influencing the level of security include the state of technological development, the cost of implementation, the potential harm of unauthorised processing or accidental loss, destruction or damage and the nature of the data. That being so, a prudent data controller will continually review his security arrangements and monitor technological improvements to security measures available.

Data controllers must take reasonable steps to ensure the reliability of staff having access to personal data. They must choose processors who provide sufficient guarantees as regards technical and organisational measures and take reasonable steps to ensure compliance with those measures. Where a processor is engaged, the processing must be carried out under a contract made or evidenced in writing under which the processor is to act only on the instructions of the data controller and which imposes equivalent security obligations on the processor. Data controllers are required to take reasonable steps to ensure that the processor complies with the security measures. Although processors do not have to notify the processing they perform on behalf of others, this mechanism is designed to make sure that they are aware of the importance of security and, in the event of a failure on the part of the processor, he will be liable for breach of contract.

EXEMPTIONS

The Data Protection Act 1998 contains a large number of exemptions from parts of the Act. First, it should be noted that there are some multiple exemptions from the 'subject information provisions' and the 'non-disclosure provisions', as follows:

■ 'subject information provisions' meaning the first principle, in as much as it requires compliance with Part II, para. 2 of Schedule 1 (providing information to the data subject on collection or in other cases) and section 7 (subject access);

■ 'non-disclosure provisions' meaning the first data protection principle (but not with respect to the requirement that one of the conditions in Schedule 2 is met and, for sensitive data, one of the conditions in Schedule 3 is also met), the second to the fifth data protection principles, section 10 (the right to prevent processing likely to cause damage or distress) and section 14(1) to (3) (right of rectification, etc. in relation to inaccurate data) *to the extent that they are inconsistent with the disclosure in question.*

These two forms of exemption do not apply in all cases and some exemptions are more extensive. Except as provided for in the exemptions, the subject access provisions are unaffected by any enactment or rule of law prohibiting or restricting the disclosure, or authorising the withholding of information.

The exemptions, some of which are set out in Schedule 7 to the Act, are numerous. Under section 38, the Secretary of State is given the power to make further exemptions to the subject information provisions and the non-disclosure provisions if he considers further exemption is necessary to safeguard the interests of data subjects or the rights and freedoms of any other individual. This is a basis for exemption in the Directive. Some of the exemptions are outside the scope of the Directive in any case, such as those relating to national security or processing by an individual for a purely personal or household activity: Article 3(2).

It should be noted that a general principle is that exemption from the relevant provisions of the Act is available only in as much as compliance would prejudice the purpose governed by the exemption or if the particular exemption is required for the purpose concerned. For example, exemption is granted from the subject access provisions for the purposes of the prevention or detection of crime. However, if subject access can be granted without prejudicing these purposes (or other exempted purposes), then it must be granted. The exemptions are not generally blanket exemptions and require a value-judgment by the data controller as to whether an exemption is available in a particular circumstance.

All the exemptions are listed in Table 31.1 and then most of the exemptions are described in more depth.

31

Data controllers and the Data Protection Act 1998

Table 31.1 Exemptions under the Data Protection Act 1998

Description	Exemption provided from	Notes
National security, section 28	■ All the Principles ■ Parts II, III and V (rights of data subjects, notification, enforcement) ■ Section 54A (inspection of personal data in certain overseas information systems by the Information Commissioner) ■ Section 55 (offences of unlawful obtaining, etc. – see later)	The exemption must be required for the purpose of safeguarding national security but a certificate signed by a Minister of the Crown (being a Cabinet Minister, the Attorney General or, in Scotland, the Advocate General for Scotland) to that effect is conclusive (as it was under the 1984 Act) – there are provisions for any person affected to appeal to the tribunal In Schedule 6, para. 6 the tribunal's jurisdiction shall be exercised *ex parte* by the Chairman or a Deputy Chairman – subject to rules made under para. 7 for regulating the exercise of the right of appeal
Crime and taxation, section 29	■ First Principle (except to the extent which it requires compliance with conditions in Schedules 2 and 3 – thus the conditions still apply) ■ Section 7 (subject access) ■ All only to the extent to which application of those provisions would be likely to prejudice matters in section 29(1)	Only for purposes of prevention/detection of crime, apprehension/prosecution of offenders or assessment/collection of any tax or duty or any imposition of a similar nature (section 29(1)) Data processed for purpose of discharging statutory function where information obtained for any purpose mentioned above are exempt from subject information provisions to the same extent Data disclosed for purposes of crime or taxation are exempt from non-disclosure provisions if those provisions would be likely to prejudice those purposes Where the data controller is a government department, local authority or other authority administering housing or council tax benefit, data are exempt from section 7 (subject access) if the exemption is required in the interests of a system of risk assessment for taxation or crime where the offence involves unlawful application for or claim in respect of public funds
Health, education and social work, section 30	Exemptions from subject access provided for by the Data Protection (Subject Access Modification) (Health) Order 2000, the Data Protection (Subject Access Modification) (Education) Order 2000 and the Data Protection (Subject Access Modification) (Social Work) Order 2000, as amended. These exemptions apply where access to the information would be likely to cause serious harm to the physical or mental health or condition of the data subject or any other person. Exemptions from the subject information provisions apply in the case of processing by courts in relation to certain types of reports in family proceedings	Leaves it to the Lord Chancellor to make orders – three have been made as noted in the preceding column. The exemptions may cover, for example, where a doctor does not want to allow a patient access to his file if it shows the patient is terminally ill and the doctor considers this knowledge would be harmful to the patient

Table 31.1 continued

Description	Exemption provided from	Notes
Regulatory activity, section 31	■ Subject information provisions	If likely to prejudice proper discharge of function covered (to protect public, charities, persons at work (as appropriate)) functions are: ■ financial loss resulting from dishonesty, malpractice, unfitness, incompetence of persons concerned in banking, insurance, investment or other financial services or management of bodies corporate; ■ financial loss resulting from the conduct of a bankrupt; ■ dishonesty, etc. by professional persons; ■ misconduct or mismanagement in administration of charities; ■ in respect of protecting property of charities; ■ in relation to health and safety at work. Exemption is extended to others such as the Parliamentary Commissioner for Administration, Health Service Commissioner, Office of Fair Trading, etc.
Journalism, literature and art, section 32	■ All the Principles (except seventh – security measures) ■ Section 7 (subject access) ■ Section 10 (right to prevent processing likely to cause damage or distress) ■ Section 12 (automated decision taking) ■ Section 14(1)–(3) (rectification, etc.)	An important exemption protecting freedom of speech Where personal data are processed for the special purposes the exemption applies if: (a) processing is with a view to publication by any person of journalistic, literary or artistic material; (b) the data controller reasonably believes it is in the public interest, having regard to the special importance of freedom of expression; (c) the data controller reasonably believes, in all the circumstances, that compliance with the provision is incompatible with the special purposes. Codes of practice may be designated by the Secretary of State and taken into account in determining reasonableness of public interest belief. A number of codes designated by the Data Protection (Designated Codes of Practice) (No. 2) Order 2000 include those of the Broadcasting Commission and the Press Complaints Commission Provision for the court to stay certain types of proceedings if data controller makes a claim that special purposes exist and he has not published the material in the preceding 24 hours – the stay is subject to the claim being withdrawn or the coming into effect of a determination by the Commissioner under section 45

31

Data controllers and the Data Protection Act 1998

Table 31.1 continued

Description	Exemption provided from	Notes
Research, history, statistics, section 33	■ Such further processing not incompatible with Principle 2 (purpose for which obtained) ■ May be kept indefinitely notwithstanding Principle 5 ■ Section 7 (subject access) – if processed in accordance with relevant conditions and results not made available in any form identifying any data subject	Research purposes includes statistical or historical purposes 'Relevant conditions' are: (a) the data are not processed to support measures or decisions with respect to particular individuals; and (b) are not processed in such a way that substantial damage or substantial distress is or is likely to be caused to any data subject. Personal data will still be treated as processed for research purposes where disclosure is to any person for research purposes, to the data subject or person acting on his behalf, at the request or with consent of data subject or person acting on his behalf or where person making disclosure has reasonable grounds for believing any of the above disclosures apply
Manual data held by public authorities, section 33A	■ First, second, third, fifth, seventh and eighth Principles ■ Sixth Principle, except for the right of access under section 7 and the right of rectification, etc. under section 14 ■ Sections 10–12, rights to object to processing and right in relation to automated decision taking ■ Section13 (right to compensation) except where it relates to damage caused by a contravention or section 7 or the fourth Principle ■ Part III (notification) ■ Section 55 (offences of unlawful obtaining, etc.)	Added by the Freedom of Information Act 2000. Applies to personal data within (e) of the definition of data under section 1(1). Where the personal data relate to appointments and removal, pay, discipline, superannuation and other personal matters in relation to employment or service in the armed forces, the Crown, local authorities, etc. further exemption from the remaining principles and the remaining parts of Part II (rights of data subjects) is given
Information available to public by or under any enactment, section 34	■ Subject information provisions ■ Fourth Principle ■ Section 12A (rights in relation to exempt manual data) – applies until 23 October 2007 ■ Section 14(1)–(3) (rectification, etc.) ■ Non-disclosure provisions	If the data controller is obliged by or under any enactment (other than one contained in the Freedom of Information Act 2000) to make the information available to the public whether by publicising it, making it available for inspection or otherwise, whether on payment of a fee or not
Disclosures required by law or in connection with legal proceedings, etc. section 35	■ Non-disclosure provisions	Where disclosure required by or under any enactment, rule of law or by court order or if necessary for legal proceedings, obtaining legal advice or establishing, exercising or defending a legal right

Table 31.1 continued

Description	Exemption provided from	Notes
Parliamentary privilege, section 35A	(a) First Principle (except to the extent which it requires compliance with conditions in Schedules 2 and 3 – thus the conditions still apply) (b) Second, third, fourth and fifth Principles (c) Section 7 (subject access) (d) Section 10 (right to prevent processing likely to cause damage or distress) (e) Section 14(1)–(3) (rectification, etc.)	Added by the Freedom of Information Act 2000. If the exemption is required to avoid an infringement of the privileges of either House of Parliament. Came into force on 1 January 2005.
Domestic purposes, section 36	■ All the Principles ■ Parts II and III (rights of data subjects and notification)	Processed by an individual only for that individual's personal, family or household affairs (including recreational purposes)
Miscellaneous exceptions in Schedule 7		
Confidential references by data controller, para. 1	■ Section 7 (subject access)	Applies to references in respect of education, employment or appointment of data subject to any office (actual or prospective) or the provisions of services by the data subject (actual or prospective)
Armed forces, para. 2	■ Subject information provisions	If likely to prejudice the combat effectiveness of any of the armed forces of the Crown
Judicial appointments, honours, para. 3	■ Subject information provisions	To assess suitability for judicial office or as a QC or the conferring by the Crown of any honour or dignity
Crown employment, etc., para. 4	■ Subject access provisions (by order of the Secretary of State – Data Protection (Crown Appointments) Order 2000 – lists the appointments, includes the Poet Laureate, Astronomer Royal, Lord-Lieutenants and Archbishops and other positions in the Church of England)	Processing to assess any person's suitability for: (a) employment by/under the Crown, (b) any office to which appointments are made by Her Majesty, by a Minister of the Crown or a Northern Ireland Authority
Management forecasts, para. 5	■ Subject information provisions	For purposes of management forecasting or planning to assist the data controller in the conduct of any business or other activity where complying would be likely to prejudice that conduct

31

Data controllers and the Data Protection Act 1998

Table 31.1 continued

Description	Exemption provided from	Notes
Corporate finance, para. 6	■ Subject information provisions	Underwriting in respect of issues, advice to undertakings on capital structure, industrial strategy and related matters, advice and services in relation to mergers and acquisitions of undertakings and underwriting such matters
		Where compliance could affect the price of an instrument in relation to investment services or if exemption required to safeguard important economic or financial interest of UK
		The Secretary of State may specify by order circumstances in which exemption is or is not taken to be required or matters to be taken into account in determining whether required for safeguarding important economic or financial interest of UK (see the Data Protection (Corporate Finance Exemption) Order 2000 – matters are the orderly functioning of financial markets and the efficient allocation of capital within the economy – data are, *inter alia*, those the data controller reasonably believes would affect a decision to deal in, subscribe to or issue an instrument)
Negotiations, para. 7	■ Subject information provisions (to extent would prejudice negotiations)	Records of intentions in relation to any negotiations with the data subject if likely to prejudice those negotiations
Examination marks, para. 8	■ Section 7 (subject access)	Simply postpones the time for compliance in cases where application made before examination results are announced
		Time for compliance is five months after request or 40 days after results announced, whichever is the earlier
		If based on the five-month period, there is a duty to supply details at the time the request was made together with subsequent versions
Examination scripts, para. 9	■ Section 7 (subject access)	Personal data recorded by candidates during academic, professional or other examination
Legal professional privilege, para. 10	■ Subject information provisions	Information in respect of which a claim to legal professional privilege (or, in Scotland, to confidentiality of communications) could be maintained in legal proceedings
Self-incrimination, para. 11	■ Section 7 (subject access)	But not in respect of offences under this Act, though such information is not admissible in criminal proceedings

▨ National security

This exemption is provided under section 28 and applies if it is necessary for the purpose of safeguarding national security. The exemption is very wide-ranging and is from all the principles, the rights of data subjects, notification and enforcement. Exemption from the provisions of section 54A is also granted. This provision allows the Information Commissioner to inspect personal data contained in the Schengen, Europol and Customs information systems. It is an offence to obstruct or fail to assist any person carrying out this power. Furthermore, the offences in section 55 in respect of unlawful obtaining, etc. do not apply if this exemption applies. A certificate signed by a Minister of the Crown who is a member of the Cabinet, the Attorney-General or, in Scotland, Advocate General, is conclusive evidence that the exemption is required. The need for this exemption is plain but the certification arrangements mean that there is little control over the scope and application of this exemption. However, there is provision for an appeal against a certificate to the Information Tribunal. Any appeal will be held before the Chairman and/or deputy Chairmen as designated by the Lord Chancellor and proceedings normally will be held *ex parte*, that is, without hearing the person appealing against the certificate. There are special procedures in respect to an appeal brought under section 28 which are set out in the Information Tribunal (National Security Appeals) Rules 2005.

Crime and taxation

This applies if the personal data are held for the purpose of the prevention or detection of crime, the apprehension or prosecution of offenders or the assessment or collection of any tax or duty or imposition of a similar nature. Under section 29, the exemption is from the first data protection principle and the subject access provisions. However, the conditions for processing under the first principle (in Schedules 2 and 3) still apply. Exemption is also given in respect of the non-disclosure provisions in relation to processing for the prevention or detection of crime. The exemption applies only in as much as the provision in question would be likely to prejudice any of the purposes covered by the exemption.

The case of *R v Chief Constables of C and D, ex parte A, The Times*, 7 November 2000 illustrates the operation of the prevention or detection of crime exemption. A local authority asked one police force to obtain information about a job applicant from another police force and to disclose the information to the local authority. It was required for a child access vetting enquiry as the job involved working with children. The information sought related to previous police investigations into allegations of inappropriate behaviour with children. The job applicant applied for judicial review of the decision taken by the police forces to disclose the information to the local authority after an offer of employment by the local authority was withdrawn. He claimed, *inter alia*, that the disclosures were a breach of the Data Protection Act 1984 and/or the Data Protection Act 1998. The court held that the 1984 Act was not applicable as the information was processed manually. As regards the 1998 Act, it was held that the processing clearly fell within the framework of the 1998 Act and the Data Protection (Processing of Sensitive Personal Data) Order 2000 (which added processing for the prevention or detection of crime in the substantial public interest to the list of conditions in Schedule 3). Therefore exemption from the non-disclosure provisions applied.

The exemption under section 29 also applies to anyone discharging a statutory function who has obtained the data from a person who held the data for any of the above purposes but here the exemption is from the subject information provisions. An example might be personal data held by the police which has been given to the Crown Prosecution Service which is considering whether to prosecute the individual concerned. As a judgment has to be made by the data controller as to whether any of the purposes covered would be prejudiced by compliance, a subjective and qualitative element is brought into the practical application of the exemption. This can be criticised as it will be the data controller who decides this, subject only to a challenge by an aggrieved person. Further exemption is granted, from the non-disclosure provisions where the disclosure is for any of the above purposes and where compliance would prejudice any of those matters.

An example of the latter is where a local authority, empowered under section 163 of the Criminal Justice and Public Order Act 1994 to use video surveillance in order to promote the prevention of crime, discloses copies of CCTV footage to the media in order to facilitate this purpose. In *R v Brentwood Borough Council, ex parte Peck* [1998] EMLR 697, an applicant for judicial review complained when the local authority disclosed a video showing him walking down the High Street, Brentwood, with a knife. He later attempted suicide by slashing his wrists but this was not caught on video. He was not charged by the police. The video was shown on television. His face had been masked at the request of the local authority but this proved to be inadequate and some of the applicant's friends and neighbours recognised him, from his distinctive hairstyle and moustache. The application was dismissed, Mr Justice Harrison confirming that the statutory provisions above empowered the local authority to take the actions it had, including distributing the footage. Furthermore, it had not acted irrationally and had not known of the objection until the video had been broadcast. The Court of Appeal refused leave to appeal and Peck brought an action before the European Court of Human Rights on the grounds that his right of privacy under Article 8 of the Human Rights Convention had been breached and he had no effective domestic remedy as required by Article 13 of the Convention; *Peck v United Kingdom* (2003) 36 EHRR 719. The Court unanimously held that there had been a violation under both Articles and awarded him €11,800 for non-pecuniary damage plus costs.

The facts of Peck happened before the Data Protection Act 1998 and the Human Rights Act 1998 came into force, hence the finding of the Court of Human Rights that Peck had no effective remedy under domestic law. Now, operators of CCTV systems have to comply with the Data Protection Act 1998 and must comply with the conditions for processing, though in the context of processing for the prevention or detection of crime, the remainder of the first data protection principle does not apply. Furthermore, the processing must be viewed in the light of the Council of Europe Convention for the Protection of Human Rights and Fundamental Freedoms and the Human Rights Act 1998 requires that so far as it is possible to do so, primary and subordinate legislation must be read and given effect in accordance with the Convention. The Act also states that it is unlawful for a public authority to act in a manner incompatible with the Convention. A claim by the UK government that the decision could undermine the right of freedom of expression under Article 10 was rejected by the European Court of Human Rights as the local authority and the media could have achieved their objectives by ensuring that Peck's identity was properly concealed. Note that, under the 1998 Act, personal data can extend to visual data (this is confirmed by the Directive) and accepted as uncontroversial by Mr Justice Lindsey in *Michael Douglas v Hello! Ltd* [2003] 3 All ER 996 in relation to photographs taken surreptitiously at the wedding of Michael Douglas and Catherine Zeta-Jones.

Where the data controller is a lawful authority (government department, local authority or other authority administering housing benefit or council tax benefit) and the personal data consist of a classification of the data subject as part of a risk assessment system, exemption from the subject access provisions is granted. This applies only with respect to the purposes of assessment of tax, duty or similar imposition or the prevention or detection of crime, apprehension of offenders or where the offence concerned involves any unlawful claim for payment out of, or any unlawful application of, public funds where the processing is for any of those purposes.

Under the 1984 Act, the Data Protection Registrar had a long-running dispute over the scope of the equivalent exemption with the Halifax Building Society. It all started when an individual complained to the Registrar that he had not received all the information he was entitled to in pursuance of a subject access request. The Society had withheld data which it considered to be 'system security data' on the basis that the crime prevention exemption applied to the data. The Data Protection Registrar issued an enforcement notice and the Society appealed to the tribunal. After many meetings and discussions and the issue of a preliminary notice in respect of the complaintant (with which the Society complied), an agreement was reached between the Halifax Building Society and the Registrar. The agreement was to the effect that the Society would not normally give details of transactions on the data subject's account, card number, computer terminal and location of the automated teller machine. However, as part of the agreement (*Agreement in the Enforcement Action against the Halifax Building Society*, 6 January 1992), the Society agreed to inform any person making a subject access request of this fact and that all other information had been made available: for example, details of address, financial circumstances, balance and the Society's views (if appropriate). The data subject would also be informed that the Society would consider requests for other information if there was a genuine need for the data subject to see it. Finally, the Society agreed to inform data subjects that they are entitled to complain to the Data Protection Registrar (now Information Commissioner) if not satisfied with the Society's response.

In relation to prevention and detection of crime, exemption is also given from the non-disclosure provisions. In *James Martin (Application for Judicial Review)*, 20 December 2002, allegations of sexual abuse of a child had been made against the applicant for judicial review in the High Court of Northern Ireland. A Health and Social Services Trust retained information about these allegations. The applicant was never charged with a criminal offence. Later, a social worker divulged information about the allegations to the applicant's new partner who had three children. The applicant and his new partner separated soon after. The applicant claimed that the retention, processing and disclosure of the information was in breach of his right to privacy under Article 8 of the Human Rights Convention and a breach of data protection law.

Article 8(2) contains a derogation from the right of privacy in accordance with the law and where necessary in a democratic society, *inter alia*, for the prevention or detection of crime. The first issue then was whether the processing by the Trust was in accordance with the law. The judge had no hesitation in accepting that the processing fell within the exemption and, therefore, the processing met the requirement of legality. The judge then went on to consider whether the Trust was justified to act as it did and he concluded it was justified. The Trust had reasonable cause to suspect that the new partner's children could be harmed and an assessment was made based on the facts and circumstances of the particular case and a pressing need for disclosure was established. Furthermore, the Trust had no blanket policy of disclosures in such cases.

Offender naming schemes are sometimes used by the police under the Crime and Disorder Act 1998. Essex police wished to introduce such a scheme, under which a photograph and name of a convicted offender would be displayed together with details of the offences committed and the sentence he was serving (only offenders with at least 12 months' imprisonment were to be selected). The first offender selected objected arguing that his right to privacy under Article 8 of the Human Rights Convention would be breached by the scheme in *R (on application of Ellis)* v *Chief Constable of Essex* [2003] 2 FLR 566. In terms of preventing and detecting crime, the actions of the police had to be proportionate. The scheme was a genuine initiative and in the public interest but more care had to be taken in appraisal and monitoring of the scheme and the effect on the offender's family must also be taken into account. There also had to be a structured assessment of the risks in the light of further information and appropriate professional advice. Only when that had been done could it be said whether the potential benefits of the scheme were proportionate to the intrusion on an offender's right to privacy. The offender also claimed a breach of the Data Protection Act 1998 but it was accepted that the combined effect of section 29 and Schedules 2 and 3 of the Act was the same as under Article 8 of the European Convention for the Protection of Human Rights and Fundamental Freedoms. Lord Woolf CJ, said that counsel accurately stated that

> ... under the 1998 Act, in order to establish the legality of the Scheme it has to be shown that the inclusion of a selected candidate is necessary for the discharge of the duty cast upon the police to

formulate and implement policies designed to reduce crime and disorder. The reference to 'necessary' in this context requires that the action on behalf of the police should be a proportionate response in precisely the same way it is described by Lord Steyn in Daly [R (on the application of Daly) v Secretary of State for the Home Dept [2001] 2 AC 532].

It now seems tolerably clear that the impact of the Data Protection Act 1998 in relation to the exemption for the prevention or detection of crime is, to all intents and purposes, identical to that under Article 8 of the Council of Europe Convention for the Protection of Human Rights and Fundamental Freedoms. Indeed, data protection law has its roots in the Convention and can be seen as protecting privacy in the context of processing personal data. In any event, the Act must be construed, as far as possible, to be interpreted and given effect in a manner compatible with the Convention.

Health, education and social work

Section 30 of the Data Protection Act 1998 empowers the Secretary of State to make orders concerning exemptions from subject access in the context of health, education and social work. Three such orders have been made:

- the Data Protection (Subject Access Modification) (Health) Order 2000;
- the Data Protection (Subject Access Modification) (Education) Order 2000; and
- the Data Protection (Subject Access Modification) (Social Work) Order 2000 (as amended).

In respect of health, exemption is from the subject access provisions under section 7 to the extent that compliance with the request would be likely to cause serious harm to the physical or mental health or condition of the data subject or any other person. Where the data controller is not a health professional, he may not withhold the information covered by the subject access request unless he has consulted a health professional, whom he thinks appropriate, on the question of whether to withhold the information. Where a person (such as a person having parental responsibility) is lawfully entitled to seek access on behalf of the data subject, the data controller must consider any expectation of confidentiality of the data subject and any wishes of the data subject as regards disclosure to that other person.

There is also exemption from the subject information provisions where processing is carried out by a court under specified circumstances, for example, where the data consist of information supplied in a report or other evidence provided by a local authority, Health and Social Services Board or Trust or probation officer in certain proceedings involving child care or criminal proceedings in relation to a child.

In terms of education, exemption from subject access is granted where disclosure of information in an educational record would be likely to cause serious harm to the physical or mental health or condition of the data subject or any other person. Where a person making a subject access request on behalf of a child for whom he has parental responsibility or on behalf of a person incapable of managing his own affairs, having been appointed by the court to manage those affairs, there is a further exemption from subject access. This is to the extent that the information indicates that the data subject, being a child or incapable of managing his own affairs, is or has been the subject of child abuse or is at risk of child abuse and complying with the request would not be in the data subject's best interests. There is also an equivalent exemption from the subject information provisions in the case of processing by a court as applies in respect of health records. Educational records are defined in Schedule 11 to the Data Protection Act 1998. In England and Wales it is any record of information processed by or on behalf of the governing body or by a teacher at a local education authority maintained school or a special school as defined in section 6(2) of the Education Act 1996. The information must relate to any person who is or has been a pupil of the school and originated from or was supplied by an employee of the local education authority or a teacher or other employee of a special school or voluntary aided, foundation or foundation special school.

There is a general exemption from the subject information provisions for social work. For some particular forms of social work, there is also an exemption from the subject access provisions except the requirement to inform the data subject whether the data controller is processing personal data relating to the data subject. It applies to the extent that access would be likely to prejudice the carrying out of social work by reason of the fact that serious harm would be likely to be caused to the physical or mental health or condition of the data subject or any other person. Where, as in relation to health and educational records, a person is entitled to make a subject access request on behalf of the data subject, that request shall not be complied with to the extent that the access would disclose information provided by the data subject, or obtained as a result of an examination or investigation, in the expectation that the data concerned would not be so disclosed or where the data subject has expressly indicated that they should not be so disclosed. The Order applies to social work set out in a Schedule to the Order, including social services work, data processed by a probation committee and by education authorities exercising their functions in relation to ensuring children of school age receive efficient education.

Any overlap between the Orders is removed. The Education Order does not apply to personal data within the Health Order and the Social Work Order does not apply where the Health or Education Orders apply.

Prior to the equivalent provision to the health exemption under the 1984 Act, it was accepted that there was no common law right of access to health data. In *R v Mid-Glamorgan Family Health Services, ex parte Martin* [1995] 1 WLR 110, a patient had been refused access to his health records going back to before 1990 on the basis that it would be detrimental for the patient to see those records directly. An offer was made to disclose the records conditionally to a medical expert appointed by the patient but was not accepted. The patient claimed that there was a right of access at common law. However, the Court of Appeal refused to grant access on the 'best interests' principle, denying that there was such a common law right.

Regulatory activity

This exemption from the subject information provisions covers a wide range of regulatory activities in order to protect the public from dishonesty, malpractice and the like by persons involved with financial services, carrying on any profession or other activity or in relation to charities. It also extends to health and safety at work. A complete list is given earlier in Table 31.1. Under section 31, the function is one conferred by or under any enactment, any function of the Crown or a Minister of the Crown or a government department or any other function of a public nature which is exercised in the public interest. This latter category is potentially very wide ranging.

Further exemption is available from the subject information provisions in respect of statutory functions of the Parliamentary Commissioner for Administration, the Commission for Local Administration, the Health Service Commission and other public bodies. The exemption also applies to certain functions of the Office of Fair Trading.

In all cases, the exemption is only available where the application of the subject information provisions would be likely to prejudice the proper discharge of the relevant function. The purpose of the exemption is to prevent, for example, a person under investigation by the Charity Commissioners for the misapplication of the property of a charity discovering that his activities are being investigated. He could find out by carrying out a subject access request or because, under normal circumstances, he is required to be informed of the disclosure of personal data relating to him to the Charity Commissioners.

Journalism, literature and art

This is an important and wide-ranging exemption protecting freedom of speech. Under section 32, exemption is from all the data protection principles (except the seventh principle on security measures), and most of the rights of data subjects including subject access. We have seen in the previous chapter how the Information Commissioner's powers are constrained in relation to the purposes of journalism and artistic and literary purposes (the special purposes). Indeed, in a court action in relation to the data subjects' rights or compensation, a claim by the data controller that he is processing only for the special purposes with a view to publication of material not previously published by him at a time 24 hours before he makes that claim, proceedings must be stayed until the Commissioner makes a determination under section 45 as to whether the special purposes do apply or the claim is withdrawn. The same applies if it appears to the court that the special purposes apply.

For the exemption to apply, the processing must be undertaken with a view to publication of any journalistic, literary or artistic material and the data controller must reasonably believe that publication is in the public interest, having regard in particular to the special importance of the public interest in freedom of expression. Furthermore, the data controller must reasonably believe that compliance with the exemption in question is incompatible with the special purposes. In making a determination as to the data controller's belief that publication is in the public interest, regard may be had to his compliance with any relevant code of practice designated by the Lord Chancellor for this purpose. Under the Data Protection (Designated Codes of Practice) (No. 2) Order 2000, the codes are those of the Broadcasting Standards Commission, Independent Television Commission, Press Complaints Commission and the Radio Authority and the Producer's Guidelines of the British Broadcasting Corporation. As noted previously, the Secretary of State can order the Information Commissioner to prepare and disseminate codes of practice after consultation with trade associations and data subjects or persons representing data subjects.

Celebrities and the section 32 exemption

The scope of the section 32 exemption came up for consideration in *Naomi Campbell v Mirror Group Newspapers Ltd* [2002] EWHC 499 (QB). The defendant had published newspaper articles which showed that the claimant, contrary to her previous false assertions, was addicted to drugs and attending meetings of Narcotics Anonymous. The articles included details of those meetings and a photograph of her leaving a meeting in Chelsea. She brought an action against the defendant for breach of confidence and for compensation under section 13 of the Data Protection Act 1998. At first instance, Mr Justice Morland in looking at the wording of the exemption under section 32 thought that the exemption only applied up to the time of publication and did not provide a defence thereafter. The wording states that processing is undertaken *with a view to publication*.

Having found that the section 32 exemption applied only up to the time of publication, the judge awarded damages for breach of confidence and under section 13 of the Data Protection Act 1998 of £3,500 including £1,000 aggravated damages. As the exemption did not apply post-publication, the judge found that the defendant could not rely on the conditions for processing data in Schedules 2 and 3 to the Act. The legitimate interests condition did not apply as the processing was unwarranted intrusion into the claimant's right of privacy. In terms of Schedule 3 (accepting that the data relating to treatment for drug addiction were sensitive personal data) the appropriate condition for processing was disclosure in the substantial public interest in connection with the commission of any unlawful act, etc. for the special purposes with a view to publication where the data controller reasonably believed publication would be in the public interest. Publishing details of the therapy (rather than simply the fact that she was having therapy) was not in the substantial public interest and the disclosure was not in connection with the commission of a criminal offence but, rather, the claimant's attempts to avoid committing criminal offences related to controlled drugs. Therefore, the processing by the defendant was in breach of the Act and the claimant was entitled to compensation under section 13 for substantial distress for a contravention of the Act by the data controller. Where the contravention relates to processing for the special purposes compensation is available for substantial distress in the absence of substantial damage. The total award could be seen as fairly small and may have been coloured by the behaviour of the claimant. The judge described her as lacking in frankness and having lied on oath.

Mirror Group Newspapers appealed against the decision of Morland J and, in *Naomi Campbell* v *Mirror Group Newspapers Ltd* [2003] QB 633, the Court of Appeal found for the defendant on both the breach of confidence issue and the section 32 defence, holding that it did apply to post-publication also. As far as the breach of confidence point, the Court of Appeal accepted that publication of the details of treatment and the photograph were acceptable as they provided credibility to the story, showing that the claimant had lied to the public when she said she did not take drugs. A claim that publication of hard copies of newspapers was outside the scope of processing for the purposes of the Data Protection Act 1998 was rejected by the Court of Appeal which said that an act carried out at the instigation of the data controller which is linked to the automated processing of personal data, such as obtaining or using (as defined in section 1(1)), should fall within the scope of the Act.

On the section 32 point, the Court of Appeal considered the Directive and the whole of section 32, which all agreed was ambiguous. The Court of Appeal thought that, if section 32 only applied up to publication, section 32(1)–(3) would be unnecessary (the main provisions for the exemption) as section 32(4) and (5) contains the provisions requiring the court to stay proceedings where the data controller claims to be within the special purposes or it so appears to the court. If the exemption only applied to pre-publication processing, section 32(4) and (5) would prevent anyone obtaining a 'gagging' order (that is, an interim injunction preventing publication) and the defence in section 32(1)–(3), with its test of reasonable belief that publication was in the public interest and the requirement to consider designated codes of practice, such as that of the Press Complaints Commission, would be irrelevant. Furthermore, the wording of the Directive and references to Hansard supported that view. The exemption was not restricted to pre-publication processing but was, therefore, of general application.

The relevant provision in the Directive is Article 9 which states that exemption or derogation may be provided if necessary to reconcile the right to privacy with the rules governing freedom of expression. This reflects the balancing act in Article 10 of the European Convention for the Protection of Human Rights and Fundamental Freedoms, paragraph 1 of which provides a right of freedom of expression subject to derogation necessary in a democratic society in paragraph 2. Of course, if section 32 gave exemption only up to the time of publication, then the freedom of the press could be seriously prejudiced for fear of an award of substantial damages. As the Court of Appeal said, if this was the case, Naomi Campbell would also have been able to obtain compensation for a story that simply mentioned the facts that she was a drug addict, contrary to her earlier claims, and was having treatment.

Naomi Campbell's appeal to the House of Lords was successful by a 3:2 majority in *Campbell* v *MGN Ltd* [2004] 2 AC 457. The House of Lords did not consider the data protection exemption as it was agreed that the outcome would be the same as under the law of confidence, taking account of Articles 8 and 10 of the Council of Europe Convention for the Protection of Human Rights and Fundamental Freedoms. The majority accepted that there had been a breach of the right to privacy which could not be justified by publication of the fact she was being treated at Narcotics Anonymous, details of her treatment and the photographs showing her leaving a meeting. The decision of the trial judge was restored.

Of course, section 32 only applies to processing under the Data Protection Act 1998 and does not affect any right to relief for breach of confidence or defamation, in appropriate cases. In *Michael Douglas v Hello! Ltd* [2003] EWHC 786 (Ch) the judge held that the reliance on the section 32 exemption as a defence was unsustainable as the defendant adduced no credible evidence of a reasonable belief that publication was in the public interest. Mr Justice Lindsay also said that what was interesting to the public was not necessarily in the public interest as many judges have also said previously. In that case, he held that some of the defendants were in breach of confidence by publishing photographs of the wedding of Michael Douglas and Catherine Zeta-Jones taken surreptitiously and that the claim to compensation under the Data Protection Act 1998 was also made out. However, in respect of the latter, he said he would make a nominal award only as this was not a separate route to recovery. The award was left over for another hearing and only a relatively small sum was awarded under data protection law. In an earlier hearing in the Court of Appeal, *Michael Douglas v Hello! Ltd* [2003] EWCA Civ 139, it was held that there was a good arguable claim that a transmission by ISDN line to London of the photographic data was processing other than for the purposes of transit through the UK, and therefore subject to the 1998 Act.

Research, history and statistics

In many cases, data processed for statistical or research purposes only will not be within data protection law as the data will be anonymous and, therefore, not personal data within the meaning in section 1(1). However, where the data remain personal data because they contain identifiers or the data controller has or may obtain other data which, together with the research data, allow individuals to be identified, section 33 allows some useful exemptions. These apply where the relevant conditions are present, being that the data are not processed to support measures or decisions with respect to particular individuals and are not processed so as to cause, or be likely to cause, substantial damage or substantial distress to any data subject. These conditions will usually be easily satisfied. If the data are being used to support measures or decisions affecting particular individuals, it may be that other exemptions are relevant – for example, in the case of research data relating to health which are now being processed to identify persons who have been exposed to some virus in the past and are now in need of an urgent inoculation.

The first exemption is simply to the effect that further processing only for research purposes is not to be regarded as incompatible with the purposes for which they were obtained, otherwise this could be a breach of the second data protection principle. The fifth principle requires that personal data are not kept for longer than is necessary and exemption from that requirement is granted in that data processed only for research purposes can be kept indefinitely. A further exemption is from the subject access provisions but only if the results of any research or any resulting statistics are not made available in a form identifying any data subject.

The exemptions are not lost merely because the data are disclosed to any person for research purposes only, to the data subject or a person acting on his behalf or at the request of, or with the consent of, the data subject or a person acting on his behalf. Nor are the exemptions lost if the person making the disclosure has reasonable grounds for believing any of these apply in the circumstances.

Sometimes research data will have been rendered anonymous by the stripping out of personal identifiers. Where this has been done, it is unlikely that the Data Protection Act 1998 applies to the data, unless the data can be later reconstituted to identify individuals or where the research data contain some entries from which an individual can be identified, for example, because the data are very unusual. In *R v Department of Health, ex parte Source Informatics Ltd* [2001] QB 244, Source Informatics Ltd attempted to persuade general practitioner doctors and pharmacists to transfer data showing the prescribing habits of doctors. The intention was that the data would be made anonymous before being supplied to Source Informatics. Processing this data would produce information about prescribing habits and trends which would prove valuable to pharmaceutical companies. The doctors and pharmacists taking part would, for a fee, download onto disks details of the quantity and identity of drugs prescribed. The Department of Health issued a policy document warning of the complex legal and policy issues and advising against such disclosures. Source Informatics sought declaratory relief in respect of the policy document arguing that disclosure after the data had been rendered anonymous would not constitute a breach of confidence.

The Court of Appeal did not consider that the planned action would involve a breach of confidence providing the identity of the patients was protected. The sole issue was the patients' right of privacy. Patients had no proprietary interest in the information and no right to control what happened to it subsequently providing his privacy was not put at stake. Thus, participation in the scheme by doctors and pharmacists would not expose them to a serious risk of successful breach of confidence actions. In terms of data protection law, the court said it was premature to try to make a definitive ruling on the data protection Directive (the 1998 Act had not been passed at the time the action accrued) but the view seems to have been that it would be unlikely to contravene the new law. Simon Brown LJ said (at paragraph 45):

> the anonymisation of data is, in my judgment, unobjectionable here under domestic law, so too, I confidently suppose, would it be regarded by other Member States.

It would appear, that supplying a copy of a database containing personal data that has been made anonymous would be acceptable. However, data subjects have rights under the Data Protection Act 1998 which include rights of compensation for breaches of the Act and, if processing was previously underway because of the data subject's express consent, it is more doubtful whether providing an anonymised copy would be within the Act. This could then take processing outside the conditions for processing. Whether removal of identifiers would also be regarded as an unauthorised erasure or loss of personal data is another point to bear in mind.

Manual data held by public authorities

This exemption applies to personal data falling within section 1(1)(e) and was inserted by the Freedom of Information Act 2000. The exemption is very wide ranging and only the fourth data protection principle still applies in full and the sixth principle applies but only in so far as data subjects' right of access and rights to rectification under sections 7 and 14 respectively are concerned. The exemption is even wider when it comes to personal data within section 1(1)(e) relating to appointments or removals, pay, discipline, superannuation or other personal matters in relation to service in the armed forces, service in any office or employment under the Crown or public authority, etc. In this case the exemption also extends to the remaining data protection principles and Part II of the Act.

The exemption under section 33A effectively gives public authorities an immunity against most forms of breach of the data protection principles and data subjects cannot object to processing likely to cause substantial damage or substantial distress and their rights to compensation under section 13 are severely curtailed, applying only to contraventions of the right of access and the fourth data protection principle (personal data required to be accurate and up to date).

Some of the exemptions for manual data held by public authorities are not really relevant anyway, such as the exemption from the right to prevent processing for direct marketing and the rights in relation to automated decision taking.

Information available to the public

This applies where the data consist of information which the data controller is required to make available to the public by or under any enactment (other than under the Freedom of Information Act 2000), whether by publication or making it available for inspection or otherwise and whether or not a fee is charged. The exemption is from the subject information provisions, the fourth data protection principle (accuracy and kept up to date), the right of rectification within section 14(1)–(3) and the non-disclosure provisions. Clearly where information has to be made available, full application of these provisions would be unnecessary. The type of information that will be within this exemption includes the electoral roll, copies of birth, marriage and death certificates and copies of specifications for patents.

Two copies of the electoral roll are now prepared. A full register is only available to credit reference agencies and, in other cases, an edited version is made available. In *R (Robertson)* v *Wakefield Metropolitan Borough Council* [2002] QB 1052, Mr Justice Maurice Kay held that supplying a copy of the full register for the purposes of direct marketing without giving individuals an opportunity to object was contrary to section 12 of the Data Protection Act 1998 and a number of provisions of the Council of Europe Convention for the Protection of Human Rights and Fundamental Freedoms. The offending parts of the Regulations that provided for copies to be made available was repealed and replaced by the Representation of the People (England and Wales) (Amendment) Regulations 2002. The provisions now allow electors to choose not to be included in the edited version of the electoral role. Further challenges were made against the new provisions, the first applicant, Robertson claimed that they did not go far enough but that was rejected by Kay J. A claim from a company offering an online credit reference service claimed that the new provisions went too far was rejected in *I-CD Publishing Ltd* v *Secretary of State* [2003] EWHC 1761 (Admin) as the company did not fall within the requirements for credit reference agencies to have access to the full register. The judge also refused to grant a declaration that, if the company changed its operations in certain ways, it would fall within the requirements.

Disclosures required by law or in connection with legal proceedings, etc.

Other exemptions in the main body of the Act are disclosures required by law or made in connection with legal proceedings or for the purpose of obtaining legal advice or otherwise necessary for the purposes of establishing, exercising or defending legal rights: section 35. A related exemption is in Schedule 7, para. 10, being exemption from the subject information provisions on the basis of legal professional privilege. Thus, there can be no barrier to disclosing personal information in connection with legal proceedings. For example, Andrew, who is a self-employed accountant, wishes to sue Brenda (one of his clients) for non-payment of accountancy fees. Andrew has a meeting with his solicitor, Carolyn, and provides her with information about Brenda and the work he did for her. Andrew is a data controller under the Act. Naturally, his notification does not mention such a disclosure but section 35 grants him exemption. As the meeting between Andrew and Carolyn is privileged, neither has to give Brenda any information about it. For example, there is no need to inform Brenda that Carolyn now has personal data relating to Brenda and, of course, any subject access request made by Brenda to Carolyn can be ignored with impunity.

Under the 1984 Act, the question of disclosure of data where the data user was exempt from registration came up for consideration in *Rowley* v *Liverpool City Council* (unreported) 24 October 1989. The judgment amply demonstrates the complexity of that Act (the 1998 Act is no less complex), and Lord Justice Woolf in the Court of Appeal said of the 1984 Act:

> ... it is right to say straightaway that the act is a complex enactment in which it is difficult to find your way about unless you are very familiar with it indeed.

In that case, the claimant brought an action against her former employer for personal injury and she had made an application for discovery (disclosure to a party in legal proceedings) of information including details of three 'comparative earners'. She wanted details of payments made to three persons employed in a similar capacity to help work out what she would have been paid had she not had to stop working because of her injury. The defendant refused claiming that such disclosure was prohibited by the Data Protection Act 1984.

The defendant was exempt from registration because the data related to payroll and is similar to the equivalent provision under the 1998 Act. Section 32(2) of the 1984 Act made it a condition of the exemption that the data are not disclosed except in limited circumstances relating to payroll and accounts. However, section 34(5) of the 1984 Act, in similar though not identical lines to the equivalent provision in the 1998 Act, allowed disclosure if required by law or in the course of legal proceedings and, therefore, the disclosure requested did not contravene the Act. Disclosure was allowed in two ways: first, because it was in the course of legal proceedings in which the defendant was a party and, secondly, in compliance with an order of the court.

The working of the exemption under section 35(1) of the 1998 Act is much simpler in many cases. For example, in *Guyer* v *Walton (Inspector of Taxes)* [2001] STC (Special Commissioners' Decisions) 75, Guyer was a solicitor who claimed he did not have to provide evidence such as his clients' ledger and cash book, copies of invoices and receipts and bank statements, cheque stubs and building society passbooks. The Revenue contended that it required such information to follow discrepancies in information provided by Guyer in his self-assessment form. Guyer claimed that the documents were not reasonably required, that he owed a duty of confidentiality to his clients, that the documents asked for were subject to legal professional privilege, that disclosure would be a breach of the right to privacy under the Council of Europe Convention for the Protection of Human Rights and Fundamental Freedoms and that disclosure of the documents would be in breach of the Data Protection Act 1998. In rejecting all those submissions, the Special Commissioner noted that, as far as data protection law was concerned section 35(1) gave exemption from the non-disclosure provisions where, *inter alia*, this was required by law. Disclosure was required by law as the Revenue had, in accordance with and as provided for by section 19A of the Taxes Management Act 1970 served a written notice requiring provision of documents, as specified in the notice, that are reasonably required for the purpose of determining whether a tax return is correct.

An order of a court requiring disclosure also falls within this exemption from the non-disclosure provisions. In *Anderson* v *Halifax plc* [2000] NI 1, the widow of a deceased man sought information from the Halifax concerning the withdrawal of £60,000 from his account with the Halifax by her husband just before his death which he had given to an unknown person. The deceased had been suffering from cancer and the heavy doses of painkillers had made him confused and his behaviour became irrational. His widow was his personal representative and applied to the court for an order for disclosure after the Halifax had refused to disclose the information sought on the grounds of confidentiality and that it would be contrary to data protection law. The court held that the appropriate remedy would be one of tracing and, being broadly equitable, within the discretion of the court. The order for disclosure was granted.

Parliamentary privilege

Section 35A grants exemption if required for the purposes of avoiding an infringement of the privileges of either House of Parliament. The exemption is from the first data protection principle (though the conditions for processing still apply), the second to fifth data protection principles and section 7 (subject access), section 10 (right to prevent processing likely to cause substantial damage or substantial distress) and section 14(1) to (3) (certain rights in relation to inaccurate personal data).

Parliamentary privilege gives immunity against libel actions as regards anything said in either House and freedom from arrest on civil (though not criminal) matters whilst at the Palace of Westminster. It is unlikely that this exemption will be relied on much if at all. The right to compensation still applies but is of much reduced scope because of the scope of the exemption. It could apply, for example, if an MP has inadequate security for his computer documents held in a computer situated at the Palace of Westminster.

Domestic purposes

The data protection Directive does not apply to processing by a natural person in the course of a purely personal or household activity. Thus, section 36 of the Data Protection Act 1998 exempts from all the data protection principles, the rights of data subjects and the requirements as to notification of personal data processed by an individual for that individual's personal, family or household affairs. This also extends to recreational purposes. The Information Commissioner may still exercise his powers of enforcement in the context of such processing if it is believed that the individual concerned is processing in such a manner as to exceed the scope of this exemption. If this is so, then the exemption will be lost to that extent. In particular, an individual who is otherwise employed but who carries on some private work in his spare time may be required to notify.

Schedule 7 exemptions

For no particular reason, a further set of exemptions is tucked away in a Schedule to the Act. All of these exemptions are listed earlier in Table 31.1, but the following are notable and discussed in more detail.

Confidential references

This exemption is from the subject access provisions only and is given under para. 1 of the Schedule. It applies where the reference is given or intended to be given by the data controller for the purposes of the education, training or employment (actual or prospective) of the data subject or the appointment or prospective appointment of the data subject to any office or the provision or prospective provision by the data subject of any service. The reference must be given, or intended to be given, in confidence. There is no distinction between the person by whom the reference is given and the person who receives it. Both will be data controllers for the purpose of this provision *if and only if* the personal data are within the scope of the Act.

To take an example, consider Harold, an employee of the Peak Accountancy Practice who now seeks employment with Flaky Financial Services. Flaky has requested a reference from Peak, which is in the form of a letter hand written by Paul, Peak's managing director. This letter is unlikely to be within the meaning of data for the purposes of the Act. It is not automatically processed nor intended so to be and is not a relevant filing system nor an accessible record. Both Peak and Flaky can refuse Harold access to it. However, if the letter is produced on a word processor by Paul, it will be within the Act but Peak can refuse Harold access to it providing it is given in confidence. Flaky is under no obligation to grant access, whether it is confidential or not, because Flaky is not processing the data automatically. If the reference is made out on a pro forma document, then both Peak and Flaky must provide access (unless it was given in confidence) providing the reference is recorded as part of or with the intention that it should form part of a relevant filing system. This will be so if Peak and Flaky keep a file of references given or received.

Management forecasts and negotiations

These two distinct exemptions are discussed together here as they may overlap and often both will apply in the context of business planning and strategy and relationships with employees. Both exemptions are from the subject information provisions. In both cases, the exemption only applies if and to the extent that compliance would be likely to prejudice the activity or negotiations, as appropriate. Both of these exemptions are new and the 1984 Act had no direct equivalent.

The first applies to personal data processed for the purposes of management forecasting or management planning to assist the data controller in the conduct of any business or other activity: para. 5. No further guidance is given but this could apply, for example, where a company is carrying out a feasibility study on some new proposed venture. It might involve personal data relating to present and potential employees and other individuals such as investors. The company may wish to gather information on individuals who are candidates for 'head-hunting' to lead the new venture. Alternatively, a company may be considering closing down some of its activities which, if carried out, will affect numerous employees. Fulfilling a subject access request could destroy the secrecy of such forecasting or planning and cause serious prejudice.

Paragraph 7 deals with negotiations with the data subject and records of intentions in respect of such negotiations by the data controller. Under the 1984 Act, statements of intentions in respect of individuals were outside the definition of personal data and, therefore, outwith the scope of the Act. This is not so under the Directive and statements of intention are personal data, providing the other requirements are met. It was thought important to grant exemption from the subject information provisions – after all, an intention is not a reality until it is carried out and the data controller may change his mind. The sort of things covered will include an intention to promote an employee or provide some person with a particular service. The exemption is not limited to negotiations between employers and employees and can apply in any context.

Examination marks and examination scripts

The exemption for examination marks gives exemption from the subject access provisions though it can only act to delay subject access. Under para. 8 of Schedule 7, the marks or other information must be held for the purpose of determining the results of an academic, professional or other examination or enabling such determination or in consequence of the determination of any such results. In the case of an undergraduate, such information might include the marks he obtained in each subject by examination (including assessed coursework) and the details of the degree classification to be awarded to the student. 'Examination' includes a process for determining the knowledge, intelligence, skill or ability of a candidate by reference to his performance in any test, work or other activity. The normal period for responding to a subject access request is 40 days. Where the period of 40 days is used below, it is to be taken to be 40 days or such other period as may be prescribed.

Normally, a data controller must comply with a data subject request within 40 days but, in respect of examination marks, the data controller does not have to respond until either the end of five months after the request has been received or 40 days after the day the results are announced (published or made available or communicated to candidates), whichever is the earlier. If the request is complied with more than 40 days after it was made, the response by the data user must include all the information held at the time of the request *and* subsequently.

The following dates provide an example of the workings of these provisions (all dates are during the same year):

1	Student sits examination	4 June
2	Marks entered on a computer	27 June
3	Student makes subject access request	2 July
4	Results published	23 July

Normally, the request must be complied with within 40 days from the request at the latest; that is, within 40 days of 2 July, which gives 11 August as being the latest date for compliance. However, in the case of examination marks, the request must be complied with by the earlier of five months after the request (2 December) or 40 days after publication (1 September). Therefore, the data controller must supply the data by 2 September. But, unlike other subject access requests which may take account of amendments, in this case the information supplied must include that held on 2 July (the request date) *and* must also include any subsequent amendments up to the date of reply. Consequently, a data controller holding examination marks must be careful to make sure that he retains copies of the personal data prior to any amendments or deletions so that he can provide all this information. For example, if the student's degree classification is changed, perhaps from a lower second honours degree to an upper second honours degree after mistakes have been found in the marking, the response must show this fact indicating the marks before and after correction. This requirement could prove very embarrassing to the data controller.

The exemption that applies to examination scripts and is granted in respect of the subject access provisions. The meaning of 'examination' is as above and the exemption relates to personal data consisting of information recorded by candidates during an academic, professional or other examination. In many cases, examination scripts will not contain personal data subject to the Act. One exception is where the examination is in the form of a multiple-choice tests performed on computers. Of course, most students have no wish to have access to their examination scripts, except where there is an issue about the mark awarded.

OBTAINING, DISCLOSING AND PROCURING OFFENCES, ETC.

Offences relating to notification and in respect of information and enforcement notices have already been mentioned. Of particular concern has been the possibility of persons obtaining personal data or procuring the disclosure of personal data, for example, by private investigators or others using a false identity or other trick to obtain the personal data without the data controller's consent. Section 55 sets out the offences under the Act that cover such activities. They do not apply to personal data exempt from section 55 by virtue of section 28 (national security) or section 33A (manual data held by a public authority). These offences are:

■ knowingly or recklessly, without the consent of the data controller, obtaining or disclosing personal data or the information contained within the personal data or procuring the disclosure to another person of the information contained within the person data: section 55(1);

■ where a person has obtained personal data in contravention of section 55(1), selling those personal data or the information contained in those data: section 55(4);

- where a person offers to sell personal data or information contained in personal data he has obtained in contravention of section 55(1) or which he subsequently obtains in contravention of that subsection: section 55(5). An offer to sell includes an advertisement indicating that the information or personal data are or may be for sale (in terms of contract law, an advertisement is usually an invitation to treat rather than an offer to sell).

There are a number of defences to the section 55(1) offences. Section 55(2) states that the offences do not apply where a person shows that:

- the obtaining, disclosure or procuring was necessary for the purpose of preventing or detecting crime or was required or authorised by or under any enactment, by any rule of law or by an order of the court;
- that he acted in the reasonable belief that he had in law the right to obtain or disclose the information or data or procure the disclosure of the information to the other person;
- that he acted in the reasonable belief that he would have had the consent of the data controller if the data controller had known about the obtaining, disclosure or procuring and the circumstances of it; or
- that in the particular circumstances the obtaining, disclosure or procuring was justified as being in the public interest. This could, for example, apply to the public interest in freedom of expression or the disclosure of an iniquity.

As with the basic definition of processing, there inclusion of information contained within data is unnecessary. It assumes that, somehow, information and data are different. The data protection Directive makes no such distinction.

Equivalent 'procuring' offences were added to the 1984 Act but only came into force on 3 February 1995. There were, however, a number of successful convictions in respect of them. For example, in July 1998, a father and son were found guilty at Horseferry Magistrates Court of a number of offences under the 1984 Act. The father operated a private investigation company and his son, who worked for the National Westminster Bank, passed on details of individuals from the bank's database to his father. The son was convicted of two charges of unauthorised disclosure and fined £500 for each. The father's company was charged with being an unregistered data user and with two charges of unlawful procuring of personal data and two charges of unlawful sale of personal data, and was fined a total of £5,000. The father was convicted of four charges of consenting or conniving with the offences committed by his company and was fined £500 for each.

The state of mind required of the accused (known as the *mens rea* to lawyers) is 'knowingly or recklessly'. For some time, it was thought that the word 'reckless' in a criminal statute required an objective test and a person behaved 'recklessly' if the risk of the relevant act or omission transpiring would be obvious to a reasonable man, whether or not the person responsible for the act or omission thought about the possibility of the risk. This was the result of the much-criticised House of Lords decision in *R v Caldwell* [1982] AC 341, a criminal damage case. This objective standard was accepted as being applicable also to data protection law in the case of *Data Protection Registrar v Amnesty International (British Section)* (unreported) 8 November 1994. However, the House of Lords overruled *R v Caldwell* in *R v G* [2004] 1 AC 1034, confirming that foresight of consequences was required. The test is, therefore, a subjective one. Did the accused consider what he did was reckless as to the prohibited consequences?

Under section 54A, inserted by the Crime (International Cooperation) Act 2003, the Information Commissioner may inspect personal data held in the Schengen, Europol and Customs information systems. Any person who intentionally obstructs the exercise of that power or fails without reasonable excuse to give any person exercising the power such assistance as he may reasonably require, commits an offence.

31

Data controllers and the Data Protection Act 1998

Table 31.2 Offences under the Data Protection Act 1998

Section	Description	State of mind (mens rea)	Defences
21(1)	Processing personal data without having notified where this is required under section 17	Strict liability	None
21(2)	Failing in the duty to notify changes in the registrable particulars or in the measures taken to comply with the security requirements under the seventh Principle	Strict liability	Where the person charged can show that he exercised all due diligence to comply with the duty
22(6)	Carrying on assessable processing unless notification has been received from the Commissioner	Strict liability	None. No order has yet been made specifying processing subject to a preliminary assessment
24(4)	In a case where processing has not been notified (because it was not required and the data controller has chosen not to notify), failing to provide relevant particulars to any person on request within 21 days	Strict liability	Where the person charged can show that he exercised all due diligence to comply with the duty
47(1)	Failing to comply with an enforcement, information or special information notice	Strict liability	Where the person charged can show that he exercised all due diligence to comply with the duty
47(2)	In purported compliance with an information notice or special information notice, making a statement which is false in a material respect	Knowing that the statement is false in a material respect or recklessly making such a statement	None
54A	Intentionally obstructing or failing without reasonable excuse to give assistance reasonably required in respect of the exercise of powers to inspect certain information systems	Intention or failing to give assistance reasonably required	None

Table 31.2 continued

Section 55 offences
Note that the section 55 offences below do not apply in relation to processing for the purposes of national security under section 28 and to manual data within the definition of data in section 1(1)(e) processed by public authorities under section 33A

Section	Description	State of mind (mens rea)	Defences

55(1) and (3)	Without the consent of the data controller –
	
	(a) obtaining or disclosing personal data or the information contained in personal data; or
	
	(b) procuring the disclosure to another person of the information contained in personal data
		Knowledge or recklessness required	Does not apply where the person shows:
			
			(a) that the obtaining, disclosing or procuring –
			
			  (i) was necessary for the purposes of preventing or detecting crime; or
			
			  (ii) was required or authorised by or under any enactment, by any rule of law or by the order of a court;
			
			(b) that he acted in the reasonable belief that he had in law the right to obtain or disclose the data or information or, as the case may be, to procure the disclosure of the information to the other person;
			
			(c) that he acted in the reasonable belief that he would have had the consent of the data controller if the data controller had known of the obtaining, disclosing or procuring and the circumstances of it; or
			
			(d) that in the particular circumstances the obtaining, disclosing or procuring was justified as being in the public interest.

55(4)	Selling personal data by a person who has obtained the data in contravention of section 55(1)	Strict liability	None

Table 31.2 continued

Section	Description	State of mind (mens rea)	Defences
55(5)	Offering to sell personal data if: (a) the person has obtained the data in contravention of section 55(1), or (b) he subsequently obtains the data in contravention of section 55(1). Note: offering to sell includes an advertisement indicating that personal data are or may be for sale	None – but require the past or future commission of an offence under section 55(1)	The defences that apply to the section 55(1) and (3) offences do not apply to this offence
55(7)	Section 1(2) does not apply for the purposes of this section; and for the purposes of this and the above offence (section 55(4)), 'personal data' includes information extracted from personal data		
56(5)	Requiring a person to supply a relevant record (enforced subject access) in connection with: (a) the recruitment of another person as an employee; (b) the continued employment of another person; or (c) any contract for the provision of services to him by another person; or Requiring a person to supply a relevant record as a condition of providing or offering to provide goods, facilities or services A relevant record is one relating to convictions or cautions or in relation to certain types of benefit	Strict liability	But not where required or authorised by or under any enactment, rules of law or by court order, or where the requirement is justified as being in the public interest. This provision is not yet in force and is unlikely to be brought into force in the foreseeable future
59(3)	The disclosure of information obtained or furnished under the Act which relates to a living individual or business and has not previously been available to the public from other sources by a present or past Information Commissioner, member of the Commissioner's staff or an agent of the Commissioner	Knowledge or recklessness as to the contravention	None

Table 31.2 continued

Section	Description	State of mind (mens rea)	Defences
61(1)	Where an offence under this Act has been committed by a body corporate and is proved to have been committed by or with the consent of, connivance of, or to be attributable to any neglect on the part of any director, manager, secretary or similar officer of the body corporate or any person who was purporting to act in any such capacity, he as well as the body corporate shall be guilty of an offence and be liable to be proceeded against and punished accordingly	Consent, connivance or neglect (the latter would seem to be based on an objective test)	None
Schedule 9, para. 12	Intentionally obstructing a person in the execution of a warrant issued under this Schedule, or failing without reasonable excuse to give any person executing such a warrant such assistance as he may reasonably require for the execution of the warrant	Intention or not having reasonable excuse as the case may be	None

All the offences under the 1998 Act are summarised in Table 31.2. The table contains the section number and a description of the offence, the state of mind required of the accused and whether there are any specific defences. Note that many of the offences are strict liability, that is to say that ignorance of the existence of the offence or of the circumstances giving rise to it will not excuse.

All the offences, apart from that under section 54A and those relating to warrants in Schedule 9, are triable either way: that is, either on indictment in the Crown Court or summarily in a magistrates' court. They are punishable on conviction on indictment by a fine or, on summary conviction, by a fine not exceeding the statutory maximum: section 60. Offences in relation to section 54A and warrants are summary only and punishable on conviction with a fine not exceeding level 5 on the standard scale. There are also provisions for forfeiture, destruction or erasure of documents or other material, subject to persons other than the offender being heard as to why the order should not be made.

Section 61 applies the usual provisions with respect to offences committed by a body corporate where it is proved that the offence was committed with the consent or connivance or was attributable to any neglect on the part of any director, manager, secretary or similar officer or person purporting to act in such a capacity. If this is so, that person as well as the body corporate is liable to prosecution. This also applies where the affairs of the body corporate are managed by its members. They are treated as directors for the purposes of this provision. In England and Wales, no proceedings for an offence under the Act can be brought except by the Information Commissioner or by or with the consent of the Director of Public Prosecutions: section 60.

The number of prosecutions remains relatively low and even seems to be declining. In the year ended 31 March 2006, there were a total of only 15 successful prosecutions brought by the Information Commissioner. There were 11 cases brought for failing to notify under section 17 and the remainder were in relation to section 55 offences. The maximum penalty was a fine of £5,000.[2]

TRANSITIONAL PROVISIONS

The Data Protection Act 1998 has much wider scope compared with previous data protection law and the data protection Directive allowed certain provisions to be delayed where processing was already underway, giving data controllers the time to bring such processing in line with the Directive. Particular exemptions were in place until the end of the first transitional period, 24 October 2001. This applied to manual and automated processing already underway before 24 October 1998 – the latest date for compliance with the Directive. The detail of these exemptions are described in detail in the previous edition of this book.

The second transitional period lasted until 24 October 2007. It applied to manual data for which processing was already underway before 24 October 1998 ('eligible manual data') and to accessible records, whenever processing started. It did not apply to eligible manual data processed only for the purposes of historical research for which there is separate provision. The exemption was from the first data protection principle (except to the extent to which it required compliance with the requirements to inform data subjects when the data was obtained from the data subject or in other cases), the second, third, fourth and fifth data protection principles, and section 14(1)–(3) which contains the basic rights to rectification, blocking, erasure and destruction. Of course, there was no requirement generally to notify manual processing (though this is a possibility where the processing in question is declared to be assessable). Data subjects still had a right of access to such data and a right to be informed in accordance with the first data protection principle. Although exemption was granted in respect of some of the rights of rectification under section 14(1)–(3), this was of little consequence as the processing is subject to section 12A instead which grants similar rights in addition to a right in relation to processing not in accordance with the legitimate interests of the data controller. Section 12A is curious as it 'self-repealed' on 24 October 2007.

Even though the new law did not fully affect manual records until 24 October 2007, some data controllers could still find it difficult and expensive to comply fully after that date. This was a particular problem where an organisation has a significant amount of archived data which it wants to retain, for example, for future research purposes or for defending legal claims. During the lead up to the Directive, the Council and Commission made a joint statement to the effect that, in certain circumstances:

> at the end of the 12-year transitional period, controllers must take all reasonable steps relating to the requirements of Articles 6, 7 and 8, which do not prove impossible or involve a disproportionate effort in terms of cost.

The manual data exemption did not prevent individuals exercising their right of subject access, their right to prevent processing and their rights to compensation. The security obligations also applied and data controllers needed to review this aspect in relation to manual files. For example, were manual files kept in secure locations and was access to them restricted to those having a genuine need to use or access them?

---

[2] Information Commissioner, *Annual Report 2005–2006*, HC1228, 2006 at p. 38.

Specific provision has been made for partial exemption during the second transitional period for personal data within the meaning of data in section 1(1)(e) processed by public authorities. The exemption is from the fourth data protection principle and section 14(1)–(3) containing some of the rights of rectification, etc. This came into force on 1 January 2005.

Processing for historical research (partial derogation)

This exemption is indefinite in time. After 23 October 2001, eligible manual data processed only for the purpose of historical research in compliance with the 'relevant conditions' and relevant automated data which are processed only for the purpose of historical research, in compliance with the relevant conditions, and otherwise than by reference to the data subject, are exempt from the first data protection principle (but not as regards informing data subjects), the second, third, fourth and fifth data protection principles, and the rights of rectification, blocking, erasure and destruction under section 14(1)–(3).

The relevant conditions are those specified in section 33 and are that the data are not processed to support measures or decisions with respect to particular individuals and that they are not processed in such a way that substantial damage or substantial distress is, or is likely to be, caused to any data subject.

Automated data (for which processing commenced before 24 October 1998 – 'eligible automated data') processed only for the purpose of historical research in compliance with the relevant conditions are exempt from the first data protection principle to the extent to which it requires compliance with the conditions in Schedules 2 and 3 (the conditions for processing). This more limited exemption applies where, in spite of the other conditions being present, the data are processed by reference to the data subject.

In respect of these exemptions, personal data are not to be treated as processed otherwise than for the purpose of historical research merely because the data are disclosed:

(a) to any person, for the purpose of historical research only,
(b) to the data subject or a person acting on his behalf,
(c) at the request, or with the consent, of the data subject or a person acting on his behalf, or
(d) in circumstances in which the person making the disclosure has reasonable grounds for believing that the disclosure falls within paragraph (a), (b) or (c).

Section 12A does not apply to eligible manual data processed for historical research.

If the relevant conditions are not met, the exemption for eligible automated data is of the more restricted variety and applies only in respect of the first data protection principle but subject to the conditions for processing.

SUMMARY

- Data controllers must notify automated processing of personal data, unless exempt.
- Manual processing need not be notified.
- There is provision for certain types of procession to be subject to a preliminary assessment.
- Data controllers must provide information about their processing:
  - if the processing in question has not been notified (for example, if exempt or manual processing);
  - to any person on request.

31

Data controllers and the Data Protection Act 1998

- Failure to notify processing that must be notified is an offence of strict liability.
- Provision exists for the introduction of in-house' data protection supervisors.
- Data subject must be informed (for example, as to the identity of the data controller):
  - upon collection of their personal data;
  - in other circumstances but not, for example, if requiring a disproportionate effort); but
  - the data controller is excused in all cases if the data subject already has the information.
- Data controllers may process personal data only if:
  - one of the conditions for processing in Schedule 2 is met; and
  - in the case of sensitive personal data, one of the conditions in Schedule 3 is also met.
- Data subjects have a right to prevent processing:
  - if likely to cause substantial damage or substantial distress;
  - for the purposes of direct marketing;
  - for certain forms of automated decision taking.
- There are no barriers to transfers of personal data throughout the EEA (providing the transfer is otherwise in accordance with data protection law).
- Transfers to third countries (outside the EEA) may take place if:
  - the country has adequate protection for the processing of personal data; or if not,
  - one of the conditions allowing transfer in Schedule 4 applies.
- Placing personal data on a passive website does not involve a transfer to third countries.
- The Data Protection Act 1998 contains a range of important exemptions from parts of the Act and the data protection principles.
- Particularly important exemptions include processing for:
  - national security purposes;
  - the prevention and detection of crime;
  - the special purposes (journalism and artistic and literary purposes);
  - health, education and social work.
- There are a number of offences under the Data Protection Act 1998.
- The offences of obtaining, disclosing or procuring the disclosure of personal data without the consent of the data controller apply:
  - if done knowingly or recklessly (the test for recklessness is a subjective one);
  - subject to a number of defences.
- Other offences include selling personal data obtained without the consent of the data controller.
- The transitional provisions only now apply in relation to:
  - eligible manual data generally but only until 24 October 2007;
  - processing for historical research.

Note: there is only one correct answer to each multiple choice question.

1 Sovereign Supplies Ltd has been in the business of supplying stationery supplies to retail shops. It has a notification as required under the Data Protection Act 1998. A few months ago, the company diversified and started a printing service for private individuals. This has involved the creation and use of a database of its individual customers which did not fall within its previous notification under the Act. The new processing activities are not exempt from the notification requirements though do not include the processing of sensitive personal data. Unfortunately, the company overlooked the requirement to notify changes to its processing activities. Which one of the following CORRECTLY describes Sovereign Supplies Ltd's actual or potential liability in relation to this failure to notify changes under section 20 of the Data Protection Act 1998?

   (a) The company has committed a criminal offence of strict liability.

   (b) As the personal data are not sensitive personal data, there is no requirement to notify the new processing activities.

   (c) The company has committed a criminal offence subject to a due diligence defence.

   (d) The company has not committed an offence providing all the data subjects consented to the processing.

2   Which one of the following is NOT CORRECT in relation to the obligation of data controllers to inform data subjects (unless falling within one of the specific exemptions under the Data Protection Act 1998)?

   (a) Where the data are obtained from the data subject, the data controller does not have to provide the information if he has made it readily available to the data subject.

   (b) In cases other than where the data are obtained from the data subject, the data controller does not have to provide the information if it would involve a disproportionate effort.

   (c) The data controller must provide information as to technical and organisational measures to be taken to ensure the security of the personal data against unauthorised or unlawful processing or accidental loss, destruction or damage.

   (d) The data controller must provide information as to his identity, his representative (if he has one), the purposes of processing and any other information to enable processing to be fair.

3   Which one of the following is NOT a condition for processing personal data under Schedule 2 of the Data Protection Act 1998?

   (a) The processing is necessary for compliance with any legal obligation to which the data controller is subject, other than an obligation imposed by contract.

   (b) The information contained in the personal data has been made public as a result of steps deliberately taken by the data subject.

   (c) The data subject has given his consent to the processing.

   (d) The processing is necessary in order to protect the vital interests of the data subject.

4   Under section 32 of the Data Protection Act 1998, processing for the special purposes is exempt from certain provisions of the Act. Which one of the following is NOT one of the requirements for the exemption to apply?

(a) The data controller reasonably believes that, having regard in particular to the special import-ance of the public interest in freedom of expression, publication would be in the public interest.

(b) The processing is undertaken with a view to publication by any person of any journalistic, lit-erary or artistic material.

(c) The data controller reasonable believes that, in all the circumstances, compliance with that pro-vision is incompatible with the special purposes.

(d) The Information Commissioner has made a determination under section 45 of the Act that pro-cessing is for the special purposes.

5   **In practice, compliance with the Data Protection Act 1998 is not onerous for data controllers. Discuss.**

.**For further resources and updates please go to the Companion Website accompanying this book at www.mylawchamber.co.uk/bainbridgeIT**

32 Data subjects' rights

INTRODUCTION

This chapter looks at the Data Protection Act 1998 from the perspective of data subjects. We have seen how the Act impacts upon data controllers, and many individuals as well as organisations in the public and private sectors (ranging from central government departments to sole traders) will be classed as data controllers, even if they do not possess a computer. But we are all data subjects. There can be very few, if any, persons in respect of whom someone, somewhere, is not processing personal data relating to them in a manner within data protection law. As information processing becomes more powerful, there is a growing need to protect the rights of individuals in that context, because of the threats to privacy and freedom. The 1998 Act significantly developed and expanded the rights of data subjects compared with the previous legislation. An example of the differences in data subjects' rights compared with those under the 1984 Act was given by Mr Justice Gray in *Lord Ashcroft* v *Attorney General* [2002] EWHC 1122 (QB) where, in a preliminary hearing, he noted that a claim for damages under the 1984 Act could only be made under section 23 where there had been loss of personal data, destruction without the authorisation of the data user or disclosure or access to personal data without such authority. A breach of a data protection principle did not, *per se*, give rise to a claim in damages. The position under the 1998 Act is entirely different and a breach of any of the data protection principles or indeed any of the requirements of the Act does give rise to a claim in damages if the data subject suffers damage as a result. A claim for distress also can be made where damage has been suffered or, where the breach relates to processing for the special purposes, a claim for distress can be made in the absence of damage.

In addition to the pre-existing rights of subject access, rectification or erasure of personal data and compensation for damage and distress, all of which have been enhanced, further rights became available under the 1998 Act being a right to prevent processing likely to cause substantial damage or substantial distress, a right to prevent processing for purposes of direct marketing, and rights in relation to automated decision taking. Data controllers also have a duty to provide data subjects with information. This duty is described in the previous chapter.

Data subjects may approach the Information Commissioner for an assessment, usually expressed as a complaint about a processing activity rather than a request for assessment as such. In some cases, individuals may be granted assistance such as the payment of legal fees. As far as enforcing their rights, data subjects may apply to a court for compensation or to ask the court to order the data controller to do something required, such as comply with a subject access request, or to refrain from doing something – for example, to comply with a notice from a data subject requiring the data controller to cease processing which is causing substantial damage to the data subject or another person. Figure 32.1 shows the relationship between the data subject, the Information Commissioner and the courts.

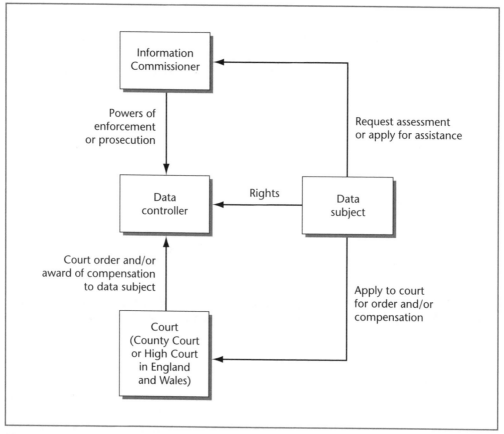

Figure 32.1 Relationship between the data subject, Commissioner and court in respect of data subjects' rights

DATA SUBJECTS' RIGHT OF ACCESS

The data subject's right of access is fundamental to the policing of data protection law by individuals. By seeing what personal data relating to a particular individual a data controller is processing, that person may, with the knowledge of other factors such as the purposes of the processing, take a view on whether the processing is fair and lawful or otherwise within the Data Protection Principles. In particular, individuals are likely to be concerned to satisfy themselves that their personal data are correct and not excessive. This may be important where the granting of credit or obtaining employment or services could depend on the data and considerable damage can be done if it is incorrect – for example, by falsely indicating that a person has a criminal record, has a county court judgment against him for debt, is an active member of an extreme political group and so on.

A right of access to personal data is possible under Article 8 of the Council of Europe Convention for the Protection of Human Rights and Fundamental Freedoms (the 'Human Rights Convention'). The right to respect for privacy and family life can impose positive obligations to provide information but is of uncertain scope. It is much more satisfactory to provide for a statutory right of access under data protection law, especially as previously there did not seem to be a right of access under common law. In *R v Mid-Glamorgan Family Health Services,*

ex parte Martin [1995] 1 WLR 110, a patient had been refused access to his health records going back to before 1990 on the basis that it would be detrimental for the patient to see those records directly. An offer was made to disclose the records conditionally to a medical expert appointed by the patient but this was not accepted. The patient claimed that there was a right of access at common law. However, the Court of Appeal refused to grant access denying that there was a right of access under common law.

Since the coming into force of the Human Rights Act 1998, effectively bringing the Human Rights Convention into UK law, there may also be a right of access under Article 8 of the Convention, as mentioned above. In *McGinley & Egan* v *United Kingdom* (1999) 27 EHRR 1, at the European Court of Human Rights, two ex-soldiers had witnessed nuclear testing carried out by the UK in 1957 and 1958 at Christmas Island in the Pacific Ocean. They later suffered health problems which they thought were caused by their exposure to radiation and they lodged claims for war pensions. These were turned down and the government did not disclose documents indicating the radiation levels at the time.

The court held that access to the documents would have either allayed their fears or allowed them to assess the danger to which they had been exposed and this raised an issue under Article 8. Although Article 8 was primarily a negative undertaking by, for example, protecting a person against arbitrary interference by public authorities, it went beyond that and could give rise to positive obligations (also recognised in *Gaskin* v *United Kingdom*: see later). Those obligations required a balance between the interests of individuals and the general interest of the community. Where a government was engaged in a hazardous activity which might have adverse consequences on the health of those involved, Article 8 required that an accessible and effective procedure was in place to enable such persons to seek all relevant and appropriate information. However, there was no breach of Article 8 in the present case as the ex-soldiers had failed to avail themselves of an appeal under Rule 6 of the Pensions Appeals Tribunals (Scotland) Rules 1981 which would have allowed them to apply for an order for disclosure of the relevant documents. The existence of that procedure meant that the UK had fulfilled its obligations under Article 8. (The UK ratified the Convention in 1951 but did not bring it into direct effect until the Human Rights Act 1998 came into force.)

There is a close relationship between data protection law and the Human Rights Convention, which is expressly mentioned in the data protection Directive. The right of privacy under Article 8(1) including the permissible derogations from it in Article 8(2) and the balancing with the right of freedom of expression form a significant basis for data protection law. Theoretically, there should be no conflict between the Data Protection Act 1998 and the Convention rights. If there is, it should be resolved in favour of the Convention rights as required by the Human Rights Act 1998.

A right of access was available under the 1984 Act but was limited simply to a statement from the data user (now data controller) as to whether he was processing data relating to the applicant and, if so, to access the data. Various rules existed to deal with the situation where access to the data would reveal information relating to another identifiable individual and the 1998 Act has provisions to deal with this situation but with some significant changes.

Statutory provisions for data subject access

Sections 7–9 and 9A of the Data Protection Act 1998 deal with data subjects' right of access. (Section 9A applies to unstructured files, within the meaning of data in section 1(1)(e), processed by public authorities and came into force on 1 January 2005.) Unless within the exemptions the subject information provisions (which include subject access and the obligations on data controllers to provide information to data subjects on collection or otherwise) have effect notwithstanding any enactment or rule of law prohibiting or restricting the disclosure, or authorising the withholding, of information: section 27(5).

Section 7(1) of the Data Protection Act 1998 provides:

(1) Subject to the following provisions of this section and to sections 8, 9 and 9A, an individual is entitled –
  (a) to be informed by any data controller whether personal data of which that individual is the data subject are being processed by or on behalf of that data controller,
  (b) if that is the case, to be given by the data controller a description of –
     (i)   the personal data of which that individual is the data subject,
     (ii) the purposes for which they are being or are to be processed, and
     (iii) the recipients or classes of recipients to whom they are or may be disclosed,
  (c) to have communicated to him in an intelligible form –
     (i)   the information constituting any personal data of which that individual is the data subject, and
     (ii) any information available to the data controller as to the source of those data, and
  (d) where the processing by automatic means of personal data of which that individual is the data subject for the purpose of evaluating matters relating to him such as, for example, his performance at work, his creditworthiness, his reliability or his conduct, has constituted or is likely to constitute the sole basis for any decision significantly affecting him, to be informed by the data controller of the logic involved in that decision-taking.

Normally the data controller has to comply within 40 days and may charge a fee up to the maximum of £10 (there are differences in respect of requests to credit reference agencies and in respect of educational records and health records, as discussed later). Notwithstanding the maximum period for complying with a subject access request, the data controller has, under section 7(8), a duty to act promptly. However, the data controller does not have to comply until he has received the request in writing and the fee, if there is one. Under section 7(3), where the data controller reasonably requires further information from the individual making the request to identify him and locate the relevant data and has informed the individual accordingly, he does not have to comply unless he is provided with that further information. Data controllers must be careful to satisfy themselves as to the identity of the person making the request and to ensure their employees and agents also appreciate the importance of this. There have been numerous examples of employees disclosing personal data to persons posing as the data subject.

Much more information is required than under the 1984 Act, although much of this additional information would be available to a data subject who examined the register entry, except for the description of the logic involved in any automated decision taking. A person making a subject access request is entitled to a copy of the information constituting the personal data of which that person is the data subject in permanent form unless the supply of such a copy would be impossible or would involve a disproportionate effort or if the individual agrees otherwise; section 8(2). Making permanent copies may be very expensive in certain cases, such as in the case of X-ray plates or where there is a substantial amount of paper files involved. In assessing whether provision of a copy in permanent form would involve a disproportionate effort, factors that may be relevant, in the Information Commissioner's view, are the cost, length of time to make the copies, the difficulty in making copies and the size of the data controller's organisation. All these factors should be balanced with the effect on the data subject. Where the information is not intelligible without an explanation, such explanation must accompany the information.

As individuals may not realise that they are entitled to more information than was the case previously, the Act allowed the Secretary of State to make regulations in particular cases so that a request for some of the above information may be treated as a request for other information required to be given. The Data Protection (Subject Access) (Fees and Miscellaneous Provisions) Regulations 2000 state that a request for information under section 7(1)(a), (b) or (c) is to be treated as a request for all the information under those provisions, though not to information under section 7(1)(d) unless there is an express intention to that effect. A request for information under section 7(1)(d) (that is, in respect of the logic in any automated decision taking) is to be treated as extending to other information under any provision of section 7(1) only if there is an express intention to that effect. A subject access request therefore should be made in terms of 'all the information under section 7(1)(a) to (d)'.

To overcome the problem of 'nuisance' subject access requests, made at frequent intervals by the same person, under section 8(3), the data controller can refuse to comply with a subsequent identical or similar request by a particular individual unless a reasonable interval has elapsed. In determining what a reasonable interval is, regard should be given to the nature of the data, the purposes of the processing and the frequency with which the data are altered; section 8(4). So, for example, where data are being updated and modified on an ongoing basis, fairly frequent requests may be deemed reasonable. The information to be given must be as it was when the request was received apart from deletions or amendments which would have been made notwithstanding the request. Therefore, if the data are inaccurate and in breach of the fourth data protection principle, the data controller must not deliberately correct the data because a subject access request has been made. However, if the data controller systematically checks the validity of the personal data as part of the management of his processing activity and, as a result of such checking, an inaccuracy is detected and corrected between the time the subject access request is made and the time when it is complied with, then the data controller need give access to the data as corrected only. As noted in the exemptions in the previous chapter, if the data are evidence that the data controller has committed an offence other than one under the Act, he is excused compliance with the subject access request to the extent that such evidence would be revealed.

The right of access is to personal data currently being processed (bearing in mind the wide definition of processing). There is no room for the 'once processed always processed' approach. Documents that were produced by word processing software and which do not otherwise fall within the meaning of data are no longer considered to be processed providing the electronic version no longer exists. The fact that such documents could be scanned into a computer and then searched for individuals' names does not bring them into the scope of the subject access provisions. An argument to the contrary was rejected by Mr Justice Laddie in *Smith v Lloyds Bank plc* [2005] EWHC 246 (Ch).

Where the processing is by automatic means and has constituted or is likely to constitute the sole basis for any decision significantly affecting him, in evaluating matters relating to the data subject such as his performance at work, creditworthiness, reliability or conduct, the data subject has the right to be informed of the logic involved in that decision taking, as mentioned above. However, this does not apply if, or to the extent that, the information constitutes a trade secret under section 8(5). 'Trade secret' is not defined but it would seem sensible to apply the meaning used in the law of breach of confidence, although it is not particularly clearly defined there. Perhaps it would be reasonable to consider a 'trade secret' here to be information the disclosure of which would harm the data controller's legitimate interests, be of benefit to a competitor or expose the data controller to a serious risk of fraud. The data protection Directive states that the data subject must not be refused all information on the basis that the logic is a trade secret.

Access where third parties identified

The provisions in the Data Protection Act 1998, dealing with the situation when compliance with a subject access request would disclose information relating to another identifiable individual, took account of a case before the European Court of Human Rights, *Gaskin* v *United Kingdom* (1990) 12 EHRR 36. The applicant for subject access claimed he had been ill-treated while a child in care of the local authority. He sought access to confidential records concerning him and his care from Liverpool City Council, which was required to keep such records. The City Council decided to give Gaskin access provided the persons who contributed to his file consented. Only 19 out of 46 of the contributors gave their consent and the relevant documents were released to him. However, the remainder, where the contributors refused consent or could not be traced, were not disclosed to him. It was held by the European Court of Human Rights that this was a breach of his right to respect for his private and family life under Article 8 of the Human Rights Convention. Although the UK could not be said to have interfered with his private life, there could be circumstances where an inherent positive obligation arose in respect for private life. Whether such an obligation arose in a particular case was a matter of balance and, on the basis of proportionality, required that an independent authority decided whether access should be granted or denied if a contributor to such records withheld consent or did not answer. That had not happened in *Gaskin*, hence the breach of Article 8.

Under section 7(4)–(6) of the Data Protection Act 1998, to comply with the request, the data controller must be satisfied that the other person (including a person who is the source of the information) has consented to the disclosure of his personal data to the person making the request. Otherwise, access can be given where it is reasonable in all the circumstances to comply without the consent of the other. In determining whether it is reasonable in all the circumstances to comply without the consent of the other, factors that may be taken into account are any duty of confidentiality owed to the other, any steps taken by the data controller to gain the consent of the other, whether the other is capable of giving consent and any express refusal of consent by the other individual.

In other cases such as where it would not be reasonable to comply, lack of consent does not excuse a data controller altogether where he can provide the access to the applicant's data without disclosing the identity of the other individual – for example, by omitting the name or other identifying particulars. This may be done by suppressing the identifying information from a computer printout which is handed to the person making the subject access request or, in the case of manual files caught by the new law, by masking the relevant information when making a photocopy to give to the person making the request. Under section 7(9), a court may order compliance with a subject access request. This is a discretionary power.

In *Durant* v *Financial Services Authority* [2004] FSR 573, the claimant had been a customer of Barclay's Bank plc and he had been involved in litigation with the bank, which he had lost. The Financial Services Authority ('FSA') investigated his complaint against the bank and he sought access to documents and information obtained from Barclay's Bank by the FSA relating to his dispute with the bank. He carried out a subject access request under section 7 of the Data Protection Act 1998. The FSA responded by providing the claimant with some data but not all the data that he thought he was entitled to gain access to. Some of the personal data were held on computer whilst other data were recorded in paper files. Of the data provided to the claimant, some had been redacted (edited for publication) by suppressing or blocking data which the FSA either did not consider to be personal data relating to the claimant or because it would disclose the name of another individual.

The Court of Appeal held that the provisions in section 7(4)–(6) suggest that data controllers should go through a two-stage process when deciding whether or not to disclose personal data relating to others when complying with a subject access request. The first issue is whether such third-party personal data are necessarily part of the data subject's personal data. If not, the data controller may redact these data. Where the third-party personal data necessarily forms part of the data subject's personal data, this requires a balancing of the data subject's interests with those of the third party who may be identified from those data. The provisions appear to raise a rebuttable presumption that third-party personal data should not be disclosed without consent. However, the data controller may consider it reasonable in the circumstances, including those set out in section 7(6), to release such data without the third party's consent.

Deciding whether to release third-party data requires a balancing of interests which might depend on balancing the importance of disclosure of third-party information where it goes to the legitimate protection of the data subject's privacy with the existence of any obligation of confidence to the third party or any sensitivity of the disclosure. Factors may be whether the third party is a recipient of the data subject's personal data and who might act on the data to the detriment of the data subject. Where the third party is the source of personal data relating to the data subject, disclosure might be important to allow the data subject the opportunity to use his rights, for example, to have inaccurate data rectified. This also must be balanced with any obligation of confidence or sensitivity relating to the disclosure.

The Court of Appeal confirmed that, with the possible exception of two redactions, the data suppressed by the FSA did not constitute personal data. In relation to the two redactions that could possibly constitute the claimant's personal data, they would have disclosed the name of an employee of the FSA who had been verbally abused by the claimant and were of little or no legitimate value to the claimant. Therefore, the redactions in question complied with the Act.

Having a blanket policy of not identifying third parties, for example, by redacting their details from the copy of personal data given to the data subject is unlikely to comply with the subject access requirements. A proper balance is required by section 7(4)(b) between the legitimate interests of the third parties and of the data subject. In *R (on application of Alan Lord)* v *Secretary of State for the Home Department* [2003] EWHC 2073 (Admin), the question of redacting came up for consideration in relation to reports prepared by prison officers and others on the classification of potentially dangerous prisoners (Category A prisoners). The interests of the authors of the reports was important and disclosure of their identity could have serious consequences. But this would not be so in every case, though in every case a prisoner's liberty was engaged. A targeted approach was called for rather than a blanket policy. Similar considerations applied to refusing access to the full text of the reports on the basis of the prevention of crime exemption under section 29(1) of the Act. Normally, prisoners were only allowed to see a 'gist' or summary of the reports. The judge, Mr Justice Munby, said (at para. 149):

> I emphasise that I am not saying that every Category A prisoner will in every case be entitled to see the full contents of his Category A reports. There will be cases – there may be many cases – in which the Secretary of State will be able to rely upon section 7(4), just as there will be cases in which he will be able to rely upon section 29(1), as justifying less than complete disclosure. All I am saying is that the Secretary of State's present policy of blanket non-disclosure cannot be justified under section 7(4), any more than it can be justified under section 29(1). What section 7(4)(b) requires, like section 29(1), is in this context a more selective and targeted approach to non-disclosure, based on the circumstances of the particular case.

Subject access may be denied under section 7 on the basis that the data to which access is sought is not personal data, the data would identify a third party and it is not reasonable to accede to the request or a court may refuse to exercise its discretion to order compliance. However, access may be obtained during legal proceedings for compensation under section 13 or in respect of inaccurate data under section 14 through the legal process of discovery: *Johnson* v *Medical*

Defence Union Ltd [2005] 1 WLR 750. The fact that a court has refused to order compliance with a subject access request may be a factor to be taken into account during the process of discovery but it is not determinative of the matter. Disclosure to a data subject may also be ordered by a court to identify persons unlawfully processing personal data. Such discovery was granted in *Hughes* v *Carratu International plc* [2006] EWHC 1791 (QB) where the claimant had been informed by the Information Commissioner that an enquiry agent who was going to be prosecuted under the Act had personal data belonging to the claimant. Discovery of the identity of the agent and the solicitor who had engaged him was ordered.

Subject access request fees and response times

As mentioned above, the basic time period for complying with a subject access request is 40 days and the maximum fee that may be charged is £10. Where the subject access request is limited to information relating to financial standing, the maximum fee is £2 (as it was previously under section 158 of the Consumer Credit Act 1974) and the maximum period for compliance is seven working days. For health records, being accessible records within the meaning of the Act, the maximum fee that can be charged is £50 if a permanent copy is provided. However, where the record has been at least partially created within the 40-day period immediately prior to the request, and no permanent copy is requested, no fee may be charged. For educational records, being accessible records for the purposes of the Act, the maximum period for compliance is 15 school days if the data controller's address is in England and Wales. Where a copy is provided in permanent form, there is a sliding scale of maximum fees in the Schedule to the Regulations, ranging from £1 for fewer than 20 pages to £50 for 500 pages or over. If the information includes material in another form to writing on paper, the maximum fee is £50, regardless of how many paper pages are also involved. This could apply, for example where the data are in the form of a photograph or on video or CD. Where health or educational records are processed by automatic means (or intended to be so processed) within section 1(1)(a) or (b), these special provisions do not apply.

Where access is sought to personal data in unstructured files held by public authorities under section 9A of the Data Protection Act 1998, a public authority is not obliged to comply if the estimated cost exceeds the prescribe limit, presently set at £600 (for authorities set out in Part I of Schedule 1 to the Freedom of Information Act 2000 which includes government departments) or £450 (for other public authorities) by the Freedom of Information and Data Protection (Appropriate Limit and Fees) Regulations 2004.

Credit reference agencies

Under section 9 of the Data Protection Act 1998, an application to a credit reference agency is taken to be limited to financial information relating to the data subject unless a contrary intention is expressed. The data controller must include a statement of the data subject's rights under section 159 of the Consumer Credit Act 1974 (a right to have wrong information corrected), to the extent required as prescribed. Section 62 of the Data Protection Act 1998 modifies section 158 of the Consumer Credit Act 1974 and the right under that section to obtain a copy of a file applies only in relation to partnerships. For other individuals the right to a copy of the file is under section 9 of the 1998 Act, although the right of correction of wrong information remains under section 159 of the 1974 Act.

Enforced subject access

Enforced subject access was perceived as an abuse of a data subject's right of access by the Data Protection Registrar under the 1984 Act and remains a concern of the Information Commissioner under the 1998 Act. This occurs where, for example, a potential employer requires a job applicant to provide a copy of his police file showing whether the data subject has been convicted or cautioned in relation to any offences. The dangers of leaving enforced subject access uncontrolled were clearly seen in *R* v *Chief Constable of 'B', ex parte R* (unreported) 24 November 1997, Queen's Bench Division.

R, who was 29 years old at the time, wanted to travel to a foreign country to teach English to adults and, to do so, he had to apply for a visa. He was required by the Consulate General of the country concerned to provide a certificate of his prosecution and conviction history. Unfortunately, R had a conviction for a minor offence of theft committed when he was 19 years old for which he received a conditional discharge and was ordered to pay compensation. However, the conviction was a 'spent conviction' under the Rehabilitation of Offenders Act 1974, the effect being that by virtue of section 4 of that Act, he was treated in law as a person who had not committed or been charged with or prosecuted for or sentenced for the offence. The time after which a sentence is considered spent depends on what the sentence was. The purpose is that a person who has not re-offended will not be prejudiced by an unwarranted disclosure of the fact of the offence to a third party. The Chief Constable to whom R applied for subject access provided a statement to the effect that R had 'no citeable convictions' but this was not on the standard form issued under the Data Protection Act 1984 and as required by the Consulate General. This form would show R's spent conviction.

The Code of Practice for Data Protection used by the Association of Chief Police Officers generally requires 'reportable' offences to be retained for 20 years, even though they may be spent convictions.[1] However, the Data Protection Act 1984 contained no discretion to exclude some information from being provided under a subject access request and, according to Lord Justice Laws, section 21 of that Act clearly required all the information constituting the personal data to be supplied. Any conflict with the Rehabilitation of Offenders Act 1974 was removed by section 26(4) of the 1984 Act which stated that the subject access provisions apply notwithstanding any enactment or rule of law prohibiting or restricting disclosure or withholding information. The judge expressed sympathy for R whom he described as having lived down his conviction, gaining a series of academic and professional qualifications and generally leading an exemplary and productive life. The judge said it was little comfort to R that enforced subject access under the new law is intended to obviate the problems he had encountered but it came too late for R. Of course, in other situations, enforced subject access can be important such as where a person applies for employment in a position of trust or authority where children or other vulnerable persons are involved.

In a late amendment to the Data Protection Bill, which became the Data Protection Act 1998, provisions were added to prevent enforced subject access, in specified cases. Section 56 of the Act (which is still not in force, apart from the power to modify it) sets out the situations where enforced subject access is prohibited, being in relation to:

■ the recruitment of another as an employee;

■ the continued employment of another person;

---

[1] The present Code of Practice allows retention of offender data on the Police National Computer for much longer periods in some cases: see Association of Chief Police Officers, *Retention Guidelines for Nominal Records on the Police National Computer*, 16 March 2006.

- any contract for the provision of services by another person; or
- the provision of goods, facilities or services to any person (this extends also to the supply of a relevant record by a third party).

The prohibition applies in relation to 'relevant records', being those showing convictions and cautions where the data controller is a chief officer of police or the Secretary of State. Also included is subject matter relating to the Secretary of State's functions under section 92 of the Powers of Criminal Courts (Sentencing) Act 2000 (detention of young persons for long periods of time for grave crimes), the Prison Act 1952, under the Social Security Contributions and Benefits Act 1992, the Social Security Administration Act 1992, the Jobseekers Act 1995 or in relation to certificates of criminal records under Part V of the Police Act 1997 (with relevant provisions for Scotland and Northern Ireland). Even if the record simply states that the data controller is not processing data relating to a particular matter, this is still to be taken as relating to that matter. For example, if the information provided under the subject access request states that the person concerned has no convictions or cautions, this will still be deemed to be within the prohibition.

Contravention of the enforced subject access provisions will be a criminal offence of strict liability. However, this will not apply where the access is authorised or required by law or court order or justified as being in the public interest. The latter will not include the ground that it would assist in the prevention or detection of crime – there must be some other public interest involved. Section 56 has not yet been brought into force, and it may be some time before it is, if it is ever brought into force.

Enforced subject access in relation to health records is also controlled but not by way of imposing criminal liability. Rather, it is a matter of making any such requirement void in contractual terms. Under section 57, any term or condition in a contract is void in as much as it purports to require the supply of, or producing to another person of, a record, copy or part of a record consisting of information contained in any health record as defined in section 68(2), which is a record consisting of information relating to the physical or mental health or condition of an individual made by or on behalf of a health professional in connection with the care of that individual. 'Health professional' is widely defined in section 69. The provisions relating to enforced subject access to health records were brought into force on 1 March 2000, when much of the remainder of the Act was brought into force.

RIGHT TO PREVENT PROCESSING LIKELY TO CAUSE SUBSTANTIAL DAMAGE OR SUBSTANTIAL DISTRESS

This right was introduced by the Data Protection Act 1998 and had no direct equivalent under the 1984 Act, although processing which had the potential to cause damage or distress might have been caught by the first data protection principle in particular and dealt with by the powers of enforcement under the Act. The right to prevent processing likely to cause substantial damage or substantial distress is a considerable improvement to the rights of the data subject in that it empowers individuals to require the data controller to stop or not commence processing that has certain consequences for the individual concerned or another. This right is backed by the power of the court to order compliance.

A data subject can require the data controller to cease or not to begin processing for a specified purpose or in a specified manner on the ground that, for specified reasons, it is unwarranted as causing or being likely to cause substantial damage or substantial distress to him or another: section 10(1). However, a limitation is that this right does not apply to processing under conditions 1–4 in Schedule 2, being processing where the data subject has given consent, where it is necessary in relation to a contract, where it is necessary for compliance with a legal obligation or where it is to protect the vital interests of the data subject. The Secretary of State may add further exceptions to the right. It can apply to the other conditions for processing 'normal' data (such as processing necessary for the legitimate interests of the data controller or a third party to whom the data are disclosed) and to all the conditions for processing of 'sensitive' data in Schedule 3 and the additional conditions provided for by Regulations.

The data subject has to give notice in writing to the data controller, specifying the purpose or manner of processing objected to and the reasons why he or another is likely to be caused substantial damage or substantial distress. Within 21 days, the data controller must give a written notice stating that he has complied with the data subject's notice or intends to do so or stating why he considers the notice unjustified to any extent and the extent, if any, to which he has complied or intends to comply.

If the data controller does not comply with the data subject's notice in whole or in part, the data subject may apply to a court for an order requiring the data controller to comply with the notice. The order will be granted if the court considers the notice justified to any extent and the data controller has failed to comply to that extent. Any failure by a data subject to exercise this right (and the right to prevent processing for the purposes of direct marketing under section 11(1)) does not prejudice any of the other rights of the data subject. An application to the court might include a claim for compensation under section 13, discussed later.

Curiously, the heading to section 10 does not contain the word 'substantial' referring only to the right to prevent processing likely to cause damage or distress. Furthermore, the word 'substantial' does not appear in section 13, which provides a right to compensation for damage or distress. The data protection Directive does not use the word 'substantial' and gives the data subject a right to object 'on compelling legitimate grounds relating to his particular situation': Article 14. The implications of all this is that, for example, a data subject will be able to obtain compensation for damage which is insufficiently substantial to give rise to the right to prevent such processing. Alternatively, or additionally, the right to compensation might apply where the data controller has already ceased the processing operation concerned. For example, this could be where a disclosure to a third party has already been made which has caused substantial damage or distress to the data subject.

RIGHT TO PREVENT PROCESSING FOR PURPOSES OF DIRECT MARKETING

The European Commission perceived direct marketing, the sending of junk mail or faxes, as a particular problem. It was decided that an individual ought to be able to prevent it in a case where the marketing material is addressed specifically to the individual. Anonymous advertising material is not affected. This is material not addressed to specific persons, such as advertising inserts in newspapers and magazines or which is simply pushed through letterboxes in a blanket mailing. In any case, such advertising campaigns of that nature do not require the processing of personal data of the recipients.

The Directive gives individuals an absolute right to prevent processing for the purposes of direct marketing and it also requires that Member States ensure that individuals are aware of this right. Thus, under section 11 of the Data Protection Act 1998, a data subject has a right, by giving written notice, to require a data controller to cease within a reasonable time in the circumstances or not to begin processing his personal data for the purposes of direct marketing. 'Direct marketing' is defined in the Act as meaning the communication by any means of any advertising or marketing material which is directed at particular individuals. The data controller must give the data subject a written notice within 21 days of receipt of the data subject's notice stating what steps he has taken or will take to comply. Again, the court has the power to order the data controller to comply, following an application by the data subject and if satisfied that the data controller has failed to comply with the data subject's notice.

Section 11(2A) contains an exception to the right in the case of processing of certain types of data held by a telecommunications provider. This provision is now meaningless. It applied to except data set out in the Telecommunications (Data Protection and Privacy) Regulations 1999. These Regulations have been revoked and replaced by the Privacy and Electronic Communications (EC Directive) Regulations 2003 which provide for rights in respect of unsolicited direct marketing communications sent through a public electronic communications network. These Regulations are described in Chapter 34. Section 11(2A) should either have been repealed or modified to mention the 2003 Regulations. As the Information Commissioner is also responsible for these Regulations to failure to repeal or modify section 11(2A) is probably of no consequence.

In the UK, the presence of the mailing preference system (MOPS), the Telephone Preference Service and the Fax Preference Service already allows individuals to indicate that they do not wish to receive marketing material. Organisations which send out marketing material are required to consult opt-out registers from time to time. Furthermore, if individuals are careful to make sure that they always tick the ubiquitous 'no marketing' box on forms and the like, this should prevent a great deal of marketing material being sent to them. However, even if advantage is taken of the above schemes and the 'no marketing' box is always ticked, some marketing material may still get through. In such cases the right to prevent marketing under the Act will prove useful, though it does require the data subject to be proactive.

It may be that the right to prevent processing for the purposes of direct marketing might go further than was originally thought. At first reading, it might seem that the right has to be exercised by an individual after he has received the offending marketing material. Under the 1984 Act, cases such as *Innovations (Mail Order) Ltd* v *Data Protection Registrar*, 29 September 1993 and *British Gas Trading Ltd* v *Data Protection Registrar*, 24 March 1998 showed that unfettered marketing activities could be in breach of the first data protection principle, which required that personal data be processed fairly and lawfully. Individuals should be allowed to object to marketing at the time data were first collected from them and not later. Such developments did not, however, give the individual a right to prevent marketing, as a breach of the principles could only be dealt with by the Data Protection Registrar (now the Information Commissioner) exercising his enforcement powers. However, by marrying the underlying rationale behind these and similar cases with the right under section 11, it is not a giant leap to accept that the right might not be confined to the ability to put a stop to further marketing from a data controller who has already sent some unsolicited marketing. It might even be a right not to be sent unsolicited marketing material at all unless the individual concerned has expressed positive consent, as now applies in relation to direct marketing using a public electronic communications network.

There is also some authority for the scope of the right to prevent processing for the purposes of direct marketing in the case of *R (Robertson)* v *Wakefield Metropolitan District Council* [2002] QB 1052. In that case, Mr Justice Kay held that the supply of the electoral register for the purposes of direct marketing without previously giving individual electors the opportunity of objecting was unlawful, being contrary to section 11 of the Data Protection Act 1998, Article 8 of the Human Rights Convention (the right to privacy) and Article 3 of the First Protocol to the Convention (the right to free elections). If this view is of general application, and there is no reason to doubt this, the impact of Article 8 of the Convention on section 11 of the Data Protection Act 1998, is to only allow the sending of unsolicited marketing material if the data subject has consented or, at least, having been given an opportunity to object, has chosen not to do so. If this is so, it has serious implications for organisations involved in list trading for marketing purposes.

One small provision in the Data Protection Act 1998 might compromise this wider view of the right. Section 10(6) states that, if a data subject does not exercise his right to prevent processing likely to cause substantial damage or substantial distress or his right to prevent processing for the purposes of direct marketing, this does not affect his other rights under Part II of the Act (the Part dealing with data subjects' rights). This suggests that the right is only available in cases where the data subject has taken positive steps to exercise it. However, this interpretation may be contrary to Article 8 of the Convention. It should be remembered that the right to privacy is subject to derogations in Article 8(2) but none of these could fairly be said to apply in the context of direct marketing.

AUTOMATED DECISION TAKING

Another concern in the lead up to the data protection Directive was automated decision taking where the decisions had or could have significant impacts on data subjects. There are obvious dangers where decisions are taken dogmatically on the basis of a number of factors without any discretion that could be used in particular cases. The potential dangers of automated decision taking were seen in decisions to grant credit being influenced by the credit record of a previous occupant of a house or flat now occupied by a person applying for credit. In *Equifax Europe Ltd v Data Protection Registrar*, 28 February 1992, Data Protection Tribunal (now Information Tribunal), a credit reference agency was using personal data relating to the financial status of individuals by reference to the current or previous address of the data subject together with financial information relating to *any other individual who had been recorded as residing at any time at the same or a similar address*. The use of such third party data was deemed to be unfair by the Data Protection Registrar (now Information Commissioner) although, in the event, the tribunal did not revoke the enforcement notice but substituted its own on much narrower terms: for example, allowing the use of such third-party data if there appeared to be a financial relationship or dependence between the applicant and the third party.

A mechanical and predetermined decision-taking process can bring unsatisfactory decisions. It could be because a factor which is a good statistical predictor is built into the logic of the decision process. The data subject's postal code is a good example but says nothing about any particular data subject. Another example is where the data subject has a foreign sounding name. The controls over automated decision taking are aimed at overcoming decisions that are unfair in a particular case. The data protection Directive took a fairly severe approach and permitted such decision taking only in the context of contracts or, subject to safeguards, where national legislation specifically allowed it.

Section 12 of the Data Protection Act 1998 deals with automated decision taking and takes advantage of the data protection Directive permitting it, subject to safeguards, in cases other than in relation to contracts. The provisions are targeted at decision taking which significantly affects an individual and which is:

> based solely on the processing by automatic means of personal data in respect of which that individual is the data subject for the purposes of evaluating matters relating to him such as, for example, his performance of work, his creditworthiness, his reliability or his conduct (section 12(1)).

Note that the definition is not exhaustive. Decisions in the context of contract or specifically permitted under legislation (known as 'exempt decisions') are treated somewhat differently to other forms of automated decision taking. In the latter case, the data subject has the right to prevent automated decisions being taken in respect of him or to require a data controller to reconsider such a decision. In terms of 'exempt decisions', the data controller must take steps to safeguard the legitimate interests of the data subject.

Exempt decisions

The precise meaning of 'exempt decisions' is given in section 12(4)–(7), being where:

- the decision is taken in the course of steps taken to consider whether to enter into a contract with the data subject or with a view to entering into such a contract or in the course of performing such a contract, or is authorised or required by or under any enactment; and
- the effect of the decision is to grant a request of the data subject or steps have been taken to safeguard his legitimate interests (for example, allowing him to make representations).

These may be added to by the Secretary of State, though none have been added as yet. However, the conditions that either the data subject's request is granted or steps have been taken to safeguard the data subject's legitimate interests do not automatically apply to any further types of decision added by the Secretary of State although, of course, any Regulations adding to the list of exempt decisions may make specific provisions for safeguards.

An example of an exempt decision can be seen below.

Consider an individual, Herbert, who has applied for hire purchase to buy a used car. The hire-purchase company, Grabbitt & Co Ltd, use an automated decision system on a computer which is based on a credit scoring formula. If Grabbitt & Co accepts Herbert's application and a hire-purchase contract is duly executed, there is no further requirement under these provisions. (Of course, if Grabbitt & Co want to disclose personal data relating to Herbert to another company, say for marketing purposes, Herbert should be told this, preferably by having a 'tick box' on the hire-purchase application form.) However, if Grabbitt & Co turns down Herbert's application, steps must be taken to safeguard his legitimate interests and, as the Act suggests, this will probably be by allowing him to make representations, that is, to respond to the failure to be granted credit. It may be that some years ago Herbert had a court judgment against him for debt and he has been open about this when completing the application form (or Grabbitt & Co have found out from a credit reference agency that he has been in default of a loan). Herbert might now want to say to Grabbitt & Co that he is a much better credit risk nowadays and that his default was at a time when he lost his job and he has since repaid the amount outstanding in full.

The Act is silent on what, if anything, the data controller should do in response to representations made by a data subject but a reasonable data controller ought seriously to consider any representations made by an individual and, in appropriate circumstances, reconsider the decision, perhaps by personal review rather than by automated decision taking.

Non-exempt decisions

As mentioned above, where the decision itself is not an exempt one, data subjects have far greater rights and can even prevent automated decision taking in respect of them where the decisions, based solely on automated decision taking, significantly affect them and are for the purpose of evaluating matters such as performance at work, creditworthiness, reliability or conduct. This is where the right not to be subject to a decision taken by automated means finds expression in the Act. However, probably the greatest proportion of automated decision taking within section 12 of the Data Protection Act 1998 will be in respect of contracts and will be exempt decisions. Other exempt decisions may be specifically authorised by or required by legislation. An example might be an automated decision taking system to determine social security payments.

It is not an easy matter to think of examples of automated decision taking which will be outside the realms of contract. One possible hypothetical candidate is where a doctor in a local NHS Trust hospital uses an automated system to decide on priority for operations where there is a long waiting list. Being an NHS Trust hospital, there is no contract between the patient and the hospital, or for that matter, between the patient and the doctor. Indeed, there are probably several other potential areas where the public sector confers benefits on individuals outside a contract. Some, such as the social security example quoted above, may be specifically provided for by legislation and thus become exempt decisions.

In respect of automated decision taking which is not exempt, under section 12(1) the data subject is given a right to prevent such decisions by serving a written notice on the data controller. There is no mention of any time limit for the notice to take effect nor that it has to be reasonable. It would seem that the intention is for the notice to take immediate effect. As with direct marketing, this right is absolute but does not, of course, apply to exempt decisions.

Where no notice has been served by the data subject, further safeguards are provided. Under section 12(2), the data controller is required to notify the data subject that the decision was taken on the basis of automated decision taking as soon as reasonably practicable. The data subject then has the opportunity to ask the data controller, by written notice, to reconsider the decision or take a new decision by other means within 21 days of receipt of the notice. Within that period, the data controller must serve a written notice on the data subject stating what steps he intends to take to comply with the data subject's notice. These rights of data subjects are backed by court powers to order compliance by the 'responsible person', being the person taking the decision in respect of the data subject. The use of the term 'responsible person' presumably is used to include the situation where the decision taking is actually carried out on behalf of a data controller by a processor, such as a computer bureau. Any court order does not affect the rights of any person other than the data subject or the responsible person.

A final point is to note that these provisions apply only where the decision is based *solely* on processing by automatic means. The word 'solely' should not be taken in a strong sense. For example, simply having the person operating the automated decision-taking software confirm or ratify the decision in an unquestioning way will not take the decision taking outside the controls on automated decision taking. Simply 'rubber-stamping' the result is not enough to escape the provisions. It would be different, however, if some aspects of the decision were actively reviewed by a human being.

RIGHT TO COMPENSATION

Individuals are entitled to compensation from the data controller for damage resulting from a contravention of *any* of the requirements in the Act. Under section 13 of the 1998 Act, compensation is available for any contravention causing damage to the data subject. Compensation for distress is available generally where there is also damage or where the contravention concerns processing for the 'special purposes' (journalism, literary or artistic purposes). Compensation for distress only in the absence of damage is available only where the contravention relates to processing for the special purposes. In *Mensah* v *Jones* [2004] EWHC 2699 (Ch), a claim for compensation for distress was rejected as no damage had been alleged and the processing in question was not for the special purposes.

Examples of situations where the data subject should be able to claim compensation for damage and/or distress under the 1998 Act are given below.

Andrew has been turned down for employment because a reference given by a former employer taken from Andrew's personnel file contained a statement that Andrew had been subject to disciplinary action for dishonesty when, in actual fact, Andrew had been cleared of the charge following an appeal within the company's disciplinary procedures. He may now have a claim for compensation for damage and, possibly, depending on the circumstances, for distress.

Brenda is a famous singer who had an illegitimate child some years before she became famous. A local newspaper published details of this last week, including the identity of the child (who was unaware of the identity of Brenda or even that they were adopted), and today the newspaper has sold the story to a national television company which intends to broadcast details in a documentary on single mothers. Brenda (and her child) may have a claim for distress. In any case, the exemption for the processing for the special purposes does not give immunity to a claim to compensation under section 13.

Colin is a self-employed management consultant. He recently submitted a quotation to carry out an in-depth management analysis for Fizkin plc, a large manufacturing company. However, the managing director of Fizkin has spoken to the company secretary of Pipkin Trading Ltd who told him that Colin used to be a member of the Communist Party. Colin used to carry out consulting work for Pipkin. Fizkin turns down Colin's quotation and tells him that the company has discovered from Pipkin that he has a dubious political background. Colin made a data subject access request to Pipkin and the printout from the computer file indeed shows that Colin was a member of the Communist Party when he was a student many years ago. Colin should have a claim for compensation for damage because, although the information is correct, it is probably in breach of the third data protection principle in that the data relating to him held by Pipkin are excessive in relation to the purposes for processing (keeping information about consultants, their work, payments to them, etc.). It is also likely that there is a breach of the first data protection principle as it is likely in the circumstances that none of the conditions for processing sensitive personal data (which such information is) apply to the processing.

Deborah recently went into hospital to have a toe amputated. Her details were sent to the hospital from her general practitioner and the hospital added further information. Her general practitioner failed to note that, in the last year or so, Brenda has developed an allergy to a certain type of anaesthetic. The information was kept in a structured paper file (a 'relevant filing system'). Unfortunately, the junior doctor entering information into her file made a mistake and this was not spotted by the surgeon. The wrong toe was amputated and, as a result, Brenda is more severely disabled physically than she would have been had the correct toe been amputated in the first place. She has also suffered minor brain damage as a result of being given an anaesthetic to which she is allergic. Brenda should have a claim to compensation for damage and possibly also for distress because the data were in breach of the fourth data protection principle in that they were inaccurate and not kept up to date (the allergy was not mentioned). Of course, Brenda will also have a claim for damages on account of negligence, apart from data protection law, and it is most likely that this will be her main claim. However, it is possible that it will be easier to prove a breach of data protection law than negligence. If both claims are successful, it is likely that the award under data protection law will be relatively small.

The right to compensation is tempered by the existence of a defence being where the data controller can prove that he took such care as was in all the circumstances reasonably required to comply with the requirement which has been contravened. Of course, compensation can only be awarded to an individual who goes to court. There are no powers for the Information Commissioner to award compensation. A data subject seeking compensation has to go to either the county court or High Court (in England and Wales). Choice of court will depend, to some extent, on the amount of compensation sought.

A person claiming compensation under the Act must still adduce evidence of the damage or distress he has suffered as a result of the breach of the Act. It is not enough to say that an average award in defamation cases is around £200,000. In *Johnson* v *Medical Defence Union Ltd* [2006] EWHC 321 (Ch) only minimal evidence was submitted by the claimant, a consultant orthopaedic surgeon, aggrieved that the defendant had terminated his membership. The judge noted that one Mr A had drawn adverse inferences but that he and the claimant were never the best of friends. There was no satisfactory evidence of others who thought less of the claimant because of the termination of membership. Although the claim to compensation failed, the judge said he would have awarded only £1,000 had it been successful.

RIGHTS IN RELATION TO INACCURATE DATA

Fundamentally, the rights of data subjects in respect of personal data that are inaccurate are similar to those that existed under the 1984 Act. However, there are some changes and the scope of the right is widened somewhat. There is also the possibility now that any court order may require that third parties to whom the data have been disclosed are informed of the inaccuracy. Another change is that, under the 1984 Act, the rights where limited to rectification or erasure. Under the 1998 Act, reflecting the fact this Act also covers certain types of manual data, rights relating to blocking and destruction are added. 'Blocking' is defined neither in the Act nor in the data protection Directive but it would seem reasonable to assume that it means suppressing the data without erasing them. For example, in a computer database, data may be suppressed from a particular form of processing or a 'flag' may be set indicating that data relating to a particular person are no longer to be processed at all or for particular purposes even though they are not deleted permanently. 'Destruction' clearly is applicable in relation to manual data.

Under section 70(2), data are inaccurate if they are incorrect or misleading as to any matter of fact. There are two forms of control in the Act, contained in section 14. The first relates to data that are inaccurate. The second relates to serious contraventions of the Act causing damage to the data subject. As with compensation, the data subject must apply to the court for an appropriate order for rectification, blocking, erasure or destruction. However, it should be noted that the Information Commissioner may also require rectification, blocking, erasure or destruction of inaccurate data as part of an enforcement notice.

Inaccurate data

Inaccurate data may be ordered by a court, on application by the data subject, to be rectified, blocked, erased or destroyed, if the court is satisfied that they are inaccurate. This extends to other data which contain an expression of opinion about the data subject which is based upon such inaccurate data: section 14(1). Paragraph 7 of Part II of Schedule 1 (interpretation of the data protection principles) states that it is not a contravention of the fourth principle (data shall be accurate and, where necessary, kept up to date) if the data accurately record information given by the data subject or a third party where:

■ having regard to the purpose or purposes for which the data were obtained and further processed, the data controller has taken reasonable steps in the circumstances to ensure the accuracy of the data; and

■ if notified by the data subject of his view that the data are inaccurate, the data indicate that fact.

Thus, where this is the case, the court may instead of ordering rectification, etc. require a supplementary statement of the true facts. If data accurately record information received or obtained from the data subject or a third party but para. 7 of Part II of Schedule 1 does not apply (for example, where the data controller has *failed* to take reasonable steps to ensure accuracy), the court may instead of ordering rectification, etc., make an order to secure compliance with or without a further order for a supplementary statement of the true facts.

The court may also order the data controller to inform third parties to whom the inaccurate data have been disclosed of the rectification, blocking, erasure or destruction.

Rectification, etc. in the case of any contravention of the Act

Under section 14(4), the court has an additional and general power to order rectification, blocking, erasure or destruction of data where the data subject has suffered damage *by reason of any contravention of the Act* in circumstances which entitle him to compensation under the Act where there is a substantial risk of further contravention in respect of those data in such circumstances. This could apply, for example, where data are accurate but excessive in breach of the third data protection principle. In such a case, the court may order erasure of the excessive data. The difference between this provision and the right of rectification, etc. under section 14(1) is that the latter applies only where the data are inaccurate.

In addition to the order above and as with inaccurate data, a court may, where it considers it to be reasonably practicable, order the data controller to notify third parties to whom the data have been disclosed of the rectification, blocking, erasure or destruction. Regard is to be had, in particular, to the number of persons involved. The data protection Directive requires third parties to be notified unless it proves impossible or involves a disproportionate effort. This provision also applies in relation to inaccurate data described above. To some extent, the ease with which third parties can be notified will be a reflection of how well the data controller keeps records of disclosures. With the use of electronic mail and a good audit trail of disclosures, notifying third parties could be quite an easy matter even if there are a large number to be informed. This could be important from the point of view of third parties as, until they have rectified, blocked, erased or destroyed the relevant data, they will probably be in breach of the Data Protection Act 1998 and vulnerable to an action for compensation.

JURISDICTION AND PROCEDURE

Under section 15, jurisdiction is conferred, in England and Wales, on the High Court or a county court. In Scotland, it is the Court of Session or the sheriff court. Where there is an issue as to whether a data subject is entitled to subject access under section 7 (including information as to the logic in any automated decision taking), the data subject or his representative will not have access to the information unless and until the court determines the matter of right of access in favour of the data subject. However, ordinary rules of discovery in court proceedings could give access in claims by data subjects based on other provisions in the Act, such as a claim to compensation or to have inaccurate data rectified or erased.

SUMMARY

- Data subjects' rights under the Data Protection Act 1998 are:
  - to access to their personal data and other information;
  - to prevent processing likely to cause substantial damage or substantial distress;

- to prevent processing for the purposes of direct marketing;
- in relation to automated decision taking;
- to compensation for any contravention of the Act;
- to rectification, blocking, erasure or destruction of inaccurate personal data.

■ Data controllers also have an obligation to inform data subjects:
- on collection of personal data from them; and
- in other cases.

■ Where data under a subject access request would identify another individual, including the source of the data, the data controller may:
- refuse access if the other does not consent if not otherwise reasonable to comply;
- grant access in redacted form;
- grant full access.

■ Enforced subject access in relation to employment or the provision of services:
- will be a criminal offence; but
- is not yet in force.

■ Contractual terms requiring access to health data are void.

■ The right to prevent processing likely to cause substantial damage or distress:
- requires the data subject to apply in writing to the data controller giving reasons;
- does not apply in relation to conditions 1 to 4 in Schedule 2.

■ The right to prevent processing for the purposes of direct marketing is absolute.

■ Rights in relation to automated decision taking depend on whether the decision is exempt:
- where not exempt, the right is to prevent it or to require the decision to be taken again, if necessary by non-automated means;
- where exempt, the right is to make representation if the data subject's request is not granted.

■ The right to compensation for damage or distress applies in respect of any contravention of the Act, but compensation for distress is available only:
- where there is also damage; or
- where processing is for the special purposes.

■ In some cases, inaccurate data may be retained if supplemented by a statement by the data controller:
- for example, where inaccurate data have been obtained from the data subject.

32

Data subjects' rights

SELF-TEST QUESTIONS

Note: there is only one correct answer to each multiple choice question.

1 **Which one of the following is NOT among the information to be provided by the data controller complying with a subject access request under section 7 of the Data Protection Act 1998?**

(a) A description of the countries or territories outside the European Economic Area to which the data controller is transferring or may transfer the personal data.

(b) A description of the recipients or categories of recipients to whom the personal data may be disclosed.

(c) A description of the purposes for which the personal data are being or are to be processed.

(d) A description of the personal data of which that individual is the data subject.

2   Mary was a patient in a psychiatric hospital for a number of years. After her discharge from the hospital, she submitted a request for access to reports made about her condition and treatment. The reports identify the individuals who wrote the reports. Which one of the following statements is CORRECT?

(a) Mary must be given unconditional access to all the reports.

(b) Mary may be given access to the reports even if their authors do not consent if it is reasonable in all the circumstance to comply with the request without the consent of the authors of the reports.

(c) Mary cannot be given access to the reports regardless of whether or not the authors of the reports consent.

(d) Mary cannot be given access to the reports as the data are health data and there is a blanket exemption on disclosure of health data to the individual who is the subject of such data.

3   Ahmed applied for a financial loan to Shark plc which assessed his application solely by automated means. His application was turned down. Which one of the following is CORRECT in relation to his rights in relation to automated decision taking under section 12 of the Data Protection Act 1998?

(a) Shark plc must have taken steps to safeguard Ahmed's legitimate interests (for example, by allowing him to make representations).

(b) Ahmed can ask Shark plc to reconsider the decision, if necessary by other means.

(c) Ahmed can ask Shark plc to provide him with information as to the logic underlying the automated decision taking.

(d) Shark plc are under no obligation to Ahmed as the decision was not to grant his request.

4   Jake applied for employment at Handy Autos Ltd. He was interviewed but failed to secure the position. A previous employer, Dodge Motors Ltd, had sent a handwritten confidential reference in the form of a letter to Handy Autos which said that Jake was dishonest. This was not true but Dodge Motors received the information from a third party in good faith and took reasonable steps to ensure its accuracy. Since then, Jake has been unable to obtain work. Eventually, Jake obtained a copy of the reference following a subject access request made to Handy Autos. Jake was very distressed when he read the reference and is threatening to sue Dodge Motors. Which one of the following statements is CORRECT in relation to any remedy Jake may have under the Data Protection Act?

(a) Jake has a claim for compensation under section 13 for the distress he has suffered.

(b) Jake has a claim for compensation under section 14 as, although Dodge Motors took reasonable steps to ensure the accuracy of the data, the fact is that the data are inaccurate.

(c) Jake has no remedy under the Data Protection Act 1998 as the reference does not contain data within the meaning of section 1(1) of the Act.

(d) Jake would have had a claim to compensation under section 13 had not the reference been exempt from the subject access provisions under Schedule 7, being a confidential reference.

5   To what extent do the subject access provisions reflect the right to privacy under Article 8 of the Council of Europe Convention on the Protection of Human Rights and Fundamental Freedoms?

For further resources and updates please go to the Companion Website accompanying this book at **www.mylawchamber.co.uk/bainbridgeIT**

32

Data subjects' rights

33 Freedom of information

INTRODUCTION

The drive to more transparency in the affairs of public authorities, sometimes described as or associated with 'open government', has led to legislation giving access to information held by public authorities under the Freedom of Information Act 2000. There is a right to request that public authorities confirm or deny whether they hold information as described in the request and, if so, to be give a copy of that information. There are a large number of exemptions, described as absolute and qualified exemptions. In the case of qualified exemptions, the applicant must be given access to the information only if the public interest in disclosure outweighs the public interest in withholding the information. A study of the exemptions shows that the principle of open government is significantly compromised, especially when it comes to the government itself. Enforcement of the Freedom of Information Act 2000 is the duty of the Information Commissioner who also has other duties, powers and functions under the Act, more or less similar to those under the Data Protection Act 1998.

A similar right of access, though of different pedigree (being based on a European Directive) is in respect of environmental information held by public authorities. This is provided for by the Environmental Information Regulations 2004 which is also enforced by the Information Commissioner.

There is an overlap between freedom of information legislation and data protection law which explains why the same authority is responsible for all three sets of legislation. We have seen that the Data Protection Act 1998 has been amended to include non-structured manual files containing personal data which are held by public authorities. The Freedom of Information Act and the Environmental Information Regulations both include exemptions or exceptions to the right of access to information which would disclose personal data. For example, information which constitutes personal data of which the applicant for access is the data subject is exempt information for the purposes of the Freedom of Information Act and the duty to provide access to environmental data does not extend to personal data of which the applicant is the data subject. The simple reason is that the data subject can make a request for access for those data under the Data Protection Act instead. Exemptions also have to be made where the information would disclose personal data relating to another person which would not be accessible under data protection law.

Freedom of information law has proved popular in relation to journalism and has bolstered the right of freedom of expression by making information available that would otherwise remain outside the public domain. As the right of access under the Freedom of Information Act has only been available for a couple of years or so, it is still early days in determining the limits of the exemptions to the right of access. There have been a number of appeals to the Information Tribunal. Probably the most contentious issue is the application of the public interest test which applies to both the Freedom of Information Act and the Environmental Information Regulations.

FREEDOM OF INFORMATION

The purpose of the Freedom of Information Act 2000 was to give persons access to information held by public authorities and could be seen as part of the move to open government. This Act applies to England and Wales and Northern Ireland. Scotland has its own Freedom of Information (Scotland) Act 2002 which is broadly similar in spirit. The scope of the Freedom of Information Act 2002 is quite enormous and it applies to an impressive list of public authorities. As far as the right of access to information held by public authorities, this came into effect on 1 January 2005.

The Act is retrospective in that access extends to information already in existence before it came into force. Public authorities are required to have publication schemes which indicate their commitment to make information available and give guidance as to how individuals may proceed to request information. Publication schemes must be approved by the Information Commissioner who has a number of powers and responsibilities under the Act. In Scotland the equivalent official is the Scottish Information Commissioner.

Public authorities

Public authorities are, under section 3, those set out in Schedule 1 to the Act, those designated by order under section 5 and publicly owned companies as defined in section 6. Schedule 1, to which there have been additions and deletions, comprises seven parts, occupies approximately 20 pages of the Act. The range is tremendous and included among the many are government departments, local authorities, national health service bodies, maintained schools, universities, police authorities and a motley host of other bodies including, by way of example only, advisory committees and panels, the BBC, British Library, the Commission for Racial Equality, Financial Services Authority, Health and Safety Executive, Intellectual Property Advisory Committee, National Museums and Galleries of Wales, Pensions Ombudsman, Strategic Rail Authority, Wine Standards Board of the Vintners' Company and the Northern Ireland Water Council.

Information is held by a public authority if it is held by the authority otherwise than on behalf of another person or if it is held by another person on behalf of the authority. This latter case would apply, for example, where the public authority uses a contractor to carry out information processing activities on its behalf such as by a facilities management company where it has outsourced its information and communications technology functions.

Under section 7, the Act is of limited application to a small number of public authorities and only applies to information of a particular description, as set out in Schedule 1. For example, for certain persons providing primary medical or dental services, the obligations apply only in respect of information relating to the provision of those services. Another example is the BBC where the information under the Act is restricted to that held otherwise than for purposes of journalism, art and literature.

Publication schemes

Under section 19 it is the duty of every public authority to which the Act applies to adopt and maintain a publication scheme approved by the Information Commissioner. The duty extends to publishing information in accordance with the scheme and to review the scheme from time to time. The scheme must specify:

33

Freedom of information

- the classes of information which the authority publishes or intends to publish;
- the manner in which information in each class is, or is intended to be, published; and
- whether the material is, or is intended to be, available to the public free of charge or for payment.

In adopting or reviewing a publication scheme, a public authority must have regard to the public interest in allowing public access to information it holds and in the publication of reasons for decisions made by the authority. The means of publication is left to the public authority to decide. Many choose to publish online. In a case where the Information Commissioner refuses to approve a publication scheme or revokes his approval, he must give a statement of his reasons for doing so.

Model publication schemes for classes of public authorities can be approved by the Information Commissioner. Under section 20, these may be prepared by the Commissioner himself or by other persons and may be approved for a limited period of time. A large number of model publication schemes have been approved in the local government, health and education sectors which may be accessed from the Information Commissioner's website. If a model scheme is adopted without modification, there is no need to submit it for approval.

Once a model publication scheme has been approved, it may be revoked by the Information Commissioner subject to six months' notice. A statement of reasons must be given. This also applies to a refusal to approve a model scheme which has been submitted for approval or the submission of modifications to a model publication scheme.

Codes of practice

Section 45 provides for the issue of codes of practice by the Secretary of State providing guidance to public authorities as to desirable practices to be followed to discharge the functions of public authorities under the Act. The codes must, in particular, provide guidance as to:

(a) the provision of advice and assistance to persons who propose to make, or have made, requests for information to them;

(b) the transfer of requests by one public authority to another public authority by which the information requested is or may be held;

(c) consultation with persons to whom the information requested relates or persons whose interests are likely to be affected by the disclosure of information;

(d) the inclusion in contracts entered into by public authorities of terms relating to the disclosure of information; and

(e) the provision by public authorities of procedures for dealing with complaints about the handling by them of requests for information.

Before making any such code of practice the Secretary of State shall consult with the Commissioner. Any code or revised code is to be laid before each House of Parliament.

Section 46 allows for the Lord Chancellor to make codes of practice providing guidance as to the keeping, management and destruction of records including in relation to public records. The Information Commissioner and the Secretary of State must be consulted and also, in Northern Ireland, the Northern Ireland Minister. Again the code shall be laid before each House of Parliament.

Basic right of access

Section 1 of the Freedom of Information Act 2000 sets out the basic right of access. Under section 1(1), any person may make a request to a public authority and is entitled to be informed in writing by the public authority whether it holds information of the description specified in the request and, if so, to have the information communicated to him. Thus, the public authority has a duty to confirm or deny that it has information of the description specified in the request and, if it has such information, must give the person making the request access to it. If the public authority communicates the information to the person making the request, it is taken to have complied with the duty to confirm or deny.

There are a large number of exemptions to the duty to comply with a request for information. Some are described as absolute exemptions and some as qualified exemptions. Where the latter applies, a public authority is required to apply a public interest test. If the public interest in withholding the information is greater than the public interest in disclosing it, the public authority can rely on the exemption. The exemptions are described later in this chapter.

How to make a request for access

The request for information must be in writing, stating the name and address for correspondence of the applicant and describing the information requested under section 8(1). The requirement for writing is satisfied if the text of the request is transmitted by electronic means, received in legible form and is capable of being used for subsequent reference. Thus, sending a request by e-mail should be satisfactory. It is, however, important that the information for which access is requested is clearly identified and a public authority may require further information so that it can identify and locate the information. Providing the request for further information is a reasonable one, the public authority does not have to comply with the request unless it is supplied with that further information. Under section 16, the public authority has a duty to provide advice and assistance, so far as is reasonable, to persons making or proposing to make access requests. This duty may be satisfied where the public authority conforms to a code of practice under section 45.

If the person who has applied for information does not consider that the duty has been dealt with in accordance with the relevant requirements of the Act, he may apply to the Information Commissioner for a decision accordingly under section 50. This could result in the Commissioner serving an enforcement notice on the public authority.

There is an 'appropriate limit' to the fees and where the cost of compliance is estimated to exceed this limit, the public authority is not required to comply, as discussed later.

Fees for access

A public authority may, within the period for complying with the request for information, give the applicant a notice in writing stating the fee (the 'fees notice') to be charged for compliance: section 9. The public authority is not obliged to comply unless the fee is paid within three months beginning with the day on which the fees notice is given to the applicant. There is no requirement that a public authority must charge a fee – it has a discretion whether to do so.

There is no set scale of fees. A public authority can charge up to a maximum fee calculated in accordance with the Freedom of Information and Data Protection (Appropriate Limit and Fees) Regulations 2004. The maximum fee is a sum equivalent to the total costs the authority expects to incur in complying with the request under section 1(1). Costs which may be taken into account include the costs as to the means of communication under section 11(1) (see later), reproducing any document containing the information and the costs of postage or other transmission of the information. This does not include the costs associated with the time any person

33

Freedom of information

carrying out the duties under section 1(1) on behalf of the public authority (informing the applicant whether the authority has the information requested and communicating that information).

Compliance with request

A public authority must generally comply with a request for information promptly and, in any event, not later than the 20th working day following receipt of the request: section 10(1). Where a fees notice has been sent the period between giving the notice to the applicant and receipt of the fee are disregarded from the 20-day rule. Where the duties under section 1(1) are subject to a qualified exemption which the public authority considers applies, a notice of refusal of access must be given to the applicant under section 17 within the normal 20-day rule. If the exemption applies only in part, compliance with the remainder of the request must be done within a reasonable time. The Act gives a limited power to the Secretary of State to modify the time for compliance. There are other time limits for compliance in particular cases, such as maintained schools, in relation to archives and information held outside the UK.

Section 11 sets out the means by which the communication is to be made. Where the applicant expresses a preference for communication by:

(a) providing the applicant with a copy in permanent or another form acceptable to the applicant;

(b) providing the applicant a reasonable opportunity to inspect a record containing the information; or

(c) providing the applicant with a digest or summary of the information in permanent or another form acceptable to the applicant;

the public authority must, as far as is reasonably practicable (taking account of all the circumstances including cost), give effect to that preference.

If the public authority determines that it is not reasonably practicable to comply with the applicant's preferred means of communication, it shall notify the applicant of its reasons for that determination. If no preference is expressed, the public authority may communicate the information by any means it considers reasonable in the circumstances.

A public authority does not have to comply with a request for information if the request is vexatious or it is identical or substantially similar to a request previously made by the same person unless a reasonable interval has elapsed between compliance with the previous request and the making of the current request: section 14. In *Attorney-General* v *Ebert (No 2)* [2005] EWHC 1254 (Admin), Ebert made more than 200 applications to set aside a bankruptcy order against him. Eventually, he was even barred from the precincts of the Royal Courts of Justice and limited to making written applications. His behaviour could be described as extreme and he had been abusive to court staff and even attempted to make a citizen's arrest of the barrister who had appeared against him. The court had no difficulty in concluding that the requests made under the Freedom of Information Act 2000 were vexatious and designed to re-open matters which must now be regarded as closed so far as litigation was concerned. His many applications to the court in relation to his challenges to the bankruptcy order could only be described as attempts to re-litigate points repeatedly decided against him.

Position where cost of compliance exceeds the appropriate limit

If the estimated cost of complying with a request under section 1(1) would exceed the appropriate limit, the public authority is not obliged to accede to the request: section 12. The appropriate limit is set out in the Freedom of Information and Data Protection (Appropriate Limit and Fees) Regulations 2004. In the case of government departments, the House of Commons and the

House of Lords, the Northern Ireland Assembly and most of the armed forces of the Crown, the appropriate limit is £600. For other public authorities the appropriate limit is £450. This does not excuse the public authority from the duty to confirm or deny unless that cost of complying with that duty alone exceeds the appropriate limit.

For the purpose of deciding whether the estimated cost would exceed the appropriate limit, the Freedom of Information and Data Protection (Appropriate Limit and Fees) Regulations 2004 allows the costs reasonably expected to be incurred in determining whether the public authority holds the information, locating the information or a document containing the information, retrieving the information or a document containing it and extracting the information from a document containing it. The costs of persons involved in these activities on behalf of the public authority are to be calculated at £25 per person-hour. Where two or more requests are made by one person or by different persons appearing to act in concert or in pursuance of a campaign, the estimated costs may be aggregated. This applies where the requests are in relation to the same or similar information and are received in a consecutive period of 60 working days.

Where the public authority is not required to comply with a request for information because to do so would exceed the appropriate limit and compliance is not otherwise required by law (an example being a data subject access request) it may still comply under section 13, charging such fee as determined by the above Regulations. This allows the addition to the costs estimated for the purposes of section 12 plus other costs associated with compliance with section 1(1) such as giving effect to a preference as to the means of communication, reproducing documents and postage or other forms of transmission.

Exemptions

There are two forms of exemption under the Act. One form is the absolute exemption. There is no value judgment to be made, on the basis of public interest or otherwise. The public authority, in some cases, does not even have to either confirm or deny that it does hold information of the description for which access is requested. An example is where the information is supplied by, or relates to, bodies dealing with security matters.

The other form of exemption is the qualified exemption, though not so described in the Act. Under section 2(1)(b) the public authority is excused from confirming or denying it has the information if the public interest in maintaining the exclusion of that duty outweighs the public interest in disclosing whether it holds the information. Section 2(2)(b) excuses the public authority from communicating the information to the applicant if the public interest in maintaining the exclusion of the duty to communicate the information outweighs the public interest in disclosing it. It is possible, therefore, for a public authority to decide if the public interest test requires it to confirm or deny that it has the information but the public interest test is against communicating the information to the applicant. The nature of the exemptions is set out below in summary form.

Absolute exemptions

The absolute exemptions are specified under section 2(3) as follows:

- information which is reasonably accessible to the applicant by other means: section 21. This includes information required to be communicated under any enactment, whether free of charge or on payment of a fee;
- information supplied by, or relating to, bodies dealing with security matters: section 23. A Minister of the Crown must certify that the information was directly or indirectly supplied by, or relates to any of the bodies specified in section 23(3) which includes the Security Service,

the Secret Intelligence Service, GCHQ and the Serious Organised Crime Agency. The certificate is conclusive of the fact that information falls within the exemption, subject to appeal to the Information Tribunal;

- information in certain documents in relation to court records, statutory inquiries or arbitration: section 32. Information in court records includes information contained in documents filed for the purposes of proceedings;

- information for which exemption is needed to avoid an infringement of parliamentary privilege: section 34. The Speaker of the House of Commons or the Clerk to the Parliaments (in the case of the House of Lords) must certify that the exemption was required to avoid an infringement of parliamentary privilege;

- information not exempt under section 35 (see below) held by a government department or the National Assembly for Wales and by any other public authority: section 36. This applies where the disclosure would be likely to prejudice, for example, the maintenance of the collective responsibility of Ministers of the Crown, or the effective conduct of public affairs or would be likely to inhibit the free and frank provision of advice or the free and frank exchange of views for the purposes of deliberation. A qualified person must be of the opinion that the duty to confirm or deny or the disclosure of the information would have caused a relevant prejudice or inhibition. A long list of qualified persons is given in section 36(5) and includes, relevant Ministers of the Crown, other heads of government departments, the Speaker of the House of Commons, the Comptroller and Auditor General of the Audit Office. There is provision for authorising public authorities, officers or employees of public authorities to be qualified persons;

- personal information constituting personal data of which the applicant is the data subject (here the applicant may have a right of access under the Data Protection Act 1998) and personal data relating to others where disclosure would contravene one of the data protection principles (including a case where section 33A of the Data Protection Act 1998 were disregarded): section 40 (part). Section 33A of the 1998 Act gives exemption, *inter alia*, to the first, second, third, fifth, sixth (part), seventh and eighth data protection principles in relation to manual data held by public authorities (see Chapter 31);

- information provided in confidence (obtained from any other person, including another public authority): section 41;

- information, the disclosure of which is prohibited by or under any enactment, is incompatible with any Community obligation or would constitute or be punishable as a contempt of court: section 44.

The public authority is exempt also from the duty to confirm or deny in most cases. For example, in relation to court records, etc., it does not arise at all. In other cases, it will depend on whether it has one of the effects for which the exemption is provided to guard against, for example, if carrying out the duty would itself result in a breach of confidence or be a contempt of court.

Qualified exemptions

Where the exemption is not absolute, under section 2(1)(b) and 2(2)(b), the obligations to confirm or deny and to communicate the information to the applicant are subject to a balancing of public interests. The duty to confirm or deny does not arise if, in all the circumstances of the case, the public interest in maintaining the exclusion of the duty outweighs the public interest in disclosing whether the public authority holds the information requested. Similarly, the duty to communicate the information does not apply if the public interest in maintaining the exemption outweighs the public interest in disclosing the information.

Where a public authority does hold the relevant information and the public interest test favours confirming that this is so, the public authority may still decide that the public interest test favours not disclosing the information itself. The two tests are independent. In a case where a public authority does not hold the relevant information, it seems bizarre that it should decided the test favours not letting the applicant know this. This is a bit like the response under the Data Protection Act 1984 to a subject access request being 'We do not hold personal data relating to you that we are required to give you access to'. This could mean that the data user did not hold any personal data relating to the applicant or, if it did, it could refuse access on the basis of an exemption. This was an unsatisfactory response because the data subject would not know whether an exemption was being relied upon, which might be open to challenge. In respect of freedom of information (and the same is true in respect of data protection law), the applicant can apply to the Information Commissioner if he thinks that his request for information has not been dealt with in accordance with the requirements of the Freedom of Information Act 2000. However, under section 17 of the Act, where a public authority relies on an exemption it must specify what it is in a notice of refusal of the request for information.

A major issue is that it is the public authority itself that applies the public interest test, subject however to a challenge by the Information Commissioner who may send a decision notice or enforcement notice (see later).

The 'qualified' exemptions are as follows:

- information intended for publication at some future date: section 22. The information may be held by the public authority or any other person with a view to its future publication (that view existing at the time of the request) and it must be reasonable in all the circumstances that it should be withheld until the future date. The duty to confirm or deny does not arise if it would involve disclosure of the exempt information;

- information for which exemption is required to safeguard national security: section 24. This applies to information which does not fall within the absolute exemption under section 23 (information supplied by, or relating to, bodies dealing with security matters). A Minister of the Crown must certify that the exemption was required and this is conclusive of that fact, subject to appeal to the Information Tribunal;

- information the disclosure of which would be prejudicial to the defence of the British Isles, any colony or the capability, effectiveness or security of any relevant forces (armed forces of the Crown or forces cooperating with those forces or any part of those forces): section 26;

- information the disclosure of which would be prejudicial to international relations and the promotion or protection of the UK's interests abroad: section 27. Also covered is confidential information obtained from a state other than the UK or from an international organisation or international court;

- information the disclosure of which would be prejudicial to relations between administrations within the UK, being the UK government, the Scottish Administration, the Executive Committee of the Northern Ireland Assembly and the National Assembly for Wales: section 28;

- information the disclosure of which would be prejudicial to the economic interests of the UK or any part thereof or the financial interests of any administration in the UK as defined above: section 29;

- information held by public authorities for a number of purposes, including investigations in relation to offences, criminal proceedings (including, for example, before a court martial) or if the information was obtained from confidential sources: section 30;

- information the disclosure of which would be prejudicial to law enforcement, such as in relation to the prevention or detection of crime: section 31;

- information relating to public authority audit functions and the examination of the economy, efficiency and effectiveness with which other public authorities use their resources in discharging their functions: section 33;

- information held by government departments or the National Assembly of Wales relating to the formulation or development of government policy, Ministerial communications, the provision of advice by and of the Law Officers (including any request for such advice) and the operation of any Ministerial private office: section 35. Once a decision as to government policy has been taken, statistical information is not to be taken as relating to the formulation or development of government policy or Ministerial communications. Thus, the exemption does not apply to such information. Furthermore, in the public interest test, account has to be taken to the particular public interest in the disclosure of factual information used, or intended to be used to provide an informed background to decision taking;

- section 36 provides an absolute exemption (prejudice to the effective conduct of public affairs) only in as much as the information in question is held by either House of Parliament (see above). In other cases, it is a qualified exemption. This could be relevant in particular where free and frank provision of advice or deliberations by public authorities are concerned. This could be prejudiced if, for example, persons might be deterred from taking up relevant positions if they thought information relating to the advice or deliberations might be made public in the not too distant future. However, in *Guardian Newspapers Ltd* v *Information Commissioner* [2007] UKIT EA/2006/001 and 0013, the Information Tribunal held that the public interest in maintaining this exemption did not outweigh the public interest in the disclosure of the minutes of a meeting of the BBC Board of Governors on 28 January 2004 (the day of the publication of the Hutton Report on the death of Dr David Kelly). The tribunal doubted that disclosure would deter persons from serving as governors on the BBC in future. Such persons were unlikely to be 'shrinking violets' and would be aware of the provisions of the Freedom of Information Act 2000;

- information relating to communications with Her Majesty, other members of the Royal family or with the Royal Household or the conferring by the Crown of any honour or dignity: section 37;

- information governed by environmental information Regulations (see the section on the Environmental Information Regulations 2004, later): section 39;

- information constituting personal data relating to a person other than the applicant where disclosure would be likely to cause damage or distress under section 10 of the Data Protection Act 1998 or where the information is exempt from subject access under section 7(1)(c) of that Act: section 40;

- information in respect of which a claim to legal professional privilege could be maintained in legal proceedings: section 42;

- information constituting a trade secret or where its disclosure would, or would be likely to, prejudice the commercial interests of any person including the public authority holding it: section 43.

The Information Tribunal considered the public interest test in *Alcock* v *Information Commissioner* [2007] UKIT EA/2006/0022. The applicant wanted information which would disclose the identity of a person who had given information in confidence to a police authority of alleged offences by the applicant. The tribunal considered the public interest in disclosure was to assist in understanding decisions of the police authority and to right any injustice to the applicant. However, the question of whether the police authority had made proper enquiries to validate the information could be done without knowing the identity of the informant. The applicant said that he wished to have the information to use in legal proceedings but he could seek an order for disclosure in any such proceedings. The public interest in disclosure was, consequently, not great. On the other hand, there was a significant public interest in maintaining the exemption under section 30 otherwise informants could be deterred from providing information to the police on a confidential basis and the prevention and detection of crime was an important public interest. The tribunal dismissed the applicant's appeal.

Public records transferred to the Public Record Office

Special provisions apply to requests for information made to Public Record Offices where the information is (or would be if it existed) in a transferred public record under section 15. A transferred public record is one transferred to the appropriate record authority and the information would be of the sort otherwise subject to a qualified exemption. The appropriate records authority is the Public Record Office, the Lord Chancellor (in respect of another place of deposit appointed by the Lord Chancellor under the Public Records Act 1958) or the Public Record Office of Northern Ireland. Before deciding whether the information is subject to the qualified exemption, the appropriate records authority must consult with the 'responsible authority', being the authority transferring the record (limited to persons who appear to be primarily concerned as set out in section 15(4)). The duty to consult is under section 66 and applies where the information has not been declared 'open information'. The final decision to confirm or deny or communicate the information lies with the responsible authority though it has a duty to consult the records authority.

Role of the Information Commissioner and enforcement

The Information Commissioner, as with data protection law, plays a pivotal role in the enforcement of the legislation and in relation to promoting good practice. The general functions of the Information Commissioner are set out in section 47. He has a duty to promote observance of the provisions of the Freedom of Information Act 2000 and the provisions of relevant codes of practice by public authorities. The Commissioner has to be consulted by the Secretary of State or Lord Chancellor, as the case may be, in relation to the issuing or revision of any code of practice. The Information Commissioner may also disseminate information about the Act regarding the operation of the Act, good practice and other matters within the scope of his functions and give advice to any person about those matters. He may, at the request of a public authority, assess whether it is following good practice and may make a charge for this service. From time to time, the Information Commissioner may consult with the Keeper of Public Records (or Deputy Keeper of the Records of Northern Ireland) about the promotion of good practice by the Commissioner in relation to public records.

Practice recommendations are provided for under section 48. These specify steps to be taken by a public authority to conform with its functions under the Act where the Information Commissioner considers that the public authority does not conform with codes of practice. Where the records are public records, the Commissioner must first consult the Keeper of Public Records or his Northern Ireland counterpart as appropriate.

The Information Commissioner must lay a report before each House of Parliament annually on the exercise of his functions under the Act and any other report in respect of those functions as he thinks fit: section 49. In practice, the annual report is combined with that for data protection and also includes a report on environmental information.

Enforcement

As with data protection law, there is provision for the serving of notices by the Information Commissioner with appeals against them going to the Information Tribunal. One form of notice, the Decision Notice, does not have a parallel under data protection law. The other forms of notice, Information Notices and Enforcement Notices are similar, with appropriate changes to the equivalent notices under the Data Protection Act 1998. Consequently, those forms of notice are not dealt with here.

Any person may apply to the Information Commissioner for a decision as to whether, in a specified respect, the public authority has dealt with a request for information in accordance with the relevant part of the Freedom of Information Act 2000: section 50. Although 'any person' may apply, in most cases, it will be the person who made the application to the public authority for information. The Information Commissioner must make a decision unless any complaints procedure provided by the public authority in accordance with a code of practice has not been exhausted, there has been undue delay in making the application, the application is frivolous or vexatious or it has been withdrawn or abandoned. In the year to 31 March 2006, the Office of the Information Commissioner received no fewer than 2,713 applications under section 50.[1]

Where the Information Commissioner considers that the public authority has failed to confirm or deny or to communicate the information where required to do so, or has failed to comply with the requirements of section 11 (the means in which the communication is to be made) or section 17 (in respect of a notice of refusal of request), the Information Commissioner must serve a decision notice on the public authority and the complainant. The notice must specify the steps to be taken to comply with the relevant requirement and the period within which the steps must be taken. The time for compliance must not expire within the period during which an appeal may be brought and, where an appeal is brought, no step affected by the appeal need be taken pending the determination of the appeal or its withdrawal. The notice must contain particulars of the right to appeal to the Information Tribunal. In the year to 31 March 2006, 187 decision notices were issued.

Exception from the requirement to comply with a decision or enforcement notice

Under section 53, there is an exception to the requirement to comply with a decision notice or an enforcement notice served on a government department, the National Assembly for Wales or any public authority designated for the purpose of this exception by the Secretary of State.

The failure to comply with the request for an information notice must be in respect of the exemptions. Any decision or enforcement notice ceases to have effect if, within 20 working days, a certificate is signed by the accountable person in the department or authority stating that he has, on reasonable grounds, formed the opinion that there was no failure to comply with the request for information. The certificate must be laid before both Houses of Parliament or the National Assembly for Wales in the case of a notice served on the National Assembly of Wales or any Welsh public authority (with equivalent provision for Northern Ireland).

The 20 days are calculated from the date the notice is given to the public authority. If there is an appeal against the notice to the tribunal, the 20 days run from the date of determination of that appeal (or subsequent appeal) or when the appeal is withdrawn.

Unless it would involve disclosure of the exempt information, in the case of a decision notice, the accountable person must give his opinion to the complainant. The accountable person is the appropriate Minister, for example, a Cabinet Minister or First Secretary of the National Assembly for Wales or the Attorney-General.

---

[1] Information Commissioner's Office, *Annual Report 2005–2006*, HC1228, The Stationery Office, 2006, p. 9.

Failure to comply with notice

If a public authority fails to comply with any of the forms of notice, the Information Commissioner may certify to the court that the public authority has failed to comply with the notice: section 54. Failure to comply includes where a public authority:

(a) makes a statement which it knows to be false in a material respect; or

(b) recklessly makes a statement which is false in a material respect.

The court may inquire into the matter and, after hearing witnesses against or on behalf of the public authority and hearing statements offered in defence, deal with the authority as if it had committed contempt of court.

There is no right of civil action against a public authority in respect of the failure to comply with any duty imposed by or under the Act: section 56. This is notwithstanding the Information Commissioner's power to certify a failure to comply to the court, above, which may result in contempt of court proceedings.

Powers of entry and inspection

Under Schedule 3 to the Freedom of Information Act 2000, the Information Commissioner has powers of entry and inspection similar to those under the Data Protection Act 1998 but with necessary changes, as appropriate. A warrant may be granted by a circuit judge if there are reasonable grounds for suspecting a failure to comply with the obligation to give a right of access to information, a decision, information or enforcement notice or an offence under section 77 has been committed (this is the offence of altering records with intent to prevent disclosure).

As with warrants under the Data Protection Act 1998, there are offences of intentionally obstructing a person executing a warrant or failing without reasonable excuse to give assistance reasonably required.

Offences

The offences in relation to the execution of search warrants have already been mentioned above. There is only one other offence in the Act, under section 77 although the offence of disclosure under section 59 of the Data Protection Act 1998, which imposes potential criminal liability on the Information Commissioner and his staff or agents also applies in respect of information under the Freedom of Information Act 2000.

Under section 77 of the Freedom of Information Act 2000, it is an offence to alter, deface, block, erase, destroy or conceal any record with the intention of preventing disclosure by the authority. This applies where a person has made a request for information under section 1 of the Freedom of Information Act 2000 or section 7 of the Data Protection Act 1998 and disclosure is prevented to all or part of the information the applicant would have been entitled to have communicated to him.

The offence can be committed by the public authority or any person who is employed by, is an officer of, or is subject to the direction of the public authority. A person guilty of the offence is subject on summary conviction of a fine not exceeding level 5 on the standard scale. Prosecutions can only be brought by the Information Commissioner or by or with the consent of the Director of Public Prosecutions (or Director of Public Prosecutions for Northern Ireland, as the case may be).

Removal of exemptions for historical records

Certain of the exemptions are removed after around 30 years. Under section 62, a record becomes a historical record at the end of the period of 30 calendar years beginning with the year following that in which it was created. Where a number of records created at different dates are kept in a file, the period is based on the latest record to be created.

Under section 63(1), information in historical records is not exempt information for the purposes of the following provisions (in most cases, these fall under the qualified exemptions):

- section 28 (relations within the UK);
- section 30(1) (information held for the purposes of investigation into offences and criminal proceedings);
- section 32 (information in court records);
- section 33 (information the disclosure of which would, or would be likely to prejudice auditing of public authority accounts, etc.);
- section 35 (information relating to the formulation of government policy, etc.);
- section 36 (information the disclosure of which would, or would be likely to prejudice the effective conduct of public affairs);
- section 37(1)(a) (information relating to communications with Her Majesty, etc.);
- section 42 (legal professional privilege);
- section 43 (commercial interests).

For historical records, compliance with the duty to confirm or deny does not have the effects of being prejudicial to a number of matters including relations within the UK, audit functions, the effective conduct of public affairs, legal professional privilege or commercial interests. This means, for example, that in relation to information relating to commercial interests, even though the public authority does not hold information of the description for which access is sought, it must inform the applicant that it does not hold such information. If it does hold such information in historical records it must confirm that this is so and communicate the information to the applicant.

Different dates apply to some forms of information. For information relating to the conferring of any dignity or honour by the Crown, it is no longer exempt after 60 years. Information which was exempt under section 31, where its disclosure would, or would be likely to, prejudice the prevention or detection of crime, etc. remains exempt information for 100 years from the beginning of the year following that in which the record containing the information was created. Exemption from the duty to confirm or deny also expires at this time.

Under section 64, information in historical records in public record offices cannot be exempt information by virtue of section 21 or 22 (information accessible to the applicant by other means and information intended for future publication). Also as regards information in historical records in public record offices relating to security matters under section 23(1) the exemption changes from absolute to qualified. In other words, the exemptions to the duties to confirm or deny and to communicate the information become qualified. Under section 65, where qualified exemption applies to a request for information in public records, there is a duty to consult the Lord Chancellor before refusing the request. (If the information is held in a public record under the Public Records Act (Northern Ireland) 1923, the duty is to consult the appropriate Northern Ireland Minister.)

Section 65 does not apply to information to which section 66 applies. This provides for a duty to consult in relation to certain transferred public records, as discussed above.

The Information Tribunal

The constitution and functions of the Information Tribunal are set out in the Data Protection Act 1998. Some changes are made, mainly in terminology but whereas the Tribunal for the purposes of the 1998 Act was required to include persons representing the interests of data controllers and data subjects, respectively, for the purposes of the 2000 Act, these are substituted with persons representing the interests of persons who make requests under the Act and persons representing the interests of public authorities.

In respect of the Freedom of Information Act, if the Tribunal considers that a notice served by the Information Commissioner was not in accordance with the law or, where it involved the exercise of discretion by the Information Commissioner, that discretion ought to have been exercised differently, it may allow the appeal or substitute such other notice as could have been served by the Information Commissioner. Otherwise the tribunal must dismiss the appeal.

The tribunal may substitute its own view on the public interest test for that of the Information Commissioner or the public authority. In *Hemsley* v *Information Commissioner* [2006] UKIT EA/2005/0026 the tribunal accepted that it was entitled, indeed obliged, to form its own view of the public interest test. In that case, the tribunal agreed with the views of the police authority and the Information Commissioner that the balance lay on the side of withholding information as to the history of speeding offences picked up by a safety camera sited along the A508 in Kelmarsh, Northamptonshire.

The Information Tribunal (Enforcement Appeals) Rules 2005 regulate the exercise of the rights of appeal and the practice and procedures of the tribunal. The Information Tribunal (National Security Appeals) Rules 2005 apply to appeals against national security certificates issued, *inter alia*, under sections 23 and 24 of the Freedom of Information Act 2000.

Appeals against decisions of the tribunal on a point of law may be made to the High Court (in England or Wales), the Court of Session in Scotland or the High Court of Northern Ireland, depending on where the public authority has its address.

Privilege against defamation

Where a public authority has obtained information from a third person which is communicated to a person applying for access to information under section 1 of the Freedom of Information Act 2000 and which contains defamatory material, the public authority has a privilege in relation to the publication of that material to the applicant under section 79. The privilege does not apply, however, if the publication is shown to have been made by the public authority with malice.

ENVIRONMENTAL INFORMATION

The Environmental Information Regulations 2004 implement Directive 2003/4/EC of the European Parliament and of the Council of 28 January 2003 on public access to environmental information and repealing Council Directive 90/313/EEC.[2] The Regulations can be seen as being parallel to the Freedom of Information Act 2000 and refer to some of the provisions of that Act.

Public authorities are under a duty to progressively make environmental information available to the public by electronic means which are easily accessible and to take reasonable steps to organise the information relevant to its functions with a view to the active and systematic dissemination to the public of the information. The duty of dissemination in electronic form and

33

Freedom of information

---

[2] OJ L 41, 14.02.2003, p. 26.

organisation does not apply to information collected before 1 January 2005 in non-electronic form.

The information must include at least the information mentioned in Article 7(2) of the Directive. This includes texts of international treaties and conventions and legislation on the environment, policies and plans relating to the environment, progress reports, reports on the state of the environment, data or summaries obtained from the monitoring of activities affecting the environment, relevant authorisations and impact studies.

There is also a duty to make environmental information available on request and obligations to make the information available in the form requested unless reasonable to make it available in another form. The general period for complying is 20 working days which may be extended to 40 working days. A charge for access may be made though not if the information is in a public register or list of environmental information held by the public authority or where the applicant requests to examine the information at the place for examination made available by the public authority.

There are provisions for dealing with the situation where further particulars are needed because the request was too general and the public authority has a duty to provide advice and assistance. It may transfer the request if it does not hold the information to another authority it believes holds it.

Exceptions

A public authority may refuse to disclose environmental information if or to the extent that its disclosure would prejudice interests, being:

- international relations, defence, national security or public safety;
- the course of justice, the ability of a person to receive a fair trial or the ability of a public authority to conduct an inquiry of a criminal or disciplinary nature;
- intellectual property rights;
- certain cases relating to confidentiality; or
- the protection of the environment to which the information relates.

Refusal may also be made if the public authority does not hold the information when the request is received, where the request is manifestly unreasonable or too general, where it is to material still in the course of completion, unfinished documents or incomplete data or where the request would involve the disclosure of internal communications. In other cases, a qualified exception applies and the public authority can refuse to disclose the information on the basis of public interest. That is, where the public interest in maintaining the exception outweighs the public interest in disclosing it. Nevertheless, a public authority must apply a presumption in favour of disclosure.

A public authority may respond to a request where an exception applies by neither confirming or denying that it holds the information if to do so would adversely affect the above interests and would not be in the public interest.

A further exception applies in relation to personal data and is equivalent to that applying under the Freedom of Information Act 2000.

Any refusal to disclose information under the exceptions must be made in writing and specify the reasons. It must be made as soon as possible but not later than 20 working days after receipt of the request for information.

Other aspects

Similar provisions apply in relation to historical records and the enforcement and appeals provisions are as they are for the Freedom of Information Act 2000 and there is also an equivalent offence of altering records with the intention of preventing disclosure. There are also provisions for the making of or revising codes of practice by the Secretary of State after consulting the Information Commissioner. Certain other aspects of the Regulations are similar to the equivalent provisions in the 2000 Act.

SUMMARY

- Freedom of information applies to public authorities.
- Scotland has its own freedom of information legislation.
- Public authorities must adopt publication schemes.
- Persons have a right of access which includes a right:
  - to be informed whether the public authority holds the information requested (confirm or deny);
  - to have the information communicated to them.
- Persons may specify the means of communication.
- Public authorities may charge and may refuse access if the cost exceeds set limits.
- There are two forms of exemption from the right of access:
  - absolute exemptions; and
  - qualified exemptions which depend on a public interest test.
- The public interest test is whether the public interest in maintaining the exemption outweighs the public interest in disclosing the information.
- In many cases, the exemptions are removed when the information is more than 30 years old.
- The Information Commissioner has powers of enforcement by way of:
  - decision notices;
  - information notices;
  - enforcement notices.
- Appeals from Information Commissioner notices go to the Information Tribunal.
- Parallel legislation concerns environmental information.
- For both sets of legislation there are offences:
  - in relation to the execution of search warrants;
  - for altering, etc. information intending to prevent access.

SELF-TEST QUESTIONS

Note: there is only one correct answer to each multiple choice question.

1 **Of the duty to inform a person making a request for information under section 1 of the Freedom of Information Act 2000 whether it holds information of the description specified**

33

Freedom of information

in the request (the duty to confirm or deny), which one of the following statements is NOT CORRECT?

(a) Where an absolute exemption applies, the duty to confirm or deny does not arise.

(b) The public authority may reasonably require further information to identify and locate the information requested.

(c) If the public authority does not hold the information, the duty to confirm or deny does not arise.

(d) Where a 'qualified' exemption applies, the duty does not arise if the public interest in maintaining the exclusion of the duty to confirm or deny outweighs the public interest in disclosing whether the public authority holds the information.

2   In relation to the exemptions under the Freedom of Information Act 2000 not declared to be absolute exemptions, which one of the following statements is NOT CORRECT?

(a) If the public authority considers that the public interest in disclosing whether it holds the information outweighs the public interest in maintaining the exclusion of the duty to confirm or deny, it must communicate the information to the applicant.

(b) As with the absolute exemptions, where the public authority relies on an exemption, the notice of refusal must specify the exemption in question.

(c) Information in respect of which the public authority is obliged to make available to the public under the Environmental Information Regulations (or would be so obliged but for an exemption in those Regulations) is exempt information.

(d) Information is exempt information if it constitutes a trade secret.

3   Under section 62 of the Freedom of Information Act 2000, which one of the following statements as to the time when a record becomes a historical record is CORRECT?

(a) At the end of the period of 30 years beginning with the year following that in which it was created.

(b) At the end of the period of 60 years beginning with the year following that in which it was created.

(c) At the end of the period of 100 years beginning with the year following that in which it was created.

(d) Information relating to communications with Her Majesty can never become a historical record.

4   In respect of the powers of the Information Tribunal under the Freedom of Information Act 2000, which one of the following statements is CORRECT?

(a) The tribunal cannot interfere with the exercise of any discretion conferred upon the Information Commissioner under the Act.

(b) The tribunal must accept the view of a public authority on whether the public interest in maintaining the exclusion of the duty to confirm or deny outweighs the public interest in disclosing whether the public authority holds the information.

(c) The tribunal must accept the view of the Information Commissioner on whether the public interest in maintaining an exemption outweighs the public interest in disclosing the information.

(d) The tribunal may substitute its own view on whether the public interest in maintaining the exclusion of the duty to confirm or deny (or maintaining an exemption) outweighs the public interest in disclosing whether the public authority holds the information (or in disclosing the information).

5   Read Directive 2003/4/EC on the public access to environmental information, available at the EUR-Lex website: http://eur-lex.europa.eu/en/index.htm

From this page select SIMPLE SEARCH,

Then search by document number (natural number),

Select Directive and enter the year 2000 and number 4.

To what extent do you consider that the Directive achieves an appropriate balance between the right of access and the exceptions to access?

For further resources and updates please go to the Companion Website accompanying this book at **www.mylawchamber.co.uk/bainbridgeIT**

33

Freedom of information

34 Privacy in electronic communications

INTRODUCTION

The advent of new technological developments in the electronic sector, such as the ability to capture information such as a caller's telephone number or to see the number from which an incoming call is made before deciding whether to answer, brought concerns about privacy. Another problem is the growing use of telephones, including mobile phones, and facsimile machines ('faxes') for marketing purposes. Other issues are the capture of data from computers, such as by the use of 'cookies', the use and storage of personal data relating to customers of electronic communications service providers, automatic call forwarding and information made available in directories, whether in paper or software form. Security and the prevention of unlawful eavesdropping are other privacy issues.

The stimulus for change and greater protection for individuals' rights to privacy came about by way of a European Directive on the processing of personal data and the protection of privacy in the telecommunications sector.[1] This was implemented in the UK by the Telecommunications (Data Protection and Privacy) Regulations 1999. Since that time, further concerns surfaced about the use of the internet for communications, such as e-mail. With a global technology, serious threats to privacy are raised and, accordingly, a further European Directive was adopted, replacing Directive 97/66/EC and extending the protection afforded to other forms of electronic communications. The Directive concerning the processing of personal data and the protection of privacy in the electronic communications sector[2] was required to be transposed into national laws before 31 October 2003. This Directive was implemented in the UK by the Privacy and Electronic Communications (EC Directive) Regulations 2003 which revoked the 1999 Regulations.

The recitals to the Directive on privacy and electronic communications make it clear that it supplements the data protection Directive and is aimed at '... protecting the fundamental rights of natural persons and particularly their right to privacy, as well as the legitimate interests of legal persons' in the context of subscribers (whether natural or legal persons) to publicly available electronic communications services. A legal person is a body such as a company, firm or other organisation, for example, a public authority or charity. The Directive does not require Member States to extend the protection afforded to natural persons under the data protection Directive to legal persons. It is intended that the protection of personal data and privacy should be the

---

[1] Directive 97/66/EC of the European Parliament and of the Council of 15 December 1997 concerning the processing of personal data and the protection of privacy in the telecommunications sector, L 24, 30.01.1998, p. 1.

[2] Directive 2002/58/EC of the European Parliament and of the Council of 12 July 2002 concerning the processing of personal data and the protection of privacy in the electronic communications sector (Directive on privacy and electronic communications), OJ L 201, 31.07.2002, p. 37.

same whatever form of technology is used in publicly available electronic communications services, for example, whether analogue or digital voice telephony systems, mobile telephones or the internet. As far as non-public communications services are concerned, the recitals to the Directive on privacy and electronic communications recognise that the data protection Directive applies to these. Harmonisation is also important to avoid obstacles to the internal market for electronic communications.

Broadcasting over a public communications network, being intended for a potentially unlimited audience, is outside the scope of the Directive, except to the extent that an individual subscriber or user can be identified, for example, in the case of video-on-demand services.

In terms of the internet, the recitals stress the fact that terminal equipment and information stored on them are part of the users' private sphere and, under the Council of Europe Convention for the Protection of Human Rights and Fundamental Freedoms, need protecting from devices that can enter the user's terminal such as 'spyware, web bugs, hidden identifiers and other similar devices' which can gain access to information stored in the terminal or store information there or trace the user's activities, such as the addresses of websites visited by the user. Such devices should only be used for legitimate purposes and then only with the user's consent. Cookies are seen as a legitimate and useful tool. They can be used to analyse the effectiveness of a website and advertising and in verifying the identity of users engaged in online transactions. These should only be used, however, where clear and precise information is provided about the purposes of cookies and similar devices and users should have a right to refuse to have them stored on the equipment they are using. The fact that access to a particular website may be prevented in the absence of informed consent is seen as acceptable.

Other aspects of the Directive relate to security and confidentiality, traffic and billing data, identification of calling and connected lines, location data (for example, in connection with the use of a mobile phone), automatic call forwarding, directories, unsolicited marketing material and technical features and standardisation.

In the main body of this chapter, reference is made to the provisions of the Directive. Particular aspects of the Privacy and Electronic Communications (EC Directive) Regulations 2003 which provide more detail than the Directive or implement options left to Member States by the Directive are discussed towards the end of the chapter.

34

Privacy in electronic communications

THE DIRECTIVE ON PRIVACY AND ELECTRONIC COMMUNICATIONS

The definitions are important to consider. Some are contained in the Directive but others are in the Directive on a common regulatory framework for electronic communications networks and services (the 'framework Directive').[3] First, the definitions contained in Article 2 of the Directive on privacy in electronic communications are listed:

(a) 'user' means any natural person using a publicly available electronic communications service, for private or business purposes, without necessarily having subscribed to this service;

(b) 'traffic data' means any data processed for the purpose of the conveyance of a communication on an electronic communications network or for the billing thereof;

(c) 'location data' means any data processed in an electronic communications network, indicating the geographic position of the terminal equipment of a user of a publicly available electronic communications service;

[3] Directive 2002/21/EC of the European Parliament and of the Council of 7 March 2002 on a common regulatory framework for electronic communications networks and services, OJ L 108, 24.04.2002, p. 33.

(d) 'communication' means any information exchanged or conveyed between a finite number of parties by means of a publicly available electronic communications service. This does not include any information conveyed as part of a broadcasting service to the public over an electronic communications network except to the extent that the information can be related to the identifiable subscriber or user receiving the information;

(e) 'call' means a connection established by means of a publicly available telephone service allowing two-way communication in real time;

(f) 'consent' by a user or subscriber corresponds to the data subject's consent in Directive 95/46/EC [the data protection Directive];

(g) 'value added service' means any service which requires the processing of traffic data or location data other than traffic data beyond what is necessary for the transmission of a communication or the billing thereof;

(h) 'electronic mail' means any text, voice, sound or image message sent over a public communications network which can be stored in the network or in the recipient's terminal equipment until it is collected by the recipient.

The relevant definitions from the framework Directive are as follow (renumbered from the Directive so as to be consecutive with those above):

(i) 'electronic communications network' means transmission systems and, where applicable, switching or routing equipment and other resources which permit the conveyance of signals by wire, by radio, by optical or by other electromagnetic means, including satellite networks, fixed (circuit- and packet-switched, including Internet) and mobile terrestrial networks, electricity cable systems, to the extent that they are used for the purpose of transmitting signals, networks used for radio and television broadcasting, and cable television networks, irrespective of the type of information conveyed;

(j) 'electronic communications service' means a service normally provided for remuneration which consists wholly or mainly in the conveyance of signals on electronic communications networks, including telecommunications services and transmission services in networks used for broadcasting, but exclude services providing, or exercising editorial control over, content transmitted using electronic communications networks and services; it does not include information society services, as defined in Article 1 of Directive 98/34/EC [any service normally provided for remuneration, at a distance, by electronic means and at the individual request of a recipient of services], which do not consist wholly or mainly in the conveyance of signals on electronic communications networks;

(k) 'public communications network' means an electronic communications network used wholly or mainly for the provision of publicly available electronic communications services;

(l) 'subscriber' means any natural person or legal entity who or which is party to a contract with the provider of publicly available electronic communications services for the supply of such services.

The definitions are fairly straightforward and not particularly controversial. It is important to note that in most cases, the protection of privacy applies to users of electronic communication services as it does to subscribers. Therefore, where the user and subscriber are different such as where an employee is using his employer's computer to send or receive e-mail messages or where a student is using a university computer to buy goods online, in most cases the rights to privacy apply also to that person as it does the subscriber. One difference is that a user can only be a natural person, that is, a living individual, whereas a subscriber can be either a natural person or a legal person such as a limited company or other organisation. The definition of value added service is important because some of the provisions of the Directive also apply to services which 'piggy-back' on the basic electronic communication service, for example, the provision of information as to congestion or weather or about the best contract for a mobile phone. A number of organisations provide information about different tariffs for telephone services and the like and indicate typical savings available by changing service providers. Location data are particularly relevant in the context of mobile phones as it is possible to find the geographic location of a mobile phone and this information could prove very important, for example, if it is important to trace the person using the mobile phone because he is injured or being attacked. Recital 14 to the Directive gives examples of location data, being data referring to longitude, latitude and altitude of the user's terminal equipment, to the direction of travel and the level of accuracy of the location information.

Security and confidentiality

The provider of a publicly available electronic communications service must take appropriate technical and organisational security measures, if necessary, in conjunction with the provider of the public communications network under Article 4. Factors to be taken into account are, as for the data protection Directive, the state of the art, cost of implementation and the risk. Where there is a particular risk of a breach of security, the provider of a publicly available electronic communications service must inform subscribers of this risk and any possible remedies including the costs involved. Where the risks lie outside the scope of the measures to be taken, the service provider must inform subscribers of any possible remedies together with an indication of the likely costs involved. Recital 32 states that where a service provider subcontracts processing, the subcontracting and subsequent processing shall be in accordance with the security obligations imposed on data controllers and processors by the data protection Directive. In particular, this means that the contract between the service provider and the subcontractor must impose the appropriate security obligations on the subcontractor and be at least evidenced in writing.

Article 5 requires that confidentiality of communications and related traffic data by means of a public communications network and publicly available electronic communications services must be ensured by national legislation. Listening, tapping, storage or other kinds of interception or surveillance must be prohibited except where such restriction is authorised by law and is a necessary, appropriate and proportionate measure in a democratic society to safeguard national security, defence and public security, or for the prevention, investigation, detection and prosecution of criminal offences, or of unauthorised use of the electronic communication system, as referred to in Article 13(1) of the data protection Directive. The Regulation of Investigatory Powers Act 2000 prohibits interception of communications and provides for surveillance in certain circumstances under carefully regulated conditions. However, recording of communications and related traffic data in the course of lawful business practice for the purpose of providing evidence of commercial transactions or other business communications which are legally authorised are unaffected. This could apply, for example, where an individual takes out car insurance over the telephone.

As regards storing information on or gaining access to information stored on a subscriber's or user's terminal equipment, this is only allowed where the subscriber or user is provided with clear and comprehensive information in accordance with the data protection Directive about, *inter alia*, the purposes of processing and an opportunity to refuse such processing must be given. However, this does not prevent technical storage or access for the sole purpose of facilitating the transmission of a communication over an electronic communications network, or as strictly necessary to provide an information society service explicitly requested by the subscriber or user.

34

Privacy in electronic communications

Traffic and billing data

Providers of public communications networks and publicly available electronic communications services need to process data relating to calls for the purpose of billing their customers. A considerable amount of information may be collected by the service provider and will include the subscriber's number, the number called, the date, start time, finish time, duration of the call, the call rate and the charge cost. Other information may be involved such as the data volume, the tariff class and data identifying the telephone exchange.

By virtue of Article 6, providers of public communications networks and publicly available electronic communications services must erase or make anonymous traffic data relating to subscribers and users when it is no longer required for the purposes set out in the remainder of the Article or when authorised by law and is a necessary, appropriate and proportionate measure in a democratic society to safeguard national security, defence and public security, etc.

Traffic data necessary for billing and interconnection payments may be processed up to the end of the period when the bill may lawfully be challenged or payment pursued (this is the limitation period for contracts, usually being six years from the date of breach of contract under section 5 of the Limitation Act 1980 but provision has to be made for legal proceedings already underway at the end of that period). With the consent of subscribers and users, as appropriate, processing may be carried out by publicly available electronic communications service providers of such traffic data, to the extent and for the duration necessary, for marketing their own services or value added services (which, according to recital 18 to the Directive, may include advice on the cheapest tariff packages, route guidance, traffic information, weather forecasts or tourist information). Information as to the type of traffic data processed and the duration of such processing must be given prior to obtaining consent. Any consent given to processing for such marketing purposes may be withdrawn at any time.

Processing of traffic data within Article 6 must be restricted to persons acting under the authority of the provider of the service or network, as the case may be, handling billing or traffic management, customer enquiries, fraud detection, marketing the provider's own services or providing a value added service. Furthermore, the processing must be restricted to that necessary for the purposes of such activities.

The above provisions are without prejudice to the possibility of competent bodies being informed of billing or traffic data under applicable legislation for settling disputes. The competent body in the UK for these purposes will be OFCOM, the Office of Communications.

Subscribers are given a right to receive non-itemised bills under Article 7. Where itemised bills are sent out, this could conflict with the right of privacy of calling users and called subscribers (outlined below). To reconcile this problem Member States must, by national provisions, for example, ensure that 'sufficient alternative privacy enhancing methods of communications or payments are available to such users and subscribers'.

Presentation and restrictions of calling and connected line identification

Article 8 of the Directive concerns calling line and connected line identification and apply where calling line or connected line is offered. The provisions are that:

- a calling user must be able, using a simple means and free of charge, to prevent the presentation of calling line information on a per-call basis and a calling subscriber must be able to do this on a per-line basis;

- a called subscriber must be able, using a simple means and free of charge, to prevent the presentation of calling line information on incoming calls (why a subscriber would want to do this is unclear although it could be relevant where the subscriber is a company and it wants to prevent employees selectively declining to answer calls from, for example, awkward customers);

■ where calling line information is presented prior to the call being established (that is, prior to connection) a called subscriber must be able, using simple means, to reject any incoming call for which calling line information has been prevented by the calling user or subscriber (an individual called at home late in the evening may prefer not to answer a call where calling line information has been suppressed);

■ a called subscriber must be able, simply and free of charge, to eliminate the presentation of calling line information to the calling user (this would prevent the automatic capture of the subscriber's telephone number, say, by a commercial organisation);

■ the elimination of the presentation of calling line identification by a calling user (on a per-call basis) or calling subscriber (on a per-line basis) must also apply to calls to third countries and the other provisions must also apply in respect of calls coming from third countries (that is, from outside the European Community).

Member States are obliged to ensure that, where presentation of calling and/or connected line information is offered, providers of publicly available electronic communications service publicise this and the possibilities of suppression as set out above.

As complete suppression of calling line information could hinder the tracing of persons making malicious or threatening calls, providers of public communications network and publicly available electronic communications service may override the elimination of presentation of calling line information in two cases and the procedures for doing must be transparent: Article 10. First, elimination of presentation of calling line identification may be overridden on the application of a subscriber requesting the tracing of malicious or nuisance calls, on a temporary basis. This will allow the storage of the data identifying the calling subscriber to be made available in accordance with national law. The second case applies to overriding the elimination of calling line information on a per-line basis for organisations dealing with emergency calls as recognised in Member States including law enforcement agencies, ambulance services and fire brigades and other organisations dealing with emergency calls for the purpose of responding to such calls.

Location data other than traffic data

It is now possible to locate the geographic position of a mobile phone with some degree of accuracy. Clearly, the misuse of location data could serious compromise privacy, particularly if a person using a mobile phone does not want the other person to know his location at a particular time. Under Article 9 of the Directive, where such data can be processed, they may only be processed if they are made anonymous or with the consent of the user or subscriber, as appropriate, to the extent and for the duration necessary for the provision of a value added service. Thus, for example, a person with a mobile phone may want an up-to-date weather forecast for the place where he is. By simply calling a number, a forecast may be sent back immediately in the form of a text message.

Again the concept of informed consent is used, the user or subscriber being given information as to the type of location data and any other traffic data to be processed, the purposes and duration of processing and whether the data will be transmitted to a third party for the purpose of providing a value added service. Consent may be withdrawn at any time. Where consent has been obtained in respect of location data other than traffic data, there must be an opportunity to temporarily refuse such processing, using a simple means and free of charge, for each connection to the network or for each transmission or communication.

34

Privacy in electronic communications

Processing must be restricted to persons acting under the authority of the provider of the public communications network or publicly available electronic communications service or of a third party providing a value added service. In the latter case, processing must also be restricted to that necessary for the purposes of providing a value added service.

The second form of exception under Article 10 also applies to location data. The temporary denial or absence of consent of a subscriber or user for processing of location data may be overridden for the purpose of responding to emergency calls. This could cover a case where, for example, the owner of a mobile phone, who has not consented to processing of location data, lends his phone to a friend who makes an emergency call after breaking his leg whilst walking on wild moor land and is unable to give an accurate location.

Automatic call forwarding

A lot of persons make use of call divert services, for example, by diverting calls to their mobile phone to their home or office telephone. This can be quite a useful service, for example, if a person is at a concert and wants to divert calls to his home answer phone or to his partner's phone. Such diversions can, however, be intrusive and prejudice the right to privacy, for example, where a business call is forwarded to a person's home late in the evening. To prevent unwelcome call forwarding by third parties, Article 11 of the Directive gives every subscriber the right to prevent automatic call forwarding by a third party to his terminal, using a simple means and free of charge.

However, this provision and those on the elimination of presentation of calling and connected line identification, and Article 10, do not apply to subscriber lines connected to analogue exchanges unless compliance is technically possible and does not require a disproportionate economic effort. Such cases must be notified to the European Commission.

Directories

Directories of subscribers to public communication services, such as telephone directories, may seem innocuous enough but may still contain information that can threaten privacy or even safety. If the directory is available electronically, especially online, it may be an easy matter to find the name of a subscriber and address from a telephone number only (which may have been captured through calling line identification). Under Article 12 of the Directive, subscribers must be informed, free of charge and before they are included in a directory personal data, of the purposes of a printed or electronic directory of subscribers available to the public or obtainable through directory enquiry services. They must also be told of possible further usages based on search functions in electronic versions of directories. Subscribers must be given the opportunity to decide whether their personal data are to be included and, if so, to what extent. They must also be given the opportunity to verify, correct or withdraw such data free of charge.

Member States may require that for any purpose of a public directory, other than a search of contact details of persons based on their name and, where necessary a minimum of other identifiers, the additional consent of subscribers must be sought. It is likely that specific consent will be required for inclusion in an electronic directory where searching by number alone is possible. It may be possible to still include an entry for a person but to suppress the search by number facility for that person. Member States must also ensure that the legitimate interests of legal persons are also sufficiently protected with regard to their entries in public directories.

Unsolicited communications

Most people find unsolicited calls from organisations trying to sell something intrusive and a nuisance. It can be very irritating to go and answer the telephone whilst in the middle of cooking a meal, reading a book or performing some other enjoyable activity only to find that it is someone 'cold-calling', trying to get you to buy double glazing, financial services or whatever. By subscribing to the Telephone Preference System, these cold-calls can be reduced to a minimum, if not eliminated altogether. Another way to reduce them is to be 'ex-directory', though this defeats the usefulness of telephone directories as a source of information and may prevent a welcome telephone contact. Things have become far worse now with marketing by e-mail and the possibility of text message marketing.

Controls over unsolicited communications are provided under Article 13 of the Directive. The use of automatic calling machines which operate without human intervention, fax machines, electronic mail for the purposes of direct marketing is only allowed where subscribers have given prior consent. However, where a natural or legal person has obtained from its customers their electronic contact details for electronic mail (e-mail address) in the context of the sale of a product or service, they may still use this for direct marketing of its own similar products or services providing the customer is clearly and distinctly given the opportunity to object, free of charge and in an easy manner when the contact details are collected and on each subsequent occasion if the customer has not initially refused such use. Member States must also ensure that the legitimate interests of legal persons are sufficiently protected with regard to unsolicited communications.

Technical features and standardisation

If different Member States adopt different technical features to comply with the Directive, this will work against the common market by impeding the placing of equipment on the market and the free circulation of telecommunications equipment. The basic rule, expressed in Article 14, is that there shall be no mandatory requirements for specific technical features imposed on terminals or other electronic communication equipment which could impede the placing of such equipment on the market and the free circulation of such equipment in and between Member States. Where the provisions of the Directive can only be implemented by requiring specific technical features in electronic communications networks, Member States are under a duty to inform the European Commission accordingly. Where required, the Commission will ensure the drawing up of common European standards in respect of such technical features in accordance with a Council Decision on standardisation in the field of information technology and communications.[4]

SPECIFIC ASPECTS OF THE REGULATIONS

The Privacy and Electronic Communications (EC Directive) Regulations 2003 restate the Directive, adding more detail where appropriate and make specific provision for matters left to Member States. For example, the Directive on privacy and electronic communications does not mention compensation for breaches of the provisions in the Directive but the data protection Directive does so provide and states that the data controller shall not be liable if '. . . he proves he

---

[4] Council Decision 87/95/EEC of 22 December 1986 on standardisation in the field of information technology and communications, OJ L 36, 07.02.1987, p. 31.

is not responsible …'. The Regulations spell this out in more detail, saying that the service provider has a defence to any claim to compensation if he proves that he has ' … taken such care as in all the circumstances was reasonably required to comply with the relevant requirement': Regulation 30(2). Other points of interest in the Regulations of interest are listed below.

1   The period of time traffic data can be kept takes into account, where proceedings are brought within the limitation period, the time when those proceedings are determined and the time allowed for an appeal, and if an appeal is brought, the time until the conclusion of the appeal. This could be a considerable time, for instance, in a matter involving Community law, where an application for a preliminary reference is made to the European Court of Justice.

2   The processing of traffic data for billing and, where allowed, for value added services is restricted to the activities of management of billing or traffic, customer enquiries, the prevention or detection of fraud, the marketing of electronic communication services or the provision of a value added service.

3   Emergency calls, allowing the overriding of elimination of calling or connected line identification is limited to 999 calls, or in Europe, 112 calls.

4   In relation to the termination of automatic call forwarding, other communications providers are required to comply with reasonable requests from the subscriber's provider to assist in the prevention of the calls being forwarded.

5   Where a term in a contract between a subscriber and the provider of an electronic communications service or between such a provider and the provider of an electronic communications network is inconsistent with the requirements of the Regulations, that term is void to the extent that it is inconsistent.

6   Nothing in the Regulations shall require a communications provider to do, or refrain from doing, anything (including the processing of personal data) if compliance would be inconsistent with requirements imposed by or under any enactment or by court order or where compliance would be likely to prejudice the prevention or detection of crime or the apprehension of offenders. Exemption from a requirement of the Regulations is also given where required in respect of legal proceedings, necessary for obtaining legal advice or establishing, exercising or defending legal rights.

7   Part V of the Data Protection Act 1998 (the Part on enforcement) and Schedules 6 and 9 (dealing with the Information Tribunal and the Information Commissioner's powers of entry and inspection) apply with appropriate modification.

8   OFCOM (the Office of Communications) or any person aggrieved by an alleged contravention of the Regulations may ask the Information Commissioner to exercise his enforcement functions, which are exercisable in any case in the absence of such a request.

9   OFCOM is required to comply with any reasonable request from the Information Commissioner for technical advice relating to electronic communications.

10 Nothing in the Regulations relieves a person of his obligations under the Data Protection Act 1988.

OFCOM maintains registers kept for the purposes of opting out of unsolicited direct marketing faxes and telephone calls. With respect to the latter, where a number listed in the register is that of a corporate subscriber, within 28 days following each anniversary of that number first being listed in the register, OFCOM must send that subscriber a written reminder that the number is listed in the register. Presumably, a corporate subscriber may wish to be reminded in case of a change of mind.

SUMMARY

- The Directive on privacy and electronic communications was implemented in the UK by the Privacy and Electronic Communications (EC Directive) Regulations 2003.
- The Regulations do not affect obligations under the Data Protection Act 1998.
- The Directive and Regulations apply to publicly available electronic communications services.
- Privacy rights are given to users and subscribers.
- Subscribers include legal persons but users must be natural persons.
- Providers of services must take appropriate security and confidentiality measures.
- Unless made anonymous, traffic data may only be processed for specific purposes, such as:
  - billing, but not kept for longer than can be legally challenged;
  - marketing or value added services but only with the subscriber's or user's consent.
- The presentation of line identification may be prevented.
- There are restrictions on the use of location data.
- Subscribers have a right to prevent automatic call-forwarding.
- Subscribers have rights in relation to directories including rights:
  - to be informed of the purposes directories are to be used for; and
  - not to be included in the directory.
- There are opt-out rights in respect of unsolicited communications.

SELF-TEST QUESTION

1 **In what ways does the Directive on privacy in electronic communications supplement to rights to privacy in respect of the processing of personal data under the data protection Directive?**

For further resources and updates please go to the Companion Website accompanying this book at **www.mylawchamber.co.uk/bainbridgeIT**

Part 6

Professional and social issues of information and communications technology

Information and communications technology has had a massive impact on society and affects virtually all aspects of society including government, business, education, medicine, travel, leisure, human relationships, privacy and freedom of expression. Almost everybody makes use of these technologies at work and at home and many persons depend upon them for their livelihood. The British Computer Society has over 50,000 members but this is only a tiny fraction of those that work in the fields of computer and software design and development and in electronic communications.

This part of the book contains two chapters. The first looks at the position of the computer professional, his duties and obligations, whistle-blowing and the role of the expert witness. The second chapter looks at issues concerning privacy and freedom of expression and the impact of ICT on society. Many of the themes discussed in the earlier parts of the book appear here also, such as piracy and counterfeiting, computer crime and privacy and data protection issues. These are discussed here in the context of their impact from a social and ethical perspective.

35 The computer professional

INTRODUCTION

Persons involved in information and communications systems, whether by teaching or specifying, designing, developing, testing or maintaining these systems hold special responsibilities. They can do great good or cause great harm by their actions and can enable or influence others so to do. It is important, therefore, that they adhere to certain standards and principles of conduct and recognise and understand the wider and social implications of what they do or enable others to do.

Because of the potential impacts and effects of what they do, computer professionals have a particular duty to make themselves aware of ethical issues relating to their work. They also have a particular duty to ensure that they have a working knowledge of laws and regulations that apply to the projects they are working on. A manager of ICT facilities must know something about intellectual property and licensing software, the legal implications of the internet, computer crime and misuse and data protection laws as a minimum. He does not need to be a legal expert but he should know how the law affects his actions and the use of the systems he is responsible for, in a practical sense. Managers are likely to be involved in the development and dissemination of codes of practice governing the use of the systems for which they are responsible.

Whether or not ICT managers are members of particular professional bodies or have relevant qualifications (as most do, of course) they should operate within recognised and accepted codes of conduct, as below.

CODES OF CONDUCT

All professional bodies have codes of conduct for their members. In terms of computers and information and communications technology, the premier professional body in the UK is the British Computer Society. Persons belonging to professional bodies are required to adhere to the code of conduct of the body on pain of disciplinary procedures or even expulsion from the body. Codes on conduct are likely to include provisions dealing with duties to employers, clients and the general public, compliance with legal requirements, conflicts of interest and duties to the profession itself.

Being a member of a professional body is an important step in an individual's career and, in some cases, membership is a prerequisite of practising a profession. For example, a person may not hold himself out as a practising barrister unless he has complied with the requirements of the Bar Council for practice and has been called to the bar. For other professions, membership of an appropriate professional body may not be legally required for practice but may be desirable, for example, in terms of indicating that the person has attained a certain level of qualification in his field of expertise and has accepted the responsibilities of being a member of that profession.

In relation to professional operating in the information and communications technology field, relevant aspects of any code of practice will include:

- an obligation to performing duties with due care and diligence and not accepting tasks beyond the individual's level of competence;
- the acceptance of full responsibility for their work and that of others working under their authority and direction;
- a duty to keep up to date by participating in continuing professional development courses – many professional bodies insist on minimum levels of training throughout an individual's career which might involve attendance at specialised courses and conferences or taking higher university degrees;
- an awareness of and compliance with legislation, codes of practice and conventions concerning health and safety, discrimination, human rights and the environment;
- having regard to important social and ethical issues such as the need to protect the environment to protect vulnerable persons from exploitation and respect for public health and safety;
- an awareness of the social and ethical implications of the work undertaken and a responsibility not to compromise basic moral and cultural values accepted as norms in society (including those belonging to or held by minority groups);
- the avoidance of conflicts of interests, such as performing duties for an organisation which conflict with duties and obligations owed to other clients or potential clients or acting in breach of confidence or contrary to a duty of fidelity;
- to uphold the reputation of the professional body and not act in any way to bring it into disrepute; to be supportive to fellow members, junior associates and trainees including acting as a role model and mentor to such persons; to generally promote the public understanding and awareness of the relevant field of activity.

Some professional bodies require practitioners to take out appropriate professional liability insurance and may even offer services in this respect. If this is not the case, any professional working in an independent capacity should consider taking out appropriate insurance against any failing on their part. This is not merely to protect that individual but is a means to ensure that clients and third parties are adequately compensated for any losses attributable to the negligence of the professional, bearing in mind that the test for whether a person has been negligent is an objective one.

One difficult problem for a professional is what to do if an employer or client wants to embark upon a venture that might be legal but is dubious from a moral standpoint. Examples, are some of the offers of free gifts or holidays that result in the 'lucky recipient' having to make telephone calls on premium rate numbers. A professional can be placed in a dilemma in such a situation, torn between his duty to comply with his employer's or client's instructions and his own judgment of the acceptability of the planned activities. He should certainly make his views known and seek the advice and guidance of colleagues or even the professional body itself in a serious conflict. One difficulty, however, is that an employed professional, in line with all other employees, owes a duty of fidelity to his employer. Where the conflict is serious and cannot be resolved, the professional should consider seeking other employment or not working again for that client. In any event, a professional should avoid involvement in any illegal activity, whether of a civil or criminal nature. Pressure from an employer to do so could be regarded as a breach of the contract of employment by an employer, giving remedies under employment law on the basis of constructive dismissal.

The professional operating in information and communications technology has an obligation to acquire and maintain knowledge of the practical implications of compliance with the relevant laws and codes of practice. For example, a manager of ICT facilities must know about data protection laws and the obligations imposed on data controllers such as duty to provide appropriate technical and organisational security measures and to understand and comply with requests for subject access and the duties to inform data subjects. Such a manager should also make it clear to persons using the facilities what are acceptable uses, contributing to the formulation and updating of conditions of use backed by disciplinary procedures. There have been many examples of employees using ICT facilities for illegal, inappropriate or undesirable uses, such as downloading pornography, making unauthorised use of the facilities or information stored therein and even bringing liability to the employer in relation to malicious falsehood by sending e-mails.

WHISTLE-BLOWING

The Employment Rights Act 1996 includes provisions protecting employees making certain types of disclosures to his employer or other responsible person. This could apply where an employee reasonably believes that a criminal offence is being, or is about to be, committed or where the employer has or will fail to comply with a legal obligation, for example, a duty under data protection or freedom of information law. Such types of disclosures are defined as qualifying disclosures under section 43B(1) of the Act and where the disclosure is made in good faith to an employer or, where applicable, some other person having responsibility, the disclosure is a protected disclosure under section 43A. This means, for example, an employee making a protected disclosure in the reasonable belief that the disclosure is a qualifying disclosure and that he makes the disclosure in good faith is protected from dismissal or other detriment as a result of the disclosure, providing he does not commit a criminal offence by making the disclosure. Indeed, if an employee is dismissed for making the protected disclosure (or that is the principal reason for the dismissal) he is to be regarded as being unfairly dismissed.

In *Bolton School* v *Evans* [2006] IRLR 500, Mr Evans was employed as a technology teacher in the school's ICT department. He was very knowledgeable about ICT matters and took an interest in the school's decision to install a new computer system. Mr Evans thought that the school should have two completely separate systems, one for the pupils and the other for the staff, and this was the original intention. However, as implemented, the new computer system had a single cable network as the head of the project group considered that, as there had been no security breaches in the past, password security would be adequate.

Mr Evans expressed concerns about the security of the system and the danger that pupils might be able to hack into confidential information stored on a central server computer with a single platform. This would mean that the school would be in breach of the seventh data protection principle which requires appropriate technical and organisational security measures to be taken by data controllers. Mr Evans decided to demonstrate that the security of the system as installed was inadequate. He informed a Mr Edmunsen, who had been designated to be the individual to whom concerns about security should be directed, that he would attempt to gain access to the administrative systems from the resources available to pupils to test security and demonstrate its shortcomings. He also informed the head of computing.

Mr Evans enlisted the help of a former pupil to decode passwords which he had copied onto a disk and taken home and, when he returned to the school, he gained access from a pupil PC in the technology department and he disabled some user accounts for the ICT services department, which was not a teaching department. He told Mr Edmunsen and others what he had done but did not inform ICT services which shut down the system, suspecting that someone had hacked into the system. It took ICT services some time to reinstate the system at a cost of around £1,000.

The school headmaster carried out an investigation and a disciplinary hearing took place. The headmaster told Mr Evans that he had deliberately hacked into the network without authority as a premeditated act. A written warning was issued. Mr Evans' appeal to the Vice-Chair of Governors was dismissed. Soon after, Mr Evans resigned as he considered that his position was untenable. He felt that he had been victimised for highlighting security concerns. He brought a successful action for constructive dismissal before the Employment Tribunal but the school appealed to the Employment Appeal Tribunal ('EAT'). Three issues were considered by the EAT, being whether there was a qualifying disclosure, did Mr Evans have a reasonable belief that there has been or is likely to be a failure to comply with a legal obligation and, finally, whether Mr Evans' conduct constituted a protected disclosure.

The EAT found that the disclosure was a qualifying disclosure but it did not consider that it was a protected disclosure. There was a distinction between making a disclosure by providing information indicating a likelihood of a breach of obligation and investigating that likelihood of a breach. In other words, the protection for whistle-blowers applies where he thinks 'something is wrong' but not where he is acting as an investigator who seeks to establish that it is wrong or that his concerns are reasonable. At the EAT, Mr Justice Elias J said (at para. 65):

> An employee cannot be entitled to break into his employer's filing cabinet in the hope of finding papers which will demonstrate some relevant wrongdoing which he can then disclose to the appropriate person. He is liable to be disciplined for such conduct, and that is so whether he turns up such papers or not. Provided that his misconduct is genuinely the reason for the disciplinary action, the employee will not be protected even if he does in fact discover incriminating papers. Success does not retrospectively provide a cloak of immunity for his actions, although he will then of course be protected with respect to the subsequent disclosure of the information itself.

The EAT held that it was not possible to sustain the finding of constructive dismissal after finding that the disclosure was not a protected disclosure. The case was remitted back to the Employment Tribunal to determine whether, in the light of the EAT's decision, there was or was not, in the circumstances, a constructive dismissal. A subsequent appeal to the Court of Appeal in *Bolton School* v *Evans* [2007] IRLR 140 resulted in the same result with the case being remitted back to the same Employment Tribunal. The Court of Appeal accepted that the original Employment Tribunal erred by not treating Mr Evans' conduct of 'hacking' into the computer system as distinct from the disclosure itself. It was plain that the warning given to Mr Evans was in relation to his conduct and not the disclosure itself.

US SARBANES-OXLEY ACT 2002

Following corporate scandals such as Enron and other companies, the US enacted the Sarbanes-Oxley Act in 2002. This voluminous piece of legislation contains new standards, *inter alia*, for financial accounting, reporting and auditing and also has impacts for corporate governance. In terms of information and communications technology, the Act has implications for those who control and manage information systems within companies used for financial reporting. It is important that where these systems are used for accounting and financial reporting they are properly understood, assessed, tested and monitored. Risk assessments should be carried out regularly and security is an important aspect together with reviewing compliance with accounting systems and any changes thereto. The Act also contains protection for corporate fraud whistle-blowers in publicly traded companies.

Publicly registered accounting firms, and persons associated with them, acting as auditors are not permitted to provide services in relation to financial information systems design and implementation, amongst other things.

In the UK, there is a Combined Code on Corporate Governance[1] which suggests that information needs and related information systems be reassessed as objectives and related risks change or as reporting deficiencies are identified.[2] Clearly information and communications technology professional dealing with or having responsibility for financial information systems must be aware of such matters. Where a computer professional is a director of a company, he will also have obligations under the legislation relating to companies.

EXPERT WITNESSES

A number of computer professionals act as expert witnesses in civil and criminal trials, in arbitrations and also in negotiations to settle disputes. The use of expert witnesses is common in trials involving complex technological issues. As with any expert witnesses, apart from being truly expert in their field, they are subject to a number of duties as well as rules of practice applicable to the giving of evidence by expert witnesses.

Professionals generally have duties towards their professional body, such as the British Computer Society, and towards their client and instructing solicitor. But the primary duty of an expert witness is to the court in which they are giving their evidence. Expert witnesses are an exception to the general rule that a witness cannot give his opinion of matter but must give evidence as to facts only. Section 3(1) of the Civil Evidence Act 1972 states that:

> ... where a person is called as a witness in any civil proceedings, his opinion on any relevant matter on which he is qualified to give expert evidence is admissible as evidence.

This puts expert witnesses in a special position but what they must not do is act as an advocate for their client. Their evidence must reflect their genuine and honestly held opinions, free from bias.

In common with other witnesses, an expert witness has immunity from civil proceedings in respect of the evidence he gives in court. This was confirmed in *Meadow* v *General Medical Council* [2006] Fam 356. This case concerned an appeal by Professor Sir Roy Meadow against the decision of a panel within the General Medical Council to strike him off the medical register. He had given evidence at the trial of Sally Clark who was subsequently convicted of the murder of her two sons. She was later acquitted on appeal after it was discovered that some important test results had been withheld. The immunity is based on public policy. It is important for there to be such a policy otherwise experts might be deterred from giving evidence. In *Meadow*, the court held that there was no reason why this immunity should not also extend to disciplinary proceedings. However, the policy was not absolute. It covered civil proceedings based on a complaint made by a party or any other person who did not like or was upset by the evidence given by the expert. However, the judge before whom an expert witness gave evidence might refer the conduct of an expert witness to a relevant disciplinary body. That was not the case here. The complaint to the General Medical Council had been made by Sally Clark's father and, accordingly, Meadow's appeal against a finding of serious professional misconduct was allowed.

Many of the communications between an expert witness and his instructing solicitor will be

---

[1] Financial Reporting Council, July 2003.
[2] At p. 41.

subject to privilege. As Lord Justice Bingham said in *Apostolos Konstantine Ventouris* v *Trevor Rex Mountain ('The Italia Express')* [1992] 2 Lloyd's Rep 216:

> In recognition of these rights [the right to seek and obtain legal advice and the right to prepare for and conduct a case], perhaps generously interpreted, proofs of witnesses, whether factual or expert, and communications with potential witnesses, have been held immune from production.

This privilege is, of course, that of the client and may be waived.

Expert witnesses in civil proceedings

We have seen above that the evidence of expert witnesses is admissible in civil proceedings under section 3(1) of the Civil Evidence Act 1972. Part 35 of the Civil Procedure Rules 1998 also applies. An 'expert' is an expert instructed to give or prepare evidence for the purpose of court proceedings. Rule 35.3 confirms that it is the duty of an expert witness to help the court on matters within his expertise. The rule goes on to state that this duty overrides any obligation to the person from whom he has received instruction or by whom he is paid. In any report submitted as evidence by an expert witness, there must be a statement to the effect that the expert understands this duty and has complied with it. The Practice Direction on Part 35 goes on to say that expert evidence must be the independent product of the expert uninfluenced by the pressures of litigation. He must provide objective, unbiased opinion on matters within his expertise and must not assume the role of an advocate. He should consider all the material facts, including those which detract from his opinion. The Practice Direction also gives the requirements as to the form and content of an expert report.

Expert evidence must be restricted to that reasonably required to resolve the proceedings and no expert witness may be called or any expert report put in evidence without the court's permission. When applying for permission, the field of expertise must be identified together, if practicable, the expert in that field on whose evidence it is sought to rely. The preference is for the expert's evidence to be given in a report. In this case, written questions can be put to the expert and the expert's answers will be treated as part of the report. Where both parties seek to call expert witnesses on a particular issue, the court may direct that the evidence shall be given by one expert only; a single joint expert. An expert witness may ask the court for directions.

Expert witnesses are common in software copyright cases and computer crime cases. An example of expert witnesses being used by both sides in a software copyright case was in *Nova Productions Ltd* v *Mazooma Games Ltd* [2006] RPC 379, discussed in Chapter 4. One of the defendant's expert witnesses was described by the judge as being:

> ... intimately involved with computer games for over 25 years and is something of a legend in the industry. He has designed, written or produced a considerable number of games.

The judge went on to say that this witness gave his evidence in a clear and objective way and that he found his evidence to be of great assistance.

Occasionally, an assessor may be appointed by the court to assist the court in dealing with a matter in which the assessor has skill and expertise. The court determines the remuneration to be paid to the assessor and this becomes part of the costs of the proceedings. Assessors are sometimes used on patent cases and personal injury cases though it is not a common practice to appoint them. One example was in *Sutton* v *Tesco Stores Ltd* (unreported) 30 July 2002 in which an experienced consultant psychiatrist was appointed as an assessor in litigation which came about as a result of someone slipping on a squashed tomato on the floor of a supermarket in New Malden.

Expert witnesses in criminal trials

Expert evidence is admissible in criminal trials under common law. This rule of law was preserved by section 118 of the Criminal Justice Act 2003. Part 33 of the Criminal Procedure Rules 2005 set out the duties of expert witnesses in criminal trials and are broadly equivalent to those for civil trials. In this context, an 'expert' is a person who is required to give or prepare expert evidence for the purpose of criminal proceedings, including evidence required to determine fitness to plead or for the purposes of sentencing. The expert's duty to the court is as with civil proceedings but with an additional express duty to help the court to achieve the overriding objective, being that criminal cases are dealt with justly. There are also detailed provisions concerning the disclosure of expert evidence.

Expert evidence may be used to prove the *actus reus* of the offence is made out where this is in issue. In *R v Whitehouse* [2000] Crim LR 172, the accused repeatedly turned on his mobile phone to send text messages in an aeroplane. He had been told on a number of occasions to switch it off as it could endanger the aircraft. When the aeroplane landed, he was arrested and charged with the offence of recklessly or negligently acting in a manner likely to endanger an aircraft, or any person therein. During the trial, the defendant argued that what he did was not likely to endanger the aircraft. Two expert witnesses were called for the Crown and the defendant called one expert witness. After hearing the expert witnesses, the judge accepted that there was a real risk that the aircraft would be endangered by the use of a digital phone and the same opinion was held throughout the world. The defendant was convicted and sentenced to 12 months' imprisonment. His appeal against conviction and sentence was dismissed. The facts of the case occurred in 1998.

In some cases, in criminal trials, expert evidence may be essential to prove a defence. For example, in *Director of Public Prosecutions v Frost* [1989] RTR 11, the defendant was charged with the offence of being in charge of a vehicle whilst unfit to drive through drink. The defendant's story was that he had fallen asleep in his car and did not intend to drive it until 9.00am the following morning. The magistrates accepted that he would not by then be over the legal limit. They did so without hearing expert evidence as to the rate of decline of breath-alcohol level over time. The appeal against that finding was allowed.

In *R v Jackson* [2006] EWCA Crim 2380, a squadron leader in the RAF was convicted of an offence of low flying (flying below 100 feet). He argued that the offence required *mens rea* and called expert evidence about the unreliability of instruments such as the altimeter in the aeroplane. However, it was held that the offence was one of strict liability and he was convicted of the offence.

Registers of expert witnesses

The British Computer Society holds a professional advice register which includes a section listing expert witnesses and the Expert Witness Institute, a body with the central objective of supporting '... the proper administration of justice and the early resolution of dispute through fair and unbiased expert evidence', also has a register of experts in all fields.

SUMMARY

- Persons who are members of professional bodies are subject to codes of conduct.
- Failure to adhere to a code of conduct can result in disciplinary action or even expulsion.

35

The computer professional

- Professionals should avoid conflicts of interests.

- Computer professionals should not work on systems that are likely to involve unlawful or dubious activities.

- Computer managers should ensure that users are aware of acceptable uses of information and communication systems and are aware of relevant legal requirements.

- There is legislation to protect whistle-blowers.

- A whistle-blower may disclose his concerns to the employer or other responsible person.

- A whistle-blower may not be protected if he carries out unauthorised acts to demonstrate his concerns.

- In the US, legislation to prevent corporate scandals may have implications for information systems used for accounting and financial reporting.

- Computer professionals may act as expert witnesses.

- Of all the duties an expert witness may have, his highest duty is to the court.

- Unlike other witnesses, opinions of expert witnesses are admissible as evidence.

- As with other witnesses, expert witnesses have immunity against civil proceedings in respect of the evidence they give.

SELF-TEST QUESTION

1   Look at the British Computer Society's Code of Conduct, available at: http://www.bcs.org/upload/pdf/conduct.pdf

To what extent could adherence to such a code of conduct result in conflicts in the work-place? Give examples of potential conflicts and how they could be resolved.

For further resources and updates please go to the Companion Website accompanying this book at **www.mylawchamber.co.uk/bainbridgeIT**

36 Privacy, freedom of expression and the impact of ICT on society

INTRODUCTION

Information and communications technology (ICT) is all-pervasive and has probably had the greatest impact on society than any other technology. We rely on ICT for all the benefits it can deliver, such as powerful information processing and storage and better quality sound and image reproduction, increased access to information, online services, electronic contracting, access to government and public bodies and mobile communications.

On the down side, there are serious concerns about the impact of ICT on property rights in information, individuals' rights to privacy, criminal and terrorist activity and the use of the internet to spread propaganda and incite racial and religious hatred. Editorial responsibility and control, which could prevent the worst abuses when material was published and distributed in paper form, is non-existent in many cases of internet publication and often the source of outrageous, compromising or harmful information is outside the jurisdiction of the courts of the country or countries to which information is targeted.

Particular issues considered in this chapter include the impact of ICT on the rights enshrined in the Council of Europe Convention for the Protection of Human Rights and Fundamental Freedoms, the desirability of property rights in information and the balance between the rights of the owners of such rights and the rights of others and whether liability for faulty information disseminated on a large scale should be the same or no weaker than that for faulty equipment or goods.

HUMAN RIGHTS CONVENTION

The Council of Europe Convention on the Protection of Human Rights and Fundamental Freedoms (the 'Human Right Convention') contains a number of rights which may be affected by ICT. The two rights that usually first come to mind are the right to privacy and the right of freedom of expression. ICT presents serious and substantial challenges to individuals' right to privacy but also increases the ability of individuals, corporations, governmental and other bodies to disseminate information and views. The two rights are not incompatible but must be balanced. Neither are the two rights absolute and both are subject to derogations.

Privacy

Individuals' privacy rights are very vulnerable in the information society. All manner of personal information is stored about us on computer systems. Some of this information may be accessed remotely from anywhere in the world. Much of the information is sensitive, such as health information, and could cause significant harm if it got into the wrong hands. Another issue is the ability of others to place information about us online. This information may or may not be true. It may, for example, be something actionable as defamation or otherwise something we might find unpleasant or distasteful. The Human Rights Convention attempts to protect privacy. Article 8 para 1 sets out the basic right but this is subject to possible derogation in para. 2. Article 8 of the Convention (right to respect for private and family life) states:

1 **Everyone has the right to respect for his private and family life, his home and his correspondence.**
2 **There shall be no interference by a public authority with the exercise of this right except such as is in accordance with the law and is necessary in a democratic society in the interests of national security, public safety or the economic well-being of the country, for the prevention of disorder or crime, for the protection of health or morals, or for the protection of the rights and freedoms of others.**

The scope of Article 8 has been interpreted liberally and it has been accepted that the basic right is not limited to public authorities and can apply to allow an individual a proactive right to obtain information that could prejudice his basic right. This will enable that person to seek appropriate redress through the law.

There are, what appear to be, wide ranging exceptions to the right as set out in para. 2. However, the interference must be 'necessary' for the interests sought to be maintained or protected. This is a question of proportionality and must take account of the importance of the goal sought to be achieved. The test may vary, therefore, depending on the degree of harm to the individual by loss of the right to privacy and the degree of harm to the interest concerned if the exception is not applied. In respect of the rights and freedoms of others, this is likely to be more of a balancing act. The sorts of rights and freedoms must include the right of freedom of expression.

We have seen how data protection law attempts to reconcile the balance between the two paras of Article 8 in the context of personal data. This has influence beyond Europe, such as in respect of the US 'safe harbors' approach to allowing transfers of personal data from Europe. Argentina is one of a growing number of countries adopting laws or codes protecting personal data. There are still numerous countries without such laws or codes, or where they have them, they are inadequate. Therein lies the problem. The internet is universal and information can be made available on the internet from anywhere in the world. With few exceptions, it can be accessed from anywhere in the world. This fact emphasises the importance of security of information systems which have a gateway to the internet, as most do. A current example is the concerns raised about the massive UK National Health Service information system for patient data. If security is breached, the implications could be very serious. One might question whether it is wise to develop such systems until and unless security can be guaranteed – an unlikely notion. If the security of US military and defence systems can be compromised by computer hackers operating in the UK, one must question whether any security measures adopted for information systems can ever be 100 per cent secure.

Privacy rights can be compromised by unauthorised access to personal and private information which is legitimately stored in information systems, whether with the consent of the individual or otherwise. But another threat to privacy comes from information which is made available for access without consent or lawful authority. There is no over-arching authority to police the internet. Service providers may adopt their own policies and take down or disable access to information they consider illegal, immoral or prejudicial to individuals but they can only realistically act on the basis of specific complaints.

It may be that the information is fairly innocuous in itself and has been placed there without malice. It may be that a person decides to write thumbnail descriptions of his friends and places these on his website but does not ask his friends for permission. It may not even occur to him that any would object or that it might be wise to ask them. The descriptions are complimentary and there is nothing about the descriptions that could be described as confidential, defamatory or a violation of privacy. Before the time when publishing used computers, he could have written the same thing by hand and submitted it to a newspaper as an article for publication. This would all have been perfectly legal. Now, by placing the information on the internet without permission, it is likely that data protection issues would arise, as in the *Lindqvist* case discussed in Chapter 31.

Some breaches of privacy may be justified under Article 8(2), for example, by publishing photographs of suspected terrorists or using offender naming schemes. But a serious consideration is whether such materials should be placed on the internet. The damage that could be done if, for example, a person had been wrongly suspected of a serious crime, could be very substantial. Offender naming schemes operated on a local basis have attracted criticism in the past. In Birmingham photographs of individuals wanted in relation to criminal activities were beamed onto the side of the police headquarters for all to see. Again, the question of proportionality is engaged. It may be proportionate to publish locally but not to publish on a website.

Another issue is that of data capture and surveillance. Clearly, the capture of data from an individual's computer, by use of cookies and other covert software, without the individual's knowledge, is a breach of the right of privacy. The same applies to intercepting and recording telephone conversations or data transmissions and to CCTV. In some cases this may be acceptable, for example, in relation to the prevention and detection of crime. But it is essential that this is done under proper lawful authority, subject to appropriate codes of practice and safeguards which take account of the Convention rights and domestic laws, such as the Regulation of Investigatory Powers Act 2000 in the UK. However, the touchstone for domestic legislation for all countries which adhere to and respect the Human Rights Convention (or any similar international agreement) is the Convention itself. The Human Rights Act 1998 makes it clear that legislation should be interpreted in accordance with the Convention rights and where this is not possible, a court can make a declaration of incompatibility which should send the message to Parliament that the legislation should be modified so as to comply.

Freedom of expression

The right to express oneself is fundamental in a free and democratic society. Again this right is not an absolute one and is tempered by the need to protect other interests which also are important in a democratic society, such as the reputation and freedoms of others. Unfortunately, governments in some countries do not recognise a right of freedom of expression and some try to interfere with what is available in their countries over the internet. For example, The People's Republic of China imposed restrictions on internet service providers and also uses firewall technology to prevent access to certain sites. Companies like Google, Microsoft and Yahoo! complied with certain restrictions. Examples included taking down blogs critical of the government and weeding out websites. It seems that access to content including words such as 'freedom' and 'democracy' was prevented.

In Europe and other democracies, there are still controls over offensive material through a wide range of national laws. Although most cover similar issues, not all are compatible. For example, in some countries though not others, it may be an offence to advertise certain types of goods. Laws such as those relating to defamation, data protection, incitement, discrimination and the stirring up of racial hatred are just some examples of those that could apply to all forms of publishing, including publishing online.

36

Privacy, freedom of expression and the impact of ICT on society

Article 10 of the Human Rights Convention sets out the right of freedom of expression thus:

1 Everyone has the right to freedom of expression. This right shall include freedom to hold opinions and to receive and impart information and ideas without interference by public authority and regardless of frontiers. This article shall not prevent States from requiring the licensing of broadcasting, television or cinema enterprises.

2 The exercise of these freedoms, since it carries with it duties and responsibilities, may be subject to such formalities, conditions, restrictions or penalties as are prescribed by law and are necessary in a democratic society, in the interests of national security, territorial integrity or public safety, for the prevention of disorder or crime, for the protection of health or morals, for the protection of the reputation or rights of others, for preventing the disclosure of information received in confidence, or for maintaining the authority and impartiality of the judiciary.

The right is without frontiers. This means, subject to para. 2, the right extends to publishing material on the internet, notwithstanding interference with the right by governments of other countries. The same point can be made about proportionality as applies to the right of privacy. Paragraph 2 also highlights the fact that the right is subject to duties and responsibilities.

There are a number of points that can be made about the right of freedom of expression. The exercise of the right might conflict with national laws in countries other than the one in which the person exercising it resides. Or the 'victim', if there is one, may be in a different country. This immediately brings into play jurisdictional issues. For example, if the exercise of the right results in the commission of a tort, in which jurisdiction is that tort actionable? We have seen issues of this nature in relation to defamation, trade marks and the internet. It may not always be possible for the person whose reputation or other rights are involved to be able to seek effective legal redress. We have also seen that, in Europe, and some other countries, laws exist to deal with the position of service providers in relation to illegal material, giving them a limited immunity. Many information society service providers have adopted their own policies to deal with material that may lie around the penumbra where freedom of expression merges into interests that need to be protected by excluding or restricting the right. Specific types of information or advertising may be prohibited by the service provider, even if not contrary to relevant laws. Even if not within the prohibited information, the service provider may take down information which he feels *may* be illegal. To this extent, service providers themselves operate a form of self-censorship which, it could be argued, further compromises the right of freedom of expression.

Decision making affecting individuals

Under Article 6 of the Human Rights Convention, everyone has a right to a fair and public trial. This applies to civil and criminal proceedings. In some cases, the trial may not be in public but held *in camera*, for example, to protect national security or where the interests of juveniles or the protection of the private life of parties so require. There is also a presumption of innocence in criminal trials.

We have not yet got to the position where computers decide guilt in a criminal trial or success in a civil trial. That is not to say that computer decision making is not possible in this arena. It is possible and certainly goes on in other matters, such as in a decision to grant or refuse an individual financial credit. Decision making by computer in trials would be extremely controversial. A computer is not able (as yet) to form a view on whether a witness is telling the truth or to assess complex evidence. On the other hand, a programmed computer may be free from some of the biases and prejudices that individuals have. It is likely to be some time before anyone seriously suggests that trials should be conducted by computer. There remains the possibility of sentencing convicted offenders using programmed computers. Research into this possibility goes back a long time, particularly in the US. In the UK, the author of this book developed such a computer system embodying an 'expert system' in the 1980s (a paper on the system is available from **www.bileta.ac.uk** under conference papers for 1990).

On the other hand, computer information is often given in evidence in court, for example, in the form of a document stored in a computer, data transmitted electronically, a mobile phone log, a read-out from a breathalyser device or a record of transactions carried out at a supermarket check-out.

To comply with the requirement of a fair trial, we must be satisfied that computer evidence is authentic, accurate, complete and verifiable. The same principles apply to voice or video evidence and other forms of hearsay evidence. At one time, there were complex rules to be used to determine whether computer evidence was admissible. If the rules were not satisfied, the evidence would be rejected. For example, in one case, a breathalyser readout was rejected, not because there was any doubt about the breath-alcohol reading, but because the time clock had been incorrectly set. These stringent rules no longer apply but, in civil and criminal trials, the court has a discretion as to whether such evidence should be admitted. If admitted, a warning may be given by the judge as to its probative value, for example, if there had been some technical problems with the computer at the relevant time.

Away from the court, less controversy applies to the use of computer in decision making. However, there are still concerns which were addressed by the data protection Directive, laying down safeguards where such decisions have legal consequence or may significantly affect the individual. Online applications for credit or other services, whether for payment or not, as a matter of good practice should be subject to the same principles, even if this is not required by law or the Human Rights Convention. It is unlikely that all do comply, particularly if established elsewhere. In some cases, the choice of jurisdiction in which to operate online from may be influenced by differences in legal regulation or lack of effective regulation in some countries. This is an issue that is by no means restricted to automated decision making.

OPEN GOVERNMENT

The internet brings opportunities for governments to place much more information in the public domain in a way which is easily located and readily accessible and downloadable. Most government departments, including local authorities, have their own websites containing significant amounts of information. A great deal of this information was available previously, for example, through Hansard, Committee Minutes and the Minutes of Local Councils. In most cases journalists attended relevant meetings and reported on them. But now, everyone can obtain, at no direct cost and relatively little indirect costs (such as the costs of equipments and a subscription to an internet service provider), all this information and much more. The Freedom of Information Act 2000 and the equivalent Act in Scotland have acted as catalysts encouraging and, in some cases, requiring government bodies and other public bodies to subscribe to the principle of open government.

Politicians individually also make use of the internet to publicise themselves and their views. This may be seen to be something of a marketing exercise but it enables them to present a more extensive and effective and, perhaps more user-friendly, face to the public than by the old tried and tested means of shaking hands, kissing babies and pushing leaflets through letterboxes.

One problem with all this is the content chosen to be made public is likely to be that most favourable except where the information is a verbatim report of proceedings or the verbatim minutes of a meeting. Vague policy intentions and soundbites may replace hard statistics and even that latter may be subject to spin. There is a danger that persons will take things at face value and not question the accuracy and completeness of the information presented. That is why political journalism continues to be a major plank in any democratic society.

In February 2007, Greenpeace won a remarkable victory over the UK government and its plans to build a new generation of nuclear power stations because of a deeply flawed consultation process. As with many government consultations, the relevant documents were available online. The judge, Mr Justice Sullivan, criticised the government for failing to carry out the 'fullest consultation' as it had promised. He said that the exercise was manifestly inadequate and procedurally unfair, adding that something had gone clearly and radically wrong. The judge said that the consultation document contained no actual proposals and the information given to the public was 'wholly insufficient for them to make an intelligent response' (*The Times*, 16 February 2007, p. 4).

On the other side of the coin, the internet enables government departments and local authorities to inform the public about services offered on an improved scale. For example, if one is not sure what days the dustmen are collecting over a bank holiday period, this can usually be found quickly and easily on the local council's website as well as much other information which may seem mundane but may be important to the local citizens.

It is also possible now to perform many tasks which previously required standing in long queues or submitting forms and other documents by post, hoping that the hoped-for response would arrive in the not too distant future. Examples of transactions which may be carried out simply and easily online include paying road fund tax, paying for a television licence and even paying income tax to HM Revenue and Customs, now much easier though still a painful experience. Of course, the tax disc and licence still are sent through the post but at least those interminable queues at the Post Office are a thing of the past.

Another benefit is that the internet can have the effect of engaging more citizens in government. For example, by accessing local planning applications online and submitting objections online. This is much easier than going to the local planning office to inspect the plans and then writing and posting a letter of objection. Many individuals who would not have taken the trouble to do this through lethargy might be prepared to do so online. In terms of the UK central government, it is now possible to sign e-petitions on the 10 Downing Street website. At the time of writing, nearly one and a half million have signed a petition against the potential introduction of road-charging. Is this an increase in the people's power or an exercise to test potential policies for their attractiveness to voters before deciding on them? Sometimes people are prepared (or relieved) to accept a lesser version of a controversial policy.

PROPERTY RIGHTS IN INTANGIBLE CREATIVE WORKS

At one time, copies of creative works existed only in tangible form, such as in a printed book, sheet music, vinyl, paint and canvas, celluloid, etc. The growth of copying technology, such as photocopying machines and video recorders, immediately brought problems of unauthorised copying of works in which property rights subsisted. But the copies were still in physical form. There were costs associated with making unauthorised copies but even if the person responsible was caught and prosecuted, the penalties were relatively light and only were really applicable to out and out pirates. Of course, monetary compensation could be awarded at civil law. In terms of individuals who made copies for themselves or to give to friends, there was little that the law could do.

In response to the growth of piracy of music, video and computer games, the criminal penalties were increased in the 1980s to include a possibility of imprisonment for up to two years.

Some, particularly copyright owners and bodies representing them, considered unauthorised copying to be equivalent to theft. After all, copyright owners could have been deprived of significant income because of the activities of pirates.[1]

The growth of the internet changed everything. No longer was there any need to have a physical carrier to make a copy of a work of copyright or a performance. Some said this would end in the demise of copyright. Unauthorised copying was almost out of control, an example being the use of peer-to-peer software allowing persons to 'share' music and video files. But the internet also did something positive for copyright owners. It clarified just what copyright is – a form of intangible property right independent of any physical carrier. It is a qualified right to prevent certain acts being done in relation to the subject matter. As a property right, the owner has a right to enjoy that property and not to be deprived of it. Article 1 of the 1952 Paris Protocol to the Human Rights Convention is titled 'Protection of property' and states:

> Every natural or legal person is entitled to the peaceful enjoyment of his possessions. No one shall be deprived of his possessions except in the public interest and subject to the conditions provided for by law and by the general principles of international law.

In terms of copyright, and the same applies to related rights such as rights in performances and the database right, the right is not absolute. It is limited in time and in relation to the acts that fall within the property right. Furthermore, there are permitted acts, things which anyone can do without infringing the right. The basic balancing of the owner's rights with those of the general public is a result of international conventions such as the Berne Convention for the Protection of Literary and Artistic Works. Very few countries in the world do not belong to this or other conventions and treaties. There are very few places where the law of the internet on intellectual property rights is not the same or similar to those in the UK and Europe. There are very few places where such intangible property rights are not respected.

One can have no sympathy for pirates. They are parasitic on the creative work and efforts of others. If a person who creates a new work by his own intellect has no control over its subsequent use and gains no reward for it because of the actions of pirates or those who facilitate unauthorised copying on a massive scale, he is little more than a slave. Of course, persons creating new works may act on altruistic grounds and be quite happy to freely distribute their work. Most academic writers and scholars are happy to publish in journals for no direct monetary gain. Property rights can be waived but that must be a result of the owner's own free will. But even authors who are happy to have their work disseminated on a wide scale by placing it on a website from where it can be freely accessed and downloaded, might be unhappy if others mutilate the work or remove the author's name before further distributing it.

There are some, possibly a large proportion of individuals, who have little sympathy for large corporations which own rights in works such as music or film and seem to exploit those rights by what is commonly seen to be excessive pricing. But that does not take account of the various persons responsible for creating the works, such as writers, composers, musicians, film directors and actors, all of whom depend for their livelihood on the ultimate commercial success of the finished work. As for the prices charged by large corporations, one thing the internet has brought is the ability to sell works online for downloading. This brings cost savings as there is no need for physical media, printing and packaging. Furthermore, the potential of reduced prices is already starting to be seen and sales are likely to increase significantly which will drive down prices even further. Market forces are likely to prevail. However, retailers and distributors of music and film CDs and DVDs are likely to see a downturn in their sales as a consequence.

---

[1] Incidentally, the use of the terms 'pirate' and 'piracy' is not of recent origin in this context and judges have used them in relation to copyright since the eighteenth century.

36

Privacy, freedom of expression and the impact of ICT on society

Legislators were relatively quick to respond to the challenges to intangible property rights brought by the internet. We have seen the European approach of clarifying the scope of the rights and infringement, protecting rights management information, making those who facilitate unauthorised acts and overcome copy-protection liable at law and providing for limited protection for service providers.

One serious issue remains which is what to do where a copyright owner makes his work available online for sale or access via subscription in a way that one or more of the permitted acts are compromised. No part of the work may be accessed or copied for fair dealing for research or private study or for criticism or review, for example. Certain free and fair uses, such as fair use for teaching purposes are permitted under the Berne Convention. The Directive on copyright in the information society was unable to deal with this apart from leaving it to the European Commission to come up with proposals to amend the Directive if, *inter alia*, the permitted acts where adversely affected by the use of effective technological measures to prevent unauthorised acts. The UK response was little better with the provision of a clumsy complaints procedure where voluntary measures did not allow access to enable the performance of the permitted acts. If ever used, this is only likely to be taken up on a piecemeal basis. Clearly, the potential for compromising the permitted acts, which lie at the root of copyright law, is serious and could shift the balance to copyright owners who choose to make their works available online only for payment.

Software patents and the internet

The patenting of software used on the internet is arguably a more controversial area. Patent rights are monopoly rights, unlike copyright, which does not prevent the independent creation of similar works. In Europe, patents are not available for computer programs and business methods as such. This limits the scope of patents affecting information on websites though does not rule it out of the question altogether. The problem is more serious in the US where there are no such exclusions and patents have, in the past, been freely available for software. Many, including the author of this book, would argue that they have been too freely available. Patents have been granted that could interfere with the design or operation of a website. In many cases, such patents have been granted to small US companies that do not exploit the patents themselves but simply seek to make money by threatening litigation. These companies are described in the US as 'patent trolls'. To give an example, in *eBay Inc* v *MercExchange LLC*, 126 S Ct 1837 (2006), MercExchange owned a number of business method patents, including a business method patent for an electronic market to facilitate the sale of goods between private individuals by the establishment of a central authority to promote trust amongst participants. eBay's website allowed sellers to list goods they wish to sell either by auction or by fixed price (Buy It Now). MercExchange attempted to license its patent to eBay but the parties failed to reach an agreement and MercExchange sued eBay for infringement of its patent.

At first instance, the jury found that the patent (and another patent) was valid, the defendants had infringed the patents and an award of damages was appropriate. However, the court refused to grant a permanent injunction. On appeal, the Court of Appeals reversed the part of the decision relating to an injunction and eBay appealed to the Supreme Court which remitted the case to the first instance court to apply the proper principles in determining whether to grant an injunction. The Supreme Court criticised the test used by the Court of Appeals in deciding it was appropriate to grant an injunction, noting that the claimant was a patent troll. It is believed that eBay has challenged the validity of the patent.

There are clear dangers in granting monopoly rights that could interfere with websites operated by others, especially as Europe seems to be moving to make software patents more readily available. As the internet is world-wide, this means that there is potential infringement in any country where there is a relevant patent, unless the website is not targeted at those countries. There are bound to be more battles ahead and the whole issue of software patents ought to be revisited to try to strike a reasonable balance between proprietors of patents and the freedom of others to do business online.

VARIOUS SOCIAL ISSUES

Information and communications technology has transformed the way we work, carry out transactions, seek information and pass our spare time. ICT now accounts for a large part of the labour force and the wealth of some nations. In the past there were worries that the technology would result in the massive loss of jobs as machines, factory and office operations became 'computerised'. Whilst many of the old traditional jobs have disappeared, ICT has been instrumental in job creation. In the US around 3 million people are employed in computer science, with around the same number in the information sector. There are over a quarter of a million computer and information systems managers.[2] There are very few people who do not now use these technologies in the workplace. The number of homes without computers is dwindling. Many persons without a computer make use of digital technology through their televisions, radios and telephones.

The paperless office seems to have been a myth, given the continued preference for hard copy, but there are some changes to working practices. ICT brings the possibility that many can work from home, at least partially. This also brings the possibility of more flexible working. Where necessary meetings can take place by video conferencing, it should no longer be essential to travel half way across the country for a meeting that lasts less than an hour. However, working practices seem unduly resistant to change. Far more people should be home-workers than is currently the case. This is something that should be addressed urgently with increasing congestion and concerns about global warming.

The benefits of ICT include the ability now to access massive amounts of information and to find out more about the workings and policies of government departments, local authorities and other public bodies. There is a danger in all this information now available online. It is not necessarily correct or complete and there is a risk that some persons who access it take it at face value. As useful as it might be, not everything in Wikipedia, the online encyclopaedia, is necessarily true. There used to be a hierarchy in the relative standing of information in the mind of some, going from the spoken word to computer print out. If it was printed out by a computer it must be right! The cynics amongst us would remind ourselves occasionally about the adage 'garbage in, garbage out'. We must be careful when confronted with information online and be prepared to question it and, preferably, verify it by independent means. Often commercial websites carry testimonials from customers. These should be read with care as they may not be genuine. It is believed that some hotels have websites carrying glowing testimonials that have been written by the staff of the hotels. Fortunately, there are some websites comparing different hotels, pubs and other establishments operated by independent persons were comments may be posted which may cast doubt on some of the testimonials.

There cannot be many persons who have yet to carry out a contractual transaction online. Online 'auction' sites such as eBay have experienced phenomenal growth. Search engines too have grown into huge businesses. It is possible to book flights, arrange holidays all over the world online. Many retailers seem to prefer selling their goods online, often offering discounts. Before

---

[2] US Bureau of Labor Statistics, 2006. Statistics for the UK are not readily available, showing some deficiencies on the move to open government in the UK. US government departments' websites seem to be far more informative.

long, many retail outlets for electronic goods in particular may be little more than stores demonstrating the goods and offering advice. Again the law has had an impact on this and consumer protection is provided for. Buying online by credit card is particularly attractive because of the protection against fraud, responsibility of the credit card company for defective products and the ability of buyers, in the case of most types of goods, to return them during the cooling off period.

The growth and development of ICT has a more serious negative side. It has been and will continue to be a vehicle for criminal activity and other activities which, although not necessarily criminal in their own right, could be seen as undesirable or objectionable. Again the law has striven to provide for appropriate penalties and civil rights of action. Whether the use of ICT has increased criminal activity is difficult to assess. It may be more a question of criminals moving away from traditional forms of crime to ICT, perhaps in the belief that detection and prosecution will be less likely. However, the greater awareness of ICT crime amongst the police and investigatory authorities together with greater international cooperation may change this view.

The impacts of ICT will continue to develop and expand into new areas of society and social interaction and relationships. It is the duty of ICT professionals and managers, governments and legislators to ensure that the benefits continue to exceed the potential for harm.

SUMMARY

- The use of ICT has particular implications for:
  - privacy rights;
  - the right of freedom of expression;
  - individuals in respect of decision taking significantly affecting them.
- Property rights in creative works may be vulnerable on the internet because of:
  - piracy;
  - peer to peer file sharing.
- Legislators have attempted to protect creative works available online.
- The sale of music and film online is likely to have significant impacts on 'brick and mortar' stores.
- Over-liberal granting of software patents may interfere with the growth of e-business.
- The growth of ICT has:
  - changed working practices and employment patterns;
  - created a large number of new jobs;
  - provides opportunities for more home-working;
  - brings increased dangers of taking online information as authoritative.

SELF-TEST QUESTIONS

1   In what ways does the use of ICT pose specific challenges to the basic rights in the Human Rights Convention?

2   The internet has spelt the death of copyright. To what extent do you agree with this statement?

3   Read the text of the Aarhus Convention (Convention on access to information, public partici-
    pation in decision making and access to justice in environmental matters) available at:
    http://www.unece.org/env/pp/treatytext.htm

    To what extent does the convention ensure that public consultations by governments are
    open, balanced and fair so that the public can make informed responses? (You may find ref-
    erence to the judgment in *Greenpeace Ltd* v *Secretary of State for the Department of Trade and
    Industry*, in the High Court (Administrative Court), 15 February 2007, of interest.)

For further resources and updates please go to the Companion Website accompanying
this book at **www.mylawchamber.co.uk/bainbridgeIT**

36

Privacy, freedom of expression and the impact of ICT on society

Selected bibliography

Note: further reading and weblinks are available on the Companion Website for this book.

GENERAL

Akdeniz, Y., Walker, C. and Wall, D. (2001) *The Internet, Law and Society*, Longman.

Edwards, L. and Waelde, C. (eds) (2000) *Law & the Internet*, 2nd edn, Hart Publishing.

Gringras, C. (2002) *The Laws of the Internet*, 2nd edn, Tottel.

Hedley, S. and Aplin, T. (2007) *Blackstone's Statutes on IT and e-Commerce*, 3rd edn, Oxford University Press.

Lim, Y.F. (2002) *Cyberspace Law*, Oxford University Press.

Lloyd, I.J. (ed.) (2004) *Butterworths E-Commerce and Information Technology Law Handbook*, 2nd edn, Butterworths.

Reed, C. and Angel, J. (eds) (2003) *Computer Law*, 5th edn, OUP.

Smith, G. (2007) *Internet Law and Regulation*, 4th edn, Sweet and Maxwell.

PART 1   INFORMATION TECHNOLOGY AND INTELLECTUAL PROPERTY

Bainbridge, D. (2007) *Intellectual Property*, 6th edn, Longman.

Bainbridge, D., (2007) *Software Copyright Law*, 5th edn, Tottel.

Cornish, W.R. and Llewelyn, D. (2003) *Intellectual Property: Patents, Copyright, Trade Marks and Allied Rights*, 5th edn, Sweet and Maxwell.

Gowers, A. (2006) *Gowers Review of Intellectual Property*, HMSO.

Philips, J. (ed.) (2005) *Butterworths Intellectual Property Law Handbook*, 7th edn, Butterworths.

Stokes, S. (2005) *Digital Copyright – Law and Practice*, Oxford University Press.

Turner, J., Halberstam, S. and Charlesworth, A. (2007) *Domain Names – A Practical Guide*, 2nd edn, Tottel.

PART 2   INFORMATION TECHNOLOGY CONTRACTS

Bainbridge, D.I. (1999) *Software Licensing*, 2nd edn, xpl publishing.

Chissick, M. and Kelman, A. (2002) *Electronic Commerce: Law and Practice*, 3rd edn, Sweet and Maxwell.

Institute of Purchasing and Supply, *Standard Form Contracts* (various), available from the Institute at Easton House, Easton on the Hill, Stamford PE9 3NZ.

Morgan, R. and Burden, K. (2005) *Morgan and Burden on Computer Contracts*, 7th edn, Sweet & Maxwell.

St Laurent, A.M. (2004) *Understanding Open Source and Free Software Licensing*, O'Reilly.

PART 3   ELECTRONIC CONTRACTS AND TORTS

Brazell, L. (2002) *Electronic Signatures: Law and Regulation*, Sweet and Maxwell.
Calow, D. (1995) 'Defamation on the Internet', *Computer Law and Security Report*, 11(4), p. 199.
Collins, M. (2005) *The Law of Defamation and the Internet*, 2nd edn, Oxford University Press.
Law Commission (2002) *Defamation and the Internet: A Preliminary Investiation*, Scoping Study No. 2, December.
Milmo, P. and Rogers, W.V.H. (2001) *Gatley on Libel and Slander*, 9th edition, Sweet and Maxwell.
Stokes, S. and Carolina, R. (2003) *Encyclopedia of E-Commerce Law*, Sweet and Maxwell.

PART 4   INFORMATION AND COMMUNICATIONS TECHNOLOGY CRIME

Audit Commission Update (2001) *yourbusiness@risk: An Update on IT Abuse*.
Computer Security Institute (2006) *CSI/FBI Computer Crime and Security Survey*.
Gowers, A. (2006) *Gowers Review of Intellectual Property*, HMSO.
HM Treasury (2002) *2001–2002 Fraud Report: An Analysis of Reported Fraud in Government Departments and Best Practice Guidelines*, October.
Law Commission (1988) *Computer Misuse* (Working Paper No. 110), HMSO.
Law Commission (1989) *Criminal Law: Computer Misuse* (Law Com. No. 186), Cm 819, HMSO.
Law Commission (2002) *Fraud* (Law Com. No. 276), Cm 5560.

PART 5   DATA PROTECTION AND FREEDOM OF INFORMATION

Bainbridge, D. (2005) *Data Protection Law*, 2nd edn, xpl publishing.
Carey, P. (2004) *Data Protection in the UK: A Practical Guide to UK and EU Law*, 2nd edn, Oxford University Press.
Jay, R. and Hamilton, A. (2004) *Data Protection Law and Practice*, 2nd edn, Sweet & Maxwell.
Report of the Committee on Data Protection (1978) *The Lindop Report*, Cmnd 7341, HMSO.

PART 6   PROFESSIONAL AND SOCIAL ISSUES IN INFORMATION AND COMMUNICATIONS TECHNOLOGY

British Computer Society (2001) *Code of Conduct*, Version 2.
Clayton, R. and Tomlinson, H. (2001) *Privacy and Freedom of Expression*, Oxford University Press.
Erman, M.D. *et al.* (eds) (2002) *Computers, Ethics and Society*, 3rd edn, Oxford University Press.
Johnson, D.G. (2003) *Computer Ethics*, Prentice Hall.
Tugendhat, M. and Christie, I. (2006) *The Law of Privacy and the Media*, Oxford University Press.
Vaidhyanathan, S. (2003) *Copyrights and Copywrongs: The Rise of Intellectual Property and How it Threatens Creativity*, New York University Press.

Answers to multiple choice questions

Note: there are no multiple choice questions for Chapters 1, 18, 22, 34, 35 or 36.

Chapter 2
1 (b)
2 (c)
3 (b)
4 (a)

Chapter 3
1 (a)
2 (a)
3 (d)
4 (a)

Chapter 4
1 (b)
2 (d)
3 (c)
4 (b)

Chapter 5
1 (a)
2 (d)
3 (b)
4 (a)

Chapter 6
1 (c)
2 (a)

Chapter 7
1 (c)
2 (a)
3 (a)
4 (d)

Chapter 8
1 (d)
2 (d)
3 (b)
4 (a)

Chapter 9
1 (a)
2 (d)
3 (a)
4 (c)

Chapter 10
1 (a)
2 (d)
3 (b)
4 (d)

Chapter 11
1 (d)
2 (b)
3 (a)
4 (d)

Chapter 12
1 (b)
2 (b)
3 (a)
4 (d)

Chapter 13
1 (b)
2 (c)
3 (a)
4 (d)

Chapter 14
1 (a)
2 (a)
3 (b)
4 (d)

Chapter 15
1 (c)
2 (b)
3 (b)
4 (a)

Chapter 16
1 (d)
2 (b)
3 (b)
4 (c)

Chapter 17
1 (b)
2 (d)
3 (c)

Chapter 19
1 (a)
2 (b)
3 (c)
4 (d)

Chapter 20
1 (c)
2 (b)
3 (d)
4 (a)

Chapter 21
1 (c)
2 (b)
3 (d)
4 (b)

Chapter 23
1 (d)
2 (b)
3 (a)
4 (d)

Chapter 24
1 (d)
2 (a)

Chapter 25
1 (a)
2 (b)
3 (a)
4 (d)

Chapter 26
1 (d)
2 (b)
3 (a)
4 (c)

Chapter 27
1 (a)
2 (d)
3 (a)
4 (d)

Chapter 28
1 (b)
2 (d)
3 (c)
4 (b)

Chapter 29
1 (c)
2 (d)

Chapter 30
1 (c)
2 (b)
3 (b)
4 (d)

Chapter 31
1 (c)
2 (c)
3 (b)
4 (d)

Chapter 32
1 (a)
2 (b)
3 (a)
4 (c)

Chapter 33
1 (c)
2 (a)
3 (a)
4 (d)

Index